Lecture Notes in Computer Science   10924

Commenced Publication in 1973
Founding and Former Series Editors:
Gerhard Goos, Juris Hartmanis, and Jan van Leeuwen

Panayiotis Zaphiris · Andri Ioannou (Eds.)

Learning and Collaboration Technologies

Design, Development and Technological Innovation

5th International Conference, LCT 2018
Held as Part of HCI International 2018
Las Vegas, NV, USA, July 15–20, 2018
Proceedings, Part I

 Springer

Editors
Panayiotis Zaphiris
Cyprus University of Technology
Limassol
Cyprus

Andri Ioannou
Cyprus University of Technology
Limassol
Cyprus

ISSN 0302-9743 ISSN 1611-3349 (electronic)
Lecture Notes in Computer Science
ISBN 978-3-319-91742-9 ISBN 978-3-319-91743-6 (eBook)
https://doi.org/10.1007/978-3-319-91743-6

Library of Congress Control Number: 2018944299

LNCS Sublibrary: SL3 – Information Systems and Applications, incl. Internet/Web, and HCI

Printed on acid-free paper

This Springer imprint is published by the registered company Springer International Publishing AG
part of Springer Nature
The registered company address is: Gewerbestrasse 11, 6330 Cham, Switzerland

Foreword

The 20th International Conference on Human-Computer Interaction, HCI International 2018, was held in Las Vegas, NV, USA, during July 15–20, 2018. The event incorporated the 14 conferences/thematic areas listed on the following page.

A total of 4,373 individuals from academia, research institutes, industry, and governmental agencies from 76 countries submitted contributions, and 1,170 papers and 195 posters have been included in the proceedings. These contributions address the latest research and development efforts and highlight the human aspects of design and use of computing systems. The contributions thoroughly cover the entire field of human-computer interaction, addressing major advances in knowledge and effective use of computers in a variety of application areas. The volumes constituting the full set of the conference proceedings are listed in the following pages.

I would like to thank the program board chairs and the members of the program boards of all thematic areas and affiliated conferences for their contribution to the highest scientific quality and the overall success of the HCI International 2018 conference.

This conference would not have been possible without the continuous and unwavering support and advice of the founder, Conference General Chair Emeritus and Conference Scientific Advisor Prof. Gavriel Salvendy. For his outstanding efforts, I would like to express my appreciation to the communications chair and editor of *HCI International News*, Dr. Abbas Moallem.

July 2018   Constantine Stephanidis

HCI International 2018 Thematic Areas
and Affiliated Conferences

Thematic areas:

- Human-Computer Interaction (HCI 2018)
- Human Interface and the Management of Information (HIMI 2018)

Affiliated conferences:

- 15th International Conference on Engineering Psychology and Cognitive Ergonomics (EPCE 2018)
- 12th International Conference on Universal Access in Human-Computer Interaction (UAHCI 2018)
- 10th International Conference on Virtual, Augmented, and Mixed Reality (VAMR 2018)
- 10th International Conference on Cross-Cultural Design (CCD 2018)
- 10th International Conference on Social Computing and Social Media (SCSM 2018)
- 12th International Conference on Augmented Cognition (AC 2018)
- 9th International Conference on Digital Human Modeling and Applications in Health, Safety, Ergonomics, and Risk Management (DHM 2018)
- 7th International Conference on Design, User Experience, and Usability (DUXU 2018)
- 6th International Conference on Distributed, Ambient, and Pervasive Interactions (DAPI 2018)
- 5th International Conference on HCI in Business, Government, and Organizations (HCIBGO)
- 5th International Conference on Learning and Collaboration Technologies (LCT 2018)
- 4th International Conference on Human Aspects of IT for the Aged Population (ITAP 2018)

Conference Proceedings Volumes Full List

http://2018.hci.international/proceedings

5th International Conference on Learning and Collaboration Technologies

Program Board Chair(s): **Panayiotis Zaphiris and Andri Ioannou,** *Cyprus*

- Ruthi Aladjem, Israel
- Carmelo Ardito, Italy
- Mike Brayshaw, UK
- Fisnik Dalipi, Sweden
- Camille Dickson-Deane, Australia
- Anastasios A. Economides, Greece
- Maka Eradze, Estonia
- Mikhail Fominykh, Norway
- David Fonseca, Spain
- Francisco J. García Peñalvo, Spain
- Preben Hansen, Sweden
- Aleksandar Jevremovic, Serbia and Montenegro
- Tomaž Klobučar, Slovenia
- Birgy Lorenz, Estonia
- Ana Loureiro, Portugal
- Efi Nisiforou, Cyprus
- Antigoni Parmaxi, Cyprus
- Marcos Román González, Spain
- Agni Stylianou, Cyprus
- Yevgeniya S. Sulema, Ukraine
- Telmo Zarraonandia, Spain

The full list with the Program Board Chairs and the members of the Program Boards of all thematic areas and affiliated conferences is available online at:

http://www.hci.international/board-members-2018.php

HCI International 2019

The 21st International Conference on Human-Computer Interaction, HCI International 2019, will be held jointly with the affiliated conferences in Orlando, FL, USA, at Walt Disney World Swan and Dolphin Resort, July 26–31, 2019. It will cover a broad spectrum of themes related to Human-Computer Interaction, including theoretical issues, methods, tools, processes, and case studies in HCI design, as well as novel interaction techniques, interfaces, and applications. The proceedings will be published by Springer. More information will be available on the conference website: http://2019.hci.international/.

General Chair
Prof. Constantine Stephanidis
University of Crete and ICS-FORTH
Heraklion, Crete, Greece
E-mail: general_chair@hcii2019.org

http://2019.hci.international/

Contents – Part I

Technological Innovation in Education

Learning and Collaboration

Contents – Part II

Technology-Enhanced Teaching and Assessment

Computing and Engineering Education

Designing and Evaluating Learning Systems and Applications

Designing for Authorship: Students as Content Creators Using Mobile Devices in Educational Settings

Patrícia B. Scherer Bassani[(⊠)] and Debora Nice Ferrari Barbosa

Feevale University, Novo Hamburgo, RS, Brazil
{patriciab,deboranice}@feevale.br

Abstract. The use of mobile devices in education brings up new possibilities of promoting the students as content producers since there are many interesting and free applications for producing images, videos, and texts, among others. The idea that students need to be creators is aligned with the studies about Personal Learning Environments (PLE). In this study, we articulated two different approaches: (a) PLE as an emergent pedagogical approach, which benefits from the affordances of digital technologies; (b) PLE as self-regulated learning. This paper presents the research path involving the use of tablets with K-12 students in formal and non-formal educational settings and also presents guidelines for the designing of learning activities with technologies based on students' authorship. The research, based on a qualitative approach, shows the results of two case studies in Brazil. The research path was divided into 3 phases: (a) the design of the learning activities; (b) the application of the proposed learning design with students; (c) the analysis of the learning activity using mobile devices based on a PLE approach and focusing on the students' authorship. In conclusion, we realized that the activities with technologies developed in the analyzed cases, emphasized the students' authorship focusing in the content production itself both in the pedagogical approach and in the self-regulated learning perspective. However, we emphasize that designing for students' authorship should involve more than content creation but experiences which can articulate reading and sharing perspectives to promote the student as a decision maker and socializer as well.

Keywords: Educational technology · Mobile learning
Personal learning environment

1 Introduction

The use of mobile devices in education such as smartphones and tablets brings up new possibilities of promoting the students as content producers. There are many interesting and free applications for producing images, videos, and texts, including social software applications, which enable collaboration between students.

The Horizon Report 2016 K-12 Edition [1], points that *students as creators* is a short-term trend in education technology adoption in K-12 education for the next one or two years. According to this report [1], there are many experiences at schools around

© Springer International Publishing AG, part of Springer Nature 2018
P. Zaphiris and A. Ioannou (Eds.): LCT 2018, LNCS 10924, pp. 3–19, 2018.
https://doi.org/10.1007/978-3-319-91743-6_1

the world where students are involved in activities to foster content creation other than consumption.

The idea that students need to be creators is aligned with the studies about Personal Learning Environments (PLE) [2–4]. Following this conception, in this study we articulated two different approaches related to PLE based on [2, 4].

According to Castañeda and Adell [2] a PLE is an emergent pedagogical approach, which benefits from the affordances of digital technologies. A PLE encompasses tools, mechanisms, and activities that each student uses to read, to produce, to share and to reflect in communities. From the reading perspective, the tools involve sites, blogs, newsletters, video channels, and others. The activities are related to reading, text revision, and conferences, among others, which are meant to exercise the use of search engines, curiosity and initiative. From the producing perspective, the tools are spaces where the student can register his process of reflection based on collected information. These tools, such as blogs, video channels, among others, allow writing, reflecting and publishing. Finally, tools for sharing and for reflection on communities allow chatting, discussion and exchange of ideas with other subjects with the purpose of forming social networks.

On the other hand, Rahimi [4] understands PLE as an activity space that encompasses tools, content, and people to support and facilitate personal learning experiences of students. In this case, each PLE represents one node connected to other nodes. Rahimi [4] proposes a framework called Learner's Control Model that defines the core principles of personal learning, based on three interrelated roles for a learner: (a) the learner as decision maker; (b) the learner as knowledge developer; (c) the learner as socializer. Rahimi's PLE concept focuses on the student and aims to enhance the student's control of his learning process [4].

Therefore, considering the PLE an emergent pedagogical approach [2] based on the student's control of their learning process [4], how can we design learning experiences using mobile devices to enhance the students as creators based on a PLE approach?

In our understanding, designing learning activities where the student can be involved in practices which promote content creation other than consumption is a way to foster the student's authorship.

This paper presents the research path involving the use of tablets with K-12 students in formal and non-formal educational settings and also presents guidelines for the designing of learning activities with technologies based on students' authorship. In this study, we understand learning design as an outcome of the process of planning learning activities, also known as the process of designing for learning [5–7].

This research, based on a qualitative approach, shows the results of two case studies involving the use of tablets in K-12 educational settings in Brazil. The first case was conducted in the context of formal education, with students from 6 to 7 years old. The second case was conducted in a non-formal educational setting, involving children from 8 and 12 years old.

This article is organized as follows: in Sect. 2 we present two different approaches of the PLE concept and the possibilities of using mobile technologies for designing learning practices to foster the student's authorship. In Sect. 3, we present the research path, describing two case studies which involve the use of tablets in K-12 educational settings in Brazil (formal and non-formal education) and its analysis based on two categories: (a) PLE as a pedagogical approach; (b) PLE as self-regulated learning. We finish the paper by presenting the findings and making recommendations for future research.

2 Personal Learning Environments and Mobile Learning

Current studies in the field of technology-enhanced learning point out the possibilities of fostering educational processes based on the Personal Learning Environment (PLE) concept [2–4]. The PLE concept appears for the first time in 2001 allied with the studies on lifelong learning [8, 9]. Since that, different approaches of the PLE concept have been found in academic literature. More recently research on PLE has moved beyond a technological approach towards a pedagogical approach [2] which can enhance the sense of control and ownership of the learners by placing them in the center of their learning process [4, 10].

The proposal of using a PLE approach in K-12 education come to light in 2011 when the Horizon Report K-12 listed the PLE as a long-term trend (time-to-adoption horizon: four to five years) [11].

According to Castañeda and Adell [2] PLE is a pedagogical approach with a strong technological base which comprises tools, mechanisms, and activities that each student uses to read, to produce, and to share and reflect in communities. Thus, a PLE also includes the social environment involving the interactions with other subjects and these interactions compose the Personal Learning Network (PLN). The PLN includes the subject-subject interactions mediated by the PLE, and characterizes the social part of the learning environment. Therefore, in a PLE the students integrate both the experiences in formal education and the new experiences with the use of web applications and services [2, 3]. Figure 1 presents the PLE components based on [2].

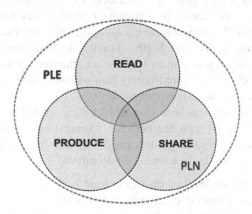

Fig. 1. PLE elements (Source: [2])

The researchers [2] highlight that the introduction of the PLE as a fundamental axis of the educational process is based on two perspectives:

(a) the teaching perspective which is meant to help teachers promote educational practices with technologies in the classroom;

(b) the student perspective which is meant to promote the students' appropriation of their learning process.

Rahimi [4] proposes a different approach for the PLE concept focusing on the self-regulated learning perspective. He developed a framework called Learner's Control Model that defines the core principles of personal learning, based on three interrelated roles for a learner: (a) the learner as decision maker; (b) the learner as knowledge developer; (c) the learner as socializer (Fig. 2).

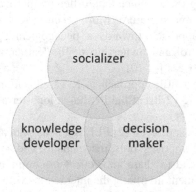

Fig. 2. Learner's Control Model components (Source: [4])

According to this model, to understand the learner as a knowledge developer means to provide him with the opportunities of using web technologies to produce different types of content with the purpose of facilitating the development of his cognitive abilities. To understand the learner as a socializer requires developing social competences and skills among the students and encouraging them to practice and strengthen these capabilities using web technologies. Finally, to understand the learner as a decision maker aims to prepare him to become an autonomous learner by providing him with appropriate choices and confronting him with situations that require decision making about his learning in an independent way.

This framework [4] was validated in a K-12 setting in Holland involving 29 students (18 girls and 11 boys) with age between 11 and 13 years old. Based on these results, Rahimi [4] suggests some guidelines to facilitate the engagement of the students in the process of building a learning environment:

(a) provide an appropriate level of student control over their learning process;

(b) facilitate the personalization of the learning process;

(c) provide mechanisms that allow students to modify and influence the structure of the learning environment.

2.1 Mobile Learning: Applications, PLE and Authorship

According to [12], mobile learning involves the use of mobile technology to promote learning anytime and anywhere, alone or in combination with other information and communication technologies (ICT).

Mobile learning is the natural evolution of e-learning and has the potential for making learning even more widely accessible since it increases the learners' ability to carry their own learning environment along with them. Besides, the use of mobile devices along with wireless technologies enables the notion of place and time to take on new dimensions related to the production and sharing of knowledge. Mobile technologies allow learners to access online educational resources, connect with others, and create content, both inside and outside classrooms. Students are therefore no longer passive elements in the educational process only receiving information, but now they have the opportunity to be active, interacting with information and other individuals in order to build their own knowledge [13, 14]. Therefore, the use of mobile devices in education brings up new possibilities for promoting the students as content producers. Thus, this technology enables that students to perform *as creators*.

We highlight two issues related to the use of mobile applications (apps) in education: (a) the selection of the appropriate app for the development of a learning activity; (b) the visibility of the content produced by students.

Regarding the selection of apps for educational use, there are studies addressing frameworks or methodologies, thus helping teachers in this task. Some of them focus on pedagogical issues but also analyze the technical characteristics of applications and their usage in education [15, 16]. On the other hand, some focuses on proposing categories to assist teachers in the selection process of mobile apps for educational use [17, 18]. Barbosa et al. [18] propose four categories to guide the selection and organization of mobile applications: support, education, entertainment, and collaborative. According to this study [18], applications classified in the Support category are those where the student can produce content such as images, text, and video, among others. Collaborative apps also promote content creation, such as blogs or social networks. Education and Entertainment apps are usually focused on a specific theme and/or content.

In an educational approach based on a PLE perspective [2], apps for content creation (Support category) focus mainly on the production component of a PLE. Collaborative apps focus mainly in the sharing perspective. However, this is not mandatory since the content produced in some app can be shared on internet and can be used from a reading perspective as well. Besides, there are many different kinds of apps that could be classified both as Educational and Entertainment - in this case, the usage depends on the app characteristics.

Regarding the visibility of the content produced by students, Heppel [19] presents an interesting framework that could be used for analyzing the audience of the content produced by students using mobile applications. He identified three possible online spaces: me, we, and see [19]. The first space - **me** - is the private one, and it is characterized by tools where the subject can organize his own contents, annotations, and other personal and private information and materials. The second space - **we** - involves tools that allow the subject to work in groups sharing the space with colleagues and friends. The third space - **see** - is the public one where all web users can see the materials published by an author. Through this perspective, when using mobile devices, the students develop their activities using apps and these can be shared in many different ways: (a) students can use some apps for the development of an individual learning activity (me); (b) for sharing within a group and practicing collaborative work (we); (c) for sharing on the public space of internet (see).

In our understanding, the selection of mobile apps and the visibility of the content produced are important issues from the perspective of teachers and of students. In relation to the teachers, it can guide them in the design of learning activities which can articulate tools and mechanisms for reading, producing, and sharing [2] with the purpose of promoting the student's PLE. As for the student, it enables him to reflect on the possibilities of using the apps for the development of leaning activities, this way enhancing their decision maker role [4].

3   The Research Path

This research, based on a qualitative approach, was guided by the following question: How can we design learning experiences using mobile devices to enhance the students *as creators* based on a PLE approach?

The research comprises two case studies involving the use of tablets in K-12 educational settings in Brazil. The first case was conducted in the context of formal education, with students from 6 to 7 years old. The second case was conducted in a non-formal educational setting, involving children from 8 and 12 years old.

The researchers had an active participation in the research process, which involved the teacher formation, the design of the learning activities, and the application of the proposed learning design with students.

The research path was divided into 3 phases:

(a) Phase 1: the design of the learning activities. In the context of formal education, the teachers in partnership with the researchers defined the activities. In this case, the teachers proposed the learning situation and the content in order to articulate the activity in the ongoing learning project and the researchers proposed the digital apps. In the context of non-formal education, the researchers proposed activities focused on linguistic and logical reasoning development.
(b) Phase 2: the application of the proposed learning design with students.
(c) Phase 3: involved the analysis of the developed learning activity using mobile devices based on a PLE approach and focusing on the students' authorship.

The data were collect from observation *in loco*, informal interviews, digital photography, and from the documents produced by students using different apps.

The results are described below.

3.1   Case 1: Tablets in Formal Education

This research was conducted in a public school in the south of Brazil, involving 6 to 7 years old students. In this section, we present three learning activities describing our experiences with mobility in the first years of elementary school. Table 1 summarizes the activities.

Table 1. Case studies in formal education

Activity	Grade	Description	Applications
1	1° (age ±6)	My alphabet. Each student had to take pictures of things which started with all the letters of the alphabet and then produce a video	Digital photography (camera app) Video Show (app)
2	2° (age ±7)	Who am I? Each student had to produce a book about his life using this theme: how I was as a baby, how I am now, and how I will be	Digital photography (camera app) Bamboo Paper (app) Aging Booth (app)
3	2° (age ±7)	Dinosaurs invaded the school. The students created images showing the dinosaurs in their school	Digital photography (camera app) Google Search Photo Collage (app)

Activity 1 involved a 1th grade class of 6-year-old students. In the activity **My alphabet** each student had to take pictures of things which started with all the letters of the alphabet and then produce a video using the Video Show app. Although the activity was individual (each student created his own video) the students collaborated all the time during the activity, sharing ideas for pictures. At the end, all individual videos were presented in a video session.

Activity 2 involved a 2nd grade class of 7-year-old students. In the activity **Who am I?** each student had to produce a book about his life using the theme "how I was as a baby, how I am now, and how I will be". They used the Bamboo Paper app for producing the book and the Aging Booth app for creating their picture as an old person (Fig. 3). This activity was individual and not shared. As well as the previous activity, the students collaborated all the time during the development. They walked around the class showing their production for colleagues, teacher and researchers.

Fig. 3. Examples of the activity Who am I? (Source: authors' database)

Activity 3 also involved a 2nd grade class of 7-year-old students. In the activity **Dinosaurs invaded the school** each student created an image showing his interaction with a dinosaur in his school (Fig. 4). The students used the Google Search app to find a dinosaur image and the Photo Collage app for the creation of the photo collage. The teacher published the images online using the class blog.

Fig. 4. Examples of the activity Dinosaurs invaded the school (Source: authors' database)

Based on our observation during the activities we realized that the mobile devices produced a new environment into a classroom. Although the number of tablets was sufficient for individual use, the students interacted all the time during the development of the proposed activities. They walked through the classroom showing their production to their colleagues, they helped each other with technical issues, and they used all the school space as their classroom (Fig. 5).

Fig. 5. Examples of mobility and collaboration (Source: authors' database)

3.2 Case 2: Tablets in Non-formal Education

With a focus on non-formal education, the research aims to identify how mobile devices, as tablets, can be used to assist in tutoring children and adolescents receiving treatment for cancer. The study is conducted in partnership with the Support

Association in Oncopediatrics (AMO) which assists children and teenagers with cancer and a vulnerable social situation. AMO offers a range of activities for cancer patients and their families, including computer workshops and tutoring. The work was developed through weekly classroom-based workshops at AMO, through activities using tablets to improve linguistic development and logical reasoning of the children between 8 and 12 years old. They are heterogeneous in terms of interests and knowledge. For example, in the same group we had students from the third, fourth, fifth, and sixth grade of elementary education. A plan was developed for each workshop, in which students were asked to develop the proposed activities, according to the themes to be addressed. Table 2 summarizes four of these activities.

Table 2. Case studies in non-formal education

Activity	Grade	Description	Applications
1	3rd–6th (age ±8–12)	My identity. In this activity, the students think and learn more about their own identity, creating comics of their daily life and the routine of their families	Digital photography (camera app) Comic Stript (app) My Family Tree (app) Supernote (app) Google search
2	3rd–6th (age ±8–12)	Producing tales - Bu: stories of fear and courage. The students create tales of horror and fantasy, writing stories about the overcoming of their fears	Evernote (app) Sketchbook X (app)
3	3rd–6th (age ±8–12)	Producing micro-stories about digital games. The students played digital games and created micro-stories about them	Evernote (app) Code.org (website)
4	3rd–6th (age ±8–12)	A Role-Playing Game (RPG) adventure with mobility. Here, we created a RPG game and narrated to students a story. So, they created their own characters and decided their actions and the end of the story	Google Drive Google Docs Autodesk Sketchbook (app) Comic Stript (app) Google handwriter Digital photography (camera app) QR Code Reader (app) Voice Changer (app) Crafting Game (app) Blogger (app)

Activity 1 involved the work with the students' identity (Fig. 6). Initially, we read to them a children's story, called "Bisa Bia Bisa Bel", about a girl and her grandmother and discussed about their daily lives. Next, we set up the student's family tree and they produced comics stories, in which they wrote about their routine using photos and drawings.

Fig. 6. Examples of the activity student's identity (Source: authors' database)

Activity 2 involved the production of tales of horror and fantasy, writing in the Evernote app. The students created stories about the overcoming of their fears.

Activity 3 involved production of micro-stories about the digital games (Fig. 7). Students used the online courses of the Code.org initiative and then created small stories inspired by the games, totaling four micro-stories per student.

Fig. 7. Production of micro-stories using write editor (Source: authors' database)

Activity 4 involved an RPG using tablets (Fig. 8). The teacher started a story and the students interacted and decided their actions. Based on the narrative proposed by the teacher, the students created their own characters for the RPG and wrote a story based on their point of view. In order to advance in the activity, they also had to perform some tasks involving drawing, speaking, and writing.

Fig. 8. Examples of the RPG activity using tablet (Source: authors' database)

3.3 Discussion

The data analysis were based on two categories involving the design of the activities and its relationship with a PLE approach to enhance the student's authorship:

(a) PLE as a pedagogical approach;
(b) PLE as self-regulated learning.

The first category, PLE as a pedagogical approach, comprises the analysis of the activities developed in both contexts (formal and non-formal) based on the PLE concept proposed by Castañeda and Adell [2]. Through this perspective, we aimed to understand how the three components of the PLE (read - produce - share) are interconnected throughout the development of educational practices with mobile technologies in K-12 settings focusing in the students' authorship.

The second category, PLE as self-regulated learning, comprises the analysis of the activities based on the PLE concept proposed by Rahimi [4] - the Learner's Control Model (decision maker - knowledge developer - socializer). Through this perspective, we aimed to understand the relationship between the students' role and authorship.

PLE as a Pedagogical Approach

Table 3 organizes the learning activities based on the PLE concept proposed by Castañeda and Adell [2], which comprises mechanisms, tools, and activities for reading, producing, and sharing.

All the activities developed in the formal educational context were articulated within a major teaching project. In this case, the learning activities with technologies comprise only a little part of a whole project. The analysis of the learning activities developed in the formal educational context (Table 3) showed an emphasis in activities based on the produce component of the PLE [2]. From the producing perspective, the tools are spaces where the student can register their process of reflection. In the analyzed cases, the activities encompassed different mobile apps for video, image, and text production. The reading perspective of a PLE, which comprises tools, activities, and mechanisms for reading, wasn't explored in the proposed activities except for one. For the development of the activity called **Dinosaurs invaded the school** the students used the Google Search app to find images of dinosaurs. We identified activities related to

Table 3. Designing for learning based on a PLE perspective [2]

Context	Activity	Read	Produce	Share
Formal education	My alphabet	——	Video using: Digital photography (camera app) Video Show (app)	Individual videos were presented in a video session
	Who am I?	—	Book using: Digital photography (camera app) Bamboo Paper (app) Aging Booth (app)	—
	Dinosaurs invaded the school	Google Search	Image using: Digital photography (camera app) Photo Collage (app)	The teacher published the images on internet (blog)
Non-formal education	My identity	Google Search	Writing using: Comic Stript (app) Supernote (app)	Individual text were presented in a reading session
	Tales of fear and courage	–	Writing using: Evernote (app) Drawing using: Sketchbook X	The stories were shared using Evernote
	Producing micro stories about digital games	—	Writing using: Evernote (app)	The stories were shared using Evernote
	A Role-Playing Game: adventure with mobility	—	Writing using: Google docs	The students shared their stories using Google docs

the sharing perspective, but they were organized by the teacher once the activities involved children aged between 6 and 7 years old.

Therefore, the analysis of the activities developed in formal education based on PLE as a pedagogical approach [2] showed that the use of mobile applications in K-12 settings enabled the students to get involved in a creative process and exercise the authorship. Considering the three analyzed activities, we identified a focus on the producing component of the PLE. The mobile apps were used as part of a major teaching project and the use of tablets were only one activity among many others developed with the students without the use of digital technologies. In this case, both reading and sharing perspectives were not emphasized in the design of learning activities.

In non-formal education, the purpose of the activities was to improve linguistic development and logical reasoning of students between 8 and 12 years old. From the producing perspective, we encouraged the students to create new materials based on their imagination and perspective, developing the writing and reading by creating their own stories. So, the students used apps which enabled them to write and save their documents.

From the reading perspective, in the development of the activity **My identity** the students used the Google Search app to find images which represented their way of life and family tree. From the sharing perspective, we encouraged the students to share their micro-stories and other productions using Evernote app.

The activities developed in non-formal education based on PLE as a pedagogical approach [2] showed that coordinating technology with the pedagogical objective to be achieved, aligned with the social context and health of the students (in this study, considering their stage of cancer treatment) is fundamental. In addition, regardless of the context, we observed students exploring the potential of tablets, making choices and using resources and applications other than those proposed for the activity. Considering the activities analyzed, we identified a focus on the producing and sharing components of the PLE. Both producing and sharing perspectives were emphasized in the design of learning activities even though the producing component was more explored.

PLE as Self-regulated Learning

Table 4 organizes the learning activities based on the PLE concept proposed by Rahimi [4] - the Learner's Control Model, which defines three interrelated roles for a learner: decision maker, knowledge developer, and socializer.

Table 4. Designing for learning based on Learner's Control Model [4]

Context	Activity	Decision maker	Knowledge developer	Socializer
Formal education	My alphabet	The students selected the images and took digital photos using the camera of the tablet	Digital photography (camera app) Video production using Video Show (app)	Individual videos were presented in a video session
	Who am I?	——	Digital photography (camera app) Book production using the apps Bamboo Paper (app) and Aging Booth (app)	—
	Dinosaurs invaded the school	The students selected the images using Google Search	Digital image using digital photography (camera app) and Photo Collage (app)	The teacher published the images on internet (blog)
Non-formal education	My identity	The students could write freely about themselves	Writing with Comic Strip (app) and Supernote (app)	Individual texts were presented in a reading session
	Tales of fear and courage	The students could create their stories as they wanted	Writing using Evernote (app)	The stories were shared using Evernote

(continued)

Table 4. (*continued*)

Context	Activity	Decision maker	Knowledge developer	Socializer
	Producing micro stories about digital games	The students could create their stories as they wanted	Writing using Evernote (app)	The stories were shared using Evernote
	A Role-Playing game adventure with mobility	The students could decide the actions of their characters and some parts of the story that the teacher narrated	Writing using Google Docs, drawing using Autodesk Sketchbook (app)	The students shared their stories using Google Docs

The analysis of the learning activities based on the Learner's Model Control [4] in the formal education context (Table 4) showed an emphasis in activities to foster the student as a knowledge developer. The students had the opportunity to use various mobile apps to produce different kinds of content: video, text, and images. The students didn't have the opportunity to act as a decision maker, since they used the app proposed by the teacher/researchers - they only had the option of choosing images for both activities **My alphabet** and **Dinosaurs invaded the school**. Furthermore, we understand that their age limited their socializer role.

In the non-formal education context, the students developed their reading and writing by creating their own and new material, thus acting as knowledge developers. So, to encourage them to write, we explored the telling of stories, playing digital games, and promoting debates. Therefore, the analysis of the learning activities based on the Learner's Model Control [4] (Table 4) shows an emphasis on activities to foster the students as a knowledge developers. Furthermore, the students had the opportunity to act as a socializer thus developing their social competences using web technologies to share their productions.

4 Conclusions

In this paper we presented and analyzed learning experiences using mobile devices in education in both formal and non-formal settings.

There are many interesting applications available for mobile devices, such as tablets, to promote the student's authorship. It is important to highlight that in this study we selected only free apps.

The research question that guided our study was: How can we design learning experiences using mobile devices to enhance the students *as creators* based on a PLE approach? Based on the literature review we defined two categories for analyzing the learning experiences developed: PLE as a pedagogical approach [2] and PLE as self-regulated learning [4].

The results pointed out important issues. In the PLE as a pedagogical approach category we perceived, in both contexts, an emphasis on activities based on the producing component of the PLE. The students produced videos, images, and texts using many kinds of apps. We realized the reading component of the PLE needs to be more explored in learning activities with the purpose of promoting reading skills which involve the use of search engines, curiosity and initiative.

On the other hand, the sharing component was explored, especially within the groups, in collaborative activities (**we** perspective [19]). We identified only one situation that explored the use of internet for sharing based on **see** perspective [19] (in formal education, the teacher posted the students' work on the classroom blog). Although the sharing perspective was applied in this situation, it is still far from a sharing perspective meant to promote a PLN as proposed by [2].

In the PLE as a self-regulated learning category we noticed that the proposed activities emphasized the learner's role as a knowledge developer in both educational settings. We identified differences between formal and non-formal activities related to the learner's role as a decision maker. Students from formal education didn't have many opportunities to choose an app - all was previously prepared by the teacher. On the other hand, students from the non-formal setting were a heterogeneous group both in terms of interests and knowledge. Consequently, the same activity needed to be adapted to different subjects, content and objectives. Therefore, the activities promoted the student's role as a decision maker.

In conclusion, we realized that the activities with technologies developed in the analyzed cases emphasized the students' authorship both in the pedagogical approach and in the self-regulated learning perspective. However, in both cases the authorship focused on the content production itself. Based on these results, articulated with data collected from observation *in loco* and interviews with teachers, we can infer that activities which involve the use of digital technologies using mobile devices are still seen as an ended-activity. This means that students produce content but the design of activities based on a PLE self-regulated approach needs also to promote the students as socializer and decision maker. Therefore, considering the differences and specificities of the two research contexts (formal and non-formal settings), the results are very similar.

Furthermore, we realized that the design of learning activities with technologies based on students' authorship, should address two important issues:

(a) mobile technologies enhance mobility and collaboration, and these characteristics need to be explored in the activities. The activities analyzed in this study used the mobile devices without exploring these possibilities;

(b) it is important to create an environment for the use of a wide variety of technology in a spontaneous way with the purpose of promoting the learner as a decision maker.

Finally, we emphasize that designing for students' authorship involves not only content creation but also experiences which can articulate reading and sharing perspectives [2] meant to enhance the student's role as a decision maker and socializer.

Future research involving the use of mobile devices in K-12 settings need to address studies articulating mobile practices and student autonomy.

Acknowledgments. We thank the National Council for Scientific and Technological Development - CNPq/Brazil (http://www.cnpq.br) for providing financial support for this study. Finally, we would like to thank Feevale University (http://www.feevale.br) for embracing this research.

References

1. Adams Becker, S., Freeman, A., Giesinger Hall, C., Cummins, M., Yuhnke, B.: NMC/CoSN Horizon Report: 2016 K-12 Edition. The New Media Consortium, Austin (2016)
2. Castañeda, L., Adell, J.: La anatomía de los PLEs. In: Castañeda, L., Adell, J. (eds.) Entornos personales de aprendizaje, pp. 11–27. Alcoy: Marfil (2013)
3. Bassani, P.S., Barbosa, D.: Experiences with the use of personal learning environments in school settings. In: 5th International Conference on Personal Learning Environments. Tallin/Estônia (2014)
4. Rahimi, E.: A design framework for personal learning environments. disponível em (2015). https://doi.org/10.4233/uuid:432bbd60-c6b9-4f08-aef4-615c2f2a101c
5. Conole, G.: Designing for Learning in an Open World. Springer, New York (2013). https://doi.org/10.1007/978-1-4419-8517-0
6. Falconer, I., Finlay, J., Fincher, S.: Representing practice: practice models, patterns, bundles. Learn. Media Technol. **36**(2), 101–127 (2011). Taylor & Francis Online
7. The Larnaca Declaration on Learning Design. https://larnacadeclaration.wordpress.com/
8. Olivier, B., Liber, O.: Lifelong Learning: The Need for Portable Personal Learning Environments and Supporting Interoperability Standards. The JISC Centre for Educational Technology Interoperability Standards. Bolton Institute, Bristol (2001)
9. Attwell, G.: The personal learning environments - the future of eLearning?. eLearning Papers, vol. 2 (2007)
10. Buchem, I., Attwell, G., Torres, R.: Understanding personal learning environments: literature review and synthesis through the activity theory lens. In: PLE Conference 2011 (2011). https://www.coursehero.com/file/24412530/PLE-SOU-Paper-Buchem-Attwell-Torressdoc/
11. Johnson, L., Adams, S., Haywood, K.: TheNMC Horizon Report: 2011 K-12 Edition. The New Media Consortium, Austin (2011)
12. UNESCO Policy Guidelines for Mobile Learning. http://unesdoc.unesco.org/images/0021/002196/219641E.pdf
13. Wagner, A., Barbosa, J., Barbosa, D.: A model for profile management applied to ubiquitous learning environments. Expert Syst. Appl. **41**(4), 2023–2034 (2014). https://doi.org/10.1016/j.eswa.2013.08.098
14. Barbosa, J., Hahn, R., Barbosa, D., Saccol, A.: A ubiquitous learning model focused on learner integration. Int. J. Learn. Technol. **6**(1), 62–83 (2011). https://doi.org/10.1504/IJLT.2011.040150
15. Deegan, R., Rothwell, P.A.: Classification of m-learning applications from a usability perspective. J. Res. Cent. Educ. Technol. **6**(1), 6–27 (2010)
16. Bassani, P., Nunes, J. Ensinar e aprender em/na rede: diferentes abordagens teórico-práticas do conceito de ambientes pessoais de aprendizagem In:. Jornada de Atualização em Informática na Educação, 1 ed, pp. 78–112 (2016). Sociedade Brasileira de Computação – SBC
17. Ipads for Learning project. Getting Started: classroom ideas for learning with the iPad. State of Victoria. Department of Education and Early Childhood Development, Melbourne (2011). http://www.ipadsforeducation.vic.edu.au

18. Barbosa, D.N.F., Bassani, P.B.S., Martins, R.L., Mossmann, J.B., Barbosa, J.L.V.: Using mobile learning in formal and non-formal educational settings. In: Zaphiris, P., Ioannou, A. (eds.) LCT 2016. LNCS, vol. 9753, pp. 269–280. Springer, Cham (2016). https://doi.org/10.1007/978-3-319-39483-1_25
19. Heppel, S.: Me, we, see. http://fuse.education.vic.gov.au/?QMS38X

Hierarchies of Understanding: Preparing for A.I.

Scott A. Carpenter[1]([⊠]), Catherine Liu[2], Weixun Cao[3],
and Allen Yao[2]

[1] Cognitive Cybernetics (CogCy), Cupertino, CA 95014, USA
ScottCarpenter@CognitiveCybernetics.com
[2] Compasspoint Mentorship, Sunnyvale, CA 94085, USA
catherinechangliu@gmail.com, allentyao@gmail.com
[3] Arixin Electronics, Wuxi, People's Republic of China
wxcao@arixin.com

Abstract. This work describes the Vision Hierarchy Model (VHM) and shows how it can inform efficient human-computer interaction (HCI) design, decision support system (DSS) design, and pedagogical design. The VHM is one member of a class of cognitive models informally called hierarchies of understanding (HoU), comprised of levels of understanding (data, information, knowledge, wisdom, vision, and possibly others) in a hierarchical fashion, with data usually at the bottom. The Vision HoU specifically informs design methodologies for HCI, DSS, and pedagogy for the age of ubiquitous artificial intelligence (U.A.I.). U.A.I. may transform civilization in turbulent ways in the 2020s. In addition to several important cognitive hierarchies, this work also describes the concept, "allocation of understanding (AoU)," which is a theoretical distribution of human understanding across the data, information, knowledge, wisdom, and vision layers of the cognitive hierarchies. The Vision HoU and the AoU together illustrate how semantic technologies are deepening human understanding, and how such trends can continue into the 2020s, an age that has many people concerned about the human workforce, among other social concerns. Illustrative examples show how the VHM and AoU elucidate the user-interface divide, the novice-expert divide, the student-teacher divide, and the coming human-A.I. divide. This work discusses two main approaches to help HCI, DSS, and pedagogical designers prepare people for the 2020s workplace: (1) complexity and simplicity are relative to the observers, and (2) simplify the source of understanding (SoU).

Keywords: AI · Artificial intelligence · Cognitive · Collaborative learning
Computer-assisted instruction · Content · Context · Cybernetics
Decision support systems · DSS · HCI · Human factors · Interface
Top-down education · Training · Semantics · Systems design · Data
Information · Knowledge · Wisdom · Vision

Acronyms and Definitions

A.I.   Artificial Intelligence, for this work, is any semantic technology that aids human cognition.

© Springer International Publishing AG, part of Springer Nature 2018
P. Zaphiris and A. Ioannou (Eds.): LCT 2018, LNCS 10924, pp. 20–39, 2018.
https://doi.org/10.1007/978-3-319-91743-6_2

AoC   Allocation of Complexity is the relative number of nodes in the information and knowledge layers. For example, a computer model having fifty knowledge nodes and fifty information nodes, in which each node is one unit of complexity, is a computer model with an even AoC across the information and knowledge layers.

AoU   Allocation of Understanding is a theoretical distribution of human understanding across data, information, knowledge, wisdom, and vision.

DSM   Decision Support Model is the computer model hidden behind the computer interface.

DSS   Decision Support Systems go by many names, such as expert management systems, knowledge management systems, and others.

FOM   Figure of Merit is a ruler of sorts used to rate the utility of individual solutions so that a wise decision (the best solution among alternatives) can be made.

FoU   Flow of Understanding indicates the directional transfer of understanding from SoU to ToU. The relative positions of the ToU and SoU with respect to each other can be top-down, sideways, or bottom-up (traditional pedagogy is bottom-up).

HCI   Human-Computer Interaction.

HoU[1]   Hierarchy of Understanding usually means a hierarchy of data, information, knowledge, wisdom, and vision (DIKWV).

%RinC   Percentage Reduction in Complexity is the percentage reduction in the number of nodes of information and knowledge within a computer model.

%RinU   Percentage Reduction in Understanding is the percentage loss in fidelity to optimize a complex system for an abridged computer model. For instance, if an optimized goal function = 100 for a reference computer model, and then 10 information or knowledge nodes are culled from the model such that the new value for the optimized goal function for the abridged model = 99, then one defines a %RinU of 1%.

SME   Subject Matter Expert is a person recognized as an expert on one particular subject.

SoU   Source of Understanding can be an SME, teacher, A.I., HCI, DSS, or other semantic technology that offers Understanding (DIKWV) to a ToU.

ToU   Target of Understanding (ToU) can be a novice, student, or User of A.I., HCI, DSS, or other semantic technology.

U.A.I.   Ubiquitous Artificial Intelligence is a predicted property of near-future (2020s) advanced societies.

VHM   Vision Hierarchy Model is synonymous with Vision HoU and Vision Hierarchy, and it is a hierarchy of data, information, knowledge, wisdom, and vision (DIKWV).

---

[1] The phrases hierarchies of understanding (HoU), cognitive hierarchies, and semantic hierarchies have similar meaning in this work. Each refers to the layers of data, information, knowledge, and beyond, and to the processes and context that transform one layer into another.

1   The Purpose of This Work

Once A.I. and other semantic technologies (i) achieve a type of global "knowledge" awareness (a semantic web), (ii) rationalize for best knowledge, information, and data (i.e., flatten the world's knowledge bases, information bases, and databases), and (iii) begin to create new knowledge (by inference reasoning), then our current paradigms of HCI design, bottom-up DSS design, and bottom-up educational pedagogy become lethargic, anachronistic, and even obsolete when compared to what U.A.I. will be able to accomplish. Already machines process data and information many orders of magnitude better than humans do in speed, quality, and quantity. Figure 1 projects a trend in cognitive cybernetics into the 2020s, 2030s, and 2040s, of which this work is only interested in the period of the 2020s, a period referred to as the "age of U.A.I." The goal of this work is to provide design principles to HCI and DSS designers and educators to inform design and pedagogy that prepares humans to maintain primacy over U.A.I. through the 2020s.

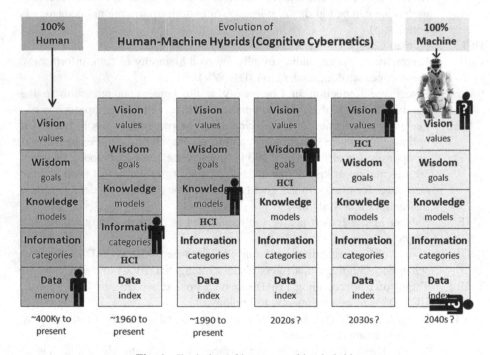

Fig. 1. Evolution of human-machine hybrids.

For most of H. sapiens existence (leftmost column in Fig. 1), humans mentally performed each layer of understanding. By the 1960s, data management systems were becoming widespread. Today, access to data, information, and knowledge is commonplace, although the Internet still treats most content as data and information. For now, the "knowledge" that is available in print media and on the Internet must be presented by the content author (the "Source") and interpreted by the content user (the "Target"); little is processed as knowledge by computing systems. But such is about to change. Soon A.I. and other semantic technologies may process knowledge as easily as computing systems process data and information today. This work assumes that such A.I. ability comes into effect in the 2020s and that A.I. quickly outperforms human knowledge management. The question is, what can humans do to maintain jobs, self-worth, and primacy over the machines in the coming age of U.A.I.? This work provides partial answers to this question.

2   Hierarchies of Understanding (HoU)

HoUs facilitate discussion about human learning (Fig. 2). Cleveland [1], Ackoff [2], and Bellinger [3] proposed a bottom-up HoU beginning with data and ending with wisdom. Tuomi [4] proposed a top-down HoU in which knowledge is first conjectured, then it is subdivided and contextualized to derive information, which, in turn, is subdivided and contextualized to derive data. Carpenter [5, 6] proposed the Vision HoU, a cognitive hierarchy based on *context-conjecture* that builds context downward (values, goals, models, categories, indexes), followed by *context-validation* in which real-world observation (content) filters upward to become data, information, knowledge, wisdom, and vision. To better understand trends in human-machine cognition, each HoU is briefly explained. Then the Vision HoU is used as a model for top-down education and top-down HCI, DSS, and pedagogical designs.

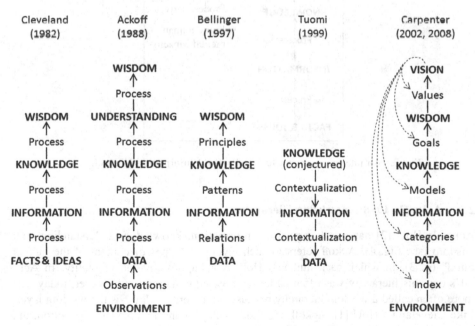

Fig. 2. Comparison of hierarchies of understanding (HoU).

2.1 Cleveland's 1982 Information Hierarchy

Cleveland [1] defines a four-level, bottom-up HoU (see Fig. 3) comprising (1) facts and ideas, (2) information, (3) knowledge, and (4) wisdom. Although Cleveland's HoU was originally referred to as an information hierarchy (consider the technology of his day), it makes sense to think of it as one of the early wisdom hierarchies, as wisdom is its top layer. Cleveland's HoU is process driven and builds from the bottom up; that is, lower layers must be developed before his unexplained learning processes can transform them into the next higher cognitive layer. Cleveland posits that human mental capacity limits the growth of human knowledge and wisdom, yet Cleveland did not see the need for an objective disambiguation of the terms information, knowledge, and wisdom. For example, Cleveland writes (p. 34), "The distinction between information and knowledge—or knowledge and wisdom—is, of course, subjective. One person's information may be another's knowledge; …" However, since Cleveland's time, Davenport and Prusak [7] wrote (p. 1), "Confusion about what data, information, and knowledge are—how they differ, what those words mean—has resulted in enormous expenditures on technology initiatives that rarely deliver what the firms spending the money needed or thought they were getting."

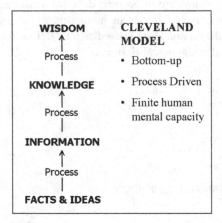

Fig. 3. An interpretation of Cleveland's 1982 Information Hierarchy [1].

2.2 Ackoff's 1988 Knowledge Hierarchy

Ackoff's HoU [2] has five layers: data, information, knowledge, understanding, and wisdom (see Fig. 4). Ackoff refers to such layers as "types of content of the human mind" (p. 3), in which each human's HoU is an approximation of reality. In Ackoff's day, his hierarchy was often called a knowledge hierarchy; however, today it is more often called a wisdom hierarchy because its uppermost layer is the wisdom layer. Like Cleveland's HoU [1], Ackoff's is process-driven and builds from the bottom up.

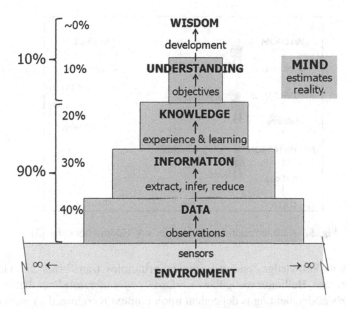

Fig. 4. An interpretation of Ackoff's 1988 Knowledge Hierarchy [2].

The base layer starts by sensing something that becomes an observation, which then somehow turns into data. Then, processes continue to build higher layers. At the top is wisdom, which Ackoff describes as akin to "effectiveness." Whereas Cleveland acknowledges that our human mental capacity is limited, Ackoff goes further to conjecture that most of our "mental space" allocates to the lower layers of his hierarchy. Ackoff develops the notion of "allocation of mental space" (p. 3) in which he mused that 40% goes to the data layer, 30% to the information layer, 20% to the knowledge layer, 10% to the understanding layer, and very little human mental space remains for the wisdom layer. Figure 4 illustrates Ackoff's allocation of mental space as a step-pyramidal shape. Ackoff's work [2] contains many important wisdomisms and foresight not covered here.

2.3 Bellinger's Wisdom Hierarchy (c.1997)

Bellinger's HoU [3] incorporates context as the key to promoting one layer of understanding into the next higher layer. Only if there is sufficient context can the observer derive meaning from content. Thus, Bellinger's cognitive hierarchy (see Fig. 5) calls out two bottom-up hierarchies that work together to create understanding; a content hierarchy (data, information, knowledge, and wisdom) and a context hierarchy (relations, patterns, and principles).

Bellinger defines data as disconnected elements, which means that a datum has no recognizable relationship (shared context) with other data or with other content. However, once an observer recognizes and understands the relationships between data and other content, then, for such observer, the relationships transform data into information. Likewise, recognizing patterns among the information transforms

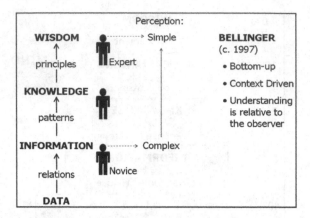

Fig. 5. An interpretation of Bellinger's Wisdom Hierarchy [3].

information into knowledge, and recognizing principles transforms knowledge into wisdom. Therefore, Bellinger recognizes a *relativity of understanding*, that the level of each observer's understanding is dependent upon context recognized by each observer. An expert may perceive a particular system as simple and easily identify information, knowledge, and wisdom; however, a novice may perceive said system as complex and only recognize data and information. Bellinger's work [3] contains many important wisdomisms and foresight not covered here.

2.4   Tuomi's 1999 Reverse Knowledge Hierarchy

Tuomi [4] defines a top-down (reverse) HoU (see Fig. 6) that posits learners acquire knowledge first. The learner applies some kind of context to the knowledge from which information emerges. Similarly, data emerges from contextualized information. When Tuomi speaks of knowledge existing before information and data, he must be speaking about conjectured knowledge or hypothetical knowledge about something that is still unknown; it is more like a hypothesis. Tuomi's work [3] contains many important wisdomisms and foresight not covered here.

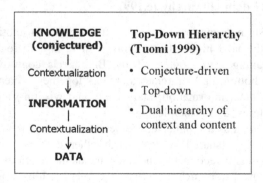

Fig. 6. An interpretation of Tuomi's 1999 Reverse Knowledge Hierarchy [4].

2.5   Vision HoU (2002)

The Vision HoU [5, 6] combines a top-down hierarchy of conjectured contexts (values, goals, models, categories, and indexes) with a bottom-up hierarchy of belief (data, information, knowledge, wisdom, and vision) (see Fig. 7). Thus, the Vision HoU combines elements of the top-down model of Tuomi [4] with the bottom-up models of Cleveland [1], Ackoff [2], and Bellinger [3]. Vision is posited to be an evolutionary adaptation that helps humans to extract increasing utility from their environments; that we are born with instincts that develop into a vision-center within the brain useful for conjecturing about the real world. In the words of Peirce [8, p. 477], "All human knowledge, up to the highest flights of science, is but the development of our inborn animal instincts." The Environment is the SoU, and human vision is the ToU. The Vision HoU explicates the process of human learning in two phases: (1) *context-conjecture* and (2) *context-validation*.

The Context-Conjecture Phase (Top-Down) (Steps 1–5 in Fig. 7). The learning process begins when we use our vision to conjecture context (human values, goals, cause-and-effect models, categories, and indexes). This phase of human learning is called the context-conjecture phase, and it represents a hierarchy of hypotheses about the real world. Values help us to decide our big purposes. Goals support achieving our purposes. In turn, cause-and-effect models support achieving our goals; categories of ideas support our models; and an index stores, organizes, and remembers the locations of the data. The context-conjecture phase is top-down. Consider that many organizations guide their workforce by first creating a vision statement and a core set of values, then goals are set, business models are developed, categories of ideas (such as words, names, and copular descriptions) are programmed in, and dynamic indexes handle the data.

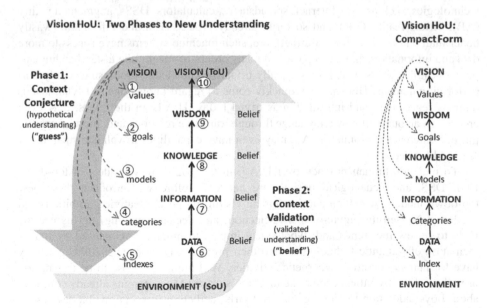

Fig. 7. The two-phase and compact forms of the Vision HoU, adapted from [5, 6].

The Context-Validation Phase (Bottom-Up) (Steps 6–10 in Fig. 7). Once the context-conjecture phase is completed, the context-validation phase begins. Context is validated once it is shown that content (a number or other type of value), having filtered into the context, represents an accurate-enough abstraction of the environment. For example, validating the context within the data layer requires only verifying that the data can be retrieved and stored without loss or unexpected transformation, and that repeated observations of the same thing under the same conditions results in the same data. As the content works its way up the layers of context (categories, models, goals, and values), content is validated at each layer by comparing the content to the environment and finding well-enough agreement. Should the context developer find that the processed content does not agree well-enough with real-world observation, then the context must be re-conjectured until it meets some criteria for accuracy as validated against the real world. Once the context is validated, conjecture turns into belief and we can say that we have learned and understand more of our environment.

3 Allocation of Understanding (AoU)

The AoU is akin to Ackoff's "Allocation of Mental Space" [2] (review Fig. 4). Figure 8 shows a hypothetical smooth lifetime AoU for a generic human under the traditional bottom-up education system of the 19th and 20th centuries, prior to the electronic computing age, say c.1870–1940. In this age, humans performed mathematics by mind and hand (finger counting, pencil and paper, slide rule, abacus—but no electronic calculators).

Traditional bottom-up pedagogy still measures today what it measured in the 19th and 20th centuries—data, information, and knowledge processing. Cognitive-cybernetic technologies, such as A.I., Internet, spreadsheets, calculators, DSSs, augmented reality (AR), virtual reality (VR), and so forth, already process data and information vastly better than humans ever have. Furthermore, such machine systems have access to more data and information, and the process it at many orders-of-magnitude faster than humans process. In the 2020s, U.A.I. may equally trivialize knowledge processing, vastly outperforming humans. Humans may quickly come to regard knowledge as trivial, just as humans regard data and information as trivial today. U.A.I., in the 2020s, may even create vast amounts of new knowledge through transitive relations and, more generally, through inference reasoning. U.A.I. may even have capabilities to validate such newly created knowledge.

To maintain human primacy over U.A.I. in the 2020s, new models of top-down HCI, DSS, and pedagogical designs are needed. Before we introduce these new top-down models, which emphasize human vision (purpose, creativity, ambition) and wisdom (goal-setting, figure-of-merit selection, and decision making), let us use the HoU to review the trends and hypothetical impact to human AoU caused by implementation of semantic technologies, and then predict what impact 2020s U.A.I. may have for human cognitive-cybernetic activities. Will humans choose to be the master, or will we, little by little, become the machine's slave? Many parents already complain about boys' addiction to video games and girls' addiction to social media devices.

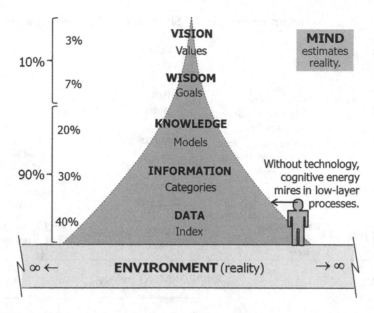

Fig. 8. Human Allocation of Understanding (AoU) across the Vision HoU.

4 The Changing Paradigm for HCI, DSS, and Pedagogy Designs

Today we exist in the age of ubiquitous computing and communication, and soon comes the age of ubiquitous artificial intelligence (U.A.I.) Let us look first at the effect that ubiquitous computing and communication have on human learning.

4.1 Brain (Data Overload) ⇒ Data Management Systems (Data Trivialization)

Our present culture classifies humans and technology as separate entities—a human and a computer with an interface (HCI). Clark [9] argues that we cannot disambiguate ourselves from our technology, that information technology is an extension of mind, that we are seamless cybernetic organisms. Thus, Clark sees no a priori limit to our cognitive ability because it expands with technology; the mind is just less and less in the head. The Vision HoU also takes this view, that humans develop computing technology, and computing technology amplifies human cognition; each iteratively amplifies the other. Figure 9 illustrates the up-shift in human AoU enabled by common data-handling technology because the human mind is relieved of mundane data handling. With data handling technology, humans can spend more of their mental energy at higher cognitive layers, to make a better estimate of reality.

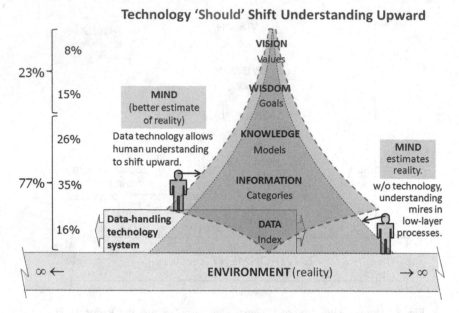

Fig. 9. Data systems (c.1960s-present) should up-shift one's allocation of understanding (AoU).

4.2   Brain (Info Overload) ⇒ Info Management Systems (Info Trivialization)

Figure 10 conceptualizes the up-shift that information-management technology SHOULD have on human AoU. Computing technology should relieve the human mind of the mundanity of data and information handling, and improve one's estimation of reality at higher layers of understanding. In the age of information systems, humans 'should' spend more time extracting knowledge from the information layer. In 2018, machines primarily handle data and information; however, humans, for the most part, still manage category-creation. Nevertheless, for many applications, category schemas and taxonomies have already been created, and weighted text searches are convenient.

4.3   Brain (Knowledge Overload) ⇒ U.A.I. (Knowledge Trivialization)

Many claim that their websites contain knowledge, but whether something is knowledge, information, or data is relative to the observer's existing AoU. For example, to a geometry student the word "sphere" should have category meaning, information, but to a toddler, the word "sphere" may be a word of unknown usage; therefore, "sphere" is only data to the toddler. Thus, most so-called web-based knowledge is actually data and information because, today, knowledge must be extracted or recognized by human observers. Today, machines do not think; they follow routines and statistics without any thought at all—calculations, yes, but thought and reflection, no.

Figure 11 extends the trend in cognitive up-shift by considering A.I. and other semantic technologies that are able to process knowledge and information with the

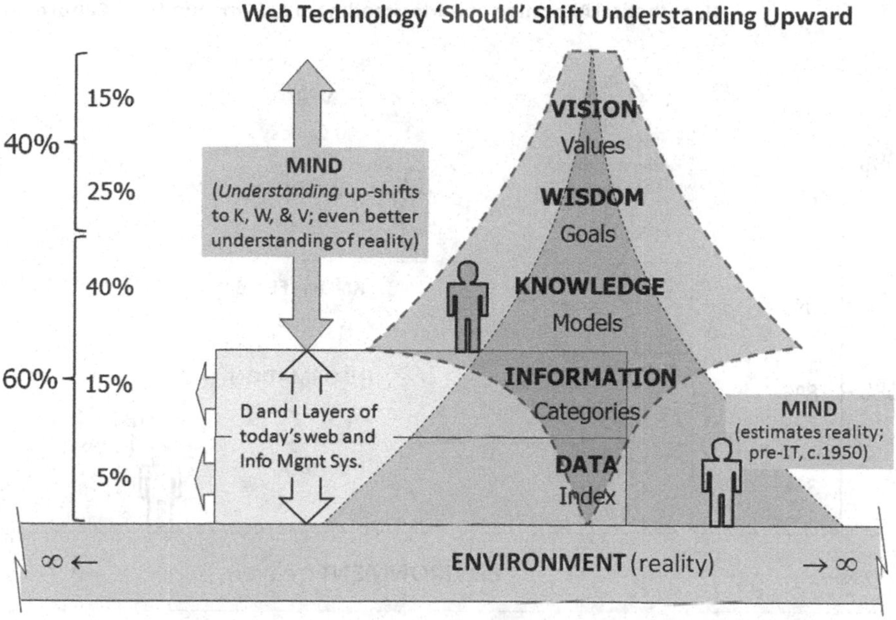

Web Technology 'Should' Shift Understanding Upward

Fig. 10. Information systems should (c.1990-present) up-shift one's AoU.

same ease as numbers are processed today. Our culture may come to view information and knowledge as mundane and as boring as data is today. In this new world of the 2020s, humans spend most of their time setting goals, choosing figures of merit (FOM), and making wise decisions (optimized to FOM) based on solutions (knowledge) supplied by U.A.I. Are such skills being taught in our 160-year-old traditional bottom-up educational system? No!

4.4 Discussion

The Vision HoU and the AoU show, hypothetically, an improvement in human AoU to the wisdom and vision layers, from 10% AoU for pre-I.T. humans (c.1950) in Fig. 8, to 23% for those using data management systems (computers, calculators, spreadsheets, and others) in Fig. 9, to 40% for information management systems (text searching, Internet, communication technology, and others) in Fig. 10, to 70% under a world of 2020s U.A.I. in Fig. 11.

Because humans cannot compete with U.A.I. at the data, information, and knowledge layers, pedagogy should immediately change to top-down, to stimulate uniquely human cognitive talents: vision (creativity and ambition) and wisdom (setting goals, choosing FOMs, and making wise decisions).

We have used the Vision HoU and the AoU to give an insightful view about where U.A.I. and humans stand in the 2020s. Recognizing and visualizing such trends in human AoU against the Vision HoU, as a function of advancing cognitive-cybernetic technologies, enables predictions about the workforce of the 2020s.

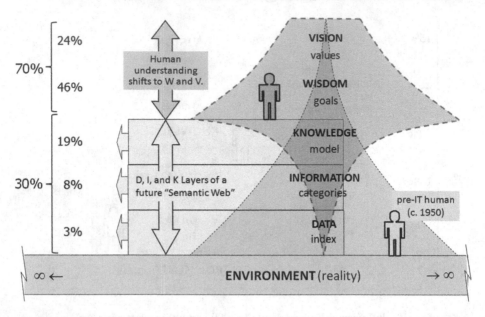

Fig. 11. The U.A.I. of the 2020s semantic technologies should up-shift one's AoU.

5   Competing with U.A.I. in the Workforce

5.1   A Century of Molding Idiot Savants

In the last one or two hundred years, our collective understanding has advanced so greatly that no longer can any one person come even close to understanding it all. Consequently, we educate and train for one or more decades to become so-called subject-matter-experts (SMEs). SMEs are, effectively, idiot savants; both SME and idiot savant know one subject well enough to be effective, but too little to be effective in any other subject in our highly competitive, specialist society. Because so much specialized understanding is required to master a given subject, one has scant time to become an expert in more than one field. Modern problems are complex and inter-disciplinary, and teams of expensive SMEs are required to resolve such complex interdisciplinary problems. Consequently, there is not much difference between a so-called scholar on one topic and an idiot, for both know too little about most other subjects. For example, take the problem of colonizing Mars. Figure 12 is an illustration of just a few of the SMEs and support staff needed to tackle such a huge, complex interdisciplinary project. How likely is it that one SME alone could successfully conclude such a project—zero!

Even if one could hire all the SMEs in the world, other problems remain, such as the communication problem (or argument problem, or even political problem) between each group. How does the superconductor-group explain their mass requirements to the system-architecture group, which demands mass reduction—the two groups may just

A Culture of Idiot Savants

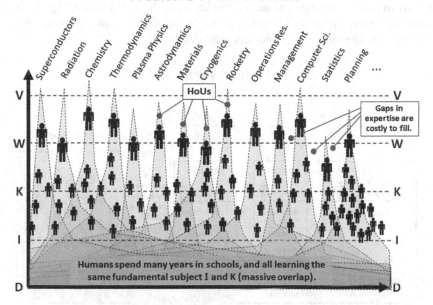

Fig. 12. The 2010s workforce, a workforce of subject-specific idiot-savants.

not understand the constraints behind each other's problems, and thus spend considerable time arguing before reluctantly settling on non-optimum goals and solutions. In summary, not only is the more expert SME more expensive, but also the more powerful and influential. Each group within a multi-group project has their own interests at heart. Each group may think it the key group, each person may think it the indispensable person. Therefore, management must resolve conflicting arguments between groups, mostly over resource control and power within the company or project, but management is often poorly able to make wise refereeing because management does not understand the technical issues involved. Furthermore, even earnest groups will not operate faithfully because each group cannot understand or see the total picture, a picture that does not even exist until the semi-optimum design is discerned, prototyped, and implemented in the market, or in space for the Mars-colonization project as indicated earlier.

5.2   The Age of U.A.I

For the workforce, the problem is about to become much worse, because no matter how many SMEs one has, U.A.I. will outperform all of them by orders of magnitude at the lower layers of understanding: data, information, and knowledge. Consider the 2020s, perhaps the late 2020s, when U.A.I. manages knowledge and information as easily as computers currently handle data, U.A.I. will not only know all that is known, it will know the best of what is known. In such a world, humans do more goal-setting and decision-making than they do information and knowledge learning, processing, and memorizing. Humans will pose goals and figures-of-merit (FOM) to U.A.I.; U.A.I. will use FOMs to propose solutions to satisfy human goals. In such a future, Fig. 13 shows that most of the expensive staff is newly unemployed; the company saves money; and the products are cheaper, better, and produced faster.

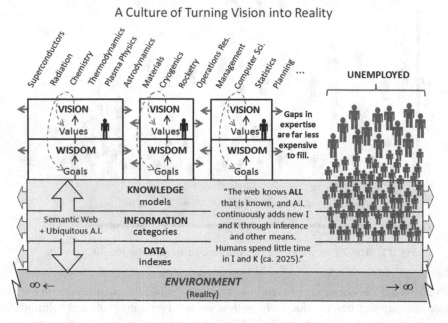

Fig. 13. A culture of visionaries, goal-setters, and decision-makers. (Color figure online)

However, the high unemployment is scary, unless the U.A.I. opens enough new opportunities to employ everyone, and everyone understands how to use U.A.I.; that is, everyone has enough vision to pose goals and to set FOMs to put U.A.I. to work. Unfortunately, our current school system is of 19th-Century design, bottom up, and it teaches primarily information and knowledge processing because that is essentially all that kindergarten through university undergraduate schools know how to measure, to grade. It is easy to grade 30 math problems taken during a one-hour test; unfortunately, integrated understanding requires vision and wisdom, which are both difficult to measure in a fair and standardized way, and this is probably why education pedagogies have remained bottom-up for 160 years, or more. Secondly, because U.A.I. is akin to a super-SME in ALL subjects, the communication and political internecine struggles for power and resources among competing departments disappear; solutions are truthfully optimized across all subjects. Thirdly, U.A.I. finds such optimizations to human-proposed goals and FOM in real-time, perhaps a million or billion or trillion times faster than could be accomplished by a team of the world's best human SMEs. The solutions are far more reliable, accurate, and fair than humans of the 2010s could ever hope to achieve. The debate about whether or not the situation in Fig. 13 is inevitable is a red herring because anyone involved in the high technology industry since 2000 has certainly seen it on small and corporate-wide scales in which only local A.I. and local semantic technologies have been applied. The 2020s, under U.A.I., are likely to see it on a massive global-wide scale.

6   What Can Be Done Now?

HCI, DSS, pedagogical designs should immediately focus on the top two layers of the Vision HoU, to prepare humans for the 2020s under U.A.I. Many authors since the 1990s consider knowledge the highest value resource to an organization. Not so anymore! In the 2020s, the workplace may look more like that of Fig. 14.

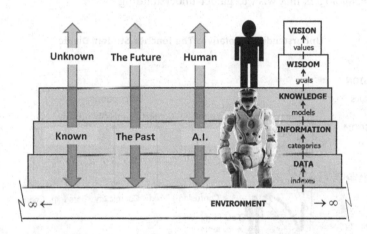

Fig. 14. A hypothetical mid-2020s U.A.I. workplace.

Organizations will logically strive to put in place as fast as possible semantic technologies that manage the bottom three layers of the Vision HoU—data, information, and knowledge—to enable their dwindling human workforce to better create, envision, set goals, establish FOMs, and make wise decisions once U.A.I. has delivered multi-dimensional solutions to goals, so that humans can make their overarching "visions" into reality. In the 2020s, and today for that matter, wisdom and vision are the highly prized layers of understanding. Albert Einstein, T.S. Eliot, Arthur C. Clarke, most CEOs, and many others have recognized the fundamental importance of wisdom and vision over knowledge, information, and data. We must avoid competing with U. A.I.; instead, we should use U.A.I. as a tool to enhance our natural human cognitive talents—vision, goal-setting, and decision-making.

Two design approaches to help HCI designers and educators to prepare humans for the 2020s workplace are (1) taking into account that complexity and simplicity are relative to the observer, and (2) simplify the source of understanding (SoU).

6.1   Understanding Is Relative to the Observer

Figure 15 represents the familiar teacher-student cognitive divide caused by the wide gap in subject-matter understanding. From the teacher's perspective, the subject matter is relatively simple, understandable, contextual, useful, and organized. However, from students' perspectives, the subject matter is complex, disconnected, unusable, and disordered. The teacher may spend years helping students to achieve expert-level understanding. Consequently, complexity and simplicity are relative to the observer. Therefore, a system can be complex, simple, and in-between because some people understand the system partly, others not at all, and still others understand it very well.

We can generalize the "teacher" as the SoU and the "student" as the ToU. Consequently, the FoU is from the SoU to the ToU. We further generalize the SoU to be a mentor, SME, U.A.I., DSS, or anything that offers understanding to a target learner. We also generalize the ToU to be a novice, a User of HCI and DSSs, and even other semantic technologies that wish to gather understanding.

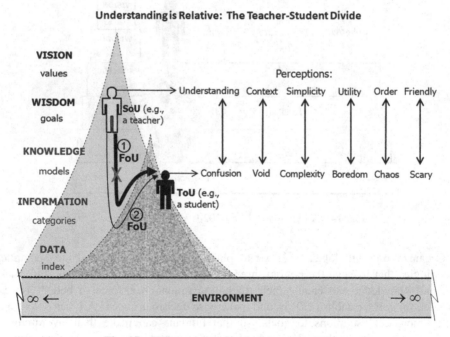

Fig. 15. Understanding is relative to the observer.

In Fig. 15, two FoUs are shown from the ToU to the SoU. FoU ① is inefficient for two reasons: (1) the expert, A.I., HCI, or DSS does not use knowledge or information (terminology) that is understood by the novice or user of the A.I., HCI, or DSS, and (2) the intended flow-RATE of understanding (FoU) from source to target is too high (thick line) for the target's cognitive capacity. The better FoU is ②, because (1) the source uses knowledge and information that is understood by the target, and (2) the rate of the FoU is low enough that it does not overwhelm the cognitive capacity of the target. How then to customize the design of HCI and DSSs to each User's cognitive ability? Sections 6.2 and 6.3 discuss approaches for doing so.

6.2   Simplify the Source of Understanding (SoU)

Because solutions to goals are unknown a priori, humans gather significantly more understanding at lesser cognitive layers than is required to exactly understand a decision space at the top. The pyramidal shape of Ackoff's (1989, p. 3) "allocation of mental space" is the result (see Fig. 16).

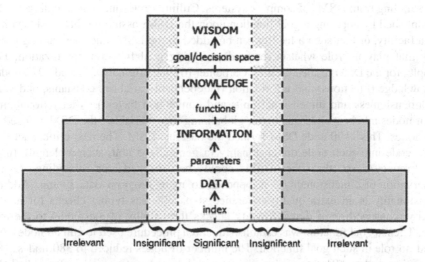

Fig. 16. An inefficient, non-parsimonious AoU results from bottom-up learning.

Filtering Irrelevant and Insignificant Understanding. Humans gather knowledge, information, and data to support making wise decisions. Figure 16 shows an inefficient AoU, which could be representative of a person's mind on a particular subject, or of the AoU as encoded in a DSS. In any case, Fig. 16 shows two regions of understanding that impede wise decision-making: irrelevant and insignificant understandings. If the irrelevant and insignificant understanding could be culled, then what remains is a perfectly efficient vertical column of understanding, each layer of data, information, and knowledge is exactly that amount of understanding that is required to support the decision space near the top, to enable making good decisions. The domain of the decision space determines the width of the vertical column. A decision support model (DSM) consisting of just the vertical column of "significant" understanding is considered a parsimonious DSM; that is, it incorporates only that quantity of understanding needed to satisfy an analysis of the decision-space at the top.

  Whereas irrelevant understanding is completely useless to the decision space, insignificant understanding is determined by the user's needs (usually established by specifying a requisite model fidelity—the representational accuracy and precision required for the complex system being modeled). Insignificant understanding may be relevant to the goal of the DSM, but (1) contributes too little to the overall under-standing of the complex system to matter to the user, in addition to its high cost to design, maintain, and to train people to use; and (2) it can possibly obfuscate significant parts of the DSM. For example, if an organization needs its DSM to model a complex system to within 1% of its true behavior, then why should the organization pay for understanding that contributes less than 1% while adding additional complexity and uncertainty to the DSM to boot? Insignificant understanding is thus defined as that subtle small quantity of understanding that is smaller than the requisite fidelity (pre-cision and accuracy) needed by an organization to make good decisions.

Carpenter [6] recently developed methodology for culling irrelevant and insignificant understanding from DSMs of complex systems. Culling irrelevant understanding can be accomplished by applying a goal function upon the DSM, assuming that the DSM has such a facility, or that such a facility can be added to the DSM, and then culling those nodes that play no role whatsoever in determining goal function optimization. For example, for the DSM testbed used by Carpenter [6], the original DSM had 1212 nodes of knowledge (functions) and information (independent variables, constants, and vari-ous dimensionless and dimensional units and conversion factors). After rationalizing similar nodes into best nodes, and after globalizing local variables, the DSM reduced to 1190 nodes. This 1190 node DSM formed the baseline DSM. The next critical activity was to code into each node dimensionality (a generalized unit, such as length, time, mass, money), so that the DSM could be checked for modeling reality (conservation-of-dimensionality), as opposed to mere program data typing. Adding dimensionality is an extra quality-assurance step. Whereas typing checks for model integrity, conservation-of-dimensionality checks the validity of the model to the real world. Then, a goal function was established, and a procedure used to cull all nodes that played no role in such goal function. The number of nodes reduced to 380 nodes: 188 information nodes, 191 knowledge nodes, and 1 goal-function node, also called the "wisdom node." At this point, irrelevant understanding has been culled from the DSM—that's 810 nodes or 68% of the DSM's complexity. Such complexity is no longer in the way of the user, and the HCI design should indicate, and possibly hide from view, such useless and possibly confusing DSM structures from the User. Still, 380 nodes remain, a lot of knowledge and information for a User to comprehend. For example, a User would want to know which pieces of information and knowledge are most important to satisfy the goal function, to make a wise decision. Many of the 380 nodes contribute insignificantly to optimizing the goal function. Consequently, using a procedure called the Knockout Methodology [6], the relevance of each node to optimizing the goal function was determined. Then, beginning with the node of least importance, nodes were removed until some reduction in fidelity limit was reached, a limit that could be set by the User. In the case of the DSM under study, 137 nodes were pruned for a further reduction in model complexity of 36%, but at only a reduction in model fidelity, or understanding, of 1%. In other words, an optimized goal function connected to 242 knowledge and information nodes, only results in a 1% deviation from an optimization of the goal function when connected to the full complement of 379 nodes. The ability to reduce nodes in complex systems models enables new DSS users to reduce the DSM to its bare minimum, which in the case of the DSM under review, was 21 nodes while maintaining conservation-of-dimensionality. These 21 nodes are the most important nodes, critical nodes to the operation of the DSM. As a new user learns the utility of these 21 nodes with respect to the goal function (the user's goal), the user can add-in the next most important nodes, and learn the relevance each new node plays as the full DSM is slowly rebuilt. Consequently, new users can come to understand the DSM as fast as their cognitive abilities allow. Voilà!, node dimensionality enables customized learning to any particular user's cognitive ability. Now consider the hypothetical situation in the 2020s when U.A.I. has "node-ified" entire subjects, such as physics, or economics. The number of discrete nodes may be in the trillions. For any given human goal posed to U. A.I., wouldn't it be nice if such U.A.I. then provided the minimum model to satisfy our goal, to which we could then add additional nodes so as to learn our subject as fast as our cognitive ability allows? I think so.

7   Conclusion

Today, semantic technologies are already automatically processing data and information, and the traditional bottom-up education paradigm is finding its bottom being chipped away. Our machines give us prodigious control over nearly limitless quantities of data. Likewise, soon semantic and A.I. technologies will give us prodigious control over unimaginable quantities of information and knowledge. As has already happened with data, knowledge will trivialize. Education must necessarily shift its emphasis to goal-setting, decision-making, value-setting, and creativity. These skills involve using our imagination in practical ways to maintain our primacy over U.A.I. through the 2020s. Later than that, who knows!

References

1. Cleveland, H.: Information as a resource. The Futurist, pp. 34–39, December 1982
2. Ackoff, R.: From data to wisdom. J. Appl. Syst. Anal. **16**, 3–9 (1989)
3. Bellinger, G.: Knowledge management—emerging perspectives. In: Circa 1997. http://www.systems-thinking.org/kmgmt/kmgmt.htm. Accessed 6 Feb 2005
4. Tuomi, I.: Data is more than knowledge: implications of the reversed knowledge hierarchy for knowledge management and organizational memory. J. Manag. Inf. Syst. **16**(3), 103–117 (1999–2000)
5. Carpenter, S.A.: Approach to assessing a space fusion transportation system (SFTS). In: American Nuclear Society Annual Meeting, Hollywood, FL, 9–13 June 2002
6. Carpenter, S.A.: New methodology for measuring information, knowledge, and understanding versus complexity in hierarchical decision support models. Ph.D. dissertation, Nova Southeastern University, FL (2008)
7. Davenport, T.H., Prusak, L.: Working Knowledge: How Organizations Manage What They Know. Harvard Business School Press, Boston (1998)
8. Peirce, C.S.: Collected Papers of Charles Sanders Peirce: Elements of Logic, vol. 2, p. 477. Harvard University Press, Cambridge (1932). Hartshore, C., Weiss, P. (eds.)
9. Clark, A.: Natural-Born Cyborgs: Minds, Technologies, and the Future of Human Intelligence. Oxford University Press, Oxford (2003)

Architecture Models for Inclusive Computational Applications, in the Treatment of Autistic Spectrum Disorder -ASD

Gustavo Eduardo Constain Moreno[1]([✉]), César Alberto Collazos[2]([✉]),
Habib M. Fardoun[3]([✉]), and Daniyal M. Alghazzawi[3]([✉])

[1] University of Cauca, National Open and Distance University,
Popayán, Colombia
gconsta@unicauca.edu.co, gustavo.constain@unad.edu.co
[2] University of Cauca, Popayán, Colombia
ccollazo@unicauca.edu.co
[3] King Abdulaziz University, Jeddah, Saudi Arabia
{hfardoun, dghazzawi}@kau.edu.sa

Abstract. This article seeks to present the initial advances found in the review of literature that analyzes the relationship between the development of skills inherent to emotional intelligence, and its usefulness in the improvement of Autism Spectrum Trash treatment-TEA, through the use of computer-human interaction techniques-IHC: In addition, a framework for the design of inclusive computational applications related to the achievement of emotional intelligence skills in children with ASD is proposed, therefore, the following are presented:- more relevant elements that could be included in the inclusive software architecture focused on people with this type of disability. It is expected that the design result will be applied in selected study cases, in order to provide rehabilitation and cognitive stimulation alternatives for this population, thus improving their quality of life.

Keywords: Inclusive applications · Emotional intelligence · Autistic spectrum disorder (ASD) · Computational solutions · MPIu+a

1 Introduction

The experience presented is part of the PhD project "Framework for the design of inclusive computational applications related to the achievement of emotional intelligence skills in children with autism spectrum disorder-ASD", in which the design of the models is contemplated Methodological and Technological for the psychoeducational intervention that allow the increase of the levels of emotional intelligence expected in the children with said disability.

Specifically, this article is related to the identification of models for the architectural design of computational applications that are inclusive and with the possibility of being used as didactic objects for training and, at the same time, provide the ability to adhere elements of autonomy that give validity the apprenticeship reached by those who use it.

© Springer International Publishing AG, part of Springer Nature 2018
P. Zaphiris and A. Ioannou (Eds.): LCT 2018, LNCS 10924, pp. 40–57, 2018.
https://doi.org/10.1007/978-3-319-91743-6_3

Therefore, the document proposes a framework that seeks to provide generalized parameters in the design of computational applications inclusive of the treatment of ASD, applied in a context of rehabilitation alternatives, compensation or cognitive stimulation for children with this type of disability, looking for in them the development of skills of emotional intelligence. The suggested computer model contemplates all the proposed implementation phases for Usability engineering and Accessibility in computer applications.

2 Antecedent

The project starts from the survey of the state of the art about the design of inclusive applications, where qualitatively it is found that this type of initiatives has been inclined mainly towards the construction of computational applications as support for motor, visual or auditory disabilities, but little has been done regarding other alterations or disorders, such as the autism spectrum, for example [1] (Fig. 1).

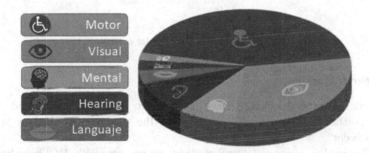

Fig. 1. Design of computer applications to support the disabled in Colombia

It is clear that technology is a great ally to help in the development of people with disorders such as autism and in this context, by deepening in the development of computer applications, there is a proliferation of initiatives tending to support of this population, but adjusted to particular cases that have generated the formulation of projects in many cases, and collections of mobile applications aimed at communities that work in the treatment of this disorder.

Taking into account various previous experiences related to pedagogical treatment interventions for cognitive stimulation, we will focus on the treatment of social story construction based on the ordered representation of pictograms to achieve sufficient stimulation in children with ASD. Lead to mental and emotional preparation that brings you closer to activities of daily life.

In this sense, we have explored the applications that are most mentioned in the therapeutic community that works with this syndrome and that has been consulted under the expression of Alternative and Augmentative Communication Systems (AACS).

3 Methodology

As it is an exploratory investigation of a mixed nature, we opt for a systematic review for the collection of information of interest in the topics considered important.

This methodology has been selected because it has all the necessary elements to carry out the search for information on the proposed topic. The importance of the mapping of the systematic review is found in the structure and in the steps it proposes to carry out the searches in an organized and methodological way, which helps to generate reliable results in the research [4].

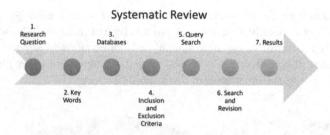

Fig. 2. Process for systematic review

3.1 Research Questions

RQ1:   What current treatments have been more accepted and used by the international therapeutic community for the treatment of Autism Spectrum Disorder?

RQ2:   What models of computational applications and especially HCI have been used for the treatment of Autism Spectrum Disorder?

RQ3:   How does the use of HCI facilitate the design of computational applications that improve the current treatments of Autism Spectrum Disorder?

3.2 Basic Definitions

To have greater clarity in the terms used in the document, a definition of the concepts table was made. The concepts are related to the search queries used in the systematic review.

Word	Definition
ASD	Autism Spectrum Disorder. Is part of permanent neurological development disorders, in which the areas related to social interaction, communication, behavior, interests, and others are deteriorated

(continued)

(continued)

Word	Definition
Model	Graphic or verbal representation or simplified version of a concept, phenomenon, relationship, structure, system or an aspect of the real world. A representation of a system that allows the investigation of the properties of the system and, in some cases, the prediction of future results
HCI	Human-Computer Interaction. Is a discipline related to the design, evaluation, development and study of the phenomena surrounding computer systems for human use
Software architecture	It is a level of design that focuses on structural aspects of software applications such as the global control structure and general organization; communication protocols, synchronization and data access; assignment of functions to design elements; physical distribution, composition of design elements; fit and performance
Emotional intelligence	It is the ability to identify, understand and manage emotions correctly, in a way that facilitates relationships with others, the achievement of goals and objectives, the management of stress or overcoming obstacles

3.3   Key Words

For the systematic review, the search for the key words in English and Spanish was defined to include greater results of the searches and to allow a more complete revision in the databases (Table 1).

Table 1. Key words for consultations

Spanish	English
Habilidades	Abilities
Autismo	Autism
Tratamiento	Treatment
Emociones	Emotions
Modelo	Model
Arquitectura	Architecture

3.4   Data Bases

For the development of the research five (5) databases were defined to perform the information search according to the systematic review. They were chosen because they are the most internationally recognized in the area of engineering, informatics and education, in addition to having good indicators for the publication of articles, conferences, book chapters and others.

Table 2. Data bases consulted

BD Name	Link	Acronym
Google Scholar	https://scholar.google.com	GS
SCOPUS	www.scopus.com	SCOPUS
Web of Science	https://webofknowledge.com	WOS
IEEE Xplore	http://ieeexplore.ieee.org/Xplore/home.jsp	IEEE Xplore
Science Direct	www.sciencedirect.com	Science Direct

3.5　Inclusion and Exclusion Criteria

The inclusion and exclusion criteria of the systematic review were defined according to the topics found in the project and the research questions for the searches.

The inclusion criteria are:

1. Articles published between the years 2013–2018;
2. Articles published in congresses, journals and book chapters;
3. Articles written in English or Spanish;
4. Articles found in the databases detailed in Table 2, and
5. Articles related to emotional skills, autism spectrum disorder, interaction and human-computer interaction.

The exclusion criteria are:

1. Document not available for download;
2. Articles in languages other than English and Spanish;
3. Articles that do not focus on the use of computational applications for the treatment of autism, and
4. Gray literature.

Once the basic inclusion and exclusion criteria have been applied, the titles and the summary of each work are reviewed. With this initial review, it is decided if the article is initially included in the accepted articles. After this process, each article is reviewed in a general way to know if it helps to answer the questions posed in the systematic review.

3.6　Search Strings

A general search query was defined based on the general concepts of the search title and which allowed answering the research questions posed. For each of the databases, we reviewed how to perform advanced searches and defined the search query for each of them, allowing more specific results according to the key words.

(("methodolog*" OR "methodological") OR ("model*")) AND ("treatment") AND ("autism*" OR "ASD" OR "syndrome")

3.7   Search Process

A general search query was defined based on the general concepts of the search title and which would allow answering the research questions posed. For each of the databases, we reviewed how to perform advanced searches in each database and defined the search chain for each of them, allowing more specific results according to the key words.

Once all the information of the searches in the databases was unified in a spreadsheet, 542 items were found in the databases and with them the review process is initiated. In the first place, a general review is carried out to find the articles, book chapters, etc., 75 articles were repeated, originated by the different searches in the databases and by different search queries.

Then, a revision of the titles and the summary of the works was carried out. This review took into account the inclusion and exclusion criteria, all the information relevant to the planned search and that will help answer the questions initially raised. The general summary of the accepted works is detailed in Fig. 3.

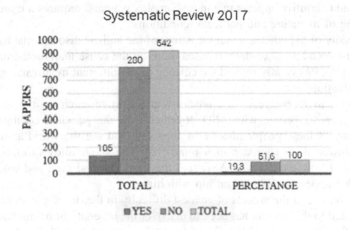

Fig. 3. Papers accepted in the systematic review

4   Partial Results Found

4.1   Related to Autistic Spectrum Disorder -ASD

The Autism Spectrum Disorder (ASD) is part of permanent neurological development disorders, in which the areas related to social interaction, communication, behavior, interests, among others, deteriorate [12] (Fig. 3).

According to [6] in the educational environment importance is given to the affective dimension of learning processes. However, this author explains that the emotional aspects in education continue to be a complex challenge in our present.

Similarly, [7] explains that emotion is composed of three components: Neuro-physiological, Behavioral and Cognitive. The neurophysiological component is man-ifested in aspects such as respiration, sweating and hypertension, which, although they are involuntary responses that the individual cannot control, clarifies that if they can be prevented by appropriate techniques. The behavioral component is related to facial expressions, non-verbal language, and tone of voice and movements of the body, among others. Unlike the neurophysiological component, these expressions are con-trollable and provide fairly accurate signals about the emotional state of the person. The cognitive component is the one that is related to the feelings, because the fear, the anguish and the rage, among other emotions are expressed in this component.

The author distinguishes the cognitive component of the neurophysiological, in terms of emotion and feeling. That is, the body state (neurophysiological) expresses emotion and is a sensation that occurs unconsciously, while the mental state (cognitive) expresses the feeling and does so consciously.

If we transfer the components proposed by [7] to a scenario where the learner is a person with particular characteristics of physical and cognitive development, such as a child with ASD, the landscape of identification and work of the neurophysiological, behavioral and Cognitive appears in a more complex way and requires a more detailed understanding of its nature and particular conditions.

The diversity of hypotheses about the nature of the autistic disorder that has existed during the last decades, all of them focused more on the cause than on the underlying mental processes, has greatly limited the efficacy of the different treatments applied for their "rehabilitation" [8].

Fortunately, in recent years, the advances made in research on the mental and cognitive aspects of people with ASD, together with the personal communications made by many of these people about how they saw and see the world around them, they have allowed us to approach their minds [8]. The above allows to have a more accurate idea of how a child with ASD sees the world around him, and what are the difficulties that appear in his relationship with him.

Particularly, one of the aspects of greatest difficulty in the development of the state of the art related to this project has been to discover the diversity of manifestations that the autistic disorder presents. This diversity is reflected in terms of the chronological age of the person, their mental age and the level of severity of the disorder presented, finding as a first element that each case of autism identified is completely different from the others, that is, that a treatment for several cases of diagnosed autism could not be generalized but that a specific one should be designed for the case studies that are selected for the experimental phase of the investigation. This circumstance has been sometimes so disconcerting that the previous experience of dealing with a person with ASD, without the accompaniment of a non-specialized professional, in some cases has prevented the recognition of this disorder in another person.

Some peculiarities [8] of people with ASD are used to identify the characteristics that must be taken into account for the design of computer solutions that contribute to the treatments currently used. Among these characteristics we have:

- Visual thinking
- Difficulty in anticipation

- Sensory alterations
- Difficulties in central coherence (Find differences between objects or people)
- Executive functions (impulse control)

4.2 Development of Emotional and Social Skills in Children with ASD

Communication is one of the most important goals in the work process of a person with autism [9], so the development of this skill must be present in all situations of their treatment. We must take advantage of any situation to promote communication, whether in a work or leisure context. The important thing is to create multiple situations to encourage the person to communicate, attending at all times to their acts and communicative reactions.

According to [10] "All autistic subjects have, to a greater or lesser degree, a failure to adequately develop their communicative and linguistic abilities." The language disorders can vary, from the total absence of speech to its late acquisition and that is accompanied by the wrong characteristics of the language.

Every communicative act consists of several components:

Table 3. Components of the communicative act

Modality	Function	Content	Context
Nonverbal:	Petition	Object	Place
Instrumental acts	Rejection	Action	Person
Natural gestures	Answer	Person	
Alternative Communication	Question		
Systems (ACS)	Commentary		

According to the components presented in Table 3, the behavior of the child with ASD is analyzed and according to the results the particular comprehensive educational intervention program is elaborated. It must be borne in mind that a person with ASD usually manifests profound and complex alterations in the area of communication, both verbal and non-verbal, presenting absence of communicative intent and/or alterations in the use of the language [10]. Therefore, within non-verbal communication, it is necessary to distinguish between instrumental acts, natural gestures and SAC (alternative communication systems).

The treatment programs that are expected to work within the research will focus mainly on alternative communication systems that are designed by computer applications under the approach of accessibility and human computer interaction.

4.3 Current Treatment and Education Programs

There are different intervention models for ASD according to the conditions of the case and the age of the sufferer. Among the most used intervention models are:

1. Denver Model: focused on children of nursing or preschool age who already have ASD or are at risk of suffering from it. It aims to acquire specific behavioral-looking

skills and invites families to use those strategies in their environment. It is effective in language, cognitive abilities, adaptive behaviors, and decreases the symptoms of autism [20].

2. Lovaas Program: is a comprehensive and structured entertainment program that improves attention, obedience, imitation and discrimination. He is criticized for problems in generalization for natural environments, for basing the results on the IQ and for not representing natural interactions [21].

3. Applied Behavior Analysis (ABA): Program that promotes behaviors through positive reinforcement and reduce unwanted behaviors through extinction, thus increasing behaviors, learning new ones, maintaining and generalizing and reducing disruptive behaviors [21].

4. Alternative communication systems: Help to understand and understand the language, for example:
   a. Complementary oral: bimodal system (combines oral language and gestural signs), and the word complemented (sounds are accompanied by hand movements).
   b. Gestural: Sign language, which uses visual transmission to express itself, and sign language that unites gestures, words and signs.
   c. Mixed, which simultaneously use oral language, signs, sign language and resources that encourage communication.

5. TEACCH Method: It has turned out to be a very effective intervention program for cases of ASD that involves the families of those who suffer from it, managing to help children to function autonomously, offer those services and transmit theoretical and practical knowledge [22].

The TEACCH program ("Treatment and Education of Autistic and Related Communication Handicapped Children") provides different services for people with autism and associated disorders, as well as for their families [11]. Its founder, Eric Schopler, has developed, through numerous publications in "The TEACCH Division", various programming and a methodology of enormous influence in the work with people with serious communication difficulties and therefore applicable to the students that are framed within the autistic spectrum [10, 11] (Fig. 4).

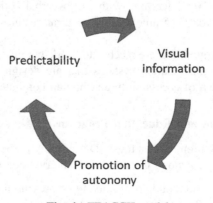

Fig. 4. TEACCH model

The use of TEACCH as a treatment model seeks to achieve, through the application of prepared activities, the child with ASD achieve an improvement in their autonomy, while avoiding communication difficulties and language comprehension [12]. The tasks for children with ASD who begin to work on this methodology are those tasks that are manipulative and that teach the principles of the task: the idea of complement, of looking for instructions, use of materials and everything that is defined for the emotional or social competences that you want to work. It is noteworthy that those who work with people with autism should know that motivation is key to learning. Attention and motivation increase when activities are clearly designed. Any activity that you want to do, you have to design it as if it were an activity with TEACCH characteristics.

Consequently, TEACCH allows the accompaniment in the treatment of ASD through specific activities such as:

- Structured learning.
- Learning without error.
- Chaining backwards.
- Incidental teaching.
- Encourage communication behaviors.
- Visual supports.
- Work systems.

For this, the physical structure of the interaction environment with the child with ASD is important. The most accurate space arrangements are:

- Face to Face: more demanding and requires student attention.
- Side by side. allows imitation and focuses on materials and instructions.
- Behind: with less adult control, encourages independence (Fig. 5).

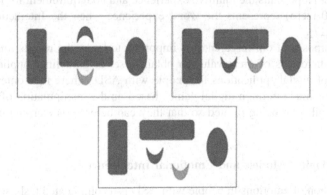

Fig. 5. Arrangement of the TEACCH method: face to face, side by side and behind

4.4 Computational Models to Support the Treatment of ASD

Children with ASD, as well as other children who do not suffer from this disorder, have an affinity for ICT information and communication technologies [13]. Taking into account this characteristic, within the treatment of ASD, the use of Natural User

Interfaces should be considered, where the user interacts without using command controls or input devices such as the mouse, keyboard, touchpad, joystick, and others [14, 15]. Instead of these controls, gestural movements such as hands or body are used, which become the command control of the application. Augmented reality is another concept that has been useful in some cases for the treatment of ASD, used to define a vision through a technological device of a physical environment of the real world, whose elements are combined with virtual elements for the creation of a mixed reality in real time [16].

In the school environment there are children with special educational needs, within these are students with ASD, with characteristics to take into account to carry out a successful and efficient intervention. Since in the school an important part of the life of the children is developed; to favor the personal and social development of these people, it is necessary that the psychoeducational intervention offers answers to individual needs, providing the necessary support in academic instruction and also favoring the integration in their peer group [17].

Regarding the use of applications of this type in the treatment of cases of ASD, it is found that there is no general intervention methodology for an objective evaluation with respect to the level of ease of use of the applications with which it has been experienced, and these must be adjusted in a particular way for each selected case of study. This means that conclusive results must be collected by running tests that evaluate usability in each case.

This is consistent with the experiences obtained by [17–19], who assess the usability of the natural user interface through tests conducted through touchless interactions oriented towards the most common actions in children with ASD. Such as clicking, dragging, moving or zooming a series of images (pictograms) on the screen. The usability level is defined by a rating scale divided into a grade of ten where the score of 9 (nine) represents the intuitive experience and no requirement for learning and the score of 0 (zero) represents the worst experience when the Interactions are not usable at all [17].

For the purposes of our research, it is important to know the results found in other experiences where it is of great value to obtain a set of guidelines applicable to the development of digital applications for people with ASD, where the context of use of the applications made through digital games based on the manipulation of pictograms with the possibility of being printed so that they can be used as learning chips in real environments.

4.5   Technological Models and Emotional Intelligence

The identification of emotions in people with ASD is a complicated task, so it has been strategic to address the issue from the treatment of the skills that are expected to strengthen. Their emotions provide us with very relevant information about their preferences in relation to people or activities and they are also an important source of information on the variables and conditions that cause them anxiety or stress and can therefore facilitate the appearance of problematic behaviors of varying degrees. It is necessary, then, to find other sources of information for the identification of emotions in these people.

Although emotion is usually understood as a multidimensional experience that encompasses three response systems: cognitive, behavioral and physiological [23], little research has been done on the physiology of emotions in people with intellectual disabilities and severe development.

The behavioral expression of emotions has been investigated more in these people [24, 25] although limitations are also found in these studies. The behavioral approach could ideally be complemented with another approach such as the physiological one, as pointed out in several pioneering studies such as those in [26, 27].

People with intellectual disabilities and severe development can have significant difficulties managing and communicating their emotions. These people can logically live situations in which they enjoy and are comfortable and situations that can cause anxiety and stress.

Due to their communicative limitations, they may have difficulties to communicate their discomfort and, in addition, they can show this in problematic ways (aggressions, self-harm, destructive behavior, etc.) for themselves and for other people. Even for the support professional it can be difficult to know in what situations the person enjoys and what situations cause discomfort or anxiety [28].

In this sense, it is very interesting the support of a system that evaluates and communicates the emotional state of the person in order that the support professional can intervene and help her to modify her emotional state or avoid situations of risk.

Among the experiences consulted, we have found options for verifying the effectiveness and usability of software solutions implemented to support TEA therapies where the same application could be used to know the emotional state of children with these characteristics in various situations, and find out which of these activities are preferred and which of them may cause anxiety or discomfort. With this knowledge you can increase the preferred activities and decrease or modify those that generate anxiety.

The study carried out by [28], was based on the use of physiological systems of emotion detection to recognize and quantify emotional values (positive, negative and neutral emotional states) using signals such as heart rate, temperature or skin conductivity, signs that have previously been used in studies of emotions in people with intellectual disabilities [27].

The information on heart rate variability was acquired using a pulsimeter (Zephyr HxM). These non-invasive and portable devices can transmit information via Bluetooth up to a distance of 30 m. Thanks to this the child with ASD could carry the sensors in the body and did not need connected cables. The data of the physiological signals were processed remotely in a mobile (in this case a HTC Nexus 1, and a Samsung Galaxy Mini) with the intention of discovering patterns that correlate with the different emotions. The mobile processor performs signal processing and uses the algorithm to measure the polarity and intensity of the person's emotional reaction at the time it occurs. The support professional of the participating child can monitor the emotional state values in real time through the mobile screen. The application for the mobile also allows the caregiver to keep track of the number of times in which the response of the system has a conflict with the user's own experience (they do not coincide). This is done through the graphical interface of the mobile.

In relation to its usability, although the pulsimeter used was designed to minimize discomfort, in some cases the sensors' bearers felt some type of discomfort when carrying the device in the chest. This is particularly important in the case of the type of children with ASD sensitive to physical contact who are expected to work and who could react adversely to the use of the system. For this reason, the study to be carried out should seek the use of non-invasive devices for data collection in selected case studies.

4.6   Alternatives of Application Design Proposed for Support from Usability Engineering

The use of computational technologies as a complement to the clinical treatment of ASD intervention brings advantages such as learning at a particular rhythm, the increase in focused attention, and behavioral changes due to the affinity of children to the development of social interactions based on digital interfaces. Facing the same process done face to face in real life.

This computational component is developed under the Usability and Accessibility Engineering Process Model MPIu+a, which seeks to cover the aspects related to the Design of Interactive User-Centric Systems (DCU) contemplating all its phases of Realization: Analysis, Design, Implementation, Launching, Prototyping and Evaluation [2] (Fig. 6).

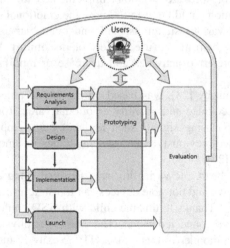

Fig. 6. MPIu+a design model

Initially, the development of the model of inclusive computer applications is framed from the concepts related to the disability linked to the ASD and specifically in the development of intrapersonal skills (motivation) and interpersonal skills (social skills) related to emotional intelligence [17]. This has to do with the conceptual organization of the project within the aspects of Software Engineering with the basic principles of Usability Engineering and Accessibility, providing a methodology that is able to guide the development teams during the process of implementation of a specific interactive and inclusive system.

Thinking about the final user of the project, it is intended that usability is a determining factor for inclusive applications that are carried out under this approach, so that the interfaces, communicative capacity and functional structure of the software developed, have to be as simple as possible. Therefore, for the design of the techno- logical model that defines appropriate software architectures, the ISO/IEC 25010 standard must be taken into account.

The application of this model is linked to the design of processes centered on the user and the evaluation of usability in each step carried out, which guarantees that both functional and non-functional requirements are met from the beginning of the design of the applications and not until the end that the tests are carried out.

According to the above, the design of computer applications interfaces that support the treatment of ASD must adapt the social histories according to the individual needs, interests and learning style of the children, for example, using the image of his favorite cartoon character, all this through collaborative construction options between the same child and his therapist, or even his own family members, thus increasing his motivation and achievement of the expected social skills.

The design of the application that builds stories with pictograms is achieved by analyzing the functionalities and the necessary tasks that allow them to be carried out, as well as modeling at a conceptual level, seeking an approximation to the mental model of the users previously analyzed to incorporate their particularities as usable elements in the same design. The design of the activity covers the space between the defined functionalities and the user interface (Fig. 7).

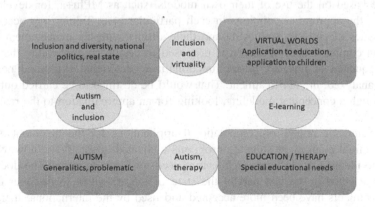

Fig. 7. Overview of story-generating application based on pictograms

Finally, the aspect of the evaluation of the solution to be obtained must be con- sidered. In this phase, the necessary techniques will be applied to receive the necessary feedback from the users and/or expert evaluators, which will be reflected in the design of the interfaces, improving their interactive processes. Therefore, for research we will talk about evaluation as: The activity that includes a set of methodologies and techniques that analyze the usability and/or accessibility of an interactive system that seeks to rehabilitate the abilities of children with ASD.

According to the above, the most appropriate method of inspection of results could be the heuristic evaluation that is used to find usability problems in an interface and can be carried out by a small group of evaluators, verifying the degree of compliance with the principles of usability and design that have been specified in the initial requirements analysis.

5 Discussion and Conclusions

Currently in countries such as Colombia is more evident the number of people with some type of disability, especially autistic spectrum disorder (ASD), which require a psychoeducational treatment adapted to their condition and especially configurable according to the progress of their cognitive stimulation therapy. The mental profile of a person with ASD is that of someone who has serious difficulties to deal with everything that is complex, subtle, ephemeral and variable, that is, the socio-mental. It is not possible to generalize a treatment for several cases of autism that have been diagnosed, therefore, a specific treatment should be designed for each case and in this sense, specific adjustments should also be made to the computational application that is designed from the perspective of the principles of interaction and accessibility. The design of computer applications to support people with disabilities in Colombia is still incipient and the software community requires greater conceptual tools that allow the design of inclusive applications in an orderly and quality manner.

The design of computer application interfaces that support the treatment of ASD should be based on the use of their own models, such as MPIu+a, for development adapted to the appropriate solutions in each particular case. Taking into account the characteristics of children with ASD and their affinity with the management of pictograms in computer applications, it is proposed to design an application that builds stories (sequence of images), where functionalities, emotional skills and necessary tasks are analyzed. in your treatment. That would be destined to be carried out by the child, through a conceptual modeling, looking for an approximation to the real life of these people.

The systematic review of computational applications for the treatment of ASD shows an initial quantity of software programs evaluated qualitatively, however, it is not easy to identify the software architecture used for these purposes. The documents that were selected in the first part of the state of the art, allow to discover that the current treatments have been more accepted and used by the international therapeutic community at present for the treatment of the Autism Spectrum Disorder [2, 4, 5]. Consequently, the TEACCH model is a didactic model for the formulation of new therapeutic initiatives and has originated programs such as the use of mobile devices with NFC technology or even the use of animals to support treatments. Notwithstanding the foregoing, no research or projects have been found related to the combined application of the above elements, that is, the use of software tools that use NFC technology for the presentation of animated pictograms of animals, as well as the inclusion of elements of serious games that support the current treatment of children with ASD or even with other functional diversity, so it would be a contribution to the new practices of inclusive education in this area of knowledge.

With respect to the model for the design of computational applications that support the treatments of ASD, although in the selected literature there is the use of applications within some treatments with important results for improving the behavior of children with ASD [3, 9], it is evident that it is not possible to generalize a treatment for several cases of autism that have been diagnosed, therefore, a specific treatment must be designed for each case and in this sense, it will also have to make specific adjustments in the computational system, application that is designed from the approach of the principles of interaction and accessibility [7]. Consequently, it is found that the design of computer application interfaces that support the treatment of ASD must be based on the use of their own models, such as MPIu+a integrated to serious game models for the development of customized and appropriate solutions in each case particular [16, 17].

A new literature review should contain the identification or design of a framework for the design of inclusive computational applications based on the use of specific software architecture standards; however, these should be adjusted to the extent that the therapeutic and technical conditions for the autistic disorder. The MPIu+a model continues to be a guide for the process of usability and accessibility engineering par excellence, however, in particular cases of disability it may require some methodological adjustment to achieve the desired objectives.

Finally, it should be taken into account that the design of computer applications to support the treatment of children with ASD should include the design of adequate interfaces (preferably non-invasive), functional diversity and guarantee an appropriate game interaction for cases of ASD. In this, the use of usability models and human-computer interaction would be of great help.

References

1. González, R.M.M., Ibarra, N.A.: Emotional intelligence in education. Complutense J. Educ. 27(2), 887–888 (2016)
2. Calle Marquez, M.G., Remolina De Claves, N.: Incidence of emotional intelligence in the learning process. Nova - scientific publication in biomedical sciences, vol. 112 (2011)
3. Villalta, R., Sánchez Cabaco, A., Villa Estevez, J.: Design of digital applications for people with ASD. Int. J. Dev. Educ. Psycol. 4(1), 291–297 (2012). National Association of Evolutionary and Educational Psychology of Children, Adolescents and Seniors Badajoz, España (2012)
4. Repeto Gutierrez, S.: Nature of autistic spectrum disorders. General developmental disorders: an approach from practice, vol. 1. Consejería de la educación. Junta de Andalucía (2010)
5. Molina Montes, A.: How to promote communication in students with autism spectrum disorder. General developmental disorders: an approach from practice, vol. 1. Consejería de la educación. Junta de Andalucía (2010)
6. Gortázar, P.: The educational response to difficulties in the field of communication and language. Educational intervention in autism. Jornadas de autismo, Tenerife (2001)

7. Martín Rodríguez, M., Del, C.: The TEACCH response in the classroom for students within the autistic spectrum. Educational intervention in autism. Jornadas de autismo. Tenerife (2001)
8. Muñoz, R., Kreisel, S.: Proyect@Emociones: software to stimulate the development of empathy in children with autism spectrum disorders. In: Conference Paper recuperado de (2012). www.researchgate.net/publication/234166847
9. University Conference on Educational Technology (JUTE 2011), Universidad de Sevilla, España. Information and Communication Technologies (ICT) in the Teaching and Learning Process of Students with Autistic Spectrum Disorder (ASD) (2011). http://congreso.us.es/jute2011/es/comunicaciones.php
10. Liddy, E., Paik, W., McKenna, M.: User interface and other enhancements for natural language information retrieval system and method (2016)
11. Liu, W.: Natural user interface- next mainstream product user interface. In: 2010 IEEE 11th International Conference on Computer-Aided Industrial Design and Conceptual Design (CAIDCD) (2011)
12. Cawood, S., Fiala, M.: Augmented Reality: A Practical Guide. The Pragmatic Bookshelf (2008). ISBN 978–1-93435-603-6
13. Contreras, V., Fernandez, D.: Gestural interfaces for children suffering from Autism Spectrum Disorder. Systems and Communications Department, National University of José C. Paz, Leandro N. Alem 4731, José C. Paz, Provincia de Buenos Aires, Argentina (2016)
14. Lara Cruz, R., Fernandez, H., Olvera, A.: Kinect interactive platform applied to the treatment of autistic children. Final report of undergraduate thesis in communications and electronics engineering. Instituto politécnico Nacional. México D.F (2013)
15. Renilla, M., Sanchez, A., Estevez, J:. Design of digital applications for people with ASD. Sci. J. Lat. Am. Carib. Spain Portugal. Scientific Information System (2012). http://www.redalyc.org/articulo.oa?id=349832337031
16. Granollers, T.: MPIu+a A methodology that integrates software engineering, human-computer interaction and accessibility in the context of multidisciplinary development teams (2007)
17. Constain Moreno, G.E.: Model proposal for architecture for inclusive computational applications, in the treatment of autista-spectrum disorder. Unplublished. Universidad del Cauca -Colombia (2018)
18. Schopler, E., Mesibov, G.: Behavioral Issues in Autism. Editorial Plenium Press, New York (1994)
19. Schopler, E., Van Bourgondien, M.E.: Preschool Issues in Autism. Editorial Plenium, New York (1993)
20. Ruggieri, V.L., Alberas, C.L.: Therapeutic approaches in autistic spectrum disorders. Neurol. J. **60**(Suplemento 1), S45–S49 (2015)
21. Mulas, F., Ros-Cervera, G., Millá, M.G., Etchepareborda, M.C., Abad, L., Tellez de Meneses, M.: Intervention models in children with autism. Neurol. J. **50**(Suplemento 3), S77–S84 (2010)
22. Mesivob, G., Howley, M.: Access to the curriculum for students with autism spectrum disorders: use of the TEACCH program to favor inclusion (2010)
23. Lang, P.J.: Emotional arousal and activation of the visual cortex: An fRMI analysis. Psychophysiology **35**(2), 199–210 (2010)
24. Adams, D., Oliver, C.: The expression and assessment of emotions and internal states in individuals with severe or profound intellectual disabilities. Clinical Psychology Review **31**(3), 293–306 (2011)
25. Petry, K., y Maes, B.: Identifying expressions of pleasure and displeasure by persons with profound and multiple disabilities. J. Intellect. Dev. Disabil. **31**(1), 28–38 (2006)

26. Lima, M., et al.: Can you know me better? An exploratory study combining behavioural and physiological measurements for an objective assessment of sensory responsiveness in a child with profound intellectual and multiple disabilities. J. Appl. Res. Intellect. Disabil. **25**(6), 522–530 (2012)
27. Vos, P., et al.: Investigating the relationship between observed mood and emotions in people with severe and profound intellectual disabilities. J. Intellect. Disabil. Res. **57**(5), 440–451 (2013)
28. Mendizábal, P., León, E.: Emotional Detection System for a better Support for People with Intellectual Disability. I Encuentro ETORBIZI de Innovación Sociosanitaria, Bilbao, 8–10 Octubre 2012

Graphical User Interface Design Guide for Mobile Applications Aimed at Deaf Children

Leidi J. Enriquez Muñoz[1], Edilson Y. Noguera Zúñiga[1],
Leandro Flórez Aristizábal[2(✉)], Cesar A. Collazos[1], Gloria Daza[1],
Sandra Cano[3], Daniyal M. Alghazzawi[4], and Habib M. Fardoun[4]

[1] IDIS Group, University of Cauca, Popayán, Colombia
{leidi,eynoguera,ccollazo,gdaza}@unicauca.edu.co
[2] GRINTIC Group, Institución Universitaria Antonio José Camacho,
Cali, Colombia
lxexpxe@gmail.com
[3] LIDIS Group, University of San Buenventura, Cali, Colombia
sandra.cano@gmail.com
[4] King Abdulaziz University, Kingdom of Saudi Arabia, Jeddah, Saudi Arabia
{dghazzawi,hfardoun}@kau.edu.sa

Abstract. The objective of this work is to establish a Graphical User Interface (GUI) design guide that will support the development of mobile applications aimed at deaf children. To achieve this goal, this research was carried out by reviewing systematic literature reviews and field research techniques. For data collection, the following research techniques were used: meetings, interviews and observation in order to define the general guidelines that are part of the guide. Based on these guidelines, we proceeded to the design and development of prototypes on paper and functional prototypes of a mobile application for deaf children of an educational institution in the city of Popayán-Colombia. These prototypes were subjected to a usability evaluation using inspection techniques by three (3) different user profiles: Specialists in children with hearing disabilities, children with hearing disabilities, designers and developers. The design guide was validated in a process that involved the teachers and students, considering criteria of identity, design, accessibility, navigation and operation. Based on the results obtained, the final guidelines were determined and, therefore, the development of the GUI design guide for mobile applications aimed at deaf children. This GUI design is a tool that can be used by developers and designers of mobile applications to create new applications that consequently allow the inclusion of this population in the use of new technologies.

Keywords: Design guide · Deaf children · Interface design
Mobile applications

© Springer International Publishing AG, part of Springer Nature 2018
P. Zaphiris and A. Ioannou (Eds.): LCT 2018, LNCS 10924, pp. 58–72, 2018.
https://doi.org/10.1007/978-3-319-91743-6_4

1 Introduction

Hearing loss affects around 32 million children worldwide and the vast majority live in low and middle income countries [1]. Taking into account that the deaf community has sign language as their mother tongue (L1), it is of great importance for them to acquire a written language (L2) through the development of literacy skills [2].

For these children the learning of reading and writing is a challenge, due to their auditory deficit and teaching strategies must be different from those used with hearing children, so it has restrictions on language proficiency at lexical, syntactic and semantic level [3].

One way to address this challenge is to use a different communication method such as sign language, as an alternative to spoken language [4]. This type of language favors the teaching-learning processes of deaf children, since they will be able to develop a complete language in an early stage that will allow them to think, plan, hypothesize, etc. In addition, it can serve as a linguistic basis for the acquisition of the written language because it facilitates its learning as a second language [3, 7].

On the other hand, the technological advance in mobile devices is creating a digital paradigm shift, especially in the way we communicate. Having a mobile device has become a necessity to communicate within a world in constant movement, so you can find a growing trend of communities and mobile social networks [6]. However, there are few studies conducted on this type of communities and networks for disabled users, particularly for the deaf community in a developing country. Taking into account the above-mentioned arguments, there is a need to establish a GUI design guide to support the development of mobile applications aimed at deaf children.

2 Background

Information and communication technologies (ICT) are a great resource for people working with deaf children, because it has characteristics such as high memory capacity, visualization capabilities, sensors, as well as sophisticated artificial intelligence techniques that can be exploited to build educational tools capable of meeting the needs of deaf children in an effective way [7]. Unfortunately, ICT tools base their content not only on images but also on text, which for reasons previously mentioned hinders the use of these by deaf children who have not yet mastered their second language (L2).

Currently, the existing educational software (national or imported) has been developed by expert programmers or systems engineers who have been mainly concerned with the technical aspects neglecting almost completely the characteristics of the user and fundamentally the pedagogical and didactic aspects of the educational goal of the developed tool [8]. However, this should not be happening on these days. The interface of a well-designed software should provide a link or relationship with users, leading them during the learning process and letting them enjoy what they are doing. It is fundamental for developers to base their designs on a set of general principles and guidelines for the design of user interfaces, agreed upon by most experts in the field [9], because when a product follows the standards and design conventions, it is more likely to direct the attention of its users and achieve their objectives while at the same time it can be innovative and attractive [10].

Before the advent of mobile devices, visual language and printed text in an interactive and visually rich format was not possible, since children with hearing problems had to look at a book and then alternate between looking at a screen (television or computer) to watch the video [11]. Now, by integrating videos and texts on the same screen will greatly enhance their learning processes.

In recent years, the design of electronic tools (e-tools) for children has increased and guidelines have been proposed for the design of this type of tools. The existing guidelines differentiate children according to their age or sex, and not according to other cognitive characteristics such as the ability to understand text, visual attention and memory skills. However, these and other skills turn out to be crucial in designing usable and accessible electronic tools for deaf people. For instance, reading skills of deaf people are lagging behind compared to their hearing peers, while visual-perceptual skills of deaf people are generally considered as equal or even more developed than their hearing peers. These differences require guidelines for the design of electronic tools that are usable and accessible for deaf people in general, and for deaf children in particular [12]. That is why the need arises to carry out the present research that proposes a guide to the design of graphical user interfaces for mobile applications aimed at deaf children.

3   Related Works

Table 1 lists some studies that contain different guidelines for designing games for deaf children, methodologies used for teaching to deaf children, applications aimed at the deaf population and the process of how those applications were developed.

Table 1. Related works

Work	Example
Applying User Interface Design Process Model for a Mobile Community Project for the Deaf [6]	DHearT design document, a mobile social network for users with hearing impairments in Malaysia to close the communication gap between deaf and hearing groups. This document illustrates and discusses the user interface design process model with its design methods and human factors techniques for a mobile community project for the deaf, specifically DHearT
Propuesta metodológica centrada en usuarios sordos [13]	This work presents a development methodology that adopts a user-centered design, with the purpose of promoting the construction of interactive environments for this community of people with different

(*continued*)

Table 1. (*continued*)

Work	Example
	capacities, realities and contexts. It proposes a model that includes the Deaf user from the beginning of the product development and throughout the process. This proposal has been validated empirically through the design of two computer systems for adolescent and young Deaf users, with medium level of literacy
Guidelines for design of a Mobile phone application for deaf people [14]	The objective of the research was getting to know the barrier of communication and a series of variables that can influence the user experience of a deaf user. Topics like user interface, usability and interaction were researched
Diseño y Responsabilidad Social: Una propuesta multimedial para niños con discapacidad auditiva [15]	This research shows that design is an important tool for real integration. The educational materials are designed for children without disabilities; and it is the disabled who must adapt to it

4 Design of the Guide

Designing interfaces that are easy to use for deaf children is not a simple task. Common interfaces are designed so that the use of audio helps users to interact easily with it, but when deaf users interact with these types of interfaces, they may face some difficulties and may need more time to perform tasks This is why the developers of applications for deaf children must understand their characteristics, capacities and needs when designing the interfaces, considering the general guidelines for their development and taking into account the specific guidelines and characteristics for these children [16]. During the process of research and construction of the GUI design guide for mobile applications aimed at deaf children, the process model of usability and accessibility engineering was integrated (MPIu+a) [17], which allowed a thorough research of important aspects of the deaf children population and thus form a set of guidelines that are reflected in the aforementioned design guide.

The research was carried out in collaboration with La Pamba Educational Institution in the city of Popayán (Colombia). This Institution has a basic classroom for the deaf, where support is provided in the educational process to children and young deaf people through the learning and use of their mother tongue. For specific reasons to the project, the case study consisted of 5 children (3 boys and 2 girls) from the first grades of school, aged between 7 and 14 years. The group of children are profound deaf.

When integrating the MPIu+a model, which is an iterative model, the phases used were: Software engineering (requirements and design analysis), prototyping and evaluation. This model is based on the user, and it is the user who decides whether a design or development is friendly or not. This model allowed the construction of the design guide, the prototype based on such guide and its validation.

4.1 Requirements Analysis

The bibliography referring to the design of interfaces for the construction of mobile applications for children was reviewed. Meetings were held with specialists and teachers responsible for teaching deaf children to obtain pedagogical recommendations that are applicable in the construction of mobile applications for this population. In addition, field work was done using the observation technique to identify the different activities that specialists, in therapies for deaf children, use in communication. In the same way, the abilities and difficulties of children when interacting with the environment were taken into account during the case study. In this way, different aspects were determined that may affect in one way or another the design of the interface for a deaf child. Based on the above, the guidelines that were part of the guide of design were presented and validated through a prototype.

4.2 Design + Prototype

The design and development of a mobile application based on the guidelines of the design guide in the previous phase was carried out. For this process, some of the previously identified activities were taken as a basis.

In the first two iterations, a prototype of low fidelity was built through the use of paper that allowed to have a first approximation of the design. In the following iterations, a functional prototype was developed in order to carry out a continuous improvement of the guidelines of the design guide. All this was done taking into account the opinions and recommendations of the experts and the case study who were involved throughout the process.

4.3 Evaluation + Prototype

In this phase, the guidelines of the design guide were validated through the prototype with the case study and the collaboration of experts in the education of deaf children, designers and developers of mobile applications.

In the process of construction of the prototype, the experts made a descriptive evaluation of each applied guideline, giving their opinions, recommendations and suggestions, and rated each guideline between 1 and 10 to determine the degree of importance as a guideline, being 1 the lowest rating and 10 the highest rating. The guidelines valued between 1 and 4 were not part of the design guide, those valued between 5 and 7 were reviewed and rethought for a second review and finally the guidelines valued between 8 and 10 were included in the design guide.

The prototype was tested in the case study so that it was observed and recorded the interaction and reactions that occurred during this process to later perform an analysis with the help of experts.

4.4   GUI Design Guide

Based on the results of the different evaluations, the design guide was divided into 6 categories which are style, components, patterns, learning, content and general. Due to the extension of all the guidelines, to have access to the final version of the guide, go to the website: https://www.guiaappssordos.com.

5   Development and Validation of the Design Guide

The process of construction and validation of the design guide was carried out in three iterations that are briefly described below.

In the first iteration through the review of the literature, suggestions from experts and related works, a set of guidelines were compiled, which would be the basis of the design guide. Three prototypes were also developed based on the above guidelines. The first prototype was on paper and was based on an existing application called *'cocosigna'*. The second version of the prototype, also on paper, contains the suggestions received and this second version of the paper prototype led to a first functional prototype for Android devices. It is noteworthy that the prototype activities were taken based on the pedagogical material called *Programa de desarrollo de habilidades básicas*[1][18] level 1 to 4. The functional prototype had 20 activities which were divided into two levels.

Among the main features of the design of the prototype are that it has a start screen, indications within the activities with videos in sign language represented by an avatar, in the same way it has the stimulation for achievements at the end of an activity and a trophy reward system. It was also added that, when finishing a task correctly, congratulate the children through the avatar.

In the second iteration the design guide was refined based on the suggestions, evaluation of the guidelines and observation of the deaf children's interaction with the application that was made in the previous iteration and a new version of the prototype was made functional, where the main changes made were the addition of a welcome screen to attract the attention of children and generate curiosity and interest, with the aim of continuing to interact with it. Indications and labels were also added to the main elements of the activities. In addition, a context interface was added, which aims to show the word and image in a specific context so that the child makes connections between the word and its meaning. In the same way, for the different activities, visual effects were added to feed the children after performing an action.

For the first iteration, the design guide was refined based on the evaluation of guide-lines in the previous iteration and the recommendations and observation of the inter-action of the application with deaf children. Based on this guide a final prototype is built to which new levels and activities were added, thus allowing to apply most of the guidelines of the guide, in the same way videos were included in sign language recorded by a certified interpreter and a linguistic model.

---

[1] This material is designed to support and encourage the development of skills in literacy and basic skills how the recognition of equal, different elements, associations between elements, among others.

The evaluation of the guide and validation through the prototype, in each one of the iterations was carried out by means of inspection techniques: cognitive walkthrough and heuristic evaluation, which were chosen taking into account the profiles of the users that would evaluate the guidelines of the guide and the prototype. These are:

- Specialists in children with hearing disabilities.
- Children with hearing disability.
- Designers and software developers

5.1   Definition of Metrics

The selected metrics that allowed to objectively measure the results that were obtained from the evaluations carried out were:

Score Guidelines: It consisted of giving a score to each of the guidelines based on the specific usability criteria taken into account to perform the heuristic evaluation, these criteria are: Identity, design, accessibility, navigation and operation. This metric is used for the heuristic evaluation.

The score for each guideline is between 1 and 10, to determine the degree of importance as a guideline, with 1 being the lowest rating and 10 the highest qualification.

The ranges proposed below are analyzed, reviewed and approved by the different experts who proposed that the first rank has greater breadth in comparison with the other ranges so that the guidelines that will be part of the design guide are filtered. The two remaining ranges are distributed equally. The ranges are posed as follows:

- The guidelines valued between 1 and 4 will not be part of the design guide.
- The guidelines valued between 5 and 7 will be reviewed and restated for a second evaluation.
- The guidelines valued between 8 and 10 will be included in the design guide.

Metrics: Number of Errors - Activities Completed. The metrics of number of errors and completed activities were selected because they are the most relevant measures when interacting with the application, since they provide important information for the validation of the usability. Therefore, completing the activities satisfactorily and a smaller number of errors can indicate the understanding of the tasks to be performed within the application. Table 2 shows the metrics with their respective description.

Table 2. Description of metrics for the evaluation of cognitive walkthrough.

Metric	Description	Interpretation
Completed activities (A)	This metric refers to the number of activities that you complete successfully without asking for help from someone else	The more activities completed successfully, the value of the metric approaches one (1)
Amount of errors (E)	This metric refers to the number of errors that the child can make when giving an answer in each of the activities and when interacting with an element within the interface	This metric refers to the number of errors that the child can make when giving an answer in each of the activities and when interacting with an element within the interface

5.2   Metric Normalization

Once the measurements associated with each metric have been obtained, the values are normalized using the formula presented in the image (see Fig. 1) in order to better analyze the data. For the formula, the maximum and minimum values of the sample must be obtained and X is the measurement obtained during the evaluation associated with the metric.

$$Z = \frac{x - min}{max - min}$$

5.3   Smiley Meter Evaluation

For the evaluation using the Smiley Meter scale [19], 3 palettes were used indicating the degree of satisfaction of the children with the application (see Fig. 1). With the help of the teacher and the linguistic model, the children were asked how they felt when interacting with each prototype in each of the iterations, and in turn, the children explained to the teacher how they felt when interacting with each using sign language and the teacher translated the responses of the children to us.

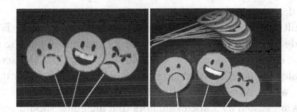

Fig. 1. Palettes used in the evaluation smiley meter.

5.4   Results of the Evaluation

Because there are two types of evaluation techniques, the result of the evaluation will be shown in each iteration of the research organized by user profile.

User Profiles: Specialists in Children with Hearing Disabilities, Designers and Developers.

Cognitive Walkthrough Analisys. The evaluation of the different prototypes in each iteration is carried out, applying the technique of cognitive walkthrough to the specialist teacher in children with auditory disability, to the designers and developers, where they are assigned a series of tasks that must be performed interacting with the different prototypes.

After completing the tasks, the evaluators make different observations and recommendations among which it is very important that all the instructions are accompanied by images or videos in sign language, since this is the mother tongue of deaf children. In the same way, they indicated that the most important information should be highlighted. On the other hand, the expert teacher recommends that when an element of an activity is shown, the image should be used accompanied by its corresponding word and a phrase that puts the word in context, since day-to-day words are used in complete sentences (e.g. "I saw a big beautiful mountain"). Designers and developers recommend making a welcome screen to capture the child's attention and make the application more eye-catching. The use of animals is proposed, since these attract the attention of the child.

The specialist teacher considered it necessary to change the avatar for a person to guide the children through the different activities in the videos shown in the prototype, since the gestures performed by the avatar are not natural compared to the gestures made by a person. In addition, the use of interpreters trained in Colombian sign language is recommended.

Heuristic Evaluation. For the heuristic evaluation, we counted on the collaboration of 5 evaluators, among them experts in children with hearing disabilities, designers and developers, who are presented with a form to fill in which each of the guidelines must be qualified based on compliance with the criteria of specific usability: design, accessibility, navigation, operation.

The heuristic evaluation of the guidelines is carried out taking into account the functional prototype built in the design phase of the second iteration and analyzed during the cognitive walkthrough, since this prototype allows to see most of the guidelines applied.

With the result of the different evaluations, a comparative table is generated for each category and subcategory to average the results and thus obtain the guidelines that will be part of the design guide, review the guidelines that obtained scores between 5 and 7 and eliminate the guidelines that are not considered necessary or do not apply for the design guide, which were rated with scores between 1 and 4.

Likewise, it is suggested by some evaluators that the guide should be restructured in terms of categories and subcategories, since some guidelines are found in categories that do not correspond and there are very extensive categories that can be divided into subcategories. On the other hand, the evaluators make recommendations on the guidelines in terms of wording and the terminology used, thus avoiding technical words and drafting guidelines that are understandable for both expert designers and developers and for inexperienced people who wish to make an application for deaf children.

User Profile: Children with Hearing Impairment

Cognitive Walkthrough Analisys. For the analysis of cognitive walkthrough tasks are assigned to deaf children with the help of the teacher and the linguistic model. Each of the deaf children performed the different activities with the functional prototype and at the same time they took note of the different difficulties they presented during the interaction with it. In the same way, the details that caught their attention and the different elements that allowed the child to interact without problems with the prototype were observed. It was noted that the elements of stimulation for each activity successfully completed and the feedback elements within the prototype caught the attention of the children and made it easier for them to understand what happened when performing an action. In the same way, the stimuli and rewards managed to capture the child's attention.

On the other hand, the videos in sign language made by trained interpreters were clear and understandable for the children, which allowed them to carry out some of the activities without asking for help from the teacher. The number of errors made within an activity decreased markedly, since they paid attention to the indication given by the interpreter in the video and then carried out the activity.

Once the cognitive walkthrough analysis is completed, the children are evaluated on the prototype by means of the Smiley Meter survey, which consisted of asking questions about aspects of the prototype with the help of the linguistic model and the teacher. The children answered with palettes indicating how they felt using the prototype of the application or if they liked or not each of the activities, colors, images, etc.

Results of the Cognitive Walkthrough for Each Iteration.

Second iteration. The prototype had the following 5 activities:

- ACT1: Find the images that look like the model
- ACT2: Find the repeated image
- ACT3: Find the differences between 2 images
- ACT4: Search for the image without a match
- ACT5: Search for specific objects

The results of the Smiley meter survey are shown below in Table 3. Even though 5 children participated in the evaluation of the prototypes, only 4 were part of the

Table 3. Survey results Smiley meter first functional prototype

Participants	Answer
Participant 1	S/he raises the palette with a happy face and answers: "I felt good. Although I did not understand very well what I had to do but it was fun. I liked dogs"
Participant 2	S/he raises the palette with a happy face and answers: "I felt good. I won many times"
Participant 3	S/he raises the palette with the happy face and answers: "I felt good, I was not angry or anything, I was happy working. I did not like the monster that appeared"
Participant 4	S/he raises the palette with a happy face and answers: "I was fine. I felt happy even though it seemed a bit complicated"
Participant 5	The child did not want to be part of this evaluation

During the execution of the cognitive walkthrough technique, the measures associated with the metrics are taken, number of errors (E) and number of times they requested help (A) and the normalization of the data obtained for each of the activities of the prototype (see Table 4) where (En) represents the normalized value of the number of errors made by each child and (An) (see Table 5) that represents each of the times the children requested help. The NAV column represents

Table 4. Errors made with the first functional prototype

Participant	ACT1		ACT2		ACT3		ACT4		ACT5		NAV	
	E	En	E	En	E	En	E	En	E	En	E	En
Participant 1	15	0,29	11	0,46	7	0,29	20	0,74	11	0,31	0	0,00
Participant 2	25	0,48	13	0,54	15	0,63	24	0,89	15	0,42	1	0,07
Participant 3	17	0,33	7	0,29	16	0,67	15	0,56	20	0,56	2	0,13
Participant 4	13	0,25	4	0,17	17	0,71	15	0,56	9	0,25	1	0,07
Participant 5	15	0,29	6	0,25	9	0,38	17	0,63	7	0,19	0	0,00

Table 5. Activities in which they requested help with the first functional prototype.

Participant	ACT1		ACT2		ACT3		ACT4		ACT5	
	A	An	A	An	A	An	A	An	A	An
Participant 1	4	0,27	1	0,07	1	0,07	2	0,13	2	0,13
Participant 2	12	0,80	6	0,40	15	1,00	3	0,20	7	0,47
Participant 3	9	0,60	4	0,27	13	0,87	4	0,27	8	0,53
Participant 4	5	0,33	3	0,20	8	0,53	1	0,07	7	0,47
Participant 5	2	0,13	2	0,13	5	0,33	2	0,13	4	0,27

In this first evaluation of the functional prototype it can be seen that the high values presented in Tables 4 and 5 are mainly due to the fact that it was the first time they interacted with the application, so it was difficult for them to understand from the beginning the dynamics of each one of the activities and had the need to ask for help to understand them.

On the other hand, the children are just beginning to familiarize themselves with the written word, therefore the texts were not very helpful to carry out the activity.

Table 4 shows that the activities in which most of the children made most of the errors were the activity of *finding the 4 differences* and *finding the image without a match*. The errors made in the activity *find the 4 differences* are due to the fact that the model image and the image they had to interact with to select the differences were not clear. On the other hand, the activity of *finding the image without a match* generates confusion in the child since the concept *"Without a match"* is not easy to explain and the signs given by the avatar were not clear to the child. For the rest of the activities the children asked a few times and with the explanation given to them, they carried out the activities. The amount of errors in general of all the activities is also due to the lack of response of the application in front of an incorrect action of the child within the activities, for instance, in the activity to *find the images equal to the model*, if the child played an element that did not correspond to the model image, the system did not take any action to inform the child that his response was incorrect, however when he selected the correct answer it was hidden implying that the option was chosen.

For the navigation within the application there were few errors made by 3 children, who used the *back button* of the device without having an answer, then they realized that there was an arrow that took them back inside the application.

Third Iteration. The children were asked how they felt with the application and everyone answered with the happy face palette. In the same way, they were asked if it was easy to use, all the children answered with the happy face palette except for one of the girls who put her face down and indicated that it was difficult for her to perform two of the activities of level 1 and 2 (see Table 6).

Table 6. Evaluation results with smiley meter scale of the second functional prototype

Participants	Answer
Participant 1	S/he raises the palette with a happy face and answers: "I felt happy doing the exercises although the video did not understand it well"
Participant 2	S/he raises the palette with a happy face and answers: "I felt good and did all the activities"
Participant 3	S/he raises his palette with a happy face and answers: "I felt good but sometimes I got confused and asked David (linguistic model)"
Participant 4	S/he raises the palette with a sad face and answers: "I felt sad because I could not do some of the activities"
Participant 5	S/he raises the palette with happy face and answers: "I felt good because I could do all the activities"

During this process, the different measures associated with the metrics of number of errors (E) and number of times they requested help (A) are taken and the data obtained in each of the activities of the prototype are normalized.

It can be seen that, for this second evaluation of the functional prototype with children, the values dropped considerably compared to the first evaluation made in the previous iteration, this is because they had already interacted one time with the application, so the number of times they asked for help was less. In addition, the feedback provided in the activities was meaningful for the children and did not need help to understand that they had selected a right or wrong answer.

The different videos with the explanations given by an avatar within the activities were not taken into account by the children, so the number of questions on the indications of the activities *Find the differences* or *find the image without a match* was high.

At the end of the activities, the children observed the context interface where they can understand the meaning of the element that is shown in each activity and associate it with a real life context, relying on the sign and the written word, which attracts a lot of attention and it generates emotion when they see it.

Final Evaluation. During the Smiley Meter survey with the support of the expert teacher and the linguistic model, the children were asked how they felt with the application and everyone answered raising the palette with the happy face and gave their opinion. Similarly, they were asked if they found it easy to use (see Table 7). Three children were part of this final evaluation.

Expert Reviews. Regarding the opinions given by the experts about the final prototype, they concluded that the videos with people trained in sign language are better than

Table 7. Survey results smiley meter with the final prototype

Participant	How did you feel about the application?	Did you find it easy or difficult to use?
Participant 1	S/he raises the palette with a happy face and responds: "I felt very happy, because for example sometimes I lost, so I could learn the right sign, I had to have a lot of patience. In the video when I could see Juan David doing the signal, then that already gave me an idea of what I had to work with, so it seemed very important to me. When the cat came out was also the interpreter with the sign, I also liked very much to see the animals and the drawings that were shown there, very beautiful, sometimes I had to repeat an exercise because I was wrong but I had many trophies, I was very patient and I I liked it very much, I was very calm doing the activity"	"It seemed very easy to me, I felt very happy doing the activity, I started to think very well what the signal was, what was the drawing, then I was able to work and it gave very well with the answer that I was asked, then I thought it was the right answer and I had it right, when the words were there, I spelled them and I also said if it is a horse, or it is another animal, then I was fine, suddenly very hot but well". He adds: For example, I could do very fast with what I was asked in the application, sometimes I asked for some explanation, but then I could work very well with the application with each of the images in the activities that were requested"
Participant 2	S/he raises the palette with a happy face and respond: "I felt very happy with the application for the tablet, I was fine, I was working on all the activities that were shown there, also when I saw the signs of Mauricio (interpreter), when I saw the signs of the animals then I could do the activities"	"When I was working with the tablet, it seemed easy, sometimes I could not, sometimes I had to repeat the activity that was requested, but anyway I tried hard and until I could get it right, it was neither so difficult nor so easy"
Participant 3	S/he raises the palette with a happy face and respond: "I felt very happy when I saw the application of the tablet, there was the rabbit, the dog, the horse, the cat, I liked it very much"	"For example, with the rabbit it seemed very, very easy, I had to think very well about what animals it was, whether the horse, rabbit or dog, but I could make it easy"

the avatar that was used previously and the improvement in the ease of interaction can be clearly observed with the prototype. In the same way, the help presented is clear and easy to understand.

Similarly, they believe that the guide can be applied to different types of content and promote different types of perceptual concepts that the deaf child should know as a first instance, for example, reading and writing, concepts of quantity, many, few, more, less, long, short.

6 Conclusions

The existing mobile apps reviewed and the existing gaps identified during the document review process, show that most of the applications that are aimed at deaf children have been developed without taking into account the specific needs of them, in addition to the content that is shown, it is not oriented to teaching or reinforcement of learning, since they mostly show images and text, without this representing any meaning for the children.

The qualitative research process was carried out to identify the needs of deaf children in terms of the GUI design needs of mobile applications aimed at these children. Through the recommendations of experts, observation of the interaction of the case study with mobile applications and review of related works, the needs of deaf children are identified and the design of inclusive tools is necessary, this can be seen in the notable lack of availability of mobile applications aimed at deaf children.

In the educational field, applications can be potentially significant in the process of acquiring new knowledge as long as the content is adequate and its graphic interfaces are designed to break the communication barriers between the child and the application.

There is a need for an artifact for developers and designers of mobile applications who wish to develop applications/games for deaf children, which allows them to cover the needs of deaf children, for which the design guide proposed in this research is oriented to cover this need.

A prototype of an application was designed and developed based on the design guide proposed for the learning or reinforcement of some subjects such as animals or objects of the house, through mini games. The validation of the prototype carried out with the case study yielded very positive approval concepts, as well as the evaluation of the experts.

The validation of the design guide was carried out along with the teachers and students, considering criteria of identity, design, accessibility, navigation and operation. From the results obtained, it can be affirmed that there was acceptance of all the aspects related to the evaluated criteria. This allows us to conclude that the GUI design for mobile applications aimed at deaf children, is a tool that can help developers and designers of mobile applications to create new tools that consequently allow the inclusion of this population in the use of these new technologies.

References

1. Organización Mundial de la salud, Pérdida de audición en la niñez, Organización Mundial de la Salud (2016). [En línea]. Disponible en: https://goo.gl/0eWSkW. Accedido 14 Oct 2016
2. Andrade Sánchez, E.M.: Diseño e implementación de un prototipo para un Centro de Relevo enfocado a personas con discapacidad auditiva. Universidad Politécnica Salesiana (2015)
3. Ruiz Linares, E.: El aprendizaje de la lectoescritura en los niños y niñas sordos, Caleidoscopio, Rev. Digit. contenidos Educ. no. 2 (2009)
4. Moya, B.S.: Aprendizaje de la lectoescritura en el alumnado con hipoacusia, Universidad de Granada (2015)

5. Alegría, J., Domínguez, B.A.: Los alumnos sordos y la lengua escrita. Rev. Latinoam. Educ. inclusiva **31**(1), 95–111 (2009)
6. Wong, C.Y., Khong, C.W., Thwaites, H.: Applying user interface design process model for a mobile community project for the deaf, iJIM **2**(4), 30–37 (2008)
7. Vettori, C., Mich, O.: Supporting deaf children's reading skills: the many challenges of text simplification. In: The proceedings of the 13th international ACM SIGACCESS conference on Computers and accessibility, pp. 283–284 (2011)
8. Montenegro, S., Saenz, G., Alvarez, E.: La importancia de evaluación de software educativo en Panamá, EDESIGN, (2008). [En línea]. Disponible en: http://emecs.blogspot.com.co/. Accedido 21 Oct 2016
9. Martínez, A.B., Cueva, J.M.: Estándares y guías. España: Universdad de Oviedo (2009)
10. Ortega Santamaria, S.: Introducción a la usabilidad y su evaluación. Universitat Oberta de Catalunya, España (2011)
11. Malzkuhn, M., Herzig, M.: Bilingual storybook app designed for deaf and hard of hearing children based on research principles. In: 12th International Conference Interaction Design and Children, pp. 499–502 (2013)
12. Di Mascio, T., Gennari, R., Melonio, A., Vittorini, P.: Designing games for deaf children: first guidelines. Int. J. Technol. Enhanc. Learn. **5**(3–4), 223–239 (2013)
13. Valenzuela, F.A., Beguerí, G.E., Collazos, C.A.: Propuesta Metodológica Centrada en Usuarios Sordos para el Diseño de Entornos Computacionale, In: Conference LACLO, vol. 5, no. 1, pp. 530–539 (2015)
14. Yeratziotis, G.: Guidelines for the Design of a Mobile Phone Application for Deaf People (2012)
15. Araya, N.J., Ahumada, M., Morales, G.: Diseño y responsabilidad social: Una propuesta multimedial para niños con discapacidad auditiva. In: Actas de Diseño N° 4 II Encuentro Latinoamericano de Diseño 2007 Diseño en Palermo, pp. 108–110 (2009)
16. Patricia, S., Mazuera, C.: Propuesta Metodológica para el Diseño de Juegos Serios para Niños con Implante Coclear, Universidad del Cauca (2016)
17. Granollers, T.: MPIu+a. Una metodologia que integra la ingeniería del software, la interacción persona-ordenador y la accesibilidad en el contexto de equipos de desarrollo multidisciplinares. Universitat de Lleida (2004)
18. Cuatroemes. Programa de Habilidades Básicas (2012). [En línea]. Disponible en: https://goo.gl/BuHHsX. Accedido 01 Feb 2018
19. Ssemugabi, S., de Villiers, R.: A comparative study of two usability evaluation methods using a web-based e-learning application, pp. 132–142 (2007)

Usability Test of WYRED Platform

Francisco J. García-Peñalvo$^{(\boxtimes)}$, Alicia García-Holgado,
Andrea Vázquez-Ingelmo, and Antonio M. Seoane-Pardo

GRIAL Research Group, Research Institute for Educational Sciences,
University of Salamanca, Salamanca, Spain
{fgarcia, aliciagh, andreavazquez, aseoane}@usal.es

Abstract. WYRED (netWorked Youth Research for Empowerment in the Digital society) is a European H2020 Project that aims to provide a framework for research in which children and young people can express and explore their perspectives and interests in relation to digital society, but also a platform from which they can communicate their perspectives to other stakeholders effectively through innovative engagement processes. It will do this by implementing a generative research cycle involving networking, dialogue, participatory research and interpretation phases centered around and driven by children and young people, out of which a diverse range of outputs, critical perspectives and other insights will emerge to inform policy and decision-making in relation to children and young people's needs in relation to digital society. The WYRED Platform is already developed, but the target group, young people, should accept it to ensure project aims. This paper presents the usability test done to evolve the Platform.

Keywords: Human interaction · Usability analysis · Digital society
Youth · Citizen science · Communication networks · Technological ecosystems

1 Introduction

WYRED (netWorked Youth Research for Empowerment in the Digital society) is a European Project funded by the Horizon 2020 programme in its "Europe in a changing world – inclusive, innovative and reflective Societies (HORIZON 2020: REV-INEQUAL-10-2016: Multi-stakeholder platform for enhancing youth digital opportunities)" Call. It is coordinated by the GRIAL Research Group [1] of the University of Salamanca (Spain) and it started at November 2016 and will be developed along three years, until October 2019.

The project aims to provide a framework for research in which children and young people can express and explore their perspectives and interests in relation to digital society, but also a platform from which they can communicate their perspectives to other stakeholders effectively through innovative engagement processes, WYRED is informed by the recognition that young people of all ages have the right to participation and engagement. It has a strong focus on inclusion, diversity and the empowerment of the marginalized. The aim is to replace the disempowering scrutiny of conventional research processes with the empowerment of self-scrutiny and self-organization through the social dialogue and participatory research [2].

© Springer International Publishing AG, part of Springer Nature 2018
P. Zaphiris and A. Ioannou (Eds.): LCT 2018, LNCS 10924, pp. 73–84, 2018.
https://doi.org/10.1007/978-3-319-91743-6_5

To support the framework for research from a technological point of view, a WYRED technological ecosystem has been defined [3]. The WYRED Platform is the component of this complex technological solution that is focused on supporting the social dialogues that take place between children, young people and stakeholders.

The Platform is already developed but it is important to ensure the acceptance by the final users, the children and young people mainly. To achieve this goal, a usability test with real users was carried out. A group of undergraduate students between 18 to 25 years old used the Platform during 3 weeks with different profiles. After the pilot the participants filled the System Usability Scale (SUS) questionnaire anonymously. This paper describes the usability study and analyzes the SUS test results.

Finally, the paper is set out in seven sections. The second and third sections provide a brief description about the WYRED ecosystem and the WYRED project. The fourth section outlines the research methodology; it explains the materials and methods used to evaluate WYRED Platform, the evaluation procedures and the involved participants. The fifth section presents the results. The sixth section is the discussion and the final section concludes the paper with its more significant contributions.

2   The WYRED Ecosystem

There are a large number of definition related to the technological ecosystem concept, but the WYRED ecosystem is based on the natural ecosystem metaphor applied to the technological context. A technological ecosystem is a set of users and software components related to each other through information flows in a physical environment that provides the support for those flows [4–7]. There are two main differences between this technological approach and the traditional information systems: the technological ecosystems have the ability to evolve in different dimensions and people are an element of the ecosystem as important as software components.

The WYRED ecosystem is composed by a set of Open Source tools and the people involved in the project, not only the partners, but also the stakeholders, children and young people. Figure 1 shows the architecture of the ecosystem and the connections among the components. This is not a final solution, the WYRED ecosystem will evolve over time to cover the new requirements provided by the project partners and solve the problems detected during the usability studies, for instance, the results of the study described in this paper.

The architecture is based on the architectural proposal for technological ecosystems defined by García-Holgado [5, 8, 9]. There are three layers that organize the different software components according to their role in the ecosystem - infrastructure, data and services - and two input streams which introduce the human factor as another element of the technological ecosystem. Currently, some components of the architecture are in development phase, in particular the document management system based on Own-Cloud and the indexing service based on ApacheSolr.

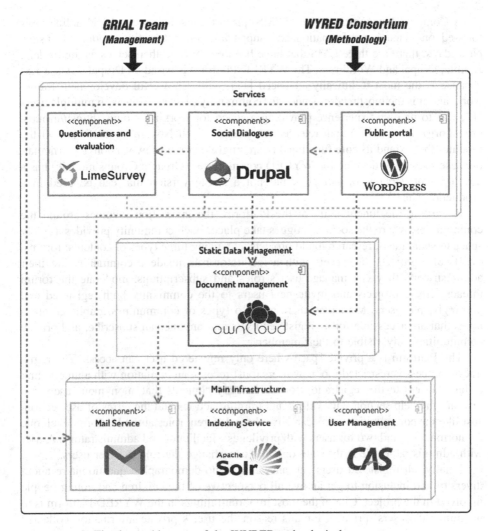

Fig. 1. Architecture of the WYRED technological ecosystem.

3 WYRED Platform

The WYRED Platform (https://platform.wyredproject.eu) is one of the services included in the WYRED ecosystem. A key aim of this project is to engage children and young people in a process of social dialogue giving them a voice to share their thoughts, fears and feelings in relation to digital society. The aim of the WYRED Platform is provided a technological support to these social dialogues.

The WYRED Platform allows an easy interaction process among the involved stakeholders; high-level engagement conditions; a secure environment in which all the participants feel comfortable enough with the privacy issues, but with a special attention to the underage ones; and a suitable dashboard for data analytics [10].

A Content Management System (CMS) provides a solid base to build online tools focused on managing information and supporting the interaction among the users. Nowadays, there are three CMS that have been established themselves as the leaders: Joomla, Drupal and WordPress. The WYRED Platform is based on Drupal (release 7.x) because is the most technically advanced [11], with a powerful development framework, and it is the most recommended for community platform sites with multiple users [12] due to its own experience providing a space for working groups (https://groups.drupal.org). Although Drupal released the version 8 on November 2015, not all the modules that extend its core functionality are migrated to the new version, in particular, the base module to develop the WYRED communities (Organic Groups module) has a development version for Drupal 8 but not a stable version that can be used in a production site.

Regarding the functionality of the Platform, the interaction revolves around the communities, where the social dialogues take place. Each community provides a safety space to share ideas, research, build projects, etc. using three types of contents: forums, events and projects. The users with a facilitator role inside a community are their administrators, they can manage user's roles and subscriptions, moderate the forum threads, create projects and invite new users to the community both registered and non-registered users. Moreover, there are two types of communities, public communities that are accessible for all registered users and anyone can subscribe; and private communities only visible to their members.

The Platform is a private space where only registered user can access. The registration process is restricted too, new users must receive an invitation with a unique link to have access to the registration form. The only contents that anonymous users can visit are the help section with videos and training actions and the terms of use section. Just like the communities, users can have three different roles at the Platform level, one for normal user and two for users with privileges - facilitator and administrator -. A user with administrator role is the only one that can change the role to other users.

Finally, all registered users can answer a socio-demographic questionnaire about diversity and inclusion to get an overall perspective of the children and young people involved in the project. One of the most important things in the WYRED Platform is to maximize the users' privacy, for this reason the user's private information collected during the registration process and with the questionnaire is saved in a different place, not in the Platform.

4   Methodology

4.1   Participants

The study was carried out in the subject of "Communication Techniques and Skills", a mandatory subject for undergraduate students that is taught in the first semester of the first year of the Degree in Social Education of the University of Salamanca (Spain) d. There were 80 students enrolled in the subject in the 2017–18 school year and the experimental group was formed by 77 students divided in 12 work groups. Only 14.29% of the students are men and 85.71% are women, these figures are due to in

Spain the number of female tertiary students that choose studies in the field of social sciences is 60% [13]. Regarding the country of birth, 68 students are from Spain and 9 are foreign (2 Dutch, 1 Argentinian, 1 Belgian, 1 Brazilian, 1 Chinese, 1 Italian, 1 Jamaican and 1 Portuguese); all of them speak Spanish. Table 1 shows the distribution of participants by role in the WYRED Platform, gender and average age.

Table 1. Participants in the usability test

Role	Female	Male	Average age
Facilitators	11	1	20.66
Students	55	10	20.02
Total	66	11	20.12

4.2 Instrumentation

The chosen tool to measure the usability of the Platform was the System Usability Scale (SUS). The SUS questionnaire provides an effective, valid and reliable [14, 15] way to score the usability of a system. In addition, it is an efficient test, given the fact that it only consists of 10 items, and it can be applicable over a wide range of systems [16].

The items of the questionnaires are positive and negative alternated statements (in order to avoid response biases) rated on a 1 to 5 Likert scale (from "strongly disagree" to "strongly agree", respectively) [17].

The validity and reliability provided by this test and the ease of its implementation made the System Usability Scale suitable for the WYRED Platform usability testing.

In addition to the 10 items of the SUS questionnaire, a set of demographic variables were also collected by the instrument: year of birth, gender, birthplace, parents' birthplace, the family's main spoken language, any eye diseases of the user that could affect the experience, the language used in the Platform and the role of the user (student or facilitator). Besides these demographic variables, an open field was provided at the end of the survey to let the users remark any relevant experience during the testing of the Platform. This field adds qualitative feedback to the SUS score (as the score itself it's not diagnostic, only provides an overall usability rating).

The instrument was implemented using a customized version of LimeSurvey (https://www.limesurvey.org), an Open Source on-line statistical survey web application. The instrument was applied in Spanish, but it is also available in English to be used for future usability studies in other partner countries.

4.3 Study Design and Data Collection

The pilot experience was carried in the last weeks of face-to-face classes of the "Communication Techniques and Skills" subject of the Degree in Social Education of the University of Salamanca (Spain) during the 2017–18 school year. One of the main goals of the subject is to address conflict resolution.

During the pilot, the students were divided in 12 work group to promote a series of social dialogues on topics that students considered of their interest and fit into the topics of the WYRED project.

The selection and configuration process of the social dialogues started with the presentation of the proposed topics in a collaborative board using the free version of Padlet (https://padlet.com), a multi-device application to make and share content with others. Then, the topics was explained in a face-to-face class with the purpose of guarantee the widest range of possible topics. Each group selected a different topic and a group member as facilitator.

The aim of the activity was argued about the selected topic using the WYRED Platform to prepare a report in which the following aspects will be reflected:

- Definition and description of the selected topic.
- To what extend the selected topic concern to young people.
- Proposals to solve or improve the state of the problem addressed.
- User experience and proposals to improve the WYRED Platform.

The topics selected by the students to work in the Platform were:

- Gender stereotypes and discrimination.
- Cyberbullying, humiliation and sexting.
- Construction and knowledge of ourselves through education and new technologies.
- Privacy on Internet.
- Stress reasons among young people.
- Young people's access to Deep Web.
- The new influencers in social networks and the false myths.
- Personality in the context of social networks.
- Gender and the digital society.
- Sexting in relation to gender violence and cyberbullying.
- Machismo in the social networks.
- Dangers of the Internet for young people.

After the first phase in classroom, the administrator of the WYRED Platform sent a registration invitation to the selected facilitators (12 students) with the data provided by the teacher. When each one of them finished the registration process, the administrator gave him/her a facilitator role in the Platform because the role cannot be assigned before the user exists in the Platform.

Each facilitator had two different tasks regarding their group mates. First, he/she had to create a community inside the Platform to carry out the activity. Second, the facilitator had to send a registration invitation to each of his/her group mates so that they had to register and start to work in the community.

The pilot experience lasted three weeks: one week to organize the activity and two weeks to use the WYRED Platform to prepare the report.

Regarding the data collection, the teacher sent by email the link to answer the questionnaire two days before the pilot experience ended, and the questionnaire was available for two weeks. During that period, two reminders were sent by the teacher to request more answers.

Moreover, the user interaction of the students was collected using Google Analytics (https://analytics.google.com), a web analytics service offered by Google to track website traffic. The WYRED Platform uses this tool principally to get information about the interactions from the different countries involved in the social dialogues and the used devices to work with the Platform. This information is complemented with the information extracted from the WYRED Platform database in order to get the number of forum threads and comments.

4.4 Analysis

The data collected by the instrument were downloaded to obtain a structured dataset with all the users' answers. This dataset was cleaned to calculate subsequently the SUS score. Although the score calculation is relatively simple [17], the analysis of the responses has been made through the Python Pandas [18] library given its high performance and easy-to-use data structures.

The individual SUS score was calculated for every participant, to finally obtain the average SUS score of the WYRED Platform.

In addition, another analysis has been made taking into account that a technical error was found in the system during the testing. The average SUS score was also calculated for both the group of users exposed to the error and the group of users that tested the Platform after the error was fixed.

The interpretation of the results is based on previous System Usability Scale studies and benchmarks [19, 20] which allow SUS score comparisons and provide insights about the perceived usability of the WYRED system.

All the source code developed for this analysis is available at https://github.com/andvazquez/wyred-sus-hci-2018 [21].

5 Results

5.1 Socio-Demographic Results

From the 70 participants that entered the questionnaire, 43 of them finalized it, with the following socio-demographic characteristics:

- 86.05% students are female and 13.95% male.
- 41 students were born in Spain, 1 in China, 1 in Belgium and 1 in Netherlands.
- 22 students have between 15 to 19 years (51.16%), 20 students have between 20 to 24 years (46.51%), 1 student has between 25 to 29 years (2.33%). The average age is 21 years, approximately.
- 33 participants used the Platform in Spanish (76.75%), 8 participants in English (18.60%) and 2 participants both in Spanish and English (4.65%).
- No users pointed out significant sight diseases that could affect their experience with the platform.

5.2 WYRED Usability Test (SUS) Results

As mentioned before 43 users completed the entire set of questions regarding the usability of the WYRED Platform. According to the literature, the System Usability Scale (SUS) is reliable with a minimum sample size of 12 participants [15]. Consequently, the 43 responses received could yield fairly reliable results.

Although the SUS was originally developed to provide a single score that indicates the (perceived) usability of a system [14], subsequent studies pointed out the two-dimensional nature of this scale [22], allowing the calculation of the system's learnability score (in addition to the usability score). Particularly, from the 10 items that conform the SUS questionnaire, items 4 and 10 can be used to score the learnability of the system being tested, while the remaining items are used to obtain its perceived usability [22].

Taking this into account, the SUS score was calculated following the scoring instructions [17] for every participant's responses. Additionally, the learnability score (from items 4 and 10) and usability score (from items 1, 2, 3, 5, 6, 7, 8 and 9) were also calculated and transformed to fit in a scale from 0 to 100 (as in the original SUS scoring method, in order to allow comparisons).

The calculations yielded the following results [21]:

- The average perceived usability of the WYRED Platform is **65.23**, which can be considered as an acceptable SUS score, as it is close to the average SUS score (68.00) and falls around the 50th percentile (interpretation based on the studies done in [19, 20]).
- On the other hand, the perceived learnability seems to be slightly higher (**66.28**) than the usability (**64.97**), both being acceptable scores.

The Fig. 2. summarizes the outcomes of the SUS questionnaire, also including the individual scores for every participant (represented by overlapping circles) across the three dimensions considered: SUS score, Usability and Learnability.

However, as mentioned in the previous sections, there are some considerations regarding these results: during the evaluation of the WYRED Platform a technical error was found. This issue was resolved over the next 8 days, meaning that some participants were exposed to that error.

Considering this situation, the users were divided into two groups (users who tested the Platform *before* the fix and users who tested the Platform *after* the fix). The SUS score was calculated for each group, reporting new results:

- Group 1 (users who tested the Platform *before* the fix): the average SUS score for the 30 participants belonging to this group is **64.67**, which is lower than the general one. Learnability and Usability scores are **65.27** and **64.48**, respectively.
- Group 2 (users who tested the Platform *after* the fix): in this case, the 13 users from this group gave an average SUS score of **66.54** (slightly higher than the SUS score obtained from the whole set of users). For these users, Learnability and Usability scores (**68.27** and **66.11**, respectively) fall closer to the average SUS score, based on the literature.

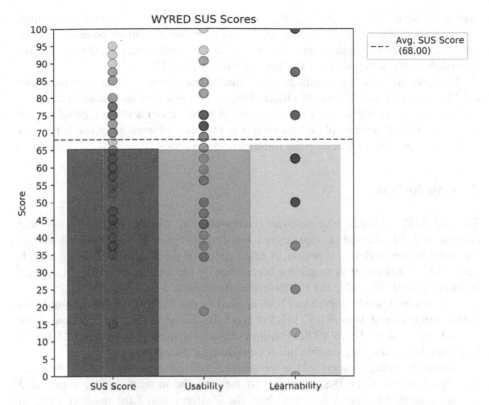

Fig. 2. Visual representation of the SUS questionnaire results regarding the WYRED Platform usability and learnability scores.

6 Discussion

The average usability of the WYRED Platform for 43 students is 65.23, which, as commented in the previous section, is an acceptable score, although it is below the average of perceived usability in web systems (68) [16]. Specifically, this score is in the "marginal high" in terms of the acceptability ranges, and falls in the "OK" and "Good" interval as defined in the SUS adjective ratings [19]. The same interpretation applies to the individual Learnability and Usability scores.

While the results can be considered as acceptable, it also reveals that the WYRED Platform usability can be improved. The SUS score gives only an overall rating for the system's usability, but the comments collected along with the survey give hints about what features to be improved or about what factors lowered the scores.

For example, there were complaints about the language of the Platform, for which translation is in progress.

In addition, some participants mentioned the technical error found during the testing (an issue that affected the login tool). This issue was mitigated and the users that completed the questionnaire after the fix rated the usability of the system better (with an average score of 66.54). Although the sample size of this set of users is lower than group that tested the Platform before the fix (13 users against 30 users, respectively), the results obtained from this segment of users is equally valid, because the sample size is enough to apply the SUS test (at least 12 participants [22]).

However, the collected comments also reflected that although some users rated low the Platform, they felt that the WYRED Platform is a practical and valuable tool.

To sum up, the application of the SUS test provided insights about the usability of the WYRED Platform and placed the system in the acceptable range of usability, with room for improvement based on the questionnaire feedback.

7   Conclusions

The WYRED Platform is a software component of the WYRED technological ecosystem that is focused on supporting the social dialogues about the digital society between children and young people. A first version of the Platform is already developed, but it is important to ensure the acceptance by the final users and to know their opinions in order to evolve the Platform and, therefore the ecosystem.

The System Usability Score has been applied to the WYRED platform in order to obtain insights about its usability. This test is not diagnostic; it gives an overview of the usability of a system. The WYRED Platform obtained an average score of 65.23, which is a score below the average (68) but is considered a decent result.

However, adding an open field in the questionnaire for comments gave hints about the improvements to be made in order to increase the usability. Also, it provided feedback about the general thoughts about the Platform, being the majority of them positive.

There are a number of important changes which need to be made in the WYRED Platform to improve the SUS score. Future works will be focus on solving some technical problems detected by the participants and the experts during the pilot experience, which could influence in the study results.

Acknowledgments. This research work has been carried out within the University of Salamanca PhD Programme on Education in the Knowledge Society scope (http://knowledgesociety.usal.es) and was supported by the Spanish *Ministry of Education, Culture and Sport* under a FPU fellowship (FPU014/04783).

With the support of the EU Horizon 2020 Programme in its "Europe in a changing world – inclusive, innovative and reflective Societies (HORIZON 2020: REV-INEQUAL-10-2016: Multi-stakeholder platform for enhancing youth digital opportunities)" Call. Project WYRED (netWorked Youth Research for Empowerment in the Digital society) (Grant agreement No 727066). The sole responsibility for the content of this webpage lies with the authors. It does not necessarily reflect the opinion of the European Union. The European Commission is not responsible for any use that may be made of the information contained therein.

This work has been partially funded also by the Spanish Government Ministry of Economy and Competitiveness throughout the DEFINES project (Ref. TIN2016-80172-R).

References

1. García-Peñalvo, F.J., Rodríguez-Conde, M.J., Seoane-Pardo, A.M., Conde-González, M.A., Zangrando, V., García-Holgado, A.: GRIAL (GRupo de investigación en InterAcción y eLearning), USAL. IE Comunicaciones: Revista Iberoamericana de Informática Educativa 85–94 (2012)
2. García-Peñalvo, F.J., Kearney, N.A.: Networked youth research for empowerment in digital society: the WYRED project. In: García-Peñalvo, F.J. (ed.) Proceedings of the Fourth International Conference on Technological Ecosystems for Enhancing Multiculturality (TEEM 2016), Salamanca, Spain, 2–4 November 2016, pp. 3–9. ACM, New York (2016)
3. García-Peñalvo, F.J.: The WYRED Project: a Technological platform for a generative research and dialogue about youth perspectives and interests in digital society. J. Inf. Technol. Res. **9**, vi-x (2016)
4. García-Holgado, A., García-Peñalvo, F.J.: The evolution of the technological ecosystems: an architectural proposal to enhancing learning processes. In: Proceedings of the First International Conference on Technological Ecosystem for Enhancing Multiculturality (TEEM 2013), Salamanca, Spain, 14–15 November 2013, pp. 565–571. ACM, New York (2013)
5. García-Holgado, A., García-Peñalvo, F.J.: Architectural pattern to improve the definition and implementation of eLearning ecosystems. Sci. Comput. Program. **129**, 20–34 (2016)
6. García-Peñalvo, F.J., García-Holgado, A. (eds.): Open Source Solutions for Knowledge Management and Technological Ecosystems. IGI Global, Hershey (2017)
7. García-Holgado, A., García-Peñalvo, F.J.: Preliminary validation of the metamodel for developing learning ecosystems. In: Dodero, J.M., Ibarra Sáiz, M.S., Ruiz Rube, I. (eds.) Proceedings of the 5th International Conference on Technological Ecosystems for Enhancing Multiculturallty (TEEM 2017), Cadiz, Spain, 18–20 October 2017. ACM, New York (2017)
8. García-Holgado, A., García-Peñalvo, F.J.: Architectural pattern for the definition of eLearning ecosystems based on Open Source developments. In: Sierra-Rodríguez, J.L., Dodero-Beardo, J.M., Burgos, D. (eds.) Proceedings of 2014 International Symposium on Computers in Education (SIIE), Logroño, La Rioja, Spain, 12–14 November 2014, pp. 93–98. Institute of Electrical and Electronics Engineers. IEEE Catalog Number CFP1486T-ART (2014)
9. García-Holgado, A., García-Peñalvo, F.J.: A metamodel proposal for developing learning ecosystems. In: Zaphiris, P., Ioannou, A. (eds.) LCT 2017. LNCS, vol. 10295, pp. 100–109. Springer, Cham (2017). https://doi.org/10.1007/978-3-319-58509-3_10
10. García-Peñalvo, F.J., Durán-Escudero, J.: Interaction design principles in WYRED platform. In: Zaphiris, P., Ioannou, A. (eds.) LCT 2017. LNCS, vol. 10296, pp. 371–381. Springer, Cham (2017). https://doi.org/10.1007/978-3-319-58515-4_29
11. http://websitesetup.org/cms-comparison-wordpress-vs-joomla-drupal/
12. http://www.rackspace.com/knowledge_center/article/cms-comparison-drupal-joomla-and-wordpress
13. Ministerio de Educación Cultura y Deporte: Datos y cifras del sistema universitario español. Curso 2015/2016. Ministerio de Educación, Cultura y Deporte (2016)
14. Brooke, J.: SUS: a retrospective. J. Usability Stud. **8**, 29–40 (2013)
15. Tullis, T.S., Stetson, J.N.: A comparison of questionnaires for assessing website usability. In: Usability Professional Association Conference, pp. 1–12 (2004)
16. Bangor, A., Kortum, P.T., Miller, J.T.: An empirical evaluation of the system usability scale. Int. J. Hum.-Comput. Interact. **24**, 574–594 (2008)

17. Brooke, J.: SUS-A quick and dirty usability scale. In: Usability Evaluation in Industry, vol. 189, pp. 4–7 (1996)
18. McKinney, W.: pandas: a foundational Python library for data analysis and statistics. In: Python for High Performance and Scientific Computing, pp. 1–9 (2011)
19. Bangor, A., Kortum, P., Miller, J.: Determining what individual SUS scores mean: Adding an adjective rating scale. J. Usability Stud. **4**, 114–123 (2009)
20. Sauro, J.: A Practical Guide to the System Usability Scale: Background, Benchmarks & Best Practices. Measuring Usability LLC, Denver (2011)
21. Vázquez-Ingelmo, A.: Code repository that supports the analysis in the paper. Usability test of WYRED Platform (2018)
22. Lewis, J.R., Sauro, J.: The factor structure of the system usability scale. In: Kurosu, M. (ed.) HCD 2009. LNCS, vol. 5619, pp. 94–103. Springer, Heidelberg (2009). https://doi.org/10.1007/978-3-642-02806-9_12

EUREKA: Engineering Usability Research Empirical Knowledge and Artifacts

An Experience-Based Expansive Learning Approach

Panagiotis Germanakos[1(✉)] and Ludwig Fichte[2]

[1] UX, Mobile & Business Services, Industry Cloud and Custom Development,
P&I, SAP SE, Dietmar-Hopp-Allee 16, 69190 Walldorf, Germany
panagiotis.germanakos@sap.com
[2] S/4HANA User Experience, P&I, SAP SE, Dietmar-Hopp-Allee 16,
69190 Walldorf, Germany
ludwig.fichte@sap.com

Abstract. Usability evaluation is accounted as a critical phase of user-centered software design and development. It is the stage where project teams can observe and measure the usability of their solutions and user interfaces, in terms of visual design, interaction, functionality, terminology, content, scenario applicability, etc. During this process, teams collect qualitative and quantitative data, or feedback items, that they have to analyze and interpret in a collaborative manner, aligning with end-users' needs and requirements and tackling specific problems or cumbersome actions. In this respect, this paper proposes EUREKA, an end-to-end Workflow-as-a-Service methodology and open tool for usability testing data analysis. It facilitates a guided expansive learning experience for the teams when applying reasoning to the collected feedback while at the same time maintains a balanced qualitative and quantitative perspective of the research results. EUREKA has been positively evaluated highlighting its added value through the maximization of outcome compared to the effort invested for empirical data analysis, in terms of a goal-directed, consistent and flexible methodology, and a modular tool that provides structured and semantically enriched content, and a smart data visualization overview.

Keywords: User experience · Usability testing · Qualitative analysis
Methodology · Tool

1 Introduction

Usability testing is considered a central phase of User Experience (UX) research and a common activity in the user-centered software design and development process. Project teams prepare and run a number of usability study sessions with end-users to validate their software by observing them, asking questions or gathering hard data. They collect feedback of how effective, efficient and satisfied [1, 2] they are while executing the given tasks which include multi-purpose interactions with a user interface, (functional) prototype, real application, system or piece of software (for the sake of simplicity, throughout this paper we will use mostly the term 'software', as an umbrella term for

© Springer International Publishing AG, part of Springer Nature 2018
P. Zaphiris and A. Ioannou (Eds.): LCT 2018, LNCS 10924, pp. 85–103, 2018.
https://doi.org/10.1007/978-3-319-91743-6_6

all these alternatives). Such feedback can be collected implicitly (with non-disruptive methods for the user) or explicitly (by asking questions), producing a number of feedback items. *Implicit* methods may include observation (i.e., what an end-user does with the testing environment; focusing on how he behaves using the different functionalities, how he navigates and reacts on the given tasks, how he searches, inputs data, or filters information, etc.), or specialized routines (quantitative methods based on key-metrics) that collect behavioral data as a result of users' interactions (e.g., time on task completion, errors, frequency of specific actions, screen flow navigation success case violation, time intervals between actions, etc.). On the other hand, *explicit* methods rely on the questions that the team asks an end-user during the execution of a task (might relate to more generic comments – what he liked and not, or more specific ones like ranking, voting, flagging or polling for a targeted topic), or post-session small-scale interviews and questionnaires that usually aim to gather the general impressions of end-users about the overall usability of a software. A combination of implicit and explicit feedback is considered an ideal mixture of information (Mixed Methods Research [3, 4]) that can be collected for a task (or interaction) under investigation since each type of feedback covers the weaknesses of the other (e.g., explicit feedback may carry more subjective and biased messages, since it relies on users' opinion, as opposed to quantitative feedback, which is more objective but does not convey 'why' an end-user is navigating in a particular way), and together provide an integrated viewpoint with an added value greater than the sum of its parts. Main aim is to create an understanding as early as possible of the interaction challenges, cumbersome situations, needs or wishes that would improve a solution in terms of usability and user experience.

However, collecting, analyzing, sorting and making sense of the collected information is a time-consuming task that requires a lot of effort. In particular, for quantitative data analysis, there are today various computational techniques and algorithms that can produce a statistical, mathematical, or numerical result, which in turn may be aligned with the objectives of a study (by e.g., establishing associations between variables, detecting patterns, recognizing similarities and differences with historical events). In contrast, for qualitative data analysis, it seems that most of the procedures (e.g., field studies, interviews and observation, focus groups, audio/video recordings, storytelling) and tools (e.g., Excel DataLogger, BitDebris, Noldus, OvoStudios, TechSmith-Morae) focus on how to gather the data and not that much on how to analyze them. It is true that qualitative data present an inherent uncertainty and fuzziness increasing the possibility of drawing different understandings, explanations or interpretations, since they cannot be easily reduced to numbers and usually express opinions, experiences, feelings, values and behaviors of people while acting in dynamic contexts. Empirically, a usability test with eight end-users might produce 130–150 feedback items of any nature. In addition, often these data are unstructured, incomplete, inaccurate, and gathered in various formats creating an overwhelming situation for a team, since many times it is not clear how to start an analysis. To our knowledge, currently there is not a consistent methodology and tool that would guide project teams through qualitative data analysis in a collaborative manner, taking advantage of the various roles' (e.g., User Researcher, Interaction and Visual Designer, Architect, Domain Expert, Product Owner, Developer) expertise and backgrounds usually involved in user-centered software development. At this point we should mention that, in this work we consider an end-to-end (E2E) qualitative data analysis as a process that starts with a pre-phase and actions that relate to e.g., data preparation, synthesis and cleaning, and ends with a post-phase that includes e.g., solutions discussion, recommendations and prioritization for future activities.

In this respect, we propose EUREKA (Engineering Usability Research Empirical Knowledge and Artifacts), an E2E Workflow-as-a-Service (WaaS) methodology and tool for analyzing empirical data collected from various usability testing sessions. It is an open solution that can be applied in any domain (e.g., educational, business) that involves the activity of usability testing of software products, tools, platforms, user interfaces, etc. EUREKA methodology adheres to well accepted theoretical perspectives like Kolb's Experiential Learning Theory [5] and Engeström's Activity Theory focusing on Learning by Expanding [6], for increasing the goal-directed learning experience and outcome while doing and exchanging. The generated knowledge is realized through the suggested modular tool for transforming the collected feedback into meaningful, semantically enriched and purposeful action items allowing a smooth and consistent transition from theory into practice.

2 Related Work and Current Challenges

During the past years, multiple tools, approaches, services, and platforms targeting usability test execution and analysis have been developed. User researchers, agencies, education facilities, and corporations offer their knowledge and expertise by providing usability research support in one way or another. A huge range can be found on the market – from open source to subscription models, from full-service providers to stand-alone applications. In order to get an understanding about what exactly is currently being offered and to which extend these available offerings support collaborative and qualitative data analysis approaches, we first conducted an extensive literature review, including e.g., conferences, journals, books, generic and targeted web searches, along with unstructured expert interviews and hands-on tool expertise. Next, we synthesized and consolidated the collected information narrowing down to a total of seventy-five tools, frameworks and services. The selection primarily was based on an empirical research analysis emphasizing on the level of completion of each solution in terms of variability of features and coverage of the usability testing process (that may be composed of distinct phases like usability method selection and planning, execution and data collection, data consolidation and analysis, and reporting). Finally, we applied a factorial analysis, comparing all the solutions based on a prioritization of factors, as a common reference point, that best express the scope, needs and requirements of the analysis as these have been obtained from the focus groups and discussions with experts. Such factors include the solutions' potential underlying model, platform applicability, supported study types, data logging functionality, quantitative and qualitative analysis capabilities, and pricing model. Even though a complete and detailed evaluation of all the tools and services is still in progress, for the scope and support of this paper we hereafter present some preliminary observations and results.

Common focal points of most available products and approaches investigated, are the (a) data logging process step (i.e., recording user actions, voice, video; capturing key strokes and mouse movements, tracking time on task, providing surveys and question-naires) and (b) quantitative data analysis (i.e., heat maps, navigation flows, task-success-rates, average ratings on multiple metrics, pattern analysis, standardized survey results). With regard to the qualitative data analysis and consolidation of feedback items gathered from the usability study sessions and the usage observations, it seems that no approach offer today, to our knowledge, adequately an E2E collaborative data analysis function-ality and support. In other words, to facilitate the data analysis process of the raw observational notes and comments (collected from multiple note takers), their consoli-dation, categorization, prioritization, and solutions recommendation.

More specifically, observing ten of the most highly scoring products, with focus on supporting formative usability testing results analysis (i.e., using the qualitative anal-ysis capabilities factor which relates to various tools' qualities like videos, pattern analysis, clustering capabilities, tagging of individual comments, etc. – see Table 1), they mainly emphasize on manual rather than automatic functionalities such as cap-turing qualitative data, either during sessions execution or shortly after a session is finished. It seems that, and in this case, they lack to structurally support comprehen-sively qualitative data analysis, promoting mutual understanding of observations and, eventually, producing findings, or following-up on recommendations agreed upon. In fact, only two of the solutions evaluated focus on supporting the creation or tracking of recommendations; a framework – User Action Framework (UAF – [7]), a structured knowledge base of usability concepts, issues and situations providing a unifying structure and tools for supporting, amongst others, usability inspection, classification and reporting of usability problems; and a method-based spreadsheet template – Usability Testing Management Tool [8], that it follows a four step process on solving usability issues that is data collection, issue prioritization, solution generation and solution prioritization.

Many scientific publications and professional usability blogs insist on the impor-tance of rigorous methodological analysis, well-formulated reports [9, 10] and meaningfully-phrased recommendations [11–13]; yet, we are missing a method-based and tool-supported solution to provide usability testing professionals as well as non-professionals and teams (such as development teams with no dedicated UX resource), a guided method to explore, understand, analyze, consolidate and learn from end-user insights, ending up with actionable findings. Below we highlight some of the most prominent challenges and problems in this domain. Today, there is:

(a) Lack of a guided user studies analysis methodology, that can bridge the gap between data collection and interpretation-based actions;
(b) Lack of a sophisticated tool that would facilitate empirical/qualitative data anal-ysis of formative usability test studies;
(c) Lack of a holistic method and tool that could tackle as a combined practice the problem focus (research data, issue consolidation) with the solution focus (rec-ommendations, follow-up, solution discussion and tracking), and potentially bridging the gap to classical project management and/or development manage-ment solutions;

Table 1. Overview of qualitative analysis capabilities of ten selected tools/frameworks which primarily support usability testing activities.

Primarily U-Test support	Qualitative analysis capabilities						
	(Highlight) Videos	Pattern analysis	Clustering issues	Filter/search comments	Combine recording with findings/notes	Categorize/tag individual comments/findings	Create/track solutions
Rapidusertests	x		x	x	x	x	
Reframer (by OptimalWorkshop)	x		x	x	x	x	
WhatUsersDo	x			x	x	x	
Userfeel	x				x	x	
Ovologger	x			x	x	x	
Usability Testing Management Tool			x	x	x	x	x
Validately	x			x	x	x	
TryMyUI	x				x	x	
Fullstory	x	x	x		x		
User Action Framework						x	x

(d) Lack of a solution that would rigorously offer an environment covering all the phases of usability study data analysis, and focusing on team collaboration for facilitating a highly synergetic and qualitative outcome;

(e) Lack of standardized reporting of usability research outcome that could enhance transparency and comparability across different solutions or domains; and

(f) High variability in the quality of usability research outcomes. Teams that cannot afford a dedicated UX resource, do not have available a method and tool that could scale to their level of expertise to apply accordingly a consistent data analysis with the expected qualitative results.

Especially in non-scientific, such as corporate, usability testing setups, multidisciplinary development teams usually are faced with different levels of usability maturity. Usability testing often is not done as a service to an external client, but rather as an inherent-process step of software development [14]. Thus, a collaborative approach not only during study execution, but also during study analysis, seems to be crucial from two perspectives: On the one hand side, it is important to minimize potential evaluator effects [15] and on the other hand side, there is the need to keep multiple team members, with different backgrounds and skill sets, engaged during all the steps of data analysis. Such an approach could be deemed beneficial in various levels for the successful data analysis and communication of the results, since participants will be able to build up commitment towards potential findings and resulting solutions as well as to share their expertise towards the same objective (collaboratively learning from the end-users, their feedback, and each other).

3 The EUREKA Methodology and Tool

In light of the abovementioned challenges, EUREKA embodies an alternative approach that could provide guidance and support through a highly synergetic environment during the analysis of the empirical data captured from the usability studies. These data represent a collection of multivariate observations, notes and testimonies either in paper or electronic format as they have been gathered by the note takers during the user studies sessions. In user research activities like field studies and interviews the analysis and outcome of the research data is more or less straight forward, since it follows well-defined processes, methods and templates that enable the classification of the data into the respective artifacts [16, 17]. Depending on the needs and requirements, a team might decide to create a e.g., persona, customer journey, activity flow, task analysis, day-in-life, or use case. However, in usability testing activities the method or tool for data analysis is not that obvious since it is highly situation-specific, driven by the data itself, and it reminds rather a clustering approach. The only solid reference point for the teams are the validation scripts that frequently provide the means for evaluating the screens and interaction flows of a prototype, application or product based on a few scenarios and tasks that the end-user has to perform.

3.1 A Workflow-as-a-Service Methodology for Guided Exploratory Analysis and Expansive Learning

In this respect, our main concern was to develop a collaborative methodology that would provide the necessary guidance to the teams to analyze their empirical data but at the same time would maintain the adequate flexibility to be adapted to its status and needs; like time constraints that might be imposed during the analysis due to the development cycles (this is a typical influencing factor for these kinds of user research activities, especially in the business sector.). In addition, we wanted to build upon a strong theoretical base that could give us the opportunity to maintain the consistency across the various process steps, would demonstrate and validate the impact during execution and would allow room for generalization and multi-applicability (e.g. educational sector).

Henceforth, we propose an E2E methodological approach that adheres to the workflow-as-a-service (WaaS) paradigm, for applying guided exploratory analysis [18] on empirical data gathered from usability studies (of e.g., educational, enterprise solutions). Unveiling hidden correlations and uncovering significant insights about empirical data requires a mix of techniques and approaches as well as an analytical perspective/approach. However, for individuals with limited technical background or analytical experience, this is often a very complex task, requiring the understanding of both the available methods and tools but also understanding the process of exploratory analysis (e.g., drilling down, creating associations, analysing frequencies, recognizing patterns and trends, etc.). To address this challenge, EUREKA methodology facilitates a structured yet flexible iterative process that consists of four interrelated phases: *Discover*, *Learn*, *Act*, and *Monitor* (see Fig. 1). The theoretical building blocks of this methodology (and each phase) are described below, in the lens of the following fundamental viewpoints.

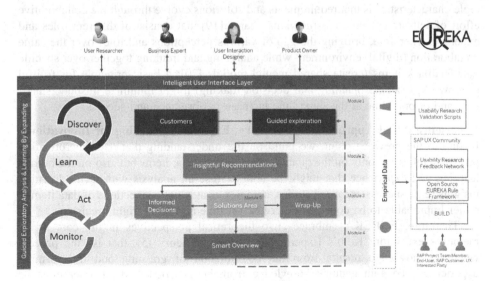

Fig. 1. The EUREKA information flow overview

Allow Data to Talk to You. Emphasize on a method that brings the generated data clusters in the center of analysis that are not visible *a priori*, through a process of gradual refinement, avoiding exercising any external influences or constraints with insufficient practices or biased interpretations (e.g. in a different scenario during data analysis from interviews, when a team creates a persona that focuses on the e.g., pain-points or the needs of end-users from the data sets, then it might guide a result). In our case, main aim is to produce a number of well-defined sources of truth e.g., individual feedback items or comments, which through the various iterations will be semantically reformed, to make sure that we will not convey abstract meaning but actionable information regarding an event.

Maintain a Balanced Qualitative and Quantitative Perspective of a Single Piece of Truth. Quantification of empirical data is always a big challenge in usability research data analysis due to the fuzziness and subjective views they present. Furthermore, applying pure algorithmic approaches (like textual analysis) that could provide a result by approximation and base future decision is not always in favor of project team members, since most of the times there is contextual information that cannot be captured or automated and need to be provided by the experts. Hence, a balanced approach that could support the feedback items on one hand with a calculated figure (e.g., frequency of references, percentage of importance, impact levels) but on the other hand would enable team members to cultivate its meaning and perspective (e.g., observations like emotional reactions, inferences, references to past experiences, political angles) would seem a rather beneficial approach for the interpretation of one datum; creating a more solid and inclusive understanding of its impact.

Diverse (Business) Roles Create a Shared Understanding About the Data at Hand. Agile development is used quite extensively today for the creation of innovative and effective software, irrespective the domain of application. One of its principle characteristics is that requirements and solutions evolve through the collaborative effort of self-organizing cross-functional teams [19] that consist of different roles and expertise. Therefore, bridging the gap of various perceptions and roles over the same collaboration (digital) environment while analyzing and thinking together over specific data/feedback items (create shared mental models [20]; a basic principle for fruitful groupwork, strategic planning and decision making) might minimize misunderstandings and errors while at the same time increase performance and success.

Experience-Based Approach for Discovery, Expansive Learning for Innovation. In line to the previous point, we build on the understanding that data interpretation primarily relies not only on the quantification of feedback items but also on the human learning and experience that might be able to fuse an analysis with tactile learning insights (e.g., success or failure stories, complex contextual connections of data items), rather improbable to be collected otherwise on time and in the right precision.

Therefore, EUREKA embraces two theoretical perspectives in the core of its method's execution: Kolb's Experiential Learning Theory [5], that is "the process whereby knowledge results from the combination of grasping and transforming experience." To gain genuine knowledge from an experience, the learner must be willing to be actively involved in the experience and be able to reflect on it, use analytical skills to conceptualize the experience and to possess problem solving and decision making skills so to use the new ideas gained from the experience [21]. A learner typically engages into four stages (as a learning cycle): The concrete experience (doing – having an experience), reflective observation (reviewing – reflecting on the experience), abstract conceptualization (concluding – learning from the experience), and active experimentation (planning – trying out what you have learned). This approach to learning, with the involved actions, differentiates experiential learning from others e.g., cognitive or behavioral learning theories that primarily regard subjective experiences as the central measurable object of analysis that is mediated during a human activity rather than the unique expressions and point of views of individuals during their actions [22]. Moreover, they emphasize in more linear, rigid paths to knowledge extraction through acquisition, manipulation and recall functional operations regarding units of information or abstract symbols. Although, most of the learning theories present their own strengths and benefits towards learning, there are some differentiating aspects that in the case of EUREKA method could not be considered as suitable comparing to the experiential learning theory (see Table 2 for a short overview of the main theories' weaknesses from the EUREKA's standpoint). Central point to EUREKA's perspective is that learning is conceived as a process that requires the resolution of conflicts between two or more dialectically opposing modes of dealing and adapting to the world, and not in terms of outcomes [5] (as a mere result of external stimuli or experiences).

Similarly, the third generation of Engeström's Activity Theory focusing on Learning by Expanding [6], by which the activity of data analysis "is not self-evident; it is typically at risk or in crisis, ambiguous, fragmented, and contested. The object is rediscovered as a result of historical and empirical work of data collection and analysis with the help of conceptual models by the participants, supported by the researcher-interventionist". The main principles of expansive learning adopted in EUREKA lie on a: (i) Horizontal movement, whereby learning is acquired through the collaboration, interaction and active reflection between the team members and the group dynamics that are generated during problem solving and decision making, as well as (ii) vertical movement, embracing the different backgrounds, motives, experiences, skills, etc., of team members, continuous negotiations are taking place for the resolution of the resultant contradictions over a feedback item. The gained shared experience and learning outcome is the product of a transformational process over the object under investigation that cannot be predicted or articulated outside the given formation [29]. All the actions (i.e. dialectics) through EUREKA stick to a top-down approach, from more generic concepts (e.g., abstract feedback items) to more concrete facts (e.g., actionable items – [30]), aiming to benefit from the knowledge acquired through the process of discovering and qualitatively modifying initial root-causes and the imminent transformation, and the resolution of inherent clashes or ambiguities [31]. The underlying forces that influence the aforementioned process principles create a scenery of expansive learning that evolves through the zone of proximal development of the (empirical data analysis) activity [32]. The main benefit resonates not only with the obvious personal development of the subjects but also with the re-conceptualization of the initial seed of information, acquiring rich interpretations and becoming a purposeful action item.

Table 2. Main learning theories' weaknesses in relation to EUREKA compliance.

Main learning theories	Weaknesses
Behaviourism *Learning is the acquisition of new behaviours based on environmental conditions, the use of instructional cues, practice, and reinforcement* [23, 24]	• Emphasizes on the perspective that a change of behaviour is a result of experience that can be measured • Uses feedback (reinforcement) to modify behaviour in the desired direction • Strict linear instructor-learner relationship in terms of stimuli presentation and passive response
Cognitivism *Learning process happens inside the human mind, acquisition of the language, and internal mental structure* [25]	• Focuses solely on the mental activities of the learner (learning is an internal brain process), neglecting other factors that may affect behaviour like individual experiences, biological structures, chemical imbalances, etc. • Instructor triggers opportunities for learning utilizing the mental processors (and data) of learners • It is based and measured on controlled environments
Constructivism *Humans construct knowledge and meaning from their experiences and their own understanding* [26, 27]	• Lack of structure, might lead to a cumbersome learning process for some individuals • Learners might not have the ability to form relationships and abstracts between the knowledge they possess and the knowledge they are learning for themselves, leading to confusion and frustration • Focuses strictly on self-evaluation of one's progress (neglecting the comparison with other learners), creating in cases a fuzzy understanding of the actual knowledge units a learner acquires or at which stages in learning process might struggle
Social learning *People could learn new behaviours and information from watching others (a.k.a. observational learning)* [28]	• Main emphasis on the environment as an influential factor that directs learning of an individual and his directs, but not on his own actions • Not direct consideration of age of individuals or developmental learning stages and growth

3.2   An Intelligent Application for Empirical Data Analysis

The EUREKA methodology could be realized with the use of the proposed tool (or better framework), that may be decomposed in five different modules (see Fig. 1). It represents primarily a native tablet application (with a desktop edition) that enables the real-time collaboration of a project team over a common interface platform, providing the necessary guidance and support based on the EUREKA methodology described above; for analyzing, validating, and sharing research outcomes (currently EUREKA runs as an Excel functional prototype, see Fig. 2). It receives empirical data collected during the usability testing sessions, with the use of dedicated validation scripts, from other tools or entered manually and generates an output of transformed semantically enriched feedback items. Those can be visualized on the intelligent user interface, can be fused to external platforms or be available as a service on demand. Furthermore, EUREKA application supports an E2E WaaS process that facilitates an effective collaboration, proactive support, knowledge sharing and learnability to the various transdisciplinary teams that participate in large-scaled projects and have the same objective: to increase the usability and user experience of user interfaces, applications and systems to the benefit of the end-users. In this respect, a number of actions could be recognized: (i) Discussion forums, where project teams can publish/share their research outcome, lessons learned and discuss related questions and issues; (ii) open source EUREKA as a service rule framework, where empirical data analysis rules and algorithms can be shared with other platforms (e.g., SAP BUILD –https://sap.build.me), extended or modified by the network community; (iii) upload EUREKA to the SAP User Experience Community (experience.sap.com), in order to run usability validation tests with customers and end-users; and (iv) invite customers for these usability testing sessions through the SAP Customer Engagement (CEI) initiative.

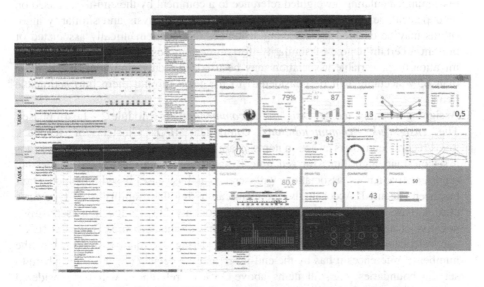

Fig. 2. The EUREKA functional prototype – example views

EUREKA presents an internal consistency regarding its methodological phases and the modules of its application; facilitating a simple and guided transition from theory to practice. Below, we briefly describe this relation, the characteristics of the five modules of EUREKA and their components (currently under development), referring to the main input and output data of each one for a better understanding of their intersection points:

1. Create understanding of *Customers* (or end-users), data empathy & clustering through *Guided Exploration* (Module 1 – Discover phase). The first module of the application is composed of two components. The **Customers** component (I/O: Profile of end-users/role-fit – generic or on task level) includes the description of the end-users and any related contextual information important for the team. It also performs a similarity analysis of the recruiting (expected) vs. the actual user profile using textual analysis algorithms. Based on the degree of association and the indicated weights of importance (e.g. specific user characteristics that should have priority in a user study) the role fit (relevance of end-users to the business role under investigation) of each end-user is dynamically calculated. This may be achieved in two levels: (a) General rule fit (background check) and (b) task-based rule fit (to what extent a task applies to the user role). The second component is the **Guided Exploration** (I/O: Raw data from validation script notes/semantic clustering of feedback items), that is responsible to collect all the feedback items per task and the related references by the end-users as well as to what extend they need assistance in order to successfully complete the task (a total success with assistance is calculated by the application making recommendations of how successful is a task). After the raw data input (from the validation script notes) and the first iteration of synthesis and consolidation, the user-by-feedback-item-matrix function is activated (assigning/calculating a weighted reference to a comment by the end-users based on their percentage of role fit). At a later stage, lexical analysis and similarity algorithms may be enabled for detecting sentences that are semantically associated or present a certain degree of similarity, for suggesting possible clustering and optimization (e.g., variable association may be used, like only similarity that is more than 65% accurate will be considered) to the team turning them into actionable items.

2. Assigning meaning and get *Insightful Recommendations* (Module 2 – Learn phase). The **Insightful Recommendations** component (I/O: Clusters of feedback items/recommendations as action items, usability issue, and judgement), at first runs a set of smart algorithms for semantically analyzing each cluster and suggesting representative names, associations with screens and use cases based on which a task has been executed. Accordingly, the team can assign the usability issue type for a cluster (based on the Usability Problem Taxonomy [33], judge if it is positive, negative or neutral and indicate the impact it has on the software. Then, EUREKA app calculates the priority of a cluster (considering the relative importance (the number of references it has by the end-users and the decision of the team where to set the boundaries, e.g., all items above 35% of references will be considered respectively) and the impact on the software) and offers recommendations to the team how to proceed (e.g., you need definitely to take an action with this feedback item). In addition, machine learning algorithms run to analyze previous recommendations by the system (i.e. based on usability issue type, relevant importance, impact on the application, and acceptance by the project team) in order to increase

the accuracy of the recommendation (e.g. by adjusting the calculation attributes and cause-effect result).

3. Meet the issues and expand on challenges by making *Informed Decisions* and inclusive *Wrap up* (Module 3 – Act phase). This module is composed of two components: The **Informed Decisions** component (I/O: Recommendations/possible solutions and decision for actions), is responsible to provide the environment so the team can collaborate for deciding which feedback items need an immediate action (assign a "Go") or could be put on hold. Therefore, it needs to make available the necessary information and setting for registering probable solutions or contextual information, and easily assign priorities and current status. Additionally, machine learning and recommender algorithms analyze the current situation (e.g. relationship of cluster recommendation, solution assigned in previous situations) and provide suggestions for possible solutions per cluster (at the same time they will receive new input, e.g., accept/reject proposal or newly inserted input by the team, for increasing the quality of the recommendation). The **Wrap Up** component (I/O: Responses on post and summary questions/clusters of responses with weighted end-users' references), contains the aftermath of a usability study, i.e. the feedback items of end-users concerning general impressions, improvement comments, what did they like more or not, as well as specialized questions by the team regarding future direction topics. Again, this component clusters the feedback items based on similarity or semantic associations and provides a weighted end-users reference per cluster.

4. Deep dive in the *Solutions* and spot the coverage and viability (Module 4 EUREKA + – Act phase). This component, *Solutions Area*, refers to the EUREKA+ edition of the application (I/O: Usability issues that have a "Go" and still in progress/coverage of usability issues from a single solution, actual impact of one solution to the affected usability issues, solutions viability), and provide the grounds for the project team to discuss and analyze in more detail the usability issues and the corresponding solutions. Accordingly, the team can indicate for a solution how many usability issues are affected and to what extent (i.e., percentage), how much effort it requires and what is the calculated implementation risk for it. EUREKA+ calculates then total coverage a solution has across the issues and the beneficial impact on them. This may help the team to make decision which one is more applicable and needs to be taken into consideration for the next stage of checking its viability. In this respect, intelligent algorithms classify the solutions of the usability issues based on the assigned effort and risk to a smart viability matrix (presenting adjustable central point that can be reconfigured depending on the distribution of the solutions on the matrix, see Fig. 3) providing insights regarding the likelihood of a proposed solution to be successful (or to fail) with respect to the estimated timeframe (i.e., 1 = high to 4 = low). Furthermore, machine learning and recommender algorithms check for possible associations of the solutions with past usability issues and backlog items and suggest in which cases they have been used and to what extent they were positively or negatively influencing an issue or functionality.

5. Keep continuous track and ease reporting with *Smart Overview* (Module 5 – Monitor phase). The **Smart Overview** component (I/O: Real-time data and formulas result from the other components/data visualizations of empirical research

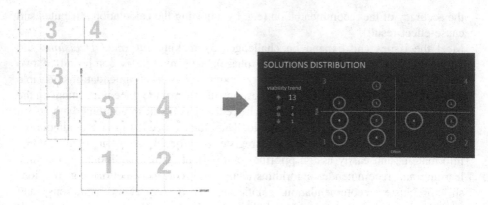

Fig. 3. Solution viability matrix example

outcome), presents the usability testing results using a variety of visually enhanced cards (see Fig. 2). The main aim of this component, apart from facilitating a quick overview of the research results, is on one hand to be used as a trigger for the project teams to perform a guided drill down on the reformulated semantic data (e.g., applying filters), for prioritizing their actions and decisions (e.g., which items to tackle first for a specific screen given the results of the analysis), and on the other hand to enable fast reporting; quick transition from data analysis and documentation to meaningful reports (e.g., making cards available in any presentation format by simply capturing them). Furthermore, this component depicts the required assistance level of each end-user by using an *assistance heat-mask* over the tested screen flows, by marking gradually more intense those screens that end-users strived more given the success with assistance protocol.

4   Benefits and Impact from Usability Tests in Real-Life Business Scenarios

The EUREKA methodology and tool have been currently evaluated internally with SAP product teams but also with co-innovation customers. More specifically, five empirical research data analysis workshops have been taken place (with an average of 4×3-h sessions each), in different time intervals, analyzing more than 800 feedback items in total. All the project teams were composed from 3–5 members (in total 19 end-users, 13 male and 6 female) with different roles and specialization satisfying all the phases of the Design-Led Development process followed in SAP [14]. During these sessions, we had the chance to make observations regarding the application of EUREKA in these real-life business settings, to conduct small scale interviews and formulate focus groups, in order to collect constructive feedback and the impression of the participants regarding the usefulness and usability of EUREKA. The results of our meta-analysis revealed a number of benefits for the teams summarized under the following evaluation criteria:

- *Effectiveness*: It is a method that facilitates a rigorous discovery of usability problems, empowering a team to synergetically transform abstract clusters and comments to concrete actionable items. It provides the necessary figures for each finding supporting any argument or decision. Also, it employs a smart overview component that steers the gradual extraction of more detailed insights into data for informed decisions, while at the same time maintains a consistent documentation and allows easy reporting and monitoring.
- *Ease of use*: It provides a guided, step-by-step approach, that can easily bring anyone on board to actively participate in decision making, no matter the background or technical expertise with data analytics. It has a clear flow and a balanced presentation of quantitative and qualitative information regarding each task under investigation, leveraging any generated cognitive overload of team members.
- *Ease of learning*: The four stepping stones of EUREKA, i.e., discover, learn, act, and monitor, frame a flexible and modular WaaS approach that can be utilized by teams depending on their needs and status. It gives the control to teams to define the breadth and depth of their analysis making its standalone elements easily consumable. Furthermore, it enhances understanding since it allows the formulation of shared mental models while teams are collaborating over a single feedback item. At the same time, it generates a total new experience in the learning process during data analysis; EUREKA's theoretical foundations follow grounded learning-theoretical perspectives like the Experiential Learning Theory and Activity Theory: Learning by Expanding, where the experiences of team members, their active participation and reflection is in the center of every action ("learning by doing") towards formulating the learning outcomes.
- *Applicability*: EUREKA constitutes an open framework of smart components/modules that could add value to existing investments, like SAP BUILD (e.g. through APIs), that lack its technologies and innovation (e.g. smart empirical data analysis, recommendations and solutions). It also generates its intelligence as a service able to be consumed by any platform.
- *New Functionality*: Intelligent algorithms and techniques contribute at each methodological step executed through the EUREKA application, simplifying the empirical data analysis process and enhancing the collaboration and user experience of the participants. Such algorithms include the assignment of weighted frequency of references to each feedback item, the formulation of semantically enriched clusters, recommendation of actions based on priorities and impact, estimation of solutions viability and coverage of issues, generation of real-time data visualizations and smart cards.

EUREKA method and tool present some unique qualities at various levels of realization. Its added value could be regarded in terms of usage and Return-On-Investment (ROI) as follows: (a) It can enrich current state-of-the-art by providing a modular approach to usability testing data analysis. It follows an E2E WaaS paradigm which facilitates knowledge transfer and enables the necessary openness and flexibility to be adopted in different platforms and scenarios as well as to the extent that a project team wants and need; and (b) it empowers a high potential for (early) success for the teams that employ EUREKA, since they can maintain a strong relationship between: tasks – feedback items – designs – use cases – usability issue types – and impact on their system. This holistic understanding and EUREKA's flexible methodological approach has a two-fold high ROI. It enables the teams to: (i) Spot any research or interaction design gaps and pitfalls through an intelligent process, supported by a structured documentation and smart monitoring of the results. This means that they can act fast with targeted actions based on informed decisions about the identified problems, saving unnecessary iterations and costs; and (ii) maintain an inclusive, consistent and semantically enriched outcome, which "outperforms" the effort invested for acquiring it; to our knowledge, no other solution today provides such a return in relation to the effort invested for empirical data analysis of user studies as EUREKA.

5   Conclusions

This paper discussed EUREKA, an E2E Workflow-as-a-Service methodology and tool for guiding the analysis of usability testing data. The big amounts of data collected from usability evaluation sessions create often an overwhelming situation for the teams which strive to analyze, sort and understand them. The fact that usually these data are unstructured, incomplete or coming from different sources, discloses a need for a rigorous methodological approach and an intelligent tool that could guide the process of their analysis, interpretation and documentation. Today, even though we are witnessing many data extraction methods and tools (either implicitly or explicitly), most of the efforts that are concentrated on qualitative data analysis present, to our knowledge, a limited scope and fragmented processing capabilities.

Accordingly, in this paper we proposed an innovative alternative solution in a core phase of user research i.e., the analysis of empirical data collected from user studies, conducted for testing the usability, interaction and functionality of software. The ingredients of EUREKA methodology reside in the fundamental principles of theoretical directions, like Kolb's Experiential Learning Theory whereby knowledge is a result of a transformational experience and Engeström's Activity Theory – Learning by Expanding, that the activity (i.e., data analysis) itself constitutes the medium for learning and development, through active collaboration, reflection and contradiction, for building shared knowledge, meaning, and concepts liable to transform any goal-directed object (i.e., feedback item) to an actionable meaningful item with purpose. On the other hand, EUREKA tool refers to a modular implementation that encapsulates a consistent transition of the scope and process of EUREKA method into practice and execution. Main characteristics are the single point of access into a digital environment that facilitates real-time collaboration, provides smart guidance and support through intelligent methods and techniques for data analysis, validation, documentation, presentation and sharing of research outcomes.

EUREKA can benefit project teams in various domains i.e., business or educational, since it provides an intelligent solution for creating data empathy through a structured and assistive data analysis guidance. EUREKA allows the data to "talk" to you, emphasizing on a balanced qualitative and quantitative perspective of feedback items and clusters of information; a collaborative setting that facilitates understanding through the generation of shared mental models among the various project roles, expertise and experiences; solutions viability analysis; smart overview and insights via semantically enriched data visualizations; consistent structured documentation; and easy reporting and monitoring. Our main concern for the teams is to develop usable and qualitative software with high ROI (in terms of e.g., coverage, effort, impact) and in this respect EUREKA provides a holistic but modular Workflow-as-a-Service with global reach towards that achievement.

Our future work includes, amongst others, the finalization of the detailed evaluation of the 75 qualified tools and frameworks, and a cross verification of the results with other experts in the area; the enhancements and formalization of the EUREKA method specifying in more detail its organizational structure, elements and relationships for easier understanding and consumption; and the development and evaluation of the EUREKA tool using latest technologies (e.g., conversational user interface based on natural language processing capabilities and text analytics for capturing and consolidating feedback items, specialized chat bots that consider the EUREKA methodology for guiding and assisting team members through the data analysis process, or machine learning algorithms providing responses to ad-hoc requests like correlations with historical data or other findings) offering the promised innovation, flexibility, consistency and ease of use.

Acknowledgements. We would like to thank our colleagues Gergely Megyesi (Product Owner), Bertram Wiest (Head of Service Industry, P&I ICD), Gergo Kondor (User Interaction Designer) for making it possible to start and evolve EUREKA through the SAP-APPLE Project Companion for Professional Services project and their encouragement throughout the process; Bernard Rummel, Alexandra Matz, Clarissa Goetz, and Beth Russel (User Researchers) for their insights and thoughts; and Timo Bess and Daphne Schimetschek for the visual advises and enhancements. Our managers Matthias Berger, Thomas Uhl, and Waltraud Germanakos for their support and allocation of resources as well as all the product organizations, teams (especially the Product & Innovation – Industry Cloud and Custom Development UX Team and S/4HANA User Experience team), customers and individuals at SAP, who have participated in the usability tests and provided their constructive comments and valuable suggestions.

References

1. Nielsen, J.: Usability Engineering. Academic Press, London (1993). ISBN 0125184069
2. Schneiderman, B.: Designing the User Interface – Strategies for Effective Human-Computer Interaction. Addison-Wesley Longman, Boston (1998). ISBN 0201694972
3. Creswell, J.W., Creswell, J.D.: Research Design: Qualitative, Quantitative, and Mixed Methods Approaches. Sage Publications, Thousand Oaks (2017)
4. Johnson, R.B., Onwuegbuzie, A.J.: Mixed methods research: a research paradigm whose time has come. Educ. Res. **33**(7), 14–26 (2004)
5. Kolb, D.: Experiential Learning: Experience as the Source of Learning and Development, p. 21. Prentice Hall, Englewood Cliffs (1984)
6. Engeström, Y.: Learning by Expanding. Cambridge University Press, Cambridge (2014)

7. Andre, T.S., Hartson, H.R., Belz, S.M., McCreary, F.A.: The user action framework: a reliable foundation for usability engineering support tools. Int. J. Hum Comput Stud. **54**(1), 107–136 (2001)
8. Rosemberg, C.: Turning usability testing data into action without going insane. Toptal (2017). https://www.toptal.com/designers/usability/turning-usability-testing-data-into-action
9. Schade, A: Making usability findings actionable: 5 tips for writing better reports. NN/g Nielsen Norman Group (2013). https://www.nngroup.com/articles/actionable-usability-findings/
10. Usability.gov: Reporting usability test results (2018). https://www.usability.gov/how-to-and-tools/methods/reporting-usability-test-results.html
11. Molich, R., Hornbaek, K., Krug, S., Scott, J., Johnson, J.: Recommendations on recommendations. Making usability usable. User Exp. Mag. **7**(4) (2008)
12. Molich, R., Jeffries, R., Dumas, J.S.: Making usability recommendations useful and usable. J. Usability Stud. **2**(4), 162–179 (2007)
13. Dumas, J.S., Molich, R., Jeffries, R.: Describing usability problems: are we sending the right message? Interactions **11**(4), 24–29 (2004)
14. Krebs, G.: Design-led development – behind the scenes in SAP. SAP User Experience Community (2016). https://experience.sap.com/basics/design-led-development-behind-scenes-sap
15. Molich, R., McGinn, J.J., Bevan, N.: You say disaster, I say no problem: unusable problem rating scales. In: CHI 2013 Extended Abstracts on Human Factors in Computing Systems, pp. 301–306. ACM (2013)
16. Geis, T.: Nutzungskontext, Erfordernisse, Anforderungen und Lösung - das Arbeitsmodell des Usability-Engineering, ProContext (2012). http://www.procontext.com/aktuelles/2012/06/nutzungskontext-erfordernisse-anforderungen-und-loesung-das-arbeitsmodell-des-usability-engineering.html
17. Geis, T., Polkehn, K.: Praxiswissen User Requirements. dpunkt.verlag GmbH (2018). ISBN 9783864905278
18. Tukey, J.W.: Exploratory data analysis (1977)
19. Collier, K.W.: Agile Analytics: A Value-Driven Approach to Business Intelligence and Data Warehousing, p. 121, Pearson Education (2011). ISBN 9780321669544
20. Converse, S., Cannon-Bowers, J.A., Salas, E.: Shared mental models in expert team decision making. In: Individual and Group Decision Making: Current, p. 221 (1993)
21. Kolb, D.A., Boyatzis, R.E., Mainemelis, C.: Experiential learning theory: previous research and new directions. In: Perspectives on Thinking, Learning, and Cognitive Styles, vol. 1(8), pp. 227–247 (2001)
22. Nagel, T.: What is it like to be a bat? Philos. Rev. **83**(4), 435–450 (1974)
23. Watson, J.B.: Behaviorism. Transaction Publishers, New Brunswick (1958)
24. Skinner, B.F.: About Behaviorism. Vintage, New York (2011)
25. Piaget, J.: Origins of Intelligence in the Child. Routledge & Kegan Paul, London (1936)
26. Vygotsky, L.S.: Mind in Society: The Development of Higher Psychological Processes. Harvard University Press, Cambridge (1980)
27. Piaget, J.: The Construction of Reality in the Child, vol. 82. Routledge, New York (2013)
28. Bandura, A., Walters, R.H.: Social Learning Theory. General Learning Press, New York (1977)
29. Engeström, Y.: From Teams to Knots: Activity-Theoretical Studies of Collaboration and Learning at Work. Cambridge University Press, Cambridge (2008)
30. Sannino, A.: Activity theory as an activist and interventionist theory. Theor. Pyschol. **21**(5), 571–597 (2011)

31. Engeström, Y., Sannino, A.: Studies of expansive learning: foundations, findings and future challenges. Educ. Res. Rev. **5**(1), 1–24 (2010)
32. Vygotsky, L.S.: Mind in Society: The Development of Higher Psychological Processes, p. 86. Harvard University Press, Cambridge (1978)
33. Keenan, S.L., Hartson, H.R., Kafura, D.G., Schulman, R.S.: The usability problem taxonomy: a framework for classification and analysis. Empir. Softw. Eng. **4**(1), 71–104 (1999)

Factors Affecting Usability of Interactive 3D Holographic Projection System for Experiential Learning

Hsinfu Huang[✉], Chin-wei Chen, and Yuan-wei Hsieh

Department of Industrial Design,
National Yunlin University of Science and Technology, 123 University Road,
Section 3, Douliou, Yunlin 64002, Taiwan, R.O.C.
hfhuang@yuntech.edu.tw

Abstract. Innovative information display/control interface is an important issue for interactive experiential learning. In this study, an interactive 3D holographic projection system was developed. And it is used in a physiologically-based experiential learning. Learners can manipulate three-dimensional learning objects (targets) through the non-touch way of somatosensory and learn the characteristics of physiological structure in 3D holographic projection environment. The learners do not need any physical button interface. The embodied function of Gesture recognition is designed in this interactive system. Further, this study explored the system's usability factors to improve the human-computer interaction and availability of this system. A total of sixty subjects (30 females and 30 males) participated in this usability experiment for the 3D interactive holographic projection learning system. These Subjects must complete an interactive experiential learning task about the physiological structure of the human organ. At the end of the task, the subject was asked to fill in the questionnaire of the five-point scale. Four important system usability factors are proposed through Principal Component Analysis (PCA). These factors include "Labeling", "Continuity", "Backlash", and "Ambiences". In addition, gender has no significant effect in each of these factors ($p > 0.05$).

Keywords: 3D holographic projection · Gesture recognition
Interactive experiential learning · Principal Component Analysis (PCA)
Design guideline

1 Introduction

Innovations in display technologies have enabled special human–computer interaction experiences such as virtual reality (VR), augmented reality (AR), and holographic projection (Brancati et al. 2016; Shin 2017; Mishra 2017). These display technologies can provide users with new three-dimensional (3D) visual experiences. AR and holographic projection differ from the closed and immersive feeling of VR by enabling users to receive complete image information projected in real environments. Mishra (2017) indicated that holographic projection can be considered a new medium for human communication.

© Springer International Publishing AG, part of Springer Nature 2018
P. Zaphiris and A. Ioannou (Eds.): LCT 2018, LNCS 10924, pp. 104–116, 2018.
https://doi.org/10.1007/978-3-319-91743-6_7

In recent years, holographic projection has gradually developed; it is currently taken seriously, and various related works are ongoing. However, most relevant studies have focused on technological developments such as new algorithms, systems with relatively few projection lenses, and the reduction of image noise (Buckley 2010; Ducin et al. 2015; Pang et al. 2017). Few studies have explored the user's experience or usability of technologies. Holographic projection is evidently a useful medium for information display in information and communications technology (ICT). In addition to technical improvements, attention should be paid to the usability of various technologies for human–computer interaction. Caggianese et al. (2018) proposed the application of holographic projection in museums. Holographic projection information provides more complete images, more messages, and more informed experiences than do static museum information boards; holographic projections can stimulate the curiosity and interest of show floor audiences. Some museums provide information to audiences on smartphones but most audiences do not want to focus on their mobiles. However, a holographic projection can provide a direct visual interface and an experience of a scene's ambience, especially in museums or exhibition halls. Mishra (2017) indicated that holographic projection techniques can be applied to medical teaching to provide students with live simulated learning programs. The advantages of remote display and guidance are the most critical features of holographic projection in learning. Therefore, we can initially observe that 3D objects offer a more stereoscopic learning experience in holographic projection than in a flat panel display. Regarding learning experiences, Pallud (2017) indicated that intuitive and interactive technology appeals to users and enables them to experience higher levels of cognitive engagement. Numerous studies have suggested that learning experiences can be enhanced through new ICT and learning technologies (Alisi et al. 2005; Liu 2008; Deng et al. 2010; Pallud 2017).

In the future, human–computer interaction is predicted to advance and the gap between holographic projection and the user should gradually close. However, the usability of holographic projection has not been discussed frequently in the literature on human–computer interaction. Holographic projection can integrate information displays into the background of an environment. This study takes advantage of this feature to further incorporate user interactive elements (functions). In this study, the holographic projection system exercises the function of human–computer interaction, which extends beyond the function of information display. User evaluations and various usability factors are investigated in this study to analyse an interactive 3D holographic projection system.

The main purpose of this study was to explore the usability factors of an interactive 3D holographic projection system in relation to experiential learning. The contents of a human physiology lesson are communicated by this 3D holographic projection system and used as stimuli for usability experiments. The 3D holographic projection system is used for experiential learning of human physiology. In addition, the 3D holographic projection system was integrated with a somatosensory interaction framework; the system detected somatosensory gestures. This 3D holographic projection system was designed so that interactive gestures can control 3D objects. The user can manipulate a 3D learning object (target) through a somatosensory noncontact method and acquire knowledge of human physiological structure within the 3D holographic projection environment. The present paper describes some vital usability factors of this interactive 3D holographic projection system. These factors can serve as design guidelines for interactive holographic projection products and related human–computer interaction interfaces.

2 Methods

2.1 Participants

A total of 66 college students participated in the usability evaluation experiment for this interactive 3D holographic projection learning experience. These college students came from design institutes and their average age was 20.2 years (standard deviation [SD] = 1.28). The participants were 30 women and 30 men, all of whom had experience in using technological products such as smartphones, game consoles, and VR devices.

2.2 Experimental Materials

In this study, the main experimental materials included an interactive 3D holographic projection system, an experiential learning interface, content regarding human physiology, and a 5-point Likert scale. The interactive 3D holographic projection system design process can be divided into hardware design and software design. The holographic projection system framework and gesture recognition mechanism are integrated at the hardware design level, and the software level includes Leap Motion interactive programming, real-time three-perspective image output, and the core content of interactive experiential learning of human physiology.

The size of this holographic projection system is $60 \times 45 \times 42 \, cm^3$ (L × W × H). A 17-in. LCD screen for projecting images is placed above the system and a transparent pyramid at the centre is used as the projection screen. The transparent projection screen is made of a 2-mm-thick acrylic sheet measuring $47 \times 30 \times 23.5 \, cm^3$ (L × W × H); each acrylic plate is glued at a 45° angle. Users can view 3D images from the front, left, and right sides. The presentation and control of holographic 3D images are delivered through self-written Unity 3D software. This interactive 3D holographic projection system is shown in Fig. 1.

2.3 Experimental Stimulus Design

The main experimental stimulus in this study is the 3D holographic projection image and its interactive experiential learning content. Holographic projection technology is based on reflected light that guides a user's attention to images on a stereoscopic transparent medium (projection screen). In our holographic projection device, the LCD screen above the pyramid provides a three-view planar image source; the images are reflected on a stereoscopic transparent medium (projection screen); the black background enhances the presentation of the reflected image. In the holographic projection environment, the user enjoys depth perception and 3D stereoscopic vision. In this

Fig. 1. Interactive 3D holographic projection system

study, a three-view projection was presented by the interactive 3D holographic projection system, as shown in Fig. 2. The three-view holographic projection involves the highly efficient use of 16:9 LCD screen and a wide range of applications can be implemented. The entire experimental stimulus design involves not only 3D holographic projection but also interactive design with gesture recognition. Users can study physiology through a special learning process through this interactive 3D holographic projection system. This interactive gesture design mainly uses Leap Motion to detect 3D coordinates of one of the user's hands and returns relevant data to control the system. The Leap Motion can recognize differences in user gestures; for example, the user can control the rotation (X-axis and Y-axis) and zoom (Z-axis) of the object when he or she makes a fist. This feature can be used to simulate the action of grasping a virtual object for control. Opening the palm can control a blue cursor in the interface. The actual interaction gestures are shown in Fig. 3.

To familiarize the study participants with gestures in the interactive 3D holographic projection system, this study provided a tutorial. Open palm hand gesture exercises were executed first in this gesture tutorial. A moveable cursor corresponded to the open palm. After a user had completed the palm gesture tutorial, he or she was automatically transferred to the next training scenario, where he or she manipulated 3D objects through fist gestures. The blue cursor changed to red when the user made a fist and transitioned to 3D object control mode. The user rotated the object by moving a fist to the left and right (X-axis) and up and down (Y-axis); the user moved his or her fist back and forth (Z-axis) to scale the size of the object. Users were allowed to practice repeatedly until they were familiar with these gestures. When a user had completed the gesture control tutorial, the system presented the core content regarding human physiology.

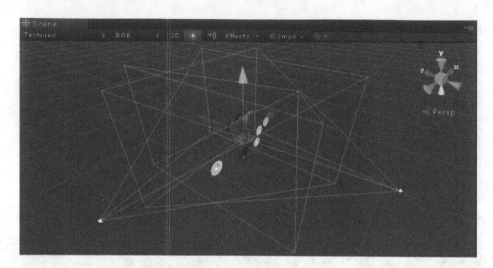

Fig. 2. Pattern of three-view projection

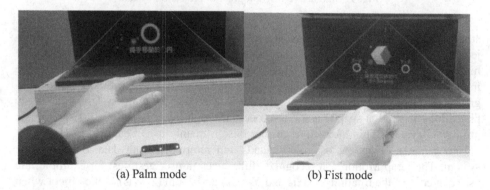

(a) Palm mode   (b) Fist mode

Fig. 3. Gesture detection with Leap Motion (Color figure online)

In the core content of interactive experiential learning, an interactive learning interface and experiential content of the physiological structure of a human organ are used as the main stimuli of the experiment. These experimental stimuli are presented on the interactive 3D holographic projection screen. A series of interactive experiential learning tasks are designed in this interface. The experiential learning interface architecture is shown in Fig. 4. Users can clearly experience the 3D human physiology structure through this interactive 3D holographic projection system. Figure 5 shows the physiology of the human body in the interactive 3D holographic projection system. Users have access to a variety of body structures through the interface of round buttons, including skin, bones, and organs. At each scene level, a user can obtain relevant knowledge through voice descriptions for each human body structure. In addition, the user can freely rotate and scale the 3D human organ object.

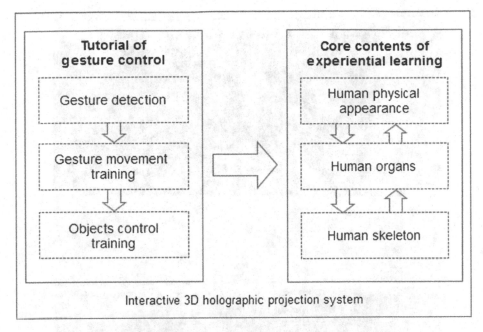

Fig. 4. Architecture of experiential learning interface for human physiology in this study

2.4 Subjective Evaluation

This experiment establishes the usability evaluation items for an interactive 3D holographic projection system in terms of Likert scales and describes these items, as shown in Table 1. In this study, the usability items were collected from related studies such as those on holographic projection (Pang et al. 2017; Mishra 2017; Caggianese et al. 2018), VR/AR interfaces (Petersen and Stricker 2015; Terzić and Hansard 2016), learning technology and experience (Liu 2008; Edirisingha et al. 2009; Finch et al. 2015; Shin 2017; Pallud 2017; Anton et al. 2018), and human–computer interface design guidebooks and human factor books (Dix et al. 2004; Paiva 2000; Shneiderman and Plasisant, 2004; Stone et al. 2005; Sanders and McCormick 1993).

2.5 Procedures

This experiment was performed in a digital ergonomic laboratory at a university. Experimental equipment was placed on a Table 75 cm above ground level. A highly adjustable chair was provided in this experiment. The participants were able to clearly see the holographic projection screen at the most appropriate posture and height, and had sufficient space to operate Leap Motion. The main steps of the experiment were as follows: (1) Explain the purpose of this study to the participant before the experiment begins. (2) The participant was asked to study the physiological structure of the human

Fig. 5. Actual situation of the physiological structure in the holographic projection system

body in an interactive 3D holographic projection system. (3) The participant's verbal expressions and movements during the experiment were recorded by a digital video camera. (4) This experiment allowed the participant to repeatedly operate the interactive 3D holographic projection system and study information until he or she fully understood the information. (5) After experiencing the learning task, the participant was required to complete a questionnaire based on a 5-point Likert scale (1 = not important at all; 5 = most important). (6) The experimenter prepared open-ended questions and the participant's thoughts and feedback were recorded. (7) Laboratory temperature and humidity were controlled to approximately 26 °C and 60%. (8) Each run of the experiment was completed in approximately 30 min.

Table 1. Items of usability

Item	Description
Image size	Image size of holographic projection
Icon shape	Shape and size of an icon on the interface
Cursor reminder	Light spot effect of a cursor on the interface
Rich contents	Complexity of learning objectives and content in the system
Level guider	Current screen with interface level position guidelines
Compatible gestures	Movement compatibility and sensitivity of gestures
Sensitive cursor	Cursor movement sensitivity on the interface (Dots Per Linear Inch)
Adjustable function	Users can adjust and set related control functions
Sound feedback	Voice instructions and click sound feedback on the interface
Background music	Background music (BGM) is provided in the system
Switching effect	Switching effects and visual animation effects on the scene level
Ambient brightness	Brightness of the surrounding environment during holographic projection

2.6 Statistical Analysis

SPSS was the main statistical analysis tool for the experimental data. Statistical analyses included reliability analysis, principal component analysis (PCA), independent sample t test, and analysis of variance.

3 Results and Discussion

3.1 Factors of Accessible Touchscreen Interfaces

This study used the Cronbach's α reliability coefficient to determine the reliability of the items listed on the 5-point Likert scale. The results revealed that the questionnaire items had high reliability (Cronbach's $\alpha = 0.796$), thereby demonstrating that the 5-point Likert scale provided appropriate and objective options for the participants. In addition, the chi-squared value of the Bartlett test was 95.936 ($p < 0.01$) and the Kaiser–Meyer–Olkin value was 0.705, thereby demonstrating suitable factor analysis (Kaiser 1974). PCA was used to extract the factors influencing the accessible interfaces from the interactive 3D holographic projection system. The factor-loading matrix was created using the varimax orthogonal rotation method and the number of factors was determined based on Kaiser's rule (Kaiser 1974) with an eigenvalue greater than 1 for factor loading. The explained variation of the six factors was 56.7%. Finally, four main factors were obtained. The PCA results are listed in Table 2.

Factor 1 is named 'Ambiences'. This factor includes background music, rich content, image size, and ambient brightness. This factor could be interpreted as the immersive nature of the environment where users interact with the 3D holographic projection system when studying the physiology of the human body. Ambiences affect

Table 2. Four main usability factors with interactive 3D holographic projection system

Factor	1		2		3		4	
Elements	Background music	0.667	Sensitive cursor	0.739	Switching effect	0.694	Sound feedback	0.796
	Rich contents	0.642	Adjustable function	0.689	Icon shape	0.630	Level guider	0.600
	Image size	0.616	Compatible gestures	0.556	Cursor reminder	0.549		
	Ambient brightness	0.552						
Cumulative %	22.49		36.43		47.44		56.70	
Eigenvalues	2.70		1.67		1.32		1.11	

a user's learning concentration and participation in a manner similar to a flow experience (Csikszentmihalyi 1990; Choe et al. 2015). Several published articles have argued that flow experiences are paramount to immersed ambiences in digital interactive learning and games (Yan et al. 2013; Hwang et al. 2014; Kaye 2016). Therefore, user immersion in an appropriate learning environment can enhance the effectiveness and efficiency of the learning experience. In the process of experiential learning, this factor should be taken seriously, especially in the interactive 3D holographic projection system. Many participants commented that the presentation of human physiology in the 3D holographic projection system seemed remarkably novel; in particular, they were impressed by how 3D-projected objects could be manipulated. In this interactive 3D holographic projection system, the brightness of the environment can be reduced to optimize stereo perception of 3D projection objects and enhance the immersion of learning through ambience.

Factor 2 is named 'Backlash'. This factor mainly indicates that an interactive 3D holographic projection system should provide a user with effective and proper control over the learning experience. This factor includes the sensitivity of the cursor, adjustable nature of functions, and compatibility of gestures. This study cites backlash in the control interface of human factors to describe the key usability of this factor. Backlash refers to ineffective space at any control position (Sanders and McCormick 1993). In this interactive 3D holographic projection system, the user controls the 3D holographic projection object through noncontact gestures (somatosensory), and the movement of each gesture affects the mobility and sensitivity of the cursor. However, the most essential requirement that the user must adapt is the control and reaction of the non-contact controller in the holographic projection system (i.e., the control-response ratio [CR ratio]). If the user's gesture involves excessive movement, the cursor moves excessively and produces more backlash. However, if the magnitude of a gesture is not sufficiently high, the degree of cursor movement is insufficient. Through the observation of actual user behaviour, this study noted that a high CR ratio setting was appropriate for this interactive holographic projection system. The high CR ratio denoted that the movements of the controller (gestures) were major and the movements of the objects in the display were minor; this was relevant to the concept of 'fine-adjustment movement'. In addition, users considered the movement compatibility of gestures to be crucial, especially when rotating 3D objects.

Factor 3 is termed 'Continuity'. This factor includes switching effects, icon shapes, and cursor reminders. These items affect a user's fluency control for the interface of the interactive 3D holographic projection system, that is, the continuity of the system control procedure. An appropriate scene switching effect can provide a user with a cue for learning object change. Moreover, obvious icon shapes and cursor reminders help to improve system usability. In qualitative interviews, the participants indicated that the cursor on the holographic projection interface should be noticeable. Some reminder effects can be applied, such as a halo cursor. In addition, the shape of the icon should resemble a simple symbol code design. Excessively complicated icon and button images tend to compress the holographic projection objects' space.

Factor 4 is named 'Labelling'. This factor includes sound feedback and level guidance. Because the interactive 3D holographic projection system is viewed as a display and control medium for experiential learning of human physiology, users must receive appropriate level indications so that they do not become lost during experiential learning in the virtual environment, especially when learning content is rich or complex. In addition, testers indicated that when a user clicks an icon or button, the system should provide sound feedback to confirm that the user has successfully performed the function in question. Therefore, an interactive 3D holographic projection system should provide adequate labelling feedback, especially in the 3D projection space.

3.2   Ranking of Usability Items

According to the results of descriptive statistics (Table 3), image size is a user's most crucial usability indicator in this interactive holographic projection system, followed by cursor sensitivity, cursor reminders, ambient brightness, and compatible gestures. These results reveal that the size of the projection object remains users' favourite item on average. The participants stated that large projection images can deliver visual impact and display numerous details of the 3D object in question. However, background music seemed to not be valued by the users, some of whom indicated that they must concentrate on receiving information concerning the physiology of the human body in this interactive 3D holographic projection system. In addition, the scene switching effect provided excessive visual animation, which may interfere with a user's gesture somatosensory operation. Generally, the users preferred to focus on the interactions of 3D holographic projection objects. The users were interested in the items related to system interactivity such as sensitive cursors, indicator reminders, and compatible gestures. This finding indicates that the holographic projection system incorporated interactive features for display and control.

Table 4 shows the mean and significance of the four factors in relation to gender. The results demonstrate no difference between genders for any factors ($p > 0.05$). Both male and female users offered similar and consistent evaluations of the usability factors of the interactive 3D holographic projection system.

Table 3. Ranking of items

Item	N	Mean	SD
Image size	60	4.73	0.446
Sensitive cursor	60	4.52	0.651
Cursor reminder	60	4.40	0.558
Ambient brightness	60	4.32	0.792
Compatible gestures	60	4.30	0.671
Sound feedback	60	4.27	0.66
Rich contents	60	4.17	0.668
Adjustable function	60	3.57	0.831
Level guider	60	3.50	0.834
Icon shape	60	3.10	0.796
Background music	60	2.83	1.011
Switching effect	60	2.68	0.833

Table 4. Independent sample t tests for usability factors in relation to gender

Factor	Male (Mean)	Female (Mean)	T value	P value
Ambiences	3.99	4.03	−0.477	0.636
Backlash	4.15	4.10	−0.676	0.502
Continuity	3.33	3.45	−0.898	0.373
Labeling	3.83	3.93	−0.565	0.547

4 Conclusion

The results of this study could be used as design guidelines for the 3D display and control of interactive experiences. These results could help to improve the effectiveness and efficiency of interactive experiential learning interfaces. Notably most of the participants opined that this 3D holographic projection interactive learning experience was fresh and vivid. They also claimed that differences in learning outcomes may exist between 3D holographic lessons and flat textbook lessons. This study indicated compatibility between users' gestures and movements of the 3D target, especially when rotating 3D objects. Furthermore, Fitt's law was evident when the user moved the cursor to the target (icon or 3D object) in this 3D operating environment; this phenomenon involves the usability of the interface; for example, the faster the required movement and the smaller the target, the greater is the error because of a speed–accuracy trade-off. The results of this study can be applied in digital learning environments such as virtual museum exhibits. Future work can be directed toward accessible user interfaces and natural speech control interface designs.

Acknowledgments. This study was partially supported by the Ministry of Science and Technology, ROC under Grant No. 106-2410-H-224 -015 MOST.

References

Alisi, T.M., Del Bimbo, A., Valli, A.: Natural interfaces to enhance visitors' experiences. IEEE Multimedia **12**(3), 80–85 (2005)

Anton, D., Kurillo, G., Bajcsy, R.: User experience and interaction performance in 2D/3D telecollaboration. Future Gener. Comput. Syst. **82**, 77–88 (2018)

Brancati, N., Caggianese, G., Frucci, M., Gallo, L., Neroni, P.: Experiencing touchless interaction with augmented content on wearable head-mounted displays in cultural heritage applications. Pers. Ubiquitous Comput. **21**, 203–217 (2016)

Buckley, E.: Holographic projector using one lens. Opt. Lett. **35**, 3399–3401 (2010)

Caggianese, G., Gallo, L., Neroni, P.: Evaluation of spatial interaction techniques for virtual heritage applications: a case study of an interactive holographic projection. Future Gener. Comput. Syst. **81**, 516–527 (2018)

Choe, K., Kang, Y., Seo, B.S., Yang, B.: Experiences of learning flow among Korean adolescents. Learn. Individ. Differ. **39**, 180–185 (2015)

Csikszentmihalyi, M.: Flow: The Psychology of Optimal Experience. Harper Perennial, New York (1990)

Deng, L., Turner, D.E., Gehling, R., Prince, B.: User experience, satisfaction, and continual usage intention of IT. Eur. J. Inf. Syst. **19**(1), 60–75 (2010)

Dix, A., Finlay, J., Abowd, G.D., Beale, R.: Human–Computer Interaction. Pearson, Prentice Hall (2004)

Ducin, I., Shimobaba, T., Makowski, M., Kakarenko, K., Kowalczyk, A., Suszek, J., Bieda, M., Kolodziejczyk, A., Sypek, M.: Holographic projection of images with step-less zoom and noise suppression by pixel separation. Opt. Commun. **340**, 131–135 (2015)

Edirisingha, P., Nie, M., Pluciennik, M., Young, R.: Socialisation for learning at a distance in a 3-D multi-user virtual environment. Br. J. Educ. Technol. **40**(3), 458–479 (2009)

Finch, D., Peacock, M., Lazdowski, D., Hwang, M.: Managing emotions: a case study exploring the relationship between experiential learning, emotions, and student performance. Int. J. Manage. Edu. **13**, 23–36 (2015)

Hwang, G.J., Wu, P.H., Chen, C.C., Tu, N.T.: Effects of the mobile competitive game approach on students' learning attitudes and flow experience in field trips. In: International Conference of Educational Innovation through Technology (EITT) (2014)

Kaiser, H.F.: An index of factorial simplicity. Psychometrika **30**, 1–14 (1974)

Kaye, L.K.: Exploring flow experiences in cooperative digital gaming contexts. Comput. Hum. Behav. **55**, 286–291 (2016)

Liu, G.Z.: Innovating research topics in learning technology: where are the new blue oceans? Br. J. Educ. Technol. **39**, 738–747 (2008)

Mishra, S.: Holographic the future of medicine–from Star Wars to clinical imaging. Indian Heart J. **69**, 566–567 (2017)

Paiva, A.: Affective Interactions: Towards a New Generation of Computer Interfaces. Springer, Heidelberg (2000). https://doi.org/10.1007/10720296

Pallud, J.: Impact of interactive technologies on stimulating learning experiences in a museum. Inf. Manage. **54**, 465–478 (2017)

Pang, H., Cao, A., Wang, J., Zhang, M.D.: Improvement of image quality of holographic projection on tilted plane using iterative algorithm. Optics Commun. **405**, 323–328 (2017)

Petersen, N., Stricker, D.: Cognitive augmented reality. Comput. Graph. **53**, 82–91 (2015)

Sanders, M.M., McCormick, E.J.: Human Factors in Engineering & Design, 7th edn. McGraw-Hill, New York (1993)

Shin, D.H.: The role of affordance in the experience of virtual reality learning: technological and affective affordances in virtual reality. Telematics Inform. **34**, 1826–1836 (2017)

Shneiderman, B., Plaisisant, C.: Designing the User Interface. Addison-Wesley, Boston (2004)

Stone, D., Jarrett, C., Woodroffe, M., Minocha, S.: User Interface Design and Evaluation. Morgan Kaufmann, San Francisco (2005)

Terzić, K., Hansard, M.: Methods for reducing visual discomfort in stereoscopic 3D: a review. Sig. Process. Image Commun. **47**, 402–416 (2016)

Yan, Y., Davison, R.M., Mo, C.: Employee creativity formation: the roles of knowledge seeking, knowledge contributing and flow experience in Web 2.0 virtual communities. Comput. Hum. Behav. **29**(5), 1923–1932 (2013)

Assessing the Usability of Urdu Learning Mobile Apps for Children

Noor Hussain, Zahid Hussain[✉], and Baqar Ali

Department of Information Technology,
Quaid-e-Awam University of Engineering, Science and Technology,
Nawabshah, Pakistan
noorhussain102@gmail.com,
{zhussain, bazardari34}@quest.edu.pk

Abstract. This study evaluated the usability of the children's Urdu learning mobile Apps for Tablet-PCs. The pre-test questionnaire based on demographic information of the participants, post-test questionnaire using the Fun Toolkit and the usability tasks were developed for collecting data from the children. The usability test was conducted by 232 participating children having age between 5 and 10 years of the primary schools. After filling the demographic questionnaire, the usability tasks were given to the children where time was recorded for each of the tasks. Afterwards, the post-test questionnaire was administered among the children in order to gather their opinion about the apps. The study result illustrated that the App3 was the best App in terms of efficiency and effectiveness. According to the Smileyometer results, the children reported more fun in using the App3. The Again-Again table results also show that the children wanted to use the App3 again and again. This study proposed the best Urdu learning mobile App from learning perspective for the children which is recommended to be complemented with the existing traditional classroom learning in the schools of the country for enhancing their learning outcomes.

Keywords: Child-computer interaction · Usability testing
Urdu Learning Mobile Apps · Fun Toolkit

1 Introduction

Information and communication technology (ICT) has been heavily utilized in education sector of the developed world. However in the developing countries, the utilization of ICT in education, specifically in primary education, is still evolving. Usability plays a crucial role for the success of an ICT system [2]. Measuring usability is difficult when it involves children [3]. However, Read and MacFarlane state that usability in this age group can be measured in terms of fun [4]. Read et al. have worked on evaluating usability of computer application, school trip and website designing [3]. They have introduced Fun Toolkit scale for measuring the children's self-reported experience of fun [3]. Read et al. have explored the Fun Toolkit as measuring tool specially designed for children aged from 5 to 10 years. They have discussed about the relationship between fun and usability [5].

This research paper is based on the master's thesis of the first author [1].

© Springer International Publishing AG, part of Springer Nature 2018
P. Zaphiris and A. Ioannou (Eds.): LCT 2018, LNCS 10924, pp. 117–126, 2018.
https://doi.org/10.1007/978-3-319-91743-6_8

Several researchers have worked on child-computer interaction and have assessed usability or fun for various technologies, i.e., fun games for children [6], mobile applications for educational purpose [7], educational software for learning English [8], the educational app for improving teaching-learning methods [9], measuring fun for Sindhi to English mobile learning App using Fun Toolkit [10], Interactive Learning System [11], measuring entertainment products [12], Child e-Learning Programs [13], and computer applications [14].

There is not much work carried out in the developing countries, specifically, in Pakistan, on evaluating the usability of the learning mobile Apps. To the best of our knowledge, no work has been carried out on the usability assessment of the Urdu learning mobile Apps for children. Therefore, this study tries to fill this gap. In this paper, the results of the usability study regarding the Urdu learning mobile Apps for children are presented.

1.1 Selection of the Urdu Learning Mobile Apps

From the Urdu learning mobile Apps available at Google Play store, four Apps were selected on the basis of their rankings, number of downloads, ratings and the reviews. Moreover, these Apps had similar activities for Urdu learning. These selected four Apps are shown in Fig. 1.

App1	Learn Urdu Free
App2	Urdu Qaida Activity Book Lite
App3	Urdu Qaida Kids Alif Bay Pay
App4	Best Urdu Qaida for Kids

Fig. 1. Selected Urdu learning mobile Apps [1, 15]

2 Methodology

The usability study was conducted at the primary schools of District Shaheed Bena-zirabad, Pakistan. A total of 232 students participated in the study. The demographic questionnaire, Fun Toolkit based post-test questionnaire and the usability tasks were developed. The questionnaires were filled by the participating children with the help of their teachers and the researchers. The following three usability tasks, which were performed by the children on each of the Apps on Tablet-PC, are shown in Fig. 2.

Task 1 Find out the Urdu alphabet letter "Pay" "پ".

Task 2 In the game, recognize the specific Urdu alphabet letter.

Task 3 Write the Urdu alphabet letter "Seen" "س".

Fig. 2. Usability tasks [1]

In the current study, two instruments from the Fun Toolkit have been used: Smileyometer and Again-Again table. In Smileyometer, five faces with meaningful labels have been given as choices of different expressions to be selected by children. These faces express children's feeling from "Awful" to "Brilliant" as shown in Fig. 3 [3].

Awful   Not very good   Good   Really good   Brilliant

Fig. 3. The Smileyometer [3]

The Again–Again table measures engagement of children [3]. This measure is based on the knowledge that people like to do fun things again. Children use the Again-Again table to answer the question if they would like to do the activities again. Figure 4 shows the Again-Again table for all the Apps used in the current study.

	Yes	Maybe	No
App1		✓	
App2		✓	
App3	✓		
App4			✓

Fig. 4. The Again-Again table [1, 3]

3   Results and Discussions

3.1   Demographic

In this study, from the test participating children, 57.33% were boys and 42.67% were girls. Among these participating children, 46.60% students were in 5–6 years age group, 23.72% students were in 7–8 years age group and 29.68% students were in 9 years or above age group.

3.2   Usability Test

In this study, the efficiency of the Apps was measured through the task completion time. The three tasks were given to the participants one by one and time was recorded for each task by the stop watch. The effectiveness of the Apps was measured by recording the tasks completion rate. Immediately after the usability test, the participating children's experience of fun was measured through the Fun Toolkit by getting their opinions about the Apps. Two instruments from the Fun Toolkit were used: Smileyometer and Again-Again table.

3.3   Tasks Completion Time

The average tasks completion time in seconds for all the Urdu learning mobile Apps was recorded. On average, the participants had completed all the tasks of the App1 in 11.95 seconds, of the App2 in 12.11 seconds, of the App3 in 9.41 seconds and they took 16.58 seconds for completing all the tasks of App4. The participants have taken minimum time in the App3 which was 9.41 seconds, as shown in Fig. 5. Hence, the App3 was more efficient App in terms of tasks completion time.

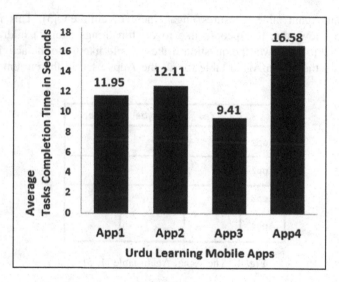

Fig. 5. Average tasks completion time for each App

Table 1 shows group differences of the Apps regarding tasks completion time. The data were analyzed using SPSS software.

Table 1. Descriptive statistics regarding tasks completion time

Urdu learning mobile Apps	Mean	Standard deviation
App1	11.95	3.25
App2	12.11	5.03
App3	9.41	3.94
App4	16.58	4.96

Table 2. One-way ANOVA

Method	Variable	Values	Significant
One-way ANOVA	Tasks_completion_time	F (3,180) = 23.201	P = 0.000

To determine whether there was a difference in the Apps in terms of tasks completion time, one-way ANOVA was used, F (3,180) = 23.201, p < 0.001 as shown in Table 2. The results show that there is statistical significant difference among the Apps in terms of tasks completion time. In Table 3, tukey post hoc pairwise statistical differences among the Apps show that there is statistically significant difference between App3 and App1 (P < 0.05), between App3 and App2 (P < 0.05), between App3 and App4 (P < 0.05). Since mean tasks completion time of the App3 was less comparing to all other Apps and the results were statistically significant, thus it can be concluded that the App3 was the most efficient App as the participants completed all the tasks in lesser time than the other Apps.

Table 3. Multiple comparisons

Tukey HSD dependent variable: Tasks_completion_time

(I) Apps	(J) Apps	Mean difference (I − J)	Std. error	Sig.	95% confidence interval	
					Lower bound	Upper bound
1	2	.00718	.90228	1.000	−2.3326	2.3470
	3	2.53902*	.88538	.024	.2431	4.8350
	4	−4.59723*	.85693	.000	−6.8194	−2.3750
2	1	−.00718	.90228	1.000	−2.3470	2.3326
	3	2.53184*	.92534	.034	.1323	4.9314
	4	−4.60440*	.89816	.000	−6.9335	−2.2753
3	1	−2.53902*	.88538	.024	−4.8350	−.2431
	2	−2.53184*	.92534	.034	−4.9314	−.1323
	4	−7.13625*	.88118	.000	−9.4213	−4.8512
4	1	4.59723*	.85693	.000	2.3750	6.8194
	2	4.60440*	.89816	.000	2.2753	6.9335
	3	7.13625*	.88118	.000	4.8512	9.4213

*The mean difference is significant at the 0.05 level.

3.4 Tasks Completion Rate

Figure 6 shows number of the participants in percentage in two categories: "Tasks Completed" and "Tasks Not Completed". Only 78.40% children have completed all the tasks for the App1 while 74.27% children have completed all the tasks for the App2. However, all the children have completed all the tasks for the App3 while only 71.59% children have completed all the tasks for the App4. Hence, the most effective App was the App3 in terms of tasks completion rate.

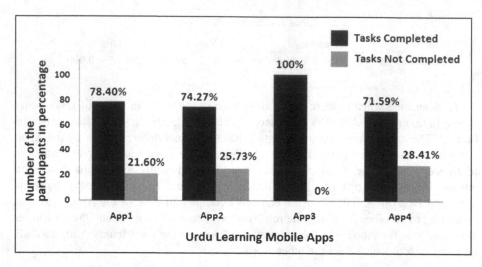

Fig. 6. Tasks completion rate of all the tasks for each App

3.5 Again-Again Table

Using Again-Again table, the participants were asked to report regarding each of the Apps: "Would you like to use this App again?" Figure 7 shows responses of the participants. For the App1, 78.22% participants' reported response was "Yes". For the App2, 81.49% participants responded as "Yes". The App3 was most rated as 95.22% of the participants rated it as "Yes". For the App4, 73.66% of the participants' response was "Yes". According to the results of the Again-Again table, most of the children wanted to use the App3 again and again.

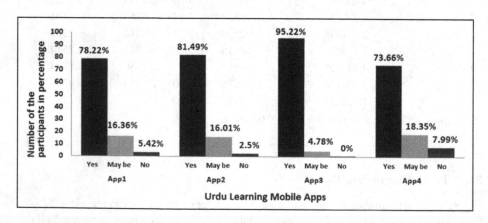

Fig. 7. Results of Again-Again table for all the Apps

The Again-Again results were coded as 3 for "Yes", 2 for "Maybe" and 1 for "No". Table 4 shows descriptive statistics of the Again-Again table responses.

Table 4. Descriptive statistics of Again-Again table

Urdu learning mobile Apps	Mean	Standard Deviation
App1	2.72	0.560
App2	2.79	0.468
App3	2.95	0.213
App4	2.66	0.618

Table 5. One-way ANOVA

Method	Variable	Values	Significant
One-way ANOVA	Again-Again table	F (3,924) = 15.319	P = 0.000

To determine whether there was a difference in the Apps in terms of the responses of Again-Again table, one-way ANOVA was used, F (3,924) = 15.319, p < 0.001 as shown in Table 5. The results show that there is statistical significant difference among the Apps in terms of Again-Again table responses. Tukey post hoc pairwise statistical differences among the Apps show that there is statistically significant difference between App3 and App1 (P < 0.05), between App3 and App2 (P < 0.05), between App3 and App4 (P < 0.05). Since mean Again-Again table responses of the App3 was less comparing to all other Apps and the results were statistically significant; hence the App3 was the App which most of the children wanted to use again and again.

3.6   Responses of Smileyometer

Using Smileyometer, the participants were asked to report regarding each of the Apps: "How much fun was it to use the App?" Figure 8 shows Smileyometer responses of the participants. For the App1, 57.56% of the participants' response was "Brilliant" and 30.56% participants' response was "Really Good". For the App2, 54.31% of the participants rated "Brilliant" and 34% rated "Really Good". 71.45% of the participants responded as "Brilliant" and 24.44% responded as "Really Good" for the App3. Finally for the App4, 46.77% of the participants' response was "Brilliant" and 25.47% of the participants' response was "Really Good". According to the Smileyometer results, the maximum positive response was reported for the App3.

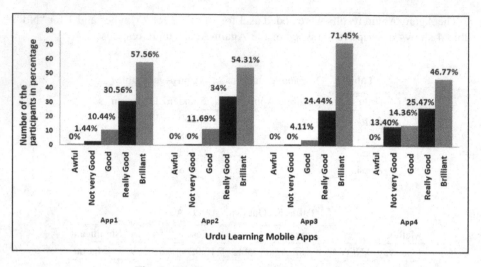

Fig. 8. Smileyometer results for each App

The Smileyometer responses were coded from 1 to 5 where 1 was used for "Awful" and 5 was used for "Brilliant". Table 6 shows descriptive statistics of the Smileyometer responses.

Table 6. Descriptive statistics of Smileyometer

Urdu learning mobile Apps	Mean	Standard deviation
App1	4.24	1.228
App2	4.43	0.692
App3	4.68	0.546
App4	4.06	1.071

Table 7. One-way ANOVA

Method	Variable	Values	Significant
One-way ANOVA	Smileyometer	F (3,924) = 18.769	P = 0.000

To determine whether there was a difference in the Apps in terms of the responses of Smileyometer, one-way ANOVA was used, F (3,924) = 18.769, p < 0.001 as shown in Table 7. The results show that there is statistical significant difference among the Apps in terms of Smileyometer responses. Tukey post hoc pairwise statistical differences among the Apps show that there is statistically significant difference between App3 and App1 (P < 0.05), between App3 and App2 (P < 0.05), between App3 and App4 (P < 0.05). Since mean Smileyometer responses of the App3 was less comparing to all other Apps and the results were statistically significant; hence the App3 was the App which most of the children reported as having most fun.

4 Conclusions

In this research four Urdu learning mobile Apps were compared from the usability perspective. According to the tasks completion time results, the App3 was the most efficient App as the participants completed all the tasks in lesser time than the other Apps. The results were statistically significant. The most effective App was the App3 in terms of tasks completion rate and the results were also statistically significant. Since mean Again-Again table responses of the App3 was less comparing to all other Apps and the results were statistically significant; hence the App3 was the App which most of the children wanted to use again and again. Since mean Smileyometer responses of the App3 was less comparing to all other Apps and the results were statistically significant; hence the App3 was the App which most of the children reported as having most fun. According to the usability perspective, the App3 is the best App. It is recommended that the App3 should be complemented with the existing traditional classroom learning in the primary schools of District Shaheed Benazirabad and other cities of the country for enhancing the learning outcomes of children. In future, more usability studies would be conducted in various schools throughout the country for getting more feedback. An experiment would also be conducted to measure the learning outcomes of the students in the primary school by introducing the App3.

References

1. Hussain, N.: Evaluating useful Urdu Qaida mobile Apps for kids, Master's thesis, Department of Information Technology, Quaid-e-Awam University of Engineering, Science and Technology, Nawabshah, Pakistan (2017)
2. Costabile, M.F., De Marsico, M., Lanzilotti, R., Plantamura, V.L., Roselli, T.: On the usability evaluation of e-learning applications. In: Proceedings of the 38th Annual Hawaii International Conference on System Sciences, pp. 1–10. IEEE (2005)
3. Read, J.C., MacFarlane, S.J., Casey, C.: Endurability, engagement and expectations: Measuring children's fun. In: Interaction Design and Children, vol. 2, pp. 1–23 (2002)
4. Read, J.C., MacFarlane, S.J.: Measuring Fun-Usability Testing for Children: Comput Fun 3. BCS HCI Group, York (2000)
5. Read, J.C., MacFarlane, S.: Using the fun toolkit and other survey methods to gather opinions in child computer interaction. In: Proceedings of the 2006 Conference on Interaction Design and Children, pp. 81–88. ACM (2006)
6. Sim, G., Read, J.C., Gregory, P., Xu, D.: From England to Uganda: children designing and evaluating serious games. Hum. Comput. Interact. 30(3–4), 263–293 (2015)
7. Masood, M., Thigambaram, M.: The usability of mobile applications for pre-schoolers. Procedia Soc. Behav. Sciences 197, 1818–1826 (2015). Chicago
8. Sim, G., MacFarlane, S., Horton, M.: Evaluating usability, fun and learning in educational software for children. In: Proceedings of World Conference on Educational Multimedia, Hypermedia and Telecommunications, pp. 1180–1187 (2005)
9. Kirci, P., Kahraman, M.O.: Game based education with android mobile devices. In: 2015 6th International Conference on Modeling, Simulation, and Applied Optimization (ICMSAO), pp. 1–4. IEEE (2015)

10. Hussain, Z., Slany, W., Rizvi, W.H., Riaz, A., Ramzan, U.: Measuring usability of the mobile learning app for the children. In: Zaphiris, P., Ioannou, A. (eds.) LCT 2017, Part I. LNCS, vol. 10295, pp. 353–363. Springer, Cham (2017). https://doi.org/10.1007/978-3-319-58509-3_28

11. Chandio, A.A., Hussain, Z., Vighio, M.S., Leghari, M.: Interactive learning system for primary schools using Tablet PC. In: Handbook of Research on Applied E-Learning in Engineering and Architecture Education, p. 446. IGI Global USA (2015)

12. Zaman, B., Abeele, V.V., De Grooff, D.: Measuring product liking in preschool children: an evaluation of the Smileyometer and This or That methods. Int. J. Child Comput. Interact. **1** (2), 61–70 (2013)

13. Alsumait, A., Al-Osaimi, A., AlFedaghi, H.: Use of survey techniques as usability evaluation for child e-learning programs. In: Proceedings of Conference ICL 2008, vol. 1(3), pp. 1–3 (2008)

14. Yusoff, Y.M., Landoni, M., Ruthven, I.: Assessing Fun: Young Children as Evaluators of Interactive Systems, pp. 11–18. University of Strathclyde, Glasgow (2010)

15. Google Play Store. https://play.google.com/store. Accessed 15 Aug 2017

The Design of Music Ear Training System in Building Mental Model with Image Stimulus Fading Strategy

Yu Ting Hwang[1] and Chi Nung Chu[2(✉)]

[1] Department of Music, Shih Chien University, No.70 Ta-Chih Street,
Chung-Shan District, Taipei, Taiwan, R.O.C.
[2] Department of Management of Information System,
China University of Technology, No. 56, Sec. 3, Shinglung Rd.,
Wenshan Chiu, Taipei 116, Taiwan, R.O.C.
nung@cute.edu.tw

Abstract. The study provides effective insights into the difficult issues related to get acquainted with the skills of music ear training. The music ear training system with image stimulus fading strategy in this design could move learners beyond basic drill exercises to a competence from vision to hearing in the music ear training process. The abstract aural skills for the novice learners can be built up through the combination of practice and immediate feedback with image stimulus fading strategy. The stimulus fading is usually used as a significant support for the special education. The concept is not new, but it is effective for improving the quality of efforts to educate learners with difficulty in music ear training. The purposes of this article are to describe the context in hearing of music ear training which could be bridged from the assistance in vision. The findings can be utilized in the design of aural skills learning with additional visual features, especially related to human computer interaction and instruction purposes.

Keywords: Music ear training · Stimulus fading strategy · Aural skills

1 Introduction

Music ear training is one of the aural skills to get into the music realm that includes identifying pitch, intervals, chords and rhythm. The inherent abstract complexity of extraction in identification of hearing variations is hard for learners to comprehend and learn. The move to use technology to support learning has become an emerging development in the recent music pedagogy. Many learners in traditional ear training exercises have faced a big burden of getting bored of repetitive or frustrating practice to develop such listening skills. Although there are a lot of ear training programs and websites which provide a related but slightly different approach to music ear taring, learners frequently stumble upon their heads with the tone that is played after they have heard a cadence to establish a key intervals. The music ear training system adopting an image stimulus fading strategy in this study is designed as an easy way for the learners to build the mental model corresponding with exercises connected to the skills of ear training.

© Springer International Publishing AG, part of Springer Nature 2018
P. Zaphiris and A. Ioannou (Eds.): LCT 2018, LNCS 10924, pp. 127–135, 2018.
https://doi.org/10.1007/978-3-319-91743-6_9

1.1 Difficulty in Music Ear Training

Music ear training is a critical skill from intonation when singing or playing an instrument to playing and transcribing by ear. It is a means for anyone to learn to be immersed into the music area [49, 72, 80]. As the music ear training which is intended for auditory studies major is quite difficult from traditional learning by visual sense. The learners have to alter their learning sense from vision to listening. Therefore music ear training confronts the challenges throughout the auditory system with learners for listening far beyond sight reading in music [33, 34, 44, 63]. Auditory music domain represents a distinct world in which well-trained learners will exhibit better memory for any kinds of sounds than visual stimuli around [15, 61, 62, 71, 84]. It is hard to establish links to previous learning experiences for the novice learners [55, 64, 83]. That is the general difficulty which is encountered by learners in their aural training course. The novice learners who lack of aural skills and some aspects of music theory are not aware of what they are doing, but practice in a mechanical way during the music ear training course. Furthermore, they are also frustrated by not having enough time and confidence to practice correctly the content of the music ear training course. It seems challenging for all novice learners to stride across the barriers of aural skills learning to be part of music realm. Thus there is a need to help them learn the rules and adapt to the new setting.

1.2 Related Strategy for Music Ear Training

The perception during music ear training includes several processing stages in identifying pitch, intervals, chords and rhythm which are the essential elements into successful music world [5, 38, 43, 45, 65]. The mentally abstract structure of auditory perception for the learners has to be marked and distinguished with relationships in temporal and spatial constitution. There are many focuses on the scientific and technological themes in the notes and the imagery of the tones, as well as the role of web sites to help learners develop the ability from intonation when singing or playing an instrument to playing and transcribing by ear.

Drill and practice based on the learning theories is one of the instructional strategies that have been used in music education software design [8, 18, 22, 47, 69, 82]. Drill and practice is the foundation to the music ear training. The accuracy of the aural skills could be achieved through performing some sequence of activities repeatedly in order to acquire or polish a specific skill. The computer assisted technology could facilitate this self-practicing characteristic in the drill and practice strategy by means of self-controlled interaction. Learners therefore could be well motivated and encouraged to learn by themselves [12, 14, 37, 70].

Cascading Strategy. The traditional way to instruct music ear training for the novices is focused on developing the ability to hear music form looking at sheet music before it is played. The strategy used in the related websites or software starts with the basics in simple notes, intervals and scales and then upgrades the difficult or complex level as learner gets better after being identified by oneself or the system assessment. All of these skills move on to navigating a specific criterion fluently [16, 21, 28, 32, 60, 74]. Learners then learn how to get advanced their work on stuff that is either atonal or near atonal. This procedure which proceeds often like the cascading style is so-called cascading strategy in this paper study. The process in cascading strategy will likely make learners in boringly learning time, and is often something interfering with their learning interests [19].

Melody Strategy. Humming a tune is really a natural way to help learners to develop the ability to overcome the trouble memorizing intervals in music ear training [4, 6, 40, 56, 77]. This melody strategy is implemented in a lot of websites and software design [25, 28, 42, 52, 75]. Once the learners hear the harmonic component of melodic sounds, the interval itself becomes much easier for them to do in isolation. After singing or playing for more than a few times, learners could see the music sheet, mark down the intervals, listen to them again and then remember what the intervals sound like. Therefore learners could tune their intonation from hearing the tonal center of the music and the harmonies.

2 The Music Ear Training System Design

2.1 Stimuli Fading Strategy

Stimulus fading is one technique to develop useful skills for learners [1, 17, 20, 48]. The strategy implemented in stimulus fading comprises gradual changes in stimulus intensity or amplitude (e.g., to "fade out" a prompt), in the shape or form of a controlling stimulus (e.g., morphing), or in the temporal relations between the onsets of prompts and target stimuli (e.g., progressive delayed cue procedures) [26, 30, 54, 66]. It is an effective and efficient way in terms of the behavioral principles that facilitate learning feedback from the skills practice [11, 36, 46, 67]. Strategical stimuli retreat during performing skills by the individual learner is the key successful mechanism for stimuli fading strategy [2, 27, 31, 39, 68].

2.2 Color Theory and Learning

Color is a ubiquitous perceptual stimulus which can enhance the user interaction mechanisms to be more intuitive and cognitive, and the user's involvement in the design of digital environment. It could attract user's attention to be involved in the application [3, 35, 57, 59]. Color itself is beyond the aesthetics, it also brings meaning for the human beings [23, 24, 51, 76, 81]. Learners' responses and emotions could be aroused as they are exposed to an environment with color [7, 10, 13, 41, 78]. Especially color red is associated with failure and evokes avoidance motivation in achievement situations. It has an exciting and stimulating hue effect [10, 41, 50, 53, 58, 73]. The color related researches show the effective potential for designing computer assisted tool in the learning environment to influence learner responses.

2.3 Architecture of Music Ear Training System

The music ear training system in this study, integrating the Microsoft Agent with Chinese Text-to-Speech Engine as a verbal tutor, is composed of piano drill engine

(Fig. 1) and ear training engine. The piano drill engine facilitates the learners in do-it-yourself to get acquainted with the sounds before advancing to ear training practice. The ear training engine provides single note and musical intervals practices which supports piano keyboards image fading in four phrases shown as Fig. 2. By applying the external stimulus fading strategy to the ear training engine, a picture of piano keyboards is presented separately in space from the practicing item, and the picture of piano keyboards is systematically and gradually faded out. Learners could thus build their own mental model from the piano keyboards fading process as the test sounds are played. Practicing listening skills in such a visual way can be useful, as it simplifies the challenge in recognizing the abstract sounds of pair notes or single note.

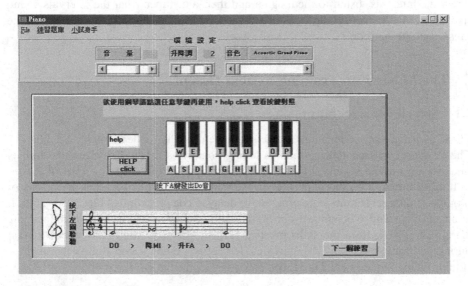

Fig. 1. Piano drill engine

3   Evaluation of Music Ear-Training System

The participants in the study consisted of 25 volunteers of senior high school students who have limited music background. The experiment involved the use of music ear training system integrated into the 8 weeks music interval instruction program. Participants were given pre and post-tests. The attitudes towards music were explored through online questionnaires.

A paired t-test was conducted to investigate the effects of ear training system with image stimulus fading strategy on interval recognition practices. The results showed a significant increase in scores from the pre to post-test (t (24) = 2.831, p = .013), indicating that the ear training system with image stimulus fading strategy could effectively achieve the learning goal of ear training. The questionnaires also showed that the learners agreed that the piano keyboards could help connect their mental model building after practicing with the piano drill engine.

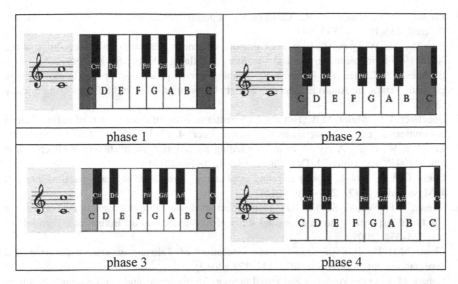

Fig. 2. Example of external stimulus fading

4 Conclusions

Ear training is a continual process of teaching your brain and ears to recognize elements in music. This does take time, and will require some persistence. The music ear training system with image stimulus fading strategy in this study could move learners beyond basic drill exercises to a competence from vision to hearing in the ear-training process. As much as this design intends that there is a way to get incredible ears to all.

References

1. Arntzen, E., Nartey, R.K., Lanny, F.: Identity and delay functions of meaningful stimuli: enhanced equivalence class formation. Psychol. Rec. **64**(3), 349–360 (2014)
2. Alberto, P.A., Troutman, A.C.: Applied Behavior Analysis for Teachers, 7th edn. Pearson Education Inc., Upper Saddle River (2006)
3. Bakar, Z.A., Long, P.: A study of visual appeal interfaces based on subjective preferences. In: Proceeding of the International Conference on Artificial Intelligence in Computer Science and ICT (AICS 2013), pp. 43–51. WorldConferences.net, Malaysia (2013)
4. Bernhard, H.C.: The effects of tonal training on the melodic ear playing and sight reading achievement of beginning wind instrumentalists. Contrib. Music Educ. **31**(1), 91–107 (2004)
5. Bigand, E.: More about the musical expertise of musically untrained listeners. Ann. N. Y. Acad. Sci. **999**(1), 304–312 (2003)
6. Blix, H.S.: Learning strategies in ear training. In: Reitan, I.E., Bergby, A.K., Jakhelln, V.C., Shetelig, G., Øye, I.F. (eds.) Aural Perspectives - On Musical Learning and Practice in Higher Education, pp. 97–115. Norwegian Academy of Music, NMH-Publikasjoner, Olso (2013)

7. Boyatzis, C.J., Varghese, R.: Children's emotional associations with colors. J. Genet. Psychol. **155**(1), 77–85 (1994)
8. Brandão, M., Wiggins, G., Pain, H.: Computers in music education. In: Proceedings of the AISB 1999 Symposium on Musical Creativity, Scotland, UK, pp. 82–88 (1999)
9. Brookes, T., Kassier, R., Rumsey, F.: Training versus practice in spatial audio attribute evaluation tasks. In: Audio Engineering Society Convention 122. Audio Engineering Society (2007)
10. Buechner, V.L., Maier, M.A.: Not always a matter of context: direct effects of red on arousal but context-dependent moderations on valence. PeerJ **4**, e2515 (2016)
11. Cengher, M., et al.: A review of prompt-fading procedures: implications for effective and efficient skill acquisition. J. Dev. Phys. Disabil., 1–19 (2017)
12. Chen, C.W.J.: Mobile learning: Using application Auralbook to learn aural skills. Int. J. Music Educ. **33**(2), 244–259 (2015)
13. Cheng, F.-F., Wu, C.-S., Yen, D.C.: The effect of online store atmosphere on consumer's emotional responses – an experimental study of music and colour. Behav. Inf. Technol. **28** (4), 323–334 (2009)
14. Chen, M.H.-P.: ICT in school music education in Taiwan: experts, experience and expectations. Int. J. Arts Soc. **6**(5), 117–127 (2012)
15. Cohen, M.A., et al.: Auditory and visual memory in musicians and nonmusicians. Psychon. Bull. Rev. **18**(3), 586–591 (2011)
16. Complete Ear Trainer Homepage. http://www.completeeartrainer.com/en/. Last accessed 20 Jan 2018
17. Corey, J.R., Shamow, J.: The effects of fading on the acquisition and retention of oral reading. J. Appl. Behav. Anal. **5**(3), 311–315 (1972)
18. Covington, K., Lord, C.H.: Epistemology and procedure in aural training: in search of a unification of music cognitive theory with its applications. Music Theory Spectr. **16**(2), 159–170 (1994)
19. Custodero, L.A.: Perspectives on challenge: a longitudinal investigation of children's music learning. Arts Learn. Res. **19**(1), 23–54 (2003)
20. Dube, W.V., Green, G., Serna, R.W.: Auditory successive conditional discrimination and auditory stimulus equivalence classes. J. Exp. Anal. Behav. **59**(1), 103–114 (1993)
21. Ear Master Homepage, https://www.earmaster.com/. Last accessed 20 Jan 2018
22. Eddins, J.M.: A brief history of computer-assisted instruction in music. College Music Symp. **21**(2), 7–14 (1981)
23. Elliot, A.J., Maier, M.A.: Color-in-context theory. In: Devine, P., Plant, A. (eds.) Advances in Experimental Social Psychology, vol. 45, pp. 61–125. Academic Press, Burlington (2012)
24. Elliot, A.J., Maier, M.A.: Color psychology: Effects of perceiving color on psychological functioning in humans. Annu. Rev. Psychol. **65**, 95–120 (2014)
25. Fetherston, M.D.: Building Memory Structures to Foster Musicianship in the Cello Studio. Diss. The Ohio State University, U.S.A. (2011)
26. Fields, L., Bruno, V., Keller, K.: The stages of acquisition in stimulus fading. J. Exp. Anal. Behav. **26**(2), 295–300 (1976)
27. Fields, L.: Enhanced learning of new discriminations after stimulus fading. Bull. Psychon. Soc. **15**(5), 327–330 (1980)
28. Functional Ear Trainer Homepage. https://advancingmusician.com/functional-ear-training. Last accessed 20 Jan 2018
29. Gil, S., Le Bigot, L.: Seeing life through positive-tinted glasses: color–meaning associations. PLoS ONE **9**(8), e104291 (2014)
30. Gollin, E.S., Savoy, P.: Fading procedures and conditional discrimination in children. J. Exp. Anal. Behav. **11**, 443–451 (1968)

31. Graaff, S., et al.: Integrated pictorial mnemonics and stimulus fading: teaching kindergart-ners letter sounds. Br. J. Educ. Psychol. **77**(3), 519–539 (2007)
32. GNU Solfege Homepage. https://gnu-solfege.en.softonic.com/. Last accessed 20 Jan 2018
33. Hannon, E.E., Trainor, L.J.: Music acquisition: effects of enculturation and formal training on development. Trends Cogn. Sci. **11**(11), 466–472 (2007)
34. Hutka, S.A.: Pitch Processing Experience: Comparison of Musicians and Tone-Language Speakers on Measures of Auditory Processing and Executive Function. Diss. University of Toronto, Canada (2015)
35. Jahanian, A., et al.: Colors-messengers of concepts: visual design mining for learning color semantics. ACM Trans. Comput.-Hum. Interact. (TOCHI) **24**(1), 2–34 (2017)
36. Jamieson, D.G., Morosan, D.E.: Training new, nonnative speech contrasts: a comparison of the prototype and perceptual fading techniques. Can. J. Psychol. **43**(1), 88–96 (1989)
37. Johnson, W.L., Rickel, J.W., Lester, J.C.: Animated pedagogical agents: face-to-face interaction in interactive learning environments. Int. J. Artif. Intell. Educ. **11**(1), 47–78 (2000)
38. Jones, M.R., et al.: Temporal aspects of stimulus-driven attending in dynamic arrays. Psychol. Sci. **13**(4), 313–319 (2002)
39. Kaplan-Reimer, H., et al.: Using stimulus control procedures to teach indoor rock climbing to children with autism. Behav. Interv. **26**(1), 1–22 (2011)
40. Kaschub, M.: Exercising the musical imagination: students can develop musical thinking skills by being guided in listening lessons and by participating in composition exercises that help them imagine sound. Music Educ. J. **84**(3), 26–32 (1997)
41. Kaya, N., Epps, H.H.: Relationship between color and emotion: a study of college students. Coll. Student J. **38**(3), 396–405 (2004)
42. Kiraly, Z.: Solfeggio 1: a vertical ear training instruction assisted by the computer. Int. J. Music Educ. **1**, 41 58 (2003)
43. Koelsch, S., Schröger, E., Tervaniemi, M.: Superior pre-attentive auditory processing in musicians. NeuroReport **10**, 1309–1313 (1999)
44. Kraus, N., Chandrasekaran, B.: Music training for the development of auditory skills. Nat. Rev. Neurosci. **11**(8), 599–605 (2010)
45. Krumhansl, C.L.: Rhythm and pitch in music cognition. Psychol. Bull. **126**(1), 159–179 (2000)
46. MacDuff, J.L., et al.: Using scripts and script-fading procedures to promote bids for joint attention by young children with autism. Res. Autism Spectr. Disord. **1**(4), 281–290 (2007)
47. McDermott, J., et al.: Should music interaction be easy? In: Holland, S., Wilkie, K., Mulholland, P., Seago, A. (eds.) Music and Human-Computer Interaction, pp. 29–47. Springer, London (2013). https://doi.org/10.1007/978-1-4471-2990-5_2
48. McIlvane, W.J., Dube, W.V.: Stimulus control shaping and stimulus control topographies. Behav. Anal. **15**(1), 89–94 (1992)
49. McPherson, G.E., Gabrielsson, A.: From sound to sign. In: The Science and Psychology of Music Performance: Creative Strategies for Teaching and Learning, pp. 99–115 (2002)
50. Meier, B.P., et al.: Color in context: psychological context moderates the influence of red on approach-and avoidance-motivated behavior. PloS One **7**(7), e40333 (2012)
51. Meier, M.A., Hill, R.A., Elliot, A.J., Barton, R.A.: Color in achievement contexts in humans. In: Handbook of Color Psychology, pp. 568–584. Cambridge University Press, Cambridge (2015)
52. MIT Musical Intervals Tutor Homepage. http://musicalintervalstutor.info/listenpg.html. Last accessed 20 Jan 2018
53. Moller, A.C., Elliot, A.J., Maier, M.A.: Basic hue-meaning associations. Emotion **9**, 898–902 (2009)

54. Moore, R., Goldiamond, I.: Errorless establishment of visual discrimination using fading procedures. J. Exp. Anal. Behav. **7**, 269–272 (1964)
55. Müllensiefen, D., et al.: The musicality of non-musicians: an index for assessing musical sophistication in the general population. PLoS ONE **9**(2), e89642 (2014)
56. Norton, A., et al.: Melodic intonation therapy. Ann. N. Y. Acad. Sci. **1169**(1), 431–436 (2009)
57. Seckler, M., Opwis, K., Tuch, A.N.: Linking objective design factors with subjective aesthetics: an experimental study on how structure and color of websites affect the facets of users' visual aesthetic perception. Comput. Hum. Behav. **49**, 375–389 (2015)
58. Okamura, Y.: The influence of the background color "red" on the appraisal of pictures. Int. J. Psychol. Educ. Stud. **4**(2), 1–9 (2017)
59. Pandir, M., Knight, J.: Homepage aesthetics: the search for preference factors and the challenges of subjectivity. Interact. Comput. **18**(6), 1351–1370 (2006)
60. Piano Play It Homepage. http://www.piano-play-it.com/index.html. Last accessed 20 Jan 2018
61. Preda-Uliţă, A.: Improving children's executive functions by learning to play a musical instrument. Bull. Transilvania Univ. Brasov, Ser. VIII: Perform. Arts **9**(2), 85–90 (2016)
62. Rodrigues, A.C., Loureiro, M., Caramelli, P.: Visual memory in musicians and non-musicians. Frontiers Hum. Neurosci. **8**(424), 1–10 (2014)
63. Schellenberg, E.G., Moreno, S.: Music lessons, pitch processing, and g. Psychol. Music **38** (2), 209–221 (2010)
64. Schellenberg, E.Glenn, Winner, E.: Music training and nonmusical abilities: introduction. Music Percept. Interdisc. J. **29**(2), 129–132 (2011)
65. Schellenberg, E.G., Trehub, S.E.: Is there an Asian advantage for pitch memory? Music Percept. Interdisc. J. **25**(3), 241–252 (2008)
66. Schlichenmeyer, K.J., Dube, W.V., Vargas-Irwin, M.: Stimulus fading and response elaboration in differential reinforcement for alternative behavior. Behav. Interv. **30**(1), 51–64 (2015)
67. Schreibman, L.: Effects of within-stimulus and extra-stimulus prompting on discrimination learning in autistic children. J. Appl. Behav. Anal. **8**(1), 91–112 (1975)
68. Schwartz, S.H., Firestone, I.J., Terry, S.: Fading techniques and concept learning in children. Psychon. Sci. **25**(2), 83–84 (1971)
69. Sidnell, R.G.: The development of self instructional drill materials to facilitate the growth of score reading skills of student conductors. Bull. Counc. Res. Music Educ., 1–6 (1967)
70. Southcott, J., Crawford, R.: The intersections of curriculum development: music, ICT and Australian music education. Austr. J. Educ. Technol. **27**(1), 121–136 (2011)
71. Snyder, J.S., Gregg, M.K.: Memory for sound, with an ear toward hearing in complex auditory scenes. Atten. Percept. Psychophys. **73**(7), 1993–2007 (2011)
72. Taebel, D.K.: Public school music teachers' perceptions of the effect of certain competencies on pupil learning. J. Res. Music Educ. **28**(3), 185–197 (1980)
73. Tello Jr., R.M., et al.: Comparison of the influence of stimuli color on steady-state visual evoked potentials. Res. Biomed. Eng. **31**(3), 218–231 (2015)
74. Tenuto. https://www.musictheory.net/products/tenuto. Last accessed 20 Jan 2018
75. The Tuning C.D. Homepage. http://raschwartz.wix.com/the-tuning-cd. Last accessed 20 Jan 2018
76. Von Castell, C., et al.: Cognitive performance and emotion are indifferent to ambient color. Color Res. Appl. **43**(1), 65–74 (2018)
77. Wallentin, M., et al.: The Musical Ear Test, a new reliable test for measuring musical competence. Learn. Individ. Differ. **20**(3), 188–196 (2010)

78. Wang, C.-H.: Exploring children's preferences and perceptions of picture book illustrations using wearable EEG headsets. World Trans. Eng. Technol. Educ. **15**(3), 212–216 (2017)
79. Wise, S.L.: Variations on the loops: an investigation into the use of digital technology in music education in secondary schools. Unpublished PhD Thesis, University of Canterbury (2013)
80. Woody, R.H., Lehmann, A.C.: Student musicians' ear-playing ability as a function of vernacular music experiences. J. Res. Music Educ. **58**(2), 101–115 (2010)
81. Xia, T., et al.: Exploring the effect of red and blue on cognitive task performances. Frontiers Psychol. (7), 784 (2016)
82. Yamada, M., Doeda, O., Matsuo, A., Hara, Y., Mine, K.: A rhythm practice support system with annotation-free real-time onset detection. In: Proceedings of the 4th International Conference Advanced Informatics, Concepts, Theory, and Applications (ICAICTA), pp. 1–6. IEEE, Kuta (2017)
83. Zaltz, Y., Globerson, E., Amir, N.: Auditory perceptual abilities are associated with specific auditory experience. Frontiers Psychol. **8**, 2080 (2017)
84. Zimmermann, J.F., Moscovitch, M., Alain, C.: Attending to auditory memory. Brain Res. **1640**, 208–221 (2016)

From Persona to Living Persona, Preliminary Data from a Pilot Study in HCI Education

Christophe Kolski[1] and Bruno Warin[2(✉)]

[1] LAMIH-UMN CNRS 8201, Univ. Valenciennes,
Le Mont-Houy, 59313 Valenciennes, France
christophe.kolski@univ-valenciennes.fr
[2] Univ Littoral Côte d'Opale, LISIC,
50 rue Ferdinand Buisson, 62100 Calais, France
bruno.warin@univ-littoral.fr

Abstract. The *Persona* technique consists in introducing, in the process of realization of a product (good or service), one or more fictitious personages representing users of the product to be designed. In this paper, we present a preliminary study on the adaptation of the *Persona* technique to promote the pedagogical quality of practical works in HCI education. These practical works concern the specification using UML and the sketching of interactive systems. We call the variant used: *Living Persona*. The teacher plays the role of the *Persona*; this *Persona* is described in paper form and provided to each student. The teacher interacts with groups of students (each simulating a company), for a better understanding of the user needs. After recalling the history of the concept of *Persona*, we explain how we develop it and introduce it into guidelines of practical works. Then we present a first study with 54 Master's degree students in Computer Science. We end the paper by presenting the implementation of a more complete study to detect other pedagogical contributions of this promising technique.

Keywords: Persona · Living persona · Interactive system · Practical work
HCI education

1 Introduction

During their university studies, students are confronted mainly with three learning modalities: the follow-up of lessons in the classroom (face-to-face teaching), the realization of student projects and internships in companies. Face-to-face teaching, i.e. periods of time with the presence of a teacher leading the session, forms the major part of the students' schedule. For example, the French national educational program of the *DUT Informatique*, an undergraduate diploma in Computer Science [1] defines the distribution of these three modalities respectively in 73,47%, 12,24% and 14,29% of the timetable academic students. Face-to-face teaching is subdivided into three sub-categories: lecture in lecture theater, directed works and practical work. During their many years of university teaching, the authors found that classroom teaching are no longer meet the expectations of students. These views are agreed with those of [2, 3].

P. Zaphiris and A. Ioannou (Eds.): LCT 2018, LNCS 10924, pp. 136–146, 2018.
https://doi.org/10.1007/978-3-319-91743-6_10

Indeed, students ask for concrete applications that are close to the professional realities of the knowledge they are studying. They ask that face-to-face teachings prepare them better for student projects, internships and ultimately for their future professional life. In this paper, we are interested in the lessons of practical work in Human-Computer Interface (HCI) in order to make them more concrete and closer to professional realities.

Several researchers have been trying to develop pedagogical techniques to make the lessons concrete and close to professional realities, see for instance [4, 5]. In keeping with this trend, the objective of this paper is to adapt the Persona technique, proposed by [6] in the HCI domain, for practical works of interactive system specification, using the UML language and sketching tools. It should be remembered that Unified Modeling Language (UML) [7] is a specification and design language often used in the development of interactive systems [8]; in this case, it is advisable to associate it with sketching and/or prototyping.

The paper is structured as follows. We first present the classical technique of the Persona and then we explain our implementation in practical works concerning specification and sketching of interactive systems. For this, we make it evolve in a variant called: Living persona. Then we present the preliminary results obtained with regard to the objective of making the practical works concrete and close to professional realities. The paper ends with a conclusion and research perspectives.

2 The *Persona* Technique

The *Persona* technique consists in introducing, in the process of realization of a product (good or service), one or more fictitious personages representing users of the product to be designed. The originality of this technique is that the *Persona* is defined by its psychological components, objectives, motivations and behaviors rather than by demographic or social data.

Cooper [6] was the first to use Persona to define a technique for analyzing end-user behavior when designing an interactive system. Cooper minimizes the involvement of users in building Personas and uses them to promote communication among the development team.

Pruitt and Grundin [9] evolved the technique by defining a 23-point method around the observation and analysis of future users to produce Personas that become descriptive models of user archetypes. They are a synthesis of several people who share the same objectives, motivations and behaviors. A Persona is then defined by two basic deliverables: a list of characteristics and a narrative about the character [10]. Following [11], researchers, such as [12–16] have proposed various techniques for identifying Personas but the Persona principle remains the same.

The use of Personas in the development of interactive systems is an alternative way used in the determination of user needs and high-level conceptual design especially when it is difficult to directly involve users [17]. For example, in the case of e-medicine, it is difficult for engineers to obtain data on patients, as this data is confidential [18]. In the design of e-services on the Web for mass markets, the wide variety of end-users also poses a problem that justifies the use of Personas [19]. During the development of an interactive system, the Persona technique comes in addition to qualitative and quantitative methods.

The use of Personas in HCI education is not new. In [11] the authors ask their students to create Personas in the context of pedagogical workshops concerning HCI design. They highlight models of effective Personas and models of bad Personas and end with advice about how inciting the students to create good Personas. Our work does not concern the creation of Personas but their use as a support to the living representation, i.e. by a teacher, of these Personas.

In [20] the authors use *Personas* to teach the issue of accessibility on ICT. They complete the textual descriptions of *Personas* by videos staging the described *Personas*. They conclude that this text-video coupling is a good communication channel to detect accessibility issues better and to promote the use of knowledge about accessibility in inclusive development.

The *Persona* technique allows project stakeholders (particularly designers) to feel empathy for the individuals they represent [9, 16]. This feature is characteristic of engaging pedagogies [21] which are not based solely on mechanisms of sanctions and arguments. Our approach is to bring the *Persona* to life through the teacher, within a framework of HCI Education.

3   Implementation of the Persona Technique: Living Persona

3.1   Structure of Our Persona

We have introduced and adapted the technique of the Persona in our practical works of specification and sketching of interactive systems. During these practical works, the Persona synthesizes the profile of a set of users. Called Living Persona, it is played by the teacher. The students must interact with the Living Persona to arrive at a product conforming to the requirements and characteristics of the Persona.

The description of the Persona is visible in Fig. 1. The psychological structure chosen for our Persona was that of [22] who architect their Personas around ten components: Identity, Status, Goals, Knowledge and experience, Tasks, Relationships, Psychological profile and needs, Attitude and motivation, Expectations, Disabilities. Details can be found in [14, 23].

A "living persona" is defined as follows: it is a physical person who plays a role corresponding to a description of objectives, motivations and behaviors in relation to the product to be developed and its contexts of use. This physical person has to interact with the learners by having reactions corresponding to the description of the Persona. The physical person has to learn the role to play with the learners because the description of the Persona is provided to the learners.

3.2   The Dual Task of the Teacher

In a typical use, the *Persona* is represented by a sheet, which is most of the time displayed on a wall. It aims to improve the communication between the stakeholders. In the case of our practical works with the *Living Persona*, we have extended the

James Dany Boonde during a demo on interactive tabletop with virtual and tangible objects at the World Play festival 2015 in Tokyo

James Dany Boonde, of Planet Entertainment Inc., is available to companies responding to a call for tender for the design of an innovative interactive kitchen system. He is 49 years old, married and has nine children (4 boys and 5 girls) who all love the conviviality of a good meal. James Dany Boonde is representative both of users of the system targeted in the invitation to tender (because his hobby is cooking), as well as analysts, designers and project managers in connection with such systems. In his various positions within the company, his aim has always been to help the company invent new systems, both innovative and profitable, allowing its users to be entertained (in the broadest sense of the term), alone or in groups. Its motto is: "Nothing beats a good user experience". But one day he witnessed an accident in connection with an innovative system of assistance for displacement (car in a ditch) and understood that any system also has to be safe for its users.

James Dany Boonde holds a Master's Degree (with distinction) in Computer Science from the University of Valenciennes, France and followed a creativity management module at Harvard University, Cambridge,

Massachusetts. He rose through the ranks of Planet Entertainment Inc. Hired as a programmer in 1990, he subsequently experienced a lot of positions, as an analyst, designer and project manager, always at the heart of innovation. He has worked in various subsidiaries of the group, both in France and abroad (Germany, United States, Netherlands and Tunisia).

As a project manager, he likes to surround himself with creative people coming from different disciplines to facilitate the brewing of ideas. It is no coincidence that his teams have deposited more than 20 patents at the international level and that he has received an Innovation Golden Globe from the INNOV'2012 show in New York in connection with a fun and personalized information system in the field of transport. Among other things, he has proposed new pedagogical simulators in the field of surgery, a card game for the blind and several applications related to interactive tabletops with tangible objects.

Even if he is appreciated for his conviviality, his colleagues know that they will always have to surpass themselves because he does not like mediocrity, or banality: each system must stand out, must bring a plus in relation to the competition. He is very demanding, but does not hesitate to spend a lot of time advising and guiding novice analysts and designers, so that they always go further in the concepts, to the service of the projects and objectives of the team. He loves his job and spends his time looking for new ideas, for new systems, whether in nature, in cinema (especially science fiction), by observing the behaviors of people on the street, at work, in means of transport, stores, etc. He would like the new systems to be everywhere, contributing to ambient intelligence, in every room and environment, under all circumstances. He also finds that his hearing is tending to decline over time, while noting that the population is aging in some countries. "It's a factor to be taken into account when it comes to innovation," he often says to his teams.

Fig. 1. Living persona played by the teacher [24]

concept by making the teacher play the role of a user of the deliverable. Thus, the teacher takes part in the experience that students will be living by playing the *Persona* role. Moreover, practical works are teaching modes during which, given the limited number of students, we can easily hold meetings between the students and the teacher in his/her second role, the *Living Persona* (Fig. 2).

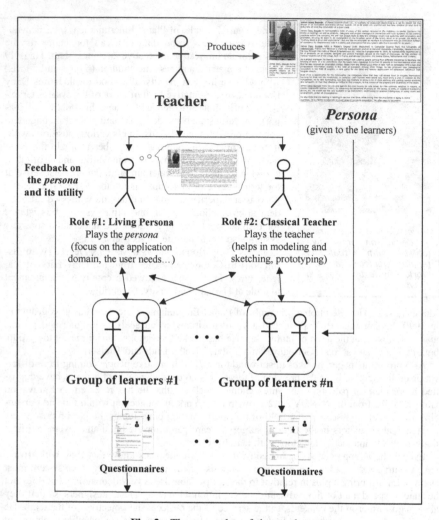

Fig. 2. The two roles of the teacher

Finally, we obtain standard practical works guidelines to which we have added two elements. First we add a description of the *Persona*, then guidelines for students that specify that the teacher will play the *Persona* to represent the archetype of users of the product they have to design. Then, they are invited to interact with the *Persona* in order to design the desired product, which is described to the students.

4 Preliminary Study of the *Living Persona* Technique

In this section describing a pilot study, we will be focusing on evaluating the pedagogic improvements made by introducing the Living Persona technique in our practical works.

4.1   Preliminary Study Goals

Adapting a concept coming from another field is a tedious operation. In other words, adapting the Persona concept to HCI teaching is not trivial. Before conducting a complete study of the Persona concept, we wanted to: (1) ensure students would understand the concept and (2) collect feedback on a Persona's capacity to make practical works concrete and close to professional realities.

4.2   Study Conception

In this pilot study, the guidelines of the practical works were given to 54 students in three different classes, composed of respectively 18, 15 and 21 students preparing a Master's degree at the University of Valenciennes, France. In each of these groups, students were split into teams of two or three. Those teams were competing between each other to win a call for tender. The guidelines were written in two parts:

- The first one described the call for tender. The assignment was to *"create an interactive system, easy to use for the whole family and naturally integrated in the kitchen. It should encourage people to cook healthy, affordable and delicious meals."* The system had also to be specified using UML diagrams.
- The second part introduced the Persona played by the teacher (Fig. 1).

As this work was a preliminary study (pilot study), we did not conduct the study on a control group. Each team received the same assignment and the same teacher played the Persona as well as performing the classical role of the teacher, helping in modeling and sketching/prototyping.

At the end of the session, a survey was conducted. Eleven questions were asked. Most of them were yes-or-no questions but justifications had to be given. Only three questions were about the preliminary study. We collected 153 surveys amongst 54*3 questions which represents a response rate of 94,5%. The results are presented in the charts shown in Figs. 3, 4 and 5. Next, we analyzed each of the written justifications given by the students according to three points of view:

1. The quality of the teacher's performance when he played the role of *Living Persona*.
2. Persona's capacity to make practical works concrete.
3. Persona's capacity to close to professional realities

We verified that the written justifications corresponded to yes/no answers given by students and whether they showed any nuances or ideas of evolution for the Living Persona. This analysis work forms the basis of the part "Sect. 6" of this paper.

5   Results

The question for Fig. 3 was: "Do you think the Persona played during your practical work was well played? Did it truly match the description given in the guidelines?". This first question is fundamental. Indeed, in the event of a negative answer, no further deduction would make any sense.

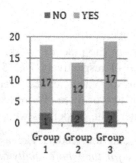

Fig. 3. Quality of the persona performance.

The question for Fig. 4 was: "Do you think the Living Persona technique enables the guidelines to be more concrete?".

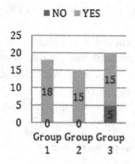

Fig. 4. Impact of the *Persona* on the concreteness of the guidelines.

The question for Fig. 5 was: "Do you think the Living Persona technique enables the guidelines to be closer to professional situations you might experience after graduating?"

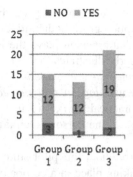

Fig. 5. Impact of the *Persona* on the professional verisimilitude.

6 Discussion

Considering the number of positive answers (46 out of 51, which is almost 90%), Fig. 3 shows that the teacher played the Persona role well for the three groups. The following justifications illustrate the overall feeling: *"I find that Mr. James Dany Boonde had a good acting, and that it well corresponded to the description..."* or *"He answered the questions and suggested some improvements which might interest the users of the app. Moreover, the acting performance was perfect."*

However, amongst the five negative feedbacks, we can read: *"We don't really know whether we are talking to James Dany Boond (Persona's name) or to the teacher who is playing the role and if we're allowed to interact with the teacher. Thus, we are not sure if the answer is from the client and has to be analyzed and interpreted or if it is the teacher's advice. That's the only black spot".*

A deep analysis of all the feedback and of the context leads us to come up with two recommendations:

- Firstly, playing the Persona role is not easy and needs the teacher to be prepared and truly involved.
- Secondly, having two teachers would be ideal. One would be playing the Persona role while the other would have a classic teacher role (nevertheless, we should consider that having two teachers available at the same time is not possible in most Universities for financial reasons). If it is not the case, the single teacher should be sure to make it clear which role is being played, when answers are given.

With 48 positive feedbacks amongst 53, which is almost 90%, Fig. 4 shows that the Persona technique makes the guidelines more concrete than the traditional guidelines. The following feedback of a student shows the interest of the *Living Persona*: *"To associate with a project a real personality to interact with him as a technical advisor makes the project more concrete. Indeed, we have worked with him by a system of questions-answers on how this project should be realized. This avoids off-topic and helps to get more precision on the task to achieve. In case of doubt the adviser can solve it. We are closer to a real case."*

However, a deep analysis on the justifications given by the students shows that it is not only the psychological description given in the guidelines that makes the guidelines more concrete but also the fact that a person plays the Persona role. The justification given by one of the students clearly illustrates that: *"It seems like we are interacting directly with the person mentioned in the guidelines and that implicitly gives the students the feeling that we are working on real projects."* This result validates the decision to make a concrete practical work: having short guidelines, three lines describes the topic, to which we add the Persona technique as we introduced it before (Fig. 1).

Another thing we learned throughout this pilot study is that students associate the word "concrete" to a situation taking place in a company: *"Thanks to this, it is easier for us to simulate a situation occurring in a company and we forget the academic environment"*.

All the negative feedback (5) came from the same group: the third one. In our future work, we will add to the survey an interview in order to explain that negative feedback.

With 43 positive feedbacks out of 49, which is more than 87%, Fig. 5 shows that the Persona technique makes the guidelines closer to professional realities encountered in the professional world than traditional practical works. The following feedback is representative of many feed-backs: *"In the job market, we will have to discuss the work to be done with a company worker, which is similar to the Living Persona technique."* However, we should note that several student feedbacks indicate that a longer practical work, and a Persona whose answers change from one session to another would bring them even closer to the professional realities.

7 Conclusion and Perspectives

The results presented in this pilot study validate our research hypothesis: the students (in this first case, preparing a Master's Degree) can understand and use a version of the *Persona*, named *Living Persona,* during practical works. They think this technique makes the practical work more concrete and closer to professional realities.

Other more complete studies are envisaged. In fact, a second one is already under progress [24]. More than a hundred students and two other teachers are involved. These two other teachers have been trained in order to keep the level as high as Fig. 3 shows.

New research questions will be added. For instance, one of them will focus on the motivation brought about by a practical work using the *Persona. Does a practical work using the Persona* technique *motivate the students more to study?* Another question will focus on the students' creativity. Indeed, one of the *Persona*'s characteristics is its tendency to innovate. *Can the Persona personality influence the students' activity? Is students' creativity boosted?* Another question will focus on the acquisition of the disciplinary competences. *Have the disciplinary pedagogic goals been reached?* The data analysis should bring insights regarding such subjects.

References

1. Ministère de l'enseignement supérieur et de la recherche, Programme Pédagogique National du Diplôme Universitaire de Technologie en informatique, France (2013)
2. Cole, M.: Using wiki technology to support student engagement: lessons from the trenches. Comput. Educ. **52**, 141–146 (2009)
3. Berret, D.: Lectures still dominate science and math teaching, Chronicle Higher Education, 25th October 2012. http://chronicle.com/article/article-content/135402/
4. Dolog, P., Thomsen, L.L., Thomsen, B.: Problem-based learning in a software engineering curriculum using Bloom's taxonomy and the IEEE software engineering body of knowledge. ACM Trans. Comput. Educ. **16**(3), Article 9 (2016)
5. Warin, B., Kolski, C., Sagar, M.: Framework for the evolution of acquiring knowledge modules to integrate the acquisition of high-level cognitive skills and professional competencies: principles and case studies. Comput. Educ. **57**, 1595–1614 (2011)
6. Cooper, A.: The Inmates are Running the Asylum: Why Hi-tech Products Drive Us Crazy and How to Restore the Sanity. Macmillan Publishing Co. Inc., Indianapolis (1999)
7. http://www.uml.org/
8. Siau, K., Halpin, T.: Unified Modeling Language: Systems Analysis, Design and Development Issues. IDEA Group Publishing, Hershey (2001)
9. Pruitt, J., Grudin, J.J.: Personas: practice and theory. In: Proceedings of the Designing for User Experiences, DUX 2003. ACM Press (2003)
10. Acuña, S.T., Castro, J.W., Juristo, N.: A HCI technique for improving requirements elicitation. Inf. Softw. Technol. **54**, 1357–1375 (2012)
11. Jones, M.C., Floyd, I.R., Twidale, F.M.B.: Teaching design with persona. Interact. Des. Architect. J. IxD&A **3**(4), 75–82 (2008)
12. Brangier, E., Bornet, C., Persona: a method to produce representations focused on consumers' needs. In: Karwowski, W., Soares, M., Stanton, N. (eds.) Human Factors and Ergonomics in Consumer Product Design, pp. 38–61. Taylor and Francis (2011)
13. Costa, A.C., Rebelo, F., Teles, J., Noriega, P.: Child-persona: how to bring them to reality? In: 6th International Conference on Applied Human Factors and Ergonomics (AHFE 2015), Procedia Manufacturing, vol. 3, 6520–6527 (2015)
14. Idoughi, D., Seffah, A., Kolski, C.: Adding user experience into the interactive service design loop: a persona-based approach. Behav. Inf. Technol. **31**(3), 287–303 (2012)
15. Schäfer, C., Zinke, R., Künzer, L., Hofinger, G., Koch, R.: Applying persona method for describing users of escape routes. In: The Conference on Pedestrian and Evacuation Dynamics 2014, Transportation Research Procedia, vol. 2, pp. 636–641 (2014)
16. Vosbergen, S., Mulder-Wiggers, J.M.R., Lacroix, J.P., Kemps, H.M.C., Kraaijenhagen, R. A., Jaspers, M.W.N., Peek, N.: Using personas to tailor educational messages to the preferences of coronary heart disease patients. J. Biomed. Inform. **53**, 100–112 (2015)
17. Anvari, F., Richards, D., Hitchens, M., Ali Babar, M., Thi Tran, H.M., Busch, P.: An empirical investigation of the influence of persona with personality traits on conceptual design. J. Syst. Softw. **134**, 324–339 (2017)
18. Jay, C., Harper, S., Calman, L.: Personas for lung cancer patients, carers and healthcare professionals, developed through the ethnographic coding of empirical data (2012). http://files.figshare.com/1027598/OSS_personas_scenarios.pdf. Accessed 26th Dec 2017
19. Hjalmarsson, A., Gustafsson, E., Cronholm, S.: Exploring the use of personas in user-centered design of web-based e-services. In: iConference Proceedings (2015)
20. Loitsch, C., Weber, G., Voegler, J.: Teaching accessibility with personas. In: International Conference on Computers Helping People with Special Needs, pp. 453–460 (2016)

21. Witchel, H.J., Santos, C.P., Ackah, J.K., Tee, J., Chockalingam, N., Westling, C.E.I.: The complex relationship between empathy, engagement and boredom. In: Proceedings of the European Conference on Cognitive Ergonomics, ECCE 2016, September 2016
22. Courage, C., Baxter, K.: Understanding Your Users: A Practical Guide to User Requirements Methods, Tools, and Techniques. Elsevier, San Francisco (2005)
23. Seffah, A., Kolski, C., Idoughi, D.: Persona comme outil de design de services interactifs: principes et exemple en e-maintenance. In: Proceedings of IHM 2009, 21ème Conférence de l'Association Francophone sur l'Interaction Homme-Machine, Grenoble, France, pp. 333–336. ACM, 13–16 October 2009
24. Kolski, C., Warin, B.: Living persona technique applied to HCI education. In: 9th conference IEEE Educon, Canary Islands, Spain, 18–20 April 2018. (accepted)

Electronic Story Book Display Method and Kindergartener Reading Behavior: An Eye-Tracking Investigation

Chia-Ning Liao[1(✉)], Yu-Ching Huang[2], Yao-Ting Sung[1],
Kuo-En Chang[2], Hsueh Chin Chen[1], Tzu-Chien Liu[1],
Yen-Hua Chang[1], Wen-Chung Kao[3], Chin-Chung Tsai[4],
and Ming-Da Wu[1]

[1] Department of Educational Psychology and Counseling,
National Taiwan Normal University, Taipei, Taiwan
artning0905@gmail.com, cyh2030@gmail.com,
{sungtc, chcjyh, tzuchien}@ntnu.edu.tw,
tarzan8720@yahoo.com.tw
[2] Department of Graduate Institute of Information and Computer Education,
National Taiwan Normal University, Taipei, Taiwan
j032400@gmail.com, kchang@ntnu.edu.tw
[3] Department of Electrical Engineering,
National Taiwan Normal University, Taipei, Taiwan
jungkao@ntnu.edu.tw
[4] Program of Learning Sciences, National Taiwan Normal University,
Taipei, Taiwan
tsaicc@ntnu.edu.tw

Abstract. If children could be enticed to pay more attention to the print area, it could help increase their print awareness and future reading ability. Along with the development of electronic technology, many books have changed to the electronic format, and storybooks are no exception. The purpose of this study was to understand which electronic storybook display method is best able to increase children's attention to the print area. To this end, we modified the electronic storybook's design and used an eye-tracker to measure children's visual attention during reading. The study included 76 children between the ages of 4–6 from two northern Taiwanese kindergartens. The kindergarteners were split into three groups: a traditional storybook group, the highlight synchronization group (implicit instruction), and the text-discussion group (explicit instruction). This study was conducted over a 6-week period: one week for pre-tests, four weeks of interventions, and one week for post-tests. The result of pre-test suggested that the northern Taiwanese children spent about 80% of their time looking at the picture area, and about 20% at the print area. The result of week 2, the first week of the intervention stage, showed that, when it came to visual attention invested in the print area, the highlight synchronization groups paid significantly more attention to the print area than the traditional storybook group.

Keywords: Electronic book · Literacy · Kindergartener · Shared book reading
Eye movements

© Springer International Publishing AG, part of Springer Nature 2018
P. Zaphiris and A. Ioannou (Eds.): LCT 2018, LNCS 10924, pp. 147–156, 2018.
https://doi.org/10.1007/978-3-319-91743-6_11

1 Introduction

Shared reading is practiced regularly by many families and is seen as helping children's literacy and language development [1]. It's well documented that children aged between 0–6 years accumulate a great deal of knowledge of the written language. The term "emergent literacy" is used to describe all the literacy related knowledge (such as recognizing letters or words), skills (such as understanding words should be read in a certain direction) and attitudes (such as reading habits or affection for reading) that children acquire from birth to the age of six, including pre-school and kindergarten [2–5]. Emergent literacy and the reading ability of older children have a significant correlation [6–8], and the most effective way to improve emergent literacy is for children to directly interact with print. Shared reading is an excellent way to increase that interaction [9, 10].

This following sections will first define the concept of emergent literacy, then introduce the concept of print awareness and how it is related to emergent literacy and follow with how different strategies in shared reading can assist emergent literacy. Finally, this study will investigate the literature surrounding eye movement and emergent literacy to understand how children's eyes behave during shared reading.

1.1 Emergent Literacy

Emergent literacy refers to the reading-and-writing associated knowledge, skills, and attitudes that children have attained before entering formal education. Previous conceptions believed that reading-and-writing ability could only be gradually cultivated after children had entered formal education. Modern conceptions recognize that, contrasting with the above view, that the beginning of reading and writing development precedes formal training. From birth to school attendance, at home children engage in activities involving reading and writing. These activities develop the child's knowledge of language, reading, and writing, and are correlated with the child's later reading and writing ability. Therefore, reading and writing learning should not be relegated to formal education, and should instead be viewed as something that continuously develops from birth onward. Because this process begins before formal education in reading and writing, "emergent literacy" has come to refer to a child's reading and writing ability before any formal schooling on the topic has begun [2–5].

It is precisely because emergent literacy takes place before formal education and accumulates from daily life that knowledge of listening, speaking, reading, writing, and their associated activities and experiences have all become important concepts within emergent literacy [2, 5], and that all of them affect children's future ability to read.

1.2 Factors of Emergent Literacy

Emergent literacy includes a great deal of influential factors, such as oral language ability, phonological awareness, and print awareness [5, 8, 11]. Of these, the latter two will be discussed herein.

Phonological Awareness. What phonological awareness refers to is an individual's sensitivity to the structure of spoken language, associated knowledge, and the ability to use this knowledge to effectively manage written or spoken words [8, 11, 12] in ways such as by rhyming words or disassembling a word into several phonemes (such as breaking up "box" into the four sounds b-o-k-s). Previous research has found that phonological awareness and reading ability are highly correlated and, especially when compared to other reading and writing abilities, that phonological awarness especially requires purposeful training, and as such has received a lot of attention.

Print Awareness. Print awareness refers to a child's sense of the written language and its uses, including text structure (such as the concept that a book should have a title and author, or that books in English are read from left to right whereas books in Chinese may be read from top to bottom and left to right, etc.), knowledge of letters (which letters they recognize) and the understanding of how the spoken word and the written word relate to one another, et cetera. Substantial previous research suggests that print awareness can predict future reading ability [7, 13–15]. Adam [16] also found that a child's understanding of the form, function, and usage of print constitutes the basis of their future reading and writing ability.

Although the research demonstrating a beneficial link between a child's ability to perceive sound and their awareness of the written language to a child's future ability to read remains inconclusive, despite controlling covariates such as intelligence, family background, and language ability, phonological awareness itself remains highly correlated with children's reading performance. However, this does not mean phonological awareness is more important than written language knowledge. The National Reading Panel, which reviews the effectiveness of various reading instructional methods for children, found in 2000 that phonological awareness must be taught at the same time as letter knowledge to improve emergent literacy [17].

Although children acquire their emergent literacy through many informal learning methods, shared reading is considered to be a key factor in promoting the cultivation of reading and writing. This is likely because shared reading does not only include print, but also provides an opportunity for social interaction. It could also be because shared reading uses picture books that simultaneously display pictures and print.

1.3   What Children Look at During Shared Reading

The comprehension process while reading storybooks that inherently contain text and figure information, as opposed to traditional pure text reading, is more complicated. To date, the eye-movement methodelogy has successfully applied to reveal the moment-to-moment activity of the mind and to provide valuable insight into readers' visual attention while learning from online text [18], science text [19] or mathematics [20]. The emergent literacy research field is no exception [21–24].

However, recent studies have discovered that preschool children spend most of their reading time attending to the picture area, rather than to the print area, of storybooks during shared reading. Only about 5% of their reading time is spent looking at the print area [21–24].

Evans and Saint-Aubin [21] examined children during a shared storybook reading experience. They changed the picture book into an electronic format and displayed it on a computer screen, and then invited five children aged 4–5 to participate in shared-readings of that storybook. Meanwhile, the researchers used an eye tracker to record the children's eye movements. The researchers used three types of picture book layouts. The first had print on the right side and pictures on the left. The second had print and pictures on every page, with print in the upper-and-bottom-most parts of the page. The third put the print in word bubbles on top of the pictures. During shared reading, the child's parent read the content of the picture books out loud for their child and were not allowed to skip or reread a page. The results showed that children spent the vast majority of their time looking at the pictures, and only spent about 6% of their time looking at the print. Even with print embedded in the pictures in the third layout, the proportion of time children spent viewing the print remained quite small.

Justice et al. [23] used two types of children's books, one emphasizing its text (print-salient) and one emphasizing its pictures (picture-salient), as their reading materials, and used an eye tracker to measure the children's visual attention. They took 10 five-year-olds and read both book types to the children. They found that although the visual attention of the five-year-olds of the print increased when reading the print-salient books as compared to when they read the picture-salient books, it still only totaled about 7% of the time spent viewing print.

Examining Chinese reading, Lai and Chen [25] used Chinese picture-books for their research. They recruited 12 4–5-year-olds and had read each five different book formats. Their results were similar to Evans [21] in that they found that children, when reading, spent the vast majority of their time attending to the pictures, and again spent only about 6% of their time looking at the text. They also found that 4- and 5-year-olds had no significant differences in their visual attentiveness to the text: They all gazed at the pictures at least ten times as long as the text. The results of this study also showed that children paid more attention to text when the pictures were black and white rather than in color, and that making the text more salient in appearance did nothing to entice the children to look at it more.

1.4 Print Referencing Strategies

If children could be enticed to pay more attention to the print area, it could help increase their print awareness and future reading ability. For example, Evans, Shaw, and Bell [26] believed that typical shared reading by family members only tended to increase a child's oral language ability and did not affect the child's ability to written language. They suggested that if parents wanted shared reading to increase the child's print knowledge, that they would have to use a print referencing strategy to guide the attention of children to the print, the names of the letters, how the letters are pronounced, and engage the child in a discussion of the text. By doing so, shared reading could develop the reading and writing skills of the child.

Evans et al. [27], researched how the "pointing" and "no-pointing" methods of shared reading differently affected 3–5 year-olds, and found that if, during shared reading, there was only reading (no-pointing), that children attended to the text at most 2% of the time; if, instead, they read and named the words (pointing) all three age groups significantly increased their attentiveness to the text. Among them, the 4-year-old children in the pointing and no-pointing groups demonstrated significantly better performance on subsequent text recognition tests over their comrades in the pure reading group. Evans et al. [27] recommended that during shared reading parents point at the words they are reading to let children become accustomed to their language's print conventions, and to entice children to look at words so they observe, name, and learn vocabulary.

Justice et al. [4] studied how adult guidance, either silent or audio-visual, affected the visual attention of children during shared reading. They recruited 44 children for an experiment where the children separately engaged in the shared reading of four storybooks. The children were divided into four groups: Pure reading, picture discussion, print discussion, and pointing. Each group was further equipped with eye-tracking hardware to measure the visual attention of the children. The results showed that the children spent about 6% of their time attending to the print, though when adults, through explicit verbal or nonverbal indicators, guided the children to pay attention to the text the children spent significantly more time attending to the print.

Roy-Charland et al. [28] recruited 36 children for a shared reading experiment, of which 10 were pre-school children, 14 were first graders, and 12 were second-graders. They selected 6 published French picture books for modification, making 3 of the books "easy" and 3 of the books "difficult." They found that preschoolers spent about 5% of their time viewing the print. First graders instead spent about 26% of their time looking at the easy books attending to the print, whereas they only spent about 16% of their time attending to the print while reading the difficult books. Meanwhile, the second graders spent about 38% of their time looking at the print. No matter their age, the vast majority of their time was spent looking at the pictures. They also separated the children into different strategy groups: pure reading, pointing, and highlighting. They found that, during shared reading, that when using a print reference strategy to help children, overall, that pointing at the print significantly increased the amount of visual attention paid to the print.

In summary, shared reading can increase children's phonological awareness and print awareness, promoting emergent literacy. However, if parents want to optimize shared reading for bolstering print knowledge, they must use a print referencing strategy to coax children to pay attention to the print and participate in discussions of the print.

Along with the development of electronic technology, many books have changed to the electronic format, and storybooks are no exception. To increase the reading and writing skills of children, many electronic storybooks have also began implementing print referencing strategies, such as pointing, highlighting, or having a bouncing ball or other multimedia focus the attention of the children on the text. For example, Guo and Feng [29] found that during shared reading if the child could follow their father's reading trajectory, then the child was able to read the story on the screen along with their parent, and doing so increased the child's overall participation in the shared reading.

2 Purpose

The purpose of this study was to understand which electronic storybook display method is best able to increase children's attention to the print area. To this end, we modified the electronic storybook's design and used an eye-tracker to measure the children's visual attention during reading.

3 Method

This study included 76 children between the ages of 4–6 from two northern Taiwanese kindergartens. Informed consent was obtained from all preschoolers' parents. Their native language was Mandarin Chinese. Before the experiment was conducted, questionnaires were distributed to evaluate the children's reading conditions at home. This study was conducted over a 6-week period: one week for pre-tests, four weeks of interventions, and one week for post-tests. The kindergarteners were split into three groups: a traditional storybook group (group 1), the highlight synchronization group (implicit instruction; group 2), and the text-discussion group (explicit instruction; group 3). Each group had 25, 25, and 26 children, respectively. The difference in each group lied in how these storybooks were displayed during the intervention stage: In the traditional storybook group, the print was simply read aloud by a recording, synchronized with the displayed page. In the highlight synchronization group, individual Chinese characters were highlighted in blue when they were being pronounced, thus implicitly teaching the children which Chinese characters were associated with which sounds. The text-discussion group added explicit instruction in the form of cuing to or discussions of the print. This study used six storybooks, each book included 16–17 pages. Half of the area of each page was picture area, and half was print area. Each child was individually presented with the same electronic storybooks. An experimenter sat next to each child during reading sessions but did not engage in shared reading. In the pre-test stage each child's print awareness and vocabulary were tested, and then all children read the same electronic storybook accompanied by its recording, meanwhile the eye-tracker was used to record how the children read their storybook. Then the 76 children were randomly assigned to the three groups, and their print awareness scores, vocabulary scores, and eye data were previewed to ensure there were no pre-existing differences between the groups. Weeks 2–5 were the intervention stage, with one session per week and two books read per session. Eye-tracking was conducted during the week 2 readings. The 6th week was the post-test stage, and, beyond merely reading an additional storybook, eye-tracking was added to the reading and post-tests (identical to the pre-tests) were administered to each child.

4 Results

For the ratio of total fixation duration (RTFD), please see Table 1.

A mixed design three-factor ANOVA was conducted on the time, area, and group variables to see their effect on RTFD, of those the time and area variables were considered as within subject variables, and group was considered as the between subject variable. The results indicate that the time variable had a significant effect (F $(1, 64) = 4.283$, p = .043, $\eta2 = .063$). The RTFD of teaching period (M = .491, SD = .304) was significantly longer than the pre-test's RTFD (M = .483, SD = .353). The area variable had a significant effect as well (F(1, 64) = 135.755, p = .000, $\eta2 = .680$). The picture area had a significantly longer RTFD (M = .747, SD = .201) than the text area's RTFD (M = .227, SD = .200). Group had no significant effect (F (2, 64) = .693, p = .504, $\eta2 = .021$).

Table 1. Ratio of total fixation duration

		Group 1	Group 2	Group 3	Total
N		22	22	23	67
		Mean (SD)	Mean (SD)	Mean (SD)	Mean (SD)
Pre-test	Picture area	.786 (.228)	.757 (.196)	.774 (.192)	.773 (.203)
	Text area	.191 (.227)	.193 (.183)	.197 (.191)	.194 (.198)
Week 2 (intervention stage)	Picture area	.826 (.176)	.599 (.177)	.739 (.173)	.722 (.197)
	Text area	.155 (.176)	.387 (.179)	.238 (.173)	.260 (.198)

The time, area, and group variables all had significant interactions (F (2, 64) = 27.001, p = .000, $\eta 2$ = .458), and so a simple effects test was conducted (F (1, 64) = 71.006, p = .000, $\eta 2$ = .526). For teaching period, group and area had a significant simple effect ($F(2, 128)$ = 8.305, p = .000, $\eta 2$ = .115). For picture area, group and time both demonstrated a significant simple effect ($F(2, 128)$ = 20.986, p = .000, $\eta 2$ = .247). For text area, group and time both had significant simple effects ($F(2, 128)$ = 28.396, p = .000, $\eta 2$ = .307).

For group 2, a further simple main effect test was conducted on the interaction between time and area. For group 2's pre-test, area had a significant simple main effect ($F(1, 128)$ = 48.920, p = .000, $\eta 2$ = .277). The mean RTFD of the picture area (M = .757, SD = .196) was significantly longer than the text area's mean RTFD (M = .193, SD = .183). For group 2's teaching period, area continued to show a significant simple main effect ($F(1, 128)$ = 6.890, p = .010, $\eta 2$ = .051). The picture area's RTFD (M = .599, SD = .177) was significantly longer than that of the text area's RTFD (M = .387, SD = .179). When it came to group 2's picture area, time had a significant simple main effect ($F(1, 128)$ = 52.495, p = .000, $\eta 2$ = .291). The pre-test's RTFD (M = .757, SD = .196) was significantly longer than the teaching period's RTFD (M = .599, SD = .177). As for group 2's text area, time had a significant simple main effect ($F(1, 128)$ = 78.377, p = .000, $\eta 2$ = .380). The pre-test's RTFD (M = .193, SD = .183) was significantly shorter than the RTFD of the teaching period (M = .387, SD = .179).

Due to the significant simple interaction between group and area under the teaching period condition, a simple main effect test was conducted. For group 1's teaching period, area had a significant simple main effect ($F(1, 128)$ = 69.272, p = .000, $\eta 2$ = .351), and the RTFD of the picture area (M = .826, SD = .176) was significantly longer than the text area's RTFD (M = .155, SD = .176). As for group 2, area had a significant simple main effect ($F(1, 128)$ = 6.890, p = .010, $\eta 2$ = .051), with the picture area's RTFD (M = .599, SD = .177) being significantly longer than the text area's RTFD (M = .387, SD = .179). As for group 3, area had a significant simple main effect ($F(1, 128)$ = 40.366, p = .000, $\eta 2$ = .240), with the picture area's RTFD (M = .739,

SD = .173) significantly longer than the text area's RTFD (M = .238, SD = .173). For the teaching period's picture area, group had a significant simple main effect (F (2, 256) = 8.011, p = .000, η2 = .059). A post-hoc analysis using Scheffe's test was run and found that group 1's RTFD (M = .826, SD = .176) was significantly longer than group 2's RTFD (M = .599, SD = .177; p < .001), and group 3's RTFD (M = .739, SD = .173) was longer than group 2's RTFD (p < .05). As for teaching period's text area, group showed a significant simple main effect (F(2, 256) = 8.381, p = .000, η2 = .061). A post hoc Scheffe's test was conducted and revealed that group 2's RTFD (M = .387, SD = .179) was significantly longer than group 1's RTFD (M = .155, SD = .176; p < .001), and group 2's RTFD was significantly longer than group 3's RTFD (M = .238, SD = .173; p < .05).

Due to the significant simple interaction between the time and group variables under the picture area condition, a simple main effect test was conducted. For group 2's picture area, time had a significant main effect (F(1, 128) = 52.495, p = .000, η2 = .291). The pre-test's RTFD (M = .757, SD = .196) was significantly longer than the teaching period's RTFD (M = .599, SD = .177). As for the picture area of the teaching period, group had a significant simple main effect (F(2, 256) = 8.011, p = .000, η2 = .059). A post hoc Scheffe's test was run and found that group 1's RTFD (M = .826, SD = .176) was significantly longer than group 2's RTFD (M = .599, SD = .177; p < .001), and group 3's RTFD (M = .739, SD = .173) was significantly longer than group 2's RTFD (p < .05).

Due to the significant simple interaction between time and group under the text area condition, a simple main effect test was conducted. For the text area of group 2, time had a significant simple main effect (F(1, 128) = 78.377, p = .000, η2 = .380). The pre-test's RTFD (M = .193, SD = .183) was significantly shorter than the RTFD of the teaching period (M = .387, SD = .179). As for the text area of the teaching period, group had a significant main effect (F(2, 256) = 8.381, p = .000, η2 = .061). A post hoc Scheffe's test demonstrated that group 2's RTFD (M = .387, SD = .179) was significantly longer than group 1's RTFD (M = .155, SD = .176; p < .001), and group 2's RTFD was significant longer than group 3's RTFD (M = .238, SD = .173; p < .05).

5   Conclusion and Discussion

The result of the pre-test suggested that the northern Taiwanese children spent 77.3% of their time looking at the picture area, and 19.6% at the print area. This is substantially higher than the findings of previous research. Meanwhile, the result of week 2, the first week of the intervention stage, showed that, when it came to visual attention invested in the print area, the highlight synchronization groups paid significantly more attention to the print area than the traditional storybook group. Any number of factors could explain the difference between our result and previous research, such as native language, nationality, socioeconomic status, and at-home reading habits, to name a few. Future research is necessary to explain this discrepancy. Meanwhile, this study did not examine the literacy skills of the children, and thus it is impossible to know whether the children's literacy skills influenced the amount of visual attention paid to the print area. Future research could add such measures to see if there is any relationship between the two. Follow-up research could also track the children two years later to examine the children's reading literacy. Due to the week 2 results, we recommend future electronic-storybook designs should not adopt a pure-speech reading design, and instead should synchronize the reading of the words with dynamic highlighting and add direct discussions of the text. Doing so will help to entice children to pay more attention to the print area.

References

1. Bingham, G.E.: Maternal literacy beliefs and the quality of mother-child book reading interactions: associations with children's early literacy development. Early Educ. Dev. **18**, 23–49 (2007). http://dx.doi.org.proxy2.cl.msu.edu/10.1080/10409280701274428
2. Teale, W., Sulzby, E.: Introduction: emergent literacy as a perspective for examining how children become writers and readers. In: Teale, W., Sulzby, E. (eds.) Emergent Literacy: Writing and Reading. Ablex Publishing Corporation, Norwood (1986)
3. Justice, L.M., Kaderavek, J.: Using shared storybook reading to promote emergent literacy. Teach. Except. Child. **34**(4), 8–13 (2002)
4. Justice, L.M., Pullen, P.C., Pence, K.: Influence of verbal and nonverbal references to print on preschoolers' visual attention to print during storybook reading. Dev. Psychol. **44**(3), 855–866 (2008)
5. Whitehurst, G.J., Lonigan, C.J.: Child development and emergent literacy. Child Dev. **69**(3), 848–872 (1998). https://doi.org/10.1111/j.1467-8624.1998.tb06247.x
6. Lonigan, C.J., Shanahan, T.: Executive Summary. A Scientific Synthesis of Early Literacy Development and Implications for Intervention. Retrieved from the National Institute for Literacy (2009)
7. Piasta, S.B., Justice, L.M., McGinty, A.S., Kaderavek, J.N.: Increasing young children's contact with print during shared reading: longitudinal effects on literacy achievement. Child Dev. **83**(3), 810–820 (2012). https://doi.org/10.1111/j.1467-8624.2012.01754.x
8. Pullen, P.C., Justice, L.M.: Enhancing phonological awareness, print awareness, and oral language skills in preschool children. Interv. Sch. Clin. **39**(2), 87–98 (2003)
9. Campana, K., Mills, J.E., Capps, J.L., Dresang, E.T., Carlyle, A., Metoyer, C.A., Urban, I. B., Feldman, E.N., Brouwer, M., Kotrla, B.: Early literacy in library storytimes: a study of measures of effectiveness. Libr. Q. **86**(4), 369–388 (2016). https://doi.org/10.1086/688028
10. Evans, M.A., Saint-Aubin, J.: Vocabulary acquisition without adult explanations in repeated shared book reading: An eye movement study. J. Educ. Psychol. **105**(3), 596–608 (2013). https://doi.org/10.1037/a0032465
11. Allor, J.H., McCathren, R.B.: Developing emergent literacy skills through storybook reading. Interv. Sch. Clin. **39**(2), 72–79 (2003)
12. Lonigan, C.J., Burgess, S.R., Anthony, J.L., Barker, T.A.: Development of phonological sensitivity in 2- to 5-year-old children. J. Educ. Psychol. **90**(2), 294–311 (1998)
13. Badian, N.A.: Phonological and orthographic processing: their roles in reading prediction. Ann. Dyslexia **51**, 179–202 (2001)
14. Clay, M.M.: Reading Recovery: A Guidebook for Teachers in Training. Heineman, Portsmouth (1993)
15. Tunmer, W.E., Herriman, M.L., Nesdale, A.R.: Phonemic segmentation skill and beginning reading. J. Educ. Psychol. **77**, 417–427 (1988)

16. Adams, M.J.: Beginning to Read: Thinking and Learning About Print. MIT Press, Cambridge (1990)
17. Cunningham, J.W.: Review: essay book reviews: the national reading panel report. Read. Res. Q. **36**(3), 326–335 (2001)
18. Sung, Y.T., Wu, M.D., Chen, C.K., Chang, K.E.: Examining the online reading behavior and performance of fifth-graders: evidence from eye-movement data. Front. Psychol. **6**, 1–15 (2015)
19. Jian, Y.C.: Reading instructions facilitate signaling effect on science text for young readers: an eye-movement study. Int. J. Sci. Math. Educ. (2018, in press)
20. Lee, W.K., Wu, C.J.: Eye movements in integrating geometric text and figure: scanpaths and given-new effects. Int. J. Sci. Math. Educ. **16**(4), 699–714 (2018)
21. Evans, M.A., Saint-Aubin, J.: What children are looking at during shared storybook reading: evidence from eye movement monitoring. Psychol. Sci. **16**(11), 913–920 (2005)
22. Evans, M.A., Williamson, K., Pursoo, T.: Preschoolers' attention to print during shared book reading. Sci. Stud. Read. **12**(1), 106–129 (2008)
23. Justice, L.M., Skibbe, L., Canning, A., Lankford, C.: Pre-schoolers, print and storybooks: an observational study using eye movement analysis. J. Res. Read. **28**(3), 229–243 (2005)
24. Roy-Charland, A., Saint-Aubin, J., Evans, M.A.: Eye movements in shared book reading with children from kindergarten to Grade 4. Read. Writ. **20**(9), 909–931 (2007)
25. Lai, M.-L., Chen, Y.-h.: Examining preschoolers' attention during storybook reading: Evidence from eye movements. J. Early Child. Educ. Res. **8**, 81–96 (2012). (in Chinese)
26. Evans, M.A., Shaw, D., Bell, M.: Home literacy experiences and their influence on early literacy skills. Can. J. Exp. Psychol. **54**, 65–75 (2000)
27. Evans, M.A., Shaw, D.: Home grown for reading: Parental contributions to young children's emergent literacy and word recognition. Can. Psychol. **49**, 89–95 (2008)
28. Roy-Charland, A., Perron, M., Boulard, J., Chamberland, J., Hoffman, N.: "If I point, do they look?": the impact of attention–orientation strategies on text exploration during shared book reading. Read. Writ. **28**(9), 1285–1305 (2015). https://doi.org/10.1007/s11145-015-9571-2
29. Guo, J., Feng, G.: How eye gaze feedback changes parent-child joint attention in shared storybook reading? In: Nakano, Y.I., Conati, C., Bader, T. (eds.) Eye Gaze in Intelligent User Interfaces: Gaze-Based Analyses, Models and Applications, pp. 9–21. Springer, London (2013). https://doi.org/10.1007/978-1-4471-4784-8_2

Reading Multiple Documents on Tablet: Effects of Applications and Strategic Guidance on Performance and Acceptance

Jordan Lombard[1(✉)], Franck Amadieu[1], Ivar Bråten[2], and Cécile van de Leemput[3]

[1] CLLE, University of Toulouse, CNRS, Toulouse, France
{jordan.lombard,amadieu}@univ-tlse2.fr
[2] Department of Education, University of Oslo, Oslo, Norway
ivar.braten@iped.uio.no
[3] Research Center for Work and Consumer Psychology,
Université libre de Bruxelles, Brussels, Belgium
cecile.van.de.leemput@ulb.ac.be

Abstract. In this experimental study, 66 undergraduate students in psychology used an iPad pro to study several documents dealing with the same topic. The study aimed to compare the effects of using two different applications on comprehension in a multiple document reading task: Adobe Reader, which is an application oriented towards linear reading, and LiquidText, which is an application designed for non-linear reading. Further, because studying multiple texts is a complex learning task that requires effective and efficient processing strategies, the study tested the effect of strategic guidance that was expected to promote both performance and acceptance of tablets. The results indicated the existence of a performance-preference paradox: while the participants guided in the use of LiquidText achieved better comprehension, they expressed less acceptance of tablets as a tool for studying multiple documents than did the participants who used Adobe Reader.

Keywords: Acceptance · Multiple document comprehension · Digital learning Tablet

1 Introduction

In 21st century societies, the comparison of multiple sources is essential in developing a well-founded, critical point of view [1]. Hence, developing multiple document literacy which concerns the ability to locate, evaluate, and use various sources of information in order to construct and communicate an integrated and reasoned representation of a particular problem, subject or situation [2]. The comprehension of multiple documents implies active and non-linear reading involving the implementation of cognitive and metacognitive strategies to meet the goals of reading. However, digital systems supporting active reading typically seek to reproduce paper affordances and, thus, seem better suited to linear than to non-linear reading [3]. This trend can be explained by learners' resistance to changing their learning habits, as the paper/pen

© Springer International Publishing AG, part of Springer Nature 2018
P. Zaphiris and A. Ioannou (Eds.): LCT 2018, LNCS 10924, pp. 157–169, 2018.
https://doi.org/10.1007/978-3-319-91743-6_12

combination is the most commonly used tool for the document study. However, this traditional tool may constrain rather than facilitate non-linear reading, such as the lack of paper flexibility, which makes it difficult to compare several parts of the same document because of the tangibility of the material [4].

Compared to paper, the tablet has its own constraints. First of all, the screen induces digital reading that provides different experiences than reading on paper [5]. Second, the size of the screen may make it difficult to simultaneously view a source document and write another document [6]. Further, the virtual keyboard of the tablet may reduce screen visibility [7]. Finally, traditional document study applications (e.g. Adobe Reader) allow only one document to be displayed at a time, which likely results in higher cognitive load when trying to compare several documents.

Tashman and Edwards [8] wanted to utilize the potential of digital technology in trying to overcome some of these constraints. Thus, these authors aimed to (a) support direct, flexible, and extensive manipulation of the visual arrangement of the original content as well as annotations; and (b) support flexibility in browsing through the content. Thy therefor developed the LiquidText application, which is an active reading system offering a substantially different approach to representation and interaction with documents. However, the availability of a tool that fits users' needs will not necessarily lead to user acceptance. In order to assess the impact of new technologies like LiquidText, research is usually framed by models of the social acceptance of technologies, such as the Technology Acceptance Model [9].

First, the present study compared the effects of two applications on comprehension in a multiple document reading task: Adobe Reader (see Fig. 4), which is a software oriented towards linear reading, and LiquidText (see Fig. 3), which is a software designed for non-linear reading. Second, because studying multiple texts is a complex learning task that requires efficient processing strategies, the study examined the effect of strategic guidance designed to promote learners' performance and, consequentially, their acceptance of tablets as a tool for studying multiple documents.

1.1   Multiple Document Comprehension

Multiple-document comprehension implies that readers study several documents in order to develop a well-informed and justified stance on an issue based on the reading of documents. In 2014, Bråten and colleagues [10, p. 10] maintained that "in multiple-text comprehension, readers need to not only comprehend each single text but also integrate information across different texts to create a global understanding of a situation or issue discussed across texts". One of the most influential model in multiple-document comprehension is the MD-TRACE model (i.e., the Multiple-Document Task-based Relevance Assessment and Content Extraction model) introduced by Rouet and Britt [11]. This model describes the use of multiple documents as a cycle of processing steps and decisions.

Specifically, the MD-TRACE model focuses on resources (internal and external) and processes involved in document-based activities (see Fig. 1). External resources are the information and materials presented to students before they begin the task, or are made available to them or created during the completion of the task. External resources manipulated in this study include task specifications in the form of a reading task scenario, a set of 5 documents dealing with the issue of sun exposure, the devices with two different applications in an iPad, and the set of task products generated by the reader via the use of the applications' functionalities. Internal resources are the cognitive resources used by the readers to achieve their reading goal. It is possible to make a distinction between permanent resources that exist prior the task (e.g., prior knowledge) and transitory resources that are generated when working on the task (e.g., representation of the task demands, representation of the document contents).

Processing steps and relevance assessment are decomposed into five steps: (1) <u>task</u>

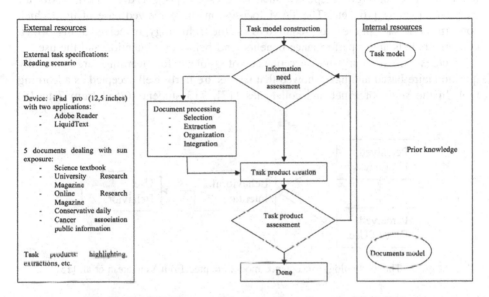

Fig. 1. The MD-Trace model adapted from Rouet and Britt [11]

<u>model construction,</u> where readers represent the activities involved in fulfilling the requirements of the task; (2) <u>information needs assessment,</u> where readers try to identify the information needs by using prior knowledge; (3) <u>documents processing,</u> where readers select, extract, and integrate relevant information from the documents in constructing a documents model, (4) <u>task product creation,</u> where readers use their document model to construct a response to the task; and (5) <u>task product assessment,</u> where readers assess whether their product fulfills the task demands. The guidance that was offered readers in this study stems directly from the document processes described in the third step of MD-TRACE, that is, the guidance consisted of instruction helping learners select/extract information and then organize extracted information for the purpose of integration. The guidance strategy is detailed in the Materials section.

1.2   Acceptance

Acceptance of a technology can be defined as an individual's perception of the value of a technology [12], as well as the extent to which an individual integrates and appropriates the technology in the context of use [13]. Acceptance addresses the potential impact of a new technology because it is based on the perceptions of future target users. In this study, acceptance concerned students' perceptions of a tablet as a tool for learning with and from multiple documents.

The best known and most widely used model for understanding acceptance of a new technology is the Technology Acceptance Model (TAM) [9] (see Fig. 2). First, this model is easy to explain and use, and, second, it is a basic model that can be easily adapted for a specific context. There are many derivatives models of TAM in the literature of technology acceptance such as UTAUT [14], TAM 3 [15], TAM for electronic reading [16], etc. The TAM focuses on the perceived ease of use, which concerns beliefs about the effort required to use the technology, perceived utility, which concerns beliefs about performance benefits, and behavioral intention and the use.

Studies investigating the acceptance of tablets for learning are generally questionnaire-based and have showed that tablets are fairly well accepted as a learning tool. In the study of Pruet and colleagues [17], 213 students (aged from 7 to 16)

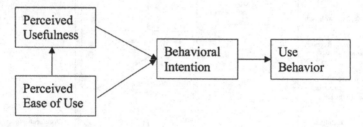

Fig. 2. The Technology Acceptance model adapted from Venkatesh et al. [15]

expressed positive attitudes towards the tablet due to the joy and productivity it provided. More specifically, participants indicated that tablets were fun, exciting, and useful for learning in class. Also, other questionnaire studies [18, 19] based on TAM and UTAUT have revealed two key variables for accepting tablets for learning: performance expectancy, that is the degree to which individuals believe that using the system will help them attain their goals, and effort expectancy, that is the degree to which individuals perceive that the system is easy to use. Further, Moran and colleagues [18] found a difference in acceptance between students who chose to use a tablet compared to those who were required to do so.

For the purpose of this study, we followed van der Linden and colleagues [20] and addressed yet another aspect of acceptance that we termed "motivational utility specific to a task". This is further described in the Materials section.

1.3   The Present Study

As far as we know, no prior study was designed to test multiple-document comprehension with tablets. Specifically, we examined the effects of specific applications and guidance of processing on performance and acceptance of tablets for such a task. The following hypotheses were tested:

(H1) Students using the application supporting multiple document processing (i.e., LiquidText) will display better comprehension performance and higher acceptance of tablets than those using Adobe Reader. The application supporting multiple document processing was expected to facilitate the extraction and integration of information from texts. Therefore, this application also was expected to promote acceptance of tablets in such a task context.

(H2) Students guided in the use of the application supporting multiple document processing (strategy group) will gain higher comprehension and higher acceptance than those who use the same application (i.e., LiquidText) without support (free group). The lack of guidance was expected to entail less efficiency, and therefore a more negative experience for learners. Consequentially, the strategy group can also be expected to report lower acceptance than the free group.

2 Method

2.1 Design - Participants

Participants were 66 undergraduate students (83% female) in psychology from the University of Toulouse with a mean age of 23 (SD = 5.60). The majority of the participants were in their third year (51 students), the others were in their first year. Only 26 participants owned their own tablets, and most of those tablets had a regular screen size (9–10 in.). Participation was anonymous and voluntary, and remuneration was 0.5 additional points for a specific course.

There were three experimental conditions with 21 participants per condition. Two groups were instructed to use the non-linear reading application LiquidText. Participants in the free group freely used LiquidText. Participants in the strategy group were instructed to use a strategy called Annotation-Extraction-Reorganization (AER) when using LiquidText. The strategy involved three phases: (1) students highlighted information during reading. (2) students selected the relevant information according to the reading goal and extracted the selected information, and (3) students organized the extracted information in the available workspace. Finally, participants in the control group freely used Adobe Reader, which means they could use any functionalities they found useful. For the writing task, the iPad screen of the students in the control group was split into two, with the Adobe Reader displayed to the left for document consultation and Notes display to the right for essay production.

LiquidText
The application LiquidText, which is available in Apple Store, is a PDF viewer designed for non-linear reading. The aim of this application is to support the processes involved in active reading: annotation, content extraction, browsing, and layout. As can be seen in Fig. 3, LiquidText displays three areas: the documents navigation panel to the left, the document viewer (up to three documents) in the middle, and a workspace to the right. In addition to the classic features, this application enables extraction of

content from the document that can be moved to the workspace. Once content is extracted and moved to the workspace, it is also possible to group and edit content from multiple documents, and to create a textbox directly in the workspace. Thus, affordances of the LiquidText application seem to fit the requirements of multiple-document comprehension tasks.

Adobe Reader

The application Adobe Reader (see Fig. 4), also available in Apple Store, is a PDF viewer oriented towards linear reading. It can display only one document at a time and

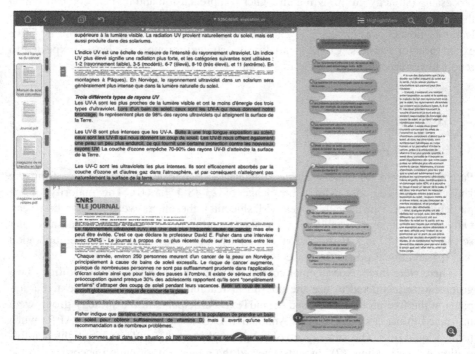

Fig. 3. LiquidText

has classic features to study a document, such as highlighting, underlining, adding comments, etc. One of the difficulties in using this application to study several documents is comparing two documents by switching from one to the other. This requires keeping the to-be-compared information in memory.

2.2   Materials

Texts

The five texts that we used presented different perspectives on sun exposure and health. For the purposes of this study, the texts have been freely translated into French from the

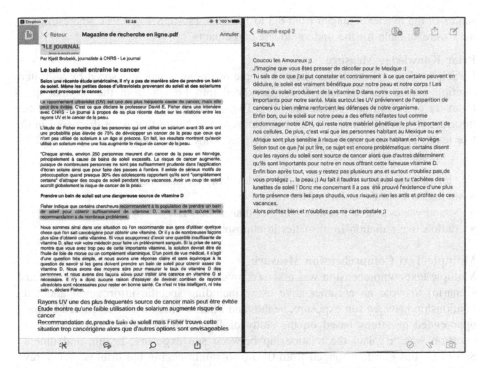

Fig. 4. Control group's screen during the writing task. To the left: AdobeReader; to the right: Notes.

original texts used by Bråten and colleagues [10]. The first text was a 469-word excerpt from a science textbook describing the nature of ultraviolet radiation, concluding that further research is needed to understand the health implications of sun exposure. In adapting the original Norwegian material, we chose "Editions Nathan" as the source of this document. The second text was a 503-word popular science article from a university research magazine arguing that sun exposure may protect against cancer. As the source of the document, we used "Exploreur", the scientific magazine of the University of Toulouse. The third text was a 473-word popular science article from an online research magazine (source: CNRS-Le journal) claiming that sun exposure is carcinogenic. The fourth text was a 414-word article from a conservative daily (source: LeMonde.fr) explaining that sun exposure provides vitamin D, which helps prevent cancer. Finally, the fifth text was a 469-word public information text published by a cancer association (source: Société Française du Cancer), which introduced different types of cancer that can result from exposure to the sun and explained how the cancer risk can be reduced.

As an indication of text difficulty, we used the Gunning-Fog index from the website www.textalyser.net to calculate readability scores for each of the texts. This index is a weighted average of the number of words per sentence, and the number of long words per word. It yields readability scores ranging from 6 (easy) to 17 (hard). The readability scores of the five texts ranged from 8.3 to 14 (M = 11.46, SD = 1.93), suggesting that they were suitable for the undergraduate participants.

Prior Knowledge Measure

Participants' prior knowledge about the topic of the texts was measured by a 20-item multiple-choice questionnaire freely translated into French from the original questionnaire of Bråten and colleagues [10]. The questionnaire focused on concepts and information central to the issue of sun exposure and health that were discussed in the five texts. This is a sample item from the prior knowledge measure:

Ultraviolet (UV) radiation is:

- electromagnetic radiation with energy level higher than visible;
- radiation from the colors of the rainbow;
- sound waves with a frequency higher than 20000 Hz;
- radioactive radiation from matter in atmosphere.

Multiple-Text Comprehension Measure

Multiple-text comprehension was assessed by asking participants (by means of a task scenario) to write an argumentative essay including specific information about the relationship between sun exposure, health, and illness. This essay was guided by three open-ended questions based on the study of Bråten and colleagues [10]. The first question was "Explain the relationship between sun exposure, health, and illness". Scores on this question ranged from 0 to 6 (6 = introducing the origins of UV rays, mentioning different perspectives on the issue, and explaining the relationship between sun exposure and different health effects). The second question was "Describe the different existing perspectives on the relationship between sun exposure, health, and illness". Scores on this question ranged from 0 to 6 (6 = explaining views in favor of versus against sun exposure with links between the two views (e.g., comparison)). The third question was "Explain, whether there can be more than one correct view on the relationship between sun exposure, health, and illness, and, if so, which one(s) is/are correct". Scores on this question ranged from 0 to 5 (5 = acknowledging the existence of different views on sun exposure and health, explain why more than one view can be correct, and presenting sun exposure recommendations). The possible range of score was thus 0–17 on the entire measure. Only participants' total scores on the entire measure were used in the statistical analysis. Two independent raters scored all the essays (Pearson intra-class correlation: ICC = 0.924; p < 0.01). The mean score of the two raters was used for the statistical analysis.

Acceptance

Participants' acceptance of the tablet as a tool for studying multiple documents was assessed by means of 4 items focusing on the motivational utility specific to a multiple-document comprehension task. The items were developed by van der Linden and colleagues [20], who targeted individual's motivation to use a certain tool for a specific type of task (sample item: The use of a digital tablet makes it more interesting to study several documents dealing with the same topic). Each item was rated on a 10-point scale (1 = not at all true for me, 10 = completely true for me). The reliability estimate (Cronbach's alpha) for participants' scores was .92.

Procedure

Participants were randomly assigned to one of the three conditions. The study sessions were individual distributed over two days.

On day one, participants answered the prior knowledge questionnaire on Qualtrics. Then, they explored all the functionalities of the LiquidText and Adobe Reader applications, respectively, by following a check-list that familiarized them with the use of the applications while given overview of the potentialities. Finally, they practiced the applications with a training task that involved studying two documents dealing with global warming in order to write a summary. This training task was designed so that the participants used the applications for collecting and organizing relevant information in a context similar to the experimental task – participants did not produce a summary during training.

On day two, participants individually completed the multiple document reading task on the tablet in their respective condition (maximum 35 min). After reading, they were asked to express their position on sun exposure and health in an essay by writing on the tablet (maximum 20 min). Finally, they answered the motivational utility specific to a multiple document comprehension task questionnaire. Before starting on the texts, participants read the following instruction on a sheet of paper: Before going on holiday, a friend of yours sends you a Facebook message. Rather cautious, this friend asks for your opinion on the effects of the sun on health. Here's the message: "Hi, how are you? As you already know, my girlfriend and I are leaving for Mexico next week. Since it's full summer at this time of the year, we're a little freaked out about the potential effects of the Mexican sun on our skin. Especially, since at home we do not agree on the issue: there is one who thinks that exposure to the sun is safe while the other thinks quite the opposite. Anyway, to close the debate we need an impartial opinion, yours". You have done a quick Internet search and selected the first five results. To make it easier to read these documents offline, you have saved them in the application. You have 35 min to study the documents in the application. At the end of this period, you will have 20 min to write a reply to your friend based on the documents you have read. The documents will remain at your disposal during the writing task. Your answer will address the following points: explain the relationship between sun exposure, health, and illness; describe the different existing perspectives of the relationship between sun exposure, health, and illness; explain, whether there can be more than one correct view on the relationship between sun exposure, health, and illness.

3 Results

3.1 Multiple-Text Comprehension

The means of the multiple-text comprehension scores are shown in Fig. 5. The descriptive statistics showed that the strategy group (M = 12.29, SD = 2.03) outperformed the free group (M = 9.92, SD = 1.37) and the control group (M = 9.40, SD = 2.25). A one-way ANOVA revealed a significant effect of condition on multiple document comprehension, $F(2, 63) = 14.78$, $p < 0.001$, $\eta^2 = 0.33$. Post-hoc comparison (Ryan-Einot-Gabriel-Welsch) indicated two subgroups: one composed of only the strategy group and the other composed of the participants in the two other conditions. This result did not support the first hypothesis, suggesting that the tool LiquidText would have no effect on comprehension compared to Adobe Reader. At the same time, this result supported the second hypothesis, which stated that guidance by the AER strategy when using LiquidText would improve comprehension.

3.2 Acceptance

The descriptive statistics (see Fig. 6) showed that the control group (M = 7.12, SD = 1.74) perceived the tablet more motivating for a multiple-document comprehension task than the free group (M = 6.42, SD = 1.52) and the strategy group (M = 5.02, SD = 2.42). A one-way ANOVA revealed a significant effect of condition on motivational utility, $F(3, 82) = 3.46$, $p < 0.05$, $\eta^2 = 0.11$. Post-hoc comparison

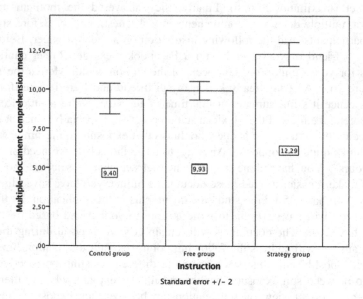

Fig. 5. Mean scores for multiple-text comprehension

(Ryan-Einot-Gabriel-Welsch) indicated a difference between the control group and strategy groups. Those perceptions contradicted our expectations and might be explained by the obligation to use the strategy.

4   Discussion

The results of this study suggested, inconsistent with hypothesis 1, that the tool LiquidText had no effect on comprehension compared to Adobe Reader. Indeed, the students using the application supporting multiple document processing did not display

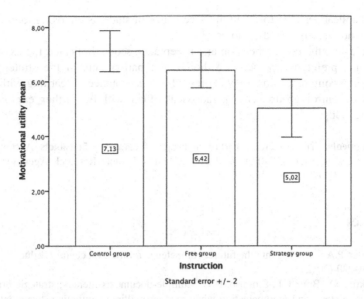

Fig. 6. Means scores for perceptions of motivational utility specific to a multiple-document comprehension task

better comprehension performance than those who used Adobe Reader. In other words, the mere provision of the tool, although adapted to a multiple document reading task, was not enough to improve performance. This result can be explained by the lack of familiarity with LiquidText, resulting in trial and error among the students in choosing which functionalities to use. This explanation is consistent with the design LiquidText, offering a substantially different (and less familiar) approach to representation and interaction with documents.

At the same time, and in accordance with hypothesis 2, the students guided in the use of the application supporting multiple document processing gained higher comprehension scores than those who used LiquidText without support. Consequentially, it would seem that students needed to be guided in their use of the tool during task completion. Thus, the instructed strategy may have compensated for the possible lack of familiarity with LiquidText. This result also suggests that LiquidText may facilitate processes such as annotation, content extraction, browsing, and layout [8], allowing the students to employ the instructed strategy. Finally, considering that the strategy was in accordance with the documents processing described by the MD-TRACE model [11], this result is in line with the literature on multiple-documents comprehension. In brief, the strategy we instructed may have helped students display forms of documents processing used by good comprehenders of multiple documents.

Contrary to our expectations, the students guided in the use of LiquidText did not express higher acceptance than those who used Adobe Reader. Those perceptions might be explained by the obligation to use the strategy, resulting in a feeling of losing control over own learning. This result can also be compared to the difference that

Moran and colleagues [18] found in the acceptance of students choosing to use a tablet and those who were required to do so.

In conclusion, the comprehension and acceptance scores indicated the existence of a performance-preference paradox. Although the participants in the strategy group achieved better comprehension, they expressed less acceptance of learning with a tablet than did the control group. This paradoxical effect will be further explored in a forthcoming study.

Acknowledgments. This research is part of the project "Learning with Tablets: Acceptance and Cognitive Processes (LETACOP)" funded by the ANR (National Research Agency) the reference "ANR-14-CE24-0032".

References

1. Alexander, P.A.: Reading into the future: competence for the 21st century. Educ. Psychol. **47** (4), 259–280 (2012)
2. Anmarkrud, Ø., Bråten, I., Strømsø, H.I.: Multiple-documents literacy: strategic processing, source awareness, and argumentation when reading multiple conflicting documents. Learn. Individ. Differ. **30**, 64–76 (2014)
3. Siegenthaler, E., Bochud, Y., Wurtz, P., Schmid, L., Bergamin, P.: The effects of touch screen technology on the usability of E-reading devices. J. Usability Stud. **7**(3), 94–104 (2012)
4. O'Hara, K.P., Taylor, A., Newman, W., Sellen, A.J.: Understanding the materiality of writing from multiple sources. Int. J. Hum Comput. Stud. **56**(3), 269–305 (2002)
5. Kostick, A.: The digital reading experience: learning from interaction design and UX-usability experts. Publ. Res. Q. **27**(2), 135–140 (2011)
6. Olive, T., Rouet, J.-F., François, E., Zampa, V.: Summarizing digital documents: effects of alternate or simultaneous window display. Appl. Cogn. Psychol. **22**(4), 541–558 (2008)
7. Mang, C.F., Wardley, L.J.: Student perceptions of using tablet technology in Post-Secondary Classes (Perceptions des étudiants quant à l'utilisation des tablettes électroniques dans les classes universitaires). Can. J. Learn. Technol. (La Revue Canadienne de l'apprentissage et de La Technologie) **39**(4) (2013). https://doi.org/10.21432/T22010
8. Tashman, C.S., Edwards, W.K.: LiquidText: a flexible, multitouch environment to support active reading. In: Proceedings of the SIGCHI Conference on Human Factors in Computing Systems, pp. 3285–3294. ACM, New York (2011). https://doi.org/10.1145/1978942.1979430
9. Davis, F.D., Bagozzi, R.P., Warshaw, P.R.: User acceptance of computer technology: a comparison of two theoretical models. Manag. Sci. **35**(8), 982–1003 (1989)
10. Bråten, I., Anmarkrud, Ø., Brandmo, C., Strømsø, H.I.: Developing and testing a model of direct and indirect relationships between individual differences, processing, and multiple-text comprehension. Learn. Instr. **30**, 9–24 (2014)
11. Rouet, J.F., Britt, M.A.: Relevance processes in multiple documents comprehension. In: McCrudden, M.T., Magliano, J.P., Schraw, G. (eds.) Text Relevance and Learning from Text, pp. 19–52. Information Age Publishing, Charlotte (2011)
12. Jamet, E., Février, F.: Utilisabilité, utilité et acceptabilité des nouvelles technologies dans l'entreprise: une approche de psychologie ergonomique. Analyser Les Usages Des Systèmes d'information et Des TIC: Quelles Démarches, Quelles Méthodes (2008)

13. Brangier, É., Barcenilla, J.: Concevoir un produit facile à utiliser (Editions Eyrolles). Editions d'organisation (2003). https://www.editions-eyrolles.com/Livre/9782708129009/concevoir-un-produit-facile-a-utiliser

14. Venkatesh, V., Morris, M.G., Davis, G.B., Davis, F.D.: User acceptance of information technology: toward a unified view. MIS Q. **27**(3), 425–478 (2003)

15. Venkatesh, V., Thong, J.Y., Xu, X.: Consumer acceptance and use of information technology: extending the unified theory of acceptance and use of technology. MIS Q. **36**(1), 157–178 (2012)

16. Hyman, J.A., Moser, M.T., Segala, L.N.: Electronic reading and digital library technologies: understanding learner expectation and usage intent for mobile learning. Educ. Technol. Res. Dev. **62**(1), 35–52 (2014)

17. Pruet, P., Ang, C.S., Farzin, D.: Understanding tablet computer usage among primary school students in underdeveloped areas: students' technology experience, learning styles and attitudes. Comput. Hum. Behav. **55**, 1131–1144 (2016)

18. Moran, M., Hawkes, M., Gayar, O.E.: Tablet personal computer integration in higher education: applying the unified theory of acceptance and use technology model to understand supporting factors. J. Educ. Comput. Res. **42**(1), 79–101 (2010)

19. El-Gayar, O., Moran, M., Hawkes, M.: Students' acceptance of tablet PCs and implications for educational institutions. Educ. Technol. Soc. **14**(2), 58–70 (2011)

20. van der Linden, J., Amadieu, F., van de Leemput, C.: L'importance de l'expérience vécue pour l'usage des tablettes à l'université. The importance of user experience for tablet usage at university. In: AIPTLF 2017 congress book (in press)

Designing and Validating Learner-Centered Experiences

Angela Payne$^{(\boxtimes)}$, John Sadauskas$^{(\boxtimes)}$, Quincy Conley$^{(\boxtimes)}$,
and Daniel Shapera$^{(\boxtimes)}$

Pearson, Boston, MA, USA
{angela.payne,john.sadauskas,quincy.conley,
daniel.shapera}@pearson.com

Abstract. Pearson is committed to offering learning products that are designed with empirical learning science research in mind and that demonstrate efficacy in enhancing learning outcomes. In applying the learning sciences to our designs, however, we must be mindful of human factors, particularly ensuring that our research-based products are designed in a way that meets the needs of our students and instructors. Accordingly, we have implemented Design-Based Research (DBR) processes to investigate student needs, iteratively test product designs, and inform design decisions. Our continually refined and scalable process has yielded many successes in both current and forthcoming products. This paper first outlines the history and theoretical underpinnings of design-based research. Additionally, the need for design-based research at Pearson is described. Subsequently, we provide an overview of our design-based research approach and processes. Finally, successes informed by design-based research are shared.

Keywords: Human-centered design · Design-Based Research
Evidence-based practice

1 Evolving Design-Based Research to Support Human Factors

In designing learning experiences, it is imperative to look to the learning sciences research for guidance on what will yield positive learning outcomes. However, much learning research is conducted in lab settings or other controlled environments ignoring the inseparable relationship of cognition and context. When applying learning principles to product design there are important considerations to be made in terms of the product's context in the learning sequence: student support needs, cognitive and noncognitive student attributes, course implementation, and numerous other human factors.

For this reason, Design-Based Research (DBR) at Pearson has been created and implemented using a set of evidence-based methodologies for integrating learning design principles to experience design using a student- and instructor-centered approach [1]. DBR is an effective way to operationalize evidence-based practice across our research and design teams. "Design-based research, which blends empirical educational research with the theory-driven design of learning environments, is an important

© Springer International Publishing AG, part of Springer Nature 2018
P. Zaphiris and A. Ioannou (Eds.): LCT 2018, LNCS 10924, pp. 170–179, 2018.
https://doi.org/10.1007/978-3-319-91743-6_13

methodology for understanding how, when, and why educational innovations work in practice" [2, p. 5]. DBR was created as a research method initially employed in classrooms to extend laboratory findings about learning to assessing instructional and contextual needs when measuring the learning impact of innovative instructional practices [3]. Our approach to DBR is focused on the same problem of bringing the evidence, context and human needs together to inform innovative design ideas and decisions. From its infancy in the early 1990s, DBR has continued to evolve as an evidence-based design practice that is now being used by researchers and designers to inform digital learning tools and hybrid learning experiences [4].

There are few defined processes for DBR in the academic literature as most experts that leverage this method develop their own set of practices, processes and tools. However, the emerging field of User Experience Design pioneered by innovators at Ideo and Stanford's d.School provide some starting point processes and toolkits that can be leveraged to further operationalize DBR, but pioneering for specific contexts and evolving these toolkits is essential to any organization looking to create DBR as an integral part of an evidence-based, experience design strategy [5].

Also, it is vital to draw on the evidence provided by psychology, anthropology, business and learning science similar to the way a cross-field approach is currently being taken in game design [6]. The main goal of creating and evolving DBR practices and tools is to develop learning-strategy oriented explanations of outcomes across the learning ecology, using specific models and tools [7]. A well-designed DBR process combines multidisciplinary evidence, student need themes, evidence-based design decisions, and context into one design and validation process.

2   Improving Learning Efficacy Using Design-Based Research

The need for an operationalized DBR process has stemmed from Pearson's stated goals to design and develop efficacious learning experiences. In recent years Pearson has become increasingly transparent about its processes and products' impacts, as demonstrated by the sharing of its Learning Design Principles and publicly conducting external-facing efficacy evaluations in cooperation with third party evaluators. In order to lay a solid foundation for efficacy measurement, Pearson's Learning Designers strive to design learning experiences that explicitly support and boost student outcomes (i.e. processes, strategies, motivation, engagement, relevance, self-monitoring, grades, etc.), as demonstrated by achievement evidence and usage analytics. To achieve these design goals, we needed processes and testing efficiencies to build a scalable capacity for rigorously and rapidly testing ideas within our design and product development process. Essentially, we wanted the ability to test (at multiple points in the design process) whether our application of learning science based principles in specific product designs was meeting student needs as intended, and to be able to do so quickly and reliably.

Accordingly, the main purpose of the Pearson DBR function and team of Learning Researchers is to support a wide-range of product creators (e.g., Learning Designers, UX Designers, User Assistance) and product owners (Product Managers and Portfolio leaders) as they seek to understand the needs of their students. While there are multiple established frameworks for design-based research [8–11], we used these frameworks to inform our own model in order to better align to our unique product portfolio and their respective business requirements and workflows.

Our team aims to build a body of evidence that the design decisions we make will support learning. We do this throughout the design process, from discovery and exploratory phases through development, testing, and market release. By systematically testing designs with students and instructors throughout this process, we create a contextualized understanding of students, learning tools, and learning environments, from which we can progressively refine learning experiences in an iterative manner. With this in mind, Sect. 3 below outlines our DBR program in greater detail, followed by Sect. 4, which highlights various student-centered successes we have experienced as a result of our DBR efforts.

3   Pearson's Design-Based Research Program

Incorporating Design-Based Research into our design process has vastly improved our capacity to apply learning science to design in ways that account for important human factors. Projects can begin and move through the process iteratively at various points in the process depending on the stakeholder and business requirements (See Fig. 1). We consistently seek an understanding of the current state of the market and specifically the key learning problems to solve, and then use a variety of methods to discover pain points and needs of students in terms of context, attitudes, skills, and behaviors to understand how to best shape a solution. Next, we consider evidence on efficacious practices from the learning sciences literature. Finally, we design and validate innovative learning experiences directly with students and seek to understand in live workshops, surveys, and focus groups how we can improve an experience and identify where we need additional evidence to inform designs. This process ensures that we base our iterative design decisions not only on the learning sciences literature, but also on real student and instructor needs to provide impactful and efficacious learning solutions. Essentially, it is how we translate research into evidence-based practice and application.

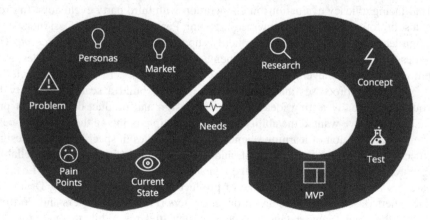

Fig. 1. Design-based research process

3.1 Discovering Learning Needs and Validating Design Decisions with Students

Our Design-Based Research process uses an iterative, mixed methods research approach to discover students' ways of working and understand their learning needs across specific learning contexts. We then use this data—aligned with learning science evidence—to inform design ideas and decisions and then iteratively validate those design ideas and decisions with students.

Since instituting our Design-Based Research program in early 2016, we have achieved a scaling capacity that sees learning ideas and design decisions being tested every day with real students. A core component of operationalizing this scaled offering is to conduct discovery and validation research with students and instructors to better understand their learning strategies and processes. Using this feedback data we conduct ongoing thematic analyses and use other qualitative research methods to curate prioritized lists of core student needs that are supported by learning science evidence and business strategies. We continually evaluate our effectiveness with our internal stakeholders to determine how to inform design investments in the most useful ways. Continuing to understand these external and internal stakeholder needs allows us to prioritize and inform business investments as well as inform learning experience design decisions that will help create digital learning tools that students want to use and that are efficacious.

Our latest prioritized needs include the following, which inform digital product design as part of a robust Higher Education DBR strategy:

- *Real-world relevance,* defined by students as overt connections provided in the learning experience between concepts, courses, skills and outcomes that demonstrate how content and activities are designed to explicitly support real-world applications including setting and achieving career goals.
- *Engagement and motivation,* defined by students as the will and skill to make prioritized decisions to get started and persist with studying especially when other alternatives of where to spend their time are more appealing.
- *Self management,* defined by students as strategies and tools for managing study time and completing assignments including preparing for class and exams in efficient and effective ways.
- *Information management,* defined by students as strategies and tools for discovering, saving, referencing, citing and combining content to generate ideas and produce quality deliverables including writing assignments.
- *21st century skills,* defined by students as career readiness and strategies needed to succeed in the modern workplace especially collaboration.

Establishing these prioritized needs informs our overall design strategy, and in turn has directly impacted efficacy and product revenue. As we continually work to understand the most pressing student needs, we partner with our Product teams to implement next-generation, student-centered design ideas and decisions, based on a nimble and customized collection of research methods.

Generally our DBR research teams gather student and instructor (i.e., user) feedback using surveys, focus groups, and interviews. Some protocols might also include co-design workshops and possible cutting edge technology like biometric testing. However, the effectiveness of our DBR strategy does not come from which methods we choose; instead it is how we use each of them in an interconnected research process within a larger product development cycle. Each method is planned and executed with scientific rigor while continually orchestrating the respective data inputs throughout a design process with multiple stakeholders. Our strength comes from how this stream of data is continually viewed through the lens of the learning sciences—the decades-long body of research regarding what has been demonstrated to reliably support learning. The following are more detailed descriptions of the research methods we are using and customizing to meet the needs of our varied stakeholders.

A first method is *ethnographies*, a staple of any social or behavior research toolkit. We only recently scaled our process to use this type of research, but it has already helped create a better understanding of our students, their needs, and how we can better support them when interacting with our products. Conducted in-person or remotely, these semi-structured interviews are conducted to allow research and design teams to take a closer look at a "week in the life of a student." What is their course load? Are they already working in the field they are studying? When do they feel the most stressed? Do they work/study with classmates, in small groups, or alone? This research is the foundation upon which student profiles (or personas) can and will be created.

Survey research is used during our DBR process for early student validation testing by gathering data (remotely, asynchronously) from our database of students. We can begin the body-of-evidence story by better understanding the current state of things such as study and reading habits, their initial impressions about a proposed enhancement or learning tool, as well as other preferences, perceptions, values, processes, and strategies. We have created a scalable process wherein a learning scientist and other stakeholders receive feedback from dozens of students within a matter of days. This efficiency empowers the design team to test out new ideas in an informative and risk-free manner. After receiving survey feedback, adjusting the design accordingly, and testing again as needed, learning scientists and designers may wish to delve deeper with students face-to-face and for an extended period of time, such as in a focus group.

Building on multiple iterations of survey feedback, *focus groups* are conducted where researchers meet with small groups of students (in-person or remotely via video chat) to continue soliciting feedback, but now on the specific areas of interest identified in prior tests. The focus group participants might be asked to describe their ideal experience or may be asked to compare their processes and strategies to the mockups or wireframes of the enhancement proposed by the moderator on behalf of the design team. The participants have multiple opportunities to compare their ideas with each other and to disagree or challenge ideas and suggestions being presented. Focus groups allow learning scientists and design teams to better understand specific aspects of the learning experiences from the student perspective and to progressively narrow their research questions accordingly.

Cognitive task analysis, conducted both in-person and remotely, provide opportunities for tasks to be observed in more authentic and contextualized ways. This affords researchers, learning scientists, and designers ways to better account for how the different elements of a learning environment are interrelated and dependent on each other. Additionally, this method brings student needs into context and is the beginning of more sophisticated, often longitudinal, testing of learning experiences.

Stemming from the field of Design [12–14], we conduct *co-design workshops* using a suite of real-world, collaborative feedback tools with students during two, full-day workshops. The goal of this tool is to explore more fully ways to support the need for real-world relevance in Higher Education and inform our design efforts with key pieces of evidence from the learning science literature. Co-designing directly with students allows us to see how they define learning challenges and what types of solutions would be most supportive to their learning goals. We expand on a tool's design internally following the co-design workshops and validate it with additional groups of Higher Education students. Moving beyond a focus on content and technology to synthesize human factors and fundamental learning needs allows us to innovate faster and generate a solution that is readily received by students.

When interested in measuring user's 'performance' during a learning experience, we use *biometrics* research methods to observe learning in action. This moves beyond self-report and leverages objective observational data [15]. Biometrics is the study of user biosignals (e.g., eye-tracking, facial expressions, galvanic skin response (GSR), electrocardiogram (ECG), electromyogram (EMG) and electroencephalography (EEG) during a user experience [16]. The benefit of using this research approach is the ability to measure unconscious biosignals that provide insights on what is happening in the user's information processing situation, reducing the potential of research biases. Triangulating the student performance and potential product improvements using biometrics, survey research, co-design, and other types of learning science research is powerful for informing the accuracy and completeness with which specific users can achieve specific instructional and learning goals in specific learning contexts.

4 User-Centered Design-Based Research Examples

Our DBR process, as described above, has informed the iterative, evidence-based enhancement of multiple market-leading learning experiences, a sampling of which are as follows.

4.1 Efficiently Integrating Writing Process Tools into Word Processing

Ongoing, iterative design-based research was instrumental to designing a writing experience in a current product that provides students with a set of tools for applying the writing process in the context of a word processor, enabling the use of research-based strategies without ever leaving their writing application. Through DBR surveys and focus groups, the design team was able to determine which features would be most valuable to students while drafting their work, and identified ways to seamlessly surface them in the context of a word processor (see Fig. 2). This included citation/bibliography creation tools, outlining, and references on topics including grammar/usage, guidance for the steps in the writing process, and idea generation for various writing genres.

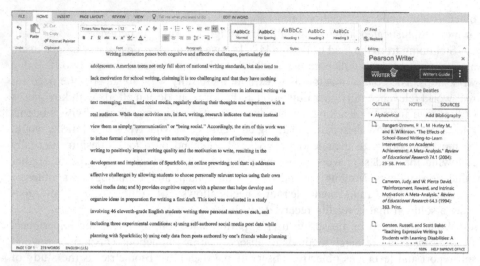

Fig. 2. Writing support tools provided in the context of a word processor.

4.2 Digital Annotation to Scaffold Studying and Review

In exploring the needs of students while they read, we discovered that they do not feel an adequate solution exists for note-taking despite the many tools available to them. Accordingly, we iteratively designed and validated a note-taking system that helps students identify and categorize important information in the moment as they read, flagging it for later review/studying. The system is designed with empirical learning science findings in mind and embodies them based on students' expressed preferences and study habits. While at face value this effort sounds simplistic, it garnered some of the most positive responses we have received from DBR participants because it was explicitly tailored to meet their needs and assist them in a task that is important to their academic success.

4.3 Algorithm-Driven Memorization Support

In hearing from students that studying for multiple exams can be both intimidating and difficult to manage, we iteratively developed an adaptive studying tool that helps them prioritize what (and when) to study. The tool determines algorithm-driven, optimal study plans based on student confidence and memory progress during practice sessions, and also leverages the benefits of spaced repetition [17].

4.4 Designing an Emoji-Inspired Reading Discussion Environment

In response to low student motivation to participate in required writing prompts, we designing a reading discussion environment intended to engage them in a way similar to social media experiences. Rather than writing with no perceived audience, the experience requires students to read and respond to each other's work, but also scaffolds high quality responses by providing guidance that is inspired in part by emoji-driven, threaded commenting. This helps students learn, in the moment, how to give each other specific, high quality feedback and drive productive discussion.

4.5   Triangulating Student Needs Using Biometrics

The use of biometrics for understand user behavior isn't new, but the majority of research using these devices are primarily focused on websites or shopping experiences. As mentioned, what is being demonstrated in this paper is not only examining products designed to help users learn, but also looking for patterns that are specific to learning—while students are acquiring new knowledge and/or skills using digital products.

For instance, to test out a new bite-size reading experience, a human communication course was tested using biometric research. In addition to improving accessibility, the concepts, theories, and trends were designed to be fun and relatable. Students found that the unique features helped them to identify and understand their own communication behaviors, as well the communication behavior of others. Specifically, taking a DBR approach, we sought to understand where students focus their attention, and what types of student journeys occur when using a sample chapter to prepare for class versus prepare for an exam. Figures 3 and 4, illustrate where students focused their attention and their observed learning paths.

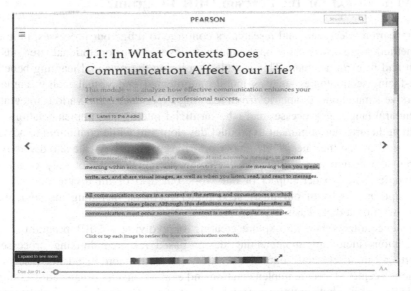

Fig. 3. Heat map of eye-tracking data from students' performance while reviewing interactive digital textbook experience.

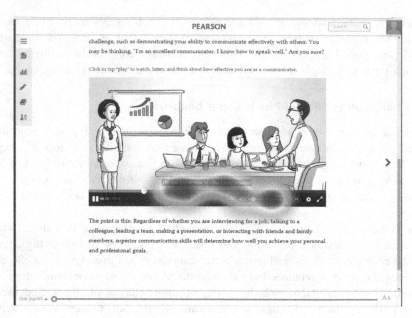

Fig. 4. A second heat map of eye-tracking data from students' performance while reviewing interactive video in a digital textbook experience.

5   What's Next for the Pearson DBR Program?

As our learning designers and researchers continue to refine our processes, protocols, and methodologies, we pursue opportunities to leverage our operational strengths and design and research acumen. This includes exploring the potential learning benefit of future-facing technologies such as mobile augmented and virtual reality, authentic, immersive simulations, biometric *driven* learning experiences, and various integrations with natural language processes and other artificial intelligence implementations.

Strengthening our alignment to product development while continuing to advocate for the student and their needs remain our priorities even as we scale and diversify our research and design capabilities. We welcome the challenges not only of the new technologies and broader impact of our work but also of improving the collective knowledge and skills of our many stakeholder partners, including the students we interact with on a daily basis.

We encourage others to explore creating or evolving a DBR program in their organizations including implementing design-based research thinking processes to support a mindset and operational shift toward more student (user) and experience-centered design, implementation and evaluation. Our organization continues to scale this service but currently our nimble team of 10–12 learning researchers support the majority of teams across Pearson responsible for product design and development. Starting small and scaling up and then collecting small wins along the way has proven to be a effective and impactful strategy. Our goal remains to shift mindsets and establish ways of working that continually improve the support of human factors in the design and validation of digital learning experiences.

References

1. Learning Design Principles. Pearson (2016)
2. Kelly, A.E.: Theme issue: the role of design in educational research. Educ. Res. **32**(1), 3–4 (2003)
3. Brown, A.L.: Design experiments: theoretical and methodological challenges in creating complex interventions in classroom settings. J. Learn. Sci. **2**(2), 141–178 (1992)
4. Payne, A.: Learning experience design thinking findings story. Pearson (2017)
5. Lanoue, S.: IDEO's 6 Step Human-Centered Design Process: How to Make Things People Want. UserTesting Blog, vol. 9 (2015)
6. Schell, J.: The Art of Game Design: A Deck of Lenses. Schell Games (2008)
7. Reimann, P.: Design-based research: designing as research. In: Luckin, R., Puntambekar, S., Goodyear, P., Grabowski, B., Underwood, J., Winters, N. (eds.) Handbook of Design in Educational Technology, pp. 44–52 (2013)
8. Fishman, B.J., Penuel, W.R., Allen, A.-R., Cheng, B.H., Sabelli, N.: Design-based implementation research: An emerging model for transforming the relationship of research and practice. In: National Society for the Study of Education, vol. 112(2), pp. 136–156 (2013)
9. Penuel, W.R., Fishman, B.J., Cheng, B.H., Sabelli, N.: Organizing research and development at the intersection of learning, implementation, and design. Educ. Res. **40**(7), 331–337 (2011)
10. Barab, S.: Design-based research: a methodological toolkit for engineering change. In: The Cambridge Handbook of the Learning Sciences, Second Edition, Cambridge University Press (2014)
11. Barab, S.A., Squire, S.A.: Design-based Research: Clarifying the Terms. A Special Issue of the Journal of the Learning Sciences. Psychology Press (2016)
12. Sanders, E.B.-N., Stappers, P.J.: Co-creation and the new landscapes of design. CoDesign **4**(1), 5–18 (2008)
13. Brown, T.: Change by Design. Harper Collins, New York (2009)
14. Sanders Elizabeth, B.N., Stappers, P.: Convivial Toolbox: Generative Research for the Front End of Design. Bis Publishers, Amsterdam (2012)
15. Farnsworth, B.: What is Biometric Research? iMotions. https://imotions.com/blog/what-is-biometric-research/. Accessed 19 Apr 2017
16. Davis, S., Cheng, E., Burnett, I., Ritz, C.: Multimedia user feedback based on augmenting user tags with EEG emotional states. In: 2011 Third International Workshop on Quality of Multimedia Experience, pp. 143–148 (2011)
17. Cepeda, N.J., Pashler, H., Vul, E., Wixted, J.T., Rohrer, D.: Distributed practice in verbal recall tasks: a review and quantitative synthesis. Psychol. Bull. **132**(3), 354–380 (2006)

Usability Evaluation of a Mobile Graphing Calculator Application Using Eye Tracking

Melanie Tomaschko$^{(\boxtimes)}$ and Markus Hohenwarter$^{(\boxtimes)}$

Johannes Kepler University Linz, 4040 Linz, Austria
{Melanie.Tomaschko,Markus.Hohenwarter}@jku.at

Abstract. This research study evaluates the usability of a mobile graphing calculator application called GeoGebra. Therefore, investigations were conducted using eye tracking and a system usability scale questionnaire. The data obtained was utilized to evaluate effectiveness, efficiency, and satisfaction in using the smartphone application of GeoGebra (version Spring 2017). The results revealed several usability issues that faced users while using the mobile application. Based on these findings, suggestions for an improved user interface and interaction design are given. These suggested improvements should help to increase educational impact of mobile graphing calculator applications in school practices.

Keywords: Usability · Eye tracking · GeoGebra

1 Introduction

The integration of Information and Communication Technology (ICT) in educational settings has gained a lot of interest. Especially the use of mobile devices can offer great potentials to complement traditional education with new technologies and enrich students' learning in various ways. Because of the increasing capabilities of these devices, they bring together a multifarious collection of software- and hardware-based functionalities and could finally also replace additionally required hardware resources such as traditional handheld calculators.

GeoGebra [1] is an open source mathematical learning tool that allows students to manipulate, explore, and experiment with mathematical concepts through different dynamically connected representation forms, which can lead to increased motivation and a deeper level of understanding [2, 3]. However, to exploit the full potential of mobile devices and related mobile applications for educational purposes, it is required to guarantee high usability [4], especially for a tool like GeoGebra which is used by millions of students and teachers worldwide. Nevertheless, a search of the literature revealed that only few studies have investigated the usability of mobile graphing calculator applications used in school practices so far. One study that could be found is described in [5]. The authors present an evaluation of the interface of an older version of GeoGebra's tablet application. However, tablets are rarely carried by students, hence smartphones should also be considered as possible learning tools. This is also confirmed by the much larger number of users of GeoGebra's new smartphone app [6] on mobile phones vs. tablets (see Fig. 1). For this reason, in this study the smartphone

© Springer International Publishing AG, part of Springer Nature 2018
P. Zaphiris and A. Ioannou (Eds.): LCT 2018, LNCS 10924, pp. 180–190, 2018.
https://doi.org/10.1007/978-3-319-91743-6_14

application of GeoGebra is investigated. The aim of this study is the identification of possible usability issues of the GeoGebra Graphing Calculator application used on smartphones. Based on the identified problems, suggestions for an improved user interface and workflow will be given. As a result, these suggested improvements should enhance the educational impact of mobile graphing calculator applications in school practices.

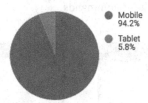

Fig. 1. Percentage of GeoGebra Graphing Calculator users on mobile phones vs. tablets (Google Analytics from Aug 2016 to Jan 2018).

2 GeoGebra

GeoGebra is a dynamic mathematics software tool that is used by millions of students and teachers worldwide. GeoGebra can support the teaching and learning of geometry, algebra, spreadsheets, graphing, statistics, and calculus. This open source math tool started out as a set of mathematical applications for the desktop operating systems Windows, MacOS X, and Linux and was later accompanied by HTML5 web applications running in all modern browsers. In 2015, a first version of a native mobile application for Android smartphones was released. This app is based on the existing source code of GeoGebra's mathematical algorithms, however the user interface was modified in order to address the special requirements of smartphones, in particular their smaller screen size.

2.1 GeoGebra Graphing Calculator

After launching the GeoGebra Graphing Calculator application the graphics and algebra view are displayed on the screen (see Fig. 2 left). At the top of the screen a toolbar is included offering possibilities for access of geometrical construction tools, settings, materials, and the main app menu. Pressing the "pen" button for construction tools in the upper left corner turns the toolbar into a panel that offers an overview of all available categories that contain one or more related tools (see Fig. 2 right). After selecting one of these tools, a subpanel is opened as a second header row, displaying the set of tools of the corresponding category. All of these tools can be used to construct new objects within the graphics view. Furthermore, the graphics view also supports familiar gestures such as one-finger pan, pinch-zooming, and long tap for moving and zooming the coordinate system. Additionally, all of the created objects are also displayed as algebraic representations within the algebra view at the bottom of the screen. It is particularly worth mentioning that the graphics and algebra view are dynamically connected. This means that manipulations in one view are always immediately shown in the other one. Aside from the graphical possibility of constructing new mathematical objects, the algebra view includes a custom formula editor for algebraic input. This editor supports input of mathematical operations as well as GeoGebra commands through a custom virtual keyboard (see Fig. 2 left). Besides, a button is included within the input bar to open a separate view that offers a list of all available mathematical functions and GeoGebra commands as well as a description and short example of how to use those commands.

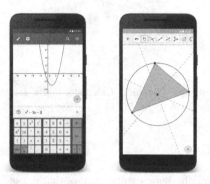

Fig. 2. GeoGebra Graphing Calculator.

3 Design of the Experiment

This study uses quantitative and qualitative analysis in order to gain insights into the usability of the mobile GeoGebra Graphing Calculator application (version of Spring 2017 as seen in Fig. 2). Eye tracking will be used to categorize user interactions with the mobile application regarding active construction, visual search, and actions that are indicative of failures. Additional data will be collected using the system usability scale (SUS) questionnaire [7], that allows to get an overall perception of the investigated application. Particularly, the study is based on the ISO 9241-11 definition of usability and evaluates effectiveness, efficiency, and satisfaction through task analysis. Effectiveness is measured by completion rate. Efficiency is based on the time spent on one task to successfully complete it and the data retrieved from eye tracking. The SUS score is used to determine user satisfaction. All of these study findings are then considered for suggestions of an improved user interface and interaction design of a mobile graphing calculator application.

3.1 Participants

The presented study collected data of 9 adult participants (6 female and 3 male). 5 of the participants had no previous knowledge in using GeoGebra or any other graphing calculator application on mobile phones. 4 of all participants were already experienced in using the desktop application of GeoGebra, but with no experience in using the mobile application.

3.2   Usability Evaluation Methods

System Usability Scale. In this study the System Usability Scale (SUS) [7] is used to quantitatively evaluate user satisfaction. SUS was created by John Brooke [7] to get a quick overall perception of an application. It is a 5-point Likert scale consisting of 10 items (see Table 1). The questionnaire consists of positive and negative formulated items, that are sorted in alternate sequence. Each of them can be answered ranging from "strongly agree" to "strongly disagree". For calculating the SUS score for all positive questions the scale position is subtracted by one. For each negative question the scale position is subtracted from 5. The average sum of all calculated scores is then multiplied by 2.5 in order to get a final overall value ranging from 0 to 100.

Table 1. System Usability Scale questionnaire.

Nr	Item
1	I think that I would like to use this system frequently
2	I found the system unnecessarily complex
3	I thought the system was easy to use
4	I think that I would need the support of a technical person to be able to use this system
5	I found the various functions in this system were well integrated
6	I thought there was too much inconsistency in this system
7	I would imagine that most people would learn to use this system very quickly
8	I found the system very cumbersome to use
9	I felt very confident using the system
10	I needed to learn a lot of things before I could get going with this system

Eye Tracking. Eye tracking allows to observe and measure eye movements of participants while they are looking at the mobile user interface. The retrieved data can be visualized as gaze plots. This enables a possibility to observe where participants are looking on a user interface. In particular, gaze plots illustrate fixations and saccades by dots and fine lines (see Fig. 3). The size of the dots depends on the duration of fixation. Small dots indicate short fixations, whereas longer fixations are indicated by larger dots.

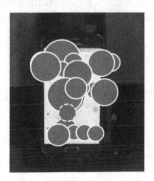

Fig. 3. Gaze plot example.

Table 2. Task scenario of this study.

Task 1	(a)	Construct any triangle ABC
	(b)	Show the angles of the triangle
	(c)	Move points A, B, and C to create a beveled triangle
Task 2	(a)	Disable the axes
	(b)	Construct any parallelogram
	(c)	Hide all objects you have used for the construction. There should only be the parallelogram visible
Task 3		Plot the function $f(x) = x^2 - sin(x)$ and determine the value of the function at position $x = 2$
Task 4		Determine the point, where function $f(x) = x^3 - 2x + 1$ and line $y = 4$ intersect
Task 5	(a)	Construct a line through points $A = (1, 1)$ and $B = (2, 3)$
	(b)	Determine the integral of the function that has been created in task a
	(c)	Determine roots of the function of task b

Task Scenarios. In order to guide the eye tracking session prepared work tasks (see Table 2) are given to the participants. These work tasks represent conventional tasks, as users would work with the application in real life situations. In addition, the exercises are defined in a way to evaluate the main features of the GeoGebra Graphing Calculator application, that are plotting and investigating function graphs and geometric constructions.

Think Aloud Method. Additional qualitative data is collected through the think aloud method. While participants conduct the task scenarios they are asked to think out loud. In this way, eye tracking can be combined with additional qualitative data that allows the correct interpretation of the gathered eye movement data.

3.3 Apparatus

For this study a Tobii Pro X2-60 [8] eye tracker was used. Since this research is based on the smartphone application of GeoGebra a special mobile device stand was used (see Fig. 4). This device stand includes a mounted high-definition scene camera to film the mobile device. This allows the recording of the user interface as well as user

Fig. 4. Mobile eye tracking setup.

interactions. Additionally, the analysis software Tobii Studio was used that superimposes the captured eye tracking data on the recording of the mounted scene camera. The mobile device used in this study was a Samsung S6 smartphone with Android operating system version 7.

3.4 Procedure

At the beginning of each experiment the motivation and goal of this study was introduced. Afterwards the workflow of the whole experiment session was explained. After this introduction each participant was asked to sit in front of the mobile device stand in a comfortable way. The eye-tracker, mobile device stand, and the calibration plate were mounted in advance. Before the calibration was started, the equipment and procedure was explained. For each participant the calibration was repeated until reliable results could be achieved.

During the eye tracking sessions participants were asked to complete a list of prepared tasks (see Table 2), that represents possible natural situations of using the GeoGebra Graphing Calculator application. After the task scenarios, participants were asked to rate their experience with the GeoGebra Graphing Calculator using the SUS questionnaire.

3.5 Data Analysis

For analyzing the gathered data from eye tracking, Tobii Studio was used to identify different segments of user interactions. This data was further analyzed using SPSS and Google Sheets for statistical analysis and graphical visualizations. The total SUS score was evaluated based on the results of the SUS questionnaire, that participants filled after the task scenarios.

4 Results

4.1 Effectiveness

In order to evaluate the effectiveness of the mobile application task completion was considered. As shown in Fig. 5 all of the participants were able to complete tasks 1, 3, and 5. Three of the participants could not successfully complete task 2. Task 4 could not be completed by two participants. The overall effectiveness of the GeoGebra Graphing Calculator application was calculated as percentage of successfully completed tasks, that is 88.89%.

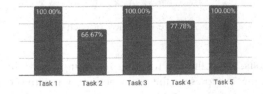

Fig. 5. Percentage of users who successfully completed each task.

4.2   Efficiency

For evaluating the efficiency of the GeoGebra Graphing Calculator application the time spent on each task as well as data that was retrieved from eye tracking were used.

The average time that was spent on each task is visualized in Fig. 6. On average task 2 took the longest amount of time to be completed, as might be expected given that constructing a parallelogram requires several steps involving different tools. On the other hand, task 3 took the shortest time to be completed by participants.

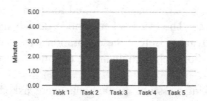

Fig. 6. Average time spent on each task.

The evaluation of the time-based efficiency of the GeoGebra Graphing Calculator application is defined as follows:

$$Efficiency = \frac{\sum_{i=1}^{N} \sum_{j=1}^{M} \frac{n_{ij}}{t_{ij}}}{NM} \tag{1}$$

Where,

N = total number of users
M = total number of tasks
$n_{ij} = 1$, if user i successfully completed task j, 0 otherwise
t_{ij} = time spent to complete task j by user I

For the mobile application an efficiency of 0.6 (tasks per minute) could be achieved. Figure 7 shows the average efficiency of each task.

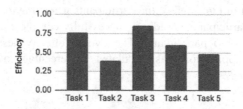

Fig. 7. Average efficiency of each task.

For further analysis, all of the eye tracking recordings were divided into multiple segments. These segments represent the main actions i.e. active construction, visual search, and repair from failure. Additionally, timestamp, duration, and a short description of the user interaction was defined for each of them. Overall 1625 segments were categorized. Considering all successfully completed tasks, participants spent 65% of total time on active construction, 31% on visual search, and 4% on repairing from failures. Figure 8 shows the average duration of the three categories for each successfully completed task. Participants spent most time on searching for specific features while they were working on task 5. Task 2 caused the most time on repairing from failures.

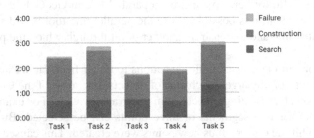

Fig. 8. Average duration that is spent on each successfully completed task based on the three action categories failure, construction, and search.

4.3 Satisfaction

In this study user satisfaction was determined by SUS score. The results of the SUS questionnaire are visualized in Table 3. The average SUS score is 63, which is below the average SUS score of 68 [9], that indicates usability issues in the investigated version of the GeoGebra Graphing Calculator application.

Table 3. SUS score results.

Nr.	1	2	3	4	5	Score
1	1	0	1	2	4	27
2	2	2	4	1	0	23
3	1	2	3	3	0	17
4	6	0	1	0	2	26
5	0	1	3	2	2	21
6	2	5	1	0	1	25
7	0	0	3	3	3	27
8	0	4	3	2	0	20
9	1	1	3	3	1	20
10	1	4	1	3	0	21
SUS score = 63						

5 Discussion and Suggestions for Improvements

Participants faced most problems while working on task 2. This may be caused as this task was more complex, requiring several steps to construct a parallelogram. Five of the participants first started to search the toolbar for a suitable tool. Therefore, they selected multiple different tools and tried what could be constructed with them. This resulted in many unused constructions that were deleted again. Three of those participants found the parallel line tool. However, one of them was not able to use it. Even the displayed tooltip was not helpful for her. To construct a parallel line in GeoGebra, first a line has to be created. After that, it is possible to use the parallel line tool in order to select the previously created line and to construct another point through which the parallel line is constructed.

Another problem that caused multiple actions to repair from failure across all tasks was caused because of the target touch area of objects. For some of the GeoGebra tools it is necessary to select existing objects from the graphics view. For example, if using the angle tool, either two segments or three points can be selected. But participants were not able to hit the objects, thus new points were created. This caused the necessity of removing the unexpected created points and repeat the construction again. Therefore, we suggest to increase the target touch area for objects within the graphics view.

Another issue that could be observed from three participants was that they have tried to zoom the graphics view by pinch-zooming while they were creating a construction, i.e. a construction tool was active. However, instead of zooming, new objects were created. For this reason, we suggest to automatically identify common gestures such as pinch-zoom and allow zooming of the graphics view even though a tool is selected.

GeoGebra uses a custom virtual keyboard that should aid users in typing mathematical expressions. From the task analysis and eye tracking recording it could be observed that participants struggled the most with the input of x^2. As shown in Fig. 9 the virtual keyboard includes a button displaying x^2, however this button only inserts power of two. Similarly, also the input of x^3 caused problems because the intended button a^x was not recognized as the correct one. As known from other custom keyboard implementations, the labeling of the buttons could be modified in a way, that it is clear to the users, which parts of the label is automatically inserted and which parts need to be entered by users.

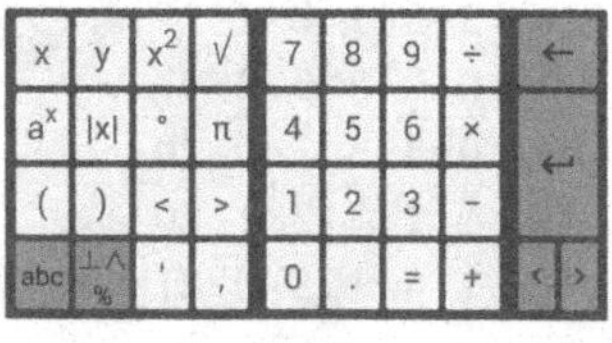

Fig. 9. Virtual keyboard.

One point that caused a lower efficiency rate for the Graphing Calculator application is the selection of a certain tool. This issue could be observed by all participants. GeoGebra provides a set of tools for constructing mathematical objects. These tools are divided into different categories that are displayed within the toolbar. After tapping one of the categories, the displayed tool is already selected and active. However, the eye tracking recordings have shown that users always selected the tool from the opened submenu, even though the tool was already selected (see Fig. 10). As the tools are only used in combination with the graphics view, the user interface could be modified in a way, that the algebra view is replaced by another view that displays all available tools. In this way, the geometric construction tools could be arranged in another way than a row with submenus. This could reduce the time spent on construction because users do not have to tap the tool icon twice.

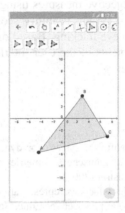

Fig. 10. GeoGebra toolbar with opened submenu.

While working on task 5 participants spent a significant amount of time on searching for a tool that can be used for calculating the integral of a function. For evaluating the integral of a function the input bar and the Integral command can be used. However, participants also searched the geometrical construction tools and the keyboard to find a proper tool that can be used for this exercise. They finally managed to complete the task after they have opened the help view of the input bar and searched for the phrase "Integral". In order to improve this issue, a button for the integral symbol could be added to the keyboard as it is already known from different other pocket calculators. Since multiple participants also searched for a construction tool, it could also be considered to add an integral tool.

Independent from the tasks, participants further searched a long time for a way to delete existing objects. GeoGebra offers two possibilities: using the delete tool from the toolbar or using the small cross displayed at the end of each algebra view row. Participants tried to select and long tap the objects and further searched within the properties view of the objects for a possibility to delete them. Therefore, we suggest to display a small context menu for each object after selecting it within the graphics view, that includes most used settings and actions such as deleting the object. This would further allow to completely remove the need for long tapping an object to open the properties view. Users were often interrupted in their construction process while moving objects or the graphics view because the touch gesture was recognized as long tap and the properties view was opened.

6 Conclusion

This paper presented a usability evaluation of the mobile GeoGebra Graphing Calculator application (version Spring 2017) using eye tracking and the SUS questionnaire, with the aim of identifying possible usability issues. To do this, usability research has been conducted involving nine participants. These users were given a set of tasks to be performed on a smartphone using the GeoGebra Graphing Calculator application. After performing the task scenarios subjective measures using SUS was collected. The result of SUS questionnaire indicated a system usability score below average, that is supported by the data gathered from eye tracking. Based on the identified usability issues several suggestions for improvements of the user interface of the GeoGebra graphing calculator application were made.

References

1. Hohenwarter, M.: GeoGebra: a software system for dynamic geometry and algebra in the plane (ein Software System für dynamische Geometrie und Algebra der Ebene). Master's thesis. University of Salzburg, Austria (2002)
2. Morgan, C., Kynigos, C.: Digital artefacts as representations: forging connections between a constructionist and a social semiotic perspective. Educ. Stud. Math. **85**(3), 357–379 (2014)
3. Heid, K.M., Blume, G.W.: Algebra and function development. In: Heid, K.M., Blume, G.W. (eds.) Research on Technology and the Teaching and Learning of Mathematics. Research Syntheses, vol. 1, pp. 55–108. Information Age Publishing, Charlotte (2008)
4. Reis, H.M., Borges, S.S., Durelli, V.H.S., Fernando De S. Moro, L., Brandao, A.A.F., Barbosa, E.F., Bittencourt, I.I., et al.: Towards reducing cognitive load and enhancing usability through a reduced graphical user interface for a dynamic geometry system: an experimental study. In: Proceedings - 2012 IEEE International Symposium on Multimedia, ISM 2012, pp. 445–450 (2012)
5. Yağmur, S., Çakır, M.P.: Usability evaluation of a dynamic geometry software mobile interface through eye tracking. In: Zaphiris, P., Ioannou, A. (eds.) LCT 2016. LNCS, vol. 9753, pp. 391–402. Springer, Cham (2016). https://doi.org/10.1007/978-3-319-39483-1_36
6. Google Play Store: GeoGebra Graphing Calculator (2017). https://play.google.com/store/apps/details?id=org.geogebra.android&hl=en. Accessed 6 Feb 2018
7. Brook, J.: SUS - a quick and dirty usability scale (1996). https://pdfs.semanticscholar.org/57d5/8f26923deab226eb3a7bcbb1dd3dd21a4b15.pdf. Accessed 5 Oct 2017
8. Tobii (2018). Official Website. https://www.tobiipro.com/product-listing/tobii-pro-x2-60/. Accessed 18 Jan 2018
9. Sauro, J.: Measuring usability with the System Usability Scale (SUS) (2011). https://measuringu.com/sus/. Accessed 1 Feb 2018

Technological Innovation in Education

Integrating MOOCs in Regular Higher Education: Challenges and Opportunities from a Scandinavian Perspective

Fisnik Dalipi[1,2(✉)], Mexhid Ferati[1], and Arianit Kurti[1,3]

[1] Linnaeus University, Växjö, Sweden
{fisnik.dalipi,mexhid.ferati,arianit.kurti}@lnu.se
[2] University College of Southeast Norway, Hønefoss, Norway
fisnik.dalipi@usn.no
[3] RISE Interactive Institute, Norrköping, Sweden
arianit.kurti@ri.se

Abstract. MOOCs are increasingly being considered by universities as an integral part of their curriculum. Nevertheless, there are several challenges that to some extent slow this process, where the most important one is the accreditation challenges and financing. These challenges are particularly important in the context of universities in Scandinavian countries where education is mostly free. In order to gain more insights on the status of proliferation of MOOCs in Scandinavian universities and understand any specific challenges, we conducted a study by analyzing two sources of data: research publications and university websites. Further on, these data have been analyzed using a framework that differentiates and categorizes MOOCs in terms of accreditation and scalability. As a result of this analysis, we have identified the remaining challenges as well as a number of opportunities regarding the full integration of MOOCs in the educational system of the Scandinavian Higher Education Institutions.

Keywords: MOOCs · Higher education · Online learning · Scandinavia
Challenges · Opportunities · Sweden · Norway · Denmark

1 Introduction

Universities are considered as key institutions for societal development and change. An important part of the societal role of such institutions is to provide knowledge and education but also to promote lifelong learning, regardless of age, place of residence, and life situation.

The current dynamics of our society increases the demand for flexible education and intends to bridge the educational journey from theory to practice. Such flexible education can be carried out regardless of time and place, and consequently is not anymore limited to campuses only. In such provisions, technology serves as a facilitating tool and component in the organization and implementation of education.

The technological innovations and their applicability in the education settings have had a tremendous impact in the way universities and other educational institutions engage in the learning practices. Nowadays, one of the most important educational

© Springer International Publishing AG, part of Springer Nature 2018
P. Zaphiris and A. Ioannou (Eds.): LCT 2018, LNCS 10924, pp. 193–204, 2018.
https://doi.org/10.1007/978-3-319-91743-6_15

innovations is the use of MOOCs (Massive Open Online Courses), which present a potential to fundamentally revolutionize the higher education. Although MOOCs face some challenges when it comes to determining the best pedagogical approaches to be based on [1, 2], they still represent a new wave of innovation for teaching and learning. Particularly, because MOOCs introduce attributes that are entirely new in higher education: cheaper, high quality content, and more accessible, both in time and space.

In general, Scandinavian countries are characterized by having a well-established higher education sector, free higher education and good educational support systems, and easy access to higher education. Besides free higher education, the Scandinavian universities are offering a vast selection of online (distance) courses, both as a single subject courses or a full study program. Despite this experience with online courses offered as part of a distance education initiative, Scandinavian universities have so far been rather moderate in the adoption of MOOCs. However, nowadays there is an increased interest and research effort on developing and promoting MOOC-supported education for many reasons: to spread knowledge and education to developing countries, for market and recruitment purposes, to support lifelong learning, or to maintain and increase the global presence [3–5].

Considering these developments in the educational landscape in Scandinavia, the focus of this paper revolves around the following questions:

- To what extent MOOCs are integrated in the Scandinavian higher education landscape?
- What are the challenges the Scandinavian universities face regarding the MOOC phenomenon?
- What are the opportunities that MOOCs can bring to the Scandinavian higher education?

To answer these questions, we have investigated existing published articles describing MOOCs in Scandinavian countries. In addition, we investigated each university website in Sweden, Norway and Denmark to see if and how many MOOC courses do they offer. The outcome is to present a detailed overview of MOOCs offerings in Scandinavian universities, with reference to instructional design, language, accreditation, and field of study. Furthermore, we highlight the challenges documented and discuss the opportunities that they provide.

This paper is structured as follows: In the next section, the research methodology is described. The third section outlines the current development of MOOCs in Scandinavian HEIs, followed by the fourth section where we discuss challenges and opportunities. The last section concludes this article.

2 Methodology

For this study, a combined methodology of literature review and web site search is used, which is partly inspired by the research strategy employed by [6]. The research strategy consists of the following three steps: (1) search for published scientific

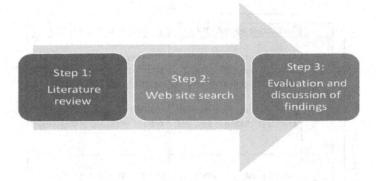

Fig. 1. Steps of methodology applied in the study.

literature discussing MOOCs development and adoption by the Scandinavian HEIs (Higher Education Institutions); (2) search for relevant information from the web sites of Scandinavian HEIs and MOOC platforms; and (3) review, evaluate and discuss the findings. In Fig. 1, we present the three steps of the strategy.

To gain a complete overview of research published within this topic, we found relevant articles using Google Scholar because of its inclusivity with major publication channels compared to specific digital libraries, e.g., ACM Digital Library, IEEEXplore. When searching, we did not consider any filtering in terms of publishing periods, but retrieved all papers that discussed MOOCs in Scandinavian countries. The list of articles retrieved and used included 26 papers in total: ten for Sweden, six for Norway, six for Denmark, and four papers discussed all three countries. The second data source comprised the detailed search of university websites, aiming to directly check whether certain HEIs offer or have produced MOOCs in national or international platforms.

In order to systematically structure, categorize and understand MOOC initiatives and developments in Scandinavian HEIs, we apply and adapt the framework for MOOCs typology proposed by [7], shown in Fig. 2. This framework is also partly grounded on many other relevant research contributions, such as [8, 9].

The typology framework describes the MOOC courses offered by the various HEIs in terms of accreditation and the target group. The model is very useful when describing and differentiating between the national mediation approach (niche-market MOOCs) and the international disruption approach (mass-market MOOCs). Thus, the national approach, i.e., the niche-market MOOCs can be associated with (i) the formal approach, when geographically targeting a narrow group of learners and occupational backgrounds and formally recognizing the obtained course certificate within one or few countries; and (ii) the informal approach, when geographically targeting a narrow group of learners and the national accreditation of the courses is not provided.

The same applies for the international approach, i.e., mass-market MOOCs, with the difference that it involves broader group of learners in terms of geographical and occupational background.

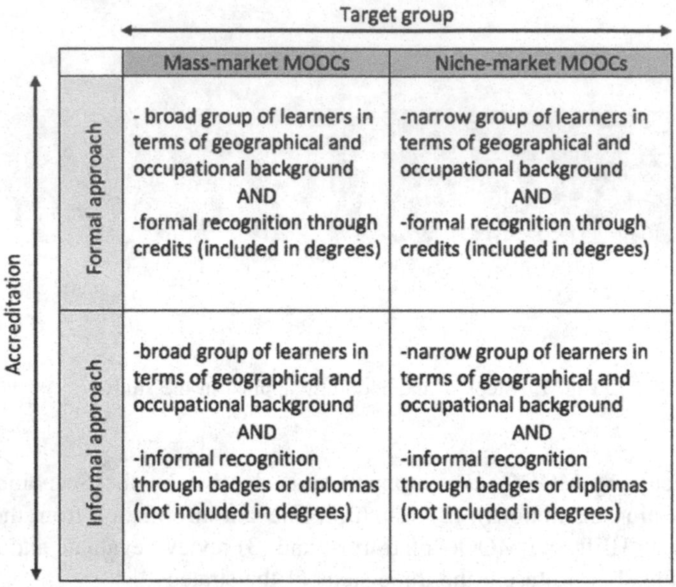

Target group

		Mass-market MOOCs	Niche-market MOOCs
Accreditation	Formal approach	- broad group of learners in terms of geographical and occupational background AND -formal recognition through credits (included in degrees)	-narrow group of learners in terms of geographical and occupational background AND -formal recognition through credits (included in degrees)
	Informal approach	-broad group of learners in terms of geographical and occupational background AND -informal recognition through badges or diplomas (not included in degrees)	-narrow group of learners in terms of geographical and occupational background AND -informal recognition through badges or diplomas (not included in degrees)

Fig. 2. MOOCs typology framework, adapted from [7].

3   The Development of MOOCs in Scandinavia

Our investigation revealed that the pace of acceptance of MOOCs in Scandinavia is slow, indicated by the low number of universities offering MOOCs across recent years. Perhaps because most of universities do not have regular funding for such initiatives, which is particularly the case in Sweden.

For the present time, the most obvious challenge is that MOOCs are not compatible with the current structural setup of the educational system (i.e., there are lack of procedures and processes that would enable a student that has finished a course in MOOC platform to include that in their regular curricula). On one hand, there is no clear guidelines on how the examination (assessment of learning outcomes) of the MOOCs should be done. On the other hand, there are difficulties in assessing the appropriate level of MOOCs to match the university basic (bachelor) and advanced (master) level courses.

There are also student admission issues in MOOCs, since in order for the university to generate governmental funding, students need to be formally enrolled at a Swedish University. Consequently, this presents a sustainability challenge from the financial point of view. This, however, is slowly changing as some of the top ranking Swedish institutions, such as Karolinska Institute and Lund University, are now providing MOOCs [10]. More recently, Chalmers University of Technology, Royal Institute of Technology, Uppsala University, Mid Sweden University, Karlstad University, Halmstad University and other young universities have adopted or have plans to run MOOCs. They are offering courses mainly from the field of engineering, medicine, and natural sciences.

Similar trends are seen in other Scandinavian countries. In Norway, the first MOOC was offered by NTNU (Norwegian University of Science and Technology) back in 2013. Since then, several other MOOCs have been established, most of them being offered in Norwegian language as they are typically linked to existing courses for Norwegian students [4].

In Denmark, even though many established educational institutions are aware of MOOCs, only few have entered the field. In addition, three universities have become partners in the Coursera platform, i.e., University of Copenhagen, Technical University of Denmark, and Copenhagen Business School [11].

To provide a general overview, in Table 1 we show MOOCs presence at Scandinavian HEIs. Detailed numbers are given for each country in terms of the number of universities offering MOOCs along with the number of courses and which platform.

Table 1. MOOCs presence at Scandinavian HEIs.

Country	MOOC platform	Number of university	Number of courses
Sweden	edX	3	31
	Coursera	1	8
	FutureLearn	1	3
	Another platform	5	7
	Total	10	49
Norway	edX	0	0
	Coursera	0	0
	FutureLearn	3	6
	Another platform	12	36
	Total	15	42
Denmark	edX	2	3
	Coursera	3	41
	FutureLearn	0	0
	Another platform	1	3
	Total	6	47

In terms of universities, Norway is leading with fifteen universities, however, in terms of courses, Sweden is leading with 49 courses in total. Denmark has a similar position with 47 courses offered, but involving only six universities.

Further details about the fields in which the courses are given are shown in Fig. 3. Courses in the field of Science comprise most of the MOOCs in Sweden and Norway, while in Denmark dominate courses in the field of Economics. Sweden is the only country offering courses in Engineering, while only Norway offers courses in Agriculture. Norway also has courses in the field of Art. In the fields of Medicine, Philosophy and History all countries offer similar number of courses.

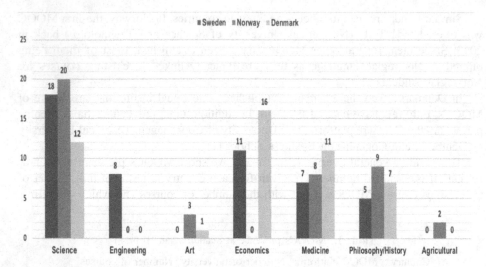

Fig. 3. Distribution of MOOCs across various disciplines at Scandinavian HEIs.

4   Challenges and Opportunities

By analyzing the collected data and the scientific literature available, we identified a number of challenges and opportunities for HEIs when it comes to embracing MOOCs in their educational settings. These challenges are mainly related to the awareness levels for MOOC integration, accreditation issues, impacts to labor market as well as legal issues. As far as the opportunities are concerned, we mainly highlight the ones dealing with possibilities for lifelong learning, educational affordance, flexibility and branding.

4.1   Challenges

Awareness. Little awareness exists among experts from educational sector and public agencies on how to integrate MOOCs in HEIs. Also, many university educators seem to lack knowledge about new learning technologies and how to produce MOOCs [12, 13]. Recently, however, MOOCs have been the topic of unprecedented discussion among researchers, educators and policy makers about their potential to transform higher education and revitalize online learning. As a result, the Swedish Higher Education Authority proposed that Swedish HEIs should, like their counterparts in other countries, be given the possibility of arranging open online courses (MOOCs) [14]. In addition, the Norwegian Government, by appointing a MOOC Commission, initiated a process aimed at establishing a knowledge base for policy decisions related to MOOCs. The main objective of this commission is to enhance the digitalization of HEIs and facilitate the strategic use of MOOCs [15]. Furthermore, in the Nordic countries, except Sweden, MOOCs are connected to existing administrative procedures for organizing continuing education (lifelong learning) within HEIs [7].

Nevertheless, when it comes to credit recognition and validation of MOOCs in the regular educational programs, no action is being taken so far in any Scandinavian country. We explain in more details such accreditation challenges in a special section below.

Labor Market Reaction. Another challenge is the reaction of the labor market towards the integration of MOOCs. For instance, in Sweden labor market is less focused on formal education, but rather on the proper skill set of the selected candidate. This is also manifested with the fact that a university graduate with a bachelor or master degree gets the same starting salary.

Furthermore, the competency development plans within companies are typically more aligned towards professional educational providers that focus very much on specific skills rather than academic level knowledge. Therefore, the introduction of MOOCs risks of being "branded" as more academic oriented, thus potentially risks of gaining sufficient attraction within the labor market. Also, MOOCs as a technology for educational content delivery has been around for a while in the professional training providers, thus it does not necessarily represent an innovation for the labor market. But in the same time, it offers the needed flexibility to the HEIs, thus providing them with opportunities of utilizing MOOCs for more professional education competence provisioning combined with flexible pedagogical approaches.

Accreditation. According to current higher education legislations of the Scandinavian countries, MOOCs do not represent a regular higher education, since participants are not legally students as they are not admitted according to the admission requirements. Therefore, the MOOC obtained credits cannot be officially recognized in the regular higher education programs or to be included in a qualification (academic degree). Thus, courses passed via MOOC platforms cannot count towards degrees.

Moreover, referring to the MOOC typology framework, which is demonstrated in Table 2, none of the Scandinavian MOOCs can be related to a formal and mass-market approach, meaning that there are no MOOCs targeted for a broad group of international students and which provide formal recognition through course credits.

Legal Challenges. Despite the fact that current legislation, for instance in Sweden, allows and promotes the use of MOOCs, there are still some undefined aspects that makes the issue of their integration in the educational offer of HEIs a bit more complicated. As a consequence, most of the universities treat these courses as distance courses, and the process of student registration goes through a standardized national portal. As a result, this to some extent reduces the flexibility of the educational offer.

Moreover, if students are not admitted and processed through the national portal and respective university admission office, they might not have the same status as other regular students in the university. This fact complicates the procedure for examination and credit award for the students, which impacts the university's ability to obtain funding from the government.

Table 2. MOOCs typology framework in Sweden, Norway and Denmark.

		Mass-market MOOCs		Niche-market MOOCs
Formal approach	S	-	S	*KU:* 3 courses, own platform
	N	-	N	UiO: 3 courses, mooc.no NTNU: 3 courses, mooc.no UiS: 2 courses, mooc.no NMBU: 1 course, mooc.no HiØ: 1 course, mooc.no HiV: 2 courses, mooc.no UiB: 1 course, mooc.no HiL: 1 course, mooc.no UiT/NTNU: 1 course, mooc.no
	D	-	D	UCZ: 3 courses, own platform
Informal approach	S	*BTH:* 1 course, Canvas *CUTs:* 16 courses, edX *KTH:* 9 courses, edX *LU:* 8 courses, Coursera *UU:* 3 courses, FutureLearn *KI:* 6 courses, edX *HU:* 1 course, Canvas *LnU:* 1 course, Canvas *MSU:* 1 course, Canvas	S	*KU:* 3 courses, own platform
	N	UiO: 3 courses, FutureLearn UiB: 3 courses, FutureLearn UiA: 1 course, Canvas NTNU: 1 course, mooc.no	N	UiO: 3 courses, mooc.no NTNU: 3 courses, mooc.no UiS: 2 courses, mooc.no NMBU: 1 course, mooc.no HiØ: 1 course, mooc.no HiV: 2 courses, mooc.no UiB: 1 course, mooc.no HiL: 1 course, mooc.no UiT/NTNU: 1 course, mooc.no WSC, 2 courses, mooc.no
	D	*CBS:* 15 courses, Coursera *TUD:* 9 courses, Coursera; 1 course edX *UC:* 16 courses, Coursera; 2 courses edX	D	UCZ: 3 courses, own platform

For the typology framework, we use the following abbreviations:
Sweden (S), Norway (N), Denmark (D), Karlstad University (KU), Blekinge Institute of Technology (BTH), Chalmers University of Technology (CUT), Royal Institute of Technology (KTH), Lund University (LU), Uppsala University (UU), Karolinska Institute (KI), Halmstad University (HU), Linnaeus University (LnU), Mid Sweden University (MSU), University of Oslo (UiO), Norwegian University of Science and Technology (NTNU), University of Stavanger (UiS), Norwegian University of Life Sciences (NMBU), University College of Ostfold (HiØ), University College of Volda (HiV), University of Bergen (UiB), University College of Lillehamer (HiL), University of Tromso (UiT), Westerdals School of Communication (WSC), Copenhagen Business School (CBS), Technical University of Denmark (TUD), University of Copenhagen (UC), University College Zealand (UCZ).

4.2 MOOC Opportunities

Lifelong Learning - Professional Development. We live in an age of abundant opportunities for acquiring new knowledge and skills through innovative learning technologies. But also, the constant technological development requires stronger and permanent connections between education and employment, thus making lifelong learning an economic imperative in our modern society. Therefore, the ongoing skill development is essential to survive in the ever-changing technological landscape.

MOOCs could be a source of lifelong learning and contribute to raising the level of knowledge in the society, by enabling people of different ages and backgrounds to engage in learning. In this way, HEIs will not only provide continuing education to strengthen workforce, but also offer opportunities to access the higher education with flexible pathways.

The Scandinavian countries are characterized by having well developed higher education sector, free higher education, and good schemes for education support. However, these are high-cost countries, and global competition means that professional life must become progressively knowledge intensive and also experience continual development and adaptation. Consequently, it is important to have opportunities for lifelong learning, where MOOCs will make knowledge and education more accessible and affordable for employees through their lives.

Educational Affordance. In large countries with small population, such as Sweden and Norway, there are areas with very sparse population, especially in the northern parts. These inland areas have lack of educational resources as most of the universities are by the coast.

In order to slow the process of brain drain, a typical issue for such areas, MOOCs can be used to help people gain knowledge and skills that the local education has difficulties to provide [10]. People needing such education could be those with extensive experience in certain field but that need new skills when new jobs emerge, and also, youth and people with disabilities who aim to enter the job market. Recently, a new target population could be helped using MOOCs; the immigrants, who need to be ready to contribute to the community. These people are also mostly sent to inland places with poor educational resources.

Supplementary Courses - Flipped Classroom. MOOCs can be instrumental in enhancing the teaching quality without increasing the number of lectures, while simultaneously supporting students in obtaining higher degrees of independence in study activities. Moreover, the utilization of MOOCs as a content delivery platform in a flipped classroom setting can free face-to-face sessions for meaningful conversations and interactive problem-solving activities that achieve deeper understanding and integrate knowing with doing [16, 17]. In this way, MOOCs can play a supplementary role in maintaining or even improving the educational standards.

Two successful experiments in a Danish university are conducted; one is concerning the usage of MOOCs for blended learning in face-to-face teaching [16], and the other is regarding a master program in "ICT-based educational design", which is offered as a MOOC to students/learners outside the university [18]. These experiments reveal that integrating MOOCs elements into a traditional face-to-face learning can significantly help teachers to efficiently use their classroom time, by using MOOCs as a resource and not spending time in producing them.

It is worth mentioning that several research works report that MOOC paradigm is appropriate for flexible learning situations, such as flipped classroom pedagogy. These studies demonstrate that student satisfaction and performance using MOOCs was high, even slightly better, compared to students in only face-to-face environments. Additionally, there were good levels of interaction reported between teachers and students [19–22].

Nonetheless, apart from the witnessed (observed) opportunities that MOOCs provide in this perspective, still more research and experiments are needed to find the balance of combining MOOCs with flipped classroom pedagogy to create far more dynamic learning environment. This will enable teachers to invest more time on planning classroom activities and bridge MOOC courses closer to the actual industry needs.

Institution Branding – Openness. Through developing MOOCs, Scandinavian HEIs have the opportunity to extend reachability and accessibility of their teaching activities, both nationally and globally. MOOCs can benefit them to develop a more strategic and flexible approach to online learning and to enhance reputation by offering innovative classroom teaching practices and developing new revenue models.

As indicated in Table 1, some of the largest and most prestigious Scandinavian HEIs already have a presence and are offering MOOCs in international platforms such as Coursera, edX, and FutureLearn. Such presence will contribute to further increase the visibility of Scandinavian HEIs and contribute to the internationalization of education.

5 Conclusions

This paper has addressed the identification of current trends of MOOCs expansion in the Scandinavian higher education landscape. It highlighted important challenges Scandinavian HEIs face today when it comes to integrating MOOCs in the regular higher education programs. Additionally, it provides several opportunities in this direction.

This study carried out an analysis using the MOOC typology framework to systematically differentiate and categorize Scandinavian MOOCs in terms of accreditation and scalability. Our investigation yielded that a considerable number of Scandinavian MOOCs have already been developed and are offered by many prestigious and top ranked HEIs. The majority of these MOOCs serve an international audience of learners, particularly those offered by Swedish and Danish HEIs. However, none of the MOOCs can be associated with a formal and mass-market approach, and by having said that, most of the Scandinavian MOOCs do not offer recognition through credits, but provide informal recognition through badges or diplomas.

The challenges included in this study provide an overview of obstacles that MOOCs face in Scandinavian countries. Despite these challenges, there are strong indications that the process of MOOC integration is moving forward and the list of opportunities included in this paper should provide a basis for discussion and inspiration.

References

1. Dalipi, F., Yayilgan, Y.S., Imran, A.S., Kastrati, Z.: Towards understanding the MOOC trend: pedagogical challenges and business opportunities. In: 3rd International Conference on Learning and Collaboration Technologies (LCT 2016), Toronto, Canada (2016)
2. Lebron, D.: Comparing MOOC-based platforms: reflection on pedagogical support, framework and learning analytics. In: International Conference on Collaboration Technologies and Systems, Atlanta, USA (2015)
3. Ljungqvist, M., Hedberg, M.: Developing a MOOC: is in the process, not just the product. In: MOOCs in Scandinavia Conference 2015, Sweden (2015)
4. Kjeldstad, B.: MOOCs for Norway: New Digital Learning Methods in Higher Education. Portland Press Limited (2016)
5. Buhl, M., Andreasen, L.B., Mondrup, H.J.: A Danish International MOOC in Indonesian Professional Care Education. KNOU (Korea National Open University) Press (2015)
6. Oliver Riera, M., Hernández Leo, D., Daza, V., Martín i Badell, C., Albó Pérez, L.: MOOCs en España. Panorama actual de los Cursos Masivos Abiertos en Línea en las universidades españolas, 33 p. (Cuaderno Red de Cátedras Telefónica. Social Innovation in Education). Universitat Pompeu Fabra, Barcelona (2014)
7. Tomte, C.E., Fevolden, A.M., Aanstad, S.: Massive, open, online and national? A study of how national governments and institutions shape the development of MOOC. Int. Rev. Res. Open Distrib. Learn. 18(5), 212–226 (2017)
8. Liyanagunawardena, T.R., Adams, A.A., Williams, S.A.: MOOCs: a systematic study of the published literature 2008–2012. Int. Rev. Res. Open Distrib. Learn. 14(3), 202–227 (2013)
9. Ross, J., Sinclair, C., Knox, J., Bayne, S., Macleod, H.: Teacher experiences and academic identity: the missing components of MOOC pedagogy. MERLOT J. Online Learn. Teach. 10 (1), 57–69 (2014)
10. Norberg, A., Handel, A., Odling, P.: Using MOOCs at learning centers in northern sweden. Int. Rev. Res. Open Distrib. Learn. 16(6), 137–150 (2015)
11. Buhl, M., Andreasen, L.B.: MOOCs beyond the c- and x-divide – the relevance of a social constructivist approach. In: MOOCs in Scandinavia Conference 2015, Sweden (2015)
12. Jacobsen, D.Y.: Dropping out or dropping in? A connectivist approach to understanding participants' strategies in an e-learning MOOC pilot. Technol. Knowl. Learn., 1–21 (2017)
13. Langseth, I., Haugsbakken, H.: Introducing blended learning MOOC – a study of one bMOOC in Norwegian teacher education. In International Conference on Stakeholders and Information Technology in Education, Portugal, 5–8 July 2016 (2016)
14. Swedish Higher Education Authority (UKÄ). http://english.uka.se/about-us/publications/reports–guidelines/reports–guidelines/2016-02-05-massive-open-online-courses-moocs.html. Accessed 27 Jan 2018
15. Official Norwegian Reports NOU. MOOCs for Norway—New digital learning methods in higher education. The Ministry of Education and Research (2014). https://www.regjeringen.no/contentassets/ff86edace9874505a3381b5daf6848e6/en-gb/pdfs/nou201420140005000en_pdfs.pdf. Accessed 27 Jan 2018
16. Nortvig, A., Gynther, K., Gundersen, P.B.: Blending MOOCs in face-to-face teaching and studies. In: Academic Conferences International Limited (2016)

17. Dalipi, F., Kurti, A., Zdravkova, K., Ahmedi, L.: Rethinking the conventional learning paradigm towards MOOC based flipped classroom learning. In: The 16th IEEE International Conference on Information Technology Based Higher Education and Training (ITHET), Ohrid, Macedonia, 10–12 July 2017 (2017)
18. Bang, J., Dalsgaard, C., Kjaer, A., O'Donovan, M.: Opening up education - some pedagogical considerations. In: EADTU 2016 (2016)
19. Sufang, A., Wenbin, L., Jichao, H., Lixiao, M., Jiwei, X.: Research on the reform of flipped classroom in computer science of university based SPOC. In: The 12th IEEE International Conference on Computer Science and Education, Houston, USA, 22–25 August 2017 (2017)
20. Muñoz-Merino, P.J., Ruipérez-Valiente, J.A., Delgado Kloos, C., Auger, M.A., Briz, S., de Castro, V., Santalla, S.N.: Flipping the classroom to improve learning with MOOCs technology. Comput. Appl. Eng. Educ. **25**(1), 15–25 (2017)
21. Israel, M.J.: Effectiveness of integrating MOOCs in traditional classrooms for undergraduate students. Int. Rev. Res. Open Distrib. Learn. **16**(5), 102–118 (2015)
22. Bralic, A., Divjak, B.: Use of MOOCs in traditional classroom: blended learning approach. In: Proceedings of the 9th European Distance and ELearning Network Research Workshop (2016)

Training Evaluation in a Learning Organization and Online Training Through the E-booklet Contribution of Game Theory and Shapley Value

Karim Elia Fraoua[✉] and Christian Bourret

Université Paris-Est Marne-La-Vallée, Equipe Dispositifs d'Information et de Communication à l'Ere Numérique (DICEN IDF), Conservatoire National des Arts et Métiers, Université Paris-Nanterre, EA 7339, Serris, France
{karim.fraoua, christian.bourret}@u-pem.fr

Abstract. This work focuses on the question of apprenticeship in French universities in relation to apprenticeship training centers and companies where the apprentice completes his internship and the definition of this new learning structure. One of the problems in this structure is the difficulty of making it work effectively through an artifact called the e-learning booklet. This brochure in the new organization should be used as a support tool for the apprentice and will contain all the knowledge and skills acquired, including know-how. This tool is relatively difficult to complete because there are few incentive tools and seems to be more a constraint when it should be an asset for the entire learning structure. In this work we will discuss the role of the lifelong learning process in France and the increased professional integration in relation to the status of apprentices and the behavior of the student-apprentice compared to a classical student. We will discuss, through game theory and Shapley's work, on what would be the value of each of the actors would be and which could lead to more effective tools to complement this electronic booklet and how to obtain greater value in terms of content that can be analyzed through textometrics and lexicometrics tools. This tool will contain both the strengths and weaknesses of the student and, above all, how it can be remedied mainly by on-line but also off-line tools, thereby improving the training process and ensuring that this tripartite organization: University - Apprentice – CFA, plays its full role as a learning organization. The student puts performance related information in a booklet which will be considered in the future in France as a companion describing his or her graduation results and skills.

Keywords: Apprenticeship · Learning organization · Game theory
Shapley value

1 Introduction

This work is part of the learning structure analysis [1] which is quite developed in France, namely the Apprenticeship Training Center. First of all, it should be agreed for structural reasons that learning is a transfer from national education to the regions, on

© Springer International Publishing AG, part of Springer Nature 2018
P. Zaphiris and A. Ioannou (Eds.): LCT 2018, LNCS 10924, pp. 205–217, 2018.
https://doi.org/10.1007/978-3-319-91743-6_16

the assumption that this new organization will be better able at measuring the needs of employment in a territory. In fact, even still now, it's the regions that decide the creation of specific training centers, whether or not in link with universities. In order to improve the professional integration of students from universities who were experiencing a real integration is a problem despite the existence in most programs of compulsory internships, it was initiated a new policy that requires the establishment of this same strategy by changing the management structures and new organizational modalities that led to the establishment of a training center for apprentices open to universities. As a result, the number of apprentices in France has risen from 100,000 in the 1980s to 400,000 today. This increase is mainly due to the additional number of vocational baccalaureates (100,000), BTS (70,000) and university (Bac + 3 to Bac + 5), which have a workforce of around 60,000, mostly in the service sector (60% of apprentices) [2]; It is clear that today the positive effects of apprenticeship has been observed in the integration of young people into the labor market, with access to employment being faster for former apprentices [3].

However, there is a contrast between training and level of training. The DUT and BTS have a highly student-oriented workforce, as well as professional licenses or master's degrees, some of which specialties have up to 80% of their enrollment in apprenticeships, particularly within University Paris Est Marne [4]. The device that is set up for the apprentice's follow-up, namely the e-booklet, would then, if properly used and filled, become a lever to transform the CFA into a learning organization. This system enables it to improve the processes put in place to monitor the apprentice and to propose areas for development to create added value beyond the administrative follow-up of apprentices. In fact, this poorly informed and little used tool in a general way will allow to create new solutions to better develop the internal competences but also their apprentices who are part of the structure during their learning. It is for this reason that we have made the decision to denote that the CFA can become a "learning organization". Indeed, this tool can become a matrix that will allow to set up new training logics through a new learning tools such as e-learning, serious or business game and which are absent from this organization nowadays.

2 The Logic of Training in the Learning Organization

The notion of learning organization is based on the idea that an organization's ability to learn is its main source of competitiveness, inferring a particular mode of organization [5]. The learning organization is built around the acquisition of professional skills and not professional qualifications and what will possible within the framework of the undertakings that are given to the CFA since it is mainly the follow-up of the apprentices. This is what allows the best professional integration compared to a traditional student who simply does an internship and who as a general rule is less valued. This new logic of learning leads to a new training landscape in which the CFA will want to play a preponderant role by its positioning and will mainly become accountant training actions. In particular, it will impose a skills-based approach on the Universities as the numbers become more and more important and the measurement tools are little or not at all adapted to this new approach. It is certain that this organizational flaw can create a dysfunction of the device and besides the tools put in place are often criticized because of their weak use and especially of their feeble analysis.

Historically and in the classical university schema, the student completes an internship at the end of his academic year and in this context few links are made with the company except at the end of internship where the student describes his work, which is evaluated by a university jury, sometimes attended by professionals. Apprenticeship, on the other hand, is a form of co-training, both in university and in business, with a shared responsibility and subject to a double evaluation, namely the knowledge acquired and the skills developed. The learning organization is characterized by the implementation of an intellectual reflection accompanying the act of production and allowing the development of the capacities of the individuals who compose it. *"An individual can be confronted with a variety of situations that engender a truly transposable experience and that generate learning and move towards competence"* [6]. In the same vein, the construction and development of skills is no longer a matter of training alone, but also of professionalization, including the passage through training situations and simple work situations made professional [7, 8].

It is therefore a matter of learning in and by the organization where the organizational framework constitutes a context that enables the learning processes. The competency approach provides a link between the explicit knowledge that comes from academic training and that can be transferred to learners and the know-how that is the result of a business practice. These two skills will form the basis of competence that the learner will acquire during his/her academic year and which should correspond to the different skill blocks that have been formally described and which will lead to the materialization of a learning action, and the integration of the learner into the world of work. Learning more in a shorter amount of time is of greater importance than the duration of the internship and allows through scenarios to build skills in action. This long and enriching experience through the various scenarios is only possible if all actors are strongly involved and implicated in the learning organization namely the company, the university and the essential role of the CFA which must be engaged in the training process, participating in the diagnosis and putting in place the necessary solutions for the production of the necessary knowledge and through the follow-up and accompaniment of the learner. The latter must be in the main agent's master plan to obtain the acquisition of these skill blocks [9].

In this process it is essential that the actors know the role that is given to them to make the necessary arrangements for the success of this action. It is important for the learner in this organization to ensure that everyone's role is fulfilled and that he becomes the master of his destiny and not merely a passive actor, which is often the attitude observed in the field. In this context, it is also necessary to explicitly define the role of the company because it must define specific objectives during this instruction and define the entrusted mission to be carried out because of the significance that the mission must have in relation to the reference system, training, skills to acquire and their validation. In this new approach in which the companies often aim, above all, to increase their performance through the performances of all actors involved but also the knowledge of the company through these actors, by increasing the knowledge and the skills of the company. These agents, it seems useful to address the notion of the actor network theory as the entire training device including actors and especially the role of e-booklet are important in this device.

3 Theory of the Network Actor

The idea is to show that the structure works in network: Apprentice-University-Enterprise and CFA but also all the tools that allow the appearance of this structure including the e-booklet. Indeed, Freeman [10] defines stakeholders as "any group or individual that affects or is affected by the achievement of the objectives of the business. As for Post, et al. [11] it is any individual or group that contribute, deliberately or not, to the creation of value for a structure, and who are its beneficiaries or who share its risks and Clarkson [12] considers an approach built on the contributions made by the actors and whose contribution can vary which is very interesting in our reading of the problem. From the perspective of the actor-network theory there is no separation-between the "human" of the "non-human" according to Callon [13]. It is even consolidated by law which defines a "meta-organization" with humans and "non-humans" who interact with each other, and consider all the elements that contribute to the final act as agents, including objects [14]. Indeed, the final act cannot take place without the contribution of each element. This approach is necessary to convince the organization that each actor has the same weight and especially that the e-booklet is also an actor of the organization. In fact, in order for the organization to become a learner organization, the fact that it is network facilitates learning since the interaction between actors is stimulated and new relationships can be established between all the actors without a hierarchical relationship. In the same way, the e-booklet will allow the conclusion of an essential concept specifically the sharing of knowledge between the actors.

4 The Role of the Apprentice and Learning Device in Learning Structures

In this very structured framework, it is useful to focus in particular on the object resulting from this device namely the apprentice. Indeed, the world of learning changes significantly and it even criticized by questioning its foundations and purposes [15]. With this in mind, the role of the CFA is more and more prominent in the approaches to learning whether from a theoretical point of view or from a point of view of practices. Indeed, learning practices have been largely impacted by these effects, as the lessons have been oriented in an approach that largely integrates operational experiences from more and more business world with case studies, or business game, or the recourse more and more often to professionals who intervene in the fields of practice. This element is interesting since the student's reception is also done through the Apprentice Training Center and it can have an influence on the student-apprentice's attitudes and actions, notwithstanding the fact that the apprentice is considered almost as an employee within the company contrary to the traditional student during his internship in the company where he will be considered trainee and ipso-facto of passage, while the first is placed in pre-employment situation and thus will act as a full-fledged employee, and is already positioning itself in this perspective as soon as he arrives, the latter will act as performing compulsory work is part of his studies. We will consider in our work that the student will make a calculation of utility related to his investment and will be able to judge that his investment will not be profitable since the company will not keep it at the end of his internship, of a point of view of the game theory this calculation, while it will be optimal for the apprentice, since he considers that the company will wish to keep it in this context and that learning is presented as being the royal road of the 'occupational integration. The e-booklet that will be presented later will have the effect of reinforcing this belief and by improving the professional integration of apprentices.

In this axis of reflection, we could consider that both these students as well as those coming from the initial formation are in a well-defined approach by Biggs [16] which shows that a student resorting to the approach «on the surface "was mainly concerned with avoiding failure at the price of a minimum commitment that would be the student in initial training and therefore performing a course unlike a student resorting to the approach" in depth», which is mainly motivated by the search for meaning and ownership and who would then be the apprentice. In the first context, the student is placed in the paradigm of teaching while the second state places it still in the paradigm of learning. The world of education has an often classical vision with definite sequences in the curriculum while in the world of learning, the evolution of students in a given field of knowledge requires new approaches to learning [17]. This reflection is reinforced by the work of Messick, who shows that there are constant individual differences in the way of organizing and processing information and experiences [18].

The role of this e-booklet will then push the apprentice to better optimize his apprenticeship in the company but also within the university to acquire the maximum amount of knowledge and skills because this tool will be the major element for measuring the graduate's actual integration skills in the world of work. It will also avoid useless arbitrations of the learner with respect to the acquisition of knowledge that will not be observed in the field, since without this knowledge, the competence cannot be validated. As an example, let us imagine the necessary skills for web site design, we can build around these skills, explicit and/or implicit knowledge acquisition needed (Table 1).

Table 1. Representation of Skills from e-booklet

Skills	Knowledge Level 1	Knowledge Level 2	Knowledge Level 3
Website design	Html	Html	Html
	CSS	CSS	CSS
	Web design	Web design	Web design
		Script language JS	Script language JS
			Php, Asp..

We will try from this perspective to consider an approach based on the notion of the need to perform an action such as making a pastry and to acquire the operational techniques such as knowledge, methods and procedures to achieve and master core practical competencies and therefore learning. We want to show in this work that the role of the apprentice is, contrary to current trends, a major element of the process of the validation of skills and we will see that the approach based on game theory will validate this hypothesis through the use of Shapley's value and show that the Shapley value of the apprentice is the greatest versus the value of the academic tutor and the company tutor.

5 Evaluation of the Apprenticeship and the Role of Booklet

The status of apprenticeship involves the enterprise both in the process of training and assessment of acquired skills. In this perspective, a pedagogical committee, which includes the companies, the university and the CFA, participates in the evaluation of the contents and encourages a better professionalization to favor the professional insertion. In addition, juries evaluating the work done and skills acquired throughout the year and no longer just at the end of the course, are of mixed composition. They include academics but also professionals including the tutor of the company. In order to make this work more efficient, an annual follow-up is done initially through a booklet that includes a theoretically active participation of the training manager, the university tutor, the apprentice and the guardian of the company. This tool is now available in digital format as e-booklet. We found that this document, whether written or digital, was not very encouraging and sometimes criticized. It was found that it was more mandatory than incentive. Few elements were present that could make it efficient from a qualitative point of view.

In this perspective of improvement, we considered two axes, first to encourage the students to give their feedback on all the courses that were followed and then to analyze the textual content and see what are the knowledge and skills that would not be acquired and by doing so, we can propose corrective actions through the provision of online courses either in the form of courses or Mooc. The apprentice himself then becomes an actor of his own learning in a constructivist approach [19] including in topics that would not be included in the pedagogical model, as better acquisitions in language related to the business needs. The latter will also be strongly associated with this approach, since it can postpone the missing skills that will be corrected either by current actions or by online training.

We then come to the essential role of the e-booklet to know the common good of all the actors that is a favorable insertion of the young person in the world of the company. Still in a perspective of improving the existing tool for a better use, we work on a modeling/anticipation of the behaviors of all the actors, starting with those of the apprentices and that the imperative need of cooperation between all the agents to know apprentice, trainer and company under the leadership of the CFA and therefore formally establish the value of Shapley [20] in order to establish that sharing this goal can lead to the common goal and that the CFA can fulfill its role of allocation of means for achieving this objective, and that the tools put in place are effective devices. The goal is to achieve a cooperative or coalition game in which players can form coalitions and act in concert and with transferable utilities where it is possible to add players' utilities and redistribute them to members of a team or a coalition. A Coalition is defined as a group of agents who decide to cooperate in order to achieve a common goal, which is the goal of the evaluation tool namely the e-booklet. To this end is associated a utility or shared reward between the different agents forming the coalition [21].

To illustrate the document, we will place ourselves in the frame in our situation with individuals having to share the benefit v(E) gained by this structure. We suppose that we know for each subset F of E, the benefit v(F) that the individuals present in F would have (a substructure can be the CFA and the university, ...). This purely individual value without the integration of the other actors would be the intrinsic value and does not take into account the contribution of each of the actors of the coalition since the agent acts alone. We seek to determine the remuneration or contribution that each actor i must receive and this is the value $\varphi(i)$ of each player [22]. The simplest way would be that the sharing is done in an equal manner namely the total value divided by 4 in our case. It is also true that our situation the overall gain would be the success and insertion of the apprentice, which is the objective of the CFA to know

$$\varphi(i) = v(E)/4.$$

In the presence of coalition, the overall value would be greater than the sum of the values of the actors. In fact, without a coalition or CFA action, which will have a coordinating role here, the overall value would be the intrinsic contribution of each of the actors. In this case all players contribute in the same way, which is obviously the conventional reasoning that all agents have the same contribution, but in fact the benefit would be higher for the apprentice and by the same his contribution should be stronger and this is the meaning of our thinking, since we will show that it will start filling the e-book under the aegis of the CFA, which as we have explained above, will have a structural evolution to do to the learning organization and in our approach to the network actor theory, the additional value of the coalition could be that of the e-booklet, except that this additional value will be shared by the other actors without forgetting the marginal contributions of the others actors.

It is useful to remember that the university sees itself playing a new role which is the accompaniment of students towards a better professional integration, with the setting up of an observatory or various indicators which influence the durability of the formations. This result, which is necessarily immaterial, is the result of the action of several actors who are the CFA, the training structure, the company and of course the apprentice, who will become the bearer of this project and the result obtained should be the most useful for him, because it will allow him to master the skills that he will need and that would have been validated by the company, and therefore by the best institution that knows best the needs for integration. Finally, the CFA will use this result to improve its knowledge and put in place tools to further improve the knowledge of all employees including the apprentice. If the apprentice's contribution to the filling of the e-booklet is the most important, his value of Shapley would be greater. To better understand this mechanism and how the apprentice will have an important role in triggering the filling of the e-booklet, we will detail the filling algorithm based on the Gale-Shapley model.

If an actor does not fill the e-booklet, it is considered transparent and has no influence on the total value, it will not validate a skill for example and therefore its value will be zero. In our system, of course it is necessary to immediately correct this situation and it is in this that the apprentice or even the CFA will have to correct this bias if it happens and must ask the actor in question to act. As much as the university will be evaluated on its ability to train collaborators and insert them professionally as the tutor of the company will have different indicators that can go towards the establishment of valuation of social and human capacities. Once integrated into the group, it can contribute to value creation such as training the apprentice and validating his skills and that will be his marginal value.

In fact the intrinsic value of the actor is not really because it depends on the intrinsic value of other players and the reality of interactions between players. In this context, pedagogical committees have a great deal of influence on expectations and needs, and there is even a training of tutors to further improve the interaction between the actors and thus increase the intrinsic values of all the actors. Without the properly completed e-booklet, each actor has only its intrinsic value and its marginal contribution would be zero and the role of the CFA, whose intrinsic value is zero without the existence of the other actors, will have a value related to the creation of the marginal value by encouraging the other actors to produce more and here in this case the filling of the e-booklet. We can of course consider the distribution of value that will benefit the apprentice more since the filling of the e-booklet will allow him to know his evaluation and therefore allow him under the aegis of the CFA to organize a training with the tools described above and/or remediation both at the level of the training organization and the company to allow it to meet 100% of the requirements of the standard and thus lead to successful insertion. We can focus on the distribution of this profit between the apprentice, the CFA, the company and the university, since each of the actors of the coalition will recover a part of the investment related to the increase of the global result. Within the university, the insertion rate of young people is a major indicator in the choice of training and this can be a form of reward.

We have seen above that the filling of the booklet becomes a real concern because it is rarely satisfactorily fulfilled and therefore it cannot serve as a tool for assessing skills and knowledge. It is certain that the obtaining of a diploma makes it possible to state that the student has been able to give satisfaction and as he has the knowledge and the competences and which are the subject of a follow-up on the part of the CFA. However, the role of the CFA remains minor if the e-booklet is not properly filled and its added value remains low or even zero, what we have called the marginal contribution. It will serve only as a place to finance training. We would like to point out that adult continuing education does not need this follow-up, adults are supposed to come from the business world and easily perceive the skills they need to acquire, they are also demanding of all the knowledge that will enable them to acquire these skills. In a lifelong learning approach, which is the leitmotif of modern and innovative societies, this document can be crucial for developing training strategies in the learner's future.

6 Situation of Actors of Learning and Game Theory

Game theory allows analyzing different situations in which agents or players interact in order to study the behavior of the various actors who participate in these interactions through a formalization of their process of cooperation, coalition or rivalry. The games can be cooperative or non-cooperative, zero sum, and in this case the gain of one is the loss of the other player or other players or non-zero sum in which the consultation between agents is desired. This cooperation can lead to a situation in which players can enter into agreements to maximize their joint profit. The notion of equilibrium is the fundamental notion in game theory. It is necessary to study and compare various strategies for which the strategy of each player is the best answer to the strategies of the other players. In fact each player has a set of actions, and the result of the game depends on the actions chosen by all players. A set of actions forms Nash equilibrium if the action of each player is the best for that player, given the actions of the other players [23]. We cannot talk about Nash equilibrium without mentioning the Pareto Optimum. One point is said Pareto optimal if it cannot be strictly dominated by another, that is to say we consider the situation where we cannot improve the utility of an agent without damaging that of at least one other and has the advantage of being acceptable to all. We see here that the interaction between actors or agents is essential and that the CFA will have a fundamental coordinating role, in order to show that the search for this common good which is the best insertion of the apprentice is the fundamental element of the creation of this coalition.

For Shapley, the marginal contribution of each player k is equal to the mathematical expectation of his marginal contributions to the gain of all the coalitions that can be formed without him. The CFA will thus be able to show the value of this marginal contribution by comparing the situations where the e-booklet is well and correctly filled and the actions taken and an e-booklet that is not completed or filled in and the result on the insertion of the apprentice [24]. To start the idea of the filling phases, we will explain the method of matching the actors in Gale and Shapley's [25] marriage model, which consists first of all in defining a finite set of women w and a finite set men m, which define the two types of individuals that we want to associate in pairs. Each individual v is characterized by a strict, transitive and complete preference relation, P_v defined on the individuals of the opposite sex and himself. Thus (m_3Pw, m_2Pw_2, w, Pwm_1) indicates that w prefers to be married to m_3 rather than m_2, and to be married to m_2 rather than remain single, and remain single rather than being married to m_1. The algorithm of Gale and Shapley privileges from the start a type of individuals, that makes proposals of marriage to the other and thus here the apprentice who will start the choice of sending the e-booklet according to the skill or knowledge that he wishes to validate. Without going into the details of this algorithm, we see clearly that the system favors the voluntary approach in obtaining the result and de facto a form of incentive to the reaction and therefore the emergence of the least of a communication process which must be a reflection to be conducted at the level of the CFA which often are in an informational approach. The dimension of communication within the organization is essential in building a learning organization.

7 Algorithm for Creating an Evaluation Tool

The agent, who starts the validation starts with all the possible sets, classifies them and sends the ones he deems acceptable to the next (Table 1). We could have in our reflection on the value of Shapley reflected on the establishment of sub-coalition that would be made up of several possibilities either the apprentice and the university tutor, or the apprentice and the company tutor. We see that here we will be able to define the process of filling the e-booklet. It is a strategy among others and this one will be more based on the construction of a coalition linked to the presence of the apprentice who is an evanescent actor of this organization unlike the university, the CFA even of the company who have more interest in being in a cooperative approach. This approach can be validated in a formal and engaging way in order to encourage the actors to be explicit and complete in their evaluations [26]. This is a process that is interesting because it will be validated at each stage. Indeed, an agent sends a set of suggestions; he signs it to indicate to the following that he has accepted. This validation will be a form of validation of skills and the role of the CFA can be a regulator of this validation, especially from the company so that it is possible. There are, of course, safeguards within the company and the CFA is supposed to check the level of the company tutor in terms of position and degree, which ultimately allows validating these skills and notwithstanding validation by the university. When an agent receives a group of sets, he sorts them into new groups and adds them to those he validated himself. If he has a group of sets that he prefers to those he has received and has not yet transmitted, he can send it to another agent, here it can be either the company or the university that will rank the skills that the learner thinks he has acquired and which will be an essential step, since this will allow to formally indicate the unfulfilled skills and the missing knowledge for this acquisition (Tables 2 and 3). At any time, an agent who has received signed sets may declare them acceptable as a solution, sign them himself and pass them on to another agent who has not signed them yet. When an agent receives a group of sets showing the skills and/or knowledge that all other agents have signed, if at least one of them is deemed acceptable, the one he deems the best is a Pareto optimum. This culmination at an optimum of Pareto, shows that in this coalition game all the actors are satisfied and none is damaged by the approach of the other actor. This last step can be devolved to the university, which by its role of diploma structure will allow beyond the diploma itself to ensure the certification of competence (Table 4).

The learner can restart the process whenever he considers that the missing knowledge or skill has been acquired. The role of other actors becomes a role of referee and not of power. The trend in the transfer of utility is also the transfer of power to all actors. If the learner realizes a website and considers that he has acquired this competence by using different languages which constitute the base of competences. The host company can validate this competence because it has responded to the specifications in terms of what has been described above in terms of compatibility with the reference system. The university can re-evaluate its arbitration towards a validation of the competence and the knowledge. It is necessary as we indicated in advance to know the establishment of a process of coordination and not of setting up the process and the CFA can fully play this role of coordinator, leaving the implementation of the process

Table 2. Step **1:** Learner filling the skills in the e-booklet

Skills	Knowledge Level 1	Knowledge Level 2	Knowledge Level 3
Website design	Html	Html	Html
	CSS	CSS	CSS
	Web design	Web design	Web design
		Script language JS	Script language JS
			Php, Asp..

Table 3. Step **2:** Company filling the skills in the e-booklet

Skills	Knowledge Level 1	Knowledge Level 2	Knowledge Level 3
Website design	Html	Html	Html
	CSS	CSS	CSS
	Web design	Web design	Web design
		Script language JS	Script language JS
			Php, Asp..

Table 4. Step **3:** Learner filling the skills in the e-booklet

Skills	Knowledge Level 1	Knowledge Level 2	Knowledge Level 3
Website design	Html	Html	Html
	CSS	CSS	CSS
	Web design	Web design	Web design
		Script language JS	Script language JS
			Php, Asp..

Acquired, Nearly acquired, Not acquired

in the hands of the apprentice in terms of start-up and validation timing, including in the reading of temporalities such as the visit of the apprentice in a company that could serve as point for the validation of skills by discussing the points of disagreement that will eventually fade away based on Aumann's theorem, that there is a satisfactory solution, [27] that in the presence of beliefs a priori common and the same information, the beliefs a posteriori are identical. This then induces the impossibility of agreeing on a disagreement, and the achievement of equilibrium. A new learning process can then be put in place to correct it. The CFA in its role of coordinator must ensure the respect of the contract indeed, the works of Harsanyi define the rules of a cooperative game, in this type of game, the commitments contracted by the agents are irrevocable and are guaranteed by an institution able to enforce them [28].

It is clearly established that the CFA will have a fundamental role to play here which is to ensure the right balance and above all to act by getting involved in the action of the cooperation between all the actors so that this balance is reached. Finally, we can also conclude since the apprentice will be the main loser of the game, to make sure that this equilibrium remains untouchable to remain of optimal use. Under this hypothesis, we look at the e-booklet to design an application that measures the equilibrium of all apprentices during the year by a systematic evaluation of the training sequences and to detect the flaws that can disrupt this training balance. In the light of this, corrective actions will be put forward to reduce this distance from a theoretical equilibrium.

8   Conclusion

The idea behind this work is to give the apprentice a greater role in evaluating learning situations and to design a tool that would be more effective. It would thus be possible to push more actors under the guidance of the apprentice to complete it and of course under the supervision of the CFA. The latter would play the role of regulator to achieve the common wealth of know how to promote professional insertion. We highlight here the role of the human factor in the learning process and how purely technical approaches such as the e-booklet completely disconnected from humane and enriching interactions, measurable thanks to the valorisation of the group, are doomed to failure. The evaluation of the group leads to the estimation of each actor through the distribution of this created value using Shapley value and thus show each agent the value created and especially that corrective actions can be implemented.

References

1. Garvin, D.A.: Building a learning organization. Harv. Bus. Rev. **71**(4), 78–91 (1993)
2. Ministère de l'éducation nationale, France. http://cache.media.education.gouv.fr/file/2015/66/6/depp_rers_2015_apprentis_454666.pdf
3. Bonnal, L., Mendes, S., Sofer, C.: School-to-work transition: apprenticeship versus vocational school in France. Int. J. Manpow. **23**(5), 426–442 (2002)
4. Université Paris-Est Marne-la-Vallée. http://www.upem.fr/fileadmin/public/UPEMLV/Guides-Plaquettes/PlaquetteUPEMGB-p-WEB.pdf
5. Ministère du travail, France. http://travail-emploi.gouv.fr/actualites/l-actualite-du-ministere/article/l-apprentissage-un-veritable-outil-d-insertion-dans-l-emploi-au-service-des
6. Zarifian, P.: Le modèle de la compétence. Wolters Kluwer, France (2004)
7. Rojewski, J.: Preparing the workforce of tomorrow: a conceptual framework for career and technical education. J. Vocat. Educ. Res. **27**(1), 7–35 (2002)
8. Le Boterf, G.: Repenser la compétence. Editions Eyrolles (2011)

9. Mallet, J.: L'organisation apprenante: l'action productrice de sens. Tome n°1. Université de Provence (1996)
10. Freeman, R.E.: Strategic Management: A Stakeholder Approach. Pitman, Boston (1984)
11. Post, J., Preston, L., Sachs, S.: Managing the extended enterprise: the new stakeholder view. Calif. Manag. Rev. **45**(1), 6–28 (2002)
12. Clarkson, M.B.E.: A Stakeholder framework for analyzing and evaluating corporate social performance. Acad. Manag. Rev. **20**(1), 92–117 (1995)
13. Callon, M., Latour, B.: Unscrewing the big Leviathan: how actors macrostructure reality and how sociologists help them to do so. In: dans Knorr Cetina, K.D., Cicourel, A.V. (dir.): Advances in Social Theory and Methodology: Toward an Integration of Micro- and Macro-Sociologies, pp. 277–303. Routledge and Kegan Paul, Boston (1981)
14. Callon, M., Law, J., Rip, A. (eds.): Mapping the Dynamics of Science and Technology. MacMillan, London (1986)
15. Moreau, G.: Apprentissage: une singulière métamorphose, Formation Emploi n° 101, janvier-mars (2008)
16. Biggs, J.: What do inventories of students learning processes really measure? A theoretical review and clarification. Br. J. Educ. Psychol. **63**, 1–17 (1993)
17. Tardif, J.: Qu'est-ce qu'un paradigme? Virage Expr. **3**(6), 4 (2001)
18. Messick, S.: The nature of cognitive styles: problems and promise in educational practice. Educ. Psychol. **19**, 59–74 (1984)
19. Perkins, D.: The many faces of constructivism. Educ. Leadersh. **57**(3), 6–11 (1999)
20. Roth, A.E. (ed.): The Shapley value: essays in honor of Lloyd S. Cambridge University Press, Shapley (1988)
21. Shehory, O., Kraus, S.: Methods for task allocation via agent coalition formation. Artif. Intell. **101**(1–2), 165–200 (1998)
22. Ieong, S., Shoham, Y.: Marginal contribution nets: a compact representation scheme for coalitional games. In: Proceedings of the 6th ACM Conference on Electronic Commerce. ACM (2005)
23. Davis, M.D.: Game Theory: A Nontechnical Introduction. Courier Corporation, North Chelmsford (2012)
24. Shapley, L.S.: A value for n-person games. Contrib. Theory Games **2**(28), 307–317 (1953)
25. Gale, D., Shapley, L.S.: College admissions and the stability of marriage. Am. Math. Mon. **69**(1), 9–15 (1962)
26. Aknine, S., Pinson, S., Shakun, M.F.: An extended multi-agent negotiation protocol. Auton. Agent. Multi-Agent Syst. **8**(1), 5–45 (2004)
27. Aumann, R.J.: Agreeing to disagree. Ann. Stat. **4**, 1236–1239 (1976)
28. Harsanyi, J.C.: A general theory of rational behavior in game situations. Econometrica **34**(3), 613–635 (1966)

Human Interaction in Learning Ecosystems Based on Open Source Solutions

Alicia García-Holgado(✉) and Francisco J. García-Peñalvo

GRIAL Research Group, Computer Sciences Department,
Research Institute for Educational Sciences, University of Salamanca,
Salamanca, Spain
{aliciagh, fgarcia}@usal.es

Abstract. Technological ecosystems are software solutions based on the integration of heterogeneous software components through information flows in order to provide a set of services that each component separately does not offer, as well as to improve the user experience. In particular, the learning ecosystems are technological ecosystems focused on learning and knowledge management in different contexts such as educational institutions or companies. The ecosystem metaphor comes from biology field and it has transferred to technology field to highlight the evolving component of software. Taking into account the definitions of natural ecosystems, a technological ecosystem is a set of people and software components that play the role of organisms; a series of elements that allow the ecosystem works (hardware, networks, etc.); and a set of information flows that establish the relationships between the software components, and between these and the people involved in the ecosystem. Human factor has a main role in the definition and development of this kind of solutions. In previous works, a metamodel has been defined and validated to support Model-Driven Development of learning ecosystems based on Open Source software, but the interaction in the learning ecosystem should be defined in order to complete the proposal to improve the development process of technological ecosystems. This paper presents the definition and modelling of the human interaction in learning ecosystems.

Keywords: Learning ecosystems · Human interaction · Metamodel
Information systems · Software engineering

1 Introduction

Nowadays most of the technological solutions to support knowledge management processes, both in companies and educational institutions, are focused on combining different technologies able to evolve in different dimensions and to include people as part of the technology, not only as mere end-users. This is due to a large extend because the evolution from Information Society to the current Knowledge Society, where the core element is not the technology, but the ability to identify, produce, process, transform, disseminate and use the information to build and apply knowledge for human development [1]. The Knowledge Society is a Learning Society, where the learning is the key factor in order to persons, business, regions and countries achieve success [2]. There is a need to be able to adapt to a world where the emphasis has

© Springer International Publishing AG, part of Springer Nature 2018
P. Zaphiris and A. Ioannou (Eds.): LCT 2018, LNCS 10924, pp. 218–232, 2018.
https://doi.org/10.1007/978-3-319-91743-6_17

moved from knowledge transfer to knowledge creation, from implicit to tacit knowledge, and where building relationships that foster trust and common benefit are the basis for sustainable, ethical progress [3]. In this context, the knowledge management emerges as a sustainable competitive advantage [4] so the organizations expend part of their resources on building their capacity to share, create and apply new knowledge continuously over time [5].

On the other hand, the advances in technology, especially those related to Internet and the mobile devices, have fostered that people build their own personal ecosystems. People select and use different technological tools to support their daily life both in the personal and professional context. Moreover, they seek a certain degree of integration between different tools and services. When these tools are provided by an institution or company two main problems arise: (1) the interoperability of these services and tools; (2) and its evolution. The technological ecosystem concept emerges as a solution to this problems, beyond a simple accumulation of technology [6, 7].

Technological ecosystems are the evolution of the traditional information systems [8, 9]. Information systems emerged in the Information Society to cover the information management needs; whereas technological ecosystems are focused on support the knowledge management typical of Knowledge Society.

The concept of natural ecosystem has been transferred to different contexts. In particular, to the computer science field [10–17] to define technological solutions composed by heterogeneous software tools connected between them to improve the user experience and the knowledge management processes inside institutions or companies. Three common elements are present in all definitions of natural ecosystem - the organisms or biotic factors, the physical environment or abiotic factors and the relationships between them - [18]. According to García-Holgado and García-Peñalvo [19–22], the natural elements appear in a technological ecosystem: the biotic factors are the users and the software components; the relationships are the information flows that establish the communication between them; and the abiotic factors are the physical environment - hardware, network, etc. - that provides support to those flows.

In the event that the knowledge management is directed on supporting learning processes, the technological ecosystem is called learning ecosystem. Llorens-Largo et al. [23] defines a learning ecosystem as a "community, with educational methods, policies, regulations, applications and work teams, which can coexist so that their processes are interrelated, and their application is based on the physical factors of the technological environment". They allow establishing learning ecologies, learning environments with a strong interactive component that allow the exchange of knowledge both in a formal and informal way.

This technological approach offers advantages over traditional learning platforms or Learning Management Systems (LMS) such as the ability to evolve in different dimensions [24, 25] or the reuse of heterogeneous tools already developed to build new systems. It provides a flexible and adaptive architecture [24, 26] to support the evolution of its components and their interconnections to achieve transparent interoperability between them. The LMS does not disappear, it becomes a software component inside the learning ecosystem.

People are not only end-users but also an important component of a learning ecosystem. They have an important role in the ecosystems life cycle as well as in the natural ecosystems. In natural ecosystems a driver is any natural or human-induced factor that directly or indirectly causes an ecosystem change [27]. For example, habitat change, climate change, invasive alien species, overexploitation and pollution, are direct drivers; and the indirect drivers are population, economic activity, and technology, as well as socio-political and cultural factors, because they influence in one or more direct drivers [28]. In technological ecosystems in general and in learning ecosystems in particular, there are also drivers; technological or human-induced factors that cause ecosystem changes. For example, direct drivers are workflows, employees or students profile, information handled; and indirect drivers are cultural factors, economic activity, organization policies, market, planned obsolescence, license changes.

Humans have a strong impact in both types of ecosystem. They produce many impacts on natural and technological ecosystems, both harmful and beneficial.

Like humans have to work to improve their role as drivers in natural ecosystems in order to mitigate many of the negative consequences of growing pressures on ecosystems [28], from a technological point of view, the tools and methods to define and develop learning ecosystems have to take into account the important role that people have in their success or failure.

The aim of this paper is to examine how the human factor in learning ecosystems has been addressed in the authors' proposal to define and develop this kind of software solutions using Open Source tools.

The paper has been organized in the following way. The second section describes how the users are part of the learning ecosystems from an architectural point of view. The third section addresses the human factor in the ecosystem metamodel. The fourth section analyses the human interaction in learning ecosystems using the Suricata Model. Finally, the last section summarizes the main conclusions of this work.

2   Human Factor from an Architectural Point of View

2.1   The Architectural Pattern for Learning Ecosystems

The early history of software engineering was heavily influenced by a highly formal and mathematical approach to specifying software components, and a reductionist approach to deriving computer software programs that correctly implemented the formal specifications. A "separation of concerns" was practiced, in which the responsibility of producing formalizable software requirements was left to others [29] one example quote that illustrates this approach is "The notion of 'user' cannot be precisely defined, and therefore has no place in computer science or software engineering" [30]. Since this statement by Dijkstra, end-user involvement has become relevant in software engineering activities such as requirement elicitation. Requirements elicitation traditionally has been focused on satisfying the needs of the majority of users [31]. However, other software paradigms, such as the services-oriented computing, introduce the identification of individual user needs as a the prerequisite for customization and tailoring of software [32].

Booher [33] summarizes the increases emphasis on human factors integration into systems engineering. He stands up for a focus on the human element to achieve both dramatic increases in system performance and productivity and dramatic reductions in problems in contexts where technology plays a fundamental role. The human element should be considered a critical component of the complex system.

Considering humans as part of the learning ecosystems, not only mere end-users, is one of the main ecosystems characteristics. Users are part of the definition and development processes of the ecosystems, not only in the requirement elicitation phase [34], but also during the whole ecosystem life cycle. They take an active role in the evolution of the ecosystem. According to Booher [33] the organization's focus should be first and foremost upon the people who, in some manner, will be directly exposed to the complex system. This idea can be applied to the learning ecosystems because they are complex tools that must adapt itself to changing users' needs, from end-users to managers and decision makers in the organization.

The software engineering processes to develop learning ecosystems should take into account the human element at the same level as technology. For this reason, the architectural pattern to define learning ecosystems [19, 20, 24, 35] includes the human factor as a key element. According to Fowler [36], a pattern is an idea that has been useful in one practical context and that will probably be useful in others. The goal of the pattern for learning ecosystems is to establish the basis for the definition and implementation of this technological solutions that can solve different knowledge management problems in any type of organization or institution.

To define the architectural pattern, several learning ecosystems [37–42] were analyzed to detect the problems associated to the definition, development and deployment of this type of software solutions. First of all, the problems were identified using a Strengths, Weaknesses, Opportunities and Threats (SWOT) analysis [19]. Then, the main problems were modelled using the Business Process Model and Notation (BPMN) and analyzed to improve the knowledge management processes and resolve the identified problems [24].

The architectural pattern is based on the Layers pattern proposed by Buschmann et al. [43] and describes the logic architecture of a learning ecosystem, regardless of the physical deployment of the system and including the methodology and the human factor as elements of the ecosystem.

The human factor is represented in the architectural pattern through three main elements: a specific layer focused on the human interaction, the fourth layer called "Presentation"; an input stream to have a strong methodological basis to support the definition and operation of the whole ecosystem; and an input stream to ensure the implementation of the methodology and the ecosystem's evolution over time. Figure 1 shows the architectural pattern with the human elements highlighted.

The heterogeneous nature of the software components that compose a learning eco-system makes end-users perceive the ecosystem as a set of parts, not as a whole. The aim of the presentation layer is to improve the usability and the user experience of the learning ecosystems fundamentally in two ways. First, it provides a unified design, not only visual but also related to interaction, for all the services or functionality provided by the lower layers in the architectural pattern. Second, nowadays, the learning ecosystems are used from different devices with distinct screen sizes (tablets, smartphones, computers), so the presentation layer must ensure accessibility to the ecosystem from any device.

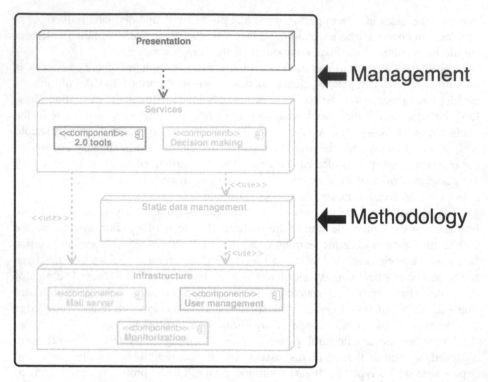

Fig. 1. Architectural pattern for learning ecosystems [24]

The role of end-users as drivers in learning ecosystems is evident, but there are other human-induced factors who cause ecosystem changes. The two input streams represent those factors in any type of organization. Both are the result of the one or several people work.

According to Cambridge Dictionary, a methodology is a system of ways of doing, teaching, or studying something [44]. In the software engineering context, Rumbaugh et al. [45] define software methodology as a process to produce software in an organized way, using a collection of predefined notation techniques and conventions. The methodology stream in the pattern represents a set of methodologies, not only a software methodology, but also learning methodologies to guide both formal and informal learning processes, or quality improvement methodologies to ensure the quality of the processes, among others. This set of methodologies provide a solid base to increase the chances of ecosystem success, as well as establishing the basis to evolve the ecosystem in the correct way.

Regarding the management stream, it is focused on ensuring the application of the methodology and providing both project and risk management to allow the evolution of the ecosystem. The people in charge of the ecosystem management aspects have to define its objectives related to technological and knowledge management in the organization. Each objective can apply one or more of the methodologies mentioned above. The learning ecosystem will evolve to meet the objectives.

2.2   Influence of Human Factor in the Success of a Learning Ecosystem

The relevance of methodology and management input streams is clearly reflected in the learning ecosystem for support the knowledge management inside a PhD Programme [46]. This learning ecosystems was defined and developed for the PhD in Education in the Knowledge Society at the University of Salamanca [47]. The main components of the ecosystem are a user-centered portal which provides most features required by the learning processes and a set of social tools centered in the dissemination of the scientific knowledge. Figure 2(a) shows the architecture with all software and human components.

This learning ecosystem (a) was transferred to other two contexts, in particular to two Mexican universities. First, the ecosystem was rolled out for supporting the scientific knowledge in a PhD Programme of the Tecnológico de Monterrey (Mexico), the PhD in Educational Innovation coordinated by the School of Humanities and Education. Figure 2(b) shows the architecture of the learning ecosystem transferred to the Tecnológico de Monterrey. The architecture was adapted to the new context. Most of the social tools were deleted, the repository was replaced although both are based on the same Open Source tool, DSpace, and the mail server was replaced by the mail server provided by the institution. Furthermore, the input stream related to the methodology is not present in this context.

On the other hand, the learning ecosystem (a) was transferred to the Behavioral Feeding and Nutrition Research Center (CICAN) at the University of Guadalajara (Mexico). The aim was to support the scientific knowledge management both in the Research Center and the postgraduate studies, the Master and PhD in Behavioral Science with Orientation to Food and Nutrition. The knowledge acquired during the first transfer to a Mexican context was applied in this new context. The main differences from the first ecosystem are that there are three different portals instead one, besides a new tool to provide institutional blogs. Regarding the human factor, this ecosystem neither has the methodology input stream. Figure 2(c) shows the architecture resulting after the transfer to this context.

The three ecosystems have many similarities:

- Same objective: scientific knowledge management in PhD studies.
- Same architecture pattern.
- The main software components: a web portal based on Drupal, one or more social tools, a repository, a mail server and a user management system based on Drupal too.

Therefore, the main differences are focused on the human factor and the cultural context. Regarding the cultural context, the ecosystem was adapted to the vocabulary and PhD studies regulations in Mexico and it was validated by end-users and directors of the PhD studies.

In relation to the human factor, the quality committee disappears in the two derived ecosystems. The quality committee in the original ecosystem is responsible of the assessment and monitoring of the PhD Programme and the learning ecosystem, it defines the methodology to support the objectives defined by the academic committee.

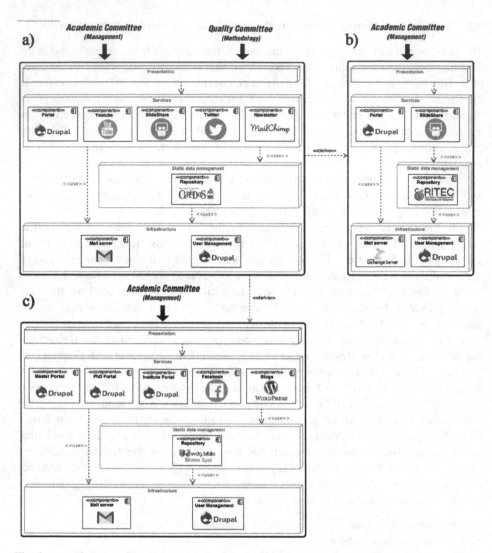

Fig. 2. Architecture of the learning ecosystem for PhD Programmes. (a) PhD in Education in the Knowledge Society at the University of Salamanca. (b) PhD in Educational Innovation at Tecnológico de Monterrey. (c) Master and PhD in Behavioral Science with Orientation to Food and Nutrition at University of Guadalajara.

In reviewing the use of the three ecosystems, no updated data was found on the derived ecosystems, only the original ecosystem continues active. The learning ecosystem (b) has updated information about the enrolled students but does not have more data related to the users' interaction and use the ecosystem. The learning ecosystem (c) was used for some months after the deployment and training to use and manage it, but there are not current data. After analyzing the situation, the main reason for this is the lack of a methodology provided by one or more persons.

3   Modeling Human Interaction in Learning Ecosystems

The definition and development of learning ecosystems is a complex process influences by many factors. Although the main goals are the same, the software components and the information flows can change, even in the same organization, mainly due to the human factor changes continuously over time. As section above shows, the transfer of an existing ecosystem involves a large number of ad-hoc developments and its success rate depends largely on how the learning ecosystem integrates the human component as one more element.

It is needed to provide a platform-independent solution to improve the definition and development of learning ecosystems which can adapt to different contexts and evolve to cover the changing needs of companies and institutions. Model-Driven Architecture (MDA) provides a framework for software development that uses models to describe the system to be built [48]. This proposal apply Model Driven Development (MDD) [49] using the standards supported by the Object Management Group (OMG). The learning ecosystem metamodel was defined in previous works to define Platform-Independent Models (PIM) of learning ecosystems, first as an instance of Meta Object Facility (MOF) and final version as an instance of Ecore [50]. The main objective of this metamodel is to provide a Computing Independent Model (CIM) for describing learning ecosystems build from software components, human elements and information flows between components which are represented by web services [22].

The human factor is one of the main concepts identified in the learning ecosystem metamodel together the different software components and the information flows to establish the relationship between the previous ones. Just like the architectural pattern for learning ecosystems, in which this metamodel is based, the human factor is highly relevant to ensure the evolution of the ecosystem. Figure 3 shows how the human factor is represented in the learning ecosystem metamodel. The full version of the metamodel in Ecore is available in high resolution on the following link https://doi.org/10.5281/zenodo.1066369 [51].

There is an abstract class that represents the human factor in the metamodel, the *People* class, from which inherit four classes that represent each of the human elements involved in a learning ecosystem. In particular, these classes represent the two input streams defined previously in the architectural patter for learning ecosystems. The methodology input stream is modelled through the *Methodology* class and the management input stream through the *Management* class. Both input streams are the result of the one or several people work, this is modelled through the *User* class. *User* has an attribute to determine the type of user – manager or computer engineer –. The relation between *User* and *Methodology* is represented by a bidirectional association which means that people can establish one or more methodologies in an ecosystem. To model that people have to ensure the application of the methodology through the management input stream, a bidirectional association between *User* and *Management* has been defined in the metamodel.

The management in a learning ecosystem is composed by a set of objectives related to technological and knowledge management in the organization. One or more methodologies are applied to achieve an objective. The aim of the learning ecosystem

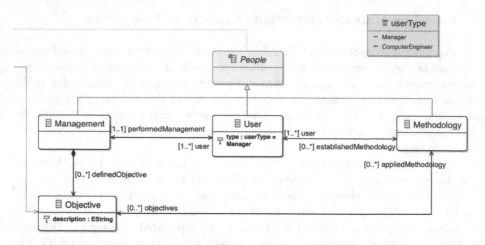

Fig. 3. Human factor in the learning ecosystem metamodel in Ecore

is to meet the defined objectives. This is modelled in the ecosystem metamodel through the *Objective* class, which compose the *Management* class. Moreover, there are two bidirectional associations. The first between *Objective* and *Methodology* classes, to model that an objective applies a methodology. The second one, between the *Objective* class and the class that represents the information flows of the learning ecosystems (*InformationFlow* class), in order to model that information flows can be defined to accomplish one or more objectives.

4 Human Factor in Knowledge Management Processes

According to King [52], knowledge management can be defined as the planning, organizing, motivating, and controlling of people, processes and systems in the organization to ensure that its knowledge-related assets are improved and effectively employed. Moreover, inside an organization, the knowledge are not only the electronic or printed documents, the knowledge in employee's mind and the knowledge embedded in the organization's processes are part of the knowledge-related assets.

The knowledge management has a life cycle as known as knowledge management process. As described above, the learning ecosystems are focused on supporting knowledge management processes inside companies and institutions. According to the architectural pattern for developing learning ecosystems, this technological approach should include methodological elements that allows the optimization of resources related to knowledge.

To ensure that the proposal for improving the definition and development of learning ecosystems take into account the human factor in the knowledge management processes, it was analyzed following the Suricata Model [53], an architectural proposal based on five layers ranging from the technological infrastructure that encompasses software, hardware and communications with an Open Source philosophy, to the personalized portal for knowledge worker, through which the user interacts with all layers of the architecture in a transparent way (see Fig. 4) [54]. This model allows to develop methods and tools to support individuals involved in the knowledge management processes, both from a personal and collective point of view, in order to promote increased productivity and innovation capacity in a context of knowledge management oriented to processes [53].

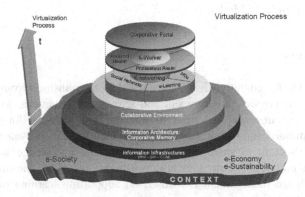

Fig. 4. Suricata model. Source: Enrique Rubio Royo [53]

First, the most basic layer of the Suricata architecture is the technological infrastructure, which aims to integrate the different software applications and facilitates their interoperability and integration. In the case of the architecture pattern for developing learning ecosystems, this layer is matched to the lower layer, the infrastructure layer, where interoperability between all components is facilitated through a set of software tools, in particular, a mail server, a tool for monitorization of the ecosystem and a user management system.

The second layer is the information architecture, which is responsible for storing digital artifacts, and allowing the content management. The proposed pattern for developing learning ecosystems has a data persistence layer in which all relevant information for the knowledge management is collected, stored and shared between the different ecosystem components, both human and software.

The third layer is the collaborative environment that enables collaboration among all the components of the architecture, ensuring the knowledge exchange. The service layer in the proposed architectural pattern is equivalent to this layer in the Suricata Model. This layer provides a set of services and information flows between them to support learning processes. Moreover, this layer supports the main knowledge management processes,

The penultimate layer of the Suricata Architecture focuses on supporting the creation of virtual communities that allow the transaction of knowledge and not just the transmission thereof between different users [55]. The transaction of knowledge is a fundamental axis in learning ecosystems. The information flows support this transactions among all the ecosystem.

The last layer in the Suricata Model corresponds to the user interface through a customized environment that allows access to all layers of the architecture. In the case of learning ecosystems, there is a layer of access to other layers, but which has directly access the different elements of the service layer. This is the presentation layer, one of the main elements which includes the human factor in the learning ecosystems based on the architectural pattern.

Therefore, the architectural pattern for defining and developing learning ecosystems accomplishes the Suricata Model.

5 Conclusions

In order to adjust to the cognitive disruption caused by the transition from a hierarchical organization of our physical environment and knowledge structures, to a networked, hyperconnected, environment we need to manage our personal knowledge in an effective, open-minded and sustainable way [3]. Technological ecosystems emerged in the Knowledge Society to share, create and apply the knowledge in any type of organization. In particular, technological ecosystems are called learning ecosystems when the knowledge management is focused on supporting learning processes, both companies and institutions.

The metaphor of natural ecosystem has been transferred to the technological area to stress the importance of human factor in technological solutions to manage knowledge. People have a main role as drivers in natural ecosystems, and they have the same role in technological ecosystems. They are not only end-users, they are an active part of the learning ecosystems.

Even though the learning ecosystems are powerful to support knowledge management processes, the definition, development, deployment and maintenance of this type of software solutions is complex and involves several problems. To solve these problems and improve the development of learning ecosystems from a software engineering point of view, an architectural pattern and a metamodel was defined in previous works [19, 20, 24, 51, 56, 57]. This paper has analyzed the human factor in these engineering proposals.

First, the human factor is one of the main parts of the architectural pattern for developing learning ecosystems. Three elements introduce this factor: a layer focused on the human interaction in the ecosystem, the presentation layer; an input stream to force the presence of one or more methodologies defined by people inside the organization; and an input stream to ensure the application of the methodologies and coordinate the evolution of the ecosystem.

Regarding the ecosystem metamodel, although usually software metamodels are focused on modelling software requirements, in the proposal the human factor was included as one of the three parts that compose the metamodel.

Finally, the Suricata Model [53] was used to analyze the human factor as a key element in the knowledge management processes supported by learning ecosystems developed with the architectural pattern and the ecosystem metamodel. In particular, the architectural pattern fulfills the Suricata Model, and also the ecosystem metamodel by transitivity because of it is based on the pattern.

Acknowledgments. This research work has been carried out within the University of Salamanca PhD Programme on Education in the Knowledge Society scope (http://knowledgesociety.usal.es) and was supported by the Spanish *Ministry of Education, Culture and Sport* under a FPU fellowship (FPU014/04783).

This work has been partially funded by the Spanish Government Ministry of Economy and Competitiveness throughout the DEFINES project (Ref. TIN2016-80172-R) and the Ministry of Education of the Junta de Castilla y León (Spain) throughout the T-CUIDA project (Ref. SA061P17).

References

1. UNESCO: UNESCO World Report: Towards Knowledge Societies. UNESCO Publishing, Paris (2005)
2. OECD: Knowledge Management in the Learning Society. OECD Publishing, Paris (2000)
3. Rubio Royo, E., Cranfield McKay, S., Nelson-Santana, J.C., Delgado Rodríguez, R.N., Ocon-Carreras, A.A.: Web knowledge turbine as a proposal for personal and professional self-organisation in complex times: application to higher education. J. Inf. Technol. Res. (JITR) **11**, 70–90 (2018)
4. Nonaka, I., Takeuchi, H.: The Knowledge-Creating Company: How Japanese Companies Create the Dynamics of Innovation. Oxford University Press, New York (1995)
5. Hargreaves, A.: Teaching in the Knowledge Society: Education in the Age of Insecurity. Teachers College Press, New York (2003)
6. Llorens-Largo, F.: Technology as driving force of the educative innovation: strategy and institutional policy at "Universidad de Alicante". Arbor **185**, 21–32 (2009)
7. Llorens-Largo, F.: University library as disseminator force of the educative innovation: strategy and institutional policy at Universidad de Alicante. ARBOR Ciencia, Pensamiento y Cultura **187**, 89–100 (2011)
8. Laudon, K.C., Laudon, J.P.: Essentials of Management Information Systems: Transforming Business and Management. Prentice Hall, Upper Saddle River (1991)
9. Langefors, B.: Information systems theory. Inf. Syst. **2**, 207–219 (1977)
10. Chen, W., Chang, E.: Exploring a digital ecosystem conceptual model and its simulation prototype. In: IEEE International Symposium on Industrial Electronics, ISIE 2007, pp. 2933–2938 (2007)
11. Dhungana, D., Groher, I., Schludermann, E., Biffl, S.: Software ecosystems vs. natural ecosystems: learning from the ingenious mind of nature. In: Proceedings of the Fourth European Conference on Software Architecture: Companion Volume, pp. 96–102. ACM, New York (2010)
12. Laanpere, M.: Digital Learning ecosystems: rethinking virtual learning environments in the age of social media. In: IFIP-OST 2012: Open and Social Technologies for Networked Learning, Taillin (2012)
13. Pata, K.: Meta-design framework for open learning ecosystems. Mash-UP Personal Learning Environments (MUP/PLE 2011), Open University of London (2011)
14. Yu, E., Deng, S.: Understanding software ecosystems: a strategic modeling approach. In: Jansen, S., Bosch, J., Campbell, P., Ahmed, F. (eds.) IWSECO-2011 Software Ecosystems 2011. Proceedings of the Third International Workshop on Software Ecosystems, Brussels, Belgium, 7 June 2011, pp. 65–76. CEUR Workshop Proceedings, Aachen (2011)

15. Mens, T., Claes, M., Grosjean, P., Serebrenik, A.: Studying evolving software ecosystems based on ecological models. In: Mens, T., Serebrenik, A., Cleve, A. (eds.) Evolving Software Systems, pp. 297–326. Springer, Berlin (2014). https://doi.org/10.1007/978-3-642-45398-4_10

16. Lungu, M.F.: Reverse Engineering Software Ecosystems. Università della Svizzera Italiana (2009)

17. Lungu, M.F.: Towards reverse engineering software ecosystems. In: IEEE International Conference on Software Maintenance, ICSM 2008, pp. 428–431. IEEE (2008)

18. Berthelemy, M.: Definition of a learning ecosystem. In: Learning Conversations, vol. 2013 (2013)

19. García-Holgado, A., García-Peñalvo, F.J.: The evolution of the technological ecosystems: an architectural proposal to enhancing learning processes. In: Proceedings of the First International Conference on Technological Ecosystem for Enhancing Multiculturality (TEEM 2013), Salamanca, Spain, 14–15 November 2013, pp. 565–571. ACM, New York (2013)

20. García-Holgado, A., García-Peñalvo, F.J.: Architectural pattern for the definition of eLearning ecosystems based on Open Source developments. In: Sierra-Rodríguez, J.L., Dodero-Beardo, J.M., Burgos, D. (eds.) Proceedings of 2014 International Symposium on Computers in Education (SIIE), Logroño, La Rioja, Spain, 12–14 November 2014, pp. 93–98. Institute of Electrical and Electronics Engineers (2014). IEEE Catalog Number CFP1486T-ART

21. García-Peñalvo, F.J., García-Holgado, A. (eds.): Open Source Solutions for Knowledge Management and Technological Ecosystems. IGI Global, Hershey (2017)

22. García-Holgado, A., García-Peñalvo, F.J.: Preliminary validation of the metamodel for developing learning ecosystems. In: Dodero, J.M., Ibarra Sáiz, M.S., Ruiz Rube, I. (eds.) Proceedings of the 5th International Conference on Technological Ecosystems for Enhancing Multiculturality (TEEM 2017), Cádiz, Spain, 18–20 October 2017. ACM, New York (2017)

23. Llorens-Largo, F., Molina, R., Compañ, P., Satorre, R.: Technological ecosystem for open education. In: Neves-Silva, R., Tsihrintzis, G.A., Uskov, V., Howlett, R.J., Jain, L.C. (eds.) Smart Digital Futures 2014, vol. 262, pp. 706–715. IOS Press (2014)

24. García-Holgado, A., García-Peñalvo, F.J.: Architectural pattern to improve the definition and implementation of eLearning ecosystems. Sci. Comput. Program. **129**, 20–34 (2016)

25. Alspaugh, T.A., Asuncion, H.U., Scacchi, W.: The role of software licenses in open architecture ecosystems. In: IWSECO@ ICSR (2009)

26. García-Peñalvo, F.J., Hernández-García, Á., Conde-González, M.Á., Fidalgo-Blanco, Á., Sein-Echaluce, M.L., Alier, M., Llorens-Largo, F., Iglesias-Pradas, S.: Learning services-based technological ecosystems. In: Proceedings of the 3rd International Conference on Technological Ecosystems for Enhancing Multiculturality, pp. 467–472. ACM (2015)

27. Chopra, K., Leemans, R., Kumar, P., Simons, H.: Ecosystems and Human Well-Being: Policy Responses. Island Press, Washington, DC (2005)

28. Millenium Ecosystem Assessment: Ecosystems and Human Well-Being: Synthesis. Island Press, Washington, DC (2005)

29. Boehm, B.: Some future trends and implications for systems and software engineering processes. Syst. Eng. **9**, 1–19 (2006)

30. Dijkstra, E.W.: Software engineering: as it should be. In: Proceedings of the 4th International Conference on Software Engineering, Munich, Germany, September 1979, pp. 442–448. IEEE Computer Society Press (1979)

31. Sutcliffe, A., Fickas, S., Sohlberg, M.M.: Personal and contextual requirements engineering. In: 13th IEEE International Conference on Requirements Engineering (RE 2005), pp. 19–28 (2005)
32. Goncalves da Silva, E., Ferreira Pires, L., van Sinderen, M.J.: Supporting dynamic service composition at runtime based on end-user requirements. In: Dustdar, S., Hauswirth, M., Hierro, J.J., Soriano, J., Urmetzer, F., Möller, K., Rivera, I. (eds.) Proceedings of the International Workshop on User-Generated Services, UGS 2009, located at the 7th International Conference on Service Oriented Computing, ICSOC 2009. CEUR Workshop Proceedings, Aachen (2009)
33. Booher, H.R.: Introduction: Human Systems Integration. In: Booher, H.R. (ed.) Handbook of Human Systems Integration, pp. 1–30. Wiley, Hoboken (2003)
34. Aparna, V., Anh Nguyen, D., Shang, G., Guttorm, S.: A systematic mapping study on requirements engineering in software ecosystems. J. Inf. Technol. Res. (JITR) **11**, 49–69 (2018)
35. García-Holgado, A., García-Peñalvo, F.J.: Patrón arquitectónico para la definición de ecosistemas de eLearning basados en desarrollos open source. In: Rodríguez, J.L.S., Beardo, J.M.D., Burgos, D. (eds.) Proceedings of 2014 International Symposium on Computers in Education (SIIE), Logroño, La Rioja, Spain, 12–14 November 2014, pp. 137–142. Universidad Internacional de la Rioja (UNIR), Logroño (2014)
36. Fowler, M.: Analysis Patterns: Reusable Object Models. Addison-Wesley Professional, Reading (1997)
37. García-Holgado, A.: GRIAL 2.0 Una propuesta de integración de servicios y aplicaciones web en un portal académico personalizable. Department of Computer Science and Automatic Control. University of Salamanca, Salamanca, Spain (2011)
38. García-Peñalvo, F.J., Rodríguez-Conde, M.J., Seoane-Pardo, A.M., Conde-González, M.Á., Zangrando, V., García Holgado, A.: GRIAL (GRupo de investigación en InterAcción y eLearning), USAL. Revista Iberoamericana de Informática Educativa, pp. 85–94. ADIE (2012)
39. Orueta, J.I., Pavón, L.M. (eds.): Libro Blanco de la Universidad Digital 2010. Ariel. Colección Fundación Telefónica. Cuaderno 11 (2008)
40. García-Peñalvo, F.J., Zangrando, V., García-Holgado, A., Conde-González, M.Á., Seoane-Pardo, A.M., Alier, M., Janssen, J., Griffiths, D., Mykowska, A., Alves, G.R.: TRAILER project overview: Tagging, recognition and acknowledgment of informal learning experiences. In: Proceedings of 2012 International Symposium on Computers in Education (SIIE), Andorra La Vella, Andorra, 29–31 October 2012, pp. 1–6. Institute of Electrical and Electronics Engineers (2012). IEEE Catalog Number CFP1486T-ART
41. García-Peñalvo, F.J., Conde-González, M.Á., Zangrando, V., García-Holgado, A., Seoane-Pardo, A.M., Alier, M., Galanis, N., Brouns, F., Vogten, H., Griffiths, D., Mykowska, A., Alves, G.R., Minović, M.: TRAILER project (Tagging, recognition, acknowledgment of informal learning experiences). A Methodology to make visible learners' informal learning activities to the institutions. J. Univ. Comput. Sci. **19**, 1661–1683 (2013)
42. García-Peñalvo, F.J., Conde, M.Á., Johnson, M., Alier, M.: Knowledge co-creation process based on informal learning competences tagging and recognition. Int. J. Hum. Capital Inf. Technol. Prof. (IJHCITP) **4**, 18–30 (2013)
43. Buschmann, F., Meunier, R., Rohnert, H., Sommerlad, P., Stal, M.: Pattern-oriented Software Architecture: A System of Patterns. Wiley, New York (1996)
44. Methodology. In: Sprachen, E.K. (ed.) Cambridge Advanced Learner's Dictionary & Thesaurus. Cambridge University Press (2013)

45. Rumbaugh, J., Blaha, M., Premerlani, W., Eddy, F., Lorensen, W.E.: Object-Oriented Modeling and Design. Prentice Hall, Englewood Cliffs (1991)
46. García-Holgado, A., García-Peñalvo, F.J., Rodríguez-Conde, M.J.: Definition of a technological ecosystem for scientific knowledge management in a PhD programme. In: Proceedings of the Third International Conference on Technological Ecosystems for Enhancing Multiculturality (TEEM 2015), Porto, Portugal, 7–9 October 2015, pp. 695–700. ACM, New York (2015)
47. García-Peñalvo, F.J.: Education in knowledge society: a new PhD programme approach. In: Proceedings of the First International Conference on Technological Ecosystem for Enhancing Multiculturality (TEEM 2013), Salamanca, Spain, 14–15 November 2013, pp. 575-577. ACM, New York (2013)
48. Mellor, S.J., Scott, K., Uhl, A., Weise, D.: Model-driven architecture. In: Bruel, J.-M., Bellahsene, Z. (eds.) OOIS 2002. LNCS, vol. 2426, pp. 290–297. Springer, Heidelberg (2002). https://doi.org/10.1007/3-540-46105-1_33
49. Atkinson, C., Kuhne, T.: Model-driven development: a metamodeling foundation. IEEE Softw. **20**, 36–41 (2003)
50. Eclipse Foundation. http://download.eclipse.org/modeling/emf/emf/javadoc/2.11/org/eclipse/emf/ecore/package-summary.html
51. García-Holgado, A., García-Peñalvo, F.J.: Learning ecosystem metamodel quality assurance. In: Rocha, Á., Correia, A., Adeli, H., Reis, L., Costanzo, S. (eds.) WorldCIST 2018. AISC, vol. 745, pp. 787–796. Springer, Cham (2018). https://doi.org/10.1007/978-3-319-77703-0_78
52. King, W.R.: Knowledge Management and Organizational Learning. In: King, W.R. (ed.) Knowledge Management and Organizational Learning, vol. 4, pp. 3–13. Springer, US (2009)
53. Rubio, E., Ocón, A., Galán, M., Marrero, S., Nelson, J.C.: A personal and corporative process-oriented knowledge manager: Suricata model. In: European University Information Systems (EUNIS) (2004)
54. Marrero, S., Ocón, A., Galán, M., Rubio, E.: Methodology for the generation and maintenance of a "base of procedures" in process-oriented knowledge management strategy. In: European University Information Systems (EUNIS) (2005)
55. Marrero, S.R., Nelson, J.C., Galán, M., Ocón, A., Rubio, E.: Metodología para organizar, recuperar y compartir recursos de información y conocimiento en un centro I+D+i en la Plataforma Suricata (2005)
56. García-Holgado, A., García-Peñalvo, F.J., Hernández-García, Á., Llorens-Largo, F.: Analysis and Improvement of Knowledge Management Processes in Organizations Using the Business Process Model Notation. In: Palacios-Marqués, D., Ribeiro Soriano, D., Huarng, K.H. (eds.) GIKA 2015. LNBIP, vol. 222, pp. 93–101. Springer, Cham (2015). https://doi.org/10.1007/978-3-319-22204-2_9
57. García-Holgado, A., García-Peñalvo, F.J.: A metamodel proposal for developing learning ecosystems. In: Zaphiris, P., Ioannou, A. (eds.) LCT 2017. LNCS, vol. 10295, pp. 100–109. Springer, Cham (2017). https://doi.org/10.1007/978-3-319-58509-3_10

Improving Engineering Education Using Augmented Reality Environment

Wenbin Guo[✉]

Department of Industrial and Manufacturing Systems Engineering,
University of Missouri, Columbia, USA
wgk95@mail.missouri.edu

Abstract. The purpose of the research is to compare the impact of students' learning performance between an augmented reality (AR) environment and in-class environment. To create an efficient AR environment, we used Microsoft HoloLens, which is the next generation of a see-through holographic computer. We developed the AR learning module: ergonomic guidelines for manual material handling (MMH). We hypothesize that AR changes the way students understand the concepts of MMH. Our analysis includes a careful evaluation of student experimental skills during the learning activities. This new AR environment could allow students to engage hands-on training of MMH and strengthen their understanding. Student test score was used as metrics for performance assessment. We found a significant improvement on student understanding of MMH lecture after they used the AR module. The findings of this study indicated the potential benefits of using AR environment interfaces in engineering education and training.

Keywords: Augmented reality · Engineering education
Learning performance

1 Introduction

Students often get bored in a classroom and take a long time to understand the engineering concepts they learned in a classroom. Although there are needs to improve engineering education, many traditional learning methods, such as power point slides, lecture notes, or videos, have shown limitations to meet the goals of future engineering education. Augmented reality (AR) is one of the advanced technologies that might meet this need and increase the student learning performances in engineering education.

AR combines virtual and real objects coexist in a common space seamlessly to reinforce human interaction. It provides the ability to develop more effective learning environment for novice workers and students. AR has many potential benefits. First, engaging and motivating students to explore class materials from different angles to help students create the spatial feeling (e.g., astronomy and geography). Second, enhancing collaboration between students and instructors. Third, fostering student creativity and imagination. Fourth, helping students control their own learning pace and path [1].

P. Zaphiris and A. Ioannou (Eds.): LCT 2018, LNCS 10924, pp. 233–242, 2018.
https://doi.org/10.1007/978-3-319-91743-6_18

Previous research related to AR has demonstrated the effect on student motivation during the learning process. According to Kim et al. [2], the materials that were designed in an AR environment could provide a positive learning effect in a computer-based training simulation. Yen and Tsai also found that AR environment could improve student interaction in class [3]. AR has applied to many educational concepts, such as earth-sun relationship [4], electromagnetism [5], and education of anatomy [6]. Their findings show that AR could provide instant feedback and improve student's academic achievement. AR also has been implemented in the various fields of medical and engineering training [7–10].

Teaching staff can take part in this new endeavor by being aware of applications in AR that can benefit students and educators [11]. AR in education is an emerging field, which exhibited the benefits in engineering education. An AR-based system designed explicitly for engineering graphics education can improve student's spatial awareness and interest in learning [12]. AR application consisting of 3D models, animations and sound help students understand the specific objects in electrical engineering. [13]. AR also enhance mechanical engineering students to learn how to sketch, design and normalize mechanical elements [14]. The study explored the impact of AR technology as used for engineering students, which influence academic performance and encourage student motivation. Besides, AR allows users to work on their own pace.

In many higher educations, AR modules have been already implemented, but have not generated any educational material for enduring use. In this study, we used Microsoft HoloLens, which is the next generation of a see-through holographic computer, to create relatively efficient and advanced AR environment.

2   Methods

2.1   Apparatus

HoloLens (see Fig. 1) is used as a head-mount teaching device with Windows 10 operating system for students which can project holograms in front of participants' eyes to combine the real and virtual worlds [15]. Participants can touch, gaze and rotate to control the holograms. HoloLens Clicker is the input device which allows students to control and interact with the holograms in the AR environment. In our experiment, we used two HoloLens interaction model Gaze and Gesture. The Gaze relates to what you are looking at (e.g. head tracking), the Gesture is an "air-tap" movement that the HoloLens will recognize and allow for selection of items. The HoloLens Clicker can be used instead of the "air-tap" gesture.

2.2   Participants

A total of thirty-two students of industrial engineering were recruited from the University of Missouri. Twenty-nine participants were male, and three participants were female. The average game level was 3.17/5 (StDev = 1.03) and the average AR level was 1.4/5 (StDev = 0.85). The game level is rating participants' previous experience level playing computer graphic video game. AR level is students' previous

Fig. 1. Microsoft HoloLens

experience level participating in an augmented reality task before. Twenty-four participants' AR level was 1, and they never knew or touched AR device before. Most students were regarded as novices for the AR experiment. Participants had an age range from 20 to 31 (Mean = 21.5, StDev = 1.50).

2.3 Engineering Education Contents

In this study, we developed the AR modules for manual material handling (MMH). It is one of the core contents of an ergonomics class. Traditionally, many students commonly make a mistake in the aspect of the meaning of asymmetric multiplier and do not know how to measure the multiplier. As a result, instructors are challenged to find new ways of presenting MMH lecture that is more beneficial for student learning.

In the MMH lecture, the revised NIOSH lifting equation is used to quantify the lifting task risk or acceptability. It contains six variables or multipliers, which are the Horizontal Multiplier (HM), the Vertical Multiplier (VM), the Distance Multiplier (DM), the Asymmetry Multiplier (AM), the Coupling Multiplier (CM) and the Frequency Multiplier (FM).

Specifically, HM is the horizontal distance of the load from the body. VM is the vertical distance of the load from the floor. DM is the vertical distance the load is lifted. AM is the angles from the sagittal line to origin or destination position. FM is the frequency and duration of the task. CM is coupling with the load about handles or handholds. All of these factors is to determine the weight of a load that can be safely handled by most people.

The revised NIOSH lifting equation shows RWL = LC * HM * VM * DM * AM * FM * CM, where RWL is the Recommended Weight Limit; LC is the Load Constant and is always equal to 51 lb (23 kg). The LC is the weight a person should be able to lift once under ideal conditions at minimal risk; The other six multipliers (HM, VM, DM, AM, FM, and CM) reduce this weight based on the actual conditions of the lift being examined. Lift Index (LI) = actual weight of the load divided by the RWL. The higher of LI, the higher the risk to the persons performing the task. The goal should be for all lifting tasks to have a Lift Index less than 1.0. The revised NIOSH equation can assist in the elimination of specific task variables of concern. The individual multipliers can identify specific aspects of the lift that are problematic and require addressing to make the lift more acceptable.

236   W. Guo

2.4   Design of Experiment

We developed the AR learning module: ergonomic guidelines for manual material handling (MMH). We hypothesize that AR changes the way students come to understand specific concepts.

In the AR MMH lecture (see Fig. 2), participants learned MMH concepts and were educated how to measure all MMH variables and assess working safety condition. In the training part, the participants was taught how to use HoloLens interaction and learn MMH lecture in AR environment. After learning the lecture, the test score was used to evaluate participant's learning performance. We can compare the test performance difference between AR group and in-class group and know more benefits with AR system.

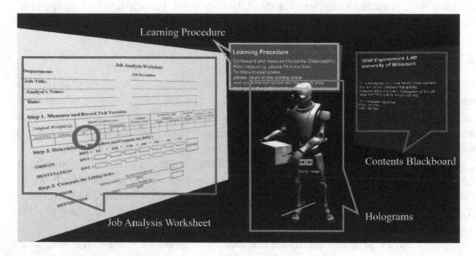

Fig. 2. Screenshot of the MMH Module

Figure 2 shows a screenshot of the MMH module. On the left side in the figure shows the job analysis worksheet that is commonly used for the observation form of MMH. The module also displays learning procedures of how to complete each module. The middle of the figure shows the primary hologram for MMH animation. Also, two arrows help students to navigate the module. The left arrow corresponds to the previous module, and right arrow corresponds to the next module. The right side of the figure displays the MMH contents that students must learn from each module, which including the definition of MMH, how to measure all multipliers (a horizontal multiplier, vertical multiplier, and asymmetric multiplier), and calculate them.

Figure 3 shows the learning module in AR environment. This scene presents all the multipliers which let participants understand clearly about MMH in a 3D space. Participants can move close to measure and observe distances in each angle.

Figure 4 presents the practice module for students and let them practice the MMH measurement and calculation to verify if they understand the MMH contents or not, meanwhile deepening their understanding of MMH content and cultivate their experimental skills.

Fig. 3. Learning module of AR MMH lecture

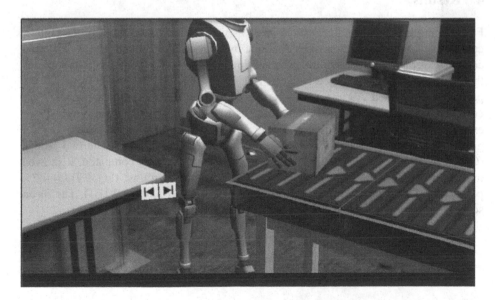

Fig. 4. Practice module of AR MMH lecture

3   Procedure

For AR group: Before the experiment, participants were asked to answer demographic questionnaires if they had computer experience level and the similar experience on AR task in the past. During the training session, participants experienced how to fit the HoloLens to get the best view, conduct gestures and modules in HoloLens, as well as how to fill in job analysis worksheet. Participants must understand how to use gestures or clicker to switch to the previous or next scene to learn MMH contents. After being trained, participants underwent the experimental test session in HoloLens. The experiment test took 40 min for learning materials. After learning materials about manual material handling, the participants needed to take a test to verify their learning performance. So the total time was expected to last one and a half hours.

For another in-class control group, the teacher explained the MMH material as in previous years. Students participated in normal activities in the classroom. The only difference was that a group of the experimental students had the AR notes available to study in the lab and the control group students used their traditional class notes to study.

To compare the learning performance in AR and in-class group, a test about MMH was taken which evaluated up to a 100 points maximum. Each multiplier (the Horizontal Multiplier (HM), the Vertical Multiplier (VM), the Distance Multiplier (DM), the Asymmetry Multiplier (AM), the Coupling Multiplier (CM) and the Frequency Multiplier (FM)) would be tested to prove if they understand. The only difference was that a group of the experimental students studied in the AR environment and the control group students learned in the classroom.

4   Results

For learning performance, a statistical analysis was carried out to identify the significant differences between the results obtained by both groups. Student test was used to compare average test score values obtained in each group. We considered hypotheses there is a significant difference between test results obtained by two groups. All the participants regarded AR use to be very interesting when educational purposes are considered. The overall opinion of the students was that studying and using AR was an excellent experience. The AR group was more motivated than the in-class control group who just studied and whose only interest was to pass the test. The two groups (Group A: augmented reality, Group B: in class) test scores were compared. It showed that there was a significant difference between two groups ($F(1, 91) = 4.39$, p-value = 0.039). The mean score of group A was 76.25/100 (SD: 30.61). The mean score of group B is 62.00/100 (SD: 31.32) (Fig. 5).

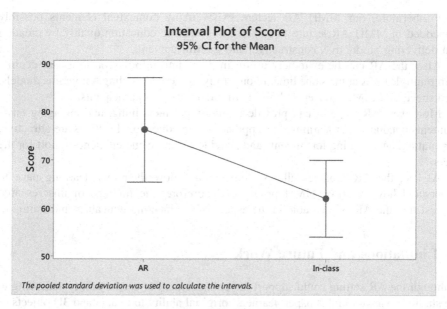

Fig. 5. Test scores (AR vs. In-class)

5 Discussion and Conclusion

According to our results, students who used the AR-based MMH lecture showed better academic performance than those using traditional class notes. 53.1% of students in the AR group marked a perfect score while only 23.3% of the students received a full credit when they used traditional learning method.

Manual material handling is a good teaching material in engineering education which can be displayed in AR environment. Successful learning MMH contents contain two aspects concepts knowledge and practical exercise. As a practical hands-on exploration, suitable design visualization and presentation are crucial for participants to understand and gain adequate knowledge. MMH AR lecture allows students to learn through three-dimensional experiences that merge the physical with the virtual and allow students to interact with the content. Through the AR environment, students can see a real human movement and objects in 3D animation. Students can measure the distance with ruler and angles with goniometer by themselves without an instructor's help. Thus, students can incorporate hands-on training for deepening the understanding of contents.

MMH is also related to safety training materials; it is definite that MMH AR lecture is much more productive and fruitful than traditional methods or medias, such as booklets, posters, videos, and other content ever before. Students might get hurt or injured in the real manual material handling environment, while AR has benefits in skills training regarding dangerous and hazardous work environments.

Furthermore, our MMH AR lecture exists many contextual elements possibly embedded in MMH AR lecture to enhance engineering education quality by creating and delivering productive, constructive, and gainful content.

Also, the AR can be extremely useful in providing information to a user dealing with multiple tasks at the same time. In our study, material handling holograms models, worksheet, and MMH concepts showed simultaneously to participants.

Moreover, AR systems can provide motivating, entertaining, and engaging environments conducive for learning. AR applications in educational settings are attractive, stimulating, and exciting for students and provide effective and efficient support for the users.

At last, the AR modules allows students to follow their own learning pace to understand how to solve MMH problems. Therefore, the findings of this research suggest that the AR is favorable in the aspect of engineering education and training.

6 Limitations and Future Work

Although the AR setting could support the enhancement of spatial ability according to the studies reviewed in this paper, learners' original ability to understand 3D objects or concepts might interfere with their learning process, learning experiences, or even learning outcomes. Moreover, students' perceived presence, which is a mental state when students participate in a virtual world, in AR-related environments may be an important learner characteristic variable to consider [16].

By detecting learning process through videotaping analysis, how students structure the scientific thinking and knowledge in AR learning activities could be better understood. Although these qualitative methods have been commonly utilized in AR-related studies, there is a need to apply mixed method analysis to attain an in-depth understanding of the learning process. For example, content analysis and a sequential analysis might be adopted to analyze students' behavioral patterns when involved in science learning with AR technology. With the aid of eye-tracking technology, researchers could collect data about eye movement sequences to represent learners' attention to AR information and further compare the quantitative data with the results of learning process analysis generated by qualitative methods.

The rise of students studying engineering degrees makes the practice's laboratories overcrowded worsening the teaching quality and reducing teacher's dedication to every student. Besides, learning and teaching procedures need to evolve for taking into account the high technological profile that most students show. In some cases, outdated teaching creates barriers for some students that are used to interact with modern technological gadgets and computers. The AR technology can accelerate the learners' acquisition of new training procedures and improve the adjustment of the training process. AR applications allow that in certain teaching/learning contexts performed by the student on his own saving the teacher's time for repeating explanations. A well-planned AR application will allow them to perform learning processes and motivate their learning desire. Students want to be empowered by technology and to apply their knowledge and experience to communicate designs that lead to improved results and higher personal satisfaction. The system can thus build a future in which students will experience competence, clarity, control, comfort, and feelings of mastery and accomplishment. We believe that AR is a cost-effective technology for providing students with more attractive contents than class paper notes.

Also, we will investigate the cognitive process flow of MMH lecture in the AR environment. The outcome of this study will improve engineering education and help students achieve their goals better. More research is required to study learning experience such as motivation and learner characteristics such as spatial ability or perceived metal state, involved in AR. Mixed methods of inspecting learning processes such as a content analysis or a sequential analysis, as well as in-depth examination of user experience beyond usabilities such as affective variables of esthetic pleasure or emotional fulfillment, should be considered. Theories including mental models, spatial cognition, situated cognition, and social constructivist learning are suggested for the profitable uses of future AR research in science education [16].

AR has compelling features for engineering educational purposes if the device is affordable for students [17]. For the future work, we will develop the advanced AR modules, which reinforce a positive learning effect of AR contents in engineering education. Besides, we hope to encourage teachers who want to motivate their students and improve student learning performance to start to take advantage of AR technologies in the classroom in their work.

References

1. Yuen, S.C.-Y., Yaoyuneyong, G., Johnson, E.: Augmented reality: an overview and five directions for AR in education. J. Educ. Technol. Dev. Exchange (JETDE) 4(1), 11 (2011)
2. Kim, J.H., Chan, T., Du, W.: The learning effect of augmented reality training in a computer-based simulation environment. In: Zaphiris, P., Ioannou, A. (eds.) LCT 2015. LNCS, vol. 9192, pp. 406–414. Springer, Cham (2015). https://doi.org/10.1007/978-3-319-20609-7_38
3. Yen, J.-C., Tsai, C.-H., Wu, M.: Augmented reality in the higher education: students' science concept learning and academic achievement in astronomy. Procedia-Soc. Behav. Sci. 103, 165–173 (2013)
4. Shelton, B.E., Hedley, N.R.: Using augmented reality for teaching earth-sun relationships to undergraduate geography students. In: The First IEEE International Workshop on Augmented Reality Toolkit. IEEE (2002)
5. Ibáñez, M.B., et al.: Experimenting with electromagnetism using augmented reality: impact on flow student experience and educational effectiveness. Comput. Educ. 71, 1–13 (2014)
6. Meng, M., et al.: Kinect for interactive AR anatomy learning. In: 2013 IEEE International Symposium on Mixed and Augmented Reality (ISMAR). IEEE (2013)
7. Webel, S., et al.: An augmented reality training platform for assembly and maintenance skills. Robot. Auton. Syst. 61(4), 398–403 (2013)
8. Fadde, P.J.: Interactive video training of perceptual decision-making in the sport of baseball. Technol. Instr. Cogn. Learn. 4(3), 265–285 (2006)
9. Radu, I.: Augmented reality in education: a meta-review and cross-media analysis. Pers. Ubiquit. Comput. 18(6), 1533–1543 (2014)

10. Damala, A., et al.: Bridging the gap between the digital and the physical: design and evaluation of a mobile augmented reality guide for the museum visit. In: Proceedings of the 3rd International Conference on Digital Interactive Media in Entertainment and Arts. ACM (2008)
11. Herron, J.: Augmented reality in medical education and training. J. Electron. Resour. Med. Libr. 13(2), 51–55 (2016)
12. Chen, H., et al.: Application of augmented reality in engineering graphics education. In: 2011 International Symposium on IT in Medicine and Education (ITME). IEEE (2011)
13. Martin-Gutierrez, J., Guinters, E., Perez-Lopez, D.: Improving strategy of self-learning in engineering: laboratories with augmented reality. Procedia-Soc. Behav. Sci. 51, 832–839 (2012)
14. Martin Gutierrez, J., Meneses Fernandez, M.D.: Applying augmented reality in engineering education to improve academic performance & student motivation. Int. J. Eng. Educ. 30(3), 625–635 (2014)
15. Tuliper, A.: Introduction to the HoloLens (2016). https://msdn.microsoft.com/en-us/magazine/mt788624.aspx
16. Cheng, K.-H., Tsai, C.-C.: Affordances of augmented reality in science learning: suggestions for future research. J. Sci. Educ. Technol. 22(4), 449–462 (2013)
17. Wu, H.-K., et al.: Current status, opportunities and challenges of augmented reality in education. Comput. Educ. 62, 41–49 (2013)

An Analysis on the Recommendation Engine of a Course Introduction Module

Toshikazu Iitaka[(⊠)]

Kumamoto Gakuen University,
Oe 2-5-1, Chuo-Ku, Kumamoto-shi, Kumamoto, Japan
iitaka2@yahoo.co.jp

Abstract. This paper is about the previously proposed recommendation engine of a course introduction module. The objective of this paper is to introduce the structure and determine the effect of the module. In addition to presenting the structure of the module, this paper presents a statistical analysis of the effect of the module, and confirms its statistically significant effect.

Keywords: Recommendation engine · Big-data · e-Learning

1 Objective

Generally speaking, information acquisition needs differ from person to person, and a recommendation engine is used to meet such needs. This paper describes the recommendation engine of a course introduction module described in [1]. The objective of this paper is to introduce the structure and effect of the course introduction module.

The paper first presents the background of this research, including related work. Then, the structure of the course introduction module is described. Finally, an analysis on the effect of the course introduction module is presented.

2 Background and Significance

This section presents the background and significance of this research. It first reviews previous studies and then describes the structure of the course introduction module and its recommendation engine.

2.1 Previous Studies

The structure of the course introduction module is based on previous studies of e-portfolios. The course introduction module in this paper and [1] can also be defined as an e-portfolio. According to [2], surveys using questionnaires seldom help improve lecture designs. The results obtained by questionnaires in general are too uniform to determine a student's satisfaction and the attainment of their goals. However, an e-portfolio allows us to check these results. An analysis based on e-portfolios reveals why students are satisfied with courses. It also shows how much students have attained their goals thanks to the course.

© Springer International Publishing AG, part of Springer Nature 2018
P. Zaphiris and A. Ioannou (Eds.): LCT 2018, LNCS 10924, pp. 243–255, 2018.
https://doi.org/10.1007/978-3-319-91743-6_19

The course introduction module of this paper was developed based on previous studies. This module unites two other e-learning modules of the content management system (CMS) Xoops. One module is an online examination and drill module, and the other is an audience response system (ARS) module. Both modules have their own portfolio functions that students can use review the material they have learned. Both modules are implemented in CMS. Moreover, CMS can be used after the students have graduated. This feature allows the modules to collect data after the end of the course. Therefore, e-portfolio functions that can use such data can reveal methods of learning that are effective long term. Moreover, CMS unites the two e-portfolio functions. The course introduction module is also designed to reinforce this unity (Fig. 1).

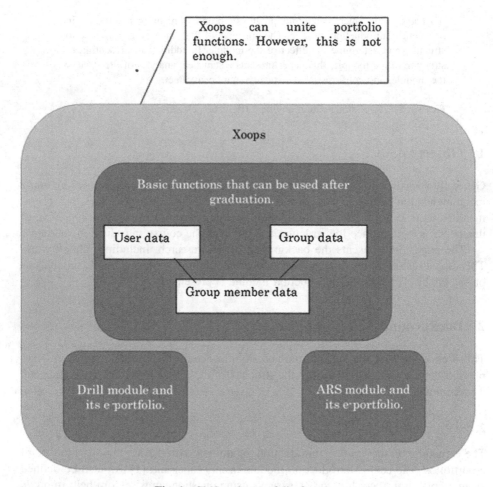

Fig. 1. CMS and e-portfolio functions

The course introduction module has a direct link with the e-portfolio pages of the two modules. Hence, the course introduction module can not only show course objectives and their attainment but also enables the students to review their learning precisely. This structure hence improves learning. In addition, this module has a recommendation engine that recommends proper courses. The function of a course introduction and e-portfolio was explained in [3]. The authors of [1] introduced the function of a recommendation engine for the course introduction module.

According to [3], a course introduction (e-portfolio) module must have the following characteristics.

1. The objectives that are checked by the course introduction module must be more abstract than those of the drill and ARS modules (concrete objectives are checked by the portfolio functions of the other two modules).
2. The module must allow students to set their own goals and level of effort.
3. The module must enable lecturers to set the objectives of their courses and the effort needed to attain them.

As [1] described, the recommendation engine can create recommendation data from the effort data and attainment data. This feature may help students formulate a learning plan.

2.2 Structure of the Module

Here, the structure of the module is described in depth. First, the main functions of the course introduction module are presented. Second, the calculation of the recommendation engine implemented in the module is shown.

The main functions of the module are shown in Fig. 2.

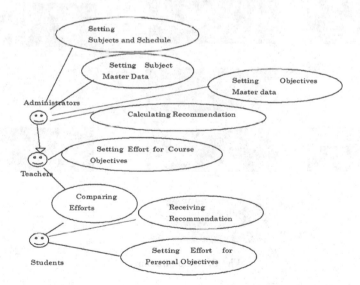

Fig. 2. Course introduction module functions

As shown in Fig. 2, the administrators can set the master data of the courses and schedule. Each lecturer can then enter the detailed data for their courses. They can then set the objectives of their courses and the level of effort needed to attain them. Students can also set their objectives and level of effort. Hence students can compare their own objectives with the course objectives. This feature can help students create a learning plan.

After a course has ended, students can evaluate the course and check the attainment of their objectives. Lecturers can also evaluate the students and check the attainment of the objectives. Hence, students can compare their evaluation with those of the lecturers, i.e., students can analyze their learning more objectively.

As shown in [1], these data allow us to create recommendations using the following items.

1. Evaluation data of the course (5 degrees)
2. Credit data (2 degrees)
3. Effort required by students to obtain the objectives of the courses (10 degrees)
4. Attainments of goal (5 degrees)

The third item is based on the master data of the objectives, which is set by the administrators. Therefore, the relationship between the students' objectives and courses' objective is indirect. The other three items relate to the course and student data.

The data structure is shown in Fig. 3.

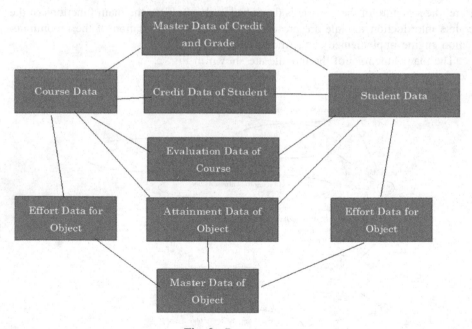

Fig. 3. Data structure

Based on these items, some recommendation items are created in the same way as in the recommendation engine for the drill module described in [4]. The recommendations are provided by the course introduction module based on the following factors.

1. Similarity of the course evaluation
2. Credit data
3. Similarity of the objectives
4. Similarity of the attainments

The recommendation based on the similarity of course evaluation is calculated by Pearson's correlation coefficient. In addition, those based on credit data are calculated by Tanimoto's correlation coefficient. These methods are almost the same as those of the drill module [4].

However, the third and fourth recommendation factors are a bit different. Similarity scores are calculated beforehand. Pearson's correlation coefficient between similarity scores is used to create the recommendation items. The similarity score for objectives is calculated as follows, which is the sum of the product of the student and course efforts:

$$\sum_{i=1}^{n} CiSi$$

Here, C1 is the effort for the first objective of the course, and S1 is the effort for the first objective of the student.

The similarity score for attainments is created in almost the same way. It is the sum of the product of student and course attainments:

$$\sum_{i=1}^{n} CiSi$$

Similarly, C1 is the first attainment of the course, and S1 is the first attainment of the student.

2.3   Use of the Module

This part describes how the module is used. An overview of its use is shown in Fig. 4.

First, the administrators must set the master data of the objectives and subjects. Then, they assign the subjects and schedule for the CMS group data.

After the master data of the objectives has been set, students can set their effort for the objectives (Fig. 5).

If the schedule has been set, the teachers and students can check the schedule of the courses from the user's page. Then, teachers can access the course information page. Teachers can then also set the effort for their course's objectives from the course information page (Figs. 6 and 7).

After the efforts have been set, students can compare their own objectives with the objectives of the course (Fig. 8).

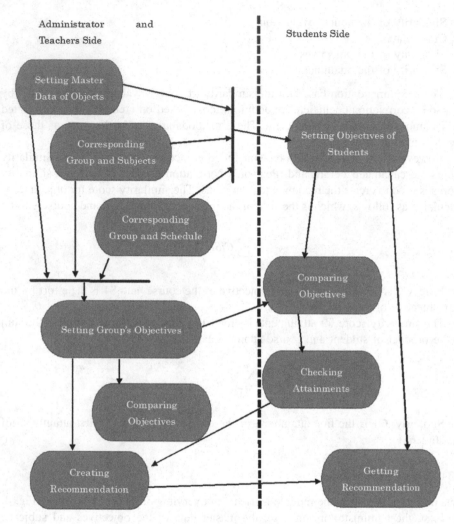

Fig. 4. Use of the course introduction module

This feature of the course introduction module helps students determine which course they should take. In addition, teachers can also check the objectives of the participants of their courses, which helps them make teaching plans.

After the course has ended, the course information pages are changed (Fig. 9).

When students access the course information page, they can set the attainment data of each objective. They can also evaluate the courses in which they have taken part.

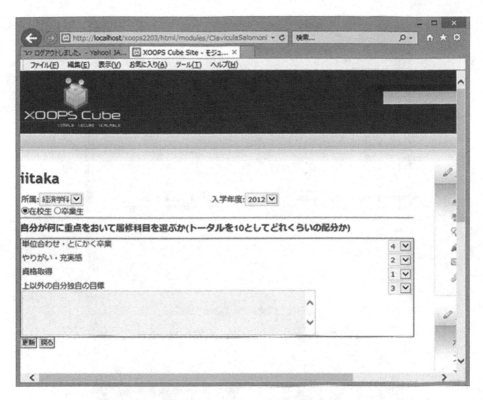

Fig. 5. Screenshot of the student's objective setting page

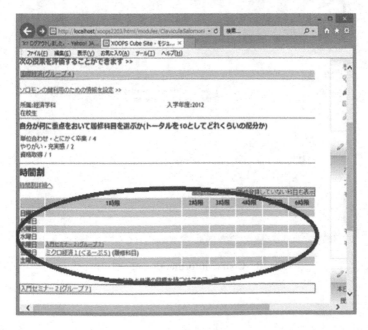

Fig. 6. Schedule page

Fig. 7. Page for setting the course objectives

Fig. 8. Course information page (1/2)

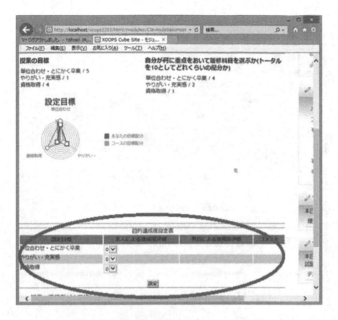

Fig. 9. Course information page (2/2)

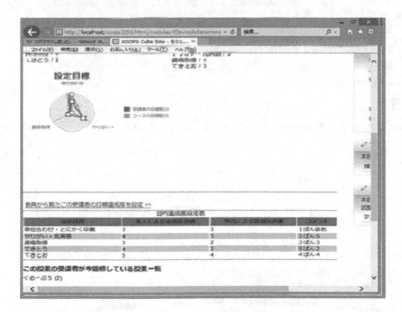

Fig. 10. Course information page for lecturers

As shown in Fig. 10, lecturers also can check the attainments of the participants. This feature helps lecturers design better courses. Moreover, lecturers can set the credit data.

Fig. 11. Recommendation setting page

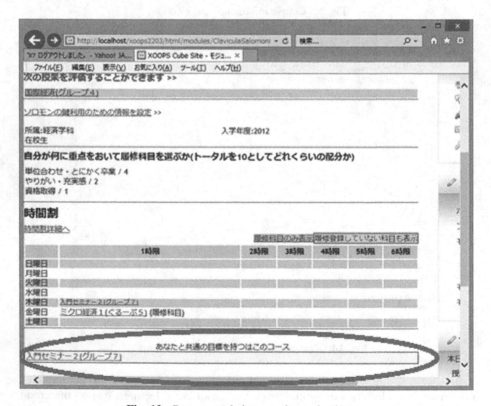

Fig. 12. Recommendations on the student's page

Based on the set of factors presented above, the administrators can determine the recommendation data.

As shown in Fig. 11, we can select from two methods: user-based or item-based methods. This method is almost the same as that of the drill module [4].

After the recommendations are created, the recommended courses are displayed for students.

As shown in Fig. 12, a list of recommended courses is shown on the students' page.

3 Method

This section describes a course for which the module was implemented and the resulting statistical analysis. First, we present the research question (RQ). We then introduce the course that provided the data for this research. Finally, the statistical analysis is presented.

3.1 Research Question and Hypothesis

As previously explained, the module allows students to compare objectives. Therefore, the module should help students to prepare for a course and ensure that the course is what the students anticipated it would be. Consequently, when the module works well, students tend not to be absent from a course or drop it.

Therefore, the following RQ and subsequent hypothesis is posited.

RQ: How does the module affect student attendance rates?
Hypothesis: The users of the module attend lectures more frequently than do students who do not use the module.

3.2 Course Characteristic

Here, we describe the characteristics of the course in which the module implemented, which are almost the same as those of the course described in [4].

As shown in Table 1, the course is an introduction to informatics for participants who do not major in informatics. The course was designed to help the class pass a qualifying examination on information technology. The number of attendees is similar

Table 1. Details of the course in which the module implemented

Course title	Introduction to informatics: preparing for a qualifying examination on information technology
Type of students	Students at the Faculty of Economics
Period	April–July 2017
Number of attendees	215
Number of module users	63
Skewness of attendance rate	−1.657
Kurtosis of attendance rate	1.788

to that in [4]. About 30% of attendees had previously used the course introduction module. Skewness and kurtosis of attendance rate are below 2.0. Hence, we can deal with the data as a normal distribution.

3.3   Statistical Analysis

Here we show the statistical analysis.

As shown in Table 2, the average attendance rate of the students who did not use the module is 68.9%. The users of the module attended 83.6% of lectures on average. Subsequently, students attended lectures more frequently when they used the module. According to the t-test, the difference is statistically significant ($t(188.1) = -4.80$, $p < 0.01$). Therefore, we can conclude that the hypothesis is confirmed.

Table 2. Average attendance rates

Module non-users	68.9%
Module users	83.6%

4   Discussion

As shown above, the module seems to have the effect that was expected. Namely, the users of the module attended lectures more frequently. However, it would be better if the module had some positive effect on examination scores. Theoretically, the module does not have a direct effect, and no such direct effect has been confirmed. As a next step, we will look for a better way of using the module to enable it to have a direct effect on student learning.

This paper have only confirmed the effect of the whole course introduction module. But we still need to confirm the effect of the recommendation engine of the module independently, although it is difficult to check this effect precisely. We must hence first determine a convincing method that will enable us to check the effect of the course recommendation engine. To check the effect of such recommendation engine may give us a hint to take advantage of big-data for education, because recommendation engine is one of the most important use of big-data.

Acknowledgement. This work was supported by JSPS KAKENHI Grant Number JP 15K12175.

References

1. Iitaka, T.: Implementation of Recommendation Engine in the Course Introduction Module (e-portfolio). IEICE Tech. Rep. **117**(83), 7–12 (2017). Tokyo
2. Hoshino, A.: 大阪府立大学におけるeポートフォリオの導入と活用について，平成25年度教育改革ICT戦略大会資料,公益社団法人私立大学情報教育協会，   Tokyo, pp. 88–93 (2013)

3. Iitaka, T.: On the connection of a course introduction module to e-learning modules. IEICE Tech. Rep. **116**(228), 31–36 (2016)
4. Iitaka, T.: Recommendation engine for an online drill system. In: Zaphiris, P., Ioannou, A. (eds.) LCT 2015. LNCS, vol. 9192, pp. 238–248. Springer, Cham (2015). https://doi.org/10.1007/978-3-319-20609-7_23

The NEON Evaluation Framework
for Educational Technologies

Michael Leitner[1]([⊠]), Philipp Hann[2],
and Michael D. Kickmeier-Rust[2,3]

[1] CREATE 21st Century, Vienna, Austria
michael.leitner@create.at
[2] University of Technology, Graz, Austria
philipp.hann@tugraz.at
[3] University of Teacher Education, St. Gallen, Switzerland
michael.kickmeier@phsg.chõ

Abstract. The evaluation of educational technology and concrete training measures is an important task to identify strengths and weaknesses, to elucidate the applicability for specific educational goals, and to make judgements about its effectiveness. This is a non-trivial task and unusually it requires lengthy inquiries with potential end users and clients. In many cases, the evaluation procedures are too much focused on usability-like criteria and superficial aspects of effectives. In this paper, we present a holistic framework based on four distinct dimensions which serves as the conceptual starting point for the set-up of evaluation activities. A special focus of the framework lies in the mutual dependence between evaluation dimensions and evaluation procedures. In order to reduce the efforts required for evaluation procedures we developed very short (10 item) instruments and compared the outcomes with those of a standard test battery of in total 231 items. The results of an exploratory study indicate that the short versions may provide sufficiently valid and reliable results which are not significantly different from the results of the long versions.

Keywords: Evaluation · eLearning · Training · NEON framework
Short scales

1 Introduction

The evaluation of educational technology is an important task to identify strengths and weaknesses, to elucidate the applicability for specific educational goals, and to make judgements about its effectiveness [5, 9]. This is a non-trivial task and usually it requires lengthy inquiries with potential end users. A comprehensive and scientifically sound evaluation is costly on the one hand, and on the other hand, not realizable for many scenarios. Thus, an approach is required that provides a short yet valid and reliable survey to evaluate an educational technology. In addition, the evaluation of technology for learning and teaching is oftentimes too focused on usability aspects, In many cases, the evaluation of educational software is reduced to 'conventional' usability and technology acceptance studies, at best it covers a superficial learning

© Springer International Publishing AG, part of Springer Nature 2018
P. Zaphiris and A. Ioannou (Eds.): LCT 2018, LNCS 10924, pp. 256–265, 2018.
https://doi.org/10.1007/978-3-319-91743-6_20

performance dimension. This is particularly true when it comes to settings of workplace learning, distance learning, or continuing qualification. Furthermore, psychological, sociological and ethical factors influence the "learner experience" too. In practice, such factors are often ignored, or evaluators are unaware of these factors' impact on the use and experience of educational software. Education as such, however, is a very complex field and a multitude of significant variables influence the quality of a product [2]. Thus, an approach is required that builds on a holistic and comprehensive view of learning scenarios.

In this paper, we introduce the NEON Evaluation Framework that has been developed in the context of an applied research project. We present the framework's dimensions, as well as a short eLearning evaluation questionnaire that has been designed and tested with a large-scale online study. We introduce a short eLearning evaluation questionnaire with 10 items. For this questionnaire, we condensed 19 evaluation tools (UX and usability questionnaires, eLearning questionnaires, etc.). We conducted a large-scale online study comparing the results of the full-scale evaluation questionnaire with a short version. The full-scale questionnaire has about 250 items covering all 19 evaluation tools. The short questionnaire has only 10 items.

In general, we experience many evaluation instruments and scales as too time consuming [7]. They are composed of too many items and questions. Due to time and budget constraints, they can hardly be applied in commercial or practical settings. Alternatively, these instruments consist of only a few superficial items, which do not reflect the characteristics of the evaluated technology.

A solid evaluation of educational technologies is a crucial, however non-trivial task. We aim to make evaluation "easier" and more "effective" without the loss of validity. Here are some of the problems we experience: Not only the quality and user-friendliness of an eLearning tool is important, also the educational effectiveness and validity must be assured. Educational effectiveness is often miss-evaluated, meaning that the effects of a single tool are not seen in a holistic educational context and thus the eLearning software's effects are either over or underestimated.

2 NEON Evaluation Framework for eLearning Technologies

As a result of our research, we introduce the NEON evaluation framework which summarizes four major dimensions for the evaluation process: the *medium of an educational goal* (this refers to the software and the hardware), the *quality of the educational contents* in itself, the *quality of the pedagogical approach*, and the aspects of the *context* within which the educational goal is to be reached. These dimensions are the result of research into existing evaluation tools and frameworks.

With these dimensions we aim to cover all relevant aspects and dimensions of educational technologies. The major dimensions are broken down into detailed sub-aspects for which we provide a catalogue of instruments, methods, scales, and items. This supports evaluators to assemble the right amount of items to keep the evaluation process short enough for real world settings. However, the selection of items aims to produce evaluation results valid enough to gain the necessary insights into the strong and weak spots of an eLearning software. The following figure gives an overview of the framework (Fig. 1).

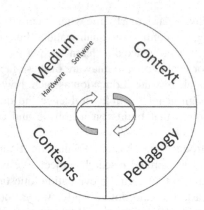

Fig. 1. Sketch of the NEON framework

We argue that a holistic approach to understanding and assessing educational measures requires building upon aspects far beyond characteristics such as usability or effectiveness. This is specifically true when evaluating with a formative approach to evaluation and technology improvement – in contrast to summative measurements.

The **first dimension** is *the medium* with which a training is presented; this refers to the hardware as such (e.g., tablets, smartphones, laptops or large screens) as well as the software (e.g., a learning management system such as Moodle, an app, or a software like *cBook* – a tool to present multimedia eLearning programs). Both hard and software must suffice the quality criteria; more importantly, these components are in a mutual dependence with the educational goal and the context conditions. Thus, statements about the quality or adequacy of the medium can only be made in the light of the other dimensions of the framework.

The **second dimension** is the *context* within which a training occurs. To develop the right educational approach, it makes a clear difference whether the learning occurs at the workplace, via mobile apps, or in form of a face-to-face workshop. More importantly, context includes the particular characteristics of the target audience, the previous knowledge, the competencies and backgrounds, as well as motivational aspects (e.g., highly motived learners do require different approaches than an audience that is not particularly interested in a training). Finally, context also includes certain constraints and limitations, e.g. in terms of course or learning time.

The **third dimension** refers to the *learning contents* as such. We argue that the contents must be seen independent from the concrete manifestation in form of a medium. The dimension refers to the correctness of the contents, the adequacy for specific learners, the syllabus (curriculum) along which it is composed, and the alignment with the educational goals. Although this seems trivial, in many trainings we could identify a gap between the actual training intentions of a customer und the concrete contents in a training. Once the right content is identified, suitable to reach the defined educational goals, these contents can be translated into the right media and the right sequence of media.

Finally, the **fourth dimension** refers to the *pedagogical (or didactic) approach*. In dependence of goals, characteristics of the target audience, certain context conditions and constraints, various pedagogical approaches may vary significantly in their effectiveness. In certain situations exploratory approaches might be useful, in others game-based/gamified approaches, social approaches, or even "talk and chalk" teaching might be the approach of choice.

3   An Exploratory Study

3.1   Aim

When it comes to evaluation of a training or an educational measure, it is evident that a complex approach - like the described framework - results in a massive battery of evaluation items. Looking at research literature, we find complete and well-elaborated, partially standardized, test instruments for all framework dimensions. To cover all NEON framework dimensions using standardized and existing tools, test subject would be presented with 231 test items. However, it is unrealistic to ask subjects to fill in hundreds of questionnaire items. This is specifically true when focusing on real-world situations, where customers wants to deploy certain educational measures and evaluate their quality and effectiveness.

The aim of this exploratory study was to investigate whether a very short questionnaire with only 15 well-chosen items could deliver valid results – comparing it with the full and extended questionnaire comprising 231 test items.

The full scales have been compiled from the following dimensions. eLearning readiness [1], user experience [8], application related aspects [10], usability [3, 6, 13, 14], esthetics [11], acceptance [12], and educational quality [4].

3.2   Study Setup

Participants. A total of 54 subjects participated in the online study. Participants were between 19 und 55 years old (M = 30.07, SD = 9.4). 38 participants were female, 16 participants were male. Regarding their use of computers 19 participants stated that they use the computer very often, 14 use it often and 21 use it on average (M = 2.04, SD = 0.87). Regarding their use of social media 17 participants stated that they use social media very often, 15 use it often, 12 use it on average and 10 use it sometimes (M = 2.28, SD = 1.11). Participants were recruited at the University of Graz and a college of education.

The Tested Self-learning Program. For the study we designed and produced an interactive 10 min self-learning program, using a technology called the "cBook". The program introduced the concept of "gamification" to participants, designed as sequential charts. Participants could browse through the charts themselves. The program included text charts, an audio speaker guiding through parts of the self-learning program, a video, a voting chart as well as an interactive video in which participants interact with a fictional character. Participants could browse through the charts (Figs. 2 and 3).

Fig. 2. Start page of the self-learning program. The program was designed on a chart-based layout. Participants could browse through the charts themselves (see arrow on the right side of the chart).

Fig. 3. As part of the self-learning program participants were presented an interactive video, in which they interacted with a fictional character called Mr. Fish (in German language).

Procedure. The first step for participants was to state their subject code, their age, their gender and their usage of computer and their usage of social media. The usage of computer and the usage of social media was measured with a 6-point Likert scale from "very often" to "never". Next the participants had to work through a short online learning course, which was created using the software "cBook" (see above). It took participants about 10 to 15 min to browse through the learning course. After finishing the online course participants were instructed to complete an evaluation questionnaire which consisted of 231 questions. It took participants about 45 min to an hour to complete the questionnaire, which contained 45 questions about the setting of the eLearning Software, 130 questions about the supporting medium, 41 questions about the contents of the eLearning Software and 15 questions about the pedagogical concept behind the eLearning Software. The answers were given with a 7-point Likert scale from "exactly" to "strongly disagree".

15 questions out of the 231 questions were part of the long questionnaire (Table 1), but also part of a shorter questionnaire, which contained seven questions about the *medium*, three questions about the *context*, two question each about the *contents* and the *pedagogical approach*. The remaining three questions were selected out of a pool of questions that covered more than one dimension. Two questions were selected to cover the dimensions *medium and contents* and one questions was selected to cover the dimensions *medium and pedagogical concept*.

Table 1. 15 questions selected out of 231. This short questionnaire was tested against the long questionnaire version (Translated from German).

Nr	Question
1	I know why I am part of this training course
2	I have the feeling that this eLearning software is following an overall concept
3	In general, I understand what eLearning is
4	During the eLearning course I sometimes did not know what to do next
5	It was a pleasure working with the eLearning software
6	The software's structure and its elements is well thought through
7	The software is visually attractive
8	The software seems to be overloaded
9	The software includes new and innovative elements
10	Working with this software is easy, considering the know-how and the resources that are required to use it
11	I have difficulties explaining why this software is useful/useless
12	The presented text content was short and precise
13	The content was presented without any errors (grammar, spelling, etc.)
14	Most of what I have learned did not seem to be related to each other
15	The course allows me to obtain new skills in realistic situations

The aim of the study was to compare the results of the longer questionnaire with the results of the shorter questionnaire in hopes that both questionnaires would evaluate a similar total score and similar scores across the four previously mentioned dimensions: medium, context, contents and pedagogical concept.

3.3 Study Results

In a first exploratory study, we compared the 4 major dimensions in long and short versions, in detail we distinguish between educational setting, pedagogical concept, contents, and the medium (technology). In addition, we separately analysed the complete short and long instruments. Table 1 shows the descriptive results for the compared tests, that is, long and short versions for all dimensions.

A t-test was used to determine whether the total score and score of each of the four dimensions of the long questionnaire matches the total score and score of each of the four dimensions of the new short questionnaire. The total score did not differ significantly between the long (M = 2.715, SD = .568) and the short questionnaire (M = 2.729, SD = .901; t(53) = −.235, p = .815). See Table 2.

Table 2. Descriptive Statistics

	N	Min	Max	Mean	SE	SD	Var
Total long	54	1,39	4,13	2,7146	,07732	,56817	,323
Context long	54	1,64	4,20	2,6522	,07299	,53636	,288
Medium long	54	1,19	4,00	2,7604	,08354	,61392	,377
Contents long	54	1,71	4,49	2,6143	,08415	,61835	,382
Pedagogy long	54	1,33	5,13	2,5506	,09599	,70535	,498
Total short	54	1,00	4,80	2,7293	,12261	,90098	,812
Context short	53	1,00	5,00	2,0472	,12678	,92298	,852
Medium short	54	1,00	5,50	3,0101	,14514	1,06657	1,138
Contents short	54	1,00	7,00	3,0710	,21270	1,56300	2,443
Pedagogy short	47	1,00	6,00	2,2979	,19455	1,33376	1,779

The same was found with the dimension pedagogical concept (Mlong = 2.521, SDlong = .704, Mshort = 2.298, SDshort = 1.334; t(46) = 1.673, p = .101), while the other three dimensions again differed significantly between the long and the short questionnaire as followed: setting (Mlong = 2.640, SDlong = .534, Mshort = 2.047, SDshort = .923; t(52) = 6.838, p = .000), medium (Mlong = 2.760, SDlong = .614, Mshort = 3.010, SDshort = 1.067; t(53) = −2.945, p = .005) and contents (Mlong = 2.614, SDlong = .618, Mshort = 3.071, SDshort = 1.563; t(53) = −2.317, p = .024).

The t-test clearly revealed that in general the mean results in short and long versions did not differ. In order to investigate the prediction quality of short version on the item basis instead of the means, we applied a linear regression model. Table 3 lists the results of the regression analysis.

The total score of the new short questionnaire significantly predicted the total score of the long questionnaire (β = .902, t = 15.063, p = .000). The regression model explained 81% of the variance of the criteria total score of the long questionnaire (R^2 = .814). Figure 4 illustrates the regression model.

In addition, we investigated the individual correlation of scales (for layout reasons we do not present the full correlation matrix). Except for the inter-correlations between the total scores and the scores of the four dimensions from both the long and the short questionnaire, there were three notable significant correlations. First, there was a *positive correlation* between the age of the subjects and the score of the dimension *contents* of the short questionnaire, which means the older the participants were the better they rated the contents of the eLearning software, but only if you look at the short questionnaire. (r(52) = .519, p = .000). Second there was a negative correlation between the age of the subjects and the score of the dimension *pedagogical approach* of the short questionnaire, which means the older the participants were the poorer they

Table 3. Regression analysis for long and short versions.

Mod. Sum.	R	R²	Adjusted R²	SE	Durbin-Watson
	.902	.814	.810	.24768	1.917
ANOVA	SS	df	Mean Square	F	Sig.
Regression	13.920	1	13.920	226.899	.000
Residual	3.190	52	.061		
Total	17.110	53			
Residual statistics	Min	Max	Mean	SD	N
Prediction	1,7310	3,8924	2,7146	,51248	54
Residual	−,5384	,60261	,00000	,24533	54
SPV	−1,919	2,298	,000	1,000	54
Std. Res.	−2,174	2,433	,000	,991	54

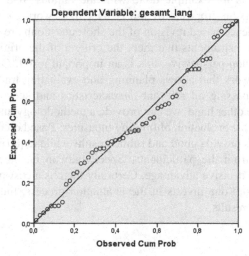

Fig. 4. Scatterplot of the linear regression between total score of the long questionnaire and total score of the new short questionnaire.

rated the pedagogical approach of the eLearning software, but also only if you look at the short questionnaire (r(45) = −.310, p = .034). Third there was a positive correlation between the usage of computers and the usage of social media, which means the more often participants use their computer the more often they use social media (r(52) = .716, p = .000).

There were no other significant correlations between the total scores and the scores of the four dimensions from both the long and the short questionnaire, the age of the participants, their gender and their computer and social media usage. Therefore, it can be assumed that both the long questionnaire and the short questionnaire can be properly used with people regardless of their age, their gender or their computer and social media usage.

4 Discussion

The aim of the NEON framework is to provide a scientifically robust, valid, and reliable approach for an evaluation of learning software and learning media that is applicable in practice. The NEON framework emphasizes the importance of taking all facets of an digital learning medium into account. It's short-sighted to believe the aspects and characteristics of the software as a carrier medium are enough for gauging its quality. A digital learning medium occurs always within certain context conditions, e.g., where and when the learning/training sessions occur, and limitations, e.g., the technology and time available. There is also a massive interaction between the content that is to be conveyed and the technological medium that is transporting the contents. With poor contents, the medium cannot be good enough to result in good learning performance and user satisfaction. The NEON framework is built around that considerations and brings together all the well-elaborated and proven tests and instruments.

Clearly it is not enough to arbitrarily select a handful of items to compose short test questionnaires, as it is for example done with the famous SUS test. As this study yielded, the short version proposed by the NEON framework showed a considerable good result. The evidence-based revision of the short questionnaire versions resulted in concise and practical instruments that meet the criteria of the original long versions.

From the application perspective, this is an important result. On the one hand, we can provide a framework that allows planning and evaluating training measures in a holistic way, encompassing all relevant characteristics and specifically their mutual dependencies. On the other hand, we can provide a methodology and concrete scales to have a handy and usable evaluation of training measures. Based on our results we argue that the short versions provide good and robust results while requiring only a minimum of time and efforts from the participants. Specifically in business-oriented learning settings this can be a decisive advantage. Certainly there is a cost-quality trade-off - in the sense that the more one invests in the evaluation process, the more detailed and reliable the obtained results.

References

1. Aydin, C.H., Tasci, D.: Measuring readiness for E-Learning: reflections from an emerging country. Educ. Technol. Soc. 8(4), 244–257 (2005)
2. Berger, T., Rockmann, U.: Quality of e-learning products. In: Handbook on Quality and Standardisation in E-Learning, pp. 143–155. Springer, Berlin (2006). https://doi.org/10.1007/3-540-32788-6_10
3. Brooke, J.: SUS: a quick and dirty usability scale. In: Jordan, P.W., Thomas, B., Weerdmeester, B.A., McClelland, I.L. (eds.) Usability Evaluation in Industry. Taylor & Francis, London (1996)
4. Entwistle, N.: Experiences of Teaching & Learning Questionnaire. ETL Project, The School of Education, University of Edinburgh (2002). www.ed.ac.uk/etl/project.html
5. Flagg, B.: Formative Evaluation for Educational Technologies. Routledge, Oxford (1990)
6. Kirakowski, J., Corbett, M.: SUMI: the software usability measurement inventory. Br. J. Edu. Technol. 24(3), 210–212 (1993)

7. Kühl, S.: Das Evaluations-Dilemma der Beratung: Evaluation zwischen Ansprüchen von Lernen und Legitimation (2009). http://www.uni-bielefeld.de/soz/personen/kuehl/pdf/Das-Evaluations-Dilemma4-Kap-4-02042008.pdf
8. Laugwitz, B., Held, T., Schrepp, M.: Construction and evaluation of a user experience questionnaire. In: Holzinger, A. (ed.) USAB 2008. LNCS, vol. 5298, pp. 63–76. Springer, Heidelberg (2008). https://doi.org/10.1007/978-3-540-89350-9_6
9. Oliver, M.: An introduction to the evaluation of learning technology. Educ. Technol. Soc. **3**(4), 20–30 (2000)
10. Oztekin, A., Kong, Z.J., Uysal, O.: UseLearn: a novel checklist and usability evaluation method for eLearning systems by criticality metric analysis. Int. J. Ind. Ergon. **40**(4), 455–469 (2010)
11. Thielsch, M.: Ästhetik von Websites. Verlagshaus Monsenstein & Vannerdat, Münster (2008)
12. Venkatesh, V., Bala, H.: Technology acceptance model 3 and a research agenda on interventions. Decis. Sci. **39**(2), 273–315 (2008)
13. Willumeit, H., Gediga, G., Hamborg, K.-C.: IsoMetricsL: Ein Verfahren zur formativen Evaluation von Software nach ISO 9241/10. Ergonomie Informatik **27**, 5–12 (1996)
14. Zaharias, P.: A usability evaluation method for e-learning courses. Unpublished PhD Dissertation, Department of Management Science and Technology, Athens University of Economics and Business (2004)

Does the Quality of Digital Teaching Materials Matter?

A Comparative Study of Art Students' Classroom Behavior and Learning Outcomes

Zhejun Liu[1](✉), Yunshui Jin[1], Shasha Liao[1], and Zheng Zhao[2]

[1] College of Arts and Media, Tongji University, Shanghai 201804, China
{wingeddreamer, jinyunshui, liaoshasha}@tongji.edu.cn
[2] Shanghai Xiandai Vocational and Technical School, Shanghai 200335, China
945595880@qq.com

Abstract. Today, digital media facilities have already become a part of the standard classroom configuration. And therefore, digital teaching materials (DTMs in short) like Powerpoint or Keynote slides are widely used by teachers from different educational organizations all over the world. A common assumption is that DTMs of higher quality would help teachers to make their students more attentive in the classroom and would lead to more rewarding learning outcomes. However, a well-designed DTM usually means a considerable amount of time and/or money investment which really needs to be justified. Trying to answer whether the quality of DTMs does matter, an experiment was designed and carried out with art students from a university and a secondary vocational school in Shanghai. In the comparative experiment, they were divided randomly into several groups to learn abstract concepts of 3D animation with either high or low-quality DTMs. Data was collected and analyzed to see whether the quality of DTM led to significant differences in three aspects: affective, cognitive and behavioral. The results of the experiment revealed that high-quality DTMs surpassed low-quality ones in most cases, but the advantages over the low-quality DTMs were not as prominent as we expected. These findings suggested a second thought before making a decision on the investment of a fancy but expensive DTM.

Keywords: Digital teaching material · Art students · Learning outcomes

1 Introduction

1.1 Background

As digital media facilities such as computers and projectors become more and more popular in all kinds of classrooms, from primary schools to universities, digital teaching materials have become an inseparable part of education all over the world. There are typically two forms of the digital learning material: auditory/verbal and visual/pictorial [1]. The common strategies to present these materials include digital slides [2], animations [3], games [4], and video clips [5] in different subject areas.

Among all types of strategies, digital slides, say Powerpoint or Keynote slides, are most popular and widely used [6]. Digital slides can be rather simple, containing only text and pictures, or very fancy and complicated when videos, animations or even interactive functions are integrated. Most teachers agreed that the beautiful and content-rich slides may attract students' attention in classrooms [7]. The problem is that better visual design, richer media types and more advanced functions usually mean more expensive development. Does the quality of digital teaching materials matter? Will it really result in more attentive students and better learning outcomes? These questions need to be answered to justify the investment on improve the quality of digital teaching materials. Unfortunately, however, qualitative and comparative researches on this question are scarce.

1.2 Target Students and Course

Art students form a special group of young people in China, large in quantity and unique in characteristics. In 2013, 271 thousand art students graduated from colleges in China, making up 8.4% of the total graduates that year [8]. They are found in secondary vocational schools, aging from 16–19 typically, and universities, aging from 18–22 typically. They usually do pretty well in painting, dancing, performing or other art ficlds, but are not very good at science subjects like math or physics.

Art students are good at emotional and affective thinking, but weak at rational thinking [9]. Digital art is a combination of art and technology, which requires a certain level of rational thinking so that one does not stop at just know how to operate a piece of software [10, 11]. 3D Abstract CG concepts, especially those related to 3D animation usually, pose a big challenge for art students because to understand these concepts usually requires more rational thinking.

Because of these reasons, art students plus abstract CG concepts should compose a typical scenario where digital teaching materials of higher quality ought to outperform those of lower quality, which means better visualization of these abstract concepts using animations could help art students to be more attentive in classrooms and understand knowledge better as well.

1.3 Overview of the Experiment

In order to have a deeper understanding of the question whether high-quality DTM can actually lead to better learning outcomes, an experiment was organized in which art students were required to learn unfamiliar and abstract CG concepts from the course named "3D Animation", using low quality and high quality digital teaching materials respectively. Topics like this were usually a challenge for most of them.

This research follows the positivism paradigm. Art students from both a secondary vocational school and a university participated in the comparative education experiment. Their performance was measured and analyzed from cognitive, affective and behavioral perspectives.

2 Hypothesis

The hypothesis is that the quality of the digital teaching materials has a positive effect on students' learning outcomes. The benefits from high-quality digital teaching materials contain both affective component and cognitive component which can be verified with evidences.

– Evidences of affective benefits:

1. Students are fonder of the high-quality materials;
2. Students are more attracted and focused;
3. Students are more aroused and excited;
4. Students begin to like and develop an interest in the subject.

– Evidences of cognitive benefits:

1. Students follow the teacher better in the classroom and answer questions correctly;
2. Students understand the content of the course more easily;
3. Students recall the content of the course better and score higher in the post-test.

3 Experiment

3.1 Subjects and Experimenters

The experiment recruited 25 students from Shanghai Xiandai Secondary Vocational School (Xiandai in short) and 20 students from Tongji University (Tongji in short). The Xiandai students majored in "Animation and Game Production", and the Tongji students majored in "Animation". All of them are art students in their first year of study. The reason why only first-year students were chosen was that they usually knew very little about the contents in the DTMs to be used as the test materials, so that the bias caused by prior knowledge was minimized.

The demographic statistics of the subjects is as follows (Table 1):

Table 1. Demographic statistics of the subjects

School	Age range	Mean age	Male	Female	Total
Tongji	17.8–21.3	19.9	6	14	20
Xiandai	15.9–19.1	17.1	14	11	25

Three teachers, two from Tongji and one from Xiandai, acted as experimenters. All of them were experienced teachers in the animation departments in both schools. Besides preparing the DTMs, they were also asked to give lessons to the subjects.

3.2   Teaching Materials

As mentioned above, "3D Animation" was chosen as the target course because it contains many abstract concepts difficult for art students to comprehend and thus may give full play to the potential of a high-quality DTM.

The experimenters carefully chose 3 topics from the course, which were:

- Topic 1: Texture Mapping and UVW Coordinates
- Topic 2: Global Illumination
- Topic 3: Parenting Hierarchy and Coordinate Systems

Topic 1 might be marginally more difficult than the other two, but the overall difficulty levels were estimated to be similar.

For each topic, a pair of DTMs were made respectively. The high-quality DTMs were standalone programs developed with Adobe Flash and/or Adobe Director, and the low-quality ones were just Powerpoint slides.

The main difference between them was the usage of animations, especially 3D animations. This was because the splendid animations commonly found in documentaries for science communication have proven their value and acceptability, but the product cost is usually beyond the budget for an in-class teaching material: a typical example of the dilemma that brought about the research question.

In the high-quality versions, 3D animations were heavily used to explain phenomena and principles in a dynamic and vivid way, while in the low-quality versions, there were only stationary pictures and texts.

It was also decided that embedded information should remain identical for both high-quality and low-quality DTMs, and the quality difference should not be deliberately exaggerated to induce positive results supporting the hypothesis. Therefore, most pictures and texts in the PPT slides were extracted directly from the animations used in the high-quality DTMs to minimized the bias (Fig. 1).

3.3   Procedures

The experiment was held in the college of Arts and Media in Tongji University in two days, one day with Xiandai students and the other day with Tongji students.

25 subjects from Shanghai Xiandai secondary vocational school were randomly divided into Xiandai Group A (n = 13) and Xiandai Group B (n = 12), and 20 subjects from Tongji university were randomly divided into Tongji Group A (n = 10) and Tongji Group B (n = 10). The lessons were taught separately in two classrooms by the 3 teachers, two from Tongji university (Teacher A and B) and one from Shanghai Xiandai secondary vocational school (Teacher C), as mentioned in Sect. 3.1. To minimize possible bias caused by personal lecturing skills, the in-classroom teaching was organized as shown in Table 2 where "L.Q." stands for "low-quality", "H.Q." stands for "high-quality".

Before the first lesson began, students were informed of the procedures of the experiment. Depending on its content and the in-class interaction, each lesson lasted for about 10 to 20 min. As soon as one lesson ended, the students were asked to finish a

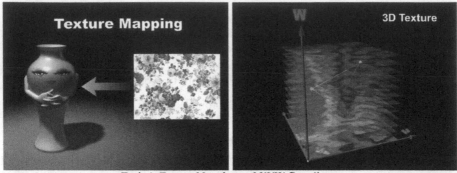

Topic 1: Texture Mapping and UVW Coordinates

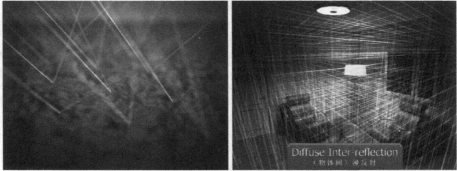

Topic 2: Global Illumination

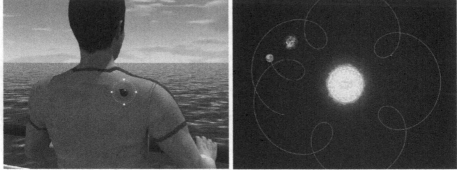

Topic 3: Parenting Hierarchy and Coordinate Systems

Fig. 1. Sample frames from the animations used in high-quality DTMs

quick test and a questionnaire (described in Sect. 3.4). After a 10-min break, the next lesson began.

3.4 Measure

Cognitive and affective learning outcomes are commonly measured to evaluate the efficacy of education [12, 13], both are equally important. Cognitive learning refers to the understanding of task-relevant verbal information and includes both factual and

Table 2. Arrangement of the experimental lessons

The "Xiandai" day

	Lesson 1	Lesson 2	Lesson 3
Xiandai Group A (n = 13) in Classroom 1	Topic 1 L.Q. DTM Teacher A	Topic 3 H.Q. DTM Teacher C	Topic 2 L.Q. DTM Teacher B
Xiandai Group B (n = 12) in Classroom 2	Topic 3 L.Q. DTM Teacher C	Topic 2 H.Q. DTM Teacher B	Topic 1 H.Q. DTM Teacher A

The "Tongji" day

	Lesson 1	Lesson 2	Lesson 3
Tongji Group A (n = 10) in Classroom 1	Topic 1 L.Q. DTM Teacher A	Topic 3 H.Q. DTM Teacher C	Topic 2 L.Q. DTM Teacher B
Tongji Group B (n = 10) in Classroom 2	Topic 3 L.Q. DTM Teacher C	Topic 2 H.Q. DTM Teacher B	Topic 1 H.Q. DTM Teacher A

skill-based knowledge [14], while affective learning means that learners generate intrinsic and extrinsic affective reactions in the learning process [15]. The reactions include personal emotion, feeling, fancy, attitude, and so on [16]. Cognitive learning outcomes are usually not difficult to assess because they deal more with factual knowledge, and in this research it could be evaluated by how well a subject understood and recalled particular information received from the lesson. To assess affective learning outcomes is more difficult, because it's much more subjective than the former one. Although questionnaires continued to be a useful tool, but its reliability is questionable when used alone. So a common practice is to supplement it with other objective measuring methods including physiological data and/or behavioral analysis [17, 18].

In order to discover the differences between high-quality and low-quality DTMs, the students' performance was inspected from 3 different perspectives, namely cognitive, affective and behavioral.

Cognitive Perspective. The cognitive component was inspected by knowing how well a subject understood the content of the lesson. The students were asked to finish a quick test form with 6 single-choice and 2 multiple-choice questions, concerning the concepts and principles just taught. Take topic 2 "Global Illumination" for instance, typical questions looked like (Table 3):

Table 3. Sample questions in the quick test form for topic 2

Q1: Which description below is correct about Global Illumination? (single choice)
  A) A rendering method in which no light casts any shadow.
  B) A rendering method that considers light from light sources and objects.
  C) A rendering method that calculates lights in world space instead of local space.

Q2: Which ones below are considered sources of indirect light? (multiple choice)
  A) Diffuse reflection   B) Sub-surface scattering   C) Reflective caustics
  D) Area light   E) Refractive caustics

Each single choice question equaled 10 marks and each multiple question equaled 20 marks, so the total marks of one test form added up to 100.

Affective Perspective. The affective component was inspected by knowing how a subject evaluated the lesson. There were 8 (for low-quality DTM) or 9 (for high-quality DTM) questions on each questionnaire in 2 categories: direct and indirect. The answers to these questions were mapped to numbers and the total marks was also 100 (Table 4).

Table 4. Description of the questions in the affective questionnaire

Category	Key information	Question type
Indirect	Fun of the lesson	Numeric scale
	Difficulty level of the lesson	Numeric scale
	Knowledge amount of the lesson	Numeric scale
Direct	Attractiveness of the DTM	Numeric scale
	Whether the DTM helped comprehension	Numeric scale
	Whether the DTM helped memorization	Numeric scale
	Whether the DTM deprived too much attention (possible negative effect)	Numeric scale
	Whether the subject like high-quality DTM more	Single choice

Behavioral Perspective. Considering that the answers to the questions in the affective questionnaires might not be objective enough, we also inspected students' in-class behavior to augment the survey data. In each classroom where the lessons were given, 2 or 3 HD video cameras were installed to capture subjects' body movement, facial expressions and voices (Figs. 2 and 3).

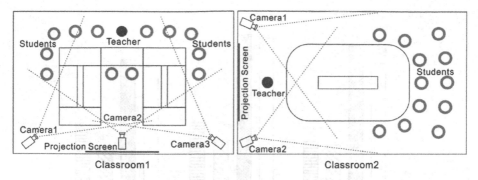

Fig. 2. Video cameras for behavior recording

Fig. 3. Sample frames of the recorded footages

To obtain meaningful and easy-to-read results, the video footages were synchronized and coded subject by subject at an interval of 10 s. Each 10-s behavior of every subject was given a score ranging from +2 to −2. The criterion was shown as below:

When coding a piece of 10-s behavior, a researcher would firstly check to see if there was any +2 (most positive) or −2 (most negative) behavior. If it was true, this period of time would be marked with the corresponding score; if no trace of "most positive" or "most negative" behavior was found, the researcher would mark that period of time with +1 or −1 according to the ratio of "positive time" against "negative time". In case a subject left the recorded area, was occluded from the camera or in a status difficult to interpret correctly as positive or negative behavior, that 10 s will be marked with 0.

4 Results

4.1 Quick Test Form Analysis Result (Cognitive Component)

A total of 135 quick test forms were collected and marked. An average score was calculated for each lesson and group as shown below (Fig. 4):

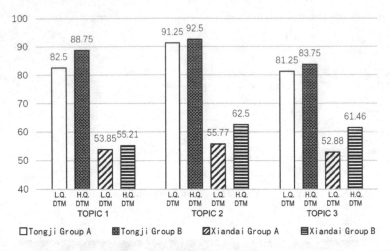

Fig. 4. Average scores of the quick test forms

As expected, every lesson taught with a high-quality DTM led to higher average score when compared with the same topic taught with a low-quality one. The average advantage was 3.33 in the case of Tongji students and 5.55 in the case of Xiandai students.

4.2 Questionnaire Analysis Result (Affective Component - Subjective)

A total of 135 questionnaires containing subjects' subjective opinions towards the lesson were collected and the answers were mapped to 0–100 scores. An average score was calculated for each lesson and group as shown below (Fig. 5):

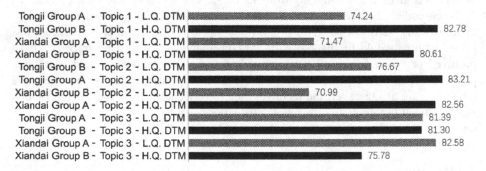

Fig. 5. Average scores of the questionnaires

Among all the 6 comparable pairs (e.g. Tongji Group A vs Tongji Group B with Topic 1 - L.Q DTM), the first 4 pairs demonstrated that high-quality DTMs outplayed the low-quality ones with big advantage. In the 5th pair, both DTMs had virtually tied. The only exception was the 6th pair, in which the low-quality DTM appeared to work better.

4.3   Behavior Analysis Result (Affective Component - Objective)

As mentioned in Sect. 3.4, subjects' behavior was recorded and coded at an interval of 10 s according to the criterion in Table 5. The number of students in different status was counted and the following figure was produced based on the result. The X axis stands for time and the Y axis stands for the percentage of students in a certain status: +2, +1, 0, −1, −2 from top to bottom (Fig. 6).

Table 5. Criterion used to code the recorded behavior

Typical behavior	Attitude	Score
– Volunteering to answer the teacher's questions – Responding actively to the teacher's assignment – Discussing about course content with classmates	Most positive	+2
– Keeping silent – Looking at the teacher or the projection – Listening to the teacher	Positive	+1
– Being distracted (for a short while) – Looking at unrelated places (for a short while) – Whispering with classmates (for a short while)	Negative	−1
– Playing with the mobile phone – Dozing – Chatting with classmates – Frolicking with classmates	Most negative	−2
– Difficult to observe or judge behavior	N/A	0

In all graphs, a grey part at the center (value = +1) occupies the biggest area, which means that the majority of the subjects were relatively positive during the lessons. As for the rest, if the students were attentive, more top black "spikes" (value = +2) and lower bottom "peaks" (value = −1 or −2) are expected to be found in the graph. By carefully comparing horizontal pairs, it's possible to conclude that most of the lessons taught with high-quality DTMs did marginally better in keeping students positive, but the advantage was not very significant.

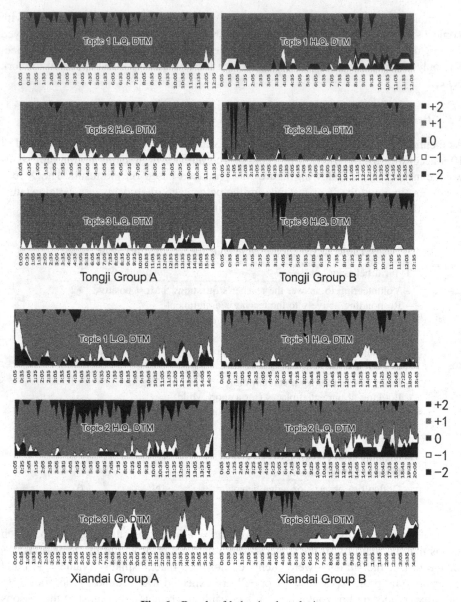

Fig. 6. Result of behavioral analysis

5 Conclusion

From the cognitive perspective, high-quality DTMs seemed to be more effective for the younger students from the secondary vocational school (with a plus of 5.5 marks) than for the university students (with a plus of 3.3 marks). The reason might be that students on higher educational level usually have better capability of comprehension and abstract thinking and need less concrete visual representations as an aid. The advantage of 3.3 or 5.5 marks was acceptable but not that impressive.

From the affective perspective, in most cases students' subjective evaluations of the lessons taught with high-quality DTM were much better than the counterparts. It's natural because teaching materials full of interesting and vivid animations do appeal to most people. But the effectiveness was undermined by the objective data from behavior observation: the students' attitude embodied in their body language did not show that much preference to the high-quality ones, which was especially true for the students from Tongji University.

According to the experiment results, though it's unfair to say that high-quality DTMs were of little value, but as far as the learning outcome is concerned, they did not work as greatly as expected. If high-quality DTMs could be obtained for free or at a low cost, they surely will not jeopardize your teaching but just add value to it. However, if a great investment of time and/or money can be foreseen, a second thought is suggested before making up your mind.

6 Limitations and Future Research Proposals

The learning behavior of human beings still remains as a black box today and no existing theory can explain how it happens in our brains. When environment and interpersonal interaction is involved, education becomes an even more complicated issue. This paper tries to bring some insight into the relationship between the quality of digital teaching materials and the learning outcomes, but there were many limitations that need to be dealt with in future researches.

Firstly, this research only inspected a certain course (3D animation) given to a specific group of students (art students), but there are many more different combinations. Besides "3D animation", other courses given to other students, say students majoring in chemistry, also involve the introduction to abstract concepts, processes and theories, which is probably much more difficult to understand than those taught in this experiment. Future researches should expand the range of students and courses to verify the conclusion given by this paper.

Secondly, this research employed a comparative educational experiment happening in a controlled environment, which was quite different from a common lesson given in a school. The experimental lesson was as long as 10–20 min, while an ordinary lesson usually lasts for 40 min or so; the experimental lesson was given to about 10 students, while an ordinary lesson is usually given to a much larger group of people; the experimental lesson only dealt with one concept while an ordinary lesson usually covers more knowledge points. Since all these factors may affect the final results, future researches are encouraged to be conducted in a real-life situation of school education.

Thirdly, in this paper, the difference between a high-quality DTM and a low-quality DTM was decided to be the use of explanatory animations and the other factors were kept as similar to each other as we could. But this is not always the real situation in teaching practice. Low-quality DTMs may also mean vague pictures, poorly designed layout, too much or too little textual information, while high-quality DTMs may also make use of videos, sounds, interactive programs and etc. These situations need to be dealt with in future researches.

Last but not least, the sample size of the experiment was 45 in total. It's a modest size but because the subjects were divided into 4 groups, there were only approximately 10 students in each group. In order to obtain a more general conclusion, future researches should consider increasing the sample size.

Acknowledgement. This research project was supported through the "Funds for Art Research Projects" given by the Shanghai Municipal Education Commission. The research team would also like to express gratitude to all the support from the College of Arts and Media in Tongji University, and the Shanghai Xiandai Secondary Vocational School.

References

1. Mayer, R.E.: Multimedia learning. Psychol. Learn. Motiv. **41**, 85–139 (2002)
2. Mayer, R.E., Johnson, C.I.: Revising the redundancy principle in multimedia learning. J. Educ. Psychol. **100**(2), 380–386 (2008)
3. Jacobs, B., Robin, B.: Animating best practice. Animation **11**(3), 263–283 (2016)
4. Moreno, R., Mayer, R.: E: Role of guidance, reflection, and interactivity in an agent-based multimedia game. J. Educ. Psychol. **97**(1), 117–128 (2005)
5. Berk, R.A.: Multimedia teaching with video clips: TV, movies, YouTube, and mtvU in the college classroom. Int. J. Technol. Teach. Learn. **5**(1), 1–21 (2009)
6. Parker, I.: Absolute PowerPoint. New Yorker **28**, 76–87 (2001)
7. Bhuvaneswari, T., Beh, S.L.: Changes in teaching and learning through digital media for higher education institutions. Int. J. Mob. Learn. Organ. **2**(3), 201–215 (2008)
8. Xie, H.: Annual Statistics of Education in China, 1st edn. Educational Press of the People, Beijing (2014)
9. Qi, W., Zheng, P.: A study on the characteristics of art students in colleges. Shizhi Acad. J. **2**, 189–190 (2010)
10. Li, Y.: A refection upon the relationship between digital art and technology. New Art **27**(2), 105–108 (2006)
11. Zhou, J., Sun, L.: The exploration of the educational principles of the computer technology lessons for the animation discipline. Acad. J. Beijing Film Acad. **3**, 41–48 (2012)
12. Titsworth, S., Mazer, J.P., Goodboy, A.K., et al.: Two meta-analyses exploring the relationship between teacher clarity and student learning. Commun. Educ. **64**(4), 385–418 (2015)
13. Witt, P.L., Wheeless, L.R., Allen, M.: A meta-analytical review of the relationship between teacher immediacy and student learning. Commun. Monogr. **71**(2), 184–207 (2005)
14. Kraiger, K., Ford, J.K., Salas, E.: Application of cognitive, skill-based, and affective theories of learning outcomes to new methods of training evaluation. J. Appl. Psychol. **78**(2), 311–328 (1993)
15. Picard, R.W., Papert, S., Bender, W., et al.: Affective learning - a manifesto. BT Technol. J. **22**(4), 253–269 (2004)
16. Wang, W.Y., Ko, L.C., Huang, Y.M., et al.: What is affective learning. Lect. Notes Electr. Eng. **260**, 177–181 (2014)
17. Glennon, W., Hart, A., Foley, J.T.: Developing effective affective assessment practices. Am. Phys. Educ. Rev. **86**(6), 40–44 (2015)
18. Marco-Giménez, L., Arevalillo-Herráez, M., Ferri, F.J., et al: Affective and behavioral assessment for adaptive intelligent tutoring systems. In: Proceedings of the ACM Conference on User Modeling (Extended), Adaptation and Personalisation, Canada. ACM (2016)

Evaluating Relevant UX Dimensions with Respect to IoT Ecosystem Intended for Students' Activities Tracking and Success Prediction

Tihomir Orehovački[1](✉), Dijana Plantak Vukovac[2], Mišo Džeko[2],
and Zlatko Stapić[2]

[1] Faculty of Informatics, Juraj Dobrila University of Pula, Zagrebačka 30,
52100 Pula, Croatia
tihomir.orehovacki@unipu.hr
[2] Faculty of Organization and Informatics, University of Zagreb,
Pavlinska 2, 42000 Varaždin, Croatia
{dijana.plantak,miso.dzeko,zlatko.stapic}@foi.hr

Abstract. The paper presents the results of research on user experience dimensions related to mobile application prototype which is a part of a complex IoT ecosystem. In the ongoing research we explore the possible use of IoT in ecosystem consisting of software, hardware and liveware employed in student's activities tracking and success prediction. By carefully reviewing pertinent current studies in the field, we determined a finite set of items and attributes that constitute the anticipated UX in the context of IoT and employed them to design a measuring instrument in the form of a questionnaire. An empirical study was carried out with an objective to examine the psychometric features of the questionnaire. University students served as a representative sample of end users. During study, participants were asked to conduct predefined scenarios of interaction with IoT ecosystem prototype and then evaluate it by completing the questionnaire. Study findings helped us identify to what extent IoT ecosystem prototype has met requirements of relevant UX dimensions and which direction should we follow when considering its design.

Keywords: IoT ecosystem · User experience evaluation · Pragmatic quality
Hedonic quality · Empirical study

1 Introduction

The Internet of Things (IoT), as a realm that enabled connection and interaction of digital and physical entities, represents global network of smart objects along with the set of supporting technologies and combination of applications and services utilizing such technologies into new functional possibilities and opportunities [12]. As rapid advances in underlying technologies are constantly opening new doors for novel applications that promise the improvement in quality of our lives [24], such global information-based network of uniquely addressable heterogeneous objects and sensors

© Springer International Publishing AG, part of Springer Nature 2018
P. Zaphiris and A. Ioannou (Eds.): LCT 2018, LNCS 10924, pp. 279–293, 2018.
https://doi.org/10.1007/978-3-319-91743-6_22

that seamlessly blend with the environment [6], quickly found its application in all aspects of human activity. Education is no exception as there are already IoT supported teaching and learning environments. On one hand, ubiquitous learning environments have been explored throughout specification of their technical framework and the system architecture [19, 25], and on the other hand by exploration of the IoT environment effectiveness in lifelong learning [3]. However, to our best knowledge, there are no reports of using a combination of software, hardware and liveware objects (which we call IoT ecosystem) with the aim of students' activities tracking and success prediction.

User experience (UX) represents an essential part of every software lifecycle that is user-centered, especially in stages of its design and evaluation. In the IoT context, user experience is not only related to active interactions with the tangible product, but also to passive confrontations with "invisible" elements in the IoT ecosystem (e.g. sensors outside the user's sight) that may provoke various perceptions of the system and resulting emotions. As such, anticipation of hedonic quality of the system plays an important role in the design of the future system. In this paper we examine anticipated UX in the context of IoT ecosystem prototype we developed for students' activities tracking. The paper capitalizes on our prior work [16] in which we introduced a set of factors that affect the academic success of students and proposed an architecture and an interactive prototype of the IoT ecosystem meant for students' activities tracking and success prediction. More specifically, it investigates relevant pragmatic and hedonic UX facets with respect to the nature of the aforementioned IoT ecosystem.

This paper is structured in six chapters, starting from introduction and chapter on research background where we bring the results of our literature review regarding the use of IoT in learning environments with the focus on evaluation of its user experience. In the third chapter we shortly introduce the design and features of an IoT ecosystem employed in students' activities tracking and success prediction. The subsequent chapters present the methodology and results of the study aiming to examine the relevant UX dimensions of the proposed prototype of the mobile component of the ecosystem.

2 Research Background

Advancements in information and communication technologies (ICT) and their integration into learning environments bring a lot of changes into the way people learn. The main purpose of the ICT usage in learning is to provide better learning experience through aligning students' interests, preferences, objectives and previous knowledge that would lead to effective knowledge acquisition and retention. While mobile devices and technologies have enhanced learning portability and mobility, IoT is contributing to construction of ubiquitous learning environments. In such environments, learners and technologies, real world and virtual worlds, are interconnected, and IoT serves as a backbone that enables recognition and identification of environmental objects, and retrieves network information to facilitate their adaptive functionality [25].

In the context of learning environments, we still do not have a clearly prescribed guidelines for development of the IoT ecosystem. Joyce et al. [8] designed the IoT ecosystem which was piloted in eight schools in England, but although it had the data collection mechanisms, its main purpose was to enable discovery-based learning with the help of supporting mobile and web technologies. Authors concluded that their learning/studying ecosystem, where environmental data is readily available, provided a new learning experience enabling students and teachers to observe the real time data and to discuss it. On the other hand, Georgescu and Popescu [5] discuss that IoT, if introduced to eLearning in person-centered design process, could open different possibilities in enhancing learning experience and learning process itself. Even more, Bandara and Ioras [1] have been using IoT to enhance gamification techniques in eLearning environments. Furthermore, the same authors state that "IoT has the ability to improve upon the learning experience by allowing for real-time and actionable insights into student performance" thus drawing a clear line connecting IoT and user experience in learning environments.

User experience (UX) consists of wide range of factors that can be classified into three categories: context around the user and system (social, physical, task, technical and information context), the user's state (e.g. motivation, emotions, expectations) and systems properties (e.g. functionalities, aesthetics, responsiveness, sustainability, etc.) [17]. Although the concept of UX was introduced in the late 80's, the consensus on its scope and definition has not been reached yet. Law et al. [11] argue this is because UX is a dynamic and subjective concept that results from interaction with a piece of software thus depending on the context of use and perceptions of individuals. When the nature of UX is taken into account, literature distinguishes two streams of researchers and practitioners. While the first one considers UX as a synonym for usability focused on the pragmatic (utilitarian) facets of software design and evaluation, the second one believes UX is a distinct concept, more recently referred to as quality of experience (QoE), dealing with hedonic (emotional) dimensions in the aforementioned respect. As an outcome of the comprehensive literature review, Bargas-Avila and Hornbæk [2] uncovered generic UX, affect and emotion, enjoyment and fun, aesthetics and appeal, hedonic quality, engagement and flow, motivation, enchantment, frustration, values, and spontaneity as the most common UX dimensions. Current studies (e.g. [9, 20, 21]) in the field indicate that learnability, usefulness, availability, attractiveness, and reliability of software as well as users' efficiency, effectiveness, and productivity are relevant antecedents of UX.

Regarding various aspects of user experience present in learning environments, Simic et al. [19] and Xue et al. [25] focused their work only on technical aspects of IoT-based learning environments development, while Cheng and Liao [3] besides that examined quality aspects of the system that includes usability. Considering complexity of ubiquitous environments, in a new product development it is essential to evaluate design concepts to "ensure predetermined design goals and to obtain design feedback" [4]. Design concepts enable users to form user experience before the user actually interacts with the real product, application or the system (anticipated UX as identified in [17]), in addition to experiences that can take place during or after the item usage. In that respect, early design concepts and actual design decisions could be drawn not only from requirements identification, but also from UX research about users' expectations and anticipated feelings that could be provoked by the future product or system. In addition, early system representations in the form of mock-ups and prototypes could be used in later design stages to evaluate proposed design.

While there is a plethora of UX evaluation methods that can be applied in various development phases [23], UX evaluation design methods for IoT ecosystem are scarce. One method can be borrowed from the product design, e.g. UX evaluation method of design concept based on multi-modal experience scenario [4], which employs semantic questionnaire and can be applied in the earlier design stages, but requires development of product usage scenarios and physical prototypes. Another approach presented in [18] is built upon integration of the quality of service (QoS) and the QoE from a user-centric perspective since IoT is provided through some form of service. The QoE model [18] gives good predictions on users' quality experiences in the use of IoT services, but might be cumbersome to use in practice due its quantitative and qualitative approach.

In that context, our approach was to create a measurement tool for evaluation of IoT ecosystem that would be feasible to use in early design stages and enable assessment of relevant UX dimensions.

3 Evaluated IoT Ecosystem

From human-computer interaction (HCI) perspective, the development of ubiquitous environments that incorporate IoT, calls for the flexibility in the design process. Main characteristics of user-centered design of new media products are: a) the design process that is based on various prototypes, from low-level to high-level, b) the design is feature-driven, where most important features are implemented first, and c) the design process is incremental and iterative [4].

Those pillars were present in the approach we took while designing IoT ecosystem for learning environment. Our main goal was to design a prototype of the IoT ecosystem meant for students' activities tracking and success prediction, as well as evaluate relevant UX dimensions in that respect. The design was materialized as an interactive prototype of mobile application as the most tangible part of the future IoT ecosystem.

A user-centered design approach, which is further elaborated in [16], consisted of the following:

(1) identification and analysis of the student needs relevant for achieving academic success by employing questionnaire, focus group, and the design of personas and storyboards,
(2) requirements definition based on needs analysis in order to propose IoT ecosystem functionalities and architecture, and
(3) design of wireframes and interactive prototypes with an aim to evaluate IoT ecosystem idea.

In the first phase, a preliminary study was conducted to effectively determine what students' features were mostly connected to academic success. The study employed two techniques for data collection, one being the focus group with university professors, and the other a student-involved questionnaire. Both techniques revealed features that were deemed important to achieve student success, but also identified means that could be used to detect or measure some of those features like motivation, goal centeredness, work related obligations, time management, etc. In addition to the results of the questionnaire and the focus group, five personas were created in order to identify student groups relevant for the learning environment. Two personas were chosen to further elaborate students' needs throughout sketching the storyboards. Outputs identified by aforementioned techniques helped in forming the idea of an IoT enabled system employed in tracking students' behavior in order to improve students' success by informing them of recognized patterns and suggesting the ways to improve their lifestyle.

In the second research phase, we built on the above mentioned study results and identified basic features that the system should implement. Thus, software requirements specification document included the requirements description of the following main components: *My classes*, *My Behaviours and Habits*, *Study Marketplace*, *Ambience* and *Analytics*. The purpose of the '*My classes*' feature was to enable student to have an insight on his/her own courses' obligations but also on the level and quality of their fulfilment. Special attention was paid to the option of enabling student to be able to compare his/her own results with the results of other groups of students without intruding their privacy. '*My Behaviours and Habits*' section described functionalities grouped either as academic (like tardiness or study time) or leisure (like sleeping habits or other routines). '*Study companion*' section includes the options of offering or seeking help in any aspect of student's life. On the other hand, section on '*Ambience*' would give the student a possibility to observe the suitability of ambient for learning in it. Finally, the overall academic lifestyle analytics were put together into specific feature named '*Analytics*'.

The usual activities of defining the system architecture and structure design followed and topological view on the system proposed in [16] is presented in Fig. 1. Faculty building areas (library, auditoriums, and teaching staff offices) and students' dormitory public areas are equipped with sensors able to track some aspects of students' behavior. Thus, the IoT ecosystem can draw conclusions based on data collected physically (via sensors) and data available on faculty services (scheduling, library records, event management and learning management system (LMS)) and finally present the data to the user via API used by the mobile application.

In the third phase, based on outputs from the first and the second phase, wireframes and an interactive prototype for an Android mobile application were created. Wireframes presented the structure and initial content of the application screens (Fig. 2) and its design was qualitatively evaluated by two members of the design team who were not involved into their creation. The interactive prototype was redesigned based on the feedbacks from the design team, and included graphic design, more elaborated content and interactivity among the screens (Fig. 3). The aforementioned one didn't have the interactive tabs on every screen in order to identify whether the students would reveal the flaws in the prototype.

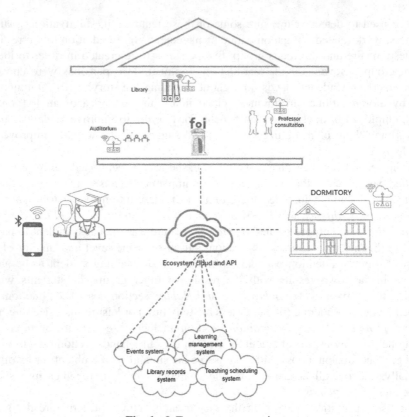

Fig. 1. IoT ecosystem overview

4 Methodology

Procedure. The study was carried out during the winter semester of academic year 2017/18. and was composed of two parts: (1) scenario-based interaction with IoT system prototype and (2) its evaluation with respect to pragmatic and hedonic facets of UX by means of the questionnaire. Upon arriving to the lab, the participants were welcomed and briefly informed about the purpose of the study. To ensure high accuracy of the gathered data, study participants were given detailed written and oral instructions on the implementation of each particular step of the research. At the beginning of the scenario performance session, every respondent received URL with the interactive prototype and URL of on online questionnaire. Participants were asked to browse throughout the prototype screens following various paths using interactive elements on the screens, and thereafter to fill out the questionnaire. At the end of the study, respondents were debriefed and thanked for their participation.

Apparatus. Data were gathered through the questionnaire which was administered online by means of the Google Forms. The questionnaire comprised 4 five-point bipolar items related to participants' demographics, 4 five-point bipolar items aimed for

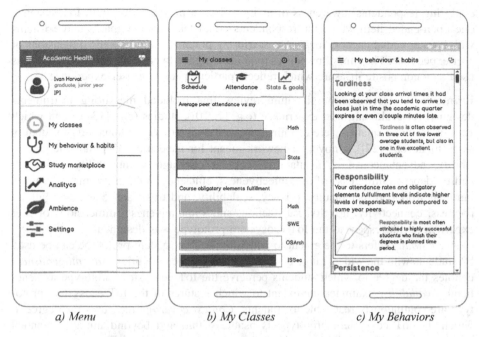

a) Menu   *b) My Classes*   *c) My Behaviors*

Fig. 2. Examples of a mobile application wireframes

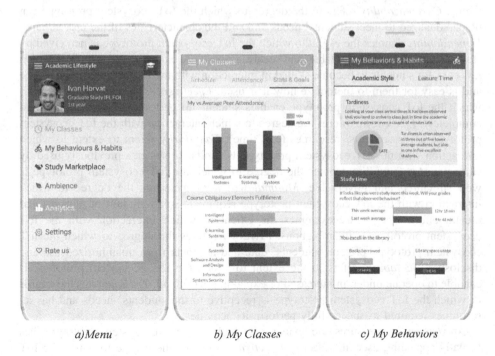

a)Menu   *b) My Classes*   *c) My Behaviors*

Fig. 3. Examples of screens of an interactive prototype

exploring respondents' awareness of and experience in interaction with IoT systems, one open-ended item where the respondents could leave their remarks and 86 items with bipolar verbal anchors meant for measuring pragmatic and hedonic dimensions of user experience. The sum of responses to items assigned to corresponding attribute was used as a composite measure which reflects particular facet of user experience.

Framework. Based on the literature review that included measuring instruments designed for evaluating user experience (e.g. [7, 10]), studies (e.g. [13–15]) in which various facets of quality were examined as well as international standards for quality assessment (e.g. [22]), a novel framework meant for measuring 17 pragmatic (accessibility, advantageousness, availability, context coverage, compatibility, customizability, dependability, ease of use, effectiveness, efficiency, familiarity, manageability, minimal workload, perspicuity, privacy, scalability, and trust) and 5 hedonic (attractiveness, connectivity, novelty, satisfaction, and stimulativeness) dimensions of user experience with respect to the IoT ecosystem prototype was designed.

Accessibility refers to the extent to which the IoT ecosystem prototype can be used by students with the widest range of characteristics and capabilities. *Advantageousness* denotes the degree to which students perceive the IoT ecosystem prototype as beneficial. *Availability* examines the extent to which features of the IoT ecosystem prototype are continuously reachable to students. *Context coverage* measures the degree to which the IoT ecosystem prototype is usable within and beyond initially intended contexts of use. *Compatibility* explores the extent to which the IoT ecosystem prototype operates properly with different types of devices and among different environments. *Customizability* refers to the degree to which the IoT ecosystem prototype can be personalized to meet students' needs and suit the characteristics of the task at hand. *Dependability* denotes the extent to which the IoT ecosystem prototype is perceived by students as unfailing, predictable, and secure. *Ease of use* examines the degree to which it is easy for students to become skilled in interaction with the IoT ecosystem prototype and is easy for them to memorize how it is used. *Effectiveness* measures the extent to which the IoT ecosystem prototype enables students to perform tasks accurately and completely. *Efficiency* explores the degree to which interaction with the IoT ecosystem prototype saves students' resources (e.g. time). *Familiarity* refers to extent to which interaction with the IoT ecosystem prototype is similar to systems previously used by students. *Manageability* denotes the degree to which the IoT ecosystem prototype is well structured and governable. *Minimal workload* measures the degree to which interaction with the IoT ecosystem prototype requires a small amount of physical and mental effort. *Perspicuity* examines the extent to which interaction with the IoT ecosystem prototype is unambiguous. *Privacy* explores the degree to which the IoT ecosystem prototype protects students' data and artefacts from unauthorized use and disclosure. *Scalability* refers to the extent to which the IoT ecosystem prototype is capable to operate under an increased or expanding workload. *Trust* denotes the degree to which the IoT ecosystem prototype is receptive to the students' needs and has all resources required to successfully perform its activities.

Attractiveness measures the extent to which the IoT ecosystem prototype has visually appealing user interface. *Connectivity* examines the degree to which the IoT ecosystem prototype is integrating, inclusive, and brings students closer to each other.

Novelty signifies the extent to which the IoT ecosystem prototype is distinctive among other ones. *Satisfaction* indicates the degree to which interaction with the IoT ecosystem prototype has met students' expectations and arouses positive emotional responses in them. *Stimulativeness* represents the extent to which interaction with the IoT ecosystem prototype is focused and encourages students' creativity.

5   Results

Participants. A total of 50 respondents took part in the study. They ranged in age from 19 to 36 years (M = 22.44, SD = 2.557). The sample was composed of 76% male and 24% female students. At the time the study was conducted, the majority (50%) of participants was in the third year of the undergraduate study, 38% of them was in the first year of the graduate study, 8% of them was in the first year of the undergraduate study whereas remaining 4% was in the second year of the graduate study. All respondents were enrolled to study programs in the field of information and communication sciences. The majority (94%) of participants were full-time students. When awareness about IoT systems was considered, 62% of students reported they are familiar with the concept of IoT while 32% of them stated they are acquainted with IoT technologies. On the other hand, when experience in interaction with IoT systems was examined, 52% of study participants reported they used at least two IoT systems while 28% of them took part in the development of at least one IoT system.

Findings. The results of data analysis revealed that 72% of study respondents reported that the IoT ecosystem prototype could be used by their peers regardless their capabilities and characteristics. More specifically, 56% of students think that the IoT ecosystem prototype can be used by everyone, while 88% of them think that the IoT ecosystem prototype is accessible. It was also found that 83.33% of study participants find the IoT ecosystem prototype advantageous. Namely, majority of students perceived the IoT ecosystem prototype as useful (88%), practical (88%), suitable (86%), functional (80%), usable (80%), and valuable (76%). Study findings also indicate that 81% of respondents agree that the IoT ecosystem prototype is continuously reachable because 82% and 80% of students find it available and disposable, respectively.

As much as 49.50% of study participants agree that the IoT ecosystem prototype is usable beyond initially intended contexts of use. More concretely, 68% of students think that the IoT ecosystem prototype has variety of possible applications, 58% of them believe that the IoT ecosystem prototype has very specific purpose, 44% of students agree that the IoT ecosystem prototype is usable only within aimed context, while 70% of study participants find it technical in nature. The analysis of gathered data also uncovered that 77% of individuals involved in the study agree the IoT ecosystem prototype operates well among diverse environments because 78% of students find it compatible and 76% supported in that respect. The same holds for the extent to which the IoT ecosystem prototype is customizable in general (77%) as well as the degree to which students' can personalize it (78%) and the IoT ecosystem prototype is adjustable to the context of its employment (76%). It also appeared that 73.60% of respondents perceived the IoT ecosystem prototype as dependable which is due to most students consider it reliable (82%), stable (80%), bug-free (56%), predictable (72%), and secure (78%).

According to the results of data analysis, 93% of study participants agree that is easy to use the IoT ecosystem prototype. Namely, 94% of students believe that is easy to become skillful in interaction with the IoT ecosystem prototype while 92% of them think that is easy to recall how to use the IoT ecosystem prototype functionalities. It was also discovered that 75.50% of study participants stated that the IoT ecosystem prototype enhances their performance in executing tasks which is because majority of students find it effective (92%), productive (90%), complete (60%), and whole (60%).

Study findings are implying that 78.50% of students believe that the IoT ecosystem prototype improves their efficacy in performing assignments owing to majority of them think that the IoT ecosystem prototype has acceptable response time (92%), is fast (86%), efficient (84%), and saves their resources (52%). As much as 51% of individuals that took part in the study reported that interaction with the IoT ecosystem prototype does not differ much from previously used applications and systems. More specifically, 64% of students found the IoT ecosystem prototype familiar whereas only 38% of students agree the IoT ecosystem prototype is similar to other systems they previously employed. The IoT ecosystem prototype was perceived by 86% of students as governable because the same proportion of them find it organized, controllable, and manageable.

A total of 80.67% of respondents agree that the interaction with the IoT ecosystem prototype requires minimal workload. Namely, it was found that majority of students reported that employing the IoT ecosystem prototype does not require a lot of physical (82%) neither mental (78%) activity nor makes students tired (82%). Moreover, 90.50% of study participants agree that interaction with the IoT ecosystem prototype was unambiguous which is due to majority of them find it understandable (96%), clear (94%), easy (92%), and consistent (80%). Only 38.67% of students think the IoT ecosystem prototype preserves their data and artefacts from unauthorized use. More concretely, 28% of respondents believe the IoT ecosystem prototype takes care about their privacy, 38% of them is convinced that the IoT ecosystem prototype would not share their personal data with third parties, while half of the study sample think that the IoT ecosystem prototype protects the privacy of their artefacts.

Study findings also indicate that 67.33% of respondents found the IoT ecosystem prototype scalable. Namely, majority of students reported that the IoT ecosystem prototype enables simultaneous work of a large number of users (80%), supports simultaneous work on a large number of tasks (66%), and allows the execution of complex tasks (56%). As much as 81% of students agree that the IoT ecosystem prototype is receptive to their needs and has all resources required to successfully perform its activities which is due to 82% of study respondents find it trustworthy while 80% of them think the IoT ecosystem prototype is competent.

All the set forth implies that in the context of IoT ecosystem prototype advantages, the most relevant pragmatic UX dimensions are ease of use, minimal workload, and perspicuity while IoT ecosystem prototype disadvantages could be mostly related to privacy, context coverage, and familiarity. Study findings related to pragmatic UX dimensions are summarized in Fig. 4.

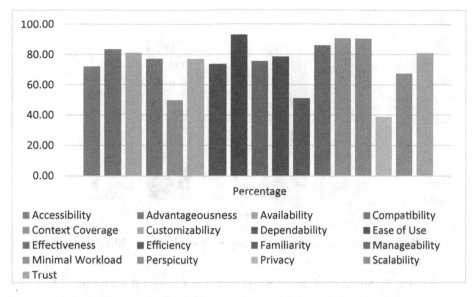

Fig. 4. Summary of study findings related to pragmatic UX dimensions

It appeared that 74.75% of study participants consider the IoT ecosystem appealing. More specifically, majority of students perceived the IoT ecosystem prototype as pleasing (88%), attractive (84%), friendly (78%), professional (76%), beautiful (74%), classy (74%), and presentable (74%) while half of the sample believe the IoT ecosystem prototype is valuable. Moreover, 78% of respondents reported the IoT ecosystem prototype encourages students networking because majority of them stated the IoT ecosystem prototype is integrating (90%), inclusive (76%), and brings students closer to each other (68%).

The results of data analysis revealed that 67.67% of study respondents reported that the IoT ecosystem prototype is distinctive among other ones. Namely, most of students find it creative (76%), innovative (72%), leading edge (70%), inventive (70%), original (64%), and unique (54%). As much as 84.29% of individuals involved in the study is happy with the IoT ecosystem prototype which is because majority of the sample agree the IoT ecosystem prototype is good (88%), likeable (88%), enjoyable (86%), pleasant (84%), meets students' expectations (84%), makes good impression (82%), and meets students' needs (78%). Finally, 72.44% of study participants agree the IoT ecosystem prototype provides stimulating effects. Namely, most of students believe the IoT ecosystem prototype encourages their concentration on task execution (90%), is supportive (86%) and interesting (86%), successfully retains students' attention (82%), is exiting (72%), motivating (72%), courageous (58%), and challenging (54%), and stimulates students' creativity (52%).

Taking into account all above, advantages of IoT ecosystem prototype with respect to hedonic UX facets are most commonly colored with satisfaction and the most sparsely with novelty. Study findings on hedonic UX aspects in the context of IoT ecosystem prototype are presented in Fig. 5.

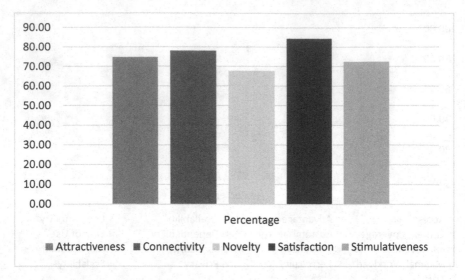

Fig. 5. Summary of study findings related to hedonic UX dimensions

When the qualitative data are considered, 38% of study participants provided 66 comments of which the same proportion (50%) were related to the benefits and to the flaws of the IoT ecosystem prototype. In the context of benefits, the IoT ecosystem prototype was perceived by study participants as all-in-one solution that includes all necessary functionalities an academic citizen requires thus representing very good idea and initiative with a potential to be employed for educational purposes and help students to achieve as much success as possible in their study. Comparison among students, monitoring sleeping pace and the quality of air, graphical representation of results, intuitive navigation and understandability, visually appealing user interface, study time average, my classes categories, and a social aspect that enables students to be better connected are the most relevant features the students reported in terms of advantages of the IoT ecosystem prototype.

On the other hand, the students expressed their concerns with respect to the privacy of data that is going to be stored in the IoT ecosystem as well as related to the functionality of comparing results with other students that could result in the opposite effect and demotivate students even further or even cause misbalance in their life habits. In addition, some of the respondents are not convinced that built-in feature of social interaction will be often used. Study participants also determined several bugs related to study marketplace, my posts, and my classes which should be addressed. Inconsistencies related to the calendar, lack of labels in active lifestyle display and graphical display of data, boring and common interface design, lack of tag search, and too much information at one place were the most often IoT ecosystem features study participants reported in terms of its disadvantages.

Finally, students suggested some additional features such as module for providing reviews on courses, faculty staff, and teaching materials, displaying each post in separate tab, schedule of lectures, digital post-it for taking notes, simplified calendar for planning learning activities, etc. All the aforementioned indicates that pros of the IoT ecosystem prototype are most commonly related to advantageousness, satisfaction, stimulativeness, and attractiveness whereas cons in the same respect are most often in relation with effectiveness, attractiveness, dependability, perspicuity, and stimulativeness. The most relevant UX facets with respect to reported advantages and disadvantages are presented in Fig. 6.

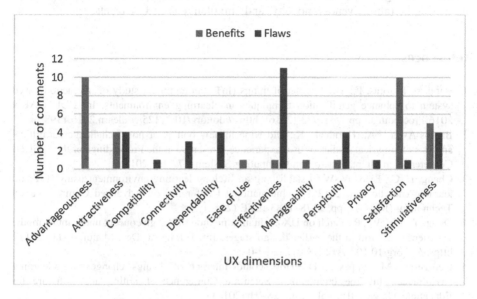

Fig. 6. Summary of study findings with respect to qualitative data obtained from students

6 Concluding Remarks

Although the IoT quickly found its application in all aspects of human activity, including education and learning, in our literature review we found no reports of using a combination of software, hardware and liveware objects (i.e. IoT ecosystem) with the aim of students' activities tracking and success prediction. Thus, in our previous research, we identified the needs, defined features and designed the architecture and structure of such system. By following the user-centered design process we also defined storyboards, wireframes and interactive prototype of Android mobile application as the only part of the ecosystem which is exposed to the end users.

As presented in this paper, the main objective of this research was to determine and examine both pragmatic and hedonic attributes that constitute UX assessment framework in the context of the introduced IoT ecosystem prototype.

Regarding evaluation of an IoT ecosystem prototype, as an outcome of literature review which included relevant studies, measuring instruments, and international standards in the field, questionnaire composed of 86 items with bipolar verbal anchors and one open-ended item was created. As a follow up, an empirical study was carried out in which students served as participants. Although there is still room for improvements, results of data analysis have shown that proposed IoT ecosystem prototype was well received by students. Taking into account together quantitative and qualitative study findings, it appears that advantages of IoT ecosystem prototype are most commonly related to 3 pragmatic (ease of use, minimal workload, and perspicuity) and 3 hedonic (attractiveness, satisfaction, and stimulativeness) UX dimensions whereas disadvantages in the same respect are associated with 6 pragmatic (context coverage, dependability, effectiveness, familiarity, perspicuity, and privacy) and 3 hedonic (attractiveness, novelty, and stimulativeness) UX facets.

References

1. Bandara, I., Ioras, F.: The internet of things (IoT): an empirical study of interaction based system to enhance gamification techniques in elearning environments. In: EDULEARN 2016 Proceedings, pp. 964–973 (2016). https://doi.org/10.21125/edulearn.2016.1198
2. Bargas-Avila, J.A., Hornbæk, K.: Old wine in new bottles or novel challenges: a critical analysis of empirical studies of user experience. Presented at the Proceedings of the SIGCHI Conference on Human Factors in Computing Systems, 7 May 2011
3. Cheng, H.-C., Liao, W.-W.: Establishing an lifelong learning environment using IOT and learning analytics. In: 2012 14th International Conference on Advanced Communication Technology (ICACT), pp. 1178–1183 IEEE (2012)
4. Dong, Y., Liu, W.: Research on UX evaluation method of design concept under multi-modal experience scenario in the earlier design stages. Int. J. Interact. Des. Manuf. 1–11 (2017). https://doi.org/10.1007/s12008-017-0393-0
5. Georgescu, M., Popescu, D.: How could Internet of Things change the e-learning environment. In: The International Scientific Conference eLearning and Software for Education, March 2016, vol. 1, pp. 68–71 (2015)
6. Gubbi, J., et al.: Internet of Things (IoT): a vision, architectural elements, and future directions. Future Gener. Comput. Syst. 29(7), 1645–1660 (2013)
7. Hassenzahl, M.: The interplay of beauty, goodness, and usability in interactive products. Hum. Comput. Interact. 19(4), 319–349 (2004)
8. Joyce, C., et al.: Building an internet of school things ecosystem. In: Proceedings of the 2014 Conference on Interaction Design and Children - IDC 2014, pp. 289–292. ACM Press (2014)
9. Kuniavsky, M.: Smart Things: Ubiquitous Computing User Experience Design. Morgan Kaufmann Publisher, Amsterdam, Boston (2010)
10. Laugwitz, B., Held, T., Schrepp, M.: Construction and evaluation of a user experience questionnaire. In: Holzinger, A. (ed.) USAB 2008. LNCS, vol. 5298, pp. 63–76. Springer, Heidelberg (2008). https://doi.org/10.1007/978-3-540-89350-9_6
11. Law, E.L.-C., Roto, V., Hassenzahl, M., Vermeeren, A.P.O.S., Kort, J.: Understanding, scoping and defining user experience: a survey approach. In: Proceedings of the SIGCHI Conference on Human Factors in Computing Systems (CHI 2009), pp. 719–728. ACM, New York (2009). https://doi.org/10.1145/1518701.1518813
12. Miorandi, D., et al.: Internet of Things: vision, applications and research challenges. Ad Hoc Netw. 10(7), 1497–1516 (2012)
13. Orehovački, T., et al.: Evaluating the perceived and estimated quality in use of Web 2.0 applications. J. Syst. Softw. 86(12), 3039–3059 (2013)

14. Orehovački, T., Babić, S., Etinger, D.: Identifying relevance of security, privacy, trust, and adoption dimensions concerning cloud computing applications employed in educational settings. In: Nicholson, D. (ed.) AHFE 2017. AISC, vol. 593, pp. 308–320. Springer, Cham (2018). https://doi.org/10.1007/978-3-319-60585-2_29
15. Orehovački, T., Babić, S.: Identifying the relevance of quality dimensions contributing to universal access of social Web applications for collaborative writing on mobile devices: an empirical study. Univ. Access Inf. Soc. (2017)
16. Plantak Vukovac, D., et al.: User experience design and architecture of IoT ecosystem employed in students' activities tracking. Presented at the 9th International Conference on Applied Human Factors and Ergonomics, Orlando, Florida (2018)
17. Roto, V., et al.: User Experience White Paper: bringing clarity to the concept of user experience. Schloss Dagstuhl-Leibniz-Zentrum fuer Informatik (2011)
18. Shin, D.-H.: Conceptualizing and measuring quality of experience of the internet of things: Exploring how quality is perceived by users. Inf. Manag. **54**, 998–1011 (2017)
19. Simic, K., et al.: A platform for a smart learning environment. Facta universitatis Ser. Electron. Energ. **29**(3), 407–417 (2016)
20. Sutcliffe, A.: Designing for user engagement: aesthetic and attractive user interfaces. Synth. Lect. Hum. Cent. Inform. **2**(1), 1–55 (2009)
21. Sward, D., Macarthur, G.: Making user experience a business strategy. In: Towards a UX Manifesto COST294-MAUSE Affiliated Workshop, Lancaster, UK, pp. 35–42 (2007)
22. Technical Committee: ISO/IEC JTC 1/SC 7 Software and systems engineering, Software and systems engineering: Systems and software engineering – Systems and software Quality Requirements and Evaluation (SQuaRE) – System and software quality models. ISO.org (2011)
23. Vermeeren, A.P.O.S., Law, E.L.-C., Roto, V., Obrist, M., Hoonhout, J., Väänänen-Vainio-Mattila, K.: User experience evaluation methods: current state and development needs. In: Proceedings of the 6th Nordic Conference on Human-Computer Interaction: Extending Boundaries (NordiCHI 2010), pp. 521–530. ACM, New York (2010). http://doi.acm.org/10.1145/1868914.1868973
24. Xia, F., et al.: Internet of Things. Int. J. Commun. Syst. **25**(9), 1101–1102 (2012)
25. Xue, R., et al.: Using the IOT to construct ubiquitous learning environment. In: 2011 Second International Conference on Mechanic Automation and Control Engineering, pp. 7878–7880 (2011)

The Digital Transformation of Teaching in Higher Education from an Academic's Point of View: An Explorative Study

Anne Thoring, Dominik Rudolph(⊠), and Raimund Vogl

University of Münster, Münster, Germany
{a.thoring, d.rudolph, r.vog}@uni-muenster.de

Abstract. The process of digitalization challenges universities worldwide, in particular the universities' IT. Qualitative interviews with lecturers were conducted to gather information on service requirements. The lecturers' experiences and suggestions demonstrate that, from their perspective, an improvement of the IT infrastructure and equipment is only secondary for the digitalization of teaching at Münster University. Instead, a centralization of information, knowledge and expertise in the field of digital teaching is required. Lecturers wish for a 'center for digitalization' which they can contact for information and practical advice on existing IT services, for counseling on digital teaching concepts, and for support in the implementation of new digitalization ideas. From the lecturers' point of view, the university's perspective on digital teaching has to change as well, overcoming baseless concerns that digitalization inevitably results in an entirely virtual university. In addition, incentive systems for excellent new forms of teaching would give more value to lecturers' efforts.

Keywords: Digitalization · Qualitative study · Higher education
Teaching

1 Introduction

While the process known as digital transformation or digitalization changes all areas of society, universities – at least in Germany – seem to be widely unaffected by now [1]. Aside from research, where the digitalization is visible in large datasets and the increasing use of informatics even in the humanities, today's studies look very similar to those in medieval times: a professor in front of his students who writes on a blackboard and students who learn from books. Even if you replace the blackboard with a beamer and books with PDFs, it is just an introduction of digital substitutes but not an alteration of the process. Nonetheless, it appears to be just a matter of time until the digital transformation fundamentally changes university life. IT services show great promise particularly for teaching and that is why the subject increasingly receives attention [2–6].

In view of the future of universities in the digital era, a discussion has started recently about the influence of social megatrends such as individualization, globalization, mobility or lifelong learning on teaching. The Internet, for example, allows for

© Springer International Publishing AG, part of Springer Nature 2018
P. Zaphiris and A. Ioannou (Eds.): LCT 2018, LNCS 10924, pp. 294–309, 2018.
https://doi.org/10.1007/978-3-319-91743-6_23

new types of courses such as MOOCs (Massive Open Online Courses) and SPOCs (Small Private Online Courses) which students can attend online wherever they are [7–11]. Lecture recordings also remove place and even time constraints [12, 13]. In consequence, every university is capable of being a global distance university and can offer courses to everyone, not just to local students [14, 15]. A higher international awareness, an intensified exchange and a better integration into the global research landscape are some of the benefits and will attract more foreign students to study on-site as well [16].

Innovative digital concepts for teaching have the potential to substantially change the way courses of studies are formed because they allow for considerably more differentiation. In an extreme case, a student could completely personalize his course of studies based on modularized teaching content [17]. Moreover, real-time feedback provides an opportunity to individually adapt the learning pace and, thereby, increase the learning success. The combination of face-to-face courses and e-learning, also known as "Blended Learning", emphasizes the lecturer's role as a trainer or moderator [18–20]. New ways of communication between students and lecturers arise and new teaching methods like serious gaming [21–23], interactive videos [24, 25] or simulation models [26, 27] enhance the learning experience.

Without doubt, the students' perspective is highly important to avoid developments that are out of touch with reality or miss the users' demands. Our first study [28] and other work in this field [e.g. 30] show that students do not expect a digital revolution of teaching but a smooth digital evolution. This is an important finding. Nonetheless, it would be a mistake to be blinkered and neglect another major player in this context: the academics. The discussion and assessment of technical capabilities and innovative ways of teaching should take into account that lecturers are heavily affected from developments in this area, too. A digital transformation in teaching would affect their everyday work and job requirements dramatically.

Therefore, this explorative study aims to give first insights into the academics' perspective on the digitalization of higher education, and – in terms of a practical purpose – identify opportunities for the improvement of existing IT services and structures at the University of Münster (WWU), one of the largest in Germany with about 50,000 students. In combination with our previous study which centers students, it also serves as a starting point to describe a full picture of different expectations and needs as well as concerns and obstacles as to the digitalization of teaching and learning.

2 Literature Review

The number of papers and studies which focus on the digitalization in higher education has increased recently. Most of them focus on the situation of students [24, 30–37]. As Cope and Ward [38] point out, not just the students' perspective is important but also the perspective of the teaching person. While a good overview of the status quo of digitalization in the US is provided by the annual ECAR studies by EDUCAUSE – quantitative surveys conducted with approximately 50,000 students [34] and 13,000 lecturers [39] –, comparable statistics from Europe are missing. In Germany, the discourse still is driven mainly by politics, not science, and in consequence publications are often working papers with a normative character or guidelines based on experts' opinions [1, 26, 40–42].

In general, most scientific studies are either very specific [27, 43, 44] or they are designed as quantitative surveys which grant an overview but no in-depth insight into the subject [34, 45, 46]. What they have in common is that they place emphasis the students' point of view on digitalization: their needs, expectations, experiences, usage behavior, preconditions, etc. This emphasis and the thought of a generation of digital natives entering university [32, 47–49] might lead to the misconception that students were the only driver behind the process of digitalization and an improvement of studying its only objective. An improvement of learning, however, is inevitably connected with an improvement of teaching – the lecturers' domain. An interesting qualitative study among Turkish academics was done by Ocak [50], who identifies eight reasons for a low usage of digital environments: complexity of the instruction, lack of planning and organization, lack of effective communication, need for more time, lack of institutional support, changing roles, difficulty of adoption to new technologies and lack of electronic means. We want to know if those problems are still relevant.

Overall, there is still a lack of studies providing insights into the experiences, wishes and opinions of academics regarding the digitalization of university life, which could, amongst other things, be harnessed for university IT.

3 Research Methodology

In the absence of recent studies describing the digitalization of universities from the students' and especially the lecturers' point of view in-depth, we planned two pilot studies to examine each perspective and subsequently compare the results. Against this background it was important to design both surveys with a parallel structure. For our first study [28], focus group interviews with students were conducted in 2017. As the method had proved successful in delivering informative results, we only had to make minor adjustments for this follow-up study which focuses on the following question: From the lecturers' point of view, to what extent is teaching in higher education already digitized and which improvements are needed?

3.1 Research Questions

To answer this question, first, it is necessary to clarify how digitized the academic studies already are from the lecturers' point of view. In order to identify concrete improvement opportunities, we need to find out which university IT services are used by academics and how they evaluate their user experience. Eventually, the study also tries to spot necessary modifications, which the university should make to stimulate the digitalization process according to its lecturers. The following three research questions (RQ) reflect these aspects:

RQ1: To what extend is teaching already digitized at present?
RQ2: How do lecturers evaluate their experience with existing IT services?

RQ3: Which changes are necessary to foster the digitalization of teaching?

Based on experiences from our first study in this field, a guided focus group interview [51–53] was chosen as a suitable research method and an existing interview guideline was adapted to structure the discussion in view of answering the research questions and produce results which are comparable with our previous findings.

3.2   Interview Instrument

The interview guideline divided the focus group interview into three sections: In the first part, the participants had to describe their experiences with the use of IT at work and for teaching purposes in particular, in order to find out which parts are already digitized and which parts are still processed offline. In this context, the lecturers also listed the IT services they used and described usage situations and problems. Finally, the participants were asked to make suggestions on how the university could simplify their work by means of IT. In the second part, the academics were asked to write down the most important IT services that the university should offer to support teaching. These suggestions were subsequently presented and classified. In the third part, the participants had to prioritize the suggested services and give reasons for their respective decisions. For this purpose, each participant could assign ten points to the mentioned services, with the possibility to assign all points to one service. A ranking list was formed based on the prioritizations.

3.3   Focus Group Interviews

Academics of Münster University were informed about the project using a mailing list aimed at all employees, the IT center's website and its Twitter profile. A sample representing the university's different departments was desired, but could not be forced due to the self-recruitment procedure. Eventually, the sample consisted of eleven academics with teaching experience from six departments, mainly natural and life sciences. The group size should not extend six persons, in order to ensure a lively exchange, enough speaking time per person and an efficient management of the discussion [51, 52]. However, due to schedule difficulties, a last minute switch had to be arranged and the final groups consisted of four and seven persons, respectively. In the run-up, participants were given very limited and general information on the subject of the study to avoid framing [52]. The survey consisted of two 1.5-h guided focus group interviews. The interviews took place on two dates within a week in December 2017. The conversations were recorded and transcribed by assistants. The data were cleansed, structured and subsequently assigned to the research questions. Significant statements were extracted and clustered into subject areas [53].

4   Findings

In this chapter, the results of the focus group interviews will be presented with regard to the research questions.

4.1   Status Quo of Digitalization

"What does the digitalization of teaching mean? What do you digitize anyway? What is the aspired goal?" Though these questions are raised by only one of the participants and not sooner than in the middle of the discussions, it is worth starting with them here. They put in a nutshell a general uncertainty about the subject as such which most of the other participants described in less concise ways as well. The university does not provide a strategy of digitalization and there are hardly any strategic or practical guidelines on the part of the departments either (with the exception of the Faculty of Medicine), leaving it up to the lecturers to find their own concept:

Participant 01: "To me, at the moment, it is the tools which you can use. But that, I think, is not per se digitalization. In fact, my vision is that teaching content can also be offered in an individualized way [...] and that can only be achieved through digital content and support."

Participant 04: "To me, digitalization is what we did analogously before. That we ported that into the digital world with the most varied possibilities."

Most participants see themselves as trailblazers who have entered largely uncharted waters. Since their orientation and testing phase is predominantly unguided, it requires a considerable investment in time and effort and, thus, dedication for the subject. Some lecturers have started to explore progressive forms of teaching on their own or are involved in small, but ambitious digitalization projects.

Participant 06: "This year, I received a Fellowship for Innovations in Digital Higher Education. Then I changed my lecture to Just-in-Time Teaching and also provided materials as open-educational resources. It was a first try for me and I am convinced that this is the way to go."

Participant 02: "I am still looking for the optimal lecture design. I always switch between chalkboard and slides, and also do online surveys and stuff like that. But I have not found the ideal way yet."

The participants also noted that the majority of their colleagues is more reluctant or even opposed to digitalization, because of nescience, insecurity or a lack of time.

Participant 05: "It is definitely something that is neglected by many and perceived as an imposition. It is very heterogeneous. Overall, it is always the most important thing that the effort is as low as possible."

Participant 02: "There will always be individuals who have been doing this in a certain way for 20 years and actually do not really understand why they should change it. I think you have to push these individuals a little, because often [their restraint is based on] ignorance and insecurity."

One thing all participants can agree on is the fact that digitalization affects all aspects of teaching – lectures, material distribution, assessment, course evaluation, communication with students and administrative task – and that the status quo of digitalization can only be described as very heterogeneous, depending on the department, the chair and the individual lecturer.

Classic lectures and seminars with PowerPoint presentations and PDF handouts are still the normal case, but video content, audience response systems (e.g. Kahoot!, PINGO, TurningPoint, and the university's own system ZIVinteraktiv) and digital devices (e.g. smartphones and tablets) have conquered many lecture rooms as well.

Lecture recordings are currently tested by some of the participants and have resulted in ambivalent opinions. On the one hand, academics value that students can choose the time and speed of reception, but on the other hand, they doubt that students understand these offers to be supplementary and use them in an efficient way.

Participant 01: "I have recorded my lecture [...] and use the extra time for exercises in form of chalk and talk. I have made very positive experiences with that. [...] Now everyone can choose their own pace and time for reception."

Participant 01: "But if you offer too much digitally, students no longer use it as an additional offer."

Participant 08: "In the week before the exam [...] [students] suddenly start to watch the lecture. This is of course extremely inefficient."

Even though lecture recordings implicate a substantial expenditure of time and effort, at least initially, they also open up time slots for alternative and more progressive forms of teaching, such as Flipped Classroom or Just-in-Time-Teaching. One participant noted changes at the department in this regard, another one had made first experiences himself.

Participant 09: "Overall, there is a lot of movement in medicine as far as teaching formats are concerned, and there is also a lot of commitment to use digital media and carry out more Inverted Classroom projects."

Participant 06: "I have tried Just-in-Time Teaching. It is like Flipped Classroom, where learning actually happens during self-study. In my opinion the lecture itself is not very suitable for knowledge transfer [...]."

While these approaches promise additional benefits in teaching and learning, lecturers do not define all tendencies of digitalization per se as progressive. They notice that not all students are digitally savvy yet and not all content is suitable for digital teaching formats.

Participant06: "Even when I thought something was easy [...], there were regularly catastrophic results. Not until then did I notice that I had already left most of the students behind and consequently there was no substantive discussion."

Participant10: "Some things have to be touched and written manually; otherwise the transfer will not take place. When you develop something digitally, students start to wait until you are done and take a photo of it."

Seemingly outdated formats or equipment, on the other hand, are not condemned but used on purpose.

Participant 02: "In introductory lectures, [...] I use the blackboard, because I have the feeling that the pace is slowed down."

When it comes to lecture materials, PDF handouts have become an established format for lecture notes and are distributed either via the university's e-learning platform Learnweb or via the department's website. Due to a special need for multimedia documents, one work group also produced e-books with iBook Author and InDesign as well as educational videos.

Participant 01: "We use Learnweb for everything in terms of communication with students. All materials are there."

Participant 07: "All videos of sports exercises that we do are uploaded to YouTube. [...] Apart from that, we implemented a lot of curricula in form of digital e-books which include videos, image series and texts, and which we distribute not through a store but via upload."

E-assessment is of little importance in most disciplines, but has become a standard at the Department of Medicine where exams are usually multiple-choice. Since there is a lot of criticism of multiple-choice test, e-assessment procedures are currently refined to be able to test practical knowledge (e.g. by using a digital microscope).

Unlike exams, course evaluations are mostly digitized, using various tools such as EVALuna, EvaSys, Unipark or Qualtrics. The conversion from paper to digital questionnaires does not always run smoothly though. While digital questionnaires can be answered quickly and comfortably on the smartphone, students feel less obliged to participate compared to paper questionnaires that are completed and handed it at the end of the course. Moreover, the existing questionnaires do not yet reflect the current transition from analogue to digital formats and are often useless in consequence.

Participant 01: "We have just switched from paper to electronic. Thereby the response rate has decreased dramatically."

Participant 01: "Due to the fact that I work with recordings now, the standard questionnaire [...] no longer fits. 'The lecturer was prepared.' Well, if it is a lecture recording, what should I tick? And now there are other forms of interaction that are not reproducible at all."

The lecturers perform administrative tasks – including exam administration, teaching reports and lecture room bookings – very reluctantly, because most bureaucratic processes are only partially digitized, and the resulting parallel structures are perceived as an additional burden and annoyance instead of a relief. Especially the booking of rooms is looked upon unfavorably, because of various systems and unclear responsibilities. The Medical Department is the only department where the administrative staff is solely responsible for allocating rooms, while lecturers are not involved in this task.

Participant 08: "Of what use is the greatest room management system, [...] if the person in charge does not use it at all or only halfway?"

Participant 01: "Booking rooms is a nightmare. I do not even do that myself, I always ask our secretary. [...] You cannot make a proper request. Instead, you must call someone who makes a request for you and who gets a reply two days later if the room is still available. I think it is a disaster."

At the end of each term, all lecturers must submit a teaching report documenting their lectures and seminars. Compiling this report is a task that has to be done digitally. Nonetheless, the administrative machinery is unable to process the report digitally as well which leads to irritation among the participants.

Participant 08: "The digitalization of the administration is a disaster. [...] When it comes to [...] teaching reports it is an idiocy: I compile a teaching report in a truly great system. [...] Then I print a few versions and send them to the deanery by internal mail. The deanery files some versions and sends the rest to the central administration by internal mail. [...] The administration completely lacks an understanding of digitalization and of IT processes."

Participant 02: "You simply have to avoid media discontinuities on such platforms. The necessity to still print and sign documents should simply not exist anymore."

In summary, the academics conclude that the digitalization at Münster University has developed inconsistently in different departments and different tasks areas, and has not progressed far enough yet (RQ1). Most participants see themselves as progressive with regard to digital teaching, despite having just entered a testing phase. This suggests that many lecturers are not yet dealing with the subject of digitalization at all. Audience response systems are increasingly used by the participants to diversify lectures and create interaction, but lecture recordings or new lecture designs such as the Flipped Classroom concept are still exceptions. Lecture materials (i.e. lecture notes and literature) are usually distributed in PDF format via e-learning platforms. E-assessment is of little importance in most disciplines, but course evaluations are mostly digitized. Administrative tasks (e.g. exam administration, teaching reports and room bookings) are only partially digitized, leading to frustration among the lecturers because they are confronted with parallel structures.

4.2 User Experiences with IT Services

Bearing in mind that most participants characterize themselves as pioneers of digitalization in their respective departments, it seems unlikely that university systems would meet all demands of their everyday work. Therefore, we were interested in their experiences and satisfaction with existing IT services.

The use of some of the university's IT tools is almost inevitable and it is no surprise that participants primarily discuss the most common services, including the e-learning platform Learnweb and the exam registration system QISPOS. Rather new offers such as the cloud storage service sciebo and the audience response system ZIVinteraktiv are mentioned as well. Other university services are of little or no importance in the discussion (e.g. standard software, printing service, e-mail service, communication infrastructure, and websites).

Overall, participants are satisfied with the e-learning platform Learnweb which they primarily use to distribute lecture notes and materials. However, they also note that they are far from exploiting the possibilities of the platform due to a lack of experience and a lack of time to familiarize themselves with its functionalities. In addition, when it comes to video material, the platform seems to meet its limits, making it questionable if it is suitable for distributing lecture recordings in the current state.

Participant 10: "Once you are familiar with it, it is relatively easy to upload something and update it. Nevertheless, you have to find the time to [...] look into it in advance. That is one reason why it may not be as widespread as it could be. At least the basics are really comprehensible, even to [...] normal end users."

Participant 07: "There is no course that is not supported by Learnweb. However, in 95% of the cases it is limited to download options, PDF and literature uploads, the assignment of tasks and the use of the mailing list. But we do not use it for interactive teaching, because we do not have any experience with it."

Participant 07: "[With regard to video content], Learnweb is complicated. It takes a long time to upload something. That is why we used YouTube."

While an intensive use of YouTube appears to be an exception, Dropbox was the most frequently used cloud service among employees until recently [54]. In 2015, the university launched the private cloud storage system sciebo to provide an alternative

302   A. Thoring et al.

that was in line with data security and privacy policies. Though the majority has adopted this alternative, two participants report that other solutions are still in use at their departments (ownCloud and Google Docs which is fully integrated into Google Drive). If sciebo is used, participants have made predominantly good experiences. However, the service seems to be more suitable for research than teaching and is sometimes neglected due to the Learnweb.

Participant 05: "Our experiences are very positive. [...] The size of our genomics data gets very big rapidly and here it is very suitable. In my opinion, sciebo is very fast and it is easy to share things – which is good and very convenient."

Participant 04: "Sciebo is a service we use a lot. It is very good. And we are allowed to store certain materials [...] for teaching there."

Participant 02: "I hardly use sciebo in teaching. If I upload stuff, then via Learnweb or websites."

While the Learnweb and sciebo receive overall positive evaluations, the exam administration system QISPOS has the greatest potential for improvement from the lecturers' point of view. At the moment, using the system is perceived as laborious and even impossible in parts. One of the departments uses FlexNow as an alternative which is not integrated into other university systems either, but perceived as convenient.

Participant 02: "QISPOS is very, very, very difficult – meaning cumbersome – to use. [...] As regards the integration of QISPOS and Learnweb: They have absolutely nothing to do with each other."

Participant 08: "I am completely doing a blind flight in QISPOS: I do not know who is registered for the exam, I cannot enter the grades, I do not see anything. I have to have my own systems inevitably. [QISPOS] does not work at all."

As regards communication services, lecturers show a significantly different user behavior than the students questioned in our previous study [28]: While students need services to coordinate groups and make use of the same commercial networks and communication tools they favor for private purposes (i.e. Facebook, WhatsApp and Skype), the participants completely withdraw from these media in their role as lecturers. Forums, wikis and blogs are not used for communication purposes either; instead e-mail and personal communication dominate.

Participant 01: "I do not want to be permanently available to students."

Participant01: "I used Skype before. I would not do that again. [...] It was an absolute chaos. The questions came so fast that I could not answer and it was pure stress."

To make lectures more interactive, all participants looked into audience response systems. Since the university's own app, ZIVinteraktiv, is widely unknown and perceived as limited in its functionalities, commercial apps, including Kahoot! and TurningPoint, as well other university's in-house developments, including PINGO and ARSnova, were heavily tested. According to the participants, Kahoot! is time-consuming in preparation and execution, and PINGO is rather complicated. ARSnova, on the other hand, was not criticized.

In summary, the discussion about the quality of existing IT systems and services (RQ2) was rather brief and focused on a limited number of tools. Overall, the users' experiences are ambivalent. The university's e-learning platform and cloud storage service are considered exemplary, even if most participant do not have the time to delve into their functionalities and use their full potential. QISPOS, the university's exam administration tool, is criticized in many ways and cited as an example for complicated administration tools and laborious bureaucratic processes. Lecturers would highly welcome an elimination of parallel structures and media disruptions as well as a reduction of bureaucracy.

4.3 Need for Improvement

The lecturers' suggestions for improvement can be divided into six categories: university strategy, information policy, lecture content, lecture administration, equipment and infrastructure, and others (Table 1). By prioritizing the suggestions, individual opinions were filtered out and a clear favorite could be identified. To foster the digitalization of teaching, lecturers need practical support in creating digital content (34 of 110 points).

Table 1. Prioritization of ideas for improvement

	G1	G2	Total
University Strategy	0	13	**13**
Incentive systems for excellent (digital) teaching			
Digital teaching strategy			
Information Policy	11	12	**23**
Central contact point			
Exchange with experts			
Exchange with other academics			
Visibility of existing tools & services			
Newsletter "Digital Teaching"			
Lecture Content	18	16	**34**
Central support office			
Support in video recording			
Support in creating digital teaching materials			
Support in legal questions (e.g. copyright)			
Lecture Administration	5	9	**11**
Equipment and Infrastructure	1	18	**19**
Software, hardware & media equipment			
Integration of central IT services			
Other	5	2	**7**
Total	40	70	**110**

Participant 07: "Many do not have the know-how. They know the content, but nothing about filming, cutting, or using InDesign – there must be support. You should be able to go somewhere with the content and say: This has to be implemented digitally."

Participant 01: "If you take the step towards a digitalization of teaching, didactic questions are raised as well – I am not trained for that. I think challenges of a very different nature will come up to the university and that should be reflected as well."

Moreover, lecturers require centralized information on existing IT tools and services, that is to say a more effective information policy (23 of 110 points). Currently, there is no overview of existing possibilities in digital teaching, no directory with contact persons, and rarely any exchange of information among lecturers. This lack of information and transparency leads to an unnecessary expenditure of work.

Participant 01: "I think that the information policy could be substantially improved. [...] I think you need central solutions."

Participant 04: "You just have to show what is possible and I can guarantee that many will say: I have always wanted it that way."

Both tasks, information and practical support, should be performed by a central contact point and support office: a 'center for digital teaching'.

Participant 02: "I would like to have such a center for digital teaching for advice. [...] It could organize the search for ideas and simple tools, and, of course, offer training and further education in this field."

Interestingly, none of the participant mentioned the ZHLdigital, the university's center for digital teaching, which was reconstituted recently and is supposed to exactly fulfill those tasks. A statement made by one of the participant in a different context fits perfectly here: "Probably it already exists and we just do not know it." It sums up that information and communication need to be intensified considerably to establish such an institution. The center needs to approach the lecturers actively to become known.

Furthermore, the participants want to initiate a rethinking of the university's appreciation of digital teaching. They consider it a cliché and an obsolete argument that digital forms of teaching would supersede classroom teaching and create a solely virtual university. On the contrary, they expect an enhancement of classroom teaching beyond basic knowledge transfer by means of an increased interaction and discussion. Therefore, teaching should be revalued by introducing incentives similar to those existing for excellent research.

Participant 01: "After 6 years, I am not measured by whether I had a great digital lecture, but by the number of my publications."

Participant 02: "I think an incentive system for improved teaching is quite appropriate – to encourage young scientists in this regard."

In summary, a digitized university is not equivalent to a virtual university but definitely implicates significant changes in teaching, from the lecturers' point of view. These changes should be reflected in the university's strategy and structure in form of incentives as well as a central point of contact, information and practical support (RQ3). These expectations already go beyond the students' picture of a digitized university which is rather pragmatic [28]: Students do not ask for a fundamental change of teaching and studying, but prioritize an integration and standardization of existing IT services. In concrete terms, they expect a portal which merges the most important information and tools. The academics agree that an integration of the basic structures could already be an enormous improvement, but they do not highlight this aspect.

5 Conclusion

This study was designed as an explorative pilot study to gain first insights into the digitalization of teaching from an academic's point of view. Naturally, these insights are subjective assessments and therefore not representative. Moreover, the results have to be evaluated in relation to the specific situation at Münster University and are not necessarily transferable to other universities. Nonetheless, we are convinced that the study complements our examination of the students' perspective [28] in a meaningful way and provides valuable information, especially for those involved in university management, administration and IT. We are aware that additional focus groups with lecturers from the humanities and social sciences are necessary to complete the picture. Subsequent quantitative surveys with both groups, lecturers and students, would allow testing the validity of the results and supporting them in a representative way.

Lecturers describe the status quo of digitalization (RQ1) as very heterogeneous, depending not only on the department, the chair and the individual lecturer, but also on the task area – a result which is generally in line with the students' experiences [28]. However, when it comes to the details, certain differences in the perceptions of both groups are revealed. Academics describe their current situation as a testing and ori-entation phase. Digital tools such as audience response systems have found their way into lectures, but lecture recordings as well as new lecture designs and formats (e.g. Flipped Classroom, Just-In-Time-Teaching) are exceptions. This coincides with the findings of Ocak [50]. Students do not elaborate on this topic, which suggests that digital lectures do rarely or not at all occur in their studies. Insofar, the experiences of both groups reflect that digitalization has not yet changed lectures fundamentally. In general, students welcome lecture recordings or interactive elements as additional possibilities, but do not claim them insistently. Academics, on the other hand, are more eager to experiment with new forms of teaching and learning, and, unlike students, do not consider classic chalk and talk lectures as future-oriented. As regards lecture materials, academics usually provide lecture notes and literature in PDF format and distribute them via e-learning platforms. In contrast, students report that digital formats and the Learnweb indeed gain in importance, but printed scripts are still very common, too. E-assessment is of little importance in most disciplines, but course evaluations are mostly digitized. When performing administrative tasks (e.g. exam administration, teaching reports, room bookings), lecturers are confronted with parallel structures, because relevant processes are only partially digitized. The students also recognize this heterogeneity, stating that the registration for exams is largely digitized, while the administration of the examination results is largely paper-based.

The academics do not discuss the quality of existing IT services (RQ2) extensively, but have quite clear opinions: The university's e-learning platform and cloud storage service are considered to be exemplary, while the exam administration tool QISPOS is criticized for being complicated and laborious. In this context, lecturers recommend an elimination of parallel structures and media disruptions. Students, on the other hand, have very high requirements due to commercial models and believe that university services cannot compete, in particular with regard to the ease of use and the interface design. As a matter of principle, university systems have an image problem among students [28] and some are not even given a try if commercial alternatives exist.

When comparing the lecturers' with the students' focus group interviews [28], it is evident that the discussions differed considerably: Students have a rather conservative opinion as to a digital university and understand digitalization primarily as the digital provision of lecture notes, the digital organization of their studies and online interaction possibilities. Since these basics already exist, their discussion of improvement opportunities (RQ3) centered on the optimization and technical integration of existing IT services. Due to their comparatively progressive attitude, lecturers, on the other hand, discussed strategical and structural changes that would facilitate a digitalization of teaching and enable new teaching formats. Their vision is much closer to a reformation of university teaching. In consequence, they do not primarily request an improvement of the IT infrastructure and equipment, but a clear direction of the university and a centralization of information, knowledge and expertise in the field of digital teaching. A 'center for digitalization' could bring together relevant players, including IT professionals and didactics experts, to provide information and practical advice on existing IT services, offer counseling on digital teaching concepts, and support lecturers in the implementation of new digitalization ideas.

Ultimately, however, the lecturers' perspective is differentiated: Even though the participants are eager to experiment with digital approaches, a digitalization of teaching is not seen per se as the future of teaching, but rather as a means to an end. To them the basic question is: "In what way do we want to teach our students in the future and what way is best?" They agree that concepts are crucial and whether they are digital or not is a completely different question. At this point, lecturers expect the university to develop and implement a future-oriented and visionary teaching strategy that also values extraordinary commitment and excellence in teaching.

References

1. Dräger, J., Friedrich, J.-D., Müller-Eiselt, R.: Digital as the New Normal - How Digitalisation is Changing Higher Education. Centrum für Hochschulentwicklung gGmbH, Gütersloh (2014)
2. Bowen, W.G.: Higher Education in the Digital Age. Princeton University Press, Princeton (2013)
3. Brown-Martin, G., Tavakolian, N.: Learning {re}imagined: How the Connected Society Is Transforming Learning. Bloomsbury Academic, an imprint of Bloomsbury Publishing Plc, London, New York (2014)
4. Craig, R.: The technology of higher education. TechCrunch (2016)
5. Hochschulforum Digitalisierung: Diskussionspapier: 20 Thesen zur Digitalisierung der Hochschulbildung. Berlin (2015)
6. Hanna, N.: Mastering Digital Transformation. Towards A Smarter Society, Economy, City and Nation. Emerald Publishing, Bingley (2016)
7. Marks, L., McFadden, D., Shuttleworth, E., Glasgow, K.: Students as educators: enhancing medical education through MOOC Creation (2017)
8. Rieber, L.P.: Participation patterns in a massive open online course (MOOC) about statistics. Br. J. Educ. Technol. **48**, 1295–1304 (2017)

9. Deng, J.: Research on Higher Vocational Students' Acceptance and Use of MOOC in Web Software Development Course. Boletín Técnico (2017). ISSN 0376-723X 55
10. Fox, A.: Can MOOCs and SPOCs Help scale residential education while maintaining high quality? In: MOOCs and Their Afterlives: Experiments in Scale and Access in Higher Education, p. 37 (2017)
11. Muñoz-Merino, P.J., Rodríguez, E.M., Kloos, C.D., Ruipérez-Valiente, J.A.: Design, implementation and evaluation of SPOCs at the Universidad Carlos III de Madrid. J. Univers. Comput. Sci. 23, 167–186 (2017)
12. O'Callaghan, F.V., Neumann, D.L., Jones, L., Creed, P.A.: The use of lecture recordings in higher education: a review of institutional, student, and lecturer issues. Educ. Inf. Technol. 22, 399–415 (2017)
13. Ollermann, F., Rolf, R., Greweling, C., Klaßen, A.: Principles of successful implementation of lecture recordings in higher education. Interact. Technol. Smart Educ. 14, 2–13 (2017)
14. Heflin, H., Shewmaker, J., Nguyen, J.: Impact of mobile technology on student attitudes, engagement, and learning. Comput. Educ. 107, 91–99 (2017)
15. Zhang, L.-C., Worthington, A.C.: Scale and scope economies of distance education in Australian universities. Stud. High. Educ. 42, 1785–1799 (2017)
16. Voogt, J., Knezek, G., Christensen, R., Lai, K.W., Pratt, K., Albion, P., Tondeur, J., Webb, M., Ifenthaler, D., Gibson, D.G. (eds.): The International Handbook of Information Technology in Primary and Secondary Education, Part 2. Association for the Advancement of Computing in Education (AACE), Chesapeake (2017)
17. Shaheen, S., Khatoon, S.: Impact of ICT enriched modular approach on academic achievement of biology students. J. Res. Reflect. Educ. (JRRE) 11, 49–59 (2017)
18. Horn, M.B., Fisher, J.F.: New faces of blended learning. Educ. Leadersh. 74, 59–63 (2017)
19. Scott, D., Ribeiro, J., Burns, A., Danyluk, P., Bodnaresko, S.: A review of the literature on academic writing supports and instructional design approaches within blended and online learning environments (2017)
20. Rodríguez-Triana, M.J., Prieto, L.P., Vozniuk, A., Boroujeni, M.S., Schwendimann, B.A., Holzer, A., Gillet, D.: Monitoring, awareness and reflection in blended technology enhanced learning: a systematic review. Int. J. Technol. Enhanc. Learn. 9, 126–150 (2017)
21. Lameras, P., Arnab, S., Dunwell, I., Stewart, C., Clarke, S., Petridis, P.: Essential features of serious games design in higher education: linking learning attributes to game mechanics. Br. J. Educ. Technol. 48, 972–994 (2017)
22. Willis, J., Greenhalgh, S., Nadolny, L., Liu, S., Aldemir, T., Rogers, S., Trevathan, M., Hopper, S., Oliver, W. (eds.): Exploring the rules of the game: games in the classroom, game-based learning, gamification, and simulations. In: Association for the Advancement of Computing in Education (AACE) (2017)
23. Barr, M.: Student attitudes to games-based skills development: learning from video games in higher education. Comput. Hum. Behav. 80, 283–294 (2018)
24. Henderson, M., Selwyn, N., Finger, G., Aston, R.: Students' everyday engagement with digital technology in university: exploring patterns of use and 'usefulness'. J. High. Educ. Policy Manag. 37, 308–319 (2015)
25. Meseguer-Martinez, A., Ros-Galvez, A., Rosa-Garcia, A.: Satisfaction with online teaching videos: a quantitative approach. Innov. Educ. Teach. Int. 54, 62–67 (2017)
26. Maurer, H., Engelmann, C.: Aktives Lernen durch EU Simulationen: Eine kritische Auseinandersetzung mit Erfahrungen an der Universität Maastricht. In: Muno, W., Niemann, A., Guasti, P. (eds.) Europa spielerisch erlernen. PB, pp. 181–202. Springer, Wiesbaden (2018). https://doi.org/10.1007/978-3-658-17463-7_10

27. Englund, C., Olofsson, A.D., Price, L.: Teaching with technology in higher education: understanding conceptual change and development in practice. High. Educ. Res. Dev. **36**, 73–87 (2016)
28. Rudolph, D., Thoring, A., Remfert, C., Vogl, R.: A requirements engineering process for user centered it services – gathering service requirements for the university of the future. In: Marcus, A., Wang, W. (eds.) DUXU 2017, Part III. LNCS, vol. 10290, pp. 275–293. Springer, Cham (2017). https://doi.org/10.1007/978-3-319-58640-3_20
29. Thoring, A., Rudolph, D., Vogl, R.: Digitalization of higher education from a student's point of view. In: EUNIS 2017 – Shaping the Digital Future of Universities, pp. 279–288. European University Information Systems Organization (EUNIS), Münster (2017)
30. Wilms, K.L., Meske, C., Stieglitz, S., Decker, H., Froehlich, L., Jendrosch, N., Schaulies, S., Vogl, R., Rudolph, D.: Digital transformation in higher education – new cohorts, new requirements? In: Proceedings of the 23rd Americas Conference on Information Systems (AMCIS) (2017)
31. Smale, M.A., Regalado, M.: Recommendations for technology in higher education. In: Smale, M.A., Regalado, M. (eds.) Digital Technology as Affordance and Barrier in Higher Education, pp. 73–87. Springer, Cham (2017). https://doi.org/10.1007/978-3-319-48908-7_5
32. Bennett, S., Maton, K.: Beyond the 'digital natives' debate: towards a more nuanced understanding of students' technology experiences. J. Comput. Assist. Learn. **26**, 321–331 (2010)
33. Chen, B., Seilhamer, R., Benett, L.: Students' mobile learning practices in higher education: a multi-year study. https://er.educause.edu/articles/2015/6/students-mobile-learning-practices-in-higher-education-a-multiyear-study
34. Dahlstrom, E.: ECAR study of undergraduate students and information technology (2015)
35. Henderson, M., Selwyn, N., Aston, R.: What works and why? Student perceptions of 'useful' digital technology in university teaching and learning. Stud. High. Educ. **42**, 1567–1579 (2015)
36. Selwyn, N.: Digital downsides: exploring university students' negative engagements with digital technology. Teach. High. Edu. **21**, 1006–1021 (2016)
37. Conole, G., de Laat, M., Dillon, T., Darby, J.: 'Disruptive technologies', 'pedagogical innovation': What's new? Findings from an in-depth study of students' use and perception of technology. Comput. Educ. **50**, 511–524 (2008)
38. Cope, C., Ward, P.: Integrating learning technology into classrooms: the importance of teachers' perceptions. Educ. Technol. Soc. **5**, 67–74 (2002)
39. Brooks, C.: ECAR study of faculty and information technology. Research Report, Louisville, CO (2015)
40. Hochschulforum Digitalisierung: Discussion Paper. 20 Theses on Digital Teaching and Learning in Higher Eduation. Working Paper No. 18, Berlin (2016)
41. Bischof, L., Friedrich, J.-D., Müller, U., Müller-Eiselt, R., von Stuckrad, T.: Die schlafende Revolution - Zehn Thesen zur Digitalisierung der Hochschullehre. Centrum für Hochschulentwicklung gGmbH, Gütersloh
42. Brown, M.: Six trajectories for digital technology in higher education. http://er.educause.edu/articles/2015/6/six-trajectories-for-digital-technology-in-higher-education
43. Delcore, H., Teniente-Matson, C., Mullooly, J.: The continuum of student IT use in campus spaces: a qualitative study. https://er.educause.edu/articles/2014/8/the-continuum-of-student-it-use-in-campus-spaces-a-qualitative-study
44. McKnight, K., O'Malley, K., Ruzic, R., Horsley, M.K., Franey, J.J., Bassett, K.: Teaching in a digital age: how educators use technology to improve student learning. J. Res. Technol. Educ. **48**, 194–211 (2016)

45. Dahlstrom, E., Brooks, C., Bichsel, J.: The Current Ecosystem of Learning Management Systems in Higher Education: Student, Faculty, and IT Perspectives, Louisville, CO (2014)
46. Dahlstrom, E., Bichsel, J.: ECAR study of undergraduate students and information technology, 2014. Research Report (2014)
47. Margaryan, A., Littlejohn, A., Vojt, G.: Are digital natives a myth or reality? University students' use of digital technologies. Comput. Educ. 56, 429–440 (2011)
48. Jones, C., Shao, B.: The net generation and digital natives: implications for higher education. York (2011)
49. Lei, J.: Digital natives as preservice teachers. J. Comput. Teach. Educ. 25, 87–97 (2009)
50. Ocak, M.A.: Why are faculty members not teaching blended courses? Insights from faculty members. Comput. Educ. 56, 689–699 (2011)
51. Prickarz, H., Urbahn, J.: Qualitative Datenerhebung mit Online-Fokusgruppen. Plan. Anal. 28, 63–70 (2002)
52. Schulz, M., Mack, B., Renn, O.: Fokusgruppen in der empirischen Sozialwissenschaft: Von der Konzeption bis zur Auswertung. VS Verlag für Sozialwissenschaften, Wiesbaden (2012). https://doi.org/10.1007/978-3-531-19397-7
53. Ruddat, M.: Auswertung von Fokusgruppen mittels Zusammenfassung zentraler Diskussionsaspekte. In: Schulz, M., Mack, B., Renn, O. (eds.) Fokusgruppen in der empirischen Sozialwissenschaft, pp. 195–206. VS Verlag für Sozialwissenschaften, Wiesbaden (2012). https://doi.org/10.1007/978-3-531-19397-7_10
54. Stieglitz, S., Meske, C., Vogl, R., Rudolph, D.: Demand for cloud services as an infrastructure in higher education. In: 35th International Conference on Information Systems. Building a Better World Through Information Systems. Auckland, New Zealand (2014)

Hierarchy Design of Online Education in Colleges and Universities

Xumin Wu[✉] and Danni Su

Wuhan University of Technology, No. 122, LuoShi Road, Wuhan, China
wu_xumin@whut.edu.cn

Abstract. Aims: Deep analysis of conditions and status of online education in Colleges and universities, combing the current China online education mode design content and features, establish the orientation of teachers' design of online education system, puts forward the hierarchical design elements of online education, the online education into virtuous circle of sustainable development. Method: Subdivide the needs of the constituents and defining the design orientation of an online education system; Design teacher needs by comparing the incentive mechanism of content providers in the network community; through the hierarchical design, decomposition level design content, and gradually realize the design elements of the system of parties from basic needs to self-value realization. Conclusion: From the system design method, analysis of the needs of the parties, in accordance with the requirements of the physical layer, security layer, respect for self-realization layer order, establish the University Online Education hierarchical design framework, especially given special attention to the demand of university teachers.

Keywords: Online education · Hierarchy design · Design elements

1 Introduction

Online education, also known as distance education, online learning, is defined as the use of information technology and Internet technology for content dissemination and rapid learning methods. In 2015, the state-supported higher education online education development [1], its core lies in the use of public service platform, the high-quality teaching resources information integration, formed mainly with disciplines for the wider audience in the form of education. Online education will break through the existing teaching mode of higher education, promote the new teaching management system, form a new teaching form, and expand the ability and means of teaching management. In online education, the classroom model and the method of communication between students and teachers turn from offline to the whole or part of the line. Network teaching, teachers are faced with more accurate content of teaching, subdivision, teaching form, self and openness combination, the teaching team needs increased, teaching experience and the past will have a big difference and other issues. The evaluation indexes of teachers and students are converted into curriculum click rate, online time length, courseware and question and answer update rate. Compared with the traditional teaching mode, online education system design needs to meet the needs of all interested parties, which not only satisfies the basic requirements of system operation, but also mobilizes all kinds of initiatives to form a virtuous cycle development of online education.

2 Online Education Background and Current Status

Online education to meet the personal development and diversification of lifelong learning, the design of online education must network around the electronic environment which includes communication technology and computer technology, computer technology, artificial intelligence, network technology and multimedia technology, Online education system design includes elements such as online education content, management environment responsible for learning process and network-based community composed by learners, content developers and experts. From MIT's online course open plan (OCW) in 2001 to the 2012 large-scale online open course (MOOC), it is popular all over the world. Many universities have done many researches on curriculum design, development and implementation. Document [2] examines the current situation of online education in China. In the analysis of existing problems, it is mentioned that interaction is not strong enough to reflect the central position of learners, but not enough attention to vertical market. It is suggested that strategies should be put forward separately from macro policy level and micro teaching methods. The study [3] of Japanese online education development present situation, pointed out that Japan's demand for online education courses must be as close as possible to the classroom teaching form, such as to ensure long, teacher-student communication, assessment report, in order to incorporate education existing laws and regulations, which makes online education setting limits. Garrison [4], a Canadian scholar, found that online education is very easy to give students a lack of social presence, cognitive Presence and teaching presence. Dr. SQE's [5] online education in the United States in the process of cultivation, set the executive sponsor, jointly undertake the guidance of online education, duty is to stimulate students' learning motivation, to guide students to determine the degree thesis, helping students to obtain facilities, data, objects of investigation and other external conditions needed for research. Compared to the large-scale MOOC education, some scholars have put forward a small range of online education curriculum [6–8]. SPOC small-scale restrictive access online courses mainly for students on college campuses, SPOC originated from teachers' dissatisfaction with the existing teaching materials and teaching methods. This model redefines the role of teachers and innovates the teaching model. Let the teachers return to the campus more, stimulate the teachers' enthusiasm for teaching and the vitality of the class. Kang [9], a Chinese scholar, analyzed the idea and practice of SPOC, and made a further exploration for the practice of online education.

Online education started earlier in Chinese training industry, through the method of the teaching methods, increase teachers number, training time and place to make relatively more flexible, reduces the cost of teaching. Online courses expand the teaching space and high-quality resource income group, are easy to achieve the personal development of different students. At present, online courses are not new courses or subjects. Under the auspices of the keynote teacher, the offline professional courses will be transformed online, which will supplement the school curriculum. The results show that the effectiveness of online courses is not high, in which teaching has a direct impact on social existence and cognitive existence [10]. The integration of online courses in Colleges and universities has obstacles in the course selection, the development mechanism and the adaptability of the new teaching model [11]. One way teaching video, teaching method single design link, interactive link and free question link, the lack of education guidance. Due to the factors of selection mechanism, interaction between teachers and students are more inclined to "Acquaintances" (with the school teachers and students) interaction, and will be through the third party communication mode; course update frequency is not high, increasing the workload of teachers, enthusiasm is not high.

3   Online Education in Colleges and Universities

Colleges and universities have more professional advantages of online education content design, and the network platform can help colleges and universities to increase the students, and is no longer limited by the time and place of learning. The most important group of online education in Colleges and universities is university teachers, learners and management organizers. There is a great difference between the three needs in the same system, but at the same time, they are closely related. This distinction between the various needs of users, design effective, in order to explore the feasible methods for the sustainable development of colleges and universities online education, to achieve convergence with the national education system, promote the University of foreign brand effect, to improve the teaching quality of the school, reduce the cost of teaching.

3.1   Orientation of Online Education Design in Colleges and Universities

As an open educational system, The online course in Colleges and universities is not only a simple way to transplant offline courses, but also an integrated service information system with content as the core, pooling of open resources and joint interaction. In this system, students will obtain resources they want; teachers will obtain a Career platform to enhance the popularity of influence to expand the impact through providing learning resources; system administrators will get more and more people participate in the quality course group. A good university online course is a comprehensive service system with a wide range of services that takes the discipline system as the center, including the discipline team, the teaching assistance team and the stable, safe network environment, which can provide valuable content for three parties. The design of the system, whether in personal growth, career planning or organizational structure, should be hierarchically and orderly designed, so that the system can enter a virtuous circle steadily and stably.

With the development of online education, the content of courses is becoming richer and richer, and the forms of expression are becoming more and more diverse. It is urgent to sort out the needs of users, the interfaces among users, and the extension mechanism. It is possible to gather high-quality curriculum resources, high-quality network resources and talent pool information resources in colleges and universities through the hierarchy design of online course system platform from the perspective of demand hierarchy. This trend conforms to the characteristics of contemporary science and technology, in the context of the integration of information network innovation, the final professional research results, through offline courses and online courses beneficial combination, faster display to the majority of scholars, thus creating a new way of learning and a good learning experience.

3.2   Teacher Design Orientation in Online Education System

A large number of online education research, from the perspective of solving curriculum settings, mobilizing students' enthusiasm and obtaining social recognition, has little direct orientation for teachers. The MOOC model pays more attention to the academic achievement of teachers, and the SPOC model turns to arouse the teachers' enthusiasm for teaching. The online education system is similar to the longer developing virtual network community, and the role of teachers in the system is similar to the network resource uploads in the community, and the teaching content, the answer design and the assessment design in the online education course are all provided and founded by the teachers. It is the identity of the opinion leader. The study of the effective positioning incentive mechanism established by the network resource uploads can be used as a reference for the design and positioning of the online education system teachers.

The intrinsic strength of individual growth and development is motivation, and the most commonly used framework for classifying motivations of virtual community is the difference between internal and external motivation (von Krogh et al. 2012) based on self-determination (SDT) (Deci and Ryan 1985). This demand from low to high level according to the ascending order, only low levels of demand satisfaction, a higher level of demand will appear, will show its incentive effect [12]. Literature [13] has studied that content providers turn from external motivation to internal motivation, which is manifested in the way of incentive from tangible money compensation to intangible reputation and self-satisfaction, while reputation motivation has a strong effect on internal motivation. The incentive design of online content providers is mainly based on the development process of online community based on user generated content. It mainly depends on the active participation of members of the community rather than the labor of the employed employee, and does not directly consider the incentive design of content providers [14]. In traditional hierarchical social network, single resource transaction involves only the transfer of ownership of virtual currency between the two parties, and does not involve the reward of the communication path and the importer, which results in the contribution of the facilitator and the original publisher [15]. Once the content publisher loses its enthusiasm, it will lead to a shrinking state of the topic in the community or the content of the community as a whole.

The literature [16] research indicates that the needs of leaders in the network community are focused on social needs and self-fulfillment needs. In the current online education, teachers do not voluntarily establish social needs through online education systems, and then realize self-respect and self-worth. Therefore, online education system, combining design and evaluation system of teachers, teachers' social occupation will encourage teachers to integrate the system, the system's attitude to internal motivation, the voluntary adoption of online education system to build social demand, in order to achieve self-value goal.

The demand and motivation of teachers' online education directly determine the role of teachers in the system, and motivation and necessity are the crux of University Teachers' ideological problems. The problem of catching the needs and motives solves the driving force and incentives of University Teachers' ideological problems. Motivation is made up of the needs of different levels, and the demand for online education teachers should be expansible. Hoppock's "Job Satisfaction" first proposed the concept of job satisfaction [17], the design of online education system needs to satisfy teachers' satisfaction with environmental factors in two aspects of psychology and physiology. This subjective response is able to meet teachers' needs and enhance teachers' career planning with the deepening of online education. According to the research results such as Guo [18], we calculated the online education propagation path, calculated the key nodes, introduced the teachers into the incentive mechanism, and encouraged the teachers to strengthen the design of each node. Online education system can add multiple roles to teachers' team in designing orientation, focusing on academic achievements, especially in teaching achievement. The system provides dynamic and open incentive mechanism for different motivational teachers in design.

3.3 The Online Course Model

Mixed Teaching Mode. Mixed teaching mode refers to the course part of the online completion of the course, part of the line to complete, this way to achieve more free time and place to learn part of the basic knowledge, and then focus on the classroom teaching complement each other to form a timely understanding of learning results, The way of learning, similar to Khan Academy "flip classroom" [19]. This model relies on the current curriculum system of colleges and universities, is the transfer of offline courses and teaching methods of the supplement, usually in the form of recording and broadcasting, through the number of clicks and replies to record learners learning trajectory, teachers in the course of recording, In the classroom to organize questions, case studies and other Q & A activities and joint test.

This model is a transitional form, the advantage is to achieve part of the freedom of learning and access to online learning network advantages, and the current university management model has a good fit, the learners have a better supervision and guidance role. The lack of learners is limited by the activities of the underline course, still based on the students.

Complete Online Teaching Mode. Completely online teaching mode refers to the completion of the online learning from the course of organization, learning and effect testing, is the online course design trend. The management system of this design pattern is very different from that of the current university, learning threshold will be set a lot of broad, the number of learners increased significantly, learning more emphasis on consciousness, There are some contradictions between the network of universal freedom and the relative mandatory university; Teachers to pay the contents of the online course content iterative update speed, a large number of online Q & A interactive discussion, their own knowledge structure learning development; The managers need to re-evaluate the teaching management and evaluation system of both sides of the teaching.

4   Hierarchy Design Elements of Online Education

By referring to Maslow's hierarchy of needs [20] and referring to Donald. A. Norman's research results on human brain activity levels [21], this paper presents a hierarchical description of user needs in online education. (Figure 1 the elements of online education). It needs to be explained that the hierarchy division of online education is not strictly related to the division of the two levels, and the demand here is more inclined to the significance of online education for users.

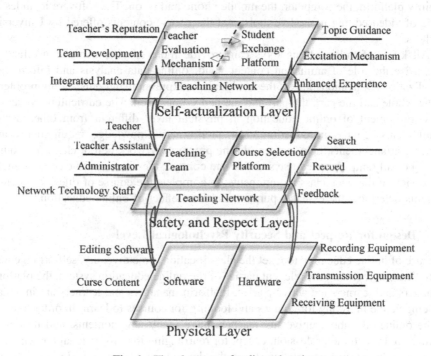

Fig. 1. The elements of online education

American psychologist Clayton Alderfer revised Malos's theory of demand and proposed ERG theory [22]. ERG theory believes that the more the lower level of demand is more satisfied, the more people desire higher levels of demand. Weil and Moore [23] believe that a person's position in a hierarchy determines his needs and behavior, and a level of demand corresponds to a demand category [24]. Therefore, online education design corresponds to teachers, elective students, network platforms and other objects. Online education design needs to meet teachers' esteem needs and self-actualization needs, and we need to satisfy students' active participation and highly recognized social practice system.

From the result evaluation method of hierarchical design, the research [25] shows that the demand hierarchy should be divided in the design research stage, and the demand collection is comprehensively targeted, which can clearly get the constraint relationship of the demand results. The relevance of all aspects of the system has been established by the use of hierarchical needs is convenient for the effective evaluation of the design system [26].

4.1   Design for Physical Level Basic Requirements

In the online education system, the physical level includes the hardware and software needed to ensure that the basic operation of the online course. The hardware includes the video camera, microphone, whiteboard and projector needed for recording video, the network needed for the transmission and reception of the course, the security and stability platform, the computer, the mobile phone and so on. The software includes all kinds of video editing tools, live tools, and the course contents offered by University teachers.

All kinds of video editing tools can provide more specific expression effect: to emphasize the role of animation content vivid, online data analysis and information visualization applications makes the intuitionistic expression and outstanding problems of the whole and the part, the part and the part comparison. The curriculum content is the core content of online education in physical layer different from other design requirements, course introduction clear preliminary knowledge requirements and teaching arrangements, help learners do the preparatory work before class; the course catalog clearly introduces course sections and content; the video specific content on the expression of the node class requirements; to complete the course of rules. The course contents determine the essence, purpose and final effect of online education.

4.2   Design for Respect and Security Psychological Level

Because of online education to meet the class location, time diversity, self-arrangement more flexibility, among the relevant parties of the online education system, the platform managers and learners are active parties. Platform managers and learners are in a state of being active in asking for courses and looking for courses to learn. In order to adapt to the online education, university teachers have many new contents, and they have nothing to do with the profession, except for rearranging the professional content, so it belongs to the passive completion. From the development of online education, online education to truly enter into a virtuous cycle, only teachers become active, play a guiding role in actively promoting the online education, so online education hierarchy design, design team of teachers, and in dynamic operation, attract teachers from entering into active passive participation and development consciousness.

As an initiative, learners have a clear purpose in finding courses: Or for the completion of academic requirements (required courses) or personal interests (optional courses). The design requirements for learners are: The course search is quick and the path is clear. It can be related to the school course selecting system, Once you choose, find the course directly; The recording process is true and the submitted work is safe and reliable; After the end of the study, the effectiveness of the feedback in a timely manner, and personal learning management system records butt. Platform managers provide stable and safe operation environment, provide guarantee for online education operation, and improve the enterprise influence of platform.

As the present passive side, the teacher has a huge workload and offers content for the core of online education. The pre-work includes the rearranging of the teaching content, the recording, the online quiz, the job feedback, the post-teaching evaluation, and the updating of the online course. And offline class lesson preparation is very different, for this change, need to be equipped with a teacher team to focus on teacher-centered, teamwork, division of labor to complete the online course work. The team can include lecturers, assistant teachers, student affairs managers, network technicians and so on. The assistant teachers may include supplementary and auxiliary personnel, such as the executive sponsor [5].

4.3   Design for Self-development Requirements

Maslow believes that self-realization is "on their own power and things always try to complete, so that they continue to tend to perfect" [27]. Although learners have the initiative to find classes and classes will, but the effect of class needs a long time to get in order to get. Very often, the experience of happiness is greater than the product itself [28]. Online education is more free than classroom education, the state high (entry rates) into low (completion rate) out easily formed, continuing to enhance the stickiness of the system design is to help the learner completed the course and achieved good learning experience effective way to self-realization. Juty suggests that web stickness is the ability of the site to retain online users and extend their per stay time [29] In the evaluation system based on user experience, pleasure, participation, acceptance, retention rate and task completion are used as evaluation parameters [27]. With the number of learners take a great leap forward, the online educational exchange platform has become an open communication circle across time zones, trans regional and inter media, In addition to the high quality of the teaching content, the stickness design also uses the online curriculum exchange platform to provide learners with professional insights and discussions. Design a number of judgment points for speech, such as the frequency of speech, the correctness of the argument, the creativity of ideas, the humor of words, and so on. Professional cases can enter the teaching content of teachers and get professional recognition.

The reason why college teachers are divided into "passive side" is that, in addition to the increase in the workload of curriculum preparation, most of the work is not related to professional progress and personal development of teachers. The integration of online education and teacher professional development and teacher evaluation system can attract university teachers and change teachers from passive to active exploration and development. Online education platform as a teacher team of the official website, can show the research results, research progress of teaching real-time updates, from the beginning of a course, the construction of online course system based on subject characteristics, forming the discipline professional guide window. The introduction of discipline experts forum, strengthen the docking with other professional platform, and cross line teaching research cross fusion, improve the teaching team evaluation mechanism of each post. The development of related fields in higher education should also be included in dynamic system design, such as the establishment of digital publishing center, the provision of digital teaching materials for teachers, etc. [30]. The teacher team "achieves the harmony, integrity and freedom of subjective feelings through the process of self-actualization" [31].

5   Application Value of Hierarchy Design of Online Education

With the development of science and technology and the change of the mode of information transfer, online education has gradually become a strong complement to the offline education, which has made changes in teaching forms at all levels, including colleges and universities. Many online education platforms are emerging, educational resources sharing, attracting more teachers and students both sides involved. The addition of colleges and universities promotes the quality of teaching resources. Among them, the participation of college teachers is an important guarantee for the online education in Colleges and universities.

The hierarchy design of online education in Colleges and universities analyzes the status of online education, and constructs the Win-win space between online education platform and participants. The system provides learning resources, personnel resources, platform for teachers' research results and research achievement transformation, and associated with career planning. At the same time, the interaction platform of learners will derive a topic circle with different themes and different directions, and form an interactive relationship of sharing, discussion and collaboration to promote the construction and development of the platform.

Big data from online education system, can integrate the demand for more personalized, accurate collection and processing recommendation, user information, mining potential users, build authentic personal network system more personalized development.

6   Conclusion

With the development of network environment and information technology, great changes have taken place in the traditional mode of teaching and learning. More and more social groups are concerned about online education. In this paper, the basic requirements, psychological safety needs and self-development needs of different groups in online education system are discussed, and the design factors are put forward. Especially, the "passive side" university teachers, due to the importance of online education, it is necessary to focus on the positioning design of the system, so as to transform the teachers in online education from "passive party" to "active party" as soon as possible.

References

1. Ministry of Education of the People's Republic of China. Opinions of the Ministry of education on strengthening the application and management of online open curriculum construction in Institutions of higher learning [EB/OL]. http://www.moe.gov.cn/publicfiles/business/htmlfiles/moe/s7056/20150层次4/186490.html. Accessed 13 Apr 2015
2. Yang, X., Zhou, X.: Research on current situation and development trend of online education in China: from analysis of NetEase open class and other 16 online education platform. E-education Res. **8**, 63–66 (2007). (in Chinese)
3. Wu, L., He, M., Miyamoto, Y., et al.: The development and characteristics of Japanese online education and it's comparative analysis with China. Technol. Educ. **9**(27), 5–11 (2017). (in Chinese)
4. Garrison, R., Arbaugh, J.B.: Researching the community of inquiry framework: review, issues, and future direction. Internet High. Educ. **10**(3), 157–172 (2007)
5. Xu, K.: The Rraining: mode and thinking of American Online Education Ph.D. Explor. High. Educ. **10**, 79–84 (2017). (in Chinese)
6. Haggard, S.: MOOCs: from Mania to Mundanity. http://www.timeshighereducation.co.uk/comment/opinion/moocs-from-maniar-to-mundanity/2007773.article. Accessed 03 Oct 2013
7. Definition of Small Private Online Course SPOC. http://lexicon.ft.com/Term=small-private-online-course-SPOC. Accessed 23 Oct 2013
8. Goral, T.: Mark Way for SPOCS: Small Private Online Courses May Provide What MOOCs Can't. University Business, vol. 16, no. 7. http://www.questia.com/library/IGI-337618040/make-way-for-spocs-small-private-online-courses
9. Kang, Y.: An analysis on SPO: post-MOOC era of online education. Tsinghua J. Educ. **1**(35), 85–93 (2014)
10. Garrison, D.R., Anderson, T., Archer, W・还用社区埋论框架模型 (Community of Inquiry Framework), Critical thinking and computer conferencing: a model and tool to assess cognitive presence. Am. J. Distance Educ. **1**, 7–23 (2001). (in Chinese)
11. Liu, H.: Integrating online courses into college curriculum teaching system: obstacles and breakthroughs. J. Higher Educ. **37**(5), 68–72 (2016). (in Chinese)
12. Han, X., Wang, C.: The Relationship between Customer Satisfaction and Loyalty in Service Enterprises, 1st edn. Tsinghua University Press, Beijing (2003). (in Chinese)
13. Lou, T., Fan, J., Yuping, L., et al.: The influence of incentive mechanism of virtual communities on members' motivation of participation, reinforce or diminish? J. Mark. Sci. **10**(3), 99–112 (2014). (in Chinese)
14. Wang, Z.: Research on Evaluating Node Influence in Social Networks. Beijing University of Posts and Telecommunications (2015). (in Chinese)
15. Chi, P., Fan, J.: On the measures to deal with ideological and political work aimed at teachers in universities and colleges under the new situation based on hierarchy of need theory. J. Jiangxi Normal Univ. (Social Sciences) **5**(49), 126–130 (2016). (in Chinese)
16. Yi, M., Song, J.-j., Yang, B., Chen, J.: Hierarchy of user needs in network knowledge community. Inf. Sci. **2**(35), 22–26 (2017). (in Chinese)
17. Hoppock, R.: Job satisfaction, 1st edn. Harper & Brother Publisher, New York (1935)
18. Guo, Z., Liu, L., Ye, M., Lei, K.: Research and design of direct marketing incentive system in hierarchical social network. Comput. Eng. Des. **8**(38), 2111–2115 (2017). (in Chinese)
19. Khan Academy. An educational nonprofit founded by Bangladeshi American Sahlman Khan, whose aim is to give free lectures using online video
20. Baidu Baike. Maslow's Hierarchy of Needs [EB/OL]. http://baike.baidu.com/view/690053.htm. Accessed 19 Mar 2012

21. Norman, D.A.: Emotional Design: Why We Love (or Hate) Everyday Things. China Citic Press, Beijing (2012). (in Chinese)
22. Alderfer, C.: An Empirical Test of a New Theory of Human Needs, pp. 142–175. Science Press, Beijing (1982). (in Chinese)
23. Tom, W.: The Continuing Question of Motivation in the Knowledge Gap Hypothesis. The Association for Education on Journalism and Mass Communication, Washington, D.C., August 1995
24. Moore, N.: A model of social information need. J. Inf. Sci. **28**(4), 297–303 (2002)
25. Li, M., Deng, X.-x.: Product Design Method Based on Hierarchy of Needs. Packag. Eng. **8**(36), 92–95 (2015). (in Chinese)
26. Yuan, Y., Li, A.: Evaluation and demonstration of the soft power of district city based on the theory of maslow's demand level. Stat. Des. **20**, 72–75 (2017). (in Chinese)
27. Maslow, A.: Chengming Translate: Maslow's Humanistic Philosophy. Jiuzhou Press, Beijing (2011). (in Chinese)
28. Joseph Pine II, B., Gilmore, J.H.: The Experience Economy. Mechanical Industry Press, Beijing (2012). (in Chinese)
29. Lin, J.C.-C.: Online stickiness: its antecedents and effect on purchasing intention. Behav. Inf. Technol. **26**(6), 507–516 (2007)
30. Shang, C., Wei, F.: An analysis on China architecture & building press: exploration and thinking on online education. View Publishing **9**(276), 15–17 (2016). (in Chinese)
31. Wu, X., Liu, M., Zheng, Q.: Quantitative evaluation method and empirical analysis of user experience in Web services. J. Comput. Appl. **S2**, 154–158 (2014). (in Chinese)

Learning and Collaboration

Teaching Discourse Markers in a Technologically-Enhanced Language Classroom

Ágnes Abuczki[1(✉)], Antigoni Parmaxi[2], and Anna Nicolaou[2]

[1] MTA-DE-SZTE Research Group for Theoretical Linguistics,
University of Debrecen,, Pf. 47, Debrecen 4010, Hungary
abuczki.agnes@gmail.com
[2] Cyprus University of Technology, PO Box: 50329, 3603 Lemesos, Cyprus
{antigoni.parmaxi,anna.nicolaou}@cut.ac.cy

Abstract. This paper reports on the methods and findings of a small-scale classroom research study focusing on the facilitation of the use of discourse markers (henceforth: DMs) by second language learners of English, at Cyprus University of Technology. In the framework of explicit teaching, mixed methods, combining traditional and digital tools, were employed in order to maximize the use of DMs in the EFL classroom. It was hypothesized that involvement in the lesson and the DM use of students along with the resulting coherence of their discourse is enhanced by and increases with the application of digital and interactive activities. In order to confirm or reject our hypothesis, an opinion questionnaire was administered to explore students' perceptions about the use of digital and traditional tools demonstrated in class and to investigate the effectiveness of the enhancement of their skills in the use of discourse markers and in composing coherent texts and participating in collaborative interaction. Our study shows that students enjoy using digital tools, and, as a result of teaching and practice, they use more DMs; consequently, their pragmatic competence increases, and their interaction and argumentation becomes more natural and easier to follow.

Keywords: Discourse markers · CALL · Digital tools

1 Introduction

The use of technology in the language classroom has driven new ways of learning and teaching. Language instructors are confronted with both challenges and opportunities when it comes to the use of new technologies for bringing students to the centre of the learning process. Computer-Assisted Language Learning (CALL) remains a phenomenon for which one can draw ambiguous conclusions. This is especially true when teaching a specific linguistic phenomenon such as discourse markers (DMs). Fraser defines DMs as metalinguistic items that provide information about the segmentation and operation of a discourse [8]. These lexical expressions (such as *so*, *well*, and *now*) have been studied in various contexts and genres and most researchers agree that their use is especially important for second language learners. More specifically, research

© Springer International Publishing AG, part of Springer Nature 2018
P. Zaphiris and A. Ioannou (Eds.): LCT 2018, LNCS 10924, pp. 323–336, 2018.
https://doi.org/10.1007/978-3-319-91743-6_25

has shown that the use of discourse markers by second language learners can convey competence in the use of a second language as well as acculturation to the target culture [5, 9]. The present study employed a variety of digital (such as interactive quizzes, Quizlet sets, authentic listening materials and videos from corpora) and traditional (such as frontal teaching and an in-class debate) tools for demonstrating the use of discourse markers and consequently engage students in their use in a real-life classroom. The study is guided by the following research questions:

- In what ways can a variety of digital (such as interactive quizzes and videos) and traditional (such as an in-class debate) tools enhance the teaching of DMs? Do they increase students' discourse marker use and their discourse coherence in EFL lessons?
- What are the students' perceptions about the use of digital and traditional tools for learning DMs?

In order to provide an answer for the above questions, we carried out a small-scale classroom study and administered a subsequent opinion questionnaire among the participating students about their perceptions of the learning methods and digital tools.

2 Literature Review

2.1 The Class of Discourse Markers

It has been illustrated in a number of previous research studies [10, 16] that discourse cohesion and coherence, which are essential for effective interpersonal communication, are maintained by various verbal and nonverbal markers. Therefore, building coherent discourse and the expression of discourse relations must be taught for second language learners as well. Coherence relations establish the link between the discourse units, and this link can be most explicitly expressed by verbal DMs, such as *and*, *however*, *so*, *well*, *I mean* or *by the way*. Although DMs have been widely studied by researchers, issues of terminology and the set of their defining properties and functions are still unresolved in the literature. In order to provide a clearer definition of DMs, Schiffrin, one of the most quoted authors in DM studies, describes them as "sequentially dependent elements which bracket units of talk" and identifies their major role as "providing contextual coordinates for ongoing talk" that indicate for the hearer how an utterance is to be interpreted [21]. It is generally agreed among most researchers that besides marking discourse structure, DMs also imply the communicative function(s) of their host units and sometimes even the attitude of the speaker, both towards the speaker and the subject (or topic) of the conversation.

In the view of Relevance Theory [22], DMs play a role in relevance understanding by reducing the processing effort needed by the hearer to uncover the intended interpretation [3]. Relevance Theory calls attention to the function of DMs facilitating the hearer's mental processes of decoding the message [22]. According to this theory, DMs contribute to "relevance understanding by reducing the processing effort needed by the hearer to reach the intended interpretation" [1]. Generally, in the framework of most hearer-oriented models of interaction, the major role of DMs is to provide instructions to the hearer(s) on how to interpret the utterance and how to integrate the host utterance of the DM into an optimally coherent discourse. From a cognitive perspective, DMs guide interlocutors to express what is not explicitly stated but is implied by the actual utterance. Because of the potential of DMs to restrict the number of possible interpretations, a segment of discourse without a DM is often more ambiguous than intended by the speaker. Fraser claims that they even "signal a sequential relationship" between discourse units [7], which means, similarly to Relevance Theory, that DMs give instructions to the hearer how to interpret the role of it and its host unit in the given context.

Weydt raised the question why, for what reasons speakers use discourse particles (Abtönungspartikeln, according to his terminology) and carried out experiments and surveys to uncover a satisfactory answer. His findings, based on the perception and intuitions of his informants, clearly suggest that the use of DMs makes our utterances sound more authentic, natural, cooperative and friendly, as well as easier to follow and understand [25]. According to Frank-Job, DMs are used by speakers in order to control turn-taking mechanisms and guarantee the smooth maintenance of interaction. Conversation participants use DMs and nonverbal cues in order to avoid problematic interruptions and too frequent overlapping speech and smoothly shift the right of speakership [6]. Furthermore, speakers employ DMs in order to inform their partner(s) about their attitude(s) as well as the intention that a new topical action is about to be performed, such as topic closing and topic change.

DM use has most frequently been studied in the language of native speakers (in first language) and in terms of their role in the organization of discourse structure, in sociolinguistic interviews [21], phone calls, and meeting conversations, dialogues of highly interactive nature. It has become evident by now that DMs can be useful devices to be employed not only in HCI (human-computer interaction) theories and technologies, including in discourse modeling, dialogue generation and discourse interpretation; but the usage and practice of DMs is beneficial in second language learning as well. As a result, effective ways must be identified to teach the appropriate use of DMs for learners as it can improve their pragmatic competence and communicative efficiency.

2.2 Approaches to Teaching Discourse Markers

Using DMs makes the language production of students less schematic and more native-like, culturally more appropriate and may contribute to the development of their communicative competence [5, 9]. Therefore, teaching the appropriate use of DMs in an effective way is necessary in communicative language teaching in order to improve the coherence and the fluency of students' discourse. Now let us refer to some of the fundamental language acquisition theories that serve as the theoretical background for our methodology to be briefly described in the next section.

According to Krashen's input hypothesis, learners acquire a language by receiving and understanding discourse which is a bit beyond their current level of competence (i + 1). Provided the proper level and amount of comprehensible input, language production ability automatically emerges, without direct teaching intervention [12]. For this reason, we selected such original, authentic discourses, including several DMs in various contexts, to be presented in lessons which are beyond the present level of the students (B1/B2) but still comprehensible for them after pre-teaching a few keywords and by relying on context.

From the perspective of Long's interaction hypothesis [14], when learners receive feedback on their production in a conversation (also referred to as negotiation), and when they are encouraged to reformulate and improve their own utterances, acquisition is facilitated. That is why group discussions and informal evaluations were promoted where both the peers could comment on each other's production and the teacher also provided corrective feedback on learners' language.

Concerning the structure and organization of our lessons, we addressed the frameworks of explicit teaching: the Illustration – Interaction – Induction (III) [15] and the Present – Practice – Produce (PPP) methodologies. With the help of pre- and post-tests, Jones and Carter [11] measured the success of the two methods in teaching DMs in two ways, in two groups of Chinese students, compared to a third, control group. The difference between employing the III and PPP frameworks was that the III groups were not provided any pre-communicative or contextualized practice of the target DMs but were given tasks which helped them analyze aspects of the DMs' uses such as the difference between the functional spectra of the DMs in English and their first language. On the other hand, the PPP groups were given contextualized and communicative demonstration and practice of the DMs in various activities, e.g. drills, dialogues and role plays which all promoted the use of the target items. Overall, based on the results of their pre- and post-tests, the PPP method was found to be more effective and more appealing to students their than the III method [11].

Similarly, Yoshimi [26] also found that presentation and the explicit explanation of DMs, followed by practice and corrective feedback, helps learners to use them within informal spoken narratives. In this experiment each group was given a pre-and post-test in which learners were asked to complete a story telling task, and the quantitative analysis of their answers confirmed that students use DMs in a much greater extent than the control group which was given no instruction, illustration or description on the same items [26].

Taking into consideration the above research findings, we decided to apply the PPP method in our classroom study. In what follows we will describe our methods and findings on a technology-enhanced implementation of teaching English DMs in a second language classroom (with non-native speakers of English).

3 Methodology

3.1 Participants and Settings

A total of thirty-eight first-year students majoring in Mechanical Engineering and Materials Science and Engineering at the Cyprus University of Technology participated in the study. The study was implemented in a span of two ninety-minute sessions (identical lesson plans on two subsequent occasions in two groups of about nineteen students each) of an English for Specific Purposes (ESP) module designed for Mechanical Engineering students, benchmarked to B1 level of the CEFR [4]. The two sessions aimed at developing the students' understanding of DMs and at enhancing the use of DMs in spoken and written interaction. Out of the thirty-eight participants, thirty-one (N = 31) completed the opinion questionnaire that was administered upon completion of the two sessions. Gender was not equally distributed in the sample as twenty-seven students (N = 27) were male and only four students (N = 4) were female. The unbalanced distribution of gender was neither unexpected nor surprising as engineering courses in Cyprus are mostly attended by male students at the specific educational context. Age groups ranged from eighteen to twenty-four years old, with eighteen to twenty being the dominant group (N = 27).

3.2   Tools and Activities

In Sects. 3.2 and 3.3 the different tools we used (digital and traditional), the kinds of activities carried out and the design of the two lessons will be described in detail. Since DMs are commonly used in spoken language for various purposes, in order to demonstrate their authentic and contextualized uses first, several excerpts were presented from BBC interviews [2], TV series and TED Talks [21], instead of relying on traditional written sources. Concerning digital tools, besides audio and video recordings, we employed web-based study applications, such as word sets created by ourselves using Quizlet [19] and multi-party competition games created in Quizizz [17]. All these tools were adopted because we believe that their use engages the students more in the lesson and enhances the acquisition of its topic and material.

Using Quizlet [19], students can learn words, expressions, terms and definitions (usually created by teachers) in several study modes: via flashcards and various games (e.g. Match or Gravity). We mostly used the Match mode in class, and Gravity was set as homework. In Match study mode students are shown a grid with expressions in it, and the task is to drag corresponding items (e.g. terms and definitions, synonyms, paraphrases or matching contexts) to make them disappear and try to match the associated items (definitions, synonyms, paraphrases or the contexts of the gapped item) in the fastest time possible, whereby students within a class can compete with each other in order to beat others' completion time. In the Gravity game, adapted from a previous popular game called Space Race, students can even set the level of difficulty and speed, and their task is to type the correct answer (in our case, a synonym we had learnt).

Quizizz [17] is a fun multiplayer game (an alternative to Kahoot) where students compete globally on live games created and shared by their teacher. Students do not need an invitation or registration to join this game; all they need is a 6-digit code provided by their teacher, which makes the use of the quiz really quick and effective in any phase of the lesson.

In the second lesson, TED Talks [13, 23, 24] were used for the analysis of the uses of DMs in semi-spontaneous, pre-planned talks (in the subject of self-driving cars). These types of talks were chosen in order to present the powerful and strategic uses of DMs in such short semi-academic talks that the students will also need to give during their future careers. After watching the talks (to collect ideas), the second lesson centered on an in-class debate session among the students (about the same, Engineering-related topic, initiated by the TED Talks) since we wanted to trigger motivated and engaged language production (in the form of a quasi-competition) and simultaneously improve their pragmatic competence and argumentation skills, which are all necessary assets in their careers.

3.3   Design of the Lessons

In order to meet the needs and interests of the students (of Mechanical Engineering) as well as fit the goals of their ESP lesson, the theme of both lessons was new types of cars, in particular, electric cars and driverless (also referred to as self-driving) cars.

Lesson 1

Our first lesson started with a presentation (or could also be referred to as an illustration) phase employing authentic listening activities (based on an interview from BBC corpus about electric cars and an episode from Big Bang Theory, an American series) followed by gap-fill listening comprehension tasks and group discussion about the attitude of the speakers towards the topic as they are expressed by the DM use of the speakers. This part was followed by some traditional frontal teaching about DMs (their definitions and functions using authentic examples of their various usages).

The upcoming practice phase involved online practice individually where students were studying Quizlet flashcards on separate computers, and afterwards, based on the previously studied flashcards, they were performing matching tasks and "gravity" games [20]. The DMs under scrutiny in both of these two activities were those expressing attitude: If you ask me, I'm afraid, I must admit, Fortunately, Obviously, Of course, Ideally, Seriously. These DMs were presented from different perspectives: with one task focusing on function and meaning (paraphrase or synonym), and the other on proper communicative context. This individual online task followed by a group discussion, in the format of the initiation-response-feedback (IRF) triad, on the uses and the cross-linguistic analysis of like as a DM (besides its verbal use) and its Cypriot Greek equivalent in different contexts, both in English and in Cypriot Greek.

Following this group discussion, in the production phase, students were working in groups of three, two of them having a conversation (for instance, a request and its polite rejection at work) with the task of involving as many of DMs and linking words as they can (e.g. *First of all, you know, I mean, Unfortunately, I must admit, The thing is*, etc.), while the third (listening) student gave a point to the student each time s/he managed to correctly use a DM. As a general rule, the one who uses more DMs wins. First, students found it difficult to get started with this activity, but then they enjoyed listening to each others' dialogues and evaluated the work presented. Finally, as a wrap-up in the closing phase, an online group competition was held, employing Quizizz, about the various meanings and uses of the overviewed DMs [18]. The winner (achieving the most points in the group, projected on the screen) was given a round of applause in the end.

One of the homework assignments set was what we call the 'Fifty shades of oh' where students need to write several mini-dialogues including oh expressing its different functions. As a hint, several functions of oh were listed, such as surprise (negative or positive), sudden realization, recalling something, exclamation (expressing sorry, disgust or horror), irony, sarcasm, general backchanneling feedback (expressing that you're listening). At a later stage, after the teacher has checked the compositions, some students will be asked to act out the conversations. Even more importantly, the other homework assignment was to watch two TED Talks [13, 24] at home, both related to the topic of the next lesson, self-driving cars, as well as the uses of DMs employed by the speakers of the talks.

Lesson 2

Our second lesson on DMs consisted of 3 phases: (1) watching excerpts, (2) group discussion and instructions for the next task, and (3) a debate (among two teams on the acceptability of the use of driverless cars). First, the group watched excerpts from the assigned TED Talks [13, 24], during which students had a twofold task: (1) to identify and note down the linking items and DMs used as well as their meaning/function/role in the particular context and discourse position, and (2) to note down reasons and arguments for and against the use of driverless cars. In the second phase, the teacher asked comprehension questions and the group discussed DM uses and collected some key words for arguments to be involved later in the debate session. Finally, in the third phase (actually, the main and longest phase), a debate was organized about (the introduction and widespread use of) driverless cars where students played different roles and they had to use DMs to make their contributions more sophisticated and sound better structured.

The debate was aided by instructions and keywords on role cards provided for the participants (see the Appendix for details), and comprised of only S-S interaction (with very little intervention by the teacher). Nineteen students participated in the debate in each of the two groups. The participants randomly picked their roles using little sheets of paper prepared by the teacher. As a result, a moderator, a timekeeper and three judges were appointed, while seven participants were assigned to argue for the use of driverless cars (PRO team), and equally, seven students were assigned to argue against the use of driverless cars thus argue for traditional cars with human drivers (CONTRA team). Each participant received a role card with prompts on it. The moderator's task was to open and close the debate, to ask for comments from the teams and for questions and evaluations from the judges. The timekeeper measured the time as well as started and stopped the preparation phase and the current team's turn. The judges monitored the use of English (during the preparatory phase as well) and made sure everyone contributed to the debate and talked. Furthermore, the judges asked questions in the final round, especially from those who had not contributed/talked much during the debate. Finally, the judges scored both teams (using rating criteria prepared by the teacher) in terms of content and discourse coherence made explicit by DMs, and consequently, they voted which team's performance was more coherent and convincing to win the debate.

Regarding the structure and timing of the debate, the session started with a preparation phase when the two teams prepared for their mini-presentation separately, based on their notes (in ten minutes). Meanwhile, the judges read the evaluation criteria, monitored the teams and took notes about the in-group use of English in both teams. The debate comprised three rounds (both teams had 2–2 min in each round), with 4-min breaks between them. In the first round of the debate, the teams presented their main ideas and arguments. The second round of debate consisted of rebuttal talks, consisting of contra-arguments in reply to the other team's arguments heard in the first round. In the third round, the teams presented a summary of their arguments in 2 min. Before closing, a question-answer session followed where judges had the chance to ask questions from both teams. In the evaluation stage, judges evaluated both sides of the debate and voted on which team won. Finally, the teacher also evaluated the session and drew the conclusions of the task, both in terms of the argumentation and the DM use of the students.

3.4 Procedure and Measure

The questionnaire was administered online via Google Forms and primarily aimed at exploring the students' opinions about the use of digital and traditional tools demonstrated in class for increasing their understanding of DMs. The secondary goal was to investigate the degree to which students felt that the two sessions contributed to the enhancement of their skills in the use of DMs. Essentially, the overarching objective of this small-scale research was to gather data on the students' perceived learning of discourse markers via various digital and traditional tools, after having participated in the designed activities during the two sessions under discussion.

The questionnaire was designed by the three researchers and it comprised three parts. The first part included nine four-point Likert-scale questions pertaining to the students' opinions about the digital tools [17, 19] which were demonstrated in class for learning DMs. This part also included three open questions which required students to provide a short definition of DMs, and also indicate what they enjoyed the most and the least in the two sessions. The second part of the questionnaire included closed questions (Yes/No/Maybe) about the students' opinions regarding the traditional activities they were involved in during the second session, namely the debate. The last part of the questionnaire included two questions on students' demographics: gender and age group.

Overall, our lesson plans and the subsequent questionnaire were designed this way in order to address and test the following two hypotheses:

- DM use and involvement increases with more student-student (S-S) interaction and less teacher-student (T-S) interaction
- DM use and involvement increases with online activities.

4 Findings

Quantitative data analyses were performed in SPSS to determine the students' degree of understanding of DMs and their perceived enhancement of their skills in using DMs. Findings demonstrate that most of the students had not used Quizlet [19] or Quizizz [17] before participating in the two sessions under scrutiny in this study; however, they found them useful in learning about and practicing DM use. In addition, the students perceived the TED talk and the TV series episode shown in class helpful for enhancing their understanding of DMs. Table 1 indicates the students' responses regarding the degree to which the aforementioned digital tools helped students understand DMs.

Table 1. Students' perceptions about the helpfulness of digital tools in understanding DMs

Digital tools	N	Mean	Std. Deviation
Quizlet	31	1,90	,700
Quizizz	31	2,16	,735
TED talk	31	1,97	,752
TV Series	31	2,00	,856

Students responded using a Likert scale from 1–4 whereby 1 meant 'Very much' and 4 meant 'Not at all':

Overall, students seem to have enjoyed practicing DMs with digital tools and they consider the use of technology in the two sessions as a useful component. Students indicated that the use of technology helped them with their learning throughout the two sessions on DMs. Students indicated their positive reactions towards the use of technology through their almost unanimous (30 out of 31 respondents) selection of 'Yes' in the respective question. In addition, responses regarding the degree of usefulness of technology point to the students' positive perceptions about the value of technology in the two sessions under discussion (Table 2).

Table 2. Students' perceptions about the degree of usefulness of technology

The use of technology in the last two sessions was	Frequency	Valid percent
Not useful at all	1	3,2
Not useful	2	6,5
Neither useful nor useless	4	12,9
Somewhat useful	15	48,4
Very useful	9	29,0
Total	31	100,0

The open question on the questionnaire which required students to provide a short definition for DMs confirms the students' understanding of the meaning and function of DMs. The fact that students provided definitions which included various uses of DMs demonstrates their deep understanding of the function of DMs in written and spoken interaction. Some of the students' definitions are provided in Table 3.

In the second part of the questionnaire, the students responded to questions about their participation in the in-class debate and indicated how this activity encouraged them to use DMs. The vast majority of students indicated that the debate encouraged them to use DMs and also to develop their verbal and critical thinking skills in English. Specifically, in the question 'Did the debate encourage you to use discourse markers?' eighteen (N = 18) students responded 'Yes', four (N = 4) students responded 'No', eight (N = 8) students responded 'Maybe' and only one (N = 1) student responded 'A little'. Finally, twenty-four (N = 24) students considered their participation in the debate session to have encouraged them to use English verbally and also to think critically in the English language.

Table 3. Students' short definitions of discourse markers (examples, extracts)

Students' short definitions of discourse markers
They are used to make a point more clear
Connection words
Express feelings
Small phrases or individual words that help start a phrase
They connect our sentences and make you not say again what you said
Express ideas feelings and thoughts
Discourses markers are being used for emphasizing
They help us describe better our thoughts
With discourse markers you can enrich your speech and connect different sentences with sophisticated vocabulary
Discourse markers are expressions we use in order to enrich our speech and tell with more accuracy what exactly we want to express
A word or phrase whose function is to organize discourse into segments
Discourse markers are words or phrases like anyway, right, okay, as I say, to begin with. We use them to connect, organize and manage what we say or write or to express attitude
Discourse markers help us to combine our sentences and also to give more information with the right attitude like agree or disagree with an argument
Help to start or contrast a sentence or a dialog

5 Conclusion

Our pilot study shows that students enjoy using digital methods in EFL classes, and, as a result of teaching and practice, they use more and more DMs with various purposes (both interpersonal and textual functions) towards the end of communicative lessons; consequently, their language production is more natural as well as easier to follow. Therefore, our methods might serve as useful guidelines for EFL teachers in connection with teaching DMs.

Naturally, further research is needed (cross-cultural as well as cross-linguistic, quantitative as well as qualitative) on classroom interaction in order to substantiate our findings about the effectiveness of our teaching methods and the long-term acquisition of DM use by students. One of our future perspectives is to expand our present small-scale study by employing an identical design of a lesson and a subsequent questionnaire in both of our home countries (Cyprus and Hungary) and consequently compare our findings (provided we have similar groups of students in terms of their level and studies). Moreover, it would also be great if we could both video record our lessons from various angles and analyze the nonverbal behavior of the students as well, including their postures, hand gestures, eye contact and pauses. Of course, it would be a question of a longitudinal study to see whether students maintained their use of DMs on the long term, which would be ideal to carry out in the future.

Acknowledgments. The research visit, a short-term scientific mission enabling the accomplishment of the lessons under scrutiny, has been supported by COST Action IS1312, in the framework of the TextLink project. The research contribution of Ágnes Abuczki to the evaluation of the study and the composition of the paper has also been supported by the National Research, Development and Innovation Office of Hungary – NKFIH research project code: PD121009.

Appendix

Role cards with prompts (for participants in the debate session, described in Sect. 3.3):

A. **Role card and prompts for the 2 debating teams:**

- Take notes during the TED talks
- During your debate, take turns talking (3 × 2–2 minutes each group)
- Use DMs in order to (1) sound more natural and sophisticated and (2) to structure your ideas and therefore make it easier for the listeners (the judges and the opposing team) to follow your ideas and logic:
  First... Second... Third... Moreover... On the other hand... On the other hand... Also... Still... Even (if) .... However... Although... It can be true that ... but .... Don't forget... We shouldn't forget about... Keep in mind... Not to mention ... So... Therefore... To put that in perspective .... Now... Anyways... In conclusion ... To sum up.... Taking everything into consideration...

B. **Time-keeper's role card:**

- The time-keeper can also act as a judge but primarily focuses on measuring time
- The task of the time-keeper is to mark the end of the preparation phrase (after 10 minutes in the beginning and then 4 minutes each round) and to stop the teams talking (after 2 minutes of speech)
- When the preparation time is over, say: "Preparation time is over."
- Then 2 minutes later, after the team's speaking time is over, say: "It's time to stop talking now. I must say that the supporting/opposing team's time is up. Thank you for your remarks."

C. **Judges' role card** (2 or 3 students + the time-keeper + the teacher):

- Read the rating criteria
- Monitor the use of English (during the preparatory phases as well) and make sure everyone contributes to the debate and talks
- Ask questions (in the final round, especially from those who hasn't contributed/talked much)
- Decide and vote which team's arguments are stronger
  Rating criteria for the judges:

Rate the teams overall on a five-point scale (from 1 to 5) based on:
1. discourse coherence: use of discourse markers and linking items
2. originality of content, creativity and number of arguments
3. team work (depending on how many group members contributed to the preparation and the presentation, in what proportion, etc.)
4. use of English (English used all the time vs. only partly during the preparation phase)
5. non-verbal behaviour of the speakers (hand gestures, eye-contact with both the judges and the opponent team)
6. presentation style, the level of involvedness, the persuasiveness, the convincing power of the argumentation

D. **Moderator's role card with the prompts**:

- Welcome the 2 teams and the judges
- Introduce the topic of the debate
- Introduce the members of the teams, the time-keeper, the judges, and yourself
- Set 10 minutes for the teams to prepare
- After 10 minutes of preparation, tell them:
  "Let me ask the supporting team to start their presentation (= first round). You have two minutes. You can start now."
- After 2 minutes of talk, say:
  "Let me ask the opposing team to start their presentation (= first round). You have two minutes. You can start now.
- After 4 minutes of preparation break between the rounds, say:
  "Let me ask the supporting team to start their rebuttal (= 2nd round). You have two minutes. You can start now."
- After 2 minutes of talk, say:
  "Let me ask the opposing team to start their rebuttal (= 2nd round). You have two minutes. You can start now."
- After 4 minutes of preparation break between the rounds, say:
  "Let me ask the supporting team to start their summary (= 3rd round). You have two minutes. You can start now."
- After 2 minutes of talk, say:
  "Let me ask the opposing team to start their summary (= 3rd round). You have two minutes. You can start now."
- When the opposing time if finished with their summary, address the judges:
  "Dear Judges, let me call you upon to ask questions from both teams."
- In the end:
  "Thank you all for your questions and answers. Now we've reached the end of the debate. It's time for the judges to evaluate their teams and vote about the winning team. Let me ask XY to share her opinion about the teams… Thank you. Now, let me ask XZ to share her opinion about the teams…"
  After counting the points and votes:

"It seems that THE WINNER of today's debate is TEAM PRO/CONTRA....
Congratulations to each and every member of the team. Here is your award.
Thank you all for your participation and contribution."

References

1. Aijmer, K., Simon-Vandenbergen, A.: Pragmatic Markers. In: Östman, Jo, Verschueren, J. (eds.) Handbook of Pragmatics. John Benjamins, Amsterdam (2009)
2. BBC Learning English homepage. http://www.bbc.co.uk/learningenglish/english/course/intermediate/unit-15/session-1. Accessed 09 Feb 2018
3. Blakemore, D.: Understanding Utterances. Blackwell, Oxford (1992)
4. Council of Europe: Common European Framework of Reference for Languages: Learning, teaching, assessment. Cambridge University Press, Cambridge (2001)
5. Flowerdew, J., Tauroza, S.: The effect of discourse markers on second language lecture comprehension. Stud. Second Lang. Acquisition 17(4), 435–458 (1995)
6. Frank-Job, B.: A dynamic-interactional approach to discourse markers. In: Fischer, K. (ed.) Approaches to Discourse Particles, pp. 359–374. Elsevier, Amsterdam (2006)
7. Fraser, B.: An approach to discourse markers. J. Pragmatics 14, 383–395 (1990)
8. Fraser, B.: What are discourse markers? J. Pragmatics 31(7), 931–952 (1999)
9. Hellermann, J., Vergun, A.: Language which is not taught: the discourse marker use of beginning adult learners of English. J. Pragmatics 39(1), 157–179 (2007)
10. Hirschberg, J., Litman, D.: Empirical studies on the disambiguation of cue phrases. Comput. Linguis. 25(4), 501–530 (1993)
11. Jones, C., Carter, R.: Teaching spoken discourse markers explicitly: a comparison of III and PPP. Int. J. Engl. Stud. 14, 37–54 (2013)
12. Krashen, S.D.: The Input Hypothesis: Issues and Implications, vol. 1, p. 985. Longman, London (1985)
13. Lin, P.: The ethical dilemma of self-driving cars (2015). https://ed.ted.com/lessons/the-ethical-dilemma-of-self-driving-cars-patrick-lin. Accessed 09 Feb 2018
14. Long, M.H.: A role for instruction in second language acquisition: Task-based language teaching. Model. Assessing Second Lang. Acquisition 18, 77–99 (1985)
15. McCarthy, M., Carter, R.: Spoken grammar: What is it and how can we teach it? ELT J. 49(3), 207–218 (1995)
16. Petukhova, V., Bunt, H.: Towards a multidimensional semantics of discourse markers in spoken dialogue. In: Proceedings of the 8th International Conference on Computational Semantics, pp. 157–168. Tilburg (2009)
17. Quizizz homepage. https://quizizz.com/. Accessed 09 Feb 2018
18. Quizizz tasks. https://quizizz.com/admin/quiz/5947f2189298cc10006ad72f, https://quizizz.com/admin/quiz/59c13fdba378ac1000769c6b. Accessed 09 Feb 2018
19. Quizlet homepage. https://quizlet.com/. Accessed 09 Feb 2018
20. Quizlet tasks. https://quizlet.com/217964122/match-the-discourse-markers-and-their-functions-expressing-the-attitude-of-the-speaker-flash-cards/, https://quizlet.com/217964431/fill-in-the-sentences-with-discourse-markers-so-that-they-best-fit-the-context-of-the-sentence-flash-cards/. Accessed 09 Feb 2018
21. Schiffrin, D.: Discourse Markers. Cambridge University Press, Cambridge (1987)
22. Sperber, D., Wilson, D.: Relevance, Communication and Cognition. Blackwell, Oxford (1986)

336   Á. Abuczki et al.

23. TED Talks homepage. https://www.ted.com/. Accessed 09 Feb 2018
24. Urmson, C.: How a driverless car sees the road (2015). https://www.ted.com/talks/chris_urmson_how_a_driverless_car_sees_the_road. Accessed 09 Feb 2018
25. Weydt, H.: (2006) What are particles good for? In: Fischer, K. (ed.) Approaches to Discourse Particles, pp. 205–217. Elsevier, Amsterdam (2006)
26. Yoshimi, D.R.: Explicit instruction and JFL learners' use of interactional discourse markers. In: Rose, K.R., Kasper, G. (eds.) Pragmatics in Language Teaching, pp. 223–244. Cambridge University Press, Cambridge (2001)

Towards a Framework Definition to Increase Collaboration and Achieve Group Cognition

Vanessa Agredo-Delgado[1,2]([✉]), Pablo H. Ruiz[1,2],
Cesar A. Collazos[1]([✉]), Daniyal M. Alghazzawi[3],
and Habib M. Fardoun[3]

[1] Department of Computing, Universidad del Cauca,
Street 5 Number. 4–70, Popayán, Colombia
{vanessaagredo, ccollazo}@unicauca.edu.co,
pruiz@unicomfacauca.edu.co
[2] Corporación Universitaria–Unicomfacauca,
Street 4 Number 8–30, Popayán, Colombia
[3] Information Systems, Faculty of Computing and Information Technology,
King Abdulaziz University, Jeddah, Saudi Arabia
{dghazzawi, hfardoun}@kau.edu.sa

Abstract. Computer Supported Collaborative Learning - CSCL is an area that focuses on how people can learn together with the computers help, it is also one of the most promising innovations to improve teaching and learning with the modern information technologies and communication help. The CSCL describes a situation in which it is expected that interaction particular forms will occur, which will produce learning mechanisms that possibly generate the planned achievement, but that there is no total guarantee that these situations will be presented effectively. For this reason, this scheme is difficult to achieve if several aspects that can really guarantee this interaction kind are considered. In addition to considering that working collaboratively is not an easy task; it is necessary to structure activities, design applications, analyze additional factors that allow achieving the planned objective, however, up to this time, there are some methodologies for the collaborative applications built that focus mainly on supporting the activity execution, leaving aside, that with these applications to achieve the group cognition through the collaborative knowledge build. As part of our previous research, we have identified that it is necessary and important to have strategies set to achieve collaboration and group cognition when participating in a collaborative learning activity. This article shows the proposal and the advances towards the framework definition that allows the collaboration increase and the group cognition construction, through the strategies centralization that allows achieving learning and collaboration.

Keywords: Computer Supported Collaborative Learning
Collaborative learning · Group cognition · Collaborative activities
Framework · Strategies

© Springer International Publishing AG, part of Springer Nature 2018
P. Zaphiris and A. Ioannou (Eds.): LCT 2018, LNCS 10924, pp. 337–349, 2018.
https://doi.org/10.1007/978-3-319-91743-6_26

1 Introduction

Today, most important decisions in organizations are made by groups who are experts in specific topics that contribute to this process and in the complex problems solution. Furthermore, the fast growth of information and communication technologies are generating new forms of work and modifying different practices in people's daily lives, in this transformation there is a progressive trend towards collaboration to achieve a common objective, where the work is organized into groups and each member interacts with the rest to obtain a better productivity [1]. Education has not been foreign to these advances and it is for this reason that one of its basic requirements in the present and future, is to prepare students to participate in networks [2]. However, working collaboratively is not an easy task; it is necessary to structure activities, design applications, analyze additional factors to achieve that objective [3]. Therefore, there is a need to define a framework that support collaborative learning activities, where these activities are designed and structured in order to ensure true collaboration and also to achieve group cognition (defined by Gerry Stahl in [4]), which is conceived as a sum of individual heads facts, rather than as a positive cognitive phenomenon of their own, which allows going beyond obtaining individual learning. It can structure activities that ensure these actions requiring approaches that must be strategically executed; it is not enough to encourage a student's group and a teacher to develop a task together to achieve a common objective, collaborative learning is more effective if participants work in well-designed scenarios [5]. As part of our research process, we have identified that it is necessary and important to have strategies set to achieve collaboration and group cognition when participating in a collaborative learning activity. This article shows the proposal and the advances towards the framework definition that allows the collaboration increasing and the group cognition construction, through the centralization of strategies that allow achieving learning and collaboration. This document is structured as follows: Sect. 2 describes the problem statement, Sect. 3 defines the proposal and Sect. 4 shows the project progress until this moment.

2 Problem Statement

Traditionally, the teaching of a topic has followed the information transmission model, where the teacher selects a learning topic, organizes it in a course and transmits it to the student in a one-way flow. The student in this model becomes a passive element, receiver of this information. For which, a new teaching-learning scheme arises, called Collaborative Learning, in which students learn by interacting and structuring their own knowledge, with the tutor guidance [6]. This model allows for the opportunity to share skills and competences in common to contrast ideas and viewpoints, wonder, question, pose challenges, discuss them, solve problems together reaching consensus and negotiate between different members. In this way and to facilitate these activities, having available technological tools within a collaborative activity can result in achieving a better performance in the task performed, that is why the concept of Computer Supported Collaborative Learning - CSCL, which is an area that focuses on how people can learn together with the computers help, is also one of the most promising innovations to improve teaching and learning with the help of modern information and communication technologies [7]. Collaborative learning describes a situation in which interaction in particular forms are expected to occur, which will produce learning mechanisms, possibly producing the planned accomplishment, but there is no total guarantee that these situations will be presented effectively. For this reason, this scheme is difficult to achieve, but different aspects that can really guarantee this interactions type are considered [2] and therefore it is necessary to consider a framework that allows the collaborative learning process, through the increase of collaboration and to achieve group cognition.

Currently, there are methodologies for the application's design that support the collaborative learning process, some of them are: CIAM [8] (Collaborative Interactive Applications Methodology), which is a methodological approach for the user interfaces development in groupware applications, Rodríguez et al. [9], define a methodology for the user interfaces design in collaborative applications from computing independent models, furthermore, AMENITIES [10] (A Methodology for aNalysis and desIgn of cooperaTIve systEmS), is a methodology focused on the system initial modeling using the user viewpoint and considering aspects related to the group (group cognition, relations between users, dynamic groups, social aspects representation, etc.), among other methodologies that focus mainly on design, leaving aside, to seek that with these applications the shared group cognition is achieved through the collaborative knowledge construction, defined by Gerry Stahl in [4], which emphasizes the support for interactions between the students themselves, with a teacher playing a role more facilitating than instructive. Furthermore, the group knowledge build implies the construction or subsequent some knowledge artifact development type. Meaning, students are not simply socializing and exchanging their reactions or personal opinions on the subject, but they could be developing a theory, model, diagnosis, concept map, mathematical proof or presentation. To achieve this group cognition, and a collaboration between the participants, it is proposed to have strategies to achieve this objective, such as: monitoring and evaluation of the participants interaction of the activity, gamification, or in the games creation, content adaptation, among other strategies to achieve this cognition and the necessary collaboration, and through a framework all these aspects are taken into account for the creation of the applications that support the proposed objectives achievement.

To achieve the above, it is necessary to analyze the problems presently present, one of the main collaborative learning problems is that in many situations it has been believed that having the technological infrastructure guarantees effective collaboration [11], but for this it is necessary to go beyond that to have a class practices set, laboratories and the respective technological tools. A deeper approach must be taken to ensure collaboration among the work teams, and also a common and egalitarian learning through some external factors analysis such as: people group, activities and technological infrastructure [12], furthermore to considering the monitoring and evaluation of the learning process by the teacher, who must be in continuous attention that the collaboration is carried out. In the same way, keep track of the interaction aspects such as technology, communication, the activity members, among others, and their relationship with the collaborative activity. The interaction ability is one of the elements that predominates in how students will develop collaborative activities, which is why

Johnson et al. [2] determine that: "it is necessary to focus more on the interaction and learning process than on the results". Furthermore, most researches on collaborative learning indicates positive effects on the participants individual learning, an increase in the group knowledge and/or the organization and an improvement in the skills to construct and generate knowledge [4, 13]. However, technological development is still very focused on individual learning models, providing few tools for collaborative knowledge management processes. Therefore, it is especially important to construct knowledge that must be generated in the process of conducting a computer-assisted collaborative activity, which allows the group cognition achievement, considering that in order to obtain learning, the usual internet environments do not work, which do not allow a true knowledge build and do not allow to link ideas, modify contributions, etc. According to Gros [14] to date, most virtual learning platforms do not facilitate the knowledge construction, "they allow an information exchange and discussion, but they are not designed to favor the knowledge construction process." For the knowledge construction are needed environments that allow ideas to arise and enter the path of continuous improvement, in such a way in community there is a shared responsibility to give life to ideas, improve them, etc. It is necessary, a shared work environment for the knowledge construction.

Taking into account the above, it is proposed to define a conceptual model that contains different strategies types, which is supported by a framework for increasing collaboration and achieving group cognition. In this way, the following research question arises: How to improve the collaborative learning process promoting collaboration and achieving group cognition among collaborative activity participants?

3 Proposal

To understand this proposal better, it is necessary to define some terms that will be important to clarify:

- Group: the focus is not on individual learning, but learning in and by small groups of students.
- Cognition: the group activity is not one of working, but of constructing new understanding and meaning within contexts of instruction and learning.
- Computer support: the learning does not take place in isolation, but with support by computer-based tools, functionality, micro-worlds, media and networks.
- Building: the concern is not with the transmission of known facts, but with the construction of personally meaningful knowledge.
- Collaborative: the interaction of participants is not competitive or accidental, but involves systematic efforts to work and learn together.
- Knowledge: the orientation is not to drill and practice of specific elementary facts or procedural skills, but to discussion, debate, argumentation and deep understanding.

The proposal presented here (see Fig. 1), is based on the concepts defined by Stahl in [4] and was added it the strategies centralization, which will allow increasing collaboration and with the execution of these strategies can also achieve group cognition, for this, it is important to have a methodological framework where the guidelines,

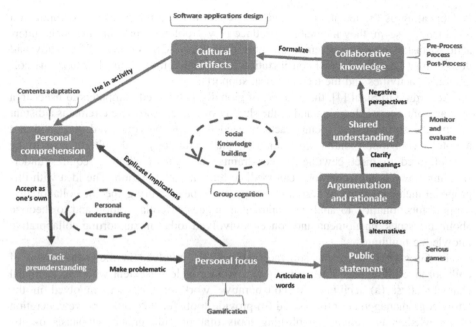

Fig. 1. Increase collaboration and achieve group cognition proposal in each phase

patterns, and other elements necessary are defined, regardless of the context in which a collaborative activity is carried out.

According to this proposal is an attempt to understand learning as a social process incorporating multiple distinguishable phases that constitute a cycle of personal and social collaborative knowledge building. This model of collaborative knowledge building incorporates insights from theories of understanding and learning within a simplistic schema in hopes of providing a useful conceptual framework for the computer supported collaborative learning, specifically collaborative knowledge-building environments with some strategies that can incorporate in activities and in the process carried out.

Considering this proposal, it is necessary to analyze first each part that composes it, in order to determine the shortcomings and determine the best elements that can give the best results. Initially, the collaboration problems will be analyzed, since the main search for cooperative knowledge work and collaborative learning according to Stahl [4], is the emergence of shared group cognition through effective collaborative knowledge building.

Collaboration. Collaborative success is hard to achieve and probably impossible to guarantee or even predict [15]. Computer-supported cooperative work (CSCW) and Computer supported cooperative learning (CSCL) represent concerted attempts to overcome some of the barriers to collaborative success, like the difficulty of everyone in a group effectively participating in the ideas development with all the other members, the complexity of keeping track of all the inter-connected contributions that have been offered, or the barriers to working with people who are geographically distant [16].

As appealing as the technological aids introduction for communication, computation and memory seem, they inevitably introduce new problems, changing the social inter-actions, tasks and physical environment. Accordingly, CSCW and CSCL study and design must take into careful consideration the social composition of groups, the col-laborative activities and the technological supports.

According to Stahl [4], the promise of globally networked computers to usher in a new age of universal learning and of the sharing of human knowledge remains a distant dream; the software and social practices needed yet to be conceived, designed and adopted. To support online collaboration, the technology and culture have to be re-configured to meet bewildering constraints set. Above all, this requires under-standing how digital technology can mediate human collaboration. The idea with this proposal includes efforts to design software prototypes featuring specific collaboration support functionality, to analyze empirical instances of collaboration and to theorize about the issues, phenomena and concepts involved today in supporting collaborative knowledge building.

To Gros [17] states that software applications involved in the management of collaborative knowledge must comply to a greater or lesser extent with two technical characteristics: (a) facilitate the collaborative work of the users involved in the knowledge management process and (b) provide tools for the collaborative generation of knowledge as well as establishing tools that provide greater emphasis on the knowledge structures generation. Knowledge management software is characterized by allowing the learning of the participants through mechanisms of integration, admin-istration and distribution of knowledge. In addition to consider that computer support can help us to transcend the limits of individual cognition. It can facilitate the formation of small groups engaged in deep knowledge building, construct forms of group cog-nition that exceed what the group members could achieve as individuals [4]. Analyzing all of the above, it is necessary to bear in mind that generating a true collaboration in an activity using a software application is not an easy task, for which several aspects must be consider, such as social, cultural, different strategies and designing well the activity that really helps in this collaboration.

Group cognition. According to Stahl [4], group cognition is achieved through the collaborative knowledge construction. As a collaborative knowledge building, the emphasis is placed on the support for interactions between the students themselves, with a teacher playing a role more facilitating than instructive, in addition to the construction or subsequent development of some knowledge artifact type. The students are not simply socializing and exchanging their personal reactions or opinions about the subject matter, but might be developing a theory, model, diagnosis, conceptual map, mathematical proof or presentation. For this reason, it is harder to understand how a small group of people collaborating online can think and learn as a group. Group cognition is conceived as a facts sum of the individual heads, rather than as a positive cognitive phenomenon of its own. An alternative conceptualization is to see group cognition as an emergent quality of the interaction of individual cognitive processes. Emerging the important question: How does a group build its collective knowledge through a software application?

Previously [18] it was thought that collaborative knowledge building consisted only of forming a group, facilitating interaction among the multiple personal perspectives brought together, and then encouraging the negotiation of shared knowledge. But when a software application was used in this process resulted in disappointing levels of knowledge building.

With this evidence we see the need to do some additional questions and try to solve them with the research that will be carried out with this proposal: Can technology help groups to build knowledge? Can computer networks bring people together in global knowledge-building communities and support the interaction of their ideas in ways that help to transform the opinions of individuals into the groups knowledge? With this questions is necessary to think that the software should support cooperative work and collaborative learning; it should be assessed at the group level and it should be designed to foster group cognition, which will be the pillars of this proposal.

There is an evolution and previous research of the group cognition concept present in [4], which helps to understand the concept presented here and the objective that is sought with the framework of application design that it wants to achieve with this proposal:

- Mediated Cognition [19]: Vygotsky's work from the 1920's and 1930's only became available in English 50 years later, when it proposed a radically different view of cognition and learning as socially and collaboratively mediated.
- Distributed Cognition: This alternative developed by a number of writers (e.g., Suchman [20], Winograd [21], Pea [22], Hutchins [23]) also stressed the importance of not viewing the mind as isolated from artifacts and other people.
- Situated Learning [24]: Lave's work applied the situated perspective to learning, showing how learning can be viewed as a community process.
- Knowledge building [25]: Scardamalia and Bereiter developed the notion of community learning with a model of collaborative knowledge building in computer-supported classrooms.
- Meaning making [26]: Koschmann argued for re-conceptualizing knowledge building as meaning making, drawing upon theories of conversation analysis and ethnomethodology.
- Group Cognition: To arrive at a group cognition theory by pushing this progression a bit further with the help of a series of software implementation studies, empirical analyses of interaction and theoretical reflections on knowledge building.

Strategies. The "collaborative learning activities" do not directly engage in the construction of collaborative knowledge, but focus on activities that are expected to lead to this [14]. Therefore, the knowledge construction that should be generated in the process of performing a computer-assisted collaborative activity is of particular importance, consider that in order to obtain learning, the usual internet environments are not useful: chats, forums, wikis, which do not allow a true knowledge build and do not allow to link ideas, modify contributions, etc. That is why it is necessary to look for strategies that achieve this knowledge build to achieve group cognition. Some possible strategies have been analyzed, such as:

To monitor and evaluate. Monitoring and evaluating of the existing process, Collazos et al. in [27] they pose: for a collaboration process to be effective, certain guidelines must be followed and some roles must be defined, so that the only definition of these guidelines and roles does not guarantee that learning will be carried out in the most efficient. It is necessary to define a collaboration scheme, where the instructor knows when and how to intervene with the objective of improving the collaboration process. For this reason, it is important not only to consider the structural design of the collaboration space, the activities set that define the collaborative task, variables that can influence collaboration (group composition, gender, etc.), use of various interaction devices, but it is also important to understand the collaborative process that occurs when developing a collaborative activity considering all these aspects. One way of understanding this process is through modeling, monitoring and evaluating it [12].

According to [2] the availability of monitoring mechanisms for participants within a group activity can be very useful to identify people with low participation or groups with an unbalanced distribution of tasks. This identification process, in turn, will allow the activity coordinator to intervene when it deems appropriate and in this way to improve the collaborative process; the availability of computer tools can give more accurate data about the people performance. Therefore, one way to evaluate the group's effectiveness is to monitor, observe and evaluate the interactions among the group members. This allows the activity coordinator and the other participants to obtain an understanding of the quality of the interactions between each member of the respective groups and their progress in the task development [28, 29].

Gamification. Consists in the use of mechanic, elements and game design techniques in the context that are not games to involve users and solve problems. Some of the gamification benefits are: activates the motivation for learning, there is a constant feedback, allows a more meaningful learning generating a greater retention in the memory to be more attractive, creates a commitment for learning and linking the student with the content and with the tasks themselves, and also generates competitiveness as well as collaboration [30].

Gamification can be a powerful strategy that promotes learning among people and a change in behavior, therefore gamification in the academic field can even create a healthy dependence state [31]. Looking for a change in the user's attitude without the need to use coercion or deception, using game elements that call the attention to the user. Several studies [32] support the idea of gamification and indicate that through games you can achieve a change in attitude in a person's behavior. These benefits are intended to serve as a strategy to achieve group cognition, and increase collaboration among the participants of a collaborative activity.

Serious games. Games designed and developed primarily for a purpose or educational finality, above entertainment [33–35], using the game characteristics to generate motivation and immersive learning experiences [36]. Serious games have a convergence between the technological, the playful and the educational or formative, but with an emphasis on the latter. In addition, they allow the multiple intuitive developments, accessible training environments for educational and training purposes [37]. Several studies [38–43] have proposed methodologies for the serious games' design, but there are no any oriented to achieve group cognition and the search for an increase in collaboration. That is why the serious games benefits can be adopted to achieve the objectives that are to be achieved in this proposal.

Contents adaptation. It is the possibility to adapt the contents and strategies methodologies to the individual characteristics of the activity participants [44]. In this sense, the computer-supported training facilitates the realization of an adjustment of the virtual environments to the different cognitive types that the students use during their formative process. These are defined as those cognitive, affective and physiological traits that serve as relatively stable indicators of how participants in an activity perceive, interact and respond to their learning environments. From this definition we can deduce that cognitive styles are relatively stable traits, although susceptible to changes and improvements, adaptable to different situations; and that if they are taken into accounting, students can learn more effectively, in such a way that a software environment adapted to the cognitive type will generate better learning results [45]. Being the content adaptation a good strategy to be applied in software applications to obtain what is desired in the collaborative activities participants.

As analyzed above, we can determine that collaborative success is difficult to achieve and probably difficult to guarantee or even predict. Concerted attempts have been made to overcome some of the barriers to collaborative success, such as the difficulty of everyone in a group that effectively participates in the ideas development with all the other members, the keeping track complexity of all the interconnected contributions that have been offered, or barriers to work with people who are geographically distant. As attractive as the technological aids introduction for communication, computing and memory, they inevitably introduce new problems, changing social interactions, tasks and the physical environment. That is why it is necessary to create conditions that are probably favorable for the interactions type we want to study. One is to create student's groups who will work well together, who get along and understand each other and contribute a healthy combination of different skills. We must also carefully design the activities that will be carried out and the contents that are lent for the development and deployment of the understanding through collaborative interactions, activities that will not be solved by an individual, but that the group can chew together in the interaction online. In addition, the technology provided to the groups must be easy to use from the beginning, while meeting the communication and representation needs of the activities.

Objectives. With the above strategies and some others that can be analyzed in the research process of the proposal presented, it is intended to generate a framework that contain the necessary elements to support these strategies that increase collaboration and generate group cognition among the participants of a collaborative learning activity.

To achieve the above, it is necessary to follow the objectives: (a) To specify and characterize the learning collaborative process elements that allow to increase collaboration and achieve group cognition; (b) To select and use a methodology for modeling the framework that contains the learning collaborative process elements that allow increases collaboration and achieves group cognition; (c) To evaluate the framework in a collaborative learning environment and to validate the framework with experts to determine the completeness and ease of use in its application.

Hypothesis. Some initial hypotheses, which can be defined from what has been analyzed until now:

- The framework definition with strategies for the increase of collaboration and the consecution of group cognition allows the collaborative learning process improvement in the activity participants.
- A student's group working in a computer-assisted collaborative activity can, sometimes and under favorable conditions build a collaborative knowledge and a shared meaning that exceeds the knowledge of the individual members of the group.
- Educational activities can be designed to encourage and structure effective collaborative learning by presenting problems that require a shared deep understanding.
- Members of collaborative groups can internalize group knowledge as their own individual knowledge and can express it through persistent artifacts.
- Group cognition and collaboration achieved in a computer-assisted collaborative learning activity are achieved through the interaction of students and the application of well-defined strategies.

4 Project Progress

The collaborative learning process is divided into three phases [46]: Pre Process, Process and Post Process, in which we have done previous work on how to increase collaboration in the collaborative learning activity development in the Process phase (was collected the studies carried out in [47]) through the monitoring and evaluation use of the process and that generates evidence of the need to apply other strategies types to achieve such collaboration and generate group cognition, through the software applications design that accomplish these objectives. In this previous work, it was possible to conclude that to increase collaboration, it is not enough to deliver an activity and a software tool. To achieve true collaborative processes, it is necessary to structure the activities, analyze the type of people that make up the groups, the external factors that can affect the collaborative work and have a tool designed for the use of control, monitoring and evaluation mechanisms activity; so that collaboration is promoted and is not simply an individual work activity and furthermore it was defined that having a software tool that contains a compendium of mechanisms that allow to evaluate and monitor collaborative learning by the teacher, is of great help so that it can generate better results of collaboration between the students who participate in the same, so that are of great benefit and allowing an active collaboration and a common and egalitarian learning.

With this evidence that collaboration can be achieved through the strategy application (in this case, monitoring and evaluation) in the students who participate in a collaborative activity, where it sees the need to define a framework that allows the design of applications software that also achieve collaboration, group cognition, through the definition of another kind of strategies that allow these objectives, regardless of the context where you want to use this applications type.

Currently, the project is in the literature search stage to determine related works and conceptual bases that generate a solid justification and clearly define the problem planning and can establish its hypothesis, furthermore the initial steps for specifying and characterize the learning collaborative process elements that allow to increase collaboration and achieve group cognition.

5 Initial Conclusion

With the previous research, we found that the collaborative learning is a complex process and the same like to obtain the collaboration and the group learning, for that reason in this work are presented the advances towards the definition of a framework to increase collaboration and achieve group cognition. As an initial result, we have identified some elements that the framework should consider like part of its content and its structure for trying to improve the collaborative learning process with the group cognition elements. With the advance of our research process, we hope to improve the proposal in its components that need to consider both in its theoretical foundation and in its several constructs.

References

1. Centro Interuniversitario de desarrollo. Las nuevas demandas del desempeño profesional y sus implicancias para la docencia universitaria (2000)
2. Johnson, D., Johnson, R., Johnson, E., Roy, P.. Circles of Learning. Cooperation in the classroom. Association for Supervision and Curriculum Development (1984)
3. Smith, K., Kaagan, S., Yelon, S.: Cooperative Learning. Age 3, 1 (1992)
4. Stahl, G.: Group Cognition: Computer Support for Building Collaborative Knowledge. MIT Press, Cambridge (2006)
5. Carreras, M.: Diseño de un entorno colaborativo y su aplicación a plataformas de aprendizaje (Doctoral dissertation, Universidad de Murcia) (2005)
6. Jacobs, G., Ball, J., Gan, S.: Learning Cooperative Learning Via Cooperative Learning: A Sourcebook of Lesson Plans for Teacher Education on Cooperative Learning. Kagan Cooperative Learning (1997)
7. Roschelle, J., Teasley, S.D.: The construction of shared knowledge in collaborative problem solving. In: O'Malley C. (ed.) Computer Supported Collaborative Learning. NATO ASI Series (Series F: Computer and Systems Sciences), vol. 128. Springer, Heidelberg (1995). https://doi.org/10.1007/978-3-642-85098-1_5
8. Molina, A.I., Redondo, M.A., Ortega, M.: CIAM: Una Aproximación Metodológica para el desarrollo de Interfaces de Usuario en aplicaciones groupware. In: VII Congreso Internacional de Interacción Persona-Ordenador (INTERACCION 2006). 2006d. Puertollano (Spain) (2006)
9. Luisa, M., Luís, J., Visitación, M., Ramón, J.: Diseño de interfaces de usuario para aplicaciones colaborativas a partir de modelos independientes de la computación. Universidad de Granada, España (2005)

10. Gea, M., Gutiérrez, F., Garrido, J., Cañas, J.: AMENITIES: Metodologia de modelado de sistemas cooperativos. In: Workshop de Investigación sobre nuevos paradigmas de interacción en entornos colaborativos aplicados a la gestión y difusión del Patrimonio cultural (2002)
11. Dillenbourg, P.: What do you Mean by Collaborative Learning? (1999)
12. Scagnoli, N.I.: Estrategias para motivar el aprendizaje colaborativo en cursos a distancia (2005)
13. Koschmann, T.: CSCL, argumentation, and deweyan inquiry. In: Andriessen, J., Baker, M., Suthers, D. (eds.) Arguing to Learn. Computer-Supported Collaborative Learning, vol. 1. Springer, Dordrecht (2003). https://doi.org/10.1007/978-94-017-0781-7_10
14. Gros Salvat, B.: Aprendizajes, conexiones y artefactos: la producción colaborativa del conocimiento (No. Sirsi) i9788497842532) (2008)
15. Grudin, J.: Why CSCW applications fail: problems in the design and evaluation of organizational interfaces. In: Proceedings of the 1988 ACM Conference on Computer-Supported Cooperative Work, pp. 85–93. ACM (1988)
16. Persico, D., Pozzi, F., Sarti, L.: Design patterns for monitoring and evaluating CSCL processes. Comput. Hum. Behav. **25**(5), 1020–1027 (2009)
17. Gros, B.: Herramientas para la gestión de los procesos colaborativos de construcción del conocimiento (2010)
18. Lewis, K., Belliveau, M., Herndon, B., Keller, J.: Group cognition, membership change, and performance: Investigating the benefits and detriments of collective knowledge. Organ. Behav. Hum. Decis. Process. **103**(2), 159–178 (2007)
19. Khan, F.A.: Classics with commentary: vygotsky on mediated cognition. Contemp. Educ. Dialogue **2**(2), 225–244 (2005)
20. Suchman, L.A.: Plans and Situated Actions: The Problem of Human-Machine Communication. Cambridge University Press, Cambridge (1987)
21. Winograd, T., Flores, F.: Understanding Computers and Cognition: A New Foundation for Design. Ablex, Norwood (1986)
22. Pea, R.D.: Practices of distributed intelligence and designs for education. Distrib. Cognitions Psychol. Educ. Considerations **11**, 47–87 (1993)
23. Hutchins, E., Klausen, T.: Distributed cognition in an airline cockpit. In: Cognition and Communication at Work, pp. 15–34 (1996)
24. Lave, J., Wenger, E.: Situated Learning: Legitimate Peripheral Participation. Cambridge University Press, Cambridge (1991)
25. Scardamalia, M., Bereiter, C.: Knowledge building environments: extending the limits of the possible in education and knowledge work. In: Encyclopedia of distributed learning, pp. 269–272 (2003)
26. Koschmann, T.: The Edge of Many Circles: Making Meaning of Meaning Making (1999)
27. Collazos, C., Muñoz, J., Hernández, Y.: Aprendizaje colaborativo apoyado por computador. J. Chem. Inf. Model, p. 66 (2014)
28. Dillenbourg, P., Baker, M. J., Blaye, A., O'Malley, C.: The Evolution of Research on Collaborative Learning (1995)
29. Webb, N.M., Palincsar, A.S.: Group Processes in the Classroom. Prentice Hall International, New York (1996)
30. Borrás Gené, O.: Fundamentos de Gamificación (2015)
31. Peris, F.: Gamificación. Educ. Knowl. Soc. (EKS) **16**(2), 13–15 (2015)
32. Díaz Cruzado, J., Troyano Rodríguez, Y.: El potencial de la gamificación aplicado al ámbito educativo. III Jornadas de Innovación Docente. Innovación Educativa: respuesta en tiempos de incertidumbre (2013)
33. Abt, C.C.: Serious Games, p. 177 (1970)

34. Michael, D.R., Chen, S.L.: Serious Games: Games that Educate, Train, and Inform. Muska&Lipman/Premier-Trade, New York (2005)
35. Marcano, B.: Juegos serios y entrenamiento en la sociedad digital. Teoría de la Educación. Educación y Cultura en la Sociedad de la Información, vol. 9(3) (2008)
36. Sellami, H.M.: An E-Portfolio to support E-Learning 2.0. In: E-Learning 2.0 Technologies and Web Applications in Higher Education, pp. 155–170. IGI Global (2014)
37. Bredl, K., Bösche, W.: Serious Games and Virtual Worlds in Education, Professional Development, and Healthcare. IGI Global, Hershey (2013)
38. Marne, B., Huynh-Kim-Bang, B., Labat, J.M.: Articuler motivation et apprentissage grâce aux facettes du jeu sérieux. In: EIAH 2011-Conférence sur les Environnements Informatiques pour l'Apprentissage Humain, pp. 69–80. Editions de l'UMONS, Mons 2011 (2011)
39. Nadolski, R.J., Hummel, H.G., Van Den Brink, H.J., Hoefakker, R.E., Slootmaker, A., Kurvers, H.J., Storm, J.: EMERGO: a methodology and toolkit for developing serious games in higher education. Simul. Gaming 39(3), 338–352 (2008)
40. McMahon, M.: Using the DODDEL model to teach serious game design to novice designers. In: ASCILITE, pp. 646–653 (2009)
41. Tran, C., George, S., Marfisi-Schottman, I.: EDoS: an authoring environment for serious games. Design based on three models. In: Proceedings of ECGBL 2010 The 4th European Conference on Games Based Learning. 4th ECGBL, pp. 393–402 (2010)
42. Marfisi-Schottman, I., George, S., Tarpin-Bernard, F.: Tools and methods for efficiently designing serious games. In: Proceedings of the 4th European Conference on Games Based Learning ECGBL, pp. 226–234 (2010)
43. Cano, S., Arteaga, J.M., Collazos, C.A., Gonzalez, C.S., Zapata, S.: Toward a methodology for serious games design for children with auditory impairments. IEEE Lat. Am. Trans. 14(5), 2511–2521 (2016)
44. Moral Pérez, M., Villalustre Martínez, L.: Adaptación de los entornos virtuales a los estilos cognitivos de los estudiantes: un factor de calidad en la docencia virtual. Pixel-Bit. Revista de Medios y Educación, vol. 26, pp. 17–25 (2005)
45. Sánchez, P., Gil, C.: La atención a la diversidad desde la programación de aula. Revista interuniversitaria de formación del profesorado 36, 107–121 (1999)
46. Collazos, C.A., Guerrero, L.A., Pino, J.A., Renzi, S., Klobas, J., Ortega, M., Redondo, M., Bravo, C.: Evaluating collaborative learning processes using system-based measurement. J. Educ. Tech. Soc. 10(3), 257–274 (2007)
47. Delgado, V.A., Collazos, Cesar A., Fardoun, Habib M., Safa, N.: Collaboration increase through monitoring and evaluation mechanisms of the collaborative learning process. In: Meiselwitz, G. (ed.) SCSM 2017. LNCS, vol. 10283, pp. 20–31. Springer, Cham (2017). https://doi.org/10.1007/978-3-319-58562-8_2

Designing a Collaborative Learning Hub for Virtual Mobility Skills - Insights from the European Project *Open Virtual Mobility*

Ilona Buchem[1]([✉]), Johannes Konert[1], Chiara Carlino[2],
Gerard Casanova[3], Kamakshi Rajagopal[4], Olga Firssova[4],
and Diana Andone[5]

[1] Beuth University of Applied Sciences,
Luxemburger Str. 10, 13353 Berlin, Germany
ibuchem@googlemail.com
[2] Cineca Consorzio Interuniversitario,
Via Magnanelli 6/3, 40033 Casalecchio di Reno, Italy
[3] Université de Lorraine, Avenue de la Foret de Hayes,
54500 Vandoeuvres les Nancy, France
[4] Open Universiteit Nederland, Valkenburgerweg 177,
6419 AT Heerlen, Netherlands
[5] Politehnica University of Timisoara, Pta Victoriei No. 2,
300006 Timisoara, Romania

Abstract. Higher education faces high requirements and challenges in today's global world, including internationalisation as a response to globalisation. Virtual Mobility (VM) has a great potential to contribute to the internationalisation, innovation and inclusion in higher education. While it is feasible to encourage outward and inward student and faculty mobility, the main limitations include high costs of travelling and living in a foreign country, diverse socio-economic, health-related and even political issues. These barriers can be reduced by adding virtual components to mobility programs and actions (e.g. virtual seminars, virtual labs, virtual internships). This paper presents an approach for designing a collaborative learning hub for promoting VM Skills of educators and students in the European Higher Education Area. The VM Learning Hub assists to enhance the Virtual Mobility readiness of higher education institutions, educators and students through achievement, assessment and recognition of VM skills. This paper introduces the concept and the architecture of VM Learning Hub – a Collaborative and Personal Learning Environment with embedded technologies for innovative forms of skill attainment (open education, gamification), skill assessment (test-based and evidence-based e-assessment), skill recognition (open credentials, linked data) and collaboration (based on algorithm-based matching of learning groups).

Keywords: Virtual Mobility · Open education · Collaborative learning
E-assessment · Open credentials · Gamification · Linked data
Matching algorithms

1 Introduction

This paper is divided into 7 parts and starts with Introduction laying out the context and background about Virtual Mobility (VM) in Europe as well as the aims and outcomes of the Open Virtual Mobility project. The next Sect. 2 introduces design approaches applied in developing the VM Learning Hub showing how the demands in European Higher Education Area (EHEA) and Open Education (OE) principles shape the design considerations at various levels of user experience design: (i) system design, (ii) interaction design, (iii) content design, (iv) learning design and (v) visual design, following the UX model by Garret [1]. The concept and the design approach of the VM Learning Hub are presented in Sect. 3. Section 4 is dedicated to the VM Learning Hub components, taking into consideration the five dimensions of UX by Garret [1]. Section 5 presents preliminary research results from the VM concept mapping study with VM experts from Europe and discussed the implications for the next design iterations of the VM Learning Hub. Finally, Sect. 6 lays out conclusions addressing specific challenges and limitations in designing collaborative learning experiences in context of Virtual Mobility. The following sections will focus on five central aspects of the collaborative learning design:

1. *Open Education* approach to promote the achievement, assessment and credentialing of VM skills (including open and flexible approaches to designing transnational online collaboration) and the UX model - both building a framework for the development of the VM Learning Hub as laid out in this paper.
2. *VM Learning Hub* as a Collaborative and Personal Learning Environment with learner-centered forms of skill recognition (e.g. open digital credentials), collaboration (e.g. algorithm-based matching tool based on psychometrics) and access (e.g. mobile app).
3. *Enhancing learner-experience* by means of meaningful gamification design, e.g. customization of goals, tracking of team performance and visual design for the enhancement of learning experience.
4. *Competency-based forms of e-assessment* such as assessing VM skills and experiences from diverse learning contexts, a quality-assured and user-friendly tool to pre-assess own VM skills and recommendations for resources to close skill gaps.
5. *Semantic description of VM skills* using machine-readable competency vocabulary and cross-referencing skills in a relational graph to allow identification of similarity between VM skills as a basis for e-assessment and recognition of VM skill sets (e.g. digital, intercultural, language, collaboration skills).

1.1 Virtual Mobility in European Higher Education Area

The European Higher Education Area (EHEA) is framework based on public international law standards such as Lisbon Recognition Convention and part of the Bologna Reform aiming at ensuring more comparable, compatible and coherent systems of higher education in Europe. The European Higher Education Area has been in operation since March 2010 and during the last eighteen years 48 countries have been continuously building this common education area by adapting their higher education systems through the implementation of reforms in higher education on the basis of common values, facilitation of fair recognition of foreign qualifications and/or study periods abroad and enhancement of mobility of students and staff. Some of the key instruments implemented in EHEA include the European Credit Transfer and Accumulation System (ECTS), the Diploma Supplement and Learning Agreements for Studies ensuring the recognition for the activities successfully completed abroad. These tools and processes have contributed to a higher compatibility, internationalisation and quality assurance in higher education in EHEA in the recent years.

Mobility of students and staff has been one of the central objectives and main policy areas of the EHEA. For example, the Communiqué of European Ministers for Higher Education in Europe from 2009 states that: "In 2020, at least 20% of those graduating in the European Higher Education Area should have had a study or training period abroad" [2]. Mobility has been considered an important part of higher education as it supports personal development and employability, fosters respect for diversity, encourages linguistic pluralism underpinning the multilingual tradition of Europe and increases cooperation and competition between higher education institutions [2]. The Erasmus program, superseded by Erasmus+, has been one of the most well-known programs promoting mobility of students and staff.

However, as the mobility statistics show, despite numerous initiatives and programs, the uptake of mobility of students and staff has been very diverse across Europe [3]. Despite acknowledging the social and cultural benefits of mobility for higher education, awareness and exploitation of mobility instruments are still not as extensive as anticipated [4]. A study about the obstacles to student mobility lists a number of reasons preventing students to be mobile [5]. These include socio-cultural background and status, disabilities and chronic diseases, family and parental obligations, the financing of the mobility period, the language proficiency, the availability of information about the mobility period and the recognition of study periods and degrees [5]. From this perspective, the concept of virtual mobility has been discussed as a non-discriminatory alternative of mobility. Through the use of ICT supported activities organized at the institutional level mobility becomes accessible to all [6]. It is important to emphasise that virtual mobility is "organized at the institutional level" which means that the activities are not ad hoc initiatives by single teachers or individual students, but are fully embedded in mainstream and core processes of the institution [6]. To conclude: Virtual mobility has a great potential to contribute to the internationalisation, innovation and inclusion in higher education, and the main obstacles to mobility can be dramatically reduced by adding the virtual component.

1.2 The Project Open Virtual Mobility

The project Open Virtual Mobility (openVM) is a strategic partnership for innovation and the exchange of good practices. The partnership is composed of nine European partner organisations from higher education, aiming at enhancing the uptake of virtual mobility in higher education by improving VM skills and in consequence VM readiness. The possibilities of virtual mobility (e.g. joint virtual seminars, virtual internships or placements, virtual campuses or virtual support activities for physical mobility before, during and after physical mobility) are still unknown to many educators and students in Europe [4]. The study by Dauksiene et al. [4] pinpoints some of the key barriers impeding VM implementation on a wider scale in higher education in Europe. These include a lack of knowledge and/or the lack of consensus about the concept of VM on the national and institutional levels, missing practical examples and applicable scenarios for VM implementations, lack of knowledge and/or experience in recognising and accrediting VM activities, and missing evidence about the effectiveness of VM at different levels (e.g. contribution to physical mobility, intercultural experience, internationalisation).

The project Open Virtual Mobility addresses these challenges and aims to create the European Virtual Mobility Learning Hub for achievement, assessment and recognition of VM skills. The VM Learning Hub is envisaged to become a central reference point for educators and students wishing to learn about the different possibilities and forms of virtual mobility, collaborate on designing VM activities, assess and recognise VM skills, i.e. skills acquire from and/or relevant for the implementation and/or participation in VM actions. The project aims to develop a set of tools, methods and guidelines to enhance achievement, assessment and recognition of skills, provide support on pedagogy and technology for the design and implementation of virtual mobility, and enhance collaborations of participating organisations, educators and students. The VM Learning Hub aims to provide engaging and effective learning experience and to provide evidence about how achievement, assessment and credentialing of VM skills contributes to the uptake virtual mobility.

The premise of the openVM project is that virtual mobility can develop its potential, provided higher education leaders, educators, students and other relevant stakeholders, such as International Offices, know about and know how to use the opportunities of virtual mobility. This means higher education staff, educators and students need the necessary skills, confidence and readiness to initiate and implement VM activities in their own organisations. The openVM project intends to enhance the readiness for virtual mobility against the backdrop with Open Education (OE) and addresses the need of creating accessible opportunities for achievement of skills, needed to design, implement and participate in VM activities in line with the principles of Open Education.

2   Overall Design Approach in the Project *Open Virtual Mobility*

The design approach in the project *Open Virtual Mobility* is based on the concept of Open Education (hence *open* in the name of the project). Open Education is an umbrella term under with many different understandings. In Europe, particularly in higher education, Open Education has been discussed as an important element of the European policy agenda. The key perspectives on open, higher education in Europe include (a) reducing or removing access barriers such as financial, geographical, time and entry requirements barriers, (b) modernising higher education in Europe by means of digital technologies, and (c) bridging non-formal and formal education, by making it easier to recognise learning achievements [7]. Both virtual mobility and open education aim to enhance participation in international knowledge flows, use of digital media, improve teaching and learning, attract and keep talents through internationalisation, but also innovate and build capacity.

The project *Open Virtual Mobility* focuses on creating readiness of educators and students for virtual mobility against the backdrop of open education. The model applied in the project is the OpenEdu framework developed by the Joint Research Centre of the European Commission. The OpenEdu framework is based on the results from four studies on OE in Europe, which included desk research, reviews of academic and grey literature (websites, blogs, newspapers, reports), consultations and validation with experts and final validation by the target audience, i.e. the decision makers at universities across Europe [7]. The framework builds on the information on the state of-the-art of OE in Europe and provides a holistic view of OE in higher education. The framework proposes 10 dimensions of OE, i.e. 6 core dimensions: access dimension, content dimension, pedagogy dimension, recognition dimension, collaboration dimension and research dimension, and 4 transversal dimensions: strategy dimension, technology dimension, quality dimension and leadership dimension. The core dimensions represent *what* is included and transversal dimensions indicate *how* to achieve it [7]. Each dimension interrelates with all other dimensions and allows for different degrees of openness in higher education. The model recommends to apply a holistic strategy for opening up higher education along these 10 dimensions and to involve various stakeholders in the process of design, i.e. education providers (institutions), teachers, researchers, students and policy makers. The design approach in the openVM project is based on the recommendations of the OpenEdu framework and applies the proposed descriptors as listed in Table 1.

Table 1. Dimensions of Open Education proposed by the OpenEdu framework [7].

Dimension	Descriptors in relation to the design of the VM Learning Hub
Access dimension	Expanding access to information and knowledge about virtual mobility is a core principle of the open project. The key focus is on granting access for learners (higher education staff and students) to engage with educational content (e.g. OER), courses (e.g. MOOC), communities of practice, networks and other types of knowledge sharing environments
Content dimension	The content dimension refers to educational material dedicated to virtual mobility, which is free of charge and available to all. The open content provided in the VM Learning Hub can be open licensed or in the public domain, is free of charge and accessible by everyone without restrictions. This grants greater permissions in the use of content, such as adaptation, translation, remix, reuse and redistribution, depending on the type of license applied
Pedagogy dimension	The pedagogy dimension refers to making the range of teaching and learning practices more open, transparent, sharable and visible. The openVM project applies pedagogical design principles for learning which help to widen participation and collaboration. To enhance the openness, the VM Learning Hub makes available the rationale for learning design, applies collaborative methods such as open learning by

(*continued*)

Table 1. (*continued*)

Dimension	Descriptors in relation to the design of the VM Learning Hub
	design and crowd creation of OER and MOOC, makes assessments and recognition of learning outcomes transparent (e.g. open credentials, evidence-based assessment)
Recognition dimension	The recognition dimension refers to the process of recognition of VM skills with the help of open credentials such as Open Badges and the process of acknowledging and accepting credentials, such as badges or certificates issued by a third-party and brought by the learners/users of the VM Learning Hub. The VM Learning Hub applies open credentials to attest that a set of learning outcomes relevant for virtual mobility and achieved by an individual has been assessed against a predefined standard specified in the competency framework. This type of recognition enables learners to make their skills visible to others in view of projects, co-operations and joint actions in line with virtual mobility, thus contributing to the uptake of VM
Collaboration dimension	The collaboration dimension refers to connecting individuals and institutions by facilitating the exchange of practices and resources. The VM Learning Hub is designed to enable collaboration, e.g. through co-development of OER and MOOC in learning groups, and peer-support, e.g. exchange of knowledge and feedback when designing own virtual mobility activities. As collaboration is a live and evolving practice which is shaped by participating individuals, the VM Learning Hub is designed to cater for such dynamics in joint practice with respect for socio-cultural differences
Research dimension	The research dimension refers to providing access to data and research on virtual mobility and enhancing participation of learners/users in research, e.g. assessing the impact of improving virtual mobility skills for the uptake of VM in practice. Researcher on VM can gain from such open research activities, because extended networks of users/learners provide a larger pool of expertise in different fields, e.g. diverse types of higher education organisations, diverse fields of study and backgrounds
Strategy dimension	The strategy dimension refers to the creation of a unique and valuable position of the VM Learning Hub about the openness of higher education, with the special focus on internationalisation as a key aspect of VM. It involved a set of activities such as communicating the values of open, higher education, providing opportunities and resources for open learning and the enhancing the capabilities of higher education institution with respect to opening up education. Basing the strategy of the VM Learning Hub on openness enhances and enriches its educational offer
Technology dimension	The technology dimension refers to the technological infrastructure of the VM Learning Hub which aims to facilitate opening up of higher education in its different dimensions. The technological solutions applied in the design and development of the VM Learning Hub focus on providing access to educational resources and activities for all, validating the identity of people being assessed for the recognition

(*continued*)

Table 1. (*continued*)

Dimension	Descriptors in relation to the design of the VM Learning Hub
	virtual mobility skills and issuing open credentials to recognise virtual mobility skills. Given the commitment to the greatest possible level of openness, the VM Learning Hub is built on open standards and open source technologies which are interoperable
Quality dimension	The quality dimension refers to the convergence of the 5 concepts of quality, i.e. efficacy, impact, availability, accuracy and excellence, with the education offer of the VM Learning Hub. The openVM project aims to measure the quality of the VM Learning Hub offer against the standards of Open Education as set out by the OpenEdu framework. Additionally, the quality of the VM Learning Hub components, such as open credentials, OER, MOOC, will be assured by experts recognised in the given field. Thus the granularity of quality assurance ranges from the overall offer to single components
Leadership dimension	The leadership dimension refers to the promotion of sustainable open education activities and initiatives. The VM Learning Hub aims to encourage individuals and organisations in creating opening up higher education through virtual mobility. The leadership of the VM Learning Hub focuses on promoting the uptake of virtual mobility by a range of stakeholders including educators and students and in supporting open education practices

The design of the collaborative VM Learning Hub in the project *Open Virtual Mobility* applies the principles of Open Education (OE) to promote achievement, assessment and recognition of VM skills. The VM Learning Hub aims to create online, open and flexible opportunities for higher education staff and students to learn about and how to plan and engage in VM, assess and recognize their VM skills and in this way increase readiness and confidence to implement virtual mobility.

3 Virtual Mobility Learning Hub Design Approach and Concept

The VM Learning Hub developed in the project *Open Virtual Mobility* is intended to become as a central reference point for achievement, assessment and recognition of virtual mobility skills. The components of the collaborative VM Learning Hub include an algorithm-based matching tool to enhance collaboration, an e-assessment tool based on rich evidence of learning from different contexts to assess VM skills, and open digital credentials to recognise VM skills with such as tools as Open Badges and Blockcerts. The VM Learning Hub is designed to cater for (a) collaborative activities as part of co-design of Open Educational Resources (OER) dedicated to virtual mobility (e.g. good practice examples and guidelines), and (b) collaborative activities as part of learning in the VM MOOC for achievement of VM skills as well as assessment and validation of VM skills (e.g. peer-reviews of evidence).

3.1 Design Approach

The approach to designing the VM Learning Hub builds on the principles of User Experience (UX) and User Engagement (UE). User engagement may be defined as the quality of the user experience as it emphasises the positive aspects of the interaction, such as being captivated and motivated to use technologies [8]. Designing for user engagement for collaborative learning means designing engaging experiences for groups of learners. User engagement has been associated with specific user characteristics which can be also applied to the field of learning, e.g. focused attention, sense of control, novel and unexpected experience, positive emotions during the interaction, willingness to repeat the experience [9]. User engagement in technology-enhanced learning setting can be evaluated by applying engagement metrics such as time spent on site, number of performed learning activities, number of comments [10].

The design of the VM Learning Hub in the project *Open Virtual Mobility* is based on the multi-layer user engagement framework proposed by Garrett [1]. The UX model by [1] is a user-centered design approach which defines the key considerations of UX design. This model has been already adapted to and applied in the field of technology-enhanced learning [10]. The design of user engagement in the VM Learning Hub takes place on all five layers as the elements affect each other to form the overall user experience, as shown in Fig. 1. Additionally, the VM Learning Hub is a suitable scenario to combine approaches for a modern web-application (task-oriented design) and a multi-medial hypertext-system (information-oriented design).

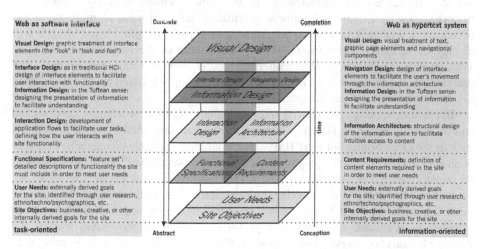

Fig. 1. UX elements in vertical layers including the horizontal duality of information-oriented vs. task-oriented design [1].

3.2 Concept

From a user perspective the VM Learning Hub is a responsive web-application with a landing page that offers solutions for the different user needs mentioned before. Technically, several components will be loosely coupled to provide the functionality, but on the front-end users primarily interact with the learning hub interface. It will be based on the Open Source Learning Management System (LMS) Moodle[1], inspired by its MOOC-oriented extension Moodle Academy[2].

As a start, users will have the choice of general information and first-step guidelines about conducting virtual mobility at their own organization (targeting teachers and administration) or about finding and participating in existing VM opportunities (targeting students). Alternatively, users can directly open e-assessment resources to assess their level of expertise and experience. In case these assessments do not require upload of artifacts as evidence, the result can be evaluated automatically. Finally, different entry points to online learning courses, depending on the users information need and level of expertise, are offered. On enrolment to a course users can voluntarily fill out the group formation questionnaires to be added to one suitable learning group. If they do not provide such personal data, they are matched randomly. Their peer learning group is created for assisting in task solving, actively responding to user forum questions, and the group is responsible for peer assessment and feedback which may be required to issue Open Credentials certifying VM skills.

All relevant activities, results and progress will be fed to an Experience API (xAPI) [11] via existing Moodle plugins [12] (or extensions to be written). The corresponding digital certification with the help of Open Credentials, such as Open Badges and Blockcerts will be provided by the partner badging platform as described in the sections below. The badging platform will watch the xAPI records and as soon as the user fulfills all criteria of a defined Open Badge, the user will be notified and the badge is issued. Official issuing organization is the Open Virtual Mobility consortium. Endorsements by national educational institutions with expertise in mobility in the EAHE are intended. To provide a consistent user experience, plugins for Moodle will display the achieved Open Credentials by connecting to the Representational State Transfer Application Programming Interface (REST-API) that provides this data. The design of the user interface and REST-API will be strongly inspired by Mozilla's Open Source Backpack for Open Badges.

Interactive learning resources for individual and collaborative learning are designed and technically based on HTML5 Package format and supported by compatible tools such as the Open Source software H5P which enables users to create interactive content in an easy way [13]. Moodle plugins for adding H5P content exist[3]. Existing OERs will be transformed to, or extended by, the HTML5-based technology such as H5P. All content will be hosted in the Moodle platform. References to the individual resources, including metadata about VM skills will be stored in the badging platform in order to calculate most suitable learning pathways for users based on their xAPI records. To inform Moodle about these pathways and display them to users within the learning hub, a plugin will access the badging platform REST-API for these suggestions. The major benefit of loosely coupling the Moodle learning hub with the badging platform via

---

[1] http://moodle.org, last accessed 2018/01/30.

[2] https://academy.moodle.net/, last accessed 2018/01/30.

[3] https://moodle.org/plugins/mod_hvp, last accessed 2018/01/30.

xAPI and REST-API is the possibility for users to easily access, display, and export their Open Credentials. Likewise, users can access recommendations for learning resources and further Open Credentials beyond the context of virtual mobility.

4 Virtual Mobility Learning Hub Components

4.1 Learning Activities and Gamification

The VM Learning Hub aims to create engaging and effective learner experience through diverse, collaborative learning activities making use of gamification as an approach to enhancing collaborative learning. Gamification means using game elements in non-game contexts [14]. The design approach builds on the concept of meaningful gamification, which focuses on providing effective incentives by helping learners find meaning in each underlying activity [15, 16]. This approach is different to some of the traditional gamification approaches which tend to provide meaningless awards which may distract or even discourage learners. The concept of meaningful gamification goes beyond providing external rewards for reaching specified thresholds or levels, which can reduce the internal motivation of the learner [15]. The goal of meaningful gamification is to enhance the internal motivation without emphasising external rewards including popular scoring systems. Studies, such as the meta-analysis by [17] show that most forms of external rewards tend to reduce internal motivation [15]. Some of the other challenges of scoring-based gamification approaches include (a) limited possibilities for an individual to make choices without external influence or control (which may have negative effects on self-determination and self-regulation), (b) the necessity to keep the user in the reward loop all the time (which may have negative effects on learner autonomy as it never frees the learner from the external control of the scoring system), and (c) enhancing negative effects through the lack of progress or weak scores compared to other users [15]. Thus the approach of meaningful gamification applied in the design of the VM Learning Hub aims to avoid the pitfalls of score-based gamification approaches and focuses on allowing users to self-identify with the goals of activities by facilitating the understanding of the importance of an activity and helping users integrate the goals of activities with personal goals [15]. The key approach here is not to create goals for learning activities without user involvement, but to involve the user in the definition and/or customization of the goals so that the goals of activities can become relevant to user background, interests and needs [15]. This also includes taking into consideration the organisational context into of learning activities [15].

The meaningful gamification design of learning activities in the VM Learning Hub is applied to create a meaningful user/learner experience in view of enhancing readiness for the uptake of virtual mobility in higher education. The meaningful gamification design is applied to key learning and collaboration activities in the VM Learning Hub, such as (a) co-design of Open Educational Resources (OER), (b) collaborative learning activities in the VM MOOC, (c) peer-assessment of evidence as part of e-assessment of virtual mobility skills. Involving learners in co-designing OER and parts of the MOOC will be accomplished by using such approaches as "Crowd Creation" [18] and "Open

Learning through Design" [19]. The co-design approach aims at creating learning activities and learning resources for educators and students wishing to develop their virtual mobility skills and enhance own readiness for effectively design and participation in virtual mobility.

The process of co-creation of learning resources and activities is driven by theory of Universal Design for Learning (UDL), which is a used as a guide to create meaningful learning experiences that are appropriate for a diverse group of learners [20]. Using UDL principles allows to design for diverse needs and interests of students by creating possibilities to demonstrate how learners have met learning outcomes, e.g. by providing evidence as part of the e-assessment. In order to take the diversity of learners' needs and interests into consideration, three strategies are recommended by [20], i.e. (a) presenting content in different ways (the "what" of learning), (b) providing different activities for the learner (the "how" of learning), and allowing different paths for learners to achieve goals and to make a meaningful connection to the activity (the "why" of learning) [15]. One practical way to support the process of co-creation of learning resources and activities by means of meaningful gamification is to allow users to set and/or customize their own goals within the VM Learning Hub: *"The design challenge here is to support and guide the user in setting long- and short-term goals such that they become achievable and provide experiences of mastery on the way"* [14, p. 37].

As any meaningful game and gamification requires not only freedom of users but also the constraints of the game, the approach of allowing learners to set and/or customise own goals also includes constraints which are placed upon learners' choices and in this way provide guidance toward making choices that are both meaningful to the learner and that meet the overall goal of the VM Learning Hub which is the enhancement of VM skills as a way to enhance readiness for the uptake of virtual mobility in higher education. The VM Learning Hub is thus designed as a flexible system which allows learners to choose from a variety of options and creates possibilities for customization. The meaningful design of the VM Learning Hub allows learners to (a) customise learning goals based on a predefined set of possible learning goals within the hub and helping learners understand how the goals of the activity connect to personal goals such as developing a particular set of virtual mobility skills, (b) choose from available open credentials which are used to mark the achievement of specific pre-identified skill-sets, which are also meaningful outside the VM Learning Hub, (c) provide own evidence to demonstrate how the learning goals/outcomes have been met as part of evidence-based assessment, (d) provide peer-assessment of the evidence attached to open credentials, (e) choose from and develop own ways of engaging with the activities such as co-design of OER, (f) create own activities and transform existing activities to match own goals and needs (e.g. defining typical obstacles in implementing and/or participating in virtual mobility and designing and/or transforming activities to overcome these obstacles (which leads to feeling satisfied and positive about own abilities by overcoming meaningful obstacles), (g) match learners into optimized groups based on individual criteria (e.g. similar goals, complementary prior knowledge, suitable combinations of personality traits for group work) so that learners can find meaning through group engagement, and (h) share the content with other users and non-users of the VM Learning Hub (e.g. colleagues and students in own organisations or in other organisations, e.g. via social media).

The approach to designing learning activities and meaningful gamification in the VM Learning Hub is in line with the theory of user-centered design which for every design decision asks and answers the question *How does it benefit the user?* and considers user needs and goals at every stage of the design process [15]. This approach is also in line with the theory of situated motivational affordances, which is a Human-Computer Interaction approach to gamification emphasising the need to consider not only artifact affordances (e.g. affordances of gamification elements) but also situational affordances (e.g. affordances of the organisational or learning context) as factors influencing a successful user interaction in a gamified context [22]. The expectation is that the user-centered meaningful gamification design as described above will result in a deeper engagement of learners and in consequence in enhanced readiness for virtual mobility.

4.2   Matching Mechanisms for Collaboration in Groups

In pedagogy, core benefits of group learning are widely agreed upon, like deeper insight into the topic, better argumentation skills and improved social competencies due to applied peer education concepts in the group learning process. Nevertheless, even in small learning scenarios teachers are overwhelmed to form optimized learning groups for certain learning goals. Consequently, mostly learning groups are formed randomly or by self-selection, while it is well known that these approaches have major drawbacks [23]. In pure online learning, like the VM Learning Hub, students and teachers may not know each other. In such learning environments, but also in larger classrooms, an algorithmic approach to form optimized learning groups is needed.

From the algorithmic perspective it is only possible to find near-optimal solutions as the brute-force calculation of optimal learner combination in groups is of complexity class $\Omega(\alpha^M)$ with $\alpha > 1$ and M as the number of participants [24, p. 646], [25, p. 90f]. Some approaches use machine learning techniques based on prior behaviour of individuals and preceding group work results. Their advantage is the incremental improvement for one certain learning goal for a specific cohort of learners. On the contrary the causality remains unclear and it cannot be didactically explained why such groups perform well. Thus the results are not transferable to other learning goals, cohorts of learners or tasks. A second group of approaches uses agent-based systems where digital agents represent learners and negotiate with each other for learning group formation. While their strength is the continuous, non-discrete dynamic formation and re-formation of groups based on changes in values the agents optimize their position for, they do not support consideration of global criteria, like similar group quality of size of groups in the while cohort. A third type of approaches is based on numerical optimization with boundary conditions and uses learner criteria vectors to find near optimal combinations satisfying a target formula for learning goals. While they can only be applied at discrete points of time to group all learners, they allow consideration of boundary conditions of the groups and the whole cohort. A more comprehensive overview of algorithms can be found in [26] or [27]. One flexible algorithm with a numerical approach is GroupAL [28] which proved already its benefits in simulations and field studies and is currently the best candidate to be applied for learning group formation in the VM Learning Hub.

The question which criteria are the most relevant ones for learning group formation, is as important as the algorithmic approach. While machine learning approaches tend to use rather unstable criteria which depend on a certain learning scenario and task types, but are quite easy to measure within a learning management system (e.g. Moodle). Such criteria are for example a degree of participation in discussions or rating of group work quality. Stable criteria, on the contrary, are defined as person-related aspects that do not change significantly when learning scenarios or group compositions switch. Therefore, if positive effects of certain combination of such stable criteria on the quality of learning groups are known, they are more likely transferable and applicable to several task types and learning goals. Which of these stable criteria are candidates for optimized learning group formation is part of the research field pedagogical psychology.

To optimize learning groups in a VM Learning Hub with participants from all over Europe, robustness against cultural differences of the selected criteria becomes a major aspect, which is rarely investigated yet. Only for personality traits, mostly referred to as the Big 5 (i.e. extraversion, conscientiousness, openness, social agreeableness, and neuroticism), it has been proven that these are stable over time for individuals and are independent of cultural backgrounds [29]. As no robust way to measure them indirectly from interaction behaviour with a learning system has been found yet, a robust questionnaire measurement has been defined [30]. Recent studies found for satisfaction with the group work, quality of group work results and cohesion within the group two aspects to be most relevant: each learning should have one member with outstanding level of conscientiousness (to align the group activities to the learning goals) and one member should have an outstanding level of extraversion (to guide the group and initiate activity continuously) [27]. Other heterogeneous or homogeneous combination of factors stayed behind in effect sizes. Still, for group cohesion, the amount of time per week, participants are willing to invest, should be matched homogeneously within a group to prevent dissatisfaction. In case when learning scenarios afford synchronous tasks to be performed by groups, even the weekly schedule could be considered.

While the mentioned criteria are found to be relevant in related literature and prior studies, the formation of learning groups for VM skills has not yet been investigated. Thus, all active members of the openVM project participate in collection, prioritization and literature research on additional criteria to consider for optimized group learning of VM skills. It is expected that no commonly agreed and proven set of criteria can be found. As a consequence one or more sets of optimization criteria will be selected based on the relevant literature base. Learners using the VM Learning Hub will be informed about the scientific research aspect of the learning group formation and they offered to opt-in for optimized learning group formation. To allow participation in group activities without agreement, participants will be grouped randomly or by self-selection.

4.3   E-Assessment of Virtual Mobility Skills

Beside the group formation tools, the e-assessment tool will be implemented in the VM Learning Hub. The main role of e-assessment will be to assess virtual mobility skills. This can take many forms including automatic self-assessments and human-supported evidence-based assessments. By using the e-assessment tool, both individuals and organizations will be able to assess and analyze the skills required for virtual mobility and will be able to identify solutions for developing those skills.

The e-assessment of VM skills is planned to be composed of two main parts: the e-assessment concept and the realization of the assessment tool. The e-assessment concept will be built in 3 phases, i.e. (1) defining the objects of the evaluation with the guiding questions in this phase being: *What will be evaluated? Who will be evaluated?*, (2) defining the purpose of assessment (e.g. formative, summative, diagnostic), and (3) defining the tools to be used which best suite according to the results of the former two phases. The main objects to be evaluated in phase one are the VM skills. These skills are defined in the first part of the project as part of the conceptual framework though applying different research methods such as Group Concept Mapping as described in the sections below. The framework will also define which VM skills are relevant for which target groups. According to the literature there are different type of e-assessment depending of the purposes: formative, summative and diagnostic [31]. Formative assessment is used to provide feedback during the learning process. Summative assessment provides a quantitative grade and is often conducted at the end of a unit or lesson to determine that the learning objectives have been met. Diagnostic assessment is a form of pre-assessment that allows a teacher to determine students' individual strengths, weaknesses, knowledge, and skills prior to instruction. It is primarily used to diagnose student difficulties and to guide lesson and curriculum planning. It can also be used after the instruction to evaluate the efficiency of learning. Diagnostic assessment will be used a priori to evaluate VM skills. It will be combined with the Open Credentials issued as part of the project summative e-assessments will be designed as part of the evidences users of the VM Learning Hub have to provide to be awarded with Open Credentials, such as VM skill badges. In the final phase, two categories must be considered for the definition of suitable e-assessment tools. These two categories are: (1) e-testing for automated e-assessment (e.g. based on the test score), and (2) e-assessments with evidence for non-automated e-assessment, i.e. e-assessment which requires the intervention of a teacher or a peer and allows for a deeper conceptual rating and more individual feedback for deep-learning (Table 2).

To support e-testing, a self-evaluation tool will be integrated into the VM Learning Hub. This tool is already used in another project (self-assessment tool in elene4work[4]). The tool consists of a survey with a Likert scale which allows users to self-evaluate their soft skills by answering a set of questions which have been defined in the competency framework in the same project. To support the e-assessment with evidence, evidence-based tools, like assignments or e-portfolios, will be offered to enable learners to demonstrate their VM skills in more qualitative ways. The evidence will be evaluated by peers or teachers and may be attached to Open Credentials such as Open Badges to form a metadata-based digital certificate. Such assessment will be useful for the individuals and organisations to adapt their practices to improve VM skills. They can also help learners to choose OERs and MOOCs recommended by the VM Learning Hub to improve less developed skills. According to the results obtained from the

---

Table 2. Categories of e-assessments applied in the VM Learning Hub.

E-testing (automated)	E-assessment with evidence (non-automated)
Multiple choice questions (with feedback or not)	E-portfolios
True or False questions	Assignment
Single choice questions (with feedback or not)	Peer assessment
Drag and drop	Cases studies
Survey (with Likert scale)	Games

three-phase of e-assessment design, a comparative study will be launched to collect different e-assessment examples. The higher education community, including project partners, will provide different examples of e-assessment forms for skill assessment. The goal is to arrive at least one e-assessment example suitable for each category of e-assessment (e.g. e-portfolio, survey, quiz) and for each type of assessment (formative, diagnosis or summative). The collection of examples will be done through an online template and will provide helpful material to build the e-assessment to evaluate VM skills. The template will include several items showing how skills are evaluated (e.g. in which forms and formats and for what kinds of skills). With the skills defined for the openVM framework, the analysis of the collected e-assessment forms and the VM Learning Hub concept, the e-assessment tools for the VM Learning Hub will be designed, implemented and tested. The e-assessment tools have to respect technical specifications defined for the VM Learning Hub as described above. The e-assessment tools must also meet quality criteria other than technical criteria such as reliability, validity and objectivity [32]. One of the most important quality criteria for e-assessment is the validity, including the construct validity, which in this context refers to whether an e-assessment measures the intended construct. In order to optimize this criterion, the evaluations will be based on the principle of scoring grids, i.e. rubrics which are scoring guides, usually in the form of a matrix or grid, with criteria and quality definitions for these criteria. A rubric for e-assessment will be applied as a tool used to interpret and evaluate learner skills demonstrated in evidence-based e-assessment against the criteria and quality standards specified in the grid. To enable users of VM Learning Hub to benefit most from the e-assessment tools, guidelines will be realized and implemented within the tools. These will also give advice to users (e.g. peers, teachers) about how to interpret the data in form of a graphic results with comparison to rubrics and/or other users means values.

4.4 Open Credentials for the Recognition of Virtual Mobility Skills

Open Credentials will be used as a component of the VM Learning Hub to recognise virtual mobility skills. Open Credentials encompass various tools and approaches, including Open Badges and Blockcerts.

Open Badges for Recognition of Skills: Open Badges are the emerging standard to digitally valorize informal and non-formal learning, or to "communicate skills and achievements by providing visual symbols of accomplishments packed with verifiable data and evidence that can be shared across the web" [33]. Initiated by the Mozilla Foundation in 2011, the Open Badge standard has been now adopted worldwide by individuals and organisations including higher education institutions to look for ways to give proper value to specific competencies, which often remain unrecognised and/or are not made transparent by formal degrees and certificates. Open Badges have a form of a Portable Network Graphics (PNG) with embedded metadata allowing the verification of the Open Badge validity and ownership [34]. Open Badges provide a digital, open and flexible way to define skills and competencies, identify them visually and issue a proof of competency mastery to learners which can be accompanied by specific evidences and outcomes, and is always completed by a clear description of criteria that needed to be met to earn that Open Badge. While Open Badges have notably been used to provide a digital, readable and quickly verifiable evidence of formal degrees (e.g. University of Milan Bicocca[5] and University of Bicocca[6]), it is significant that the most enthusiasm has been drawn to the field of soft skills, especially important for an ever changing contexts and lifelong learning [35, 36]. Soft skills, which comprise a large part of the virtual mobility skill-set, are also difficult to identify [37]. The problem of agreeing on competency definitions will be avoided by making the definition and the alignment to the competency frameworks used to define VM skill-sets transparent. The same will be done for criteria: each Open Badge issuer will be able to define own criteria, and Open Badge readers will be able to choose how an Open Badge should be evaluated based on those criteria and the related evidences. The openVM project will apply the Open Badge concept to the Virtual Mobility domain, leveraging the Bestr[7] platform developed by one of the project partners. The project will identify which competencies would benefit from being represented with an Open Badge, also with reference to the user experience and the gamification approach that the use of Open Badges enables. Having a visual representation of a goal to be achieved by collecting a series of learning experiences or evidences is of course a basic element for gamification, but an extremely important added value for all learners is represented by the fact that such achievement will also be valid outside the learning experience and can actually be inserted in CVs, where it will provide instant verification not only of the validity of the Open Badge but also of the criteria and institution who issued the badge. The VM Learning Hub will therefore represent relevant examples of institution (hub of institutions) providing assessment in the soft skills field, an activity currently more required than performed given the intrinsic complexity of evaluating such skills. Lastly, it must be noted that Open Badges can also contribute to a formal learning path being recognised by a school or university, action made simpler by the digital status of the Open Badge as shown by the experience of automatic recognition of badges by the Student Information System [38].

Open Assessment Though xAPIs and Learning Record Store: The key to the recognition of skills developed in different contexts is the ability to gather learning information from a variety of sources where learning and assessment can happen:

---

[5] https://www.unimib.it/node/9485, last accessed 2018/01/28.

[6] https://www.unimib.it/node/11113, last accessed 2018/01/28.

[7] https://bestr.it, last accessed 2018/01/28.

instead of designing – with a top-down approach typical of formal learning – a single main learning path where learning experiences should happen, multiple and diverse learning experiences need to be recognised and read in the light of relevant competencies they are developing. Technically, this can be achieved through the use of the Experience API, more commonly called Experience API (xAPI). The xAPI is an open specification designed to allow the interoperable exchange of learning and performance activity data between various systems and applications [11]. The xAPI standard aims at opening up the way learning experiences can be captured, stored and used. With xAPI any system can express a learning experience through a statement describing how a learner (the subject) has performed an action (the verb, e.g. answered), with reference to an object (e.g. questionnaire). Statements are captured in xAPI format and stored in a Learning Record Store that acts as a specialized database for xAPI data generated by different systems (e.g. LMS, apps, blogs, forums), called activity providers. The Bestr platform, used in the openVM project to provide Open Badges, has its own Learning Record Store and is capable of collecting xAPI statements from any platform integrated with it [39, 40]. Criteria for issuing Open Badges in Bestr are defined according to verbs and objects of learning statements which the learner must accomplish in order to gain a specific Badge. When the platform identifies that a set of statements for a given subject (the learner) is matching the criteria required for a badge, the Open Badge is issued to the learner. Having obtained an Open Badge is a new learning statement (a new learning achievement), which can be used as a starting point for issuing a new Open Badge. Leveraging this system based on open standards, the openVM Learning Hub will be able not only to express its own learning statements connected to the use of its own OER, but also to convey learning statements from any other compliant and authorised platform towards the LRS, and use any set of such information to activate the automatic issuing of a Badge and perform useful analytics for the project.

Blockcerts for Encrypted Certification: The openVM project will also evaluate the opportunity to introduce, besides Open Badges, the Blockcerts as a Blockchain-based technology for digitally certifying skills. Blockcerts, in the words of JRC report *Blockchain in education* [41] can be defined as follows: *"The cornerstone of the Blockcerts open standard is the belief that people should be able to possess and prove ownership of their important digital records. [..] Within this context, the Blockchain is considered to be a technology that allows individuals to own their official records and share them with any third-party for instant verification, all the while precluding any attempt to tamper with or edit the records."* The openVM project will consider the benefits of a permanent and encrypted recording of achievements such as those that will happen through the VM Learning Hub, as well as costs related to integrating the technology into the VM Learning Hub and to using it on a publicly available Blockchain, where writing transactions requires a constantly increasing fee.

4.5   Competency Directory for Referencing of Virtual Mobility Skills

In the preceding chapters major components of the targeted VM Learning Hub and there benefits based on literature research and practical evidences were described. Some of them will benefit from an alignment to competency definitions. This especially refers to the e-assessment and to open digital credentials which will be both combined with the competency directory to identify certain levels of skills in different domains in order to personalize the learning experience and recommended suitable resources. The freely available resources (such as VM MOOC, OERs) are the second part benefiting of alignment to competency definitions in order to express the skills intended to be learned while using the resources. The major benefit of adding metadata to such components of the VM Learning Hub is the algorithmic ability to recommend more suitable resources for identified skills to be improved, adapt the learning paths more flexible and after passing a certain assessment for competencies to be awarded directly with (all) Open Badges which need (a subset of) these competencies as criteria a learner has to evidence. The Open Bade Specification [42] allows the use of extended Uniform Resource Locators (URLs) as Internationalized Resource Identifiers (IRIs) to avoid ambiguities in referencing the same competency in different Open Badges (e.g. languages versions align to the same competency). Specific data formats in the VM Learning Hub will need yet to be decided to support IRI-based referencing. While it is already a great benefit to have unambiguous IRIs for competencies that allows algorithms to easily detect same reference to same competencies, it would be of additional advantage to be able to identify levels of competencies, similarities and prerequisites as well as successors of competencies. Thus, web servers, hosting competency definitions, deliver a response in a machine readable format via Hypertext Transfer Protocol (HTTP) as answer to a HTTP client request for the IRI. While not yet one open format is established, JavaScript Object Notation-Linked Data (JSON-LD) or Resource Description Framework (RDF) are promising candidates. Beside information about competencies themselves (name, description, translations, levels) they allow cross referencing other IRIs by semantic tuples (resource, property, value), e.g. IRI1 is part of IRI2 where IRI{1|2} represent competencies. The same concept is used to store activities in xAPI as described above.

While manifold competency frameworks exist, each is defined for a certain (narrow) domain and only a few provide unique referencing to competencies based on IRIs. Even worse, most existing competency frameworks do not provide machine readable formats, but publish their competency definitions as PDFs containing self-made IDs of competencies. To solve these problems for better machine-based processability, efforts exist to centralize and define the one competency framework to contain them all [43, 44]. It can be questioned that such efforts will ever succeed as competency definitions change over time, new competencies arise due to evolution and others fade. Additionally, different cultural backgrounds add ambiguity, e.g. for competencies like cooperativity [43]. Consequently, a more feasible goal is to keep and maintain manifold competency frameworks but cross-reference among them in a meaningful, semantic format to allow algorithms to deduct similarities and detect connections (i.e. paths) from one competency definition to the other. Thus, VM Learning Hub will provide its own hosted competency framework containing the definitions of all VM related skills needed for the hub. These are to be provided in a machine-readable format via a Representational State Transfer Application Programming Interface (REST-API) using unique IRIs per competency. Beside the format (JSON-LD or RDF) the vocabulary to express semantic data needs to be decided. While InLOC [45] is an open and well-defined vocabulary for skills, competencies, knowledge and evidences of competencies, it lacks implementation in practice. Since 2017 the European Union encourages the use of European Skills Competency and Occupation framework (ESCO) vocabulary, which is less precise in abilities to express competency frameworks but a first implementation exists containing more than 8000 competencies and their relations as used within the European union for job descriptions [44]. In case of using ESCO vocabulary it is an optional add-on to cross-reference VM Learning Hub competency definitions to similar or superset competencies defined by ESCO. The vocabulary of Competency and Skills System (CASS) defined since 2015 is less complex in variations of expressible relations than ESCO, but provides Open Source licensed client and server applications with the ability to decentrally host several interconnected CASS instances [43]. First pilot additions of ESCO defined competencies exists. In case requirement analysis for the VM Learning Hub competency directory reveals editing and cross-referencing needs, using CASS as a basis might be suitable. Developed in the former project Open Badge Network Europe[8], Competency Directory supports the automatic crawling and updating of competency framework data and provides unique URLs with a web-based search interface [46]. It was designed for light-weight searching for IRIs of competencies to use them in Open Badge alignment and criteria fields. Beside CASS it is a valuable alternative code base to be used, but offers no front-end editing yet as it automatically fetches competency frameworks from their servers.

5   OpenVM Study and Design Implications

5.1   Aims and Methods of the OpenVM Study

As the experiences with and knowledge of the concepts of Virtual Mobility and Open Education vary greatly, depending on individual implementations, one of the first steps in the openVM project is to develop a shared understanding of the concept of Open Virtual Mobility and to establish the core characteristics of Virtual Mobility activities against the backdrop op Open Education. This is achieved through a series of research studies leading to establishing the conceptual framework. Given the focus of the openVM project on credentialing learner skills, a particular focus was placed within this study on the learner skills and competences that can be developed in Open Virtual Mobility contexts. For this purpose, the Group Concept Mapping (GCM) methodology was applied. GCM supports knowledge construction through collecting and organizing ideas of individuals so that a visual geography of a concept can be created to be further analyzed, interpreted and used to feed understanding, design and/or decision or policy making [47, 48].

The GCM follows several distinct phases, in which all or a selection of participants take part. It starts with idea generation which can be based on the input of different stakeholders and/or literature reviews. Idea generation is followed by involving participants in organizing collected ideas and evaluating them on a number of relevant dimensions, e.g. importance and feasibility [49]. Thereafter, the input is analyzed with

---

[8] http://www.openbadgenetwork.com.

two advanced multivariate statistical techniques - multidimensional scaling (MDS) and hierarchical cluster analysis (HCA) to identify patterns in the data. The output of this analysis are maps representing collective standpoints on an issue or a concept under research together with individual positions. Such maps can be used to validate the shared understanding and to formulate further actions or strategies [47].

In order to understand the views on learning in an Open Virtual Mobility context a range of stakeholders, including representatives of research community as well as educators, students, internationalisation officers, higher education leaders and policy-makers were invited to participate in a GCM study. All project members of the openVM project contributed as experts on both Virtual Mobility and Open Education. The majority of participants were university professors and/or researchers with at average 20 or more years experience in education and affinity with the concepts of Virtual Mobility and Open Education. In total 101 statements were generated in phase 1 of the study. Statements were checked whether they contained repetition or ambiguity issues by two project members. All duplicates were removed. The final 90 statements were grouped by study participants based on their similarity in meaning, provided with meaningful labels and evaluated on dimensions of importance and feasibility by the first nine representatives of the VM expert community (initial stage). While the participation of more experts both from practice and from the research community is to follow, first results of the GCM study provide insights into the way experts understand VM skills which form a basis for further development of the VM Learning Hub and its components.

5.2   Preliminary Results of the OpenVM Study

The preliminary results of the GCM study are based on the clustering and rating of the 90 statements by the first 9 participants. The point map of the 90 collected statements has the stress value of 0,333 which indicates that this map is a good representation of the raw data [50]. Based on a combination of cluster analysis suggested by the tool and a discussion of the clusters by the two researchers, a nine cluster configuration was selected. Bearing in mind, that this is preliminary data based on the input of 9 first participants, the configuration as presented in Fig. 2 was considered sufficiently differentiating and meaningful. The preliminary character of the results is, however evident: the clusters differ in average bridging values of constituent statements from extremely low (0,001) to extremely high (0,99). The bridging values (from 0 to 1) point to the extent of coherence in the way individual participants group statements. A low bridging value indicates that participants agree relatively easily on the content of the cluster. A high bridging value means that a statement has been grouped together with statements farther apart.

Only one cluster, Intercultural Literacy, has a really low bridging value, indicating a great deal of agreement between the 9 participants over the underlying statements. We can therefore deduce that this cluster even at this preliminary stage of the study points to a clear learner skill that can be supported and developed through Open VM. Table 2 shows an overview of the statements in this cluster, with their related bridging values and also with average values of ratings on dimensions of importance and feasibility (Table 3).

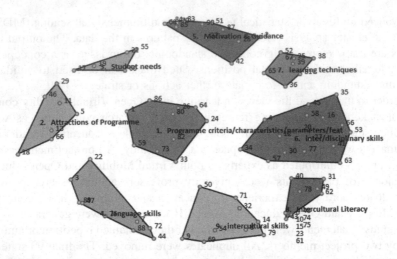

Fig. 2. Cluster map with statements from the preliminary phase of the openVM GCM study.

Table 3. Cluster intercultural literacy and constituent statements.

	Statements	Bridging value	Average rating
74	Gain knowledge about the culture they visit	0.00	3.44
48	Become self-aware of their cultural prejudices	0.00	3.67
75	Getting a feeling of how learning (or teaching) is like in a different country	0.00	3.11
6	Become self-aware of their own cultural identity during the VM activity	0.01	3.33
23	Improve their understanding of intercultural issues at the general and disciplinary level	0.01	3.89
10	Get to know other cultural-based perspectives of formal education	0.01	3.88
15	Gain knowledge about their own culture	0.01	3.44
61	Learn to reserve judgment on the people they work with in case of intercultural misunderstandings	0.01	3.89
43	Can experience different cultural settings in all its facets	0.03	3.88
40	Interact with libraries and databases in a foreign language	0.15	3.56
78	Learn to work and cooperate in an international setting with the use of ICT and social platforms	0.22	3.67
31	Exposure to different working and cultural backgrounds which could raise both new potentials and barriers at the same time	0.24	3.78
62	Through the VM activity learn about dealing with ambiguity	0.25	3.22

(*continued*)

Table 3. (*continued*)

	Statements	Bridging value	Average rating
49	A chance to develop trans-boundary skills and competences	0.27	4.11
	Cluster	0.08	M 3.63 (SD 0.28)

The five clusters have medium bridging values. These are: Interdisciplinary skills (0.34), Programme characteristics (0.35), Intercultural skills (0.38), Motivation and Guidance (0.42) and Learning Techniques (0.47). The remaining 3 clusters Language Skills (0.80), Student Needs (0.70) and Attractions of Programme (0.87) show high bridging values, indicating a higher possibility of coincidence in sorting. Taking into consideration that only 9 participants performed the sorting and rating phases of the GCM, we do not discuss these clusters here. We do expect these clusters to evolve with the participation of more experts.

5.3   Implications of the OpenVM Study for VM Learning Hub Design

Intercultural literacy emerges as a clear learner skill from the preliminary results of the GCM study. A closer look at the cluster reveals that the statements deal with cultural aspects of an Open Virtual Mobility activity, more specifically, about the potential intercultural learning that a learner in OpenVM can experience. Four aspects of intercultural theories are covered in this cluster [51–53] (and IEREST[9] platform): knowledge (74, 75, 23, 10, 15, 43, 40), attitude (61, 62), self-awareness (48, 6, 31) and skills (78, 49) Interestingly, statements relating to gaining knowledge of other cultures show 0 or near-0 bridging values. Statements relating to self-awareness also score relatively low. There is more divergence in opinion within our 9 participants on intercultural skills and attitudes. One key implication from this initial stage of the GCM study for the design of the VM Learning Hub is that it necessarily needs to focus the development of intercultural literacy skills. Further completion of the study will show which other skills are deemed relevant for Open Virtual Mobility.

6   Conclusions

This paper has presented the concept, approaches, considerations and first study results relevant for designing a collaborative learning hub for promoting VM Skills of educators and students in the European Higher Education Area. While the development of the VM Learning Hub to enhance the Virtual Mobility readiness through achievement, assessment and recognition of VM skills is still at an early stage, the authors of this paper aimed to demonstrate the complexity of designing such as collaborative learning

---

[9] http://www.ierest-project.eu/, last accessed 2018/01/31.

hub with the view of helping in planning and decision-making in similar projects. The considerations presented here may be interesting for other projects and contexts which aim to apply technologies for collaborative forms of skill attainment, skill assessment and skill recognition.

Acknowledgement. This paper is based on the joint work and research conducted by partner organisations in the Erasmus+ Project Open Virtual Mobility, Cooperation for Innovation and the Exchange of Good Practices, Strategic Partnerships for higher education, (partially) founded by the European Union, Project Number 2017-1-DE01-KA203-003494.**Disclaimer**The creation of these resources has been (partially) funded by the ERASMUS+ grant program of the European Union under grant no. 2017-1-DE01-KA203-003494. Neither the European Commission nor the project's national funding agency DAAD are responsible for the content or liable for any losses or damage resulting of the use of these resources.

References

1. Garrett, J.: The Elements of User Experience: User-Centered Design for the Web. New Riders Publishing, Thousand Oaks (2002)
2. European Commission: Communiqué of the Conference of European Ministers Responsible for Higher Education, Leuven and Louvain-la-Neuve (2009). http://europa.eu/rapid/press-release_IP-09-675_en.htm Accessed 25 Jan 2018
3. Eurostat: Learning Mobility statistics, Eurostat Homepage (2017). http://ec.europa.eu/eurostat/statistics-explained/index.php/Learning_mobility_statistics. Accessed 25 Jan 2018
4. Dauksiene, E., Tereseviciene, M., Volungeviciene, A.: Virtual mobility creates opportunities. In: Application of ICT in Education 2010: Experience, Issues and Perspectives of E-studies. Conference Proceedings, Kaunas, Lithuania, pp. 30–35 (2010). https://www.researchgate.net/publication/317549367_VIRTUAL_MOBILITY_CREATES_OPPORTUNITIES. Accessed 25 Jan 2018
5. Bruns, S., Scholz, C.: Promoting mobility—study on obstacles to student mobility. ESIB— The National Unions of Students in Europe (2007). http://media.ehea.info/file/ESU/85/9/ESIB_study_mobiity_582859.pdf. Accessed 25 Jan 2018
6. Op de Beeck, I., Van Petegem, W.: Virtual mobility: an alternative or complement to physical mobility? In: ERACON 2011 & 2012 Dual Year Proceedings, pp. 151–160, Romania (2013). http://i2agora.odl.uni-miskolc.hu/i2agora_home/data/P3_D6_ERACON_Virtual%20mobility_paper.pdf. Accessed 25 Jan 2018
7. Inamorato dos Santos, A., Punie, Y., Castaño-Muñoz, J.: Opening up education: a support framework for higher education institutions. JRC Science for Policy Report, JRC Homepage (2016). http://publications.jrc.ec.europa.eu/repository/bitstream/JRC101436/jrc101436.pdf. Accessed 25 Jan 2018
8. Hart, J., Sutcliffe, A.G., di Angeli, A.: Evaluating user engagement theory. In: CHI 2012, 5–10 May 2012, Austin, TX, USA (2012). http://di.ncl.ac.uk/uxtheory/files/2011/11/5_Hart.pdf. Accessed 25 Jan 2018
9. Attfield, S., Kazai, G., Lalmas, M., Piwowarski, B.: Towards a science of user engagement (Position Paper). In: WSDM Workshop on User Modelling for Web Applications (2011). http://www.dcs.gla.ac.uk/∼mounia/Papers/engagement.pdf. Accessed 25 Jan 2018

10. Buchem, I., Merceron, A., Kreutel, J., Haesner, M., Steinert, A.: Designing for user engagement in wearable-technology enhanced learning for healthy ageing. In: iLRN Conference 2015, Workshop Proceedings of the 11th International Conference on Intelligent Environments (2015). http://ebooks.iospress.nl/volume/workshop-proceedings-of-the-11th-international-conference-on-intelligent-environments. Accessed 25 Jan 2018

11. Johnson, A.: xAPI specifications (2017). https://github.com/ADLNET/XAPI-SPEC. Accessed 30 Jan 2018

12. Hruska, M.: Integrating xAPI into a learning ecosystem using Moodle LMS. eThink (2017). http://ethinkeducation.com/integrating-xapi-into-a-learning-ecosystem-using-moodle-lms/. Accessed 30 Jan 2018

13. H5P: Package Definition (h5p.json) (n.d.). https://h5p.org/documentation/developers/json-file-definitions. Accessed 30 Jan 2018

14. Deterding, S.: Meaningful play: Getting « gamification « right. Google Tech Talk (2011). http://www.slideshare.net/dings/meaningful-play-getting-gamification-right. Accessed 25 Jan 2018

15. Nicholson, S.: A user-centered theoretical framework for meaningful gamification. In: Paper Presented at Games + Learning + Society 8.0 (2012a). http://scottnicholson.com/pubs/meaningfulframework.pdf. Accessed 25 Jan 2018

16. Nicholson, S.: Strategies for meaningful gamification: concepts behind transformative play and participatory museums. In: Presented at Meaningful Play 2012, Lansing (2012b). http://scottnicholson.com/pubs/meaningfulstrategies.pdf. Accessed 25 Jan 2018

17. Deci, E., Koestner, R., Ryan, R.: Extrinsic rewards and intrinsic motivations in education: reconsidered once again. Rev. Educ. Res. 71(1), 1–27 (2001)

18. Solemon, B., Ariffin, I., Din, M.M., Anwar, R.M.: A review of the uses of crowdsourcing in higher education. Int. J. Asian Soc. Sci. 3(9), 2066–2073 (2013)

19. Bartoletti, R.: Learning through design: MOOC development as a method for exploring teaching methods. Curr. Issues Emerg. eLearning, 3(1), Article 2 (2016). http://scholarworks.umb.edu/ciee/vol3/iss1/2. Accessed 25 Jan 2018

20. Rose, D., Meyer, A.: Teaching Every Student in the Digital Age: Universal Design for Learning. ASCD, Alexandria (2002)

21. Deterding, S., Dixon, D., Khaled, R., Nacke, L.: From game design elements to gamefulness: defining gamification. In: Proceedings of the 15th International Academic MindTrek Conference: Envisioning Future Media Environments, 28–30 September 2011, pp. 9–15, Tampere, Finland. ACM (2011b)

22. Deterding, S.: Situated motivational affordances of game elements: a conceptual model. In: Presented at Gamification: Using Game Design Elements in Non-Gaming Contexts, a workshop at CHI 2011 (2011c). http://gamification-research.org/wp-content/uploads/2011/04/09-Deterding.pdf. Accessed 25 Jan 2018

23. Mitchell, S.N., Reilly, R., Bramwell, F.G., Lilly, F.: Friendship and choosing groupmates: preferences for teacher-selected vs. student-selected groupings in high school science classes. J. Instr. Psychol. 31(1), 1–6 (2012). http://web.centre.edu/plummer/readings/228readings/mitchell.pdf. Accessed 25 Jan 2018

24. Henry, T.R.: Creating effective student groups. In: Proceedings of the 44th ACM Technical Symposium on Computer Science Education - SIGCSE 2013 (2013)

25. Konert, J.: Interactive Multimedia Learning: Using Social Media for Peer Education in Single-Player Educational Games. Springer, Heidelberg (2014). http://www.springer.com/engineering/signals/book/978-3-319-10255-9. Accessed 25 Jan 2018

26. Srba, I., Bielikova, M.: Dynamic group formation as an approach to collaborative learning support. IEEE Trans. Learn. Technol. 8(99), 173–186 (2014)

27. Bellhäuser, H., Konert, J., Müller, A., Röpke, R.: Who's the perfect match? Effects of algorithmic group formation using personality traits. i-com J. Interact. Media (2018, accepted)
28. Konert, J., Burlak, D., Steinmetz, R.: The group formation problem: an algorithmic approach to learning group formation. In: Rensing, C., de Freitas, S., Ley, T., Muñoz-Merino, P.J. (eds.) EC-TEL 2014. LNCS, vol. 8719, pp. 221–234. Springer, Cham (2014). https://doi.org/10.1007/978-3-319-11200-8_17
29. McCrae, R.R., Costa, P.T.: The stability of personality: observations and evaluations. Curr. Dir. Psychol. Sci. 3(6), 173–175 (1994)
30. Rammstedt, B., John, O.P.: Kurzversion des Big Five Inventory (BFI-K): Entwicklung und Validierung eines ökonomischen Inventars zur Erfassung der fünf Faktoren der Persönlichkeit. Diagnostica 51, 195–206 (2005)
31. JISC InfoNet. Effective use of VLEs: e-Assessment (2006). http://tools.jiscinfonet.ac.uk/downloads/vle/eassessment-printable.pdf. Accessed 29 Jan 2009
32. HR-Guide: Chap. 3: Understanding test quality-concepts of reliability and validity (2015). https://hr-guide.com/data/G362.htm. Accessed 1 Feb 2018
33. Mozilla Foundation: About Open Badges, Open Badges Homepage (2016). https://openbadges.org/about/. Accessed 30 Jan 2018
34. Open Badges v2.0 IMS Candidate Final/Public Draft (2017). https://www.imsglobal.org/sites/default/files/Badges/OBv2p0/index.html. Accessed 30 Jan 2018
35. McKinsey & Company: education to employment: getting Europe's Youth into work (2014). https://www.mckinsey.com/industries/social-sector/our-insights/converting-education-to-employment-in-europe. Accessed 29 Jan 2018
36. OECD: Getting Skills Right: Italy. OECD Publishing, Paris (2017). https://doi.org/10.1787/9789264278639-en
37. Presant, D.: Recognizing soft skills is hard work (2016). https://littoraly.wordpress.com/2016/06/05/recognizing-soft-skills-is-hard-work/. Accessed 23 Jan 2018
38. Bertazzo, M., Carlino, C., Giacanelli, F., Ravaioli, S.: Bestr: open badges and SIS to empower Lifelong & Lifewide Learning, EUNIS (2016). http://www.eunis.org/eunis2016/wp-content/uploads/sites/8/2016/03/EUNIS2016_paper_15.pdf. Accessed 29 Jan 2018
39. Fiumana. F., Bertazzo, M., Giacanelli, F., Carlino, C.: xAPI to integrate eLearning platforms and Open Badge issuing, OPENEPIC (2016). http://www.epforum.eu/sites/www.epforum.eu/files/ePIC%202016%20Proceedings_0.pdf. Accessed 29 Jan 2018
40. Fiumana, F., Cacciamani, S., Bertazzo, M.: xAPI per integrare piattaforme e-learning e rilasciare Open Badge, EMEMITALIA (2016). https://www.ememitalia.org/archivio/2016/atti-ememitalia-2016. Accessed 29 Jan 2018
41. Grech, A., Camilleri, A.F.: Blockchain in education. In: Inamorato dos Santos, A. (ed.) JRC Publication Repository, EUR 28778 EN (2017). http://publications.jrc.ec.europa.eu/repository/bitstream/JRC108255/jrc108255_blockchain_in_education%281%29.pdf. Accessed 29 Jan 2018
42. Otto, N., Gylling, M.: Open badges V2.0. (2017). http://www.imsglobal.org/Badges/OBv2p0/index.html. Accessed 18 Mar 2017
43. Robson, R.: Competency and skills system (CASS) components. (2017). http://docs.cassproject.org/index.html?doc=1z1OUZtX1lfgGunfD1djjDr5xUqZncpjphvHbvYsDiuY#h.o0ljbgmdbnu8. Accessed 29 Jan 2018
44. De Smedt, J., le Vrang, M., Papantoniou, A.: ESCO: towards a semantic web for the European Labor Market. In: WWW 2015 Work. Linked Data Web (2015)
45. European Committee for Standardization: InLOC - Part 1: Information Model for Learning Outcomes and Competences (CWA 16655-1) (2013)

46. Konert, J., Buchem, I., Lewis, L., Hamilton, G., Riches, T.: Competency alignment of open badges. In: World Learning Summit of Future Learning Lab., Kristiansand, Norway (2017, accepted)
47. Kane, M., Trochim, W.M.K.: Concept Mapping for Planning and Evaluation. Sage Publications, Thousand Oaks (2007)
48. Kane, M., Rosas, S.R.: Conversations About Group Concept Mapping: Applications, Examples, and Enhancements. Sage Publications, Thousand Oaks (2018)
49. Trochim, W.M.K., McLinden, D.: Introduction to a special issue on concept mapping. Eval. Prog. Plann. **60**, 166–175 (2017)
50. Rosas, S.R., Kane, M.: Quality and rigor of the concept mapping methodology: a pooled study analysis. Eval. Prog. Plann. **35**, 236–245 (2012)
51. Deardorff, D.K.: Identification and assessment of intercultural competence as a student outcome of internationalization. J. Stud. Int. Educ. **10**(3), 241–266 (2006)
52. Deardorff, D.K. (ed.): The SAGE Handbook of Intercultural Competence. Sage, Thousand Oaks (2009)
53. Byram, M.: Language awareness and (critical) cultural awareness–relationships, comparisons and contrasts. Lang. Awareness **21**(1–2), 5–13 (2012)

Towards the Use of Social Computing for Social Inclusion: An Overview of the Literature

Vaso Constantinou[1]([✉]), Panagiotis Kosmas[1]([✉]),
Antigoni Parmaxi[1]([✉]), Andri Ioannou[1]([✉]), Iosif Klironomos[2]([✉]),
Margherita Antona[2]([✉]), Constantine Stephanidis[2,3]([✉]),
and Panayiotis Zaphiris[1]([✉])

[1] Department of Multimedia and Graphic Arts,
Cyprus University of Technology,
30 Archiebisopou Kyprianou Street, 3036 Limassol, Cyprus
va.constantinou@edu.cut.ac.cy,
{panayiotis.kosmas, antigoni.parmaxi, andri.i.ioannou,
panayiotis.zaphiris}@cut.ac.cy
[2] Institute of Computer Science, Foundation for Research and Technology –
Hellas (FORTH), N. Plastira 100, Vassilika Vouton, 70013
Heraklion, Crete, Greece
{iosif, antona, cs}@ics.forth.gr
[3] Department of Computer Science, University of Crete, Heraklion, Greece

Abstract. Social computing constitutes a new computing paradigm in an interdisciplinary research community which will strongly influence informatics systems and applications in the years to come. Indeed, from a social perspective, considerable interest in examining the influences of Social Computing (SC) for Social Inclusion (SI) arises from researchers and designers. This paper addresses the existing literature on the use of SC for SI. Previous studies have been reviewed to report affordances of SC design in five different areas: (a) for the elderly, (b) for people with disabilities, (c) for gender studies, (d) for societal change, and (e) for the preservation of cultural heritage. Results from the literature overview provide some examples of applications of new technologies that were designed to reduce social exclusion. Our review further shows that the use of different tools used by different groups of people has a positive impact for those people who are either socially included or excluded from their use. However, further research is needed in these five directions, which are analysed in this document and direct research into the gaps identified.

Keywords: Social computing · Social inclusion · Social exclusion
Assistive technologies · Disabilities · Elderly · Gender inequalities
Educational technology · Peace

1 Introduction

With the advance of Computing, Informatics and Web technologies, the accessibility of computing resources and mobile devices, the massive use of media, and the world's changes, social computing applications have evolved quickly over the past decade.

© Springer International Publishing AG, part of Springer Nature 2018
P. Zaphiris and A. Ioannou (Eds.): LCT 2018, LNCS 10924, pp. 376–387, 2018.
https://doi.org/10.1007/978-3-319-91743-6_28

Nowadays, the general aim of Social Computing (SC) has expanded greatly influencing many aspects of computing practice and research. Wang et al. (2007) define SC as a "computational facilitation of social studies and human social dynamics as well as the design and use of ICT technologies that consider social context" (p. 79) [14]. Social Exclusion (SE) is further characterized as a broad, complex and longstanding social problem which exists and has existed regardless the progress of ICTs. Levitas et al. (2007) offered the following definition: "Social exclusion is a complex and multi-dimensional process. It involves the lack or denial of resources, rights, goods and services, and the inability to participate in the normal relationships and activities, available to the majority of people in society, whether in economic, social, cultural, or political arenas. It affects both the quality of life of individuals and the equity and cohesion of society as a whole" (p. 9) [28].

Additionally, the idea of SE has the same characteristics with the idea of Social Inclusion (SI). According to Hayes, Gray, and Edwards (2008), the concepts of SE and SI are closely related, and it is difficult to separate them as two different theories or frameworks [17]. SE cannot be discussed without also discussing SI. Throughout this study, we report and discuss social exclusion and inclusion as two ends of a single dimension.

In recent days, besides the negative examples of technologies that endorse SE, there are a lot of different positive examples of applications of new technologies that were designed to reduce SE. From this perspective, our overarching aim is to gather the recent most essential SC initiatives regarding SE/SI. In particular, in this manuscript, we discuss the use of different technologies used by different groups of people who are either socially included or excluded from their use. Five main research directions, regarding the use of SC, were generated:

(a) Design in SC for the elderly,
(b) Design in SC for people with disabilities,
(c) The use of SC to fill the gender gap in the computer science field,
(d) The use of SC for societal change, and
(e) The use of SC to preserve cultural heritage.

In the sections below, we first state the related work that has been implemented in the field of SC for SE/SI in the abovementioned five different areas of interest. Subsequently, the closing remarks and future implications in the field are described.

2   SC for SE/SI

2.1   SC Research and Design for the Elderly

It is a fact that the elderly may face different types of health issues (e.g. difficulty in breathing), mobility problems (e.g. they cannot walk) and diseases, chronic or not (e.g. cancer, heart problems, weak cognitive functioning, etc.). In our days, the focus on Ambient Assisted Living (AAL) is important and obvious [44]. Pieper et al. (2011, p. 19) stated that the roots of AAL are in traditional Assistive Technologies for people with disabilities, Design for All approaches to accessibility, usability and ultimately acceptability of interactive technologies, as well as in the emerging computing paradigm of Ambient Intelligence, which offers new possibility of providing intelligent, unobtrusive and ubiquitous forms of assistance to older people and to citizens in general. AAL can be best understood as age-based assistance systems to address a healthy and independent life [42]. Furthermore, AAL is concerned with people in their living environment; offering different types of user-friendly equipment in the home and outside, considering at the same time that many older people have mobility, vision, hearing problems or dexterity [42]. The development of AAL products and services should be focused on enhancing the quality of life, reducing at the same time the health costs [55]. AAL systems can be developed with the combination of ubiquitous computing and context awareness. For example, the activity of elderly at home could be tracked through the sensors placed in their house [6, 55]. They could also reduce the stress of the elderly and their families, creating at the same time the feeling of safety as they will stop thinking that if something terrible happens to them, nobody will notice. Some examples of different AAL products are mobile wearable sensors, home sensors, smart fabrics, health applications and assistive robots [45]. One practical example to demonstrate the usefulness of AAL products and services is the creation of a robotic platform and a smart environment (connected to the robot) that provides healthcare management services to the elderly with the goal to improve their independent living [5].

It is also necessary for the elderly to be able to find correct information about a health problem that they may face on the Internet. Therefore, the need for reliable healthcare websites, blogs and online communities is important, as is the need for web-based platforms that are built with the consideration of Universal design and access. Besides the web platforms for supporting the elderly about their health issues, it is important to allow these people to be socially involved in the world of social networks and give them the opportunity to meet online communication technologies such as Facebook. Norval et al. (2014) investigated possible measures to make Social Networking Sites (SNS) more inclusive for the elderly. The study explored the positive and negative aspects of SNS usage, and provided recommendations for developers to avoid common barriers that make older adults avoid using SNS [35].

Social networks can also be used to maintain and enhance the cognitive function of elderly persons. Various studies have indicated that the elderly who have a better cognitive function are those who are socially active and cognitively engaged, in contrast to the elderly who are isolated and disengaged [34]. Myhre et al. (2016) examined the effect of learning through the use of the social network Facebook, on maintaining or enhancing the cognitive function of the elderly. Moreover, many researchers have carried out extensive research in HCI issues related to the analysis, the design and the evaluation of interactive systems for the elderly [34]. Zaphiris et al. (2008) focused on inclusive design for web navigation and online support communities for the elderly [60]. With regards to the online support communities, researchers emphasized on the importance of message sequences in the sustainability of an online support community for the elderly [41], the social network patterns within an empathic online community for older people [38], the elderly perceptions and experiences of online social support [40], the existence of social roles for the elderly in an online support community [39], and the challenges and opportunities of the elderly on the web [59]. Besides the online support communities for the elderly, Kurniawan and Zaphiris (2003) described an efficient information architecture for web-based health information for the elderly. Further, researchers focused on the computer-based learning for senior citizens by examining the opportunities and challenges within this field [26]. Moreover, Siriaraya et al. (2013) examined the supporting social interaction for the older users in game-like 3D virtual worlds [53]. Last, Lanitis and Tsapatsoulis (2011) have focused on the quantitative evaluation of the effect of ageing on biometric templates [27].

2.2   Design and Inclusion of People with Disabilities

In the last few years, many researchers in the HCI field have tried to examine different technologies for learning goals and social inclusion for students with special needs. A number of studies in SC and Educational Technology have been conducted to support both children and adults with different health problems and impairments. Many technologies, under the field of game-based learning, such as motion-based interactive games, appear to enhance the academic, cognitive and motor skills of children with disabilities [24, 25]. The study of Constantinou et al. (2016), examined the personal tour of cultural heritage for deaf museum visitors through a mobile application. The findings showed high levels of user satisfaction and usefulness of the application in allowing deaf museum visitors to have a fun tour, using their mobile devices as the only means of support [11]. Furthermore, in another study, a system was developed for hearing impaired users, for immediate access to emergency services via a mobile application [9]. Moreover, researchers investigated the use of virtual reality to train designers to develop friendly interfaces for achromatic vision patients [10].

In the study conducted by Henderson et al. (2013) with students with disabilities ranging from learning difficulties, social/communication impairment, mental health conditions to physically impaired students or students with mobility issues, blind or partially sighted, and deaf or hearing-impaired students. The study focused on the above students and the use of technology to improve their experience in learning and studying, making use of different applications on iPads (e.g. iBooks, MindNode, Speak it, AudioNote, PDfReader, Stanzain) in a higher education context [18]. Another study [51] focused on the inclusion of children and youths with disabilities regarding advancing their computer skills and using ICT for social leisure. Results showed that participants improved considerably in most of their computer skills. Access to ICT increased the rate of participants' engagement in a variety of activities involving ICT use. Additionally, the study showed that the computer serves in various ways, mainly in their social, academic, and leisure activities. Moreover, the younger participants focused mostly on leisure activities and games where the older ones used the computer for improving academic achievements, retrieving information, shopping, dealing with authorities, and connecting with friends.

Along the same lines, many studies have focused on design for different groups of people with disabilities, ranging from autistic, people with dementia to people with dyslexia, students with special needs, hearing impairment and visual impairment. In the recent study of Kosmas et al. (2017), the use of motion-based technology in classroom facilitates children with disabilities motor skills and emotional engagement [24]. Also, Ioannou et al. (2015) studied the effect of participation of the humanoid robot NAO in therapeutic conferences in children with autism [21]. Also, Polycarpou et al. (2016)

investigated the potential of using the humanoid robot, NAO, as a playful tool for assessing the listening and speaking skills of seven hearing impaired students who use cochlear implant(s) and sign language as their main communication modality [43].

Furthermore, Loizides et al. (2015) described the project entitled "Minority Language Applications" in which with the use of interactive multimedia, they studied the application's effect in children with autism in a multilingual environment [30]. In regard to studies related to dementia, Savitch and Zaphiris (2005) investigated the accessibility of web-based information for people with dementia [48], and explored the navigation design needs when developing a website for people with dementia [49]. Further, Savitch et al. (2006) explored the participation of people with dementia in the development of a web-forum [50]. Moreover, Al-Wabil et al. (2008) examined the visual attention with the use of eye tracking in navigation structures on six different websites for people with and without dyslexia. In the particular study, the authors provided information on how to apply eye tracking to evaluate the usability [2]. Based on people with hearing impairment, Yeratziotis and Zaphiris (2015) described the development of research in HCI, with the focus on accessibility for the deaf users [58]. Finally, Michailidou et al. (2012) carried out a web accessibility evaluation based on the websites of different Cypriot universities, and they have found that all the websites have accessibility issues which make it hard for the students with disabilities to use [32].

2.3   SC Research for Filling the Gender Gap in the Computer Science Field

Another group of people who are discriminated from an important field of study are women. Many studies [13, 33, 47] indicated that women are under-represented in the Computer Science (CS) education. Further, different research studies have displayed the unbalanced participation between male and female students in CS degrees [1, 15, 31].

Nowadays, there is an increased research interest in exploring why girls or women do not enter CS education and why they do not advance or remain in the field [57]. Researchers also explore the view of female and male students regarding computer culture [54]. In addition, few studies have been conducted with the focus on the university level to explore gender differences within an introductory module in programming [47]. Different studies have stated that male university students can program more easily, and they may also have higher intention to program than female students [54, 57]. Male students and in general the male IT professionals and programmers are assumed to be more competent in programming and the IT sector. This increases the "fear" of women to enter this field and study CS or other IT degrees.

In general, female students in society are not supported to study CS/IT in the same level as male individuals [33], and a negative message that women are not capable enough to enter the field is promoted within our society. Paloheimo and Stenman (2006, p. 14) explained that "the society does not actually prevent girls from accessing computers, but it has failed to introduce computer science as a viable option for them" and therefore it is promoted that the CS field is a men's field [36]. Although besides the men's stereotype in the CS/IT fields there are women who have showed that female can also be equally capable and successful in the fields of CS/IT, such as Ginni Rometty, the president and CEO of IBM [19] and Marissa Mayer, president and CEO of Yahoo [23].

According to Varma (2010), many students believe that the two main reasons that explain why fewer women than men select to study CS/IT are the gendered socialisation and technical anxiety [56]. Vitores and Gil-Juárez (2015) specified that during the middle school years the terms "exclusion" and "disaffection" about the CS field are promoted and by high school the gender differences in CS are very well established, and therefore girls have limited interest in CS or IT [57].

In this direction, some recent research provides an active engagement in the area of enhancing gender equality, mainly through the implementation of the Womenpower platform. WomenPower is an online platform that looks at online mentoring for allowing women to fight discrimination and rise to the upper ranks of the corporate ladder. It has the intention to link women mentors and mentees from different fields such as technology, academia, business and healthcare [37]. Finally, it is important to consider CS as important as math and physics, and therefore it would be good if nations were including in their educational curriculum, even from primary education the CS concept. In this way, female students will be involved in CS from a very young age, and therefore they would not follow a negative stereotype. The UK (since 2014) has imposed CS in primary school through their STEM (Science, Technology, Engineering, Mathematics) education which indicates remarkable progress [23]. External non-profit international organisations such as Robogals aims to increase female participation (primary and secondary school) in Technology, Engineering and Science through the use of programmable robots which it is also an essential step towards the support of female students in the CS field [46].

2.4   SC for Societal Change

How could social networks help in reaching social change? How could we take advantage and use new technologies such as computer-based simulations or serious games, in the direction of conflict management and peace promotion? Carmichael and Norvang (2014) carried out a pedagogical pilot study supported by the annual Nobel Peace Prize Forum (NPPF) in which students using technology and social media are brought together (SI-connecting people) to engage learning practices through a global dialogue on important issues [7].

Several studies explored the use of different technologies to reduce conflicts and promote peace between different people from various nations. Cuhadar and Kampf (2014) evaluated the use of the game "PeaceMaker" as a pedagogical tool in teaching about conflict and its resolution. Participants included 39 American, 38 Turkish, 50 Israeli-Jewish, and 20 Israeli-Palestinian students. All students played the game that simulates the Israeli-Palestinian conflict in both Israeli and Palestinian decision-maker roles. The results showed that after playing the game, American students got closer to thinking that both Israeli and Palestinian sides were equally right when they had a more pro-Israeli view before playing the game. Similarly, results show that Turkish students got closer to thinking that both sides were equally right when they had a more pro-Palestinian view before playing the game. In contrast, Israeli & Palestinian students did not change their perspective regarding the rightness of their side. The game affects students (Turkish and American) with less salient and weaker attitudes concerning the conflict, as opposed to Palestinian and Jewish participants who have stronger and more salient attitudes. Results showed that further studies are necessary to investigate under which conditions technology can be used as an effective conflict resolution intervention [12].

Various studies have explored over the past years, various technological aspects that led to societal change. Specifically, some researchers have investigated how the use of different technologies could promote different forms of peacemaking. For example, Ioannou et al. (2013) designed a collocated brainstorming tabletop activity to facilitate dialogue and consensus decision making in groups of college students discussing sensitive and controversial topics, including peace-building in a country of long-term ethnic conflict. The authors found that discussion around the tabletop was fluent with no evidence of tension, anxiety or strong disagreement among the participants [22]. Moreover, Ioannou and Antoniou (2016) conducted an empirical investigation of technology enhanced peacemaking in a conflict-stressed school environment. The peacemaking intervention required students in conflict-laden groups to collaborate on various game-like learning activities on a multitouch interactive tabletop, over the span of three weeks. Students' interviews and video observations provided evidence that tabletops can become a means of communication and collaboration giving a chance for students in conflict to share a common space, shifting attitudes and improving their relationships. The results showed that the use of the tabletops can increase cooperation between students in conflict and it can change attitudes and improves the students' relationships [20].

2.5   SC for SE/SI and Cultural Heritage

Hansen, Postmes et al. (2012, p. 223) stated that "Culture is not a stable set of beliefs or values that reside inside individuals. Instead, it is located in society, in patterns of practices, ideas, institutions, products, and artefacts" [16]. Different studies have been conducted with the aim to preserve the cultural heritage of various countries with the use of technology, indicating the importance of presenting to the new generation the cultural heritage of their country. Different types of technologies ranging from websites, archaeological databases, touch screens with interactive applications to virtual environments, virtual reality, augmented reality, serious games for cultural heritage, commercial, historical games and pervasive cultural heritage serious games have been used to illustrate the cultural heritage of different countries. These technologies are often placed in museums and archaeological sites and monuments visited by schools and other visitors [3, 8, 52].

In recent days, Virtual Reality (VR) has been used in many cases to present the cultural heritage of a country. Different projects were based on virtual reconstructions to educate and train their users. Some examples of virtual reconstructions systems are "Roma Nova: the Rome Reborn project", "Ancient Pompeii" and "Parthenon project" [3]. Other VR systems are being used in different museums. Bergamasco et al. (2002) presented a VR system called "Museum of Pure Form" that allows the user to interact through sight and touch with digital models of 3D art forms and sculptures [4]. Loizides et al. (2014) carried out a user evaluation of two virtual museums where items of the Cypriot cultural heritage were placed. Visitors were able to use a stereoscopic Powerwall projection or a Head Mounted Display to experience 3D immersion [29]. Furthermore, different interactive virtual exhibitions that can be visited in real-world museums are facilitating games technologies in order to provide a digital representation of cultural heritage playfully and educationally to engage better the students and other visitors who visit the museums. Some examples of serious games in the context of cultural heritage, specifically designed for educational purposes are the "Virtual Egyptian Temple" and "Revolution" [3]. Pervasive cultural heritage serious games are also being used in some museums. Coenen et al. (2013) described a case study on MuseUs pervasive cultural heritage serious game. This game is used in museums exhibitions where visitors can use their smartphone to download its app. During their visit to the museum, players are guided to create their exposition, and this application aims to provide learning outcomes during the visit in a museum exhibition [8].

3 Discussion and Future Implications

This paper has highlighted some of the essential theoretical and practical implications of SC in the concept of SE or SI. It has summarized both the applications and achievements of SC applications over the past years. Thus, the overall goal of this paper is to address the state of the art of SC for SE/SI aiming to contribute, support, and facilitate the future application and adoption of the principles of Design for All and Universal Access in the context of the Information Society. SC research can serve as an opportunity to help people to engage in social activities and the community without any issues. Future efforts could include the development and evolution of methodologies, techniques and tools supporting the application of Design for All in HCI or the development of interaction techniques for specific target user groups, supported through user interface development toolkits. In that respect, future research in this area should focus on five research directions as described in the following.

1. Design in SC for the elderly.

This research direction could investigate the use of several technology initiatives designed to improve the quality of life of the elderly. Consequently, two main research questions in this direction are: (1) "How can SC based solutions (including products, systems, or services) enhance older adults' quality of life?" and, (2) "How can technology (e.g. health technologies, virtual communities, etc.) promote, facilitate and sustain SI for specific populations such as the elderly)?"; specifically, this research direction could focus on online support communities, social communities and health-care communities and examine their usability in terms of standards of the universal web design and accessibility. In addition, this research direction could also examine the use of various AAL systems as well as the use of Internet of things at home.

2. Design in SC for people with disabilities.

The second research direction deals with the technological initiatives aiming to improve the quality of life of people with disabilities. It should focus on supportive equipment, Universal web design and accessibility, online healthcare communities and online support communities. The main research question of this RT is "How can technology (e.g. health technologies, virtual communities, applications, etc.) promote, facilitate and sustain SI for specific populations such as people with disabilities?";

3. The use of SC to fill the gender gap in the Computer Science field.

Gender issues in the field of CS and the use of SC could focus on the discrimination that women often face in the CS field. It will further examine ways to fill the gap between men and women in the CS field by (i) adopting innovative methods to inspire female computer scientists and, (ii) by creating online platforms/communities and face-to-face workshops for mentoring and supporting women in CS.

3. The use of SC for societal change.

This research direction should focus on several aspects that negatively affect our society. Specifically, it could explore the use of different technological tools to address conflict management, antisocial behavior, peace-making and bringing people together.

5. The use of SC to preserve cultural heritage.

For cultural heritage, SC should focus on the awareness and promotion awareness of cultural heritage through the use of different technologies. This research direction could examine the use different innovative technologies with the aim to engage young children in an environment designed to inform them about their country's cultural heritage.

Closing, this paper discusses the literature on the use of SC for SI and SE. Results from previous theoretical and empirical studies in the area revealed affordances and implications for SC design in five different areas, which are (a) the elderly, (b) people with disabilities, (c) gender studies, (d) societal change, and (e) the preservation of cultural heritage. The literature overview shows that the use of different technological tools used by different groups of people has a positive impact for those people who either socially included or excluded from their use. However, further research is needed in these five directions, which are analysed in this document and direct research into the gaps identified.

Acknowledgments. The authors would like to acknowledge travel funding from the European Union's Horizon 2020 Framework Programme through NOTRE project (H2020-TWINN-2015, Grant Agreement Number: 692058).

References

1. Adam, A.: Gender, Ethics and Information Technology. Springer, Heidelberg (2005)
2. Al-Wabil, A., Zaphiris, P., Wilson, S.: Examining visual attention of dyslexics on web navigation structures with eye tracking. In: International Conference on Innovations in Information Technology, IIT 2008, pp. 717–721. IEEE, December 2008
3. Anderson, E.F., McLoughlin, L., Liarokapis, F., Peters, C., Petridis, P., de Freitas, S.: Developing serious games for cultural heritage: a state-of-the-art review. Virtual Reality **14**(4), 255–275 (2010)
4. Bergamasco, M., Frisoli, A., Barbagli, F.: Haptics technologies and cultural heritage applications. In: Proceedings of Computer Animation, pp. 25–32. IEEE (2002)

5. Bonaccorsi, M., Fiorini, L., Cavallo, F., Esposito, R., Dario, P.: Design of cloud robotic services for senior citizens to improve independent living and personal health management. In: Andò, B., Siciliano, P., Marletta, V., Monteriù, A. (eds.) Ambient Assisted Living. Biosystems & Biorobotics, vol. 11, pp. 465–475. Springer, Cham (2015). https://doi.org/10.1007/978-3-319-18374-9_43

6. Botia, J.A., Villa, A., Palma, J.: Ambient assisted living system for in-home monitoring of healthy independent elders. Expert Syst. Appl. **39**(9), 8136–8148 (2012)

7. Carmichael, T., Norvang, R.: A global dialogue on peace: creating an international learning community through social media. Int. J. Teach. Learn. High. Educ. **26**(3), 445–452 (2014)

8. Coenen, T., Mostmans, L., Naessens, K.: MuseUs: case study of a pervasive cultural heritage serious game. J. Comput. Cult. Heritage (JOCCH) **6**(2), 8 (2013)

9. Constantinou, V., Ioannou, A., Diaz, P.: Inclusive access to emergency services: an action research project focused on hearing-impaired citizens. Univ. Access Inf. Soc. **16**(4), 929–937 (2017)

10. Constantinou, V., Lanitis, A., Ioannou, A.: Using virtual reality to train designers to develop friendly interfaces for achromatic vision patients. In: Proceedings of the 22nd International Conference on Intelligent User Interfaces Companion, pp. 77–80. ACM, March 2017

11. Constantinou, V., Loizides, F., Ioannou, A.: A personal tour of cultural heritage for deaf museum visitors. In: Ioannides, M., Fink, E., Moropoulou, A., Hagedorn-Saupe, M., Fresa, A., Liestøl, G., Rajcic, V., Grussenmeyer, P. (eds.) EuroMed 2016, Part II. LNCS, vol. 10059, pp. 214–221. Springer, Cham (2016). https://doi.org/10.1007/978-3-319-48974-2_24

12. Cuhadar, E., Kampf, R.: Learning about conflict and negotiations through computer simulations: The case of PeaceMaker. Int. Stud. Perspect. **15**(4), 509–524 (2014)

13. DuBow, W.: Attracting and Retaining Women in Computing. Computer **47**(10), 90–93 (2014)

14. Wang, F.Y., Carley, K.M., Zeng, D., Mao, W.: Social computing: from social informatics to social intelligence. IEEE Intell. Syst. **22**(2), 79–83 (2007)

15. Farmer, L.: Teen girls and technology: what's the problem, what's the solution? ALA Editions. American Library Association, Chicago (2008)

16. Hansen, N., Postmes, T., van der Vinne, N., van Thiel, W.: Information and communication technology and cultural change. Soc. Psychol. **43**(4), 222–231 (2012)

17. Hayes, A., Gray, M., Edwards, B.: Social inclusion: origins, concepts and key themes, Social inclusion, Social Inclusion Unit, Canberra (2008). http://pandora.nla.gov.au/pan/142909/20130920-1300/www.socialinclusion.gov.au/sites/default/files/publications/pdf/si-origins-concepts-themes.pdf. Accessed 01 Feb 2018

18. Henderson, K., Gibson, C., Gibb, F.: The impact of tablet computers on students with disabilities in a Higher Education setting. Technol. Disabil. **25**(2), 61–76 (2013)

19. IBM (2016). http://www.ibm.com/ibm/ginni/speeches.html

20. Ioannou, A., Antoniou, C.: Tabletops for peace: technology enhanced peacemaking in school contexts. Educ. Technol. Soc. **19**(2) (2016)

21. Ioannou, A., Kartapanis, I., Zaphiris, P.: Social robots as co-therapists in autism therapy sessions: a single-case study. In: Tapus, A., André, E., Martin, J.C., Ferland, F., Ammi, M. (eds.) Social Robotics, ICSR 2015. LNCS, vol. 9388. Springer, Cham (2015)

22. Ioannou, A., Zaphiris, P., Loizides, F., Vasiliou, C.: Let's talk about technology for peace: a systematic assessment of problem-based group collaboration around an interactive tabletop. In: Interacting with Computers, iwt061 (2013)

23. Kermarrec, A.M.: Computer science: too young to fall into the gender gap. IEEE Internet Comput. **3**, 4–6 (2014)

24. Kosmas, P., Ioannou, A., Retalis, S.: Using embodied learning technology to advance motor performance of children with special educational needs and motor impairments. In: Lavoué, É., Drachsler, H., Verbert, K., Broisin, J., Pérez-Sanagustín, M. (eds.) Data Driven Approaches in Digital Education (2017)

25. Kosmas, P., Ioannou, A., Retalis, S.: Moving bodies to moving minds: a study of motion-based games in Special Education. J. Tech Trends. (2017, accepted)

26. Kurniawan, S.H., Zaphiris, P.: Web health information architecture for older users. IT Soc. 1(3), 42–63 (2003)

27. Lanitis, A., Tsapatsoulis, N.: Quantitative evaluation of the effects of aging on biometric templates. Comput. Vis. IET 5(6), 338–347 (2011)

28. Levitas, R., Pantazis, C., Fahmy, E., Gordon, D., Lloyd, E., Patsios, D.: The multi-dimensional analysis of social exclusion (2007)

29. Loizides, F., El Kater, A., Terlikas, C., Lanitis, A., Michael, D.: Presenting cypriot cultural heritage in virtual reality: a user evaluation. In: Ioannides, M., Magnenat-Thalmann, N., Fink, E., Žarnić, R., Yen, A.-Y., Quak, E. (eds.) EuroMed 2014. LNCS, vol. 8740, pp. 572–579. Springer, Cham (2014). https://doi.org/10.1007/978-3-319-13695-0_57

30. Loizides, F., Kartapanis, I., Sella, F., Papadima-Sophocleous, S.: Mi.L.A: multilingual and multifaceted mobile interactive applications for children with autism. In: Critical CALL–Proceedings of the 2015 EUROCALL Conference, Padova, Italy, p. 368. Research-Publishing.Net, December 2015

31. Margolis, J., Fisher, A.: Unlocking the Clubhouse: Women in Computing. MIT press, Cambridge (2003)

32. Michailidou, E., Mavrou, K., Zaphiris, P.: eInclusion@ cyprus universities: provision and web accessibility. In: CHI 2012 Extended Abstracts on Human Factors in Computing Systems, pp. 1637–1642. ACM, May 2012

33. Mirjana, I., Zoran, P., Anja, S., Zoran, B.: The IT gender gap: experience, motivation and differences in undergraduate studies of computer science. Turk. Online J. Distance Educ. 12(2), 170–186 (2011)

34. Myhre, J.W., Mehl, M.R., Glisky, E.L.: Cognitive benefits of online social networking for healthy older adults. J. Gerontol. Ser. B Psychol. Sci. Soc. Sci. 72(5), 752–760 (2016). gbw025

35. Norval, C., Arnott, J.L., Hanson, V.L.: What's on your mind? Investigating recommendations for inclusive social networking and older adults. In: Proceedings of the SIGCHI Conference on Human Factors in Computing Systems, pp. 3923–3932. ACM, April 2014

36. Paloheimo, A., Stenman, J.: Gender, communication and comfort level in higher level computer science education-case study. In: 36th Annual Frontiers in Education Conference, pp. 13–18. IEEE, October 2006

37. Parmaxi, A., Vasiliou, C.: Communities of interest for enhancing social creativity: the case of Womenpower platform. In: Proceedings of INTED 2015 Conference, pp. 2838–2847 (2015)

38. Pfeil, U., Zaphiris, P.: Investigating social network patterns within an empathic online community for older people. Comput. Hum. Behav. 25(5), 1139–1155 (2009)

39. Pfeil, U., Svangstu, K., Ang, C.S., Zaphiris, P.: Social roles in an online support community for older people. Int. J. Hum. Comput. Interact. 27(4), 323–347 (2011)

40. Pfeil, U., Zaphiris, P., Wilson, S.: Older adults' perceptions and experiences of online social support. Int. Comput. 21(3), 159–172 (2009)

41. Pfeil, U., Zaphiris, P., Wilson, S.: The role of message-sequences in the sustainability of an online support community for older people. J. Comput. Mediated Commun. 15(2), 336–363 (2010)

42. Pieper, M., Antona, M., Cortés, U.: Ambient assisted living. In: ERCIM News, vol. 87 (2011)

43. Polycarpou, P., Andreeva, A., Ioannou, A., Zaphiris, P.: Don't read my lips: assessing listening and speaking skills through play with a humanoid robot. In: Stephanidis, C. (ed.) HCI 2016. CCIS, vol. 618, pp. 255–260. Springer, Cham (2016). https://doi.org/10.1007/978-3-319-40542-1_41

44. Queirós, A., Silva, A., Alvarelhão, J., Rocha, N.P., Teixeira, A.: Usability, accessibility and ambient-assisted living: a systematic literature review. Univ. Access Inf. Soc. **14**(1), 57–66 (2015)

45. Rashidi, P., Mihailidis, A.: A survey on ambient-assisted living tools for older adults. IEEE J. Biomed. Health Inform. **17**(3), 579–590 (2013)

46. Robogals (2016). http://www.robogals.org

47. Rubio, M.A., Romero-Zaliz, R., Mañoso, C., Angel, P.: Closing the gender gap in an introductory programming course. Comput. Educ. **82**, 409–420 (2015)

48. Savitch, N., Zaphiris, P.: An investigation into the accessibility of web-based information for people with Dementia. In: 11th International Conference on Human-Computer Interaction, Las Vegas, July 2005

49. Savitch, N., Zaphiris, P.: Accessible websites for people with Dementia: a preliminary investigation into information architecture. In: Miesenberger, K., Klaus, J., Zagler, W.L., Karshmer, A.I. (eds.) ICCHP 2006. LNCS, vol. 4061, pp. 144–151. Springer, Heidelberg (2006). https://doi.org/10.1007/11788713_22

50. Savitch, N., Zaphiris, P., Smith, M., Litherland, R., Aggarwal, N., Potier, E.: Involving people with dementia in the development of a discussion forum: a community-centred approach. In: Designing Accessible Technology, pp. 237–247. Springer, London (2006). https://doi.org/10.1007/1-84628-365-5_24

51. Schreuer, N., Keter, A., Sachs, D.: Accessibility to information and communications technology for the social participation of youths with disabilities: a two-way street. Behav. Sci. Law **32**(1), 76–93 (2014)

52. Silberman, N.A · Beyond Theme Parks and Digitized Data: What Can Cultural Heritage Technologies Contribute to the Public Understanding of the Past? (2005)

53. Siriaraya, P., Zaphiris, P., Ang, C.S.: Supporting social interaction for older users in game-like 3D virtual worlds (2013)

54. Stoilescu, D., Egodawatte, G.: Gender differences in the use of computers, programming, and peer interactions in computer science classrooms. Comput. Sci. Educ. **20**(4), 283–300 (2010)

55. van den Broek, G., Cavallo, F., Wehrmann, C.: AALIANCE Ambient Assisted Living Roadmap, vol. 6. IOS press, Amsterdam (2010)

56. Varma, R.: Why so few women enroll in computing? Gender and ethnic differences in students' perception. Comput. Sci. Educ. **20**(4), 301–316 (2010)

57. Vitores, A., Gil-Juárez, A.: The trouble with 'women in computing': a critical examination of the deployment of research on the gender gap in computer science. J. Gender Stud. **25**(6), 1–15 (2015)

58. Yeratziotis, A., Zaphiris, P.: Interactive software technology for deaf users: mapping the HCI research landscape that focuses on accessibility. In: Antona, M., Stephanidis, C. (eds.) UAHCI 2015, Part I. LNCS, vol. 9175, pp. 253–264. Springer, Cham (2015). https://doi.org/10.1007/978-3-319-20678-3_25

59. Zaphiris, P., Kurniawan, S., Ellis, R.D.: Web and aging: challenges and opportunities. Univ. Access Inf. Soc. **4**(1), 1–2 (2005)

60. Zaphiris, P., Sustar, H., Pfeil, U.: Inclusive Design for Older People. Centre for HCI Design City University London (2008)

Lessons Learned: Engaging Older Adults in Generative Design Sessions for a Digital Messaging System

Abena Edugyan$^{(\boxtimes)}$, Andreas Papallas, and Panayiotis Zaphiris

Cyprus University of Technology, Limassol, Cyprus
abena@abenaedugyan.com

Abstract. The global population continues to age within an increasingly digitally connected society. Because of the ubiquity of technology, the needs, experiences and values of older adults should be considered to ensure they are not excluded from any advantages the digital society may provide. Engaging in generative design research allows users to collaborate with designers to uncover those needs as well as discover creative solutions to design problems. This paper explores the results of three generative design sessions conducted with older adults to gain insight into the feasibility of a digital messaging system designed to foster their inclusion in the digital society. Immersion and card sort sessions revealed the value placed in face-to-face communication with peers, while the card sort and brainstorm sessions highlighted health as a possible theme to be further explored. Additionally, the brainstorm session concluded with the creation of a rudimentary prototype, reinforcing the creativity older adults can bring to the design process. While the feedback generated from the sessions may not have supported the initial idea, they showed that the contribution of older adults in the design research process should not be understated.

Keywords: Generative design · Older adults · Digital society

1 Introduction

Generative design research can help designers explore people's values and needs and uncover solutions to design problems which may not be initially evident [1]. This type of research can be especially insightful to address the design of digital products, systems or services for older adults. Although technology adoption is increasing among older adults, they continue to face hurdles, including lacking confidence in their abilities to perform tasks effectively and needing to be shown how to use new devices due to ineffective usability [2].

Because technology has become so pervasive, concrete steps should be taken to foster the inclusion of older adults into the digital society. To help overcome the aforementioned hurdles, older adults should be involved in all stages of technology design as a means of understanding their needs via insight into their social influences, experiences, preferences and usage patterns [3].

© Springer International Publishing AG, part of Springer Nature 2018
P. Zaphiris and A. Ioannou (Eds.): LCT 2018, LNCS 10924, pp. 388–399, 2018.
https://doi.org/10.1007/978-3-319-91743-6_29

This paper discusses the results of three generative sessions used to explore the viability of a proposed solution to address the problem statement: "Design a product, system or service to foster inclusion of older adults in our digital society." After a brief review of the literature on the use of generative or participatory design methods with older adults, the paper will describe the methods employed in this study and the data collected. Finally, the paper closes with a discussion of the findings, including lessons learned, and offers conclusions.

1.1 Generative Design and Older Adults

In the generative design research process, the researcher becomes a facilitator of collective creativity, where designers and non-designers collaborate to explore problems and opportunities [1]. Gatsou [4] viewed designers and researchers as facilitators who helped users express their ideas and become creators of artifacts. Incorporating generative design methods can help designers identify themes they may not have previously considered; it also fosters user creativity and buy-in.

Lindsay, Jackson, Schofield, and Olivier [5] argued that older adults should be engaged in the design process from the beginning as partners and active participants, not as an afterthought. Though older adults' potential lack of experience with technology may result in technologically impossible designs, this should not preclude them from being involved in the creative design process [6]. In fact, Kristensson and Magnusson [7] found that everyday users have the ability to produce cutting-edge ideas. Accordingly, Ostlund [cited in 8] advised designers to capitalize on the older adult's capacity to learn new technologies because of their exposure to a multitude of technological changes.

1.2 Older Adults and Technology

In 2017, adults aged 60 and over made up 13% of the global population; the United Nations projects this number to increase to 21.5% by 2050 [9]. It should be noted that as the world's population ages, older adults are becoming increasingly more digitally interconnected. For example, in 2013, 23% of American seniors reported owning a smartphone; this number rose to 42% in 2017 [2]. This increase is not geographically limited; for example, in 2013, 36% of Russians and 43% of Chileans aged 50 and over reported accessing the internet or owning a smartphone [10]. The benefits of engaging older adults in the digital society are increasingly positive.

And they want to be included. Fifty-eight percent of adults aged 65 and older agreed that technology's impact on society has been mostly positive [2]. Lewis and Neider [11] and Satariano et al. [12] highlighted how technology can reduce social isolation by increasing the number of avenues older adults can use to connect with family and friends. Finally, the results of a 2016 study by Juárez et al. [13] showed that older adults who used technology had greater socialization and more intergenerational communication with their family and acquaintances.

1.3   Problem Statement and Proposed Solution

As part of the Design Theory and Methodology module for the M.Sc. in Interaction Design at Cyprus University of Technology/Tallinn University, students were tasked with tackling the problem statement: "Design a product, system or service to foster inclusion of older adults in our digital society."

The results of ethnographic and observational research guided the features of the proposed solution targeted in this paper: it would offer a non-intimidating interface, take advantage of existing community structures and provide prompts for users to engage with others within a social network. Tentatively titled RAPP Connections (Responsive Application for Peer to Peer Connections), the tablet-based digital messaging system would allow the older adults living within a retirement community to connect directly with each other. The objective of the system would be to integrate messaging technologies into everyday living, foster the creation and nurturing of social networks, and reduce social isolation. It would also facilitate both online and face-to-face social interactions via calendars on the interface detailing upcoming activities within the community, along with prompts for residents to invite friends who have similar interests.

2   Methods

The generative sessions focused on informing the viability of the digital messaging system by observing older adults' day to day living and exploring what is valuable to them.

2.1   Participants

Three participants were recruited through family members and acquaintances. The only screen for inclusion was age.

P1 is a 71-year old retired female living in an independent living retirement community. She is comfortable using her laptop, Smart TV and cell phone.

P2 is a 77-year old male, who is semi-retired and lives alone. He has worked in electronics for over 30 years and is very comfortable with personal computers and laptops. He is comfortable using basic functions on his cell phone.

The final participant, P3, is a 66-year old male, who is also semi-retired and lives alone. He is comfortable using a laptop and cell phone and is a judicious user of mobile communications applications such as WhatsApp.

2.2   Procedure

The generative design sessions were guided by the methods outlined in IDEO's Field Guide to Human-Centered Design [14]. The first author acted as facilitator, conducting and recording all sessions.

Immersion. The immersion technique requires spending time observing and listening to the intended user of the design, essentially gaining a view of their everyday life [14].

The method was chosen for two reasons: the environment was a direct match for the scope of the digital messaging system and the data gathered could directly inform whether it would satisfy an actual or perceived need.

P1 was observed both within her home and in the common area of her independent retirement living complex, allowing for physical details and routines to be observed. Upon entering the building, photographs of the common areas were taken; photos were also taken of the main living area in her home. The next 60 min were spent visiting and talking about her life.

Card Sort. Card sorts can provide insight into what is important to a user [14]. This session focused on discovering the participants' top personal values and exploring why their choices resonated most with them. A secondary goal was to see if their values aligned with the words best describing the perceived benefits of the digital messaging system.

P2 and P3 were given 50 cards from the Personal Values Card Sort [15]. A sampling of the cards is shown in Fig. 1. They were asked to sort them into three categories: Not Important to Me, Important to Me and Very Important to Me, as displayed in Figs. 2 and 3. If more than 10 cards were placed in the Very Important to Me category, participants were asked to narrow down their choices. Once each sort was completed, the results were photographed and the top three common choices in each category were identified. The participants then discussed the reasoning behind their final selections.

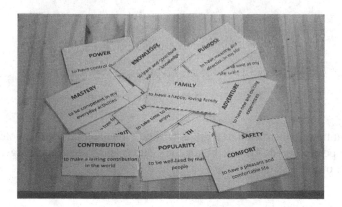

Fig. 1. Sampling of cards for card sort session

Brainstorm. Brainstorms stimulate creativity from collaboration and are fueled by the goal of generating a multitude of unfettered ideas and solutions [14]. The focus of this sixty minute session was to generate as many ideas as possible related to the design problem and to gain insight into the problem statement from the perspective of the users. Participants had access to a number of tools to encourage creativity, including paper, pens, pencils and markers. They were also given Post-It notes on which to record their ideas. The problem statement was written on a poster board and placed in the middle of the table. We began with a review of the basic rules (i.e., there are no right or wrong answers; judgement should be reserved until the end of the session) [14],

Fig. 2. P2 completing the card sort

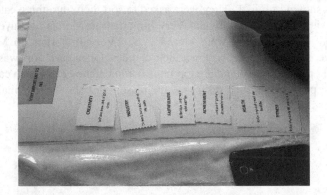

Fig. 3. P3 completing the card sort

and participants were instructed to write down their ideas on the Post-It notes and stick them on the poster board. The facilitator took audio and video recordings, as well as photographs, of the session.

3   Results and Discussion

The main observations of each session and key findings are discussed.

3.1   Immersion

Observations. P1 lives in a one-bedroom apartment within a managed building for independent seniors. The common areas within the building include, among other dedicated spaces, a large TV room and Arts & Crafts room. The bulletin board near the main entrance featured flyers advertising upcoming events within the building and messages outlining rules and safety.

After entering P1's home, the facilitator observed a smartphone, laptop, printer, and Smart TV. P1 immigrated to Canada 20 years ago and remains connected to her country of origin via family members and online. During the observation, she turned on the television and Apple TV and searched YouTube for news from "back home". We watched news stories and discussed current events. She prepared a traditional snack for the facilitator and we continued to discuss her experience living in the retirement community.

Findings. The immersion session helped inform thoughts around social interaction within the environment. In spite of P1's comfort with technology, communicating digitally within a closed environment did not appear to be important or useful to her. When asked how she connected with her neighbors, she stated that she would go to their apartments to see them in person to chat or see them around the building in the common areas. Accordingly, she preferred face-to-face interactions with her friends in the city as well. And when asked about the building's organized activities, she stated that she enjoyed participating in them and checked the bulletin board every week to plan her time. For P1, the value of the features of the digital messaging system may be minimal. A product, system or service which would enhance communication with loved ones who are far away may be more beneficial.

Ideally, the session should have been conducted over the course of several hours to a day, but time constraints did not allow for that to occur. In the future, it is also recommended that more immersion sessions be completed with other residents within that same community or residents living in other, similar environments.

3.2 Card Sort

Observations. As shown in Fig. 4, Health, Faithfulness and Achievement were the top three shared choices in the Very Important to Me category. Table 1 features the participants' explanations of why these particular values are very important to them.

Fig. 4. Top three selections common to both participants

Table 1. Reasoning for card sort selections

Very important values	P2	P3
Health - To be physically well and healthy	"My back and knees hurt when I don't exercise. I do 10–15 min of weights every day. I want to live as long as my mother!"	"I have friends who take meds for every little thing. I don't want that."
Faithfulness - To be loyal and true in relationships	"I have some good friends. (Name redacted) took me for lunch this week and paid - I paid last week."	"I hang out with my buddies all the time. Some of these guys I've known for years and years."
Achievement - To have important accomplishments	"I've done a lot in my life…but I still have another 20 years left in me!"	"I have all these business ideas…so many. I had that one cool business that made a lot of money. I need to do that again."

Findings. Words in the card sort aligning most closely with the proposed solution included: Family, Autonomy, Communication, Friendship, and Commitment. While P2 categorized family as being Very Important, P3 viewed it as Important. None of the other words were deemed very important by either participant. Research has shown that the personal values someone adopts or finds significant can reveal insight into their consumer behavior [16].

Both participants mentioned friends when discussing faithfulness and when asked to elaborate stated they valued face-to-face communication with their network when possible. If he could not communicate in person, P2 preferred phone calls, followed by email. P3 also preferred phone calls as a second means of communication, followed by texting. Therefore, if within close proximity to their networks, they would take the time to travel and meet in person.

Though these two participants currently live independently, their input regarding preferred communication methods was valuable. One could surmise that even if their living arrangements change as they age, faithfulness as a personal value will remain very important to them - as will the significance they place on face-to-face communication - and they would continue to seek out in-person interactions for as long as they could.

With only two participants, the captured data were clearly limited. However, it would be relatively easy to expand the reach of this session (for example, by offering the card sort online) to increase the number of participants and collect more data.

3.3 Brainstorm

Observations. P2 and P3 participated in this session. They did not follow the convention of writing their ideas and thoughts down on the Post-It notes, and instead expressed their ideas in a stream-of-consciousness manner. The facilitator ended up recording the main ideas on Post-It notes and posting them on the poster board while simultaneously taking photos and videos. Audio was continuously recorded throughout the entire session.

After visually defining the problem statement, P3 kicked off the session by discussing the computerized version of the Solitaire game:

P3: You know the games that are on computers? Have you looked at them? They had games like solitaire and different kinds...FreeCell...do you know why they had those games on there? Lots of people know how to play those games just using ordinary cards, you know. But they were trying to teach people how to drag and drop. In the process, these guys thought they were playing a game...

P2: But they were actually learning a skill...

P3: They were learning a skill...and also some of these things were to make them not afraid of the computer. But actually, that's the whole idea behind solitaire and FreeCell.

P2: Because then you're masking it under something else.

P3: You know this thing - castor oil? It was nasty. My mom used to give it to us in... ginger [ale] or whatever so it would go down easily. But then someone came up with a brilliant idea - put it into a capsule. You just swallow the darn thing and you don't taste it. They drink water and it does its job.

P2: Same with garlic.

P3: If you're trying to create a product...if they find it intimidating - but something that they're doing without even knowing that they're doing it. So, what do seniors do now...?

The participants continued to discuss instances where friends came up with creative solutions to problems. The highlight of the brainstorm session occurred near the end.

P3: One thing might be to think of a difficulty they are having and come up with something for them.

P3: What happens [when we age]? Sometimes the memory goes. Generally, as you get older you take more meds...sometimes people forget so they have those dishes for pills for days of the week. So, on Sunday you fill the whole thing and every day you take one. But you're also thinking digital world. You could come up with something like...Yes, we're going to build the product.

He proceeded to pick up nearby objects and build the rudimentary prototype shown in Fig. 5.

P3: So, these holes are the days of the week. Say they have to take it at 12 but if it's after 12, and they don't take the pills - if they don't take it, an alarm goes off. If this is filled, the alarm goes on. As soon as the pill's out, it goes off.

P2: A medicine cabinet alarm...yeah - it can have a light too for people who don't hear well.

P3: Exactly. And to go even further, maybe it can send a text message to my phone if I forget to take my pill.

Fig. 5. P3 making a rudimentary prototype from everyday objects

Findings. The brainstorm session became a "making, telling, enacting" session [1], with P3 making a prototype and using it to tell a story about how it might solve the design problem. Ultimately, the session concluded with a creative solution which capitalized on a schema, or existing behavior or thought pattern, to create the digitized version of a familiar product.

The entire exchange also reinforced the importance of patience in facilitation: the facilitator sat back and did not interject and judgment was reserved until the session reached its natural conclusion. It would have been interesting to see what other ideas could have transpired from a larger, more heterogeneous group.

4 Lessons Learned

A number of salient points emerged from the generative sessions. First, the proposed solution was based solely on the results of ethnographic/observational studies and a literature review. However, it became apparent that further exploration was needed to determine whether enhancing digital communication between older adults was truly a problem to be addressed. For instance, these three participants all valued face-to-face communication more than communicating digitally. In addition, they were comfortable and satisfied with existing technological tools. Even for P1, who is living within the environment in which the digital messaging system would be used, the perceived usefulness could be considered low. Perceived usefulness is one of the key variables related to pre-implementation technology acceptance, or a person's intention to use a technology that has yet to be used [17]. The results of the generative design sessions demonstrated that the messaging system may not be as useful as was assumed.

Second, the characteristics of the target audience could have been more clearly defined beyond the age demographic. During the brainstorm session, P3 reflected on the phrase "inclusion in digital society":

P3: How would a person be classified as being already included? For example, if an older adult plays a lot of video games, does that include them? If a person owns a computer and goes on the Internet, are they already included?

Narrowing down the scope at the beginning would have provided more guidance to the project, including outlining more specific criteria for participant inclusion in the generative sessions.

Finally, although the results of the sessions did not appear to support the proposed solution, the experience was not unsuccessful. The sessions ultimately identified a new theme for further exploration: health. Health featured prominently in both the card sort and brainstorm sessions. Moreover, in the card sort, the word Fitness was deemed Very Important to P3 and as Important to P2, reinforcing the theme. Based on the feedback from these sessions, a solution encompassing this concept could be more suitable. Figure 6 summarizes the process starting with the proposed solution, incorporating the design sessions, highlighting the common preferred mode of communication and culminating with the shared theme of health.

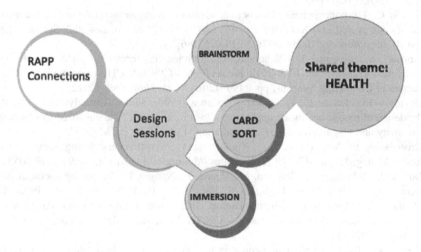

Fig. 6. Big picture summary of the generative design sessions

5   Conclusion

The feedback from the generative design sessions with older adults reinforced the importance of engaging users in the design process. The sessions generated valuable information about experiences, preferences and influences which could not have been gleaned from observational studies, leading to greater insight into the problem statement and the proposed solution of a closed digital messaging system. A number of themes materialized, including the value placed on face-to-face communication, which could potentially invalidate the proposed solution. However, another theme emerged – health – which the facilitator concluded warrants further exploration. The findings also triggered the consideration of complementary factors such as technology acceptance and cognitive schemas, both pertinent to design research.

Overall, the sessions tapped into the older adults' wisdom and creativity [18], yielding imaginative ideas and artifacts that would not have been generated without their participation.

Acknowledgments. We thank the participants, who generously volunteered their time to share their thoughts, perceptions and creativity.

References

1. Sanders, E.B.-N., Stappers, P.J.: Convivial Toolbox: Generative Research for the Front End of Design. BIS Publisher, Amsterdam (2013)
2. Pew Research Center: Tech Adoption Climbs Among Older Adults, May 2017
3. Das, A., Bøthun, S., Reitan, J., Dahl, Y.: The use of generative techniques in co-design of mhealth technology and healthcare services for COPD patients. In: Marcus, A. (ed.) DUXU 2015, Part III. LNCS, vol. 9188, pp. 587–595. Springer, Cham (2015). https://doi.org/10.1007/978-3-319-20889-3_54
4. Gatsou, C.: From inexperienced users to co-creators: an exploration of a generative method. In: Marcus, A. (ed.) DUXU 2014, Part IV. LNCS, vol. 8520, pp. 244–252. Springer, Cham (2014). https://doi.org/10.1007/978-3-319-07638-6_24
5. Lindsay, S., Jackson, D., Schofield, G., Olivier, P.: Engaging older people using participatory design. In: CHI 2012 Proceedings of the SIGCHI Conference on Human Factors in Computing Systems, pp. 1199–1208. ACM, New York (2012)
6. Davidson, J.L., Jensen, C.: Participatory design with older adults: An analysis of creativity in the design of mobile healthcare applications. In: Proceedings of the 9th ACM Conference on Creativity and Cognition, Sidney, Australia, pp. 1199–1208. ACM (2013)
7. Kristensson, P., Magnusson, P.R.: Tuning users' innovativeness during ideation. Creat. Innov. Manag. **19**(2), 147–159 (2010). https://doi.org/10.1111/j.1467-8691.2010.00552.x
8. Durick, J., Robertson, T., Brereton, M., Vetere, F., Nansen, B.: Dispelling ageing myths in technology design. In: Shen, H., Smith, R., Paay, J., Calder, P., Wyeld, T. (eds.) Proceedings of the 25th Australian Computer-Human Interaction Conference on Augmentation, Application, Innovation, Collaboration - OzCHI 2013, Adelaide, Australia, pp. 467–476. ACM Press (2013)
9. United Nations, Department of Economic and Social Affairs, Population Division World Population Prospects: The 2017 Revision, Key Findings and Advance Tables. Working Paper No. ESA/P/WP/248 (2017)
10. Pew Research Center: Emerging Nations Embrace Internet, Mobile Technology, February 2014
11. Lewis, J.E., Neider, M.B.: Designing wearable technology for an aging population. Ergon. Des. **25**(3), 4–10 (2017). https://doi.org/10.1177/1064804616645488
12. Satariano, W.A., Scharlach, A.E., Lindeman, D.: Aging, place, and technology: toward improving access and wellness in older populations. J. Aging Health **26**(8), 1373–1389 (2014). https://doi.org/10.1177/0898264314543470
13. Juárez, M.R., González, V.M., Favela, J.: Effect of technology on aging perception. Health Inform. J. (2016). https://doi.org/10.1177/1460458216661863

14. IDEO Field Guide to Human-Centered Design. http://www.designkit.org/resources/1. Accessed 07 Jan 2018
15. Personal values card sort. https://casaa.unm.edu/inst/Personal%20Values%20Card%20Sort. pdf. Accessed 29 Nov 2017
16. O'Cass, A.: An exploratory study of the influence of personal values on purchase decision & advertising involvement. In: Tidwell, P.M., Muller, T.E. (eds.) AP - Asia Pacific Advances in Consumer Research, pp. 67–72. Association for Consumer Research, Provo (2001)
17. Peek, S.T.M., Wouters, E.J.M., van Hoof, J., Luijkx, K.G., Boeije, H.R., Vrijhoef, H.J.M.: Factors influencing acceptance of technology for aging in place: a systematic review. Int. J. Med. Inform. **83**, 235–248 (2014). https://doi.org/10.1016/j.ijmedinf.2014.01.004
18. Rogers, Y., Marsden, G.: Does he take sugar? Moving beyond the rhetoric of compassion. Interactions **20**, 48–57 (2013). https://doi.org/10.1145/2486227.2486238

Micro Flip Teaching with Collective Intelligence

Ángel Fidalgo-Blanco[1], María Luisa Sein-Echaluce[2(✉)],
and Francisco J. García-Peñalvo[3]

[1] LITI Laboratory, Technical University of Madrid, Madrid, Spain
angel.fidalgo@upm.es
[2] GIDTIC Research Group, University of Zaragoza, Zaragoza, Spain
mlsein@unizar.es
[3] GRIAL Research Group, University of Salamanca, Salamanca, Spain
fgarcia@usal.es

Abstract. One of the main objectives within the educational context is that the students must be active during the learning process, and one of the indicators of this activity is the production of content by the students themselves. There are methods such as Micro Flip Teaching that promote active learning. However, achieving that the students generate content is not enough; these contents should also be used in the learning process itself and, for this, they should be managed appropriately. This article presents a method of management of the resources generated by the students and the professors as well, through the use of collective intelligence. A model of collective intelligence was developed, based on four pillars: the utility of the created contents, technology, methodology and the strategy of use. This work shows that the main factor needed so that the students generate knowledge was the strategy of use.

Keywords: Collective intelligence · Flip teaching · Knowledge management
Social networks

1 Introduction

The organization, management and access to knowledge are vital for the development of society. For this, the appearance of technologies that allow for the creation, communication and access to knowledge has changed in the world. The Information and Communication Technologies (ICT) have contributed to the creation of present society, the society where we live: the society of knowledge.

One of the most characteristic products-services of this new society is the internet, which offers us the possibility of being connected to the rest of the people and the accessing of the content that is created at any time, place and immediately, synchronously or asynchronously.

But the manner of creating, organizing and utilizing internet content has two formats: Web 1.0 and Web 2.0. The Web 1.0 format is the heir to the classic communication media (newspaper, radio, cinema, television, etc.), where a set of people (frequently with a great reputation) create, select, organize and classify the content so

© Springer International Publishing AG, part of Springer Nature 2018
P. Zaphiris and A. Ioannou (Eds.): LCT 2018, LNCS 10924, pp. 400–415, 2018.
https://doi.org/10.1007/978-3-319-91743-6_30

that it is accessible for everyone. In this format, the person who accesses the content acts in a similar fashion as a radio listener; his or her degree of freedom consists on "changing the station". The Web 2.0 format, on the contrary, tries to liberate and democratize the creation and organization of knowledge. In this case, the former "listeners" rebel, gain prominence, and are creators at the same time that they are consumers of knowledge. A new figure is created, the spectator now becomes the "prosumer" (producer and consumer).

This atomization of the creation of knowledge leads to knowledge now having different sources of creation that are distributed in nodes with multiple flows between themselves. This is what is known as distributed and networked knowledge [1].

To optimally manage distributed knowledge, its own characteristics should be taken into account: knowledge created by different people, distributed in different nodes and with multiple fluxes and connections. The tools that allow for this management belong to the denominated Web 2.0, and the most common are the so-called social networks.

Likewise, the organizations of the industrial sector have applied this same approach as the method of management of the organization itself. This is what is known as knowledge management within the organizations, which is based on the generation, identification, classification, organization and use of the knowledge created not only by a single person, who is usually the one with the most expertise in the organization, but all the people that comprise it [2].

On the other hand, the educational context should not be set aside from the communication media utilized by the students, and should take into account the multiple channels and varieties of these media [3]. Likewise, the "school", as an organization whose main objective is the creation of knowledge, should not remain detached from the new ways of managing it [4]. In other words, the social networks as a means of communication between people and their organizations, as well as knowledge management (KM), produced by these people, should be taken into account. The integration of social networks with KM is possible, as these networks allow for the sharing of information and promoting of the creation of scenarios that are suitable for the diffusion of knowledge [5].

Thus, at school as well as in organizations, the knowledge created by their members should be taken into consideration. If this condition is transferred to the context of the classroom, it is about the managing of the knowledge created by the professors and students to bring about learning, as the collective capacity always exceeds that of an individual member of this same collective [6]. This consideration is necessary, as it is usually the professors who provide the knowledge in the classroom, and the students only create knowledge to pass the evaluations, not for learning to take place.

History and evolution of humanity has been based on the cooperation of individuals, and has been the object of numerous studies, such as collective intelligence (CI), based on sociology and computer sciences. CI has been applied to diverse areas within the educational context, such as in medicine to improve diagnosis [7] or for the making of decisions [8]. Independently of its denomination, a common characteristic of all the applications is that their success depends on the capacity to activate the intelligence of all its members [9].

Thus, if CI is to be used between the students and the professors of a specific school subject, the following conditions must be met:

- That the students are willing to cooperate.
- That the students collaborate in the creation of knowledge.
- That knowledge is useful for the common objective of the students (to favor learning).
- That said knowledge is managed efficiently.
- That said knowledge is used.

The principles of CI can be applied to any group of students enrolled in the same course, as the students have many common characteristics: their main objective is to pass the course, they have different degree of knowledge on the subject matter, they have access to the same channels of cooperation, and they can share tasks and processes.

The management of knowledge, as well as collective intelligence, require that the students be active, and also that the students create content during the learning process. These two characteristics (activity and creation of knowledge) are conducted through the active method of Micro Flip Teaching (MFT). This method combines the Flip Teaching method (the students have to conduct a pre-activity before the in-class session) with the believe that the students are able to create knowledge, the product of learning, and that this knowledge can be used as a resource for learning as well [10,11, 12].

In the present work, a model of action is proposed, named "Active Cooperative Collective Intelligence (ACCI), which was devised so that students in a course create knowledge in a cooperative manner through an active methodology (such as MFT), which could be used under the principles of CI. For this, a model of action was proposed that included the use of:

1. Social networks as the communication channel between persons.
2. Active methodology (MFT) so that the students create knowledge.
3. Knowledge management systems (KMS) for its organization.
4. Strategic methodology that favors CI.

Items 2 and 3 have already been investigated by the authors of the present work, resulting in validated models of action within the university context [11, 13]. The two main contributions of this present work are:

- The validation of a strategic methodology that favors CI (items 1 and 4)
- Integration of the result with other aspects validated in previous works to generate a model that integrates CI with MFT.

As for the strategy, the main approach of this work is the successful creation of knowledge (by the students) that neither depends only on the use of a social network (web 2.0), nor granting a perspective of usefulness to the students (planning of the KM as an organizational method), but the creation of an inertia among the students of the course for the creation and management of collective intelligence.

The proposed ACCI model integrates CI, learning communities (using social networks), the active method MFT, a KMS and the creation of knowledge by the students. For this, the following aspects will be measured:

- Capacity of the students to contribute contents during the learning process
- Type of knowledge provided by the students
- Use of knowledge
- Organization and search for knowledge
- Usefulness of knowledge

In the following sections, the ACCI model, the research context, the results and the conclusions will be presented.

2   Proposed ACCI Model

The proposed ACCI model is based on the integration of three lines of educational innovation that are currently considered as tendencies: MFT, KMS and CI. Figure 1 shows the integration of 4 main sub-models: (a) MFT, (b) the student as the generator of didactic resources, (c) KMS and (d) CI.

In previous studies, the sub-models (a), (b) and (c) were validated in asynchronous situations; meaning that the students from a specific course contributed knowledge that was posteriorly used by students of other courses, or the same course, but in a different semester or academic year. In this case, the knowledge created was produced at the end of the learning process.

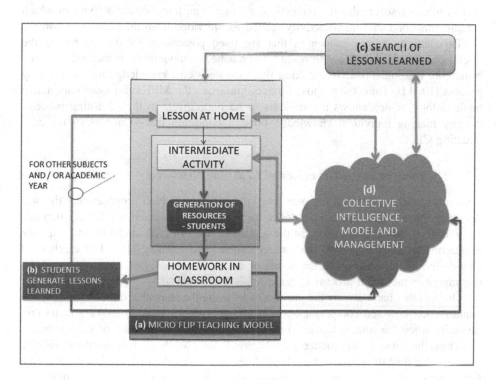

Fig. 1. Design of the ACCI model

For example, creating a learned lesson that only the students from the subsequent courses could benefit from this knowledge; this method was named "collective intelligence in asynchrony". However, the students who were participative, active and cooperative did not benefit from this action (although they did benefit from the one conducted by the ex-students of said subject). The sub-model (d), related to CI is proposed so that the students benefit from their action and cooperation in real-time through the organized management of the resources as they are generated. This article presents the validation of sub-model (d).

2.1 Micro Flip Teaching

The Flip Teaching (FT) model is based on changing the place where the two main generic activities of the learning process take place: the lesson and homework. In the traditional model, the lesson is conducted in the classroom, and later, the homework is done at home. However, the FT model proposes that the lesson be done at home, and the homework in the classroom. This favors that the student study the theoretical lesson, and later, their presence in the classroom is exploited for conducting more practical activities [14–16].

The main problem of the FT model is that the inactivity of the students is transferred from the classroom to the home, and there seems to be a disconnection between the activities "at home" and the ones in "the classroom" [17]. The Micro Flip Teaching (MFT) model resolves this disconnection, as it adds an intermediate activity in which the students conduct a micro activity related to the video from the "lesson at home".

This activity creates evidences that are used posteriorly by the teacher in the in-class session [18]. In previous research, it has been shown that this method succeeds in making the students active, making them create useful knowledge for the learning process [10, 11]. Thus, the proposed model integrates the MFT sub-model with active methodology, which allows the students to be participants in their learning process, thereby making individual knowledge flow, a condition that is necessary for constructing CI.

2.2 The Student as the Generator of Learning Resources

This sub-model is based on the peer learning approach, which proposes that the students are able to create useful knowledge for the students themselves [18] and, that this knowledge is varied (depending on the academic level of each student), and thus, the production of knowledge and the variety can lead to learning [19]. The creation of knowledge by the students is the result of active methodologies where the students participate in their own process of learning.

On the other hand, during the process of learning the student acquires experience in contents, abilities and competencies on a specific school subject, arriving at its culmination when the student has finished the learning of a specific bit of knowledge.

Thus, the student can produce useful knowledge [20] that can be used by students in another course or academic year [12]. The students explain (through a video) what they have done, and how they have conducted a specific learning activity. To prove the validity of the lesson learned, a previous research study was conducted where an experimental group only used the lessons learned by the students, and a control group used the knowledge created by the teachers. The results did not show significant differences in the learning results, showing the validity of the knowledge created by the students as didactic resources [11].

2.3   KMS

In the proposed ACCI model proposed, a KMS is needed, as the combination of the previous two sub-modules succeeds at having the student create a great quantity of knowledge, as the result of different learning activities. If the resources that are created by the students during the different courses (with common materials) are added to the different academic courses where they are produced, then the amount of knowledge that is able to be used as a didactic resource increases. But this process and accumulation presents two problems: the degree of validity of the knowledge created by the students and its organization so that it is easy to find.

The KMS is a repository named the BRACO repository (Collaborative Academic Resource Finder, or Buscador de Recursos Académicos Colaborativos in Spanish) [19, 20] designed so that the students can find knowledge from another student based on the activity that will be conducted with this knowledge, meaning, based on the final aim of the use of said knowledge [12, 21].

2.4   CI Sub-Model

The objective of this sub-model is to achieve, in an environment that is participative and active, that the student from a specific course share the knowledge created continuously during the learning process and allow for the creation of CI. It is based on 4 pillars: technology, the content to be shared, the methodology and the strategy for its use.

- *Technology.* a social network was chosen as it is a communication channel that is very utilized by the students, who have the habit of use and the necessary technical skills. Google+ was chosen as the social network due to its characteristics of content organization. In other popular networks, the contents are organized as a list where the last contents introduced appear at the top of the page, and the older ones at the bottom of the page. However, Google+ allows the establishing of categories that work as an index where the content can be organized, and within each section of the index, the organization works as in other social networks.
- *Content to be shared.* Any information is considered as content as long as it contributes didactic value to the learning process, such as, for example, a doubt, an answer to this doubt, an example, a thought, resolution of a problem, notes, etc.
- *Methodology.* The methodology, which is shown in Fig. 2, should provide the necessary support so that the knowledge can be shared as it is created. For example, a question or doubt can appear previous to an in-class session, in class or after class. Thus, the concept is that the social network can be used everywhere and under every circumstance where learning is produced such as, for example, allowing the students to use their mobile devices during the in-class sessions.

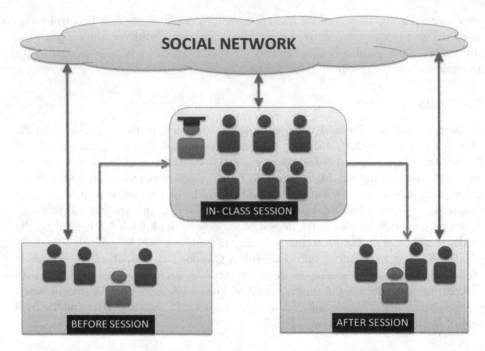

Fig. 2. Methodology of creation and utilization of CI

- *The strategy.* It is about establishing a procedure for the use of the aforementioned elements. The strategy, described in the next section, should have in mind the student's habits of use of social networks in the academic context. One of the objectives of this work was to determine the influence of this habit for creating collective intelligence.

Likewise, the professors include, in the social network, all the didactic resources, scripts, examples, etc. that can be used in each in-class session before it is conducted, so that the students can use it during the in-class session. The objective of this research is to validate this CI sub-model and to integrate it into the ACCI model, so that it will be possible to work synchronously; thus, during the learning process itself, and so that the beneficiary is the CI's own creator.

3 Research Context

The research was conducted in the "Informatics and Programming" course, which corresponded to the first academic year of the Energy Engineering and Mine Engineering degrees. The model was applied in 2017, in the first semester, to a laboratory group from the Energy Engineering degree, and to two laboratory groups during the second semester of the Mine Engineering degree.

The course included 6 laboratory classes on Matlab programming. Each laboratory was organized into 9 sessions lasting 2 h each, so that the sections created in the

Google+ social network coincided with each in-class session. The professor created the sections through the option "filters", and each filter was equivalent to the name of each session (see Fig. 3-a). For example, the link with the name "session 3" only showed the resources that had been created in that session.

Likewise, the type of resource that each member contributed to the network was classified into three categories: "Action, Subject and Source", and each category, at the same time, was decomposed into a set of tags: Syllabus, Petition, Doubt, Answer and Contribution (for Action), Matlab and Algorithm (for Subject), Professor and student (for Source). The list is shown in Fig. 3-b.

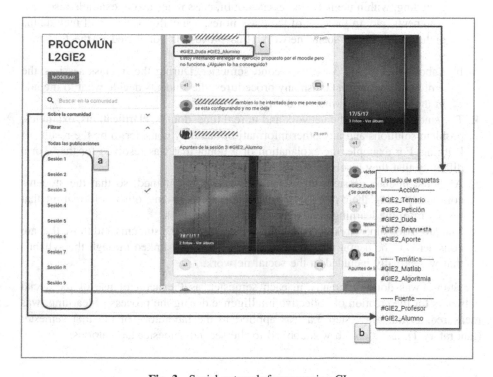

Fig. 3. Social network for managing CI

In conclusion, each time that a student contributed a resource to the social network, the following information was created: user (generated by the network by default), filter (the network obliges the choosing of a filter before making the resource public) and the tags (optional). Thus, when a resource was included (Fig. 3-c), the session (Fig. 3-a) and its tags (Fig. 3-b) that only the professor had included according to the content that the student included, could be observed.

The strategy of the ACCI model (Sect. 2.4) is described through the following procedure:

1. On the first day of the course, the mission and objectives of the creation and the use of the CI is explained, the functioning of the network is explained and the student's membership is verified.
2. Previous to the session, the professors includes the planning of the session and the resources that will be used in the social network. The tag "syllabus" is assigned.
3. During the in-class session:
    a. Laboratory 1, first semester. The professor establishes the procedure for including, within the network, every doubt, class notes taken, example resolved, comments, etc. In the case of the class notes, a specific student will include his or her notes in the social network (this process is conducted in the first four sessions).
    b. Laboratories 2 and 3 of the second semester. During the in-class session, the professor does not establish any procedures, the students decide what to include in the network and when to do it.
4. The students share, in the network and in real time, doubts, clarifications, examples, problem solutions and any other information that they consider to be the results of learning. For example, the explanation of a doubt that was resolved for them, or a difficulty that they resolved themselves.
5. After the in-class session, the social network is maintained, so that the students continue posting their doubts, sharing their notes or any other information that results from the learning conducted outside of the class.
6. The professor supervises the resources contributed by the students and those that are considered to be useful for the rest of the students are linked through the syllabus that was initially included in the social network.

Step 3 was done differently in each semester, as the habit of use of the social networks for the creation of collective intelligence during the process of learning, was measured. In this way, step 3.a was applied to the laboratory of the first semester (laboratory 1), and step 3.b was applied to the second semester laboratories.

4   Results

The gathering of data was conducted from two sources: the evidences contributed to the network (shared knowledge) and from a perception questionnaire.

4.1   Evidences Contributed to the Social Network

The quantification of knowledge, shared by the students, was obtained from the sum of the resources included in the social networks: shared class notes, doubts mentioned, responses to these doubts, examples solved, etc.

Figure 4 shows the distribution of the contributions created in each group/ laboratory. Figure 4(a) corresponds to the students from laboratory 1 (31 students) during the in-class sessions, and the Figs. 4(b) and (c) correspond to the two groups

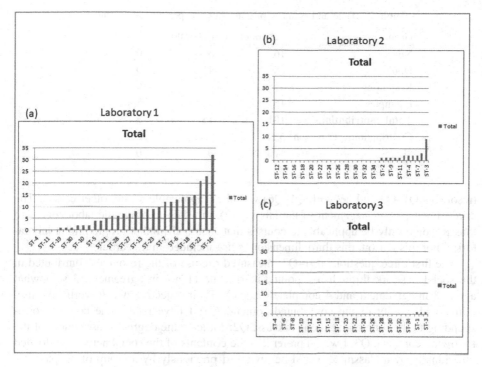

Fig. 4. Number of contributions per group/laboratory

(35 students in each group) from laboratories 2 and 3. The difference between laboratory 1 and laboratories 2 and 3 is that laboratory 1 conducted step 3.a from the ACCI strategy (presented in the research context section), while the other two laboratories conducted step 3.b.

Table 1 shows the percentage of participation, i.e., the number of students who contributed at least one type of content with respect to the total number of students, and Table 2 shows the type of knowledge and the number of contributions from each group. The "Likes" are not considered contents, but show that this contribution was useful for the students.

Table 1. Percentage of participation per group/laboratory

Group	Laboratory 1	Laboratory 2	Laboratory 3
Percentage of participation	87.09	31.42	8.57

4.2 Qualitative Data

The qualitative data were obtained from a questionnaire that was by comprised by 9 questions, and was structured in three dimensions: the resources included in the social network, the management of the network itself and the academic management of the laboratory itself. Each dimension had three associated questions. The first two dimensions

Table 2. Type and quantity of contributions per group/laboratory

Group	Laboratory 1	Laboratory 2	Laboratory 3
Notes	16	6	0
Doubts	28	4	0
Responses	41	9	0
Examples	16	6	3
Total contributions	**101**	**15**	**3**
Contributions per person	3.25	0.71	0.08
"Likes"	170	0	0

(resources Q1–Q3 and network Q4–Q6) would be applicable to any other course. The third dimension (management of the laboratory) aimed to improve the laboratory, and thus it would only be applicable to courses that included Matlab programming laboratories. For this reason, this third dimension is not included in this article.

The first three questions (Q1–Q3) measured the use of the resources contributed in the social network through a 4 point Likert scale (1 not in agreement, 2 somewhat agree, 3 in agreement and 4 completely agree). Their objective was to verify the use, utility and quality of the contributed content. Q1: I have read some content corresponding to the different sessions in class. Q2: Indicate the degree of usefulness of the following contents. Q3: I would prefer that the contents of the social network uploaded individually by a classmate would be reviewed previously by a group of people.

Next, the 31 answers from laboratory 1 are presented. These results have been published in a previous research study [4] to analyze the perception of the students of this laboratory. Tables 3 and 5 show this data as a percentage of answers (Table 4).

Table 3. Percentages of responses to question Q1 (resources)

Q1. I have read some content corresponding to the different sessions in class.

	1	2	3	4
Notes contributed by other classmates	13	28	41	19
Doubts and responses	6	31	31	31
Professor's syllabus	0	3	47	50
Programs solved by classmates	9	13	41	38

Table 4. Percentages of responses to question Q2 (resources)

Q2. Indicate the degree of usefulness of the following contents.

	1	2	3	4
Notes contributed by other classmates	16	50	28	6
Doubts and responses	0	19	56	25
Professor's syllabus	0	13	41	47
Programs solved by classmates	0	19	38	44

Table 5. Percentages of responses to question Q3 (resources)

Q3. I would prefer that the contents of the social network uploaded individually by a classmate would be reviewed previously by a group of people.	1	2	3	4
Notes	6	31	34	28
Doubts and responses	16	25	38	22
Programs solved (its proper functioning verified by the professor)	9	13	31	47

Questions Q4–Q6 are open-ended questions used to verify the efficiency of the CI sub-model (through the social network), as well as its improvement: Q4-indicate what you liked the most of the social network, Q5- indicate what you liked the least of the social network and Q6- indicate what you would improve about the social network. An analysis of the open-ended questions was conducted, and these were later grouped into diverse categories: What I liked the most (collaboration, content, accessibility, organization, teacher relationship and novelty), What I liked the least (types of content, difficulty finding content, quality control, nothing and technical problems) and Improvements (organizations and search, specific content, nothing, other applications – help with recovering missed classes, involvement of the professor and quality control). Figure 5 shows the evaluations of the students from laboratory 1 for the five most valued answers.

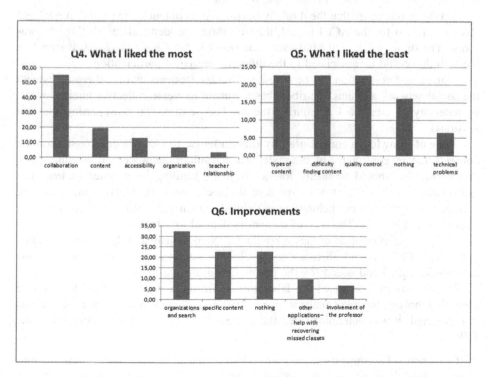

Fig. 5. Evaluation questions Q4, Q5 and Q6 of the CI sub-model

5 Conclusions

From the results gathered, the following conclusions are drawn, grouped into the following sections that contribute with the validation of the ACCI model:

- Capacity of the students to contribute content during the process of learning
- Type of knowledge contributed by the students
- Use of the knowledge
- Usefulness of the knowledge
- Organization and search of knowledge

Capacity of the students to contribute content during the process of learning. This refers to the capacity of the students to generate the elements of knowledge necessary to construct the process of collective intelligence. That is, the elements of knowledge that they contribute during the process of learning. The laboratory 1 group had a high capacity for creating contributions in the contents of the social network (101 in Table 2) as well as in the verification of the usefulness of said content (170 "likes" in Table 2). Likewise, in this same lab, 87.1% of the students contributed at least one type of content (Table 1).

However, the laboratories 2 and 3 had a low contribution of resources (15 in lab 2 and 3 in lab 3, Table 2), with 0 "likes", which could be a sign of the low interest of both groups. The percentages of participation of the persons that contributed content were very low, with 31.42 for lab 2 and 8.57 for lab 3.

Taking into account that the 4 pillars (technology, content to be shared, model and strategy of use) for the ACCI model, the first three are identical for all three laboratories. The strategy of use, the only variation between lab 1 and labs 2–3 was step 3, is the step that could be associated to the different degree of participation.

Thus, a first conclusion can be stated: so that the students involve themselves with the social network and thus contribute basic content to create collective intelligence, it is necessary to create a habit during the in-class sessions (at least during the first sessions).

Type of knowledge contributed by the students. The knowledge consists on the contents that are contributed by the students as a result of the process of learning. Also, this knowledge should be useful for favoring the learning by another student. The information on the content is mirrored in the social network. On the one hand, the section where the content belongs to is defined, which indicated the in-class session related to it (Fig. 3-a). The type of content is defined as a tag.

The process of creation of tags is conducted continuously and dynamically, so that at the start of laboratory 1, there are no tags, but as content is added by the students, the tags are identified and added (by the professors, in this case).

Due to this process, once the laboratory is finished, the type of content can be identified through the mere analysis of the different tags contributed. After the analysis is conducted, it was determined that the content contributed by the students was the following:

- *Class notes.* Photographs of the notes taken by the students in the in-class sessions (they have the professor's permission, according to the intellectual property norms).

- *Doubts.* The doubts that arise during the in-class session or outside of the classroom.
- *Responses to the doubts.* These are solutions contributed to the doubts asked by the students. Some students answer their own doubts; meaning that the students who posted a doubt have already solved it through their own means.
- *Examples resolved.* As these are programming laboratories, these are examples that are done in a different manner as those conducted in class, and that the students have conducted to understand specific concepts or proposed problems.

Use of knowledge. The most significant contribution comes from laboratory 1, as it is the most reliable group as there are quantitative data (the use of the social network, Tables 1 and 2) that back the utilization of knowledge. Question Q1 provided information on the utilization of the knowledge contributed to the social network, in relation to values 3 and 4 of the scale (in agreement and complete agreement): 97% used the contents contributed by the professors, 79% the examples resolved, 62% the contents of type doubts and responses, and 60% the notes taken by other classmates. Thus, there is a greater use of the contents contributed in the social network.

Utility of the knowledge. This data was obtained from question Q2. The perception of the utility of the content, as related to the students that had answered "in complete agreement" or "in agreement", was almost 90% of the cases for the content contributed by the professors (88%), doubts and responses (81%) and examples (81%). However, it was very scarce for the notes contributed by other classmates (34%). Thus, it was shown that the contents contributed by other people in the network were useful for learning, however, the contents contributed that coincided with the contents that was already possessed by the students (as in the case of class notes), were not considered useful.

Organization and search for information. It was evident that if there are little resources in a social network, it would be difficult to find them (due to their scarcity), but when there is a great number of resources, the organization is closely linked to the ease of searching, identification and utilization. In the open-ended questions, it was observed that one of the aspects that was least liked by the students (open-ended question Q5) was the difficulty in finding contents in the network, and on the other hand, this was complemented by the open-ended answers provided for Q6 (improvements), where the students considered that the most important was the organization and search for content. This justifies the utilization of component (c) within the ACCI model (Fig. 1-c): the knowledge management system, where in other research studies, the ease of its system of searching was evaluated.

In this work, the strategy of use of the CI sub-model was validated and defined. The next step of the research study will be to apply the complete ACCI model; meaning, including all the sub-models.

References

1. Siemens, G.: Connectivism: A Learning Theory for the Digital Age. Int. J. Instr. Technol. Distance Learn. **2**, 3–10 (2005)
2. Nonaka, I., Takeuchi, H.: The Knowledge-Creating Company: How Japanese Companies Create the Dynamics of Innovation. Oxford University Press, New York (1995)
3. Lee, A., Lau, J., Carbo, T., Gendina, N.: Conceptual Relationship of Information Literacy and Media Literacy in Knowledge Societies, Paris (2013)
4. Fidalgo-Blanco, Á., Sein-Echaluce, M.L., García Peñalvo, F.J.: Inteligencia colectiva en el aula. Un paradigma cooperativo - [Collective Intelligence in the classroom. A cooperative paradigm]. In: La innovación docente como misión del profesorado : Actas del IV Congreso Internacional sobre Aprendizaje, Innovación y Competitividad. CINAIC 2017, 4–6 de Octubre de 2017, Zaragoza, España, pp. 599–603. Zaragoza, España: Servicio de Publicaciones Universidad de Zaragoza (2017). https://doi.org/10.26754/cinaic.2017.000001_125
5. Altinay, Z., Saner, T., Bahçelerli, N.M., Altinay, F.: The role of social media tools: accessible tourism for disabled citizens. Educ. Technol. Soc. **19**, 89–99 (2016)
6. Mann, R.P., Helbing, D.: Optimal incentives for collective intelligence. Proc. Natl. Acad. Sci. USA **114**, 5077–5082 (2017)
7. Kämmer, J.E., Hautz, W.E., Herzog, S.M., Kunina-Habenicht, O., Kurvers, R.H.J.M.: The potential of collective intelligence in emergency medicine: pooling medical students' independent decisions improves diagnostic performance. Med. Decis. Mak. **37**, 715–724 (2017)
8. De Vincenzo, I., Giannoccaro, I., Carbone, G., Grigolini, P.: Criticality triggers the emergence of collective intelligence in groups. Phys. Rev. E **96**, 22309 (2017)
9. Pör, G.: Collective Intelligence and Collective Leadership: Twin Paths to Beyond Chaos. All Sprouts Content (2008). http://aisel.aisnet.org/sprouts_all/207. Accessed 20 Feb 2018
10. García-Peñalvo, F.J., Fidalgo-Blanco, Á., Sein-Echaluce, M.L., Conde, M.Á.: Cooperative micro flip teaching. In: Zaphiris, P., Ioannou, A. (eds.) LCT 2016. LNCS, vol. 9753, pp. 14–24. Springer, Cham (2016). https://doi.org/10.1007/978-3-319-39483-1_2
11. Fidalgo-Blanco, A., Sein-Echaluce, M.L., García-Peñalvo, F.J.: APFT: active peer-based flip teaching. In: ACM International Conference Proceeding Series Part F132203, vol. 83 (2017)
12. Sein-Echaluce, M.L., Fidalgo-Blanco, A., García-Peñalvo, F.J.: Students' knowledge sharing to improve learning in academic engineering courses. Int. J. Eng. Educ. (IJEE) **32**, 1024–1035 (2016)
13. Fidalgo-Blanco, Á., Sein-Echaluce, M.L., García-Peñalvo, F.J.: Ontological flip teaching: a flip teaching model based on knowledge management. Univers. Access Inf. Soc. 1–15 (2017). https://doi.org/10.1007/s10209-017-0556-6
14. Lage, M.J., Platt, G.J., Treglia, M.: Inverting the classroom: a gateway to creating an inclusive learning environment. J. Econ. Educ. **31**, 30–43 (2000)
15. Bergmann, J., Sams, A.: Flip Your Classroom: Reach Every Student in Every Class Every Day. International Society for Technology in Education, New York (2012)
16. Baker, J.W.: The "Classroom Flip": using web course management tools to become the guide by the side. In: Chambers, J.A. (ed.) Selected Papers from the 11th International Conference on College Teaching and Learning, pp. 9–17. Florida Community College at Jacksonville. Jacksonville (2000)
17. Strayer, J.F.: How learning in an inverted classroom influences cooperation, innovation and task orientation. Learn. Environ. Res. **15**(2), 171–193 (2012)

18. Fidalgo-Blanco, A., Martinez-Nuñez, M., Borrás-Gene, O., Sanchez-Medina, J.J.: Micro flip teaching - An innovative model to promote the active involvement of students. Comput. Human Behav. (CHB) **72**, 713–723 (2017)
19. Lambert, C.: Eric Mazur on new interactive teaching techniques. Harvard Magazine, http://harvardmagazine.com/2012/03/twilight-of-the-lecture. Accessed 20 Feb 2018
20. Fidalgo-Blanco, Á., García-Peñalvo, F.J., Sein-Echaluce, M.L., Conde-González, M.Á.: Learning content management systems for the definition of adaptive learning environments. IEEE-Xplore International Symposium on Computers in Education (SIIE), pp. 105–110 (2014)
21. Sein-Echaluce, M.L., Fidalgo-Blanco, A., Esteban-Escaño, J., García, F.: The learning improvement of engineering students using peer-created complementary resources. Int. J. Eng. Educ. **33**(2B), 927–937 (2017)

Mapping Teaching Authorship and Learning Practices in Higher Education Settings: First Step in Creating a Knowledge Base Through Sharing

Cláudio Felipe Kolling da Rocha[✉], Cristina Ennes da Silva,
Guilherme Thiesen Schneider, Inajara Vargas Ramos,
Luis Henrique Rauber, Marshal Becon Lauzer,
and Patrícia B. Scherer Bassani

Feevale University, Novo Hamburgo, RS, Brazil
{claudiodarocha, crisennes, gts, iramos, luishenrique,
marshal, patriciab}@feevale.br

Abstract. Learning Design (LD) is a research field developed to help teachers to create pedagogically effective learning interventions using digital technologies. LD as a research area is based on three core concepts: guidance, representation, and sharing. This study focuses on the sharing perspective and aims to add to the current knowledge on teaching authorship and learning practices in higher education settings. The present study is based on a qualitative-quantitative and exploratory approach aiming to identify the authorship profile of undergraduate teachers in a university in south Brazil, as a survey to verify the viability of creating a knowledge base to foster innovative practices development. Data were collected using an online questionnaire answered by 243 teachers (46.7% of the total). The answers were analyzed on two major categories: authorship profile and pedagogical practice representation. The evaluation of the authorship profile revealed two characteristics: (a) teachers produce their own teaching resources and (b) teachers are open to a process of sharing educational resources. In the pedagogical practice representation category, we identify the majority of the teachers did not describe the sequence, resources and tools of the proposed activities in a clear way. Therefore, we highlight the importance of defining a framework for documentation of learning practices that will allow sharing of pedagogical know-how among educators. In conclusion, the present scenario is impeditive for the adoption and adaptation of learning practices. A series of interventions must be formulated to foster authorship of innovative educational resources as well as standardization of pedagogical practices documentation.

Keywords: Learning design · Authorship · Pedagogical practices

1 Introduction

Studies in the Learning Design area aim to foster the use of digital technologies in teaching and learning processes. The core concepts of Learning Design are: (a) guidance (ways for helping teachers to learn new methods and technologies); (b) representation

© Springer International Publishing AG, part of Springer Nature 2018
P. Zaphiris and A. Ioannou (Eds.): LCT 2018, LNCS 10924, pp. 416–429, 2018.
https://doi.org/10.1007/978-3-319-91743-6_31

(tools and models for representing practices); (c) sharing (a way of enhancing the use of digital technologies in education) [1].

This study focuses on the sharing perspective and aims to add to the current knowledge on teaching authorship and learning practices in higher education settings [1–10].

In our understanding, the teaching community can collaborate, inside a learning design perspective [10], sharing their teaching products, including resources such as presentations, videos, and others, and also pedagogical practices.

One way of spreading the design workload is to use Open Educational Resources (OER) repositories such as Merlot, in North America, or Portal do Professor, in Brazil [4]. Nonetheless, they are still underused by the majority of teachers. According to Laurillard [10] educators still don't have a strong culture of remix, that is, building on the work of others while designing their own teaching.

Laurillard [10] proposes that teachers, as learning design scientists, should be able to build on the work of others, which means, find the design of others, adopt and adapt them for their context. Furthermore, they should be able to represent their pedagogical practices in a formal way which can be understood by others. Laurillard [10] emphasizes that this has to be done collaboratively in order to improve teaching practices through building a knowledge base for the academic teaching community.

This study is part of an ongoing project called Rethinking: educational resources for the teaching-learning process (in Portuguese, *Repensar: recursos educacionais para o processo ensino-aprendizagem*). It aims to map the pedagogical practices developed at Feevale University[1] and also identify the authorship profile of its teachers, in order to verify the possibilities of creating a knowledge base which can improve innovative practices in higher education. In our understanding, the comprehension of teachers' authorship profile and the identification of their pedagogical practices could guide us in the development of a model to foster authorship and collaborative practices in the classroom.

What is, though, their authorship behavior? Do they share the learning contents they produce? What methodologies and learning practices have they been developing in their classrooms? Can they describe their pedagogical practices in a way that another instructor can replicate or be inspired by?

In order to answer these questions, it is important to take back what is presented as the background when it comes to the authorship category. It is necessary to understand how the construction of teaching professionalism is given so that we can infer what facilitates or hinders sharing and authorship. In such case, could we talk about co-authorship (collaboration in authorship)?

Studies on teacher education have undergone numerous changes of focus since the 1960s. If in that decade the emphasis was on the teaching process and on the products derived from it, in the following decade the political role of teachers was the great discussion. The 80s were marked by the refined analysis of academic formation as reference for the professional practice, which was ruled by the technical rationality. In the following decades, the valorization of the knowledge and experiences of teachers

---

[1] http://www.feevale.br/.

leverages another type of thinking which gives protagonism and authorship to the teacher in the construction of his career, with a focus on understanding how it is constructed.

According to Gimeno Sacristán [11], throughout his career, a teacher creates or appropriates different practical schemes, transforms them or combines them in a new way. In this approach, the professional practice of the teacher is considered as an intellectual and autonomous practice, not merely technical. It is a cooperative process of action and reflection, of inquiry and experimentation, in which the teacher learns to teach and teaches because he learns [12].

From the 1990s to 2000 it is possible to see the role of the teachers formation evolving to reach the consciousness of the educator as someone historically committed to the interests of the working class, valuing the micro-social aspect, with emphasis on the cultural constitution of the subject [13]. This thought defines that the professional learning and the acquisition of knowledge that guides the teaching practice are not restricted to specific moments of its formation, but it rather reveals itself as a dynamic and continuous process that includes the relations established with different subjects, contexts, experiences and relationships [14].

It is well known that the construction of professionalism requires a set of knowledges that distinguish the professions from the occupations. Tardif [15] argues along with authors like Bourdoncle [16] and Gauthier and Tardif [17] that the professionals need to support themselves in specialized and formalized knowledge acquired through a solid high-level training based on scientific disciplines considered "pure". It is also a professional's requirement to have the capacity to adapt and improvise in front of the new, which require a continuous feedback process, since they progressively evolve. As professional, teachers are submitted to the same process.

It is considered, therefore, that the teaching knowledge is temporal, composite, plural, heterogeneous, personalized and located. From this set of knowledges, it is important to highlight the one that directly influences the apparently installed difficulty in sharing collaborative practices between peers: personalized and localized knowledges. This relationship is what we can approach to the process of composition of an authorial teaching practice, since it disregards personal culture, relies on knowledge derived from formal learning, is based on experience.

We understand the curriculum as the activities and relationships that take place in the classroom and in the school space, in general, where not only the content but also the pedagogical relationships that are created in its development stand out [18]. This conception broadens the scope of the curriculum, bringing it closer to a critical vision that allows and accepts creative participation, flexibility, disruption of disciplinarity, dialogicity, knowledge arising from work and, fundamentally, warns that content does not come from neutral choices [19]. In this process, the curriculum becomes a field of struggles, where the diversity of interests disputes what, how and for what purpose we teach. And it is in this teciture of the different acts of a pedagogical process that the struggle for the duality of sharing/reservation the teacher is constantly submitted, and that says much of the postures and processes of learning in a academic career.

From this perspective, we understand that teachers' understanding of the authorship profile can guide institutional actions and strategies in order to enable the recording and sharing of pedagogical practices in the context of the Feevale University [10].

This article is organized as follows: Sect. 2 presents a reflection on Learning Design and the matter of sharing; in Sect. 3 we present the course of the research, including the research methodology, results and discussion. Then we close with the final considerations, pointing out new research perspectives.

2 Designing for Learning

Learning Design (LD) is a research field which has developed as a means to help teachers in creating pedagogically effective learning interventions using digital technologies [1, 2].

LD has two different research pathways within the field of technology-enhanced learning: (a) a technical perspective, involving the development of computer systems for the delivery of learning resources and activities; (b) a pedagogical perspective, involving the need for finding effective ways for sharing good and innovative practices [3].

Teaching is often a very personal activity [10] and usually a learning design exist only in the head of the teacher who implemented it, especially in higher education [3]. In order to be shared with others this idea needs to be represented through a mediation artifact. There are different mediation artifacts that can be used for representing practices such as models, narratives, case studies among others [2, 4]. The use of a mediation artifact enables teachers to document and share teaching practices. This way, LD encompasses both the process of designing a learning experience as well as the product which is an artifact representing a learning practice [2].

Some authors suggest the use of the term designing for learning for representing the research area and the term learning design for the artifact which is the document produced as an output of the design process [1–3].

LD as a research area is based on three core concepts: guidance, representation, and sharing [1]. Guidance encompasses many ways that educators can be assisted to think about their teaching and learning decision-making such as promoting workshops and study groups about digital tools, innovative methodologies, analysis of learning designs available online in different repositories and the possibilities of reuse.

These materials, among others. Representation encompasses the use of mediation artifacts for representing learning practices. In this case, the essence of a learning activity is abstracted into a mediation artifact [2]. There are different mediation artifacts that can be used for representing learning practices such as models, narratives or case studies, vocabularies, diagrammatic or iconic presentations [2]. Different mediation artifacts represent different aspects of learning activities. Although there isn't a general consistent notation system for learning design, there are many studies focusing on it [3–10]. Sharing is another central element in the LD. The reason for representing learning activities is to propagate these ideas among educators to foster innovative teaching and learning practices. Thus, representation is central for the purpose of sharing and reuse designs.

Learning design as an artifact represents an individual example of a sequence of teaching and learning activities. The implementation of a learning design with a particular group of students is called a running learning design or a running sequence [3]. The key elements of a learning design are [7–9]: learning tasks, learning resources, and leaning support. The tasks comprise the activities proposed. The learning resources encompass the content and the information needed for the development of a learning task (e.g. papers, documents, books, web links). These resources could be produced especially for a course, and also open educational resources, available online in repositories. Lastly, the learning support comprises assistances, scaffolds, structures, and encouragements. The support is necessary to guide the student and to provide feedback. From this perspective, a learning design, as an artifact, describes the student learner experience.

The authoring of a learning design is different from the task of monitoring the student's progress throughout a running learning design [10]. Laurillard [10] highlight two situations: (a) an educator can evaluate a learning design authored by another educator; (b) an educator can analyze data from a running version of a learning design produced by another educator (or across multiple running versions of the same learning design).

Dalziel [20] emphasize the importance of sharing pedagogical know-how among educators. According to him [20], if we can represent great teaching practices in the form of runnable learning designs and make these documents shareable through a collective effort, we can have a teaching knowledge base to enhance learning experiences.

3 The Research Path

The present work aimed to answer the following questions, having Feevale University undergraduate teachers as research target: What is their authorship behavior? Do they share the learning contents they produce? What methodologies and learning practices have they been developing in their classrooms? Can they describe their pedagogical practices in a way another instructor can replicate or be inspired by?

To address the questions above, a qualitative-quantitative and exploratory approach was used. Data were collected using an online questionnaire answered by 243 teachers (46.7% of the total undergraduate teachers at Feevale University). The answers were analyzed on two major categories: (a) authorship profile; (b) pedagogical practice representation.

The first category comprised the identification of the educational resources produced by the teachers for their classes and those of third party origin. The respondent had to state the relevance each resource (Table 1) has in their practice, first when made by themselves and second when gathered from third party source. The answers were given in a 0 to 4 scale, 0 corresponding to DO NOT USE THE CURRENT RESOURCE and 4 to OF MAJOR IMPORTANCE. Using a 1 to 5 scale, teacher should also state if the majority of the learning resources they use were 1 - FROM THIRD PARTY SOURCE or 5 - AUTHORIAL SOURCE. Finally, we also investigated their willingness to share the learning resources they produced and their knowledge of authorship attribution. Willingness to share was measured through a simple choice question were the answers were WOULD SHARE WITH ANYONE; WOULD SHARE WITH COLLEAGUES; WOULD NOT SHARE. Knowledge of means of authorship attribution was measured

Table 1. Educational resources presented to the respondents

Presentation	Audio	Blog	Picture	Games
Paper/Text	Site	Software/APP	Video	Other

through self-declaration in a simple answer question were the possible answers were HAVE NO KNOWLEDGE ABOUT; KNOWS IN DETAILS; GOOD; AVERAGE; BAD.

The second category comprised the analysis of an open-ended question were the respondent should describe a pedagogical practice he considered relevant, identifying the methodology and educational resources used. The analysis of the open-ended question was performed by four independent investigators and the mean result was computed as well as the standard deviation of the mean. First, the answers were analyzed based on two characteristics:

(a) possibility of adoption/replication (Based on the provided description, can we reuse this practice in another context?);
(b) possibility of adaption/remix (Based on the provided description, can we remix and reuse this practice in another context?).

The answers considered sufficient to allow adoption were further analyzed for the description of educational resources used and statement of authorship.

3.1 Results

We evaluate authorship profile through a quantitative approach. When asked about the importance of authorial resources in their practice, in a scale from 0 to 4, we found Presentations (3.18) to be the most important authorial resource. In order of importance, presentations were followed by Paper/Text (2.63), Picture (2.56), Video (1.93), Site (1.58), Software/APP (1.35), Audio (1.27), Games (0.81), Other (0.72) and Blog (0.46). Results are summarized in Fig. 1.

For third-party resources, the respondents declared Paper/Text (2.84) as the most important, closely followed by Pictures (2.5), Video (2.49) and Site (2.11). Software/APP (1.64), Presentation (1.35), Audio (1.22), Games (0.72), Blog (0.6) and Other (0.28) followed. Third party results are shown in Fig. 2 and a comparison between authorial and third-party resources importance is presented at Fig. 3. In a scale of 1 to 5, 1 as mainly third-party resources and 5 mainly authorial resources, our teachers declared, in average, their used resources to be more authorial then third party (mean score 3.86 of 5).

As for the willingness to share we also took a quantitative approach. From the 243 respondents, 63 (26%) would share with anyone, 164 (64%) would share with colleagues at the University and 16 (7%) would not share. Data is graphically presented in Fig. 4.

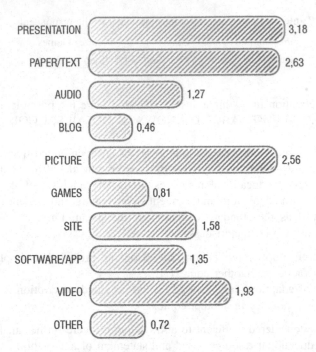

Fig. 1. Importance of each resources when produced by the teacher (Source: created by authors) 0 = DO NOT USE THE CURRENT RESOURCE; 4 = OF MAJOR IMPORTANCE. The number represents the mean score from the 243 respondents.

When evaluating authorship attribution knowledge from 243 participants 111 (46%) declared to have no knowledge about, 61 (25%) declared their knowledge as insufficient (BAD), 39 (16%) as average, 27 (11%) as good and 5 (2%) declared to know it in details. Data is graphically presented in Fig. 5.

We evaluate **pedagogical practice representation** through an open-ended question were the respondents should describe a pedagogical practice they considered relevant, identifying the methodology and educational resources used. The question was analyzed by four independent investigators. From 243 answers we found only 27.5 ± 14.6 (mean ± standard deviation) present enough information to allow replication/adoption, corresponding to only 10.5% of the answers. When looking for practices that inspire remix/adaption we found 35 ± 10.5 answers (mean ± standard deviation), corresponding to 14.4% of the total. Data is summarized in Fig. 6.

The answers considered sufficient to allow adoption were further analyzed for the description of the educational resources involved and statement of instructors' authorship. We found 72.1% ± 9.6 (mean ± standard deviation) of the included answers to describe the educational resources involved. When looking for statement of authorship by the instructor only 20.2% ± 14 (mean ± standard deviation) of the included answers were considered to have it. The data is summarized in Fig. 7.

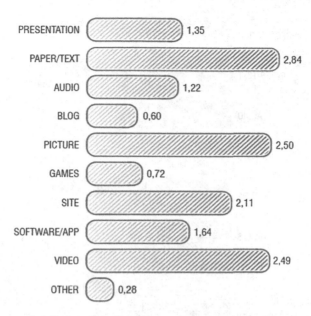

Fig. 2. Importance of each of the bellow resources when produced by others. (Source: created by authors) 0 = DO NOT USE THE CURRENT RESOURCE; 4 = OF MAJOR IMPORTANCE. The number represents the mean score from the 243 respondents.

3.2 Discussion

The results pointed out important issues. In the authorship profile category, presentations, such as PowerPoint slides, are the most important educational resource produced by teachers, followed by papers/text and images. On the other hand, papers/texts created by others are the most important educational resource used by them in their classes, followed by images and videos. According to the data, we verified that resources produced by teachers for their own use are more relevant to them than those produced by others.

PowerPoint slides usually are developed based on the author's comprehension of a text or subject. Besides, some of them are constructed with many images and examples. These features make slides a difficult resource for reusing. Thus, this meets the studies of Tardif [15], Bourdoncle [16], and Gauthier and Tardif [17], which indicate that teaching knowledge is personalized and located, and therefore, reveals a limitation in the collaborative exchanges between teachers.

Gimeno-Sacristán [11] states that the teaching authorship is always under construction throughout the teaching career and during this process the teacher creates based on the knowledge of others. In this case, teaching authorship can be understood as a collaborative construction as well.

When the teachers were asked about their interest in sharing their educational resources, 93% answered affirmatively (sharing with somebody: 26%; sharing only with colleagues: 67%). Furthermore, sharing rules and authorship attribution, like creative commons licenses, are still vaguely known (only 2% claimed to already

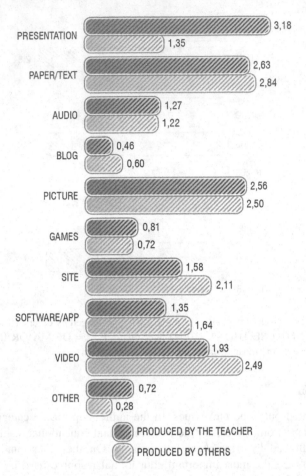

Fig. 3. Comparison between Authorial vs Third Party resources importance in each category (Source: created by authors) 0 = DO NOT USE THE CURRENT RESOURCE; 4 = OF MAJOR IMPORTANCE. The number represents the mean score from the 243 respondents.

know). Based on these data we can infer the faculty has openness to a process of sharing educational resources, but they prefer to do it with their university partners. We suggest as one of the possible explanation for the unwillingness to share with an open audience the low knowledge about authorship attribution (creative commons).

The evaluation of the authorship profile revealed two characteristics of Feevale faculty: (a) teachers produce their own teaching resources; (b) teachers are open to a process of sharing educational resources. The authorship profile is represented in Fig. 8.

In the **pedagogical practice representation** category, we identify that 66% of the teachers did not described the sequence, resources and tools of the proposed activities. From the 108 valid answers, only 27 presented sufficient data to allow reproducibility and 35 inspired remix. Furthermore, most of the answers did not state the instructors' authorship.

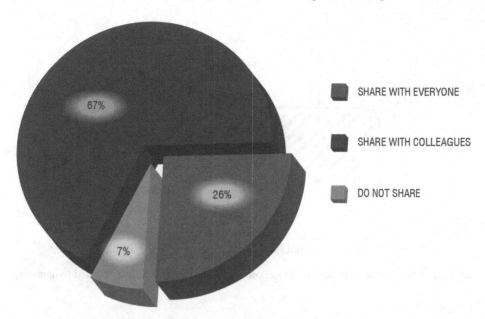

Fig. 4. Willingness to share authorial resources (Source: created by authors)

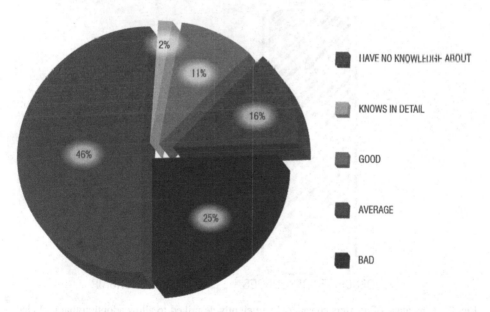

Fig. 5. Knowledge about authorship attribution (Source: created by authors)

Regarding the learning design components (tasks, resources, and support) [7–9], data revealed the teachers emphasized the description of the learning task. The indication of resources was present only in 72,12% (Fig. 7) of the answers which presented sufficient data to allow reproducibility (Fig. 6). Therefore, we highlight the importance

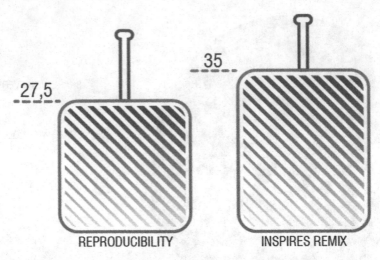

Fig. 6. Practices sufficiently described to allow adoption or remix (Source: created by authors)

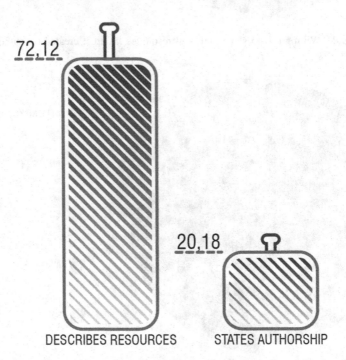

Fig. 7. Percentage of answers considered sufficiently described to allow adoption that included the description of the educational resources used and a those that included a statement of authorship by the instructor (Source: created by authors)

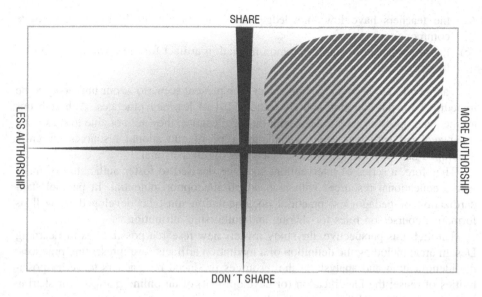

Fig. 8. Authorship profile (Source: created by authors)

of defining a framework for documentation of learning practices that will allow sharing of pedagogical know-how among educators [20].

4   Conclusion

This study is part of an ongoing project which aims to map teaching authorship and learning practices in higher education settings with the purpose of creating a knowledge base through sharing. The first stage in this research was to understand the authorship profile of the teachers (What is their authorship behavior? Do they share the learning contents they produce?) and identify the methodology and educational resources used in learning practices based on an open and personal description (What methodologies and learning practices have they been developing in their classrooms? Can they describe their pedagogical practices in a way another instructor can replicate or be inspired by?)

The data collected through an online questionnaire revealed:

(a) the teachers use resources produces from third part but mainly they use their own resources;
(b) Power Point slides are the most important educational resource produced by teachers for their classes;
(c) the teachers indicated they are willing to share the resources they produce especially with their university colleagues;

(d) the teachers have low knowledge about authorship attribution (e.g. creative commons);
(e) the importance of using a common mediation artifact for the documentation of a learning practice [5–9].

Taking all in to account, we understand the present scenario at our university to be impeditive for the adoption and adaptation [10] of learning practices. Although our teachers are open to share, at least with their colleagues, they are not able to do so in a organized and sufficient way. Second, the type of educational resources currently developed has very low reusability, since it is highly personal.

Therefore, a series of interventions must be devised to foster authorship of innovative educational resources with high adaption/adoption potential. In parallel standardization of pedagogical practices documentation must be developed as well as formative courses on rules for sharing and authorship attribution.

Through this perspective, the study reveals new research possibilities in Learning Design area, including the definition of a mediation artifacts for representing practices; the identification and analysis of the resources produced by teachers to verify possibilities of reuse; the identification (or development) of an online platform for sharing learning practices and resources as well.

Thus, in our understanding, with adequate guidance, our teaching community can collaborate sharing their know-how inside a learning design perspective [10], expanding and improving the teaching-learning experience.

Acknowledgments. We would like to thank Feevale University (http://www.feevale.br) for making the present research possible.

References

1. The Larnaca Declaration on Learning Design. https://larnacadeclaration.wordpress.com
2. Conole, G.: Designing for Learning in an Open World. Springer, UK (2013). https://doi.org/10.1007/978-1-4419-8517-0
3. Falconer, I., Finlay, J., Fincher, S.: Representing practice: practice models, patterns, bundles. Learn. Media Technol. **36**(02), 101–127 (2011)
4. Bassani, P., Lima, C., Dalanhol, D.: Documentação e compartilhamento de atividades de aprendizagem: um estudo sobre repositórios de prática e artefatos de mediação. Revista e-Curriculum **14**, 1423–1453 (2016). PUCSP, São Paulo
5. Bassani, P., Bassani, R.: Production and sharing of learning activities with technologies: designing for learning in teacher formation courses. In: ATINER'S Conference Paper Series, No: EDU2016-1901. Atiner, Atenas (2016)
6. Scherer Bassani, P.B., Escalante Casenote, I., Albrecht, E.G., Mergener, D.: The development of a mediation artifact for representing teaching practices: a study connecting the areas of design and learning design. In: Zaphiris, P., Ioannou, A. (eds.) LCT 2017. LNCS, vol. 10295, pp. 158–172. Springer, Cham (2017). https://doi.org/10.1007/978-3-319-58509-3_14
7. Oliver, R., Herrington, J.: Teaching and learning online: a beginner's guide to e-learning and e-teaching in higher education. Edith Cowan University. Centre for Research in Information Technology and Communications (2001)

8. Oliver, R., Harper, B., Hedberg, J., Wills, S., Agostinho, S.: Formalising the description of learning designs, in quality conversations. In: Proceedings of the 25th HERDSA Annual Conference, Perth, Western Australia, 7–10 July 2002
9. Learning Design. http://www.learningdesigns.uow.edu.au/project/learn_design.htm
10. Laurillard, D.: Teaching as a Design Science. Routledge, New York (2012)
11. Gimeno Sacristán, J.: Consciência e ação sobre a prática como libertação profissional dos professores. In: Nóvoa, A. (ed.) Profissão professor, 2nd edn., pp. 63–92. Porto Editora, Porto (1995)
12. Gimeno Sacristán, J., Gómez, P.: Compreender e transformar o ensino, 4th edn. Artmed, Porto Alegre (1998)
13. Santos, L.L.C: Formação do professor e pedagogia crítica. In: Fazenda, I. (ed.) A pesquisa em educação e as transformações do conhecimento, pp. 17–18. Papirus, Campinas (1995)
14. Ferenc, A.V.F., Saraiva, A.C., Dalben, A., et al.: Os professores universitários, sua formação pedagógica e suas necessidades formativas. In: Dalben, A., et al. (eds.) Convergências e tensões no campo da formação e do trabalho docente. Autêntica, Belo Horizonte (2010)
15. Tardif, M.: Saberes profissionais dos professores e conhecimentos universitários. Revista Brasileira de Educação, Jan/Fev/Mar/Abr No. 13, pp. 5–24 (2000)
16. Bourdoncle, R.: Savoir professiionnel et formation des enseignants: une typologie sociologique. No. 13, pp. 77–96 (1994)
17. Gauthier, C., Tardif, M.: Pour ou countre un ordre professionnel des enseignantes et des enseignantes au Quebéc? Laval, Quebéc, Presses del'Université (1999)
18. Aranha, A.V.S.: A abordagem por competência como paradigma e política de currículo. In: Dalben, A., et al. (eds.) Convergências e tensões no campo da formação e do trabalho docente. Autêntica, Belo Horizonte (2010)
19. Ramos, I.V.: Estágios curriculares: autonomia inconteste e protagonismo discente revelados. UNISINOS, Doctorate thesis (2013)
20. Dalziel, J.: Learning design: sharing pedagogical know-how. In: Liyoshi, T., Kumar, M.S.V. (eds.) Opening Up Education. The Collective Advancement of Education Through. Open Technology, Open Content, and Open. Knowledge. The MIT Press, Cambridge (2010)

Social Learning and Social Design Using iPads and Groupware Technologies

Aekaterini Mavri[1(✉)], Andri Ioannou[1], Fernando Loizides[2], and Nicos Souleles[3]

[1] Cyprus Interaction Lab, Department of Multimedia and Graphic Arts,
Cyprus University of Technology, 30 Archbishop Kyprianou Street,
3036 Limassol, Cyprus
{aekaterini.mavri,andri.i.ioannou}@cut.ac.cy
[2] School of Computer Sciences and Informatics,
Cardiff University, 5 The Parade, Cardiff CF24 3AA, Wales, UK
LoizidesF@cardiff.ac.uk
[3] Art + Design: eLearning Lab, Department of Multimedia and Graphic Arts,
Cyprus University of Technology, 30 Archbishop Kyprianou Street,
3036 Limassol, Cyprus
nicos.souleles@cut.ac.cy

Abstract. Over the past few years we have seen the uptake of the iPad into the Higher Education (HE) curriculum, in purpose of encouraging active social learning. This is augmented through direct-input interfaces, multi-touch interactions and portable, ubiquitous, formal and informal learning, aligning ably with the social constructivist model.

Its widespread integration across multiple epistemological domains has been the subject of considerable research, yet more vertical and targeted understanding of its potential within specialized domains, used with typical context-specific software, is still in need. Its affordances for collaboration, a primary concept in higher education, rooted in the shift from individualistic to richer collective learning paradigms [1], also warrants further investigation.

In this case study we examine the contribution of the iPad in a tertiary design course which focuses on User Experience (UX) design, a socially-aware collaborative design area. Through the collective activity of co-located and remote student dyads aiming to co-create artefacts such as sitemaps and mind maps, this study seeks to observe the impact of mobile devices on the students' social learning process and perceived outcomes.

The findings suggest and confirm the device's ability to extend social learning beyond the classroom, its suitability and positive role, particularly in the early exploratory stages of the design lifecycle, as well as the necessity for promoting learner-autonomy particularly in the co-configuration of the software tools and peripheral equipment in order to suit the discipline-specific (UX design) and phase-specific activities.

Keywords: Collaborative learning · Social learning · Groupware
Usability · Courseware · Shared workspaces

© Springer International Publishing AG, part of Springer Nature 2018
P. Zaphiris and A. Ioannou (Eds.): LCT 2018, LNCS 10924, pp. 430–445, 2018.
https://doi.org/10.1007/978-3-319-91743-6_32

1   Introduction

The iPad is closing in on a decade of incorporation and use in multiple phases of K12 and Higher Education (HE). It's acknowledged potential to transform education by promoting motivation, engagement and deep learning, is stated in numerous studies [2–8]. Furthermore, its role in the initiation and proliferation of the ubiquitous learning paradigm, is evident [9, 10]; that is flexible, autonomous, student-managed, situated learning (where applicable) without restrictions of time, place, load or status [11].

Although investigation in its role in various disciplines (mainly in STEM, Humanities, Social and Applied sciences) is widespread, more vertical and exhaustive research on the interaction between device and learners, using collaborative software applications that are characteristic of a particular domain, is still limited; this creates a gap of specialized implications for designers and educators. Adding to this gap are additional parameters which are inherent in today's complex learning contexts: physical or digital, co-located, remote or blended/hybrid, synchronous or asynchronous.

In this paper, we seek to examine the role of the iPad in supporting both co-located and distant Computer Supported Collaborative Learning (CSCL) in a HE UX Design module, during the early design stages of sitemapping and mind-mapping of concepts. By observing the collaborative activity and investigating the perceived outcomes (experience and learning) of groups of student dyads, we seek to outline the implications for instructional designers and educators and propose ways to support the implementation of m-learning in similar design topics.

We are primarily interested in the utility and usability of the iPad as a device embedded in the social learning process, yet we hypothesize that the perceived experience of hardware and software is intertwined and often difficult to isolate. Through comparison with a control group (laptop users), we anticipate to extract those outcomes that are specific to the use of the device.

This research is guided by the following questions:

1. What is the role and contribution of the iPad to the experience and learning outcomes of co-located and remote groups of students in the design field?
2. How do the iPad's affordances affect the social learning process in the design field?

In the following sections, we provide related research concerning the use of iPads in CSCL, describe the research context, explain the methodology employed for data collection and analysis, outline and discuss the findings as well as propose instructional guidelines for m-learning in design disciplines.

2   Related Work

Portability, a concept that is important in modern-day education [12], is the iPad's primary asset [13] which supports ubiquitous and situated learning in multiple contexts (lecture hall, laboratory, home, office/workplace, outdoors, public places) [9, 14], in different conditions such as formal (lectures, workshops, meetings), and informal social (coffee, gatherings, travelling, events) learning settings [11, 15], and in different times and states (day/night, on the move, at leisure, at rest etc.).

Up to date, the iPad has been incorporated in various educational fields such as STEM [16–18], architecture, art, design [19–22], language learning [15, 23], health and physical education [24, 25] and many more. Amongst others, they have been used for the purposes of information seeking, research and analysis, resource management and sharing digital content generation, presentation and assessment [9, 22] and have been particularly important in Computer Supported Collaborative Learning (CSCL) contexts [26–28].

We haven't yet seen studies focusing on the area of UX design, a socially responsible design philosophy, which focuses on empathizing with users in the development of products that support users and have implicit or explicit social implications [71]. This study focuses on the early design stages of analysis and prototyping, that amongst others, involve collective externalizations, mind maps and sitemaps, as part of the conceptual planning and the information (application) architecture. Subsequent stages, such as prototyping, are investigated in a few studies only, which primarily look at collaborative sketching through the use of multiple devices [29, 30]. However, substantial research on the role of m-learning in design education, especially in the creation of social design artefacts, compared to the spread and importance of this field, is scarce.

Mind mapping, is described as memorizing, accessing, processing, connecting and outputting information stored in our brains "in a visually expressive way" [31–33]. In team-driven terms, it is a visual form of brainstorming, which "serves as an extension of the mind" [34]. Karakaya and Demirkan [35] state its importance by reporting an increasingly strong focus on such processes in the digital creative industries domain today.

Sitemapping is similar in the sense that it externalizes information but it has a different goal; that is to organize and structure information to reflect the hierarchical flow of a digital application [36]. This is typically initiated on paper, using pens and markers, through the contribution of one or all team members; the iPad has been known to be an effective alternative to the paper and pen media [37], yet, to the best of our knowledge, no site or mind-mapping-specific studies have been reported up-to-date.

Collaboration is a vital prerequisite for the generation of sitemaps and mindmaps and can be realized in co-located environments, remotely or in a blended setting, that is a mixture of both modalities [38–40].

The advantages of face-to-face collaboration are indisputably notable, as proximity facilitates "interpersonal interaction and awareness" especially in small groups [41]. Kraut et al. [42] for example, report that pairs of researchers accommodated in near-by offices, are four times more likely to produce published research collaboratively than in remote teams. Technology, can augment this process further, for both co-located and remote collaborative teams, through the synergistic use of PCs (desktops, laptops), tabletop surfaces, wall-mounted displays, motion-sensing systems and handhelds [43–45]. Interestingly, despite being primarily intended for personal use, handhelds may reportedly encourage better face-to-face collaboration, since they are smaller and easier to handle in close proximity, than PCs [46]. Even so, they do invite concerns about visibility due to screen size, angle and distance as well as restrictions in "multi-touch interactions" that may lead to user redundancy [47].

These devices' contribution in the interaction of geographically distributed teams of learners, teachers and other stakeholders, cannot be overlooked [15, 34, 48]. Mobile devices are unique in facilitating synchronous collective work, on shared artefacts, strengthening flexibility through the "mobility of learning and the mobility of learners" [10]. The sum of the hardware features and online multi-user apps, can augment learning by transferring it outside of traditional classrooms [26], if only designed effectively. Falloon [49] notes that the design and content of apps can heavily impact the overall user experience: the absence of provisions for distant communication & coordination, material organization, negotiation, interactivity, mobility and peer awareness at the software-level, can severely hinder the perceived quality of learning with technology [50–52]. Early and iterative formative usability evaluation of these, as well as their interaction with specialized hardware, is thus essential for designing successful instructional interventions whose outcomes depend on such synergies [38].

3   Method

3.1   Study

Eleven (11) out of 22 second-year multimedia students were provided an iPad each to complete assignments collaboratively throughout weeks two to four of the semester, for a unit of study (13-week UX design module). All students had used the iPads extensively in their first-year modules. The rest of the students were asked to collaborate using their laptops or desktops in the lab.

Following a short lecture session in class, each dyad used a single iPad or laptop, to create an account and work on building a sitemap for a website, using Lucid Chart sitemap builder app. Students were also provided a printout of a step-by-step procedure of (a) the deliverables for each of the following weeks and (b) a brief software manual and sharing-setup guide.

At the end of the lesson, the owner of the sitemap file in each dyad invited their partners to register, in order to continue collaborating on the project remotely, in – ideally - a synchronous manner, to complete the assignment. Since all of the students had Gmail accounts, all teams were prompted to use Google Hangouts (already installed on the iPads) for communication and coordination during the process. Following the iPads' return back to the instructor on the following week, the students participated in an online survey and a focus-group session.

In lesson/week four, students were assigned a semester-long group project – that was to re-design the Cyprus Red Cross Society website with an aim to enhance the experience of users who visit with different backgrounds, purpose, expectations as well as limitations. The project required them to collaborate on building a mind-map, as part of the initial brainstorming phase. An alternative software, Coggle (freeware mind mapping app), was used in place of Lucid Chart for this assignment, following student reports of interface and resource limitations of the former. While still in the same teams as week two, the remaining half of students, got hold of the iPads and worked jointly on their mind-maps in class, using a single device. Like week two, they were asked to share their mind-map and continue collaborating from home, returned the devices on the following week, and completed a second survey and focus group session.

3.2 Analysis

This study uses the ACAD (Activity Centered Analysis and Design) framework for the design and analysis of the collaborative network, process and outcomes. ACAD is based on the notion that collaborative learning is activity which is "physically, socially and epistemically situated" [53]. More particularly, it seeks to investigate a learning network and the interactions that occur within that, rather than a single device or a tool. Instead, multi-faceted assemblies are taken into account, planned for, captured and analyzed: components such as the physical or digital, blended/hybrid learning spaces, the social dynamics and the activities that are shaped based on the synergies between them, form the units of research [54].

Likewise, in this work, the facets of these components refer to a multi-dimensional Set, that is the equipment, materials and resources used, on physical and digital levels, the Social, that is the group structure and particular work arrangements i.e. divisions of labor and interaction amongst the members, and the Epistemic, that is the assignments that are supposed to generate knowledge outcomes, in this case, the sitemapping and mind mapping subjects. The instructional design should be flexible in allowing changes that could originate both from the outside (top-level action – i.e. instructional designers, instructor) and from within (participatory action i.e. the group members), what ACAD proposes as the Co-configuration component. These components are entangled and overlap one another, in practice. Isolated analysis is therefore feasible on a theoretical - rather than on a practical level.

As we are primarily investigating the usability of the iPad and its effects on learning in a domain-specific context, to further analyze the Set component (the digital in this case), we draw from five primary usability principles for the design and evaluation of products, systems or services [55–57]. These are: (a) Learnability – the ease by which novices become accustomed to the system (b) Memorability – experience of the system's functionality by users who haven't used it for some time, (c) Efficiency – the speed and level of accuracy and completeness achieved by users reaching their goals, (d) Satisfaction – the emotional or physiological attitude of users during the use of the system and (e) Error incidence and recovery – the occurrence of errors and the ease by which users regain control. Memorability did not apply in this case, due to the uninterrupted use of the device throughout the study. The abovementioned principles were explored, largely based on the general user perception of the system as a whole, rather than the particular device per-se, for two reasons:

(a) We were aware of the difficulty in eliciting explicit outcomes for hardware and software separately, as these are rarely understood in isolation
(b) We could retrieve such findings indirectly through comparison between the two groups from both the quantitative and qualitative data collected.

4   Results

In this work, we triangulate the results from (a) two questionnaires employing 5-point-likert scale questions (1 = highest and 5 = lowest) and open-ended comments and (b) four focus groups (two for each device groups) carried out in weeks three and five of the semester.

Quantitative data was not normally distributed. Non-parametric tests, such as the Wilcoxon signed-rank test [58] were thus used to conclude on significant statistical differences between the two groups and between in-class and remote conditions. Findings are analyzed according to the four components of the ACAD framework.

4.1   Set Component: Usability Factors

Learnability. The iPad cohort reported significantly longer in-class learnability times than in remote settings following a within-groups comparison test ($Z = -2.111$, $p = .035$). This was admittedly an anticipated effect, for both iPad and Laptop groups, as the learning process for the particular task was instigated during the lesson and progressed outside class, producing a decreasing learning curve over time. The laptop group, however, did not report such results, due to a greater level of familiarity with their device. This outcome disputes the "duality" of hardware and software in user experience, as the two are typically perceived as one - acting in favor or against each other, depending on the case [59, 60]. In this case, hardware unfamiliarity transferred onto and hindered the software experience.

Efficiency. Device-specific differences were detected, regarding the perceived effectiveness in creating the sitemaps/mind-maps, in the classroom, weighing negatively for iPad users ($Z = -2.449$, $p = .014$) (Table 1). Such were not recorded for out-of-class settings. Coinciding with results from the previous section, disparate in-and out-of-class outcomes can be connected and attributed to the gradually lessening residuals of the learnability process.

Table 1. iPad versus PC in-class and remote usability results

	iPad			PC			Z	p
	N	Mean	S.D.	N	Mean	SD.		
In class time to learn	14	2.5	1.092	11	2.27	1	−.302b	.763
Remote time to learn	14	2	1.038	11	2.09	1.04	−.632c	.527
In class efficiency	14	2.21	.699	11	1.73	.647	−2.449b	.014
Remote efficiency	14	2.43	.756	11	2	.775	−1.730b	.084
Time to complete tasks	14	1.73	1.1	11	4	1.6	−2.061b	.039
In class error occurrence	14	1.93	.829	11	1,45	.820	−1.748b	.080
Remote error occurrence	14	2.07	1.072	11	2	1.183	−.551b	.582
In class user experience	14	2.3	1.089	11	2.2	0.700	−1.469b	.142
Remote user experience	14	2.9	1.177	11	2.7	0.809	−1.933b	.053

a. Wilcoxon Signed Ranks Test, b. Based on positive ranks, c. Based on negative ranks.

Further investigation into efficiency indicated that iPad users agreed to needing significantly more time (M = 1.73, SD = 1.1) to resolve the exercises than those who worked on laptops (M = 4, SD = 1.6), a phenomenon recorded more prominently during the first cycle of the experiment, weeks two to three (Z = −2.061, p = .039).

Interestingly, the effect was minimized when the second group took hold of the iPads in week four as most of the students appeared undecided - yet - not negative - in this question. This indicates that since the second group had the chance to familiarize themselves - not with the device - but with the software instead, reinforces the point that hardware and software usability was not perceived in isolation. In other words, in this case the experience gained in using the software tool for two weeks, affected the perceived iPad usability in the second group of users.

Error Incidence. Although the two groups had similar quantitative responses concerning the errors encountered, iPad users mentioned a wider range than those of laptop users.

Open-ended comments referring to in-class use fixated on software issues - such as problematic user interface affordances which were amalgamated with hardware affordances (i.e. the touch interface). In the case of remote use, adding to the poor interface affordances, connectivity issues caused delays and prolonged response times: unsynchronized activity caused confusion and insecurity in users who commented that they were 'blind' as to their peers' contributions (edits) in the shared workspace:

> "There was no indication as to what my partner was doing and I didn't know if I should add new elements because maybe they would end up appearing twice… I didn't know what was old or new…"

Expectations were set, based on the functionality provided by such synchronous collaborative tools and when these failed to perform as anticipated, students were confused and felt doubtful as to their own and peers' actions. Collaboration compromised due to lack of timely response and feedback, is not new in CSCL. Users cannot evaluate their activities against those of others and therefore 'awareness information' becomes insufficient in these shared spaces [51, 61].

Although mentioned by both groups, such problems were heightened in using the iPad', caused by parallel delays of failed struggles for accurate onscreen actions - especially in the sitemap design case; erratic selection, accidental activation, unsatisfactory target selection precision, also dubbed 'read-to-tap asymmetry' phenomenon [62], failure to draw straight lines or to align elements, plus the constant pinching and spreading to zoom in for detailed views [63], further compromised the poor experience due to connectivity issues:

> "But I prefer it (laptop) because I can point somewhere with the mouse and I don't have to zoom in and out …"

> "…with the touch… it is extremely sensitive, you might touch something and something else gets activated on the sitemap…"

> "…you couldn't easily select the small lines so you can play with them …it was annoying".

Difficulties with sharing content between linked accounts also surfaced, and together with aforementioned issues, lead to a stronger preference towards co-located collaboration, especially in the case of iPad users.

User Experience. Outcomes of the study in relation to user experience indicated no significant differences between the two devices, for both in class ($Z = -1.469$, $p = .142$) and remote collaboration ($Z = -1.933$, $p = .053$) (Table 1), although use of the iPad was more adverse in the case of remote settings due to the extent of problems described in the previous section. When probed whether they would use - or not - the devices to work on similar assignments in the future, a question directed to iPad users, the responses were either neutral or negative: students were not sure or tended to disagree with the prospect of using it again for future projects.

4.2   Social Component

According to qualitative outcomes, the predominant choice of working mode for both groups, was co-located, rather than remotely. However, the tendency to continue this mode of collaboration for learning in more social, out-of-class setting was only observed in the iPad group's case.

The majority of participants commented that should circumstances allow it, they would rather work with their peers and "resolve problems there and then" than remotely. In their point of view, distant collaboration was helpful but should be utilized only if a face-to-face alternative was not feasible. For them it was important to be proximally close, while having the chance to talk and elaborate on their opinions, "think together", make mistakes together, verify correctness and reach consensus for solutions collectively.

"... when you are together, you are close, you think together, you tell one another..."

Literature also refers to the advantages of co-located collaboration, due to proximity allowing for real social interaction and contextual understanding [41] the unrestricted articulation of comments, questions, negotiation over common goals [64], and prevention of challenges which often affect remote settings [48, 65]. However, when it comes to iPads, this was a surprising outcome. Working with a small screen, excludes everyone but one user from operating with the device while the rest typically observe or provide verbal feedback in a co-located setting [37]. Yet that did not seem to have a negative impact on the social aspect of learning.

To confirm this finding, the iPad group added that not only did they prefer class-based face-to-face collaboration but also transferred this working mode to other informal environments, such as cafés, outdoors and in unconventional physical settings such as on the move or at rest:

"...an example: I am working with C. in the park cause I like to do so – being outside in the open – and as I walk we talk about this and at the same time we are watching it on the iPad... but with the laptop, I need to plug it in.... you need an office to do that..."

"...you can both lie down and work on it...", "...Its far more restful...", "...you feel more comfortable with it...".

Although, no statistical differences were recorded between the two groups with regards to informal learning, qualitative data ascertains that the device's distinctive portability traits [37] can foster learning through extended social interaction beyond the classroom. That, in effect, prolongs group interaction through discourse, reciprocal decision-making and negotiation, all of which contribute towards better learning [66].

Agreeing with previous literature, negative feedback for co-located collaboration stemmed from delays, superfluous conversations and other sidetracking activities both in and out of class [67].

4.3   Epistemic Component

Epistemic refers to the activities or results that are closely linked to learning. Quantitative results revealed significant differences in the students' perceived learning outcomes in the thematic area of diagrams ($Z = -2.326, p = .02$). Laptop users agreed that the specific exercise process had a positive impact on their learning in the scope of sitemap/mind-map design ($M = 1.6$, $SD = .69$), whereas iPad users were skeptical about this ($M = 2.55$, $SD = .82$). Subject-centric skills like "developing practical experience in the development of flow diagrams" were rated low in this case. However, the social learning skills rates such as "collective problem solving" and "remote communication and collaboration" were elevated for iPad users. Agreeing with literature, technology that supports both formal and informal social learning methods, can expand time-on-task, enhance engagement, trigger incidental learning and allow for more interpersonal experimentation [51, 66]. Indeed, the socio-physical process of collective "trial and error" and iterative experimentation was practiced and remarked heavily on by co-learners in this study. Reportedly this enables learners to perceive this type of tacit learning as deepening their understanding of the subject matter [68, 69].

"And as soon as we would finish one category – the other one would check to see if ok…when one makes a mistake, the other will see it and will try to solve it…"

"It was a way to make sure (ensure) that whatever we were thinking was correct… it's much better to collaborate from the point of view of errors/mistakes… rather than being alone…"

Adding to the informality of learning, we were also able to infer that students implicitly associated touchscreen devices with specific types or levels of learning activities. Our findings indicate a consensus towards the device's affordances for spontaneous and experimental types of tasks, like brainstorming, quick sketching and online research.

"It's easy for searching purposes to find it at the time… so not to setup the 'whole' laptop thing…"

"Use it like for illustration… not using an extra device – since it is touch…. And it is more direct… for drawing…"

"I can work with brainstorming yes… but in a much more abstract and loose way… it's flexible".

As the project lifecycle progressed, the need for finer manipulation and control, target precision and advanced functionality (Fig. 1) warranted more stable and accurate equipment (personal computer, larger screens, pointing/input devices), that could also maintain the focus on the task-at-hand rather than dealing with the quirks of the device.

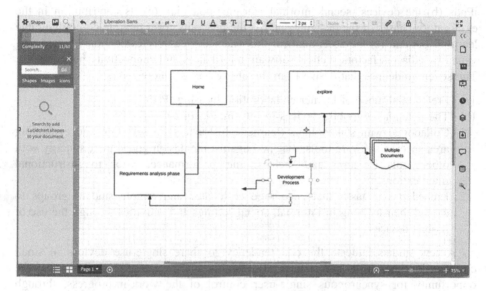

Fig. 1. Lucid chart user interface for sitemap design

4.4 Co-configuration Component

The learning network in this study was modified to ensure that the goals of the assignments could be accomplished (epistemic) and that efficient group collaboration was feasible (social). Two run-time interventions on the software tools (Set) were necessary to resolve problems that arose from (a) combination of poor tool interface affordances and bad internet speeds and (b) preferred method of communication for coordination purposes – in remote collaboration.

In phase one of the study, negative feedback was received regarding the tool used (Lucid Chart) from participants. Reportedly the lack of visual cues of their collaborators' actions caused disorientation while working online (4.1 Error Incidence). In addition, the students had already reached the maximum amount of shapes allowed by the software. Following search for alternatives and agreement from all stakeholders (researchers, instructor, and students), the next assignment was implemented using a different tool (Coggle).

Likewise, in supporting their need of communication and coordination during remote collaboration, and although another software tool was installed, students switched to other favored tools to expedite the process, as they claimed it was "faster for them" to work in that way. They used Skype or Facebook messenger to either chat but mostly conduct video calls while working on the shared artefact.

5 Discussion

Based on the results, this study has derived seven important m-learning guidelines for instructional designers and educators in UX design and related areas. These stemmed from outcomes concerning: (a) the preferential mode of learner collaboration in using iPads (b) the devices' social informal learning potential, (c) its contribution in the exploratory phases of the design cycle (d) the necessity for a flexible co-configurable learning Set and (e) the ascertainment that exact device-only evaluation is often pervaded by adjacent factors such as software affordances and connectivity performance. The seven guidelines that derive from the above are as follows:

(a) Preferential mode of learner collaboration in using iPads
(b) The potential of mobile devices in informal learning
  1. Collaborate with stakeholders (learners, instructors) in selecting and evaluating area-specific software tools, matched against the design goals, their synergy with other tools (if any) and their online performance, prior to instructional interventions.
  2. Embed design tasks that encourage co-located and remote student groups to extend their learning in informal, social settings and activities through the use of mobile devices.

A few studies indicate the odd tendency to share single-use devices in small co-located groups [70], nonetheless, it was this study's initial hypothesis that the opportunity for synchronous single-user control of the work-in-progress, through online collaboration, would be of preference to users. In agreement with prior research, its findings present the preferred work approach as the immediate, "there-and-then", single-screen type of co-located - versus - online collaboration. Close-proximity, face-to-face communication and coordination, even when working with small displays which might prevent active participation by everyone, were the dominant factors for this. Most interestingly, learners were initially prompted to use a single device in their groups in class – however – this approach was also taken to out-of-class settings and in various states (being sedentary, on the move, lying down etc.), a phenomenon occurring with iPad only. This indicates the device's key potential in promoting social ubiquitous learning and knowledge that is both implicitly and explicitly acquired in informal conditions and environments.

The possibility that the co-located behavior was chosen over low network speeds, cannot be ignored. We therefore seek to run additional investigations on the quality and extend of distance collaboration - relying on stable infrastructures – versus the co-located method, in order to obtain more accurate results.

(c) The iPad's role in the exploratory phases of the design cycle
  3. Incorporate iPads predominantly in the early, exploratory stages of the design lifecycle, such as brainstorming, sketching and research to enhance intuitive collective experimentation
  4. Ensure that intermediary input devices (i.e. stylus pen, apple pencil etc.) are incorporated in later development and refinement stages of the design lifecycle

In regards to the pedagogical (epistemic) outcomes, this study elicits that (a) the device had not explicitly augment learning in the students' perception and (b) that the type and state of the task dictates the working approach, which in-turn specifies the choice of appropriate device on two stages: exploratory and refinement. The stricter, more refined and greater-detailed visual artefacts to be produced, the more accurate selection and handling mechanisms are required. These are far from the fingertip-sized target manipulation offered by tablets and smartphones which are evidently a better fit for earlier experimental steps in the process; these being online research, brainstorming, mind-mapping and sketching. On the other hand, the design and fine-tuning of site-maps with hairline-width connector lines and arrows, tiny transform vertices and pixel-perfect positioning, call for advanced precision tools, which are lacking in these devices.

(d) The importance of a flexible co-configurable learning Set (hardware, software, physical)
5. Engage into thorough, run-time observation and investigation of all instructional system components (Set, Social, Epistemic) throughout the design lifecycle, and allow for or reconfigure accordingly if required.

In this study, we are able to confirm that the instructional design should be malleable enough to expect and adopt ad-hoc restructurings on any of the three components of a learning network (Set, Social or Epistemic). Likewise, the software constituent of the Set component, was co-configured twice, both externally (top-down) from the instructional researchers and internally (within) from the team members, to accommodate concerns regarding (a) tool UI complexity and (b) preferred method of communication. Such a design directed participants along a well-defined learning path while at the same time encouraged learner autonomy and self/team-management to counterbalance pragmatic limitations at the time of execution.

(e) Specific Set component usability evaluation is often difficult to isolate
6. Design specialized methods of investigation – depending on the context - for the evaluation of m-learning, in order to elicit targeted findings for each separate unit of interest (i.e. hardware vs software)

Lastly, this study infers that users are most often unable to have distinct hardware and software experiences. This reinforces the view of the inter-dependency and the cross-impact of the two major constituents of CSCL, hardware and software.

We sought to investigate participants' experience in building sitemaps and mind-maps using the specific device, yet responses referred predominantly to software. Undeniably the software UI "impacts experience more than the underlying hardware" and this by itself calls for more specialized human factors-driven research [60].

6 Conclusion

This study provides findings regarding the impact of incorporating iPads in the curriculum to support UX design activities for the creation of socially-responsible products, during the early design stages of sitemapping and mind-mapping. The outcomes denote that these devices can be suitably utilized in the early exploratory stages of the design lifecycle, their unique potential in extending learning beyond the classroom into informal social settings and that additional manipulation devices (i.e. apple pencil) are categorically required in the more advanced and refinement stages of the design cycle.

References

1. Resta, P., Laferrière, T.: Technology in support of collaborative learning. Educ. Psychol. Rev. **19**(1), 65–83 (2007)
2. Martin, F., Ertzberger, J.: Here and now mobile learning: an experimental study on the use of mobile technology. Comput. Educ. **68**, 76–85 (2013)
3. Kinash, S., Brand, J., Mathew, T., Kordyban, R.: Uncoupling mobility and learning: when one does not guarantee the other (2011)
4. Diemer, T.T., Fernandez, E., Streepey, J.W.: Student perceptions of classroom engagement and learning using iPads. J. Teach. Learn. Technol. **1**(2), 13–25 (2012)
5. Ciampa, K.: Learning in a mobile age: an investigation of student motivation. J. Comput. Assist. Learn. **30**(1), 82–96 (2014)
6. Wang, B.T., Teng, C.W., Chen, H.T.: Using iPad to facilitate English vocabulary learning. Int. J. Inf. Educ. Technol. **5**(2), 100 (2015)
7. Psiropoulos, D., Barr, S., Eriksson, C., Fletcher, S., Hargis, J., Cavanaugh, C.: Professional development for iPad integration in general education: staying ahead of the curve. Educ. Inf. Technol. **21**(1), 209–228 (2016)
8. Minty-Walker, C., Wilson, N.J., Ramjan, L., Glew, P.: Unleashing the potential and pitfalls of the iPad on undergraduate nursing students in tertiary education. JANZSSA-J. Aust. New Zeal. Stud. Serv. Assoc. **25**(2) (2017)
9. Nguyen, L., Barton, S.M., Nguyen, L.T.: Ipads in higher education—hype and hope. Br. J. Educ. Technol. **46**(1), 190–203 (2015)
10. Traxler, J.: Defining, Discussing and Evaluating Mobile Learning: The moving finger writes and having writ.... Int. Rev. Res. Open Distrib. Learn. **8**(2) (2007)
11. Melhuish, K., Falloon, G.: Looking to the future: M-learning with the iPad (2010)
12. Beldarrain, Y.: Distance education trends: integrating new technologies to foster student interaction and collaboration. Distance Educ. **27**(2), 139–153 (2006)
13. Laurillard, D.: Pedagogical forms of mobile learning: framing research questions (2007)
14. Sharples, M., Taylor, J., Vavoula, G.: Towards a theory of mobile learning. Proc. mLearn **1**(1), 1–9 (2005)
15. Hargis, J., Cavanaugh, C., Kamali, T., Soto, M.: A federal higher education iPad mobile learning initiative: triangulation of data to determine early effectiveness. Innov. High. Educ. **39**(1), 45–57 (2014)
16. Hesser, T.L., Schwartz, P.M.: iPads in the science laboratory: experience in designing and implementing a paperless chemistry laboratory course. J. STEM Educ. Innov. Res. **14**(2), 5 (2013)
17. Johnson, A.M., Reisslein, J., Reisslein, M.: Representation sequencing in computer-based engineering education. Comput. Educ. **72**, 249–261 (2014)
18. Kearney, M., Maher, D.: Mobile learning in maths teacher education: using iPads to support pre-service teachers' professional development. Aust. Educ. Comput. **27**(3), 76–84 (2013)
19. Cochrane, T., Narayan, V., Oldfield, J.: iPadagogy: appropriating the iPad within pedagogical contexts. Int. J. Mob. Learn. Organ. **7**(1), 48–65 (2013)

20. Souleles, N.: iPad versus traditional tools in art and design: a complementary association. Br. J. Educ. Technol. **48**(2), 586–597 (2017)
21. Mavri, A., Loizides, F., Souleles, N.: A case study on using iPads to encourage collaborative learning in an undergraduate web development class. In: 1st International Conference on the use of iPads in Higher Education 2014, pp. 267–290 (2014)
22. Page, T.: Application-based mobile devices in design education. Int. J. Mob. Learn. Organ. **8**(2), 96–111 (2014)
23. Demouy, V., Jones, A., Kan, Q., Kukulska-Hulme, A., Eardley, A.: Why and how do distance learners use mobile devices for language learning? EuroCALL Rev. **24**(1), 10–24 (2016)
24. Rosenthal, M.B., Eliason, S.K.: 'I Have an iPad. Now What?' Using mobile devices in university physical education programs. J. Phys. Educ. Recreat. Danc. **86**(6), 34–39 (2015)
25. Nuss, M.A., Hill, J.R., Cervero, R.M., Gaines, J.K., Middendorf, B.F.: Real-time use of the iPad by third-year medical students for clinical decision support and learning: a mixed methods study. J. Commun. Hosp. Intern. Med. Perspect. **4**(4), 25184 (2014)
26. Falloon, G.: What's the difference? Learning collaboratively using iPads in conventional classrooms. Comput. Educ. **84**, 62–77 (2015)
27. Jahnke, I.: Informal learning via social media: preparing for didactical designs (2013)
28. Furuya, T., Mizuochi, Y., Yatsushiro, K., Mizukoshi, K.: A study regarding the effects of synchronous CSCL use involving tablet-type terminals in arithmetic class and through practical experience with fractions using edutab. In: 2016 IEEE/SICE International Symposium on System Integration (SII), pp. 658–663 (2016)
29. Spitzer, M., Ebner, M.: Collaborative learning through drawing on iPads. In: EdMedia: World Conference on Educational Media and Technology, pp. 806–815 (2015)
30. Colombo, L., Landoni, M.: Low-tech and high-tech prototyping for eBook co-design with children. In: Proceedings of the 12th International Conference on Interaction Design and Children, pp. 289–292 (2013)
31. Buzan, T.: Modern Mind Mapping for Smarter Thinking. BookBaby (2013)
32. Hornbæk, K., Frøkjær, E.: Reading of electronic documents: the usability of linear, fisheye, and overview+detail interfaces. In: Proceedings of the SIGCHI Conference on Human Factors in Computing Systems, pp. 293–300 (2001)
33. Lin, H., Faste, H.: Digital mind mapping: innovations for real-time collaborative thinking. In: Extended Abstracts on Human Factors in Computing Systems, CHI 2011, pp. 2137–2142 (2011)
34. Hwang, G.-J., Shi, Y.-R., Chu, H.-C.: A concept map approach to developing collaborative Mindtools for context-aware ubiquitous learning. Br. J. Educ. Technol. **42**(5), 778–789 (2011)
35. Karakaya, A.F., Demirkan, H.: Collaborative digital environments to enhance the creativity of designers. Comput. Hum. Behav. **42**, 176–186 (2015)
36. Mears, C.: (2013). http://theuxreview.co.uk/sitemaps-the-beginners-guide
37. Pearson, J., Buchanan, G.: Real-time document collaboration using iPads. In: Proceedings of the Third Workshop on Research Advances in Large Digital Book Repositories and Complementary Media, pp. 9–14 (2010)
38. Tsiatsos, T., Konstantinidis, A., Pomportsis, A.S.: Evaluation framework for collaborative educational virtual environments. Educ. Technol. Soc. **13**(2), 65–77 (2010)
39. Graham, C.R.: Blended learning systems. The handbook of blended learning, pp. 3–21 (2006)
40. Nason, R., Woodruff, E.: Supporting online collaborative learning in mathematics. In: Encyclopedia of Distance Learning, pp. 1725–1731. IGI Global (2005)

41. Kraut, R.E., Fussell, S.R., Brennan, SE., Siegel, J.: Understanding effects of proximity on collaboration: Implications for technologies to support remote collaborative work. In: Distributed Work, pp. 137–162 (2002)
42. Kraut, R., Egido, C., Galegher, J.: Patterns of contact and communication in scientific research collaboration. In: Proceedings of the 1988 ACM Conference on Computer-Supported Cooperative Work, pp. 1–12 (1988)
43. Seifert, J., et al.: MobiSurf: improving co-located collaboration through integrating mobile devices and interactive surfaces. In: Proceedings of the 2012 ACM International Conference on Interactive Tabletops and Surfaces, pp. 51–60 (2012)
44. Hawkey, K., Kellar, M., Reilly, D., Whalen, T., Inkpen, K.M.: The proximity factor: impact of distance on co-located collaboration. In: Proceedings of the 2005 International ACM SIGGROUP Conference on Supporting Group Work, pp. 31–40 (2005)
45. Evans, M.A., Rick, J.: Supporting learning with interactive surfaces and spaces. In: Spector, J., Merrill, M., Elen, J., Bishop, M. (eds.) Handbook of Research on Educational Communications and Technology, pp. 689–701. Springer, New York (2014)
46. Zurita, G., Nussbaum, M.: A constructivist mobile learning environment supported by a wireless handheld network. J. Comput. Assist. Learn. **20**(4), 235–243 (2004)
47. Greenspan, S.: Collaborating through shared displays and interacting devices. CA Technol. Exch. Post-PC Era **5**, 61–64 (2012)
48. Nicolaescu, P., Derntl, M., Klamma, R.: Browser-based collaborative modeling in near real-time. In: 2013 9th International Conference on Collaborative Computing: Networking, Applications and Worksharing (Collaboratecom), pp. 335–344 (2013)
49. Falloon, G.: Young students using iPads: app design and content influences on their learning pathways. Comput. Educ. **68**, 505–521 (2013)
50. Paul, S.A., Bolinger, J.W.: Ask an expert: mobile workspaces for collaborative troubleshooting. In: 2015 48th Hawaii International Conference on System Sciences (HICSS), pp. 442–451 (2015)
51. Chickering, A.W., Ehrmann, S.C.: Implementing the seven principles: technology as lever. AAHE Bull. **49**, 3–6 (1996)
52. Vavoula, G.N., Sharples, M.: Challenges in evaluating mobile learning (2008)
53. Martinez-Maldonado, R., et al.: Learning about collaborative design for learning in a multi-surface design studio. In: Proceedings of the International Conference on Computer-Supported Collaborative Learning, pp. 174–181 (2015)
54. Goodyear, P., Carvalho, L.: Activity centred analysis and design in the evolution of learning networks. In: Tenth International Conference on Networked Learning, Lancaster University, Lancaster (2016)
55. Nielsen, J.: Usability 101: Introduction to Usability. Nielsen Norman Group (2012). http://www.nngroup.com/articles/usability101introductiontousability
56. Bevan, N., Carter, J., Harker, S.: ISO 9241-11 revised: what have we learnt about usability since 1998? In: International Conference on Human-Computer Interaction, pp. 143–151 (2015)
57. Nielsen, J., Landauer, T.K.: A mathematical model of the finding of usability problems. In: Proceedings of the INTERACT 1993 and CHI 1993 Conference on Human Factors in Computing Systems, pp. 206–213 (1993)
58. Woolson, R.F.: Wilcoxon Signed-Rank Test. Wiley Encyclopedia of Clinical Trials (2008)
59. Barlow, M.: When Hardware Meets Software - How the Internet of Things Transforms Design and Manufacturing. 1005 Gravenstein Highway North. O'Reilly Media, Sebastopol (2015)
60. Nielsen, J.: Hardware Specs vs. User Experience (2012). https://www.nngroup.com/articles/hardware-specs-vs-user-experience

61. Dourish, P., Bellotti, V.: Awareness and coordination in shared workspaces. In: Proceedings of the 1992 ACM Conference on Computer-Supported Cooperative Work, pp. 107–114 (1992)
62. Budiu, R., Nielsen, J.: iPad App and Website Usability (2011)
63. Mavri, A., Loizides, F., Photiadis, T., Zaphiris, P.: We have the content now what? The role of structure and interactivity in academic document triage interfaces. Inf. Des. J. 20(3) (2013)
64. Olguín, C.J.M., Delgado, A.L.N., Ricarte, I.L.M.: An agent infrastructure to set collaborative environments. Educ. Technol. Soc. 3(3), 65–73 (2000)
65. Kirschner, P.A., Erkens, G.: Toward a framework for CSCL research. Educ. Psychol. 48(1), 1–8 (2013)
66. Stallings, J.: Allocated academic learning time revisited, or beyond time on task. Educ. Res. 9(11), 11–16 (1980)
67. Wakefield, J., Smith, D.: From Socrates to satellites: iPad learning in an undergraduate course. Creat. Educ. 3(5), 643 (2012)
68. Marsick, V.J., Volpe, M.: The nature and need for informal learning. Adv. Dev. Hum. Resour. 1(3), 1–9 (1999)
69. Marsick, V.J., Volpe, M., Martin, F., Ertzberger, J.: Here and now mobile learning: an experimental study on the use of mobile technology. Adv. Dev. Hum. Resour. 68(3), 1–9 (2013)
70. Rogers, Y., Lim, Y., Hazlewood, W.R., Marshall, P.: Equal opportunities: do shareable interfaces promote more group participation than single user displays? Hum. Comput. Interact. 24(1–2), 79–116 (2009)
71. Tromp, N., Hekkert, P., Verbeek, P.: Design for socially responsible behavior: a classification of influence based on intended user experience. Des. Issues 27(3), 3–19 (2011)

Evaluating the Use of Groupware Technologies in Support of Collaborative Learning in an ESP Tertiary Education Course

Aekaterini Mavri[1]([✉]) and Stavroula Hadjiconstantinou[2]

[1] Cyprus Interaction Lab, Department of Multimedia and Graphic Arts,
Cyprus University of Technology, 30 Archbishop Kyprianou Str. 3036,
Limassol, Cyprus
aekaterini.mavri@cut.ac.cy
[2] Language Centre, Department of Multimedia and Graphic Arts,
Cyprus University of Technology, 30 Archbishop Kyprianou Str. 3036,
Limassol, Cyprus
s.hadjiconstantinou@cut.ac.cy

Abstract. ESP (English for specific purposes) refers to English teaching and learning with a strong emphasis on discipline-specific competencies and skills. Collaboration provides key benefits in ESP education, in terms of stronger linguistic gains and better written artefacts. Dedicated learning platforms as well as knowledge management and social networking tools, have become central in supporting collaboration in educational settings, yet sufficient evidence of their in-depth contribution and usability, with regards to ESP, is limited.

This study seeks to evaluate the perceived usability of two web-based collaborative learning and productivity platforms: (a) Moodle Elgg and (b) Google Drive, Docs & Hangouts, as well as investigate their distinct pedagogical impact on the students' perceived learning.

Results indicate that the affordances of each tool are accountable for the type and extend of activities performed within them, and - consequently – the respective learning outcomes achieved. Significant differences were recorded between the tools and the outcomes render Google Drive as a more appropriate option than Moodle Elgg for the ESP requirements in this study.

Keywords: Collaborative learning · Groupware · Usability · Courseware
Shared workspaces

1 Introduction

The present study seeks to evaluate the usability and suitability of two online collaborative learning and productivity platforms, as well as investigate their pedagogical impact in terms of the students' perceived learning outcomes within the context of an ESP (English for specific purposes) course in higher education. ESP refers to English teaching and learning with a strong emphasis on discipline-specific competencies and skills, whether these relate to the particular field of studies or workplace setting [1]. It seeks to motivate learners to self-direct their studies according to their needs and

© Springer International Publishing AG, part of Springer Nature 2018
P. Zaphiris and A. Ioannou (Eds.): LCT 2018, LNCS 10924, pp. 446–465, 2018.
https://doi.org/10.1007/978-3-319-91743-6_33

goals, through purpose-related, in-and-out of class activities, which are methodically planned by educators and instructional designers, as part of a learner-centered approach.

Over the past few years, higher education has generated a great demand for technological tools that can sustain such a shift, from the traditional "teacher-centered" to more student-oriented, "inquiry-based" pedagogy [2]. According to this, learners are expected to take control of their knowledge management, through information capturing, sharing and transferring, as well as develop work artefacts in collaboration with their peers. Collaborative learning, through the use of dedicated, web-based educational platforms has proven to benefit learners in terms of enhanced knowledge acquisition and better interpersonal skills development [2]. Students are able to maximize their learning and reach higher accomplishments, by sharing perspectives and through collective knowledge scaffolding [3]. Collaboration, in the context of English as a foreign Language has been shown to steer motivation and active student participation, benefit learners in achieving a "better vocabulary gain" [4] and enable them to produce better written constructs [5].

In support of collaborative learning, inclusive web-based Course Management Systems (CMS) and Learning Management Systems (LMS), such as Blackboard and Moodle, have emerged over the last two decades [6] and became central for the dissemination of learning materials, student collaboration (embedded wikis and forums), and assessment. Moreover, there is increasing interest in the use of commercial knowledge-management, productivity, blogging and social networking products such as DropBox, Google Docs, WordPress and Facebook, in order to cater for such educational practices [7] as well as benefit from the enhanced communicative features provided [8].

However, sufficient evidence about these tools' role and contribution in pedagogical practices as well as their level of usability, when compared to traditional LMSs, for foreign language education and especially ESP, is limited. We do not currently know how the particular user activities, behaviors and interactions, based on the capabilities and behavior of different environments, may impact the students' experience and their specific knowledge outcomes within this context.

This study incorporates two types of web applications, Moodle, a prevalent traditional e-learning platform and Google Drive, a commercial groupware product, in an undergraduate ESP course. In doing so it seeks to investigate their distinct implications on student experience and learning performance. More specifically, two groups of students are asked to use either Moodle Elgg, Moodle's social learning platform or a combination of Google's Drive, Docs and Hangouts to collectively gather, organize material and collaborate in co-authoring an article on a pre-assigned topic. We asked students to (a) evaluate the perceived usability and suitability of the tools in performing required collaborative activities within the context of ESP and (b) report on the perceived pedagogical impact of these tools on their knowledge development outcomes in regards to linguistic competencies, critical thinking and collaborative article writing.

The next section begins with an overview of studies concerning relate to educational approaches followed by usability evaluation guidelines and practices. Then we proceed by an outline of the design and research methodology used in the study. The analysis section then looks at the two main areas of research interest, the usability and suitability of the tools for this study, as well as their impact on the students' learning performance, followed by an overview and discussion of the findings, as well as a final report of the study's results, limitations and future work prospects.

2 Related Work

2.1 English for Specific Purposes (ESP) Approach

The term English for Specific Purposes (ESP) has been in use since at least the mid-1980s to describe a learner-centered branch of ESL/EFL (English as a Second/Foreign Language) that caters for the study- or work-related needs of individuals which are not properly attended to by General English [9]. It can be characterized, amongst other things, by curriculum development based on the target-situation needs and wants of stakeholders, by a focus on specialized vocabulary and authentic materials as well by as a strong emphasis on learner autonomy [10]. Self-direction is sustained through specially-designed purpose-related activities in the classroom, in which learners, aware of the demands placed on them, assume responsibility for their learning. From an instructional point of view, the analysis of needs of learners in specific contexts especially in higher education is a key process of the ESP approach and so educators and course designers always make decisions on content, material and activities based on these needs.

In line with the principles behind the ESP approach, the courses offered to the students in tertiary education are especially designed based on those skills that are considered essential for individuals in each discipline. Language competence, critical thinking and ICT skills are among the most important. The English for Media and Communication Studies course - under investigation in this study - is organized around the kinds of tasks that students in the areas of Communication and Media would be expected to perform as part of their future academic or professional engagements.

2.2 Critical Media Literacy Skills

Periodic evaluation of the course including detailed needs analysis has highlighted a certain type of skills, directly related to the field of Communication and particularly important for future professionals in this field, which could have been more adequately covered in the curriculum as they could both facilitate and benefit from linguistic development. Among these were Critical media literacy skills, highlighted for their importance in empowering learners to effectively perform and excel in Communication, Media and Information infused digital contexts. Critical Media Literacy, refers to learners' everyday literacy practices in the 21st century, and more specifically the immense influence of Mass Media and popular culture in the everyday comportment of younger generations. Critical Media Literacies in this sense would include the sets of language and skills required for participating in such digitally mediated contexts. These might include the ability to search vast online databases, retrieve and process large quantities of information, communicate online with other people in various places and for different purposes, collaborate through online platforms with the purpose of sharing or constructing knowledge through the creation of multimedia texts [11].

Students at tertiary education and especially learners in the fields of Communication and the Media - need to be endorsed with these types of skills in order to cope with the abundance of information they receive and which they need to process and manipulate for various purposes. As future Media people, then and as information mediating agents these students need to develop sophisticated skills of individual and collective 'text' creation using their own selection of materials from a variety of sources, and this goes beyond decoding texts, or understanding them, to the more demanding processes of re constructing and synthesizing information to accommodate a vast range of online texts.

2.3   Social Constructivism and Collaborative Learning

This study has been borrowing from Vygotskian theory or social constructivism, an approach to learning and teaching that emphasizes not only individual learners but also the social and material environment with which they interact in the course of their development [12]. A second fundamental feature of Vygotskian stresses the role of artifacts that are shaped and mastered in activity and interaction with others. Belonging to a community seems to increase learner's self-confidence making the learning experience easier, more pleasant and motivating for most participants in a course [13–15].

Transferring these considerations to the context of the present study, called for a reconceptualization of the curriculum, methodology and activities to include collaboration at various levels, between communities of learners with shared interests. Harasim defines online collaborative learning as "a learning process where two or more people work together to create meaning, explore a topic, or improve skills [7]. Consequently, an important characteristic of the activities was that they were organized and supported in ways that enabled learners to draw on multiple sources of assistance (peers, technology, and instructor) in creating their artifacts and in developing the necessary skills and competencies in the process.

2.4   Technology Enhanced Learning

In support of the development of skills and competencies and of course the collaborative requirements of the curriculum, a number of ICT tools have been integrated into various components of the course to serve a number of purposes over the last few years.

Initial attempts were based on a number of factors. Among these were student's previous experience with technology, affordances of the various tools as well as the academic and professional needs and collaboration requirements these tools would be facilitating Technology employed to accommodate such needs has highlighted strengths and weaknesses related to the various linguistic, contextual and communicative demands placed on the learners and has led to the need for a more detailed investigation of the perceived effect of specific tools on critical media literacy development and collaboration.

The question of how students interact at and with the computer has been addressed in a number of studies [16, 22] the type of software and the tasks teachers set for students had a large effect on the type and quality of student interaction with each other when working in pairs or small groups. In general, "software that requires a minimum of verbal interaction generates very little, while having students write a joint report or otherwise produce something collaboratively results in a substantial amount of inter-action" [23].

Moreover, there is recognition that group size depends on the scope, duration, and complexity of the task. The learning group, however, needs to be small enough to enable students to participate fully and to build group cohesion [24, 25]. Bean (2011) asserts a group size of five may be optimal for many learning situations because larger groups may dilute the experience for the learner [26].

2.5 Usability of Collaborative Learning Platforms

Tools that can assist in the development of the abovementioned skills and competen-cies are widely available today, and depending on context and functionality, come in various labels: collaboration software [27], computer supported cooperative work systems [28], e-learning landscapes or platforms [29, 30] or real time distributed groupware [31]. Groupware is a term initially defined as the "intentional group pro-cesses plus software to support them" [32]. The latter will be used or the purposes of this paper.

In assessing such tools' effectiveness, amongst others, researchers and analysts draw from a set of predefined criteria for usability evaluation purposes. Fundamental usability metrics include a product's learnability - how easily users learn to perform tasks, efficiency - how fast users can perform tasks, memorability - how proficient returning users are after a period of inactivity, errors - the amount of errors and ways to recover, and satisfaction - how pleasant the experience is in performing desired tasks [33]. Furthermore, there is well-documented methodology for conducting usability evaluations on digital products – involving users in controlled and not-controlled experiments, field studies, formatively and/or predictively, such as heuristic evaluation [34]. However, these alone may not be sufficient for the evaluation of groupware, as they tend to focus on single-user applications. In fact, Baker, Greenberg and Gutwin mention that although commercial real-time groupware has become widely available over the recent years, it is under-utilized due to serious issues, which can go undetected from the scope of individual-user usability evaluation models [31].

Research attempts to answer this problem, by identifying the main components of collaboration – namely context, support, tasks, interaction processes, teams, individuals and overarching factors (psychological factors, trust, incentives, experience) and sug-gests these as a foundation to support, evaluate and improve systems for collaborative, co-located and distributed work [35]. More elaborate frameworks have emerged in the process, which attempt to augment the existing, more generic usability guidelines [36–38] where groupware is concerned; a set of adapted heuristics, directed towards the mechanics of "teamwork", rather than the single-user "taskwork". They derive from face-to-face collaboration, and evolve to fit the particularities of virtual collaboration, focusing on the crucial activities, tasks and processes within this context, namely communication, planning, monitoring, assistance, coordination and protection [31].

The above considerations guide the research objectives set by the present study and consequently inform the design of activities, the selection of supporting tools and the thematic data requirements and guidelines upon which analysis is conducted and conclusions are inferred.

3   Study and Methodology

3.1   Participants

The study recruited second-year students of the department of Communication and Internet Studies, part of the faculty of Communication and Media Studies at the Cyprus University of Technology. A total of twenty-eight students (sixteen male and twenty-one female students) took part in the two-week study, after agreeing to participate. The students' English language proficiency was of an intermediate level. Students had prior knowledge and adequate experience with the groupware tools they were instructed to use.

3.2   Procedure and Materials

The study involved firstly the use of Elgg, Moodle's learning-oriented social networking application which combines features of file repositories, e-portfolios and weblogging to form a "personal learning landscape" [29]. For the purpose of this research, tools providing similar functionality to Elgg, from Google's Productivity Suite [39] were also employed: Google Drive, Docs and Hangouts. Although distinct through different features (interface, behavior, synchronous/asynchronous editing, communication and version control), yet both tools facilitate information-structuring and management (folders, documents), sharing, communication, and collaborative writing of artefacts. These tools will be referred to as Moodle Elgg and Google Drive throughout the course of this paper.

Based on the program structure, students were naturally sampled into two independent groups, A and B. Group A (twelve students) was instructed to work with Moodle Elgg and group B (sixteen students) with Google Drive. The instructor formed several, mixed-ability teams of students within each group. Both the team and instructor had access to each team's work-folder on both tools. An initial hands-on session was performed to inform students about various tool technicalities and ensure that they were fully familiar with utilizing tool functionality for the purposes of the assignment.

The assignment required students to attend a lecture on the subject of "Concepts in Communication", in which a number of important concepts in the area of Communication were discussed and related to personal experiences. Simulating a real life situation, students - in teams of five- as members of an editorial board for an online magazine- were asked to first take notes from the lecture and then use these and other related material to collaboratively write a short article (around 200 words) discussing one of the concepts using the same approach - (personal) examples from real life. All activities could be performed both in-and-out of classroom, on documents in their shared online folders and by communication through Google's Hangouts or Moodle Elgg's blogging tool.

Drafts of the article were submitted at specific times during the completion process so that the instructor could provide corrective feedback. The final artefact should have the structure and format of an online article as it would appear on the University's student website. The assignment was part of student's summative assessment scheme.

3.3 Data Collection and Analysis

Following completion of the assignment, students were asked to participate in an online survey consisting of twenty-two close-ended questions as five-point Likert scales, rating matrices and multiple choice forms, as well as, open-ended responses – as supplementary commentary. The survey enquired about subject-driven activities that, amongst others, have been classified into three key areas which are characteristic of online collaboration for educational purposes: (a) information structuring and sharing (b) collaborative learning and writing and (c) knowledge building and management [40].

Although the two activities, 'Document/folder/notes management' and 'Sharing material' might appear similar, they are distant in the sense that 'documents, folders and notes management' involves primarily the structuring of resource taxonomies (i.e. folder-and-file hierarchies) whereas 'sharing material' presupposes the existence of such an infrastructure, in order to take place.

Table 1. Specific activities and classifications

Information structuring and sharing	1. Collecting material in various formats
	2. Document/folder/notes management
Collaborative learning and writing	3. Collaboration with team members for work material processing
	4. Exchanging feedback and comments on artefact development
	5. Communication/chat for coordination purposes
	6. 'Like' functionality
Knowledge building and management	7. Studying text and audiovisual material
	8. Sharing material

Survey Monkey was used for the data collection with regards to the above dimensions and activity items. The close-ended results were quantitatively analyzed using SPSS (Version 23.0.0.0). Contingent to the type of question and based on the small data set size, non-parametric, exact statistical tests were conducted to compare the two groups.

Open-ended data was qualitatively analyzed using nVivo (Version 11.0.0.317). Initial codes were recorded by two researchers who worked separately, using an inductive thematic analysis approach [41], until saturation of codes and themes was reached. Next, the researchers jointly refined and finalized the data structure into a total of two major categories and nine thematic groups and proceeded with further individual coding cycles, achieving an inter-rater agreement result of k = 0,9 based on Cohen's Kappa coefficient measure. This constitutes as an 'almost perfect agreement', according to Viera and Garrett [42].

4   Results

Results from survey were classified based on the research objectives, in two major thematic categories:

1. Usability: tool affordances, functionality, suitability and user experience within the scope of the assignment.
2. Context-specific (Language) collaborative learning: tool support for collaborative English learning and writing and the perceived impact on student learning outcomes.

4.1   Tool Usability, Tool Affordances and User Experience

Through the study participant assessment was collected in regards to the usability and the degree of suitability in performing specific activities.

According to adopted usability metrics (single and group interaction) [31, 33, 35], we were looking into the following areas:

(a) Ease of use: the level of ease by which learners perform tasks
(b) Tool suitability: suitability of the tool in facilitating various learning tasks?
(c) Error incidence and recovery: the occurrence of errors and how easy it was for learners to recover from them through the support of the system
(d) Time to learn: how fast users learn how to perform tasks using the tool
(e) User experience: how pleasant was the experience is in performing desired collaborative learning tasks

Ease of Use. Participants were asked to rate separate activities facilitated by the tool and by amalgamation of these ratings, generic usability evaluations were concluded. The rating options ranged from 1 to 5, with 1 being Very Bad and 5 Very Good.

The totals suggest that Google Drive (N = 16, M = 4,1, SD = 0,01) was overall perceived as more usable compared to Moodle Elgg (N = 12, M = 3,5, SD = 0,3), within the context of this study. Statistical tests were performed to examine the exact relationships between all rated activities, amongst the two groups. Significant differences were detected in two activities: (a) Using the tools to 'Collect material in various formats' ($p = 0.026$ by Fisher's exact test) and (b) Using the tools to 'Study textual or audiovisual material' ($p = 0.026$ by Fisher's exact test). These are discussed below.

The results from the two groups coincided as far as the three top-most preferred options were concerned (Table 3). 'Sharing material' was the easiest activity to perform for Moodle Elgg users, followed by 'Collaborating with team members in work material processing' and then 'Document/folder/notes management'. Although in different order, Google Drive users also elected the same easiest activities, namely

Table 2. Easiest collaborative activities supported by the two tools -

Activities	Moodle Elgg				Google Drive			
	Rank	Median	Mean	SD	Rank	Median	Mean	SD
Document/folder/Notes management	3	4	3,5	1	1	4,5	4,2	1
Sharing material	1	4	4	0,8	2	4,5	4,1	1
Collaborating with team members for work material processing	2	4	3,7	0,9	3	4,5	4	1,3
1 = Very Bad - 5 = Very Good usability								

'Document/folder/notes management' and 'Sharing material' as first and second-best. The differences, lay with the remaining activities which although received equal usability ratings in both tools, were generally higher in Google Drive, than Moodle Elgg (Moodle Elgg: M < 4, Google Drive: M > 4) (Table 2).

It was anticipated for Google Drive to best support the creation and management of documents, folders and notes for users, as it primarily is a file storage and synchronization service that seamlessly integrates Google Docs. Moodle Elgg, on the other hand, an education-centric social networking tool, presents far less sophisticated file-repository capabilities bearing distinct limitations outlined in the following sections.

As mentioned above, '|Collecting materials in various formats' and 'Studying text and audiovisual material' were significantly lower in usability scores for Moodle Elgg than for Google Drive. As next section (Tool suitability) explains, this result coincides with feedback concerning Moodle Elgg's suitability for collecting, managing and studying material in various forms (i.e. text, imagery, video, audio). Due to a technical glitch of the software release, the 'Embed content' option in the Files repository, did not allow for a thumbnail preview - a typically useful feature in image-filtering and selection, especially when traversing large image file volumes [43]. File embedding, also available in Google Drive ('Insert' menu), came with an additional file preview tool, which enabled easier file selection. However, aside from the filtering issue, problems in Moodle Elgg mostly fixated on within-document image manipulation (moving or resizing). Evidently, this forced students to abandon their efforts and leave images unaltered.

Tool Suitability. The groupware tools were not consistently evaluated in terms of their suitability in performing various activities (Table 4) within the scope of the lesson - the two most contradictory being the 'Communication/chat for coordination purposes' and the 'Like' option. An analysis of the four most suitable and the two less suitable activities, per tool, follows. We remind the reader that low scores indicate positive suitability in the following Sects. (0% = Most Suitable, 100% = Most Unsuitable).

Communication/Chat for Coordination Purposes. Despite the fact Moodle Elgg is a primarily social networking learning tool, the majority of its users found it not fitting for communication and chat whereas, this very feature was perceived as most suitable in Google Suite. The relation between the two group proportions was validated using a

Fisher's exact test and provided significant differences between the two (Moodle Elgg: 66,6%, Google Drive: 7,6%, $p = 0.004$).

This was an expected finding; while the Moodle platform offers a set of e-tools, namely forum, email and online chat, as part of its communication platform, Elgg, however, provides only weblogging activities instead – which were evidently under-exploited in this study. Typically, a weblog or forum allows for communication through asynchronous posts and replies, rather than real time messaging. Although generally seen as more structured, in that conversations involve a single threated, archived and searchable topic [44], they are typically asynchronous, slower-paced and require additional user actions than instant chat. They are thus limited in enabling users to become truly engaged into the discussion process, by projecting themselves "socially and emotionally as real people" [45], since they lack immediacy.

On the contrary, Google Hangouts, seamlessly paired with Google Drive - allows for more direct and flexible forms of dialogue between logged-in users. These outcomes are congruent with past findings that substantiate the valuable contribution of instant communication for collaborative learning, aside of its ability to encourage better peer relationships and social interactions outside of classroom [31, 46]. Students do not only deem this important, but also expect its direct incorporation into their e-learning environments.

'Like' Functionality. Apart from communication issues, significant suitability results were contradictory for the 'Like' functionality, with almost two thirds (61,5%) of Google Drive group members asserting that the tool was inapt for such an option, as opposed to a mere 11,1% in the case of Moodle ($p = 0.020$ by Fisher's exact test). Results are not surprising as Moodle's Elgg offers a 'Like' button embedded in its blogging tool. On the other hand, although Google users were advised to reward someone by text – similar to the 'like' button, whenever they wished, they failed to do so.

Studying Text and Audiovisual Material. Interestingly, 'Studying text & audiovisual material' was deemed as another less suitable activity for both groups (Moodle Elgg: 44,4% - Google Drive: 30.7%), despite the difference in percentages. This also agrees with user ratings regarding Moodle Elgg's ease-of-use from previous section.

Exchanging Feedback and Comments on Artefact Development. An examination of Google Doc's revision history, showed a complete lack of suggestions and comments, and justifies the participants' negative assessment of this activity as the second less suitable. Although students were informed and prompted to switch to the in-document 'Suggesting' mode, it appears that they have used the 'Editing' mode to make direct changes instead, hence the lack of constructive feedback. Blau and Caspi explain that it is common, amongst collaborators, to prefer offering and receiving productive suggestions, rather than seeing their work being modified by others [5]. In fact, Raman et al. propose that educators could establish corresponding grading schemes to motivate students to post comments rather than intrusive arbitrary edits, promoting a more considerate and effective form of online collaboration [47]. The activity was also found unsuitable in Moodle Elgg, albeit, in significantly lower ratings than Google Docs.

Document/Folder/Notes Management. Overall, although in varied proportions, both groups were in agreement, in jointly rating 'Document/folder/Notes management', as their most suitable feature. Previous work, investigating online collaboration in design education, also indicates that students attribute the autonomy to create and populate shared online repositories with relevant material, as highly useful, facilitating better design processes as well as enhanced learning outcomes [48]. This is an illustrative example of how tools and systems can generate or enable and shape different inter-actions within them, and how these interactions can positively impact the students' overall learning process [49].

Table 3. Weighted averages and ranks of tool unsuitability for various activities

The tools were ranked as suitable for the following activities:	Moodle Elgg		Google Drive		Sig.
	Rank		Rank		
Document/folder/Notes management	1	0%	1	7,7%	1
Sharing material	3	22,2%	3	23%	0.963
Collaborating with team members for work material processing	2	11,1%	2	15,4%	0.779
Studying text & audiovisual material	4	44,4%	4	30,7%	0.521
Exchanging feedback and comments on artefact development	3	22,3%	4	30,7%	0.665
'Like' option	2	11,1%	5	61,5%	0.020
Communication (chat) and coordination purposes	5	66,6%	1	7,6%	0.004
0% = Most Suitable - 100% = Most Unsuitable					

Error Incidence and Recovery. Feedback in regards to the perceived amount, type and recovery from errors, a dichotomous question, was equally positive and negative in the case of Moodle Elgg. In contrast, the vast majority of Google Drive users reported not facing any problems with the tool. By employing a Fisher's exact test, we were able to conclude on significant differences between the two groups ($p = 0,023$).

These results agree with outcomes from the "Ease of Use" section, in performing various activities, as far as Google Drive is concerned. Users rated the tool's usability as 'Good to Very Good' on average.

On the contrary, although Moodle Elgg was generally assessed as of mostly 'Fair to Good' usability level, users reported on encountering several problems - irresoluble in certain cases. Issues related mainly to loss of orientation, poor navigation and prob-lematic interaction with the interface. Participants reportedly felt that they found it '*difficult to comprehend how to use the tool*', that '*it was confusing*' and '*in some cases*', '*the state and presentation of the site was chaotic*'. They were also unable to 'locate the tools' and 'work with imported images'.

According to usability principles, users typically expect to understand the way a system works, navigate it and perform tasks within it, preferably without prior training [33]. In contrast, Moodle evaluations expose a series of usability issues which also evolve around bad layout, poor navigation, unattractive interface design, confusing information structure, duplicate elements and inconsistent visual graphics such as symbols and icons [30].

Moreover, in accordance to other findings (Tool Suitability section) the tool's limitation in providing necessary means for effective team communication was heavily criticized. Finally, users employed unorthodox error recovery methods according to usability heuristics (that is, native system support for automatic error recovery) [50, 51]. These were: technical support phone calls, instructor's assistance and giving up on their image manipulation goals altogether.

Time to Learn. The time required in learning how to use the tool for collaborating in module activities was perceived as normal for participants in both groups A (N = 12, M = 2,59, SD = 0,84) and B (N = 16, M = 1,57, SD = 0,5) based on an ordinal scale of 1 to 5, with 1 being Very Short and 5 being Very Long. No statistical differences were detected between the two tools.

User Experience. The perceived experience in using the tool to complete the assignment was considered to be 'Neutral to Pleasant' for Moodle Elgg (N = 12, M = 2,26, SD = 0,59) and 'Pleasant' for Google Drive (N = 16, M = 1,57, SD = 0,5) users respectively. On a scale from 1 to 5, with 1 being Very Pleasant and 5 being Very Unpleasant, the groups had significant statistical differences between them by Fisher's exact test ($p = 0,04$).

The user experience results agree and reflect the sum of others, such as usability and suitability evaluations. Conforming to previous studies, the overall outcomes indicate a clear predominance of Google Drive versus Moodle Elgg, in positive user-experience in performing online collaborative tasks [3, 29, 30]. The biggest concerns, in regards to Moodle Elgg, derive largely from interface design issues: poor presentation and layout and 'lack of finish', conspicuous properties that were found insufficient by users, through comparisons to similar, more effective tools (i.e. Flickr, in regards to image management functionality). In agreement to this study's outcomes, Google Drive & Docs have been recurrently linked to 'enjoyment' from a user-experience perspective, due to the user-friendly layout and an overall ease-of-use [2].

4.2   Context-Specific Language Learning Outcomes

This section analyzes the role and contribution of the two tools for the development of context-specific outcomes: linguistic and related competencies, critical thinking, learning English and producing written artefacts in English through collective effort.

Development of Linguistic and Other Competencies. The entirety of responses in both groups selected the capability to '5. Exchange feedback and comments on artefact development', rendering it as essential for developing linguistic competencies and skills (Table 4). As previously stated, feedback and suggestions are preferred rather than directly editing others people's work, in collective work, especially when content semantics are modified [5]. Direct alterations are tolerable only on the language level (i.e. grammar and spelling corrections) or when "adding rather than deleting sentences". Although, as previously stated, students did not utilize the in-document suggestion tools, alternative (external) communication tools were employed as they were deemed important for the development of linguistic skills.

The fact that group B (Google drive) rated '7. Communication/chat for coordination purposes' as highly important, a view not shared by group A – also coincides with previous outcomes, denoting the lack of instant messaging as one of Moodle Elgg's main disadvantages.

Groups A and B agreed in rating '1. File/folder/note management' as the second most important activity, equally with '3. Team collaboration' only in Google Drive. The importance of student-induced information and resource structuring is highlighted in related literature [52]. This emphasizes that it is actually necessary for learners to organize information as well as knowledge (concepts and ideas) themselves, in order to achieve true competency and expertise in a specific subject.

Participants in this study also justified that 'Team collaboration' was central in this context, in that it "can improve their writing skills" and that "consulting others was much easier in this way". In fact, related research concludes that working and communicating through online collaborative environments, versus single-user desktop applications (i.e. Microsoft Word) encourages the creation of longer and better-written artefacts [3, 53].

Finally, both groups agreed that the '6. Like' functionality is the least suitable feature for supporting the development of 'linguistic and other competencies'.

From an overview perspective, we are able to report on significant statistical differences in regards to the negative evaluations (Moodle Elgg: 50% - Google Drive: 12,5% - $p = 0.03$ by Fisher's exact test) indicating that students perceived Google Drive as by far, a more efficient tool in supporting the development of 'linguistic and other competencies' within the context of this study.

Table 4. Top-most positive and negative preferences for tool activities supporting the *development of linguistic and other competencies*

Activities assisting in: The development of linguistic and other competencies?	Positive preferences		Negative preferences	
	Moodle Elgg	Google Drive	Moodle Elgg	Google Drive
	5	5, 7	6, 4	6
	1	1, 3	7, 2	4

1. Document/Folder/Notes management **2.** Sharing material **3.** Collaboration with team members for work material processing **4.** Studying text & audiovisual material **5.** Exchanging feedback and comments on artefact development **6.** "Like" functionality **7.** Communication/chat for coordination purposes

Development of Critical Thinking. In accordance to the previous variable (Linguistic and other competencies section), the topmost activities in support of critical thinking development were 'Exchanging feedback and comments on artefact development' and '1. File/folder/note management' for both groups unanimously (Table 5).

Google users also deemed '3. Collaboration with team members' and, expectedly, '7. Chat/communication' as the next two preferred variables for critical thinking. The majority of the Google group, were nonetheless consistent with previous evaluations in downgrading the 'Like' facility as not important for this ability. In general, suggesting, feedback, communication and collaboration amongst peers are themes that have been found central in promoting critical thinking abilities. This relies in the fact that it is nearly impossible for one person to have all the knowledge and competencies required to achieve highly sophisticated tasks, requires critical thinking processes, without the help of others [54, 55].

In conclusion, there were no significant statistical differences recorded between the positive and negative feedback from the two groups, in relevance to critical thinking development.

Table 5. Top-most positive and negative preferences for tool activities supporting the *development of critical thinking*

Activities assisting in: The development of Critical thinking	Positive preferences		Negative preferences	
	Moodle Elgg	Google Drive	Moodle Elgg	Google Drive
	1, 5	3, 5	6, 4	6
	–	1, 7	–	4

1. Document/Folder/Notes management **2.** Sharing material **3.** Collaboration with team members for work material processing **4.** Studying text & audiovisual material **5.** Exchanging feedback and comments on artefact development **6.** "Like" functionality **7.** Communication/chat for coordination purposes

Learning English. Results were - to some extent - subversive in examining this variable – especially in the case of Moodle Elgg users, indicating that the 'Study of audiovisual material' was considered primary in supporting the learning of English language (Table 6). This was rated as the second most important activity for Google users, following their previous consistent selection of three activities, namely, 'File/Folder/Notes management', 'Exchanging feedback and comments on artefact development' and 'Collaboration with team members'.

Evaluations from both groups were again, in agreement in denoting the 'Like' option, as not supportive of Learning English activity.

Table 6. Most positive and negative preferences for activities that contribute to *learning English*

Activities assisting in: Learning English	Positive preferences		Negative preferences	
	Moodle Elgg	Google Drive	Moodle Elgg	Google Drive
	4	1, 3, 5	6	6
	1	4	–	–

1. Document/Folder/Notes management **2.** Sharing material **3.** Collaboration with team members for work material processing **4.** Studying text & audiovisual material **5.** Exchanging feedback and comments on artefact development **6.** "Like" functionality **7.** Communication/chat for coordination purposes

Collaboration in the Development of Written Artefacts in English. Participant evaluations were confidently positive (Moodle Elgg: 91.67%, Google Drive: 81.2%) in regards to the assistive role of both tools in collective article-writing within the context of ESP. Qualitative feedback produced themes relating to – primarily - time flexibility and remote collaboration and secondly, problem-solving support. The fact that students could work together or independently, regardless of time and location constraints, was thought of as exceptionally useful in the study: "*...we don't all need to be in the same place for working on the assignment*", "*...we could edit the article at any time*" and "*... because it was easy to use... a very good application for co-op with my team for instant results in a document...*" were some of the responses from the survey. This agrees with multiple studies that also illustrate these tools' synchronous/asynchronous collaboration and communication potential as favorable by learners [56, 57].

Moreover, rapid collective problem-solving, through corrections and suggestions from the team, in real-time, can evidently help overcome challenges of traditional educational settings; one of these being the increased number of students versus limited instructional support in higher education [58]. As a participant explained, "*other people from my team could help me anytime in case I had trouble doing something...*". Evidently, the lack of timely support may cultivate bad time-management behavior, such as procrastination and extended completion times, consequently leading to overall poor learning outcomes for students [59].

The relation between the two groups in for this activity, showed no significant differences. These results suggest that producing a written artefact collectively is perceived as generally well-supported by online collaborative platforms, regardless of the tool used.

5 Discussion

This study was conducted with the aims to (a) Evaluate usability and suitability factors for two groupware products – Moodle Elgg and Google Drive and (b) Investigate the effect of these tools through various activities, on the perceived student learning outcomes within the scope of ESP in tertiary education.

Based on the findings we are able to infer that outcomes from research aim **a** were mostly related - either positively or negatively - to activities that fall under the '*Information collection, structuring and sharing*' and '*Knowledge building and management*' categories (Table 1), while outcomes from research aim **b** were more associated with activities involving '*Collaborative learning and writing*' followed by '*Knowledge building and management*'.

With regards to the *usability* and *tool affordances* evaluation results, Google Drive was overall perceived as a significantly better option than Moodle Elgg as far as ease of use, error incidence and user experience were concerned (Table 7).

Google Drive, primarily a file storage service, offering seamless document-management integration, justifiably received higher usability scores where 'document, folder and notes management' activities were concerned. Equally, the activity of 'sharing material' was rated as the top-most usable facility for Moodle Elgg. This also agrees with earlier research indicating that a wiki-based environment– similar to

Table 7. Top-most positive and negative preferences for easily supported activities based on *tool affordances*, *usability* and *suitability* evaluations

Tool usability and suitability in relation to specific activities	Positive preferences		Negative preferences	
	Moodle Elgg	Google Drive	Moodle Elgg	Google Drive
	2, 1	1, 2	8, 7	4, 6

1. Document/Folder/Notes management **2.** Sharing material **3.** Collaboration with team members for work material processing **4.** Studying text & audiovisual material **5.** Exchanging feedback and comments on artefact development **6.** "Like" functionality **7.** Communication/ chat for coordination purposes **8.** Collecting material in various formats (Q1 only)

Moodle Elgg - (interlinked webpages) constitutes a very appropriate means for information sharing, particularly in the early stages of learning [52].

With respect to the tools' *suitability* in facilitating various key activities in this context, outcomes were contradictory, mainly in terms of communication as well as attribution and acknowledgement purposes. In regards to communication, while Google Hangouts was evidently utilized constructively and rated as the top-most suitable option, Elgg's asynchronous blog-posting service was negatively received. Conversely, based on the latter's social networking nature, functionality such as the 'Like' option was principally favored and employed by group members, which was not the case for Google Drive. Aside from these disparities, the tools were consistently assessed for 'studying text and audiovisual material', as the second worst suitable activity, agreeing with the usability evaluation results. Based on responses, this was largely due to lack of direct manipulation (moving, resizing) issues with the images, rather than the textual elements within the documents.

Participant response for activities regarding context-specific - *language learning* - outcomes, such as the development of *'linguistic skills'* and *'critical thinking competencies'*, *'learning English'* and *'producing written artefacts collaboratively'*, show consistent acceptance for both groupware products.

Overall, students considered the 'exchange of feedback' and 'comments on the written artefact' as primary for the development of such skills. Apart from rapid problem-solving activity, reciprocal feedback lies at the heart of effective knowledge construction and the building of specific competencies, necessary for achieving sophisticated field-centric tasks [54]. Agreeing with usability outcomes, creating and maintaining 'Online documents, folders' and notes' followed as fundamental, from a context-specific (language learning) perspective. Similarly, learners also considered the 'study of audiovisual material' and 'collaboration with team members for work material processing' as essential, while (by marginal difference) 'communication and chat for coordination purpose's as equally important in the case of Google Drive use only (Table 8).

In the case of *linguistic and other competencies development*, Google Drive was perceived as, by far a more efficient tool for performing related activities. Additionally, responses concerning the role of Google Drive's collaboration and feedback facilities

Table 8. Top-most positive and negative preferences for activities supporting *general context-specific (language learning) outcomes*

Tool evaluation in regards to activities assisting in:	Positive preferences		Negative preferences	
The development of linguistic and other competencies, critical thinking and learning English	Moodle Elgg	Google Drive	Moodle Elgg	Google Drive
	5, 1, 4	5, 1, 3	6	6

1. Document/Folder/Notes management **2.** Sharing material **3.** Collaboration with team members for work material processing **4.** Studying text & audiovisual material **5.** Exchanging feedback and comments on artefact development **6.** "Like" functionality **7.** Communication/chat for coordination purposes **8.** Collecting material in various formats (Q1 only)

for the development of context-specific (language learning) competencies, appear to be more consistent and less dispersed, compared to those on Moodle Elgg.

Based on the findings we are able to infer that outcomes from research aim a were mostly related - either positively or negatively - to activities that fall under the 'Information collection, structuring and sharing' and 'Knowledge building and management' categories (Tables 10 and 11), while outcomes from research aim b were more associated with activities involving 'Collaborative learning and writing' followed by 'Knowledge building and management' (Tables 10 and 12).

6 Conclusion

This study examines the usability and suitability of Moodle Elg and Google Drive as technologies that can support collaborative learning processes within the context of an undergraduate ESP course, as well as investigate the pedagogical impact on the participants' perceived learning outcomes.

With regards to the tool affordances, usability and suitability evaluation results, Google Drive is perceived as a significantly better option to Moodle Elgg as far as ease of use, error incidence and user experience are concerned. The three easiest activity areas are the 'creation and management of folder, files and notes', 'sharing material', and 'collaborating with team members for work material processing'. In regards to tool suitability evaluation, outcomes indicate that Google Drive is most suitable for communication purposes (instant chat) and 'document management' facilities. Results relating to the role of specific activities in context-specific (Language learning) outcomes, mainly involve the 'exchange of feedback and comments on written artefacts' and the 'management of folders, documents and notes' for the purposes of the lesson, while attribution features ('Like' option) were not deemed important by learners, from this perspective.

This study is limited by the small participant sample and the context of research in terms of subject specificity (ESP) and therefore lacks an adequate level of generalizability to the larger population.

References

1. Byram, M.: Routledge Encyclopedia of Language Teaching and Learning. Psychology Press, London (2017)
2. Chu, S.K.W., Kennedy, D., Mak, Y.K.: MediaWiki and Google Docs as online collaboration tools for group project co-construction. In: Proceedings of the 2009 International Conference on Knowledge Management (2009)
3. Zhou, W., Simpson, E., Domizi, D.P.: Google Docs in an out-of-class collaborative writing activity. Int. J. Teach. Learn. High. Educ. 24(3), 359–375 (2012)
4. Liu, S.H.-J., Lan, Y.-J.: Social constructivist approach to web-based EFL learning: collaboration, motivation, and perception on the use of Google Docs. Educ. Technol. Soc. 19(1), 171–186 (2016)
5. Blau, I., Caspi, A.: What type of collaboration helps? Psychological ownership, perceived learning and outcome quality of collaboration using Google Docs. In: Proceedings of the Chais Conference on Instructional Technologies Research, vol. 12 (2009)
6. Bold, M.: Use of wikis in graduate course work. J. Interact. Learn. Res. 17(1), 5 (2006)
7. Harasim, L.M.: Learning Networks: A Field Guide to Teaching and Learning Online. MIT Press, Cambridge (1995)
8. Forment, M.A., Guerrero, M.J.C., Mayol, E., Piguillem, J., Galanis, N., García-Peñalvo, F.J., González, M.Á.C.: Docs4Learning: getting Google Docs to work within the LMS with IMS BLTI. J. UCS 18(11), 1483–1500 (2012)
9. Huchinson, T., Waters, A.: English for Specific Purposes: A Learning-Centered Approach. Cambridge University Press, Cambridge (1987)
10. Csizér, K., Kontra, E.H.: ELF, ESP, ENL and their effect on students' aims and beliefs: a structural equation model. System 40(1), 1–10 (2012)
11. Hafner, C.A., Chik, A., Jones, R.H.: Engaging with digital literacies in TESOL. TESOL Q. 47(4), 812–815 (2013)
12. Lee, C.D., Smagorinsky, P.: Vygotskian Perspectives on Literacy Research: Constructing Meaning Through Collaborative Inquiry. Cambridge University Press, Cambridge (2000)
13. Vygotsky, L.S.: Mind in Society: The Development of Higher Mental Process. Harvard University Press, Cambridge (1978)
14. Wenger, E.: Communities of practice: learning as a social system. Syst. Thinker 9(5), 2–3 (1998)
15. Swan, K., Shea, P.: The development of virtual learning communities. In: Learning Together Online: Research on Asynchronous Learning Networks, pp. 239–260 (2005)
16. Abraham, R.G., Liou, H.-C.: Interaction generated by three computer programs: analysis of functions of spoken language. In: Computer-Assisted Language Learning: Research and Practice. Newbury House/Harper Row, New York (1991)
17. Dudley, A.: Communicative CALL: student interaction using non-EFL software. CÆLL J. 6(3), 25–33 (1995)
18. Dziombak, C.E.: Searching for collaboration in the ESL computer lab and the ESL classroom. Diss. Abstr. Int. A Humanit. Soc. Sci. 51(2296–A) (1991)
19. Levy, M., Hinckfuss, J.: Program design and student talk at computers. Comput. Assist. English Lang. Learn. J. 1(4), 21–26 (1990)
20. Meskill, C.: ESL and multimedia: a study of the dynamics of paired student discourse. System 21(3), 323–341 (1993)
21. Murillo, D.: Maximizing CALL effectiveness in the classroom. CÆLL J. 2(2), 20–25 (1991)
22. Pujol, M.: ESL interactions around the computer. CÆLL J. 6(4), 2–11 (1995)

23. Warschauer, M., Healey, D.: Computers and language learning: an overview. Lang. Teach. **31**(2), 57–71 (1998)
24. Barkley, E.F., Cross, K.P., Major, C.H.: Collaborative learning techniques: a handbook for college faculty. Wiley, Hoboken (2014)
25. Schellens, T., Valcke, M.: Fostering knowledge construction in university students through asynchronous discussion groups. Comput. Educ. **46**(4), 349–370 (2006)
26. Bean, J.C.: Engaging Ideas: the Professor's Guide to Integrating Writing, Critical Thinking, and Active Learning in the Classroom. Wiley, Chichester (2011)
27. Klemm, W.R.: Benefits of Collaboration Software for On-Site Classes (1997)
28. Dekeyser, S., Watson, R.: Extending Google Docs to collaborate on research papers, vol. 23, p. 2008. University of Southern Queensland, Australia (2006)
29. Werdmuller, B., Tosh, D., Files, F., Free, P.: Elgg–A personal learning landscape. TESL-EJ **9**(2), 1–11 (2005)
30. Tee, S.S., Wook, T., Zainudin, S.: User testing for moodle application. Int. J. Softw. Eng. Its Appl. **7**(5), 243–252 (2013)
31. Baker, K., Greenberg, S., Gutwin, C.: Empirical development of a heuristic evaluation methodology for shared workspace groupware. In: Proceedings of the 2002 ACM Conference on Computer Supported Cooperative Work, pp. 96–105 (2002)
32. Johnson-Lenz, P., Johnson-Lenz, T.: Post-mechanistic groupware primitives: rhythms, boundaries and containers. Int. J. Man Mach. Stud. **34**(3), 395–417 (1991)
33. Nielsen, J.: Usability 101: Introduction to Usability. Nielsen Norman Group (2012). http://www.nngroup.com/articles/usability101introductiontousability
34. Nielsen, J., Molich, R.: Heuristic evaluation of user interfaces. In: Proceedings of the SIGCHI Conference on Human Factors in Computing Systems, pp. 249–256 (1990)
35. Patel, H., Pettitt, M., Wilson, J.R.: Factors of collaborative working: a framework for a collaboration model. Appl. Ergon. **43**(1), 1–26 (2012)
36. Crumlish, C., Malone, E.: Designing Social Interfaces: Principles, Patterns, and Practices for Improving the User Experience. O'Reilly Media Inc., Sebastopol (2009)
37. Luna-García, H., Mendoza-González, R., Vargas Martin, M., Muñoz-Arteaga, J., Álvarez-Rodríguez, F.J., Rodríguez-Martínez, L.C.: Validating design patterns for mobile groupware applications by expert users: a USAER case. Comput. Sist. **20**(2), 239–250 (2016)
38. Pinelle, D., Gutwin, C., Greenberg, S.: Task analysis for groupware usability evaluation: modeling shared-workspace tasks with the mechanics of collaboration. ACM Trans. Comput. Interact. **10**(4), 281–311 (2003)
39. Herrick, D.R.: Google this!: using Google apps for collaboration and productivity. In: Proceedings of the 37th Annual ACM SIGUCCS Fall Conference: Communication and Collaboration, pp. 55–64 (2009)
40. Chu, S.K.-W.: TWiki for knowledge building and management. Online Inf. Rev. **32**(6), 745–758 (2008)
41. Patton, M.Q.: Qualitative Evaluation and Research Methods. SAGE Publications Inc., Thousand Oaks (1990)
42. Viera, A.J., Garrett, J.M.: Understanding interobserver agreement: the kappa statistic. Fam. Med. **37**(5), 360–363 (2005)
43. Shneiderman, B.: Reflections on authoring, editing and managing hypertex (1998)
44. Farmer, R.: Instant messaging–collaborative tool or educator's nightmare. In: The North American Web-based Learning Conference (NAWeb 2003) (2003)
45. Garrison, D.R., Anderson, T., Archer, W.: Critical inquiry in a text-based environment: computer conferencing in higher education. Internet High. Educ. **2**(2), 87–105 (1999)

46. Nicholson, S.: Socialization in the 'virtual hallway': instant messaging in the asynchronous web-based distance education classroom. Internet High. Educ. 5(4), 363–372 (2002)
47. Raman, M., Ryan, T., Olfman, L.: Designing knowledge management systems for teaching and learning with wiki technology. J. Inf. Syst. Educ. 16(3), 311 (2005)
48. Bubaš, G., Orehovački, T., Kovačić, A.: E-learning with Web 2.0 tools: what can ('t) go wrong. In: 18th European University Information Systems (EUNIS) Congress-A 360° Perspective on IT/IS in Higher Education (2012)
49. Farmer, R.: Instant messaging: IM Online! RU? Educ. Rev. 40(6), 49 (2005)
50. Preece, J.: Sociability and usability in online communities: determining and measuring success. Behav. Inf. Technol. 20(5), 347–356 (2001)
51. Ardito, C., Costabile, M.F., De Marsico, M., Lanzilotti, R., Levialdi, S., Roselli, T., Rossano, V.: An approach to usability evaluation of e-learning applications. Univers. Access Inf. Soc. 4(3), 270–283 (2006)
52. Nicol, D., Littlejohn, A., Grierson, H.: The importance of structuring information and resources within shared workspaces during collaborative design learning. Open Learn. J. Open Distance e-Learn. 20(1), 31–49 (2005)
53. Apple, K.J., Reis-Bergan, M., Adams, A.H., Saunders, G.: Online tools to promote student collaboration. In: Getting connected: Best Practices for Technology Enhanced Teaching and Learning in High Education, pp. 239–252 (2011)
54. Wang, Q.: Using online shared workspaces to support group collaborative learning. Comput. Educ. 55(3), 1270–1276 (2010)
55. Liaw, S.-S.: Investigating students' perceived satisfaction, behavioral intention, and effectiveness of e-learning: a case study of the Blackboard system. Comput. Educ. 51(2), 864–873 (2008)
56. Emmer, E.T., Liu, M., Reimer, T.C.: Student perceptions of a collaborative online learning environment (2005)
57. Bower, M., Richards, D.: Collaborative learning: some possibilities and limitations for students and teachers. In: 23rd Annual Conference of the Australasian Society for Computers in Learning in Tertiary Education: Whos Learning, pp. 79–89 (2006)
58. Lahtinen, E., Ala-Mutka, K., Järvinen, H.-M.: A study of the difficulties of novice programmers. In: Proceedings of the 10th Annual SIGCSE Conference on Innovation and Technology in Computer Science Education - ITiCSE 2005, p. 14 (2005)
59. Mavri, A., Loizides, F., Souleles, N.: A case study on using iPads to encourage collaborative learning in an undergraduate web development class. In: 1st International Conference on the use of iPads in Higher Education 2014, pp. 267–290 (2014)

Measuring Teamwork Competence Development in a Multidisciplinary Project Based Learning Environment

Francisco J. Rodríguez-Sedano[1], Miguel Á. Conde[2(✉)],
and Camino Fernández-Llamas[2]

[1] Department of Electric, Systems and Automatics Engineering,
School of Engineering, University of León,
Campus de Vegazana S/N, 24071 León, Spain
francisco.sedano@unileon.es
[2] Department of Mechanics, Computer Science and Aerospace Engineering,
Robotics Group, University of León,
Campus de Vegazana S/N, 24071 León, Spain
{miguel.conde, camino.fernandez}@unileon.es

Abstract. Nowadays the development of teamwork competence is a key issue in several contexts. It is highly valued both in educational institutions and in business. However, measuring how it is acquired is a difficult task and specially when it is not developed in a traditional classroom context. In this paper authors have explored the evaluation of teamwork competence acquisition during the development of projects by teams with members coming from different contexts. These members have different knowledge, skills and not the same way to work. In addition, there is not a teacher continuously checking what they are doing or not. Given this context, and to guarantee the success of these multidisciplinary projects and evaluate teamwork competence development, several methodologies were studied. CTMTC methodolgy was adapted and complemented with other tools in order to check if it can work in this specific context. The aim of this adaption is that the methodology allows measuring individually and as group teamwork acquisition in multidisciplinary contexts. The methodology was successfully applied in an experiment and it was possible to see that it works properly although some improvements can still be done.

Keywords: Multidisciplinary projects · Teamwork competence
Project based learning · Competence acquisition measurement

1 Introduction

Nowadays the society requires better prepared professionals that must be able to work with others to succeed in their work. In this sense, many initiatives have been developed to promote teamwork for developing projects and address challenges. Companies and Educational institutions are giving to teamwork competence special relevance [1] and try to support its acquisition by applying methodologies such as collaborative learning and more specifically Project Based Learning (PLE) [2] or Challenge Based Learning (CBL) [3].

© Springer International Publishing AG, part of Springer Nature 2018
P. Zaphiris and A. Ioannou (Eds.): LCT 2018, LNCS 10924, pp. 466–479, 2018.
https://doi.org/10.1007/978-3-319-91743-6_34

With the aim of promoting teamwork competence and entrepreneurship the authors of this paper have launched in the University of León a laboratory for developing collaborative projects. The idea is to define an open and common space where any student and/or teacher could exchange knowledge and collaborate in order to perform multidisciplinary projects. Projects that aim to promote issues such as of creativity, innovation and collaboration and that can be developed with different proposes as: final degree projects, products for companies, prototypes to be applied as proofs of concepts, etc.

Some of the individuals involved in the project development could have some previous knowledge in project management issues. This is because most teachers have participated in projects previously and most of engineering students have taken subjects related to project management or have used project management methodologies to address problems or assignments in their subjects (some examples can be found in [4–6]). However, not all the lab users have the same educational/professional background (they are not only coming from engineering degrees) and should solve problems from different areas that are not always related to their expertise. Moreover, the projects in the lab could not be associated to a subject, so the way in which the team members deal with the project tasks is something they should manage by themselves if they want to succeed. This means that common project management methodologies should be adapted.

Given this context the present work aims to assess three main issues: (1) the success of the lab for producing useful projects; (2) the possibility to adapt a project management methodology to such heterogeneous context; and (3) the evaluation of the individual acquisition of team work competence (TWC) by each project team member.

With this information it is possible to know if the lab is working as expected, if it is useful for students and teachers and if it is promoting the acquisition of teamwork competence by the users.

This research work is then focused in clarifying and supporting these assertions. In order to do so the paper is structured as follows. Section 2 describes the research context, especially the lab and how it works and the methodologies employed by the lab users. Section 3 describes how the previous described issues where measured. Section 4 presents the results and discuses about them. Finally, in Sect. 5 some conclusions are posed.

2   Research Context

2.1   The Lab

The lab was equipped and launched in 2016/17 academic course. In the kick off several teachers and researchers both from the Department of Electronic Engineering and the Department of Mechanical, Computer Science and Aerospace Engineering were involved. The main goal for this space is to develop collaborative projects in which can be involved students from different areas, teachers, researchers and professionals.

The lab, that has around 120 m^2, is divided in two parts. One is employed for prototype development. This part includes two 3D printers, a numerical control milling machine and several toolkits (Fig. 1).

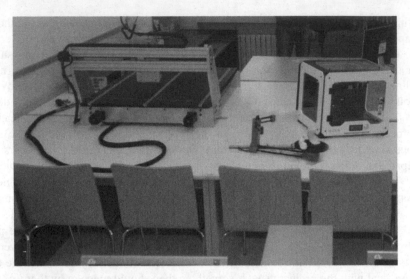

Fig. 1. The numerical control milling machine

The other part is used for academic activities such as workshops and courses related with the lab activities, there are 10 computers, a video projector and an electronic board for this aim (Fig. 2).

Fig. 2. Students working in the computers and with the 3D printers.

Regarding the staff in charge of the lab include the researchers mentioned above and two grantees that made managerial tasks during 2016/17 academic course (related to access control, equipment maintenance and description of the supplies required for the normal operation of the lab). Also, two students' associations have supported the use of the lab by promoting it and developing out several workshops and roundtables.

Given this context two type of actions were carried out:

- Academic activities. Several actions of this type have been developed. Specifically: 3 free workshops related to software use and software engineering; 4 additional courses for students; and an optional subject in the 4th year of the Degree in Computer engineering, Specific and Embedded Architectures, that uses this lab for developing projects.
- Projects. Beyond those developed during the subject described above, students/teachers and researchers. 29 projects were developed in this sense. These projects and the methodology applied in them is described in the following subsection.

2.2   The Projects and the Methodologies Used

As commented in the previous section, one of the main activities of this Lab is to support the development of research projects. These projects are all developed by teams, and the methodology applied depends on the type of project we are dealing with. The possible categories of projects are the following:

- Projects related to subjects. In this case the project can be the final or partial outcome of a subject. The lab provides tools and materials to develop these projects. The groups that addresses the project are formed by students (from 4 to 8) and applied a project management methodology. Their work is supervised by teachers. During 2016/17 academic year 8 projects were presented and in 2017/18 they were 13.
- Final Degree projects (FDP). This is an activity located at the end of the studies and it integrates the skills assessment that a professional must have once he/she finishes the degree. The lab provides tools and materials to implement these projects, that in this case are developed in pairs. The methodology applied for teamwork and for project managing use to be suggested and assessed by the FDP advisor. 8 FDPs have been developed in the collaborative lab.
- Free projects (FP). This type of projects is developed not only by students but also by teachers and professionals. In this case the projects are carried out by a team of people that could have a different educational context and work together in order to obtain a research output or a product. For instance, veterinary researchers and computer scientist can work together in order to develop a product or a solution to a specific problem. 4 projects of this type have been carried out and 3 of them were granted by different Spanish prototype calls (Results are shown in Fig. 3). These are:
  - Development of a robotic arm controlled by brain activity and muscular sensors. This involves health professionals and Computer Scientists. It has been granted by several Spanish Universities (Part A of Fig. 3).
  - Development of a system for low cost manufacturing of prosthesis for healing animal injuries. It involved researchers from veterinary, mechanical engineering

and Computer Science engineering. It has been granted by the regional government of Castilla y León in Spain and the Veterinary Hospital of the University of León (Part B of Fig. 3).
- System of uninterrupted feeding of material for 3D printers by means of pellets. It has been granted by the regional government of Castilla y León within the TCUE 2015-2017 Plan (Part C of Fig. 3).
- Low cost software prototype to measure vertical jump in smartphones. This project was awarded a prize in the competition of prototypes of the University of León (Part D of Fig. 3).

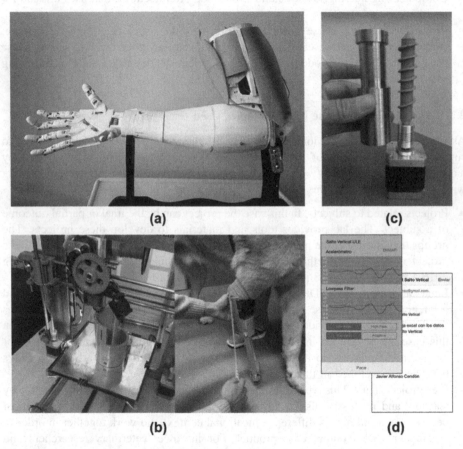

Fig. 3. The four granted projects. A is the robotic arm, B the system for prosthesis manufacturing, C the system for interrupt feeding of material for 3D printers and D the app for measuring vertical jumping

In these projects it is also necessary to apply teamwork and project management methodologies. However, the activities carried out are unattended, they are not linked to a specific subject or degree. It is necessary to define/adapt methodologies that help to guarantee the project success.

By exploring the learning programs of the subjects and asking the teachers involved in several subjects that carry out learning activities we find out that two main methodologies were applied.

The first methodology is an adaptation of the integrated model of effective teamwork, IMO [7], developed for nonacademic organizational environments but accepted in academia as a valid conceptual framework with high value. This model represents teamwork as a set of processes conditioned by some previous factors that lead to results. It also incorporates the cyclical and dynamic nature as results become new process inputs. The above model has been adapted and completed to include other skills and promoting employability of students. Specifically, the work proposed by Viles et al. [7] used a questionnaire to provide feedback to teams on their performance. To do this, they created a chart radar called "footprint" with the scale of assessment for each operating process. In this way each team could analyze the strengths and weaknesses. The methodology in the University of León was applied in the optional subject of Specific and Embedded Architectures that develops the projects in the collaborative lab. As the subject has a few students and lectures deal with them daily, the feedback was immediate. It involves a verbal communication of those deficiencies that were observed in the laboratory sessions and tutorials, considering the detailed aspects in "Direct Observation" section.

Other teamwork methodology applied in several subjects of different degrees of university of León was Comprehensive Training Model of the Teamwork Competence (CTMTC) [6]. CTMTC explore the group results and how each individual has acquired the competence. The methodology relics on the analysis of learning evidences from data generated by the use of IT-based learning tools by teams during a project development [5]. Moreover CTMTC application entails that teams develop the project in several stages adapted from the International Project Management Association (IPMA) [8]. CTMTC is a proactive method that draws on three aspects of group-based learning: teamwork phases (mission and goals, responsibility maps, planning, implementation and organization of documentation), collaborative creation of knowledge, and cloud computing technologies (wikis, forums, social networks and cloud storage systems) [5]. In the CTMTC, faculty continuously monitors team members' collaboration and individual evidences along the teamwork phases. Monitoring also enables teachers to guide students' individual learning. CTMTC allows teachers to do partial summative assessments of TWC [9]. This method has been tested in prior settings [9–12]. The methodology was applied and adapted for its application in different degree subjects of the University of León (between them Specific and Embedded Architectures) with a high rate of success and acceptation [4, 6, 13].

Given these two options, and taking into account that the projects in which this research are focused are not going to be continuously tracked, it is necessary to use a methodology flexible enough; which, given the previous experiments in different subjects makes CTMTC the most suitable one. With this methodology it is possible to measure not only the final outcome produced by a team during a project but how their members acquire teamwork competence. Although, also the methodology requires some adaptation.

3   CTMTC Adaptation

First of all, we should say that CTMTC methodology is a very flexible methodology. It has been applied in very different subjects and adapted to them as shown in other works [4, 6, 13]. In fact, it has been applied in the lab during the subject Specific and Embedded Architectures with a high participation rate [4].

CTMTC have associated a rubric that allows measuring both the group work and each member work in the group tasks [13]. The rubrics is applied over the evidences gathered during the project development, and theses evidences are mostly stored in forums (group members interactions), wiki (group outcomes) and sometimes cloud technologies (to store final results). However, in case of the FPs the team members are not always employing a learning platform or this kind of tools to carry out their work, so if we aim to employ this methodology both the tools employed to gather evidences and the rubrics should be adapted.

For compiling evidences three actions were carried out:

1. Each group will have a meeting every two week during the project development. In this weeks, the members should describe what they have done in this two weeks and what are they going to do in the following, describing the problems they have found and if the planning has been affected. This is similar to the meetings employed in agile methodologies for software development [14]. But in this meeting the members are also surveyed individually and asked about what they have done during this two weeks and what their partners have done.
2. Every month there will be a meeting with the results obtained since then. During these meetings the team members should present what the group has done, specifying the mission and goals, how they have distributed works, how team members interact between them and the results obtained until this meeting.
3. A final presentation. At the end of the work, the team should present their outcomes to other students/teachers working in the lab and to their advisors.

With these three actions and as commented above the rubric needs to be adapted. Tables 1 and 2 shows how this is done.

Table 1 shows the different issues that were evaluated about the team work developed. It is adapted taking into account how information is now gathered and stored. Explicit references to forums and wikis were removed.

Table 2 shows the part of the rubric employed to assess individual work of team members. It was adapted for this our FPs. The advisor should attend to team member behavior when they are developing the project, during the meetings and in the surveys. However, as not all the interaction could be gathered as it happens by employing other tools, this table should be supported by other tools. This is done by applying the self-perception of students about the acquisition of TWC using Team Work Behaviour Questionnaire (TWBQ) [15]. The students involved in the experiences should fulfil a questionnaire before and after the development of the projects (one sample of the questionnaire can be accessed here: https://goo.gl/kHYskM). TWBQ has two parts: one in which students have to assess their own ability, TWBQ (Self), and another in which they assess the ability of the group as a whole, TWBQ (Others). In each item

Table 1. Questions employed in the rubric to measure group evidences

Rubric for group evidences	
Mission and goals	• Is the final aim of the work described? • Is target audience identified? • Is the necessity of the work described? • Is the utility of the work described? • Is it possible to match the goals with the final results?
Team normative	• Are there rules to manage individual work? • Are there communication procedures for the team to follow when an emergency happens? • Are there rules that describe what happens when team members break the rules?
Responsibility map	• Are responsibilities distributed among members? Are team members reviewing team outcomes? • Is work equally distributed?
Planning	• Are exams, holidays, or other non-working days taken into account? • Are related tasks groups in milestones? • Is there a kick-off and closure date for each milestone? Are they briefly described? • Is there a work schedule? • Is work distribution realistic (more job when end is nearer) • Is there some estimated time for the review and integration of the work?
Implementation	• Is it possible to check individual responsibilities? • Is it possible to compare the implementation with the defined planning? • Is it possible to see what the team is carrying out week by week?
Final outcomes	• Is it easy to access and test the final work? • Is the documentation well organized?

Table 2. Questions employed in the rubric to measure individual work of team members

Individual work rubric	
Responsibility and engagement	• Is team member participating actively in all group tasks? How is doing this? • Does the member participate more or less than other team members? • Do team members interact properly in meetings?
Tracking	• Are team members aware of what are other members doing? • Do they help them? Are students visiting all the threads? • Is this described during the meetings? • Does each member describe properly what he has done since last meeting?
Discussion	• Are team members commenting and giving suggestions to help their peers?
Leadership	• Who is starting the debate during meetings? • Who is solving problems? • Who is making decisions?

(statement), participants have to evaluate their own behavior or the other members' behavior in terms of an appropriate behavior, on a 7 points Likert-type scale (l= "not at all"; 7 = "very much"). The test gives each part a total grade [16]. Although this test is based on self-appraisal opinion, research has found that a person's beliefs about teamwork behavior predict the generic teamwork behavior that this person displays as a team member [15].

In order to check how is this methodology working we have applied it as a proof of concept in the 9 projects that are being developed during 2017/18 academic year, results can be seen in the following section.

4   Results and Discussion

4.1   Experiment Description

For this experiment 13 FPs were studied, they involved 34 researchers (2 or 3 per FP). The projects began in September of 2017. The researchers were requested to answer the TWBQ at the beginning, later each group developed their work with the associated meetings (8 2-weekly meetings and 4 outcomes presentation). After the second presentation the researchers have fulfilled the TWBQ as if they would have finished the project. This is done for this proof of concept although projects will last at least until June 2018.

4.2   Results

The advisor has been observing the team members during their work and had surveyed them in the 2-weekly meetings. With this it was possible to apply the rubric to evaluate TWC acquisition, which results are shown in Tables 3 and 4.

Table 3. Average grades taking into account each group outcomes

	Mission & goals	Team norm.	Resp. map	Planning	Imp.	Final outcomes	Average group grade
GP01	10	2	6	6	10	8	7.00
GP02	10	2	10	10	10	8	8.33
GP03	8	2	10	6	6	6	6.33
GP04	8	2	10	10	6	6	7.00
GP05	10	2	8	10	6	6	7.00
GP06	10	2	6	6	10	8	7.00
GP07	8	2	10	6	6	6	6.33
GP08	8	2	10	6	6	6	6.33
GP09	8	2	10	10	6	6	7.00
GP10	10	2	8	10	6	6	7.00
GP11	10	2	10	10	10	8	8.33
GP12	8	2	10	6	6	6	6.33
GP13	10	2	8	10	6	6	700

Table 4. Average grades taking into account individuals work in each team

Researcher group	Responsibility and engagement	Tracking	Discussion	Leadership	Average grade
R1-GP1	10	10	10	10	10
R2-GP1	8	8	10	10	9
R1-GP2	10	10	10	10	10
R2-GP2	8	7	6	6	6.75
R1-GP3	6	6	8	6	6.5
R2-GP3	0	8	10	6	6
R1-GP4	6	8	8	6	7
R2-GP4	10	10	10	10	10
R3-GP4	8	10	10	10	9.5
R1-GP5	6	6	8	7	6.75
R2-GP5	6	7	8	7	7
R1-GP6	1	5	7	6	4.75
R2-GP6	10	10	10	10	10
R3-GP6	10	10	10	10	10
R1-GP7	10	10	10	10	10
R2-GP7	8	8	6	6	7
R3-GP7	10	8	8	10	9
R1-GP8	1	4	7	6	4.5
R2-GP8	10	8	10	10	9.5
R3-GP8	8	6	8	7	7.25
R1-GP9	1	5	7	6	4.75
R2-GP9	10	10	10	10	10
R3-GP9	5	6	7	6	6
R1-GP10	10	10	10	10	10
R2-GP10	5	6	7	6	6
R3-GP10	10	10	10	10	10
R1-GP11	10	10	10	10	10
R2-GP11	0	5	10	6	5.25
R3-GP11	10	8	10	6	8.5
R1-GP12	6	8	8	7	7.25
R2-GP12	10	10	10	10	10
R1-GP13	10	10	10	10	10
R1-GP13	6	7	8	6	6.75
R1-GP13	10	10	10	10	10

Table 3, shows each of the rubric elements valued a 0–10 points scale. The last column includes the final grade associated to the work each group has done.

Table 4 shows the individual work by each team member taking into account the rubric. It is possible to that not all the members of a team have the same grade.

Another analysis that is carried out is to compare the perception of teamwork behavior by using TWBQ. Students are asked to score several items regarding their TWC development and the other members in their teams. To do so, a 7 value Likert scale was used. Table 5 shows the average results for each of the groups before and after the experiment.

Table 5. TWBQ with answers per each group about own and others perception before and after the experiment

	OWN-Before (Std dev)	Other-Before (Std dev)	Own-POST	Other-POST
GP01	4.83 (1.586)	5.00 (1.483)	4.92 (1.975)	5.55 (1.968)
GP02	4.54 (0.177)	5.09 (0.643)	5.29 (0.177)	5.55 (0.000)
GP03	4.17 (0.589)	2.82 (2.571)	5.33 (0.118)	5.41 (0.193)
GP04	4.94 (0.966)	5.21 (0.757)	5.97 (0.674)	5.91 (0.506)
GP05	4.19 (0.718)	4.61 (0.292)	5.50 (0.144)	5.45 (0.000)
GP06	5.17 (2.406)	5.09 (2.508)	6.42 (1.730)	6.18 (1.834)
GP07	4.86 (0.914)	4.97 (0.555)	4.94 (1.400)	5.00 (0.396)
GP08	5.19 (1.347)	5.82 (3.078)	5.36 (0.268)	6.00 (0.091)
GP09	5.88 (0.412)	5.59 (0.193)	5.92 (0.707)	6.09 (0.900)
GP10	4.88 (0.059)	5.45 (0.643)	5.29 (0.530)	5.50 (0.064)
GP11	4.71 (0.530)	5.32 (0.707)	4.83 (0.589)	5.45 (0.514)
GP12	5.29 (1.237)	5.64 (0.129)	5.38 (1.120)	5.73 (0.129)
GP13	5.08 (1.528)	5.61 (1.241)	5.42 (1.732)	5.91 (1.417)

It is interesting to explore if the difference between self and others perception before and after the experiment is significant. In order to check this, first normality is explored to define if parametric or non-parametric test can be applied. Normality is explored taking into account the answers of the whole sample before and after the experiment, which imply more than 50 answers to be explored, this means that Kolmogorov-Smirnof tests can be applied. Both for the own perception of TWC (with a signification of 0.475) and the perception about others work (with a signification of 0.065) null hypotheis is retained, which means that the answers distribution is normal. Taking this into account we have selected a Student' T test for related samples, because the same students answer the same questions before and after the experiment. Table 6 show the results for the whole sample.

Table 6. Results of the student T test for related samples, with self-perception and other perception about teamwork behavior compared before and after the experiment

		t	Sig. (2 tailed)
Pair 1	OWNBEFORE - OWNAFTER	−2.920	0.007
Pair 2	OTHERBEFORE - OTHERAFTER	−2.864	0.008

4.3   Discussion

The adaptation of CTMTC methodology has allow us gathering some results as shown in previous section. When exploring group results in Table 3 it is possible to see that the work per each team is correct with an average grade of 7 over 10. These grades were assigned by the project advisor in the outcomes meetings. Grades are based in the difficulty of the project compared with other carried out previously in the laboratory and the necessity of support by experts and teachers to finish it successfully. It should be noted that grades could have been better if students had described the normative they were using in the group. As this was not clear in any of the projects the grade assigned was 2 over 10 which has a negative impact in the group average grade. For future projects the advisor will clarify the necessity of the specification of team normative.

Regarding the individual grades, and as in other applications of the methodology [4, 13], it is possible to differentiate which team members are working more and which less. However in this case the grade assigned is based on advisor perception as has also happened in other project based learning initiatives [17] and not only in objective data. This could be a problem if the same advisor should review an important number of projects.

Regarding the results shown in Tables 5 and 6, it is possible to say that self-perception and others-perception about TWC development has been increased for all the groups after the experiment which is something positive. In addition, when taking into account the whole sample we can see that the difference is significant. TWBQ has been used in other works with different results. In [16] several subjects TWBQ results are compared in order to see how specific training improves students teamwork capacity. Other works such as [18] also use TWBQ but do not find differences in teamwork acquisition before and after the application of two methodologies. In Conde et al. work [13] this is compared in a compulsory subject and in an elective one. In this case we are exploring other possibility by comparing not different subjects but projects.

5   Conclusions

The development of projects that involve people from different contexts is not easy. The researchers involved could have not the same knowledge, could not work in the same way, have different aims, etc. This makes necessary using methodologies that guarantee the project success in such context. One of the key issues to explore during the project development is teamwork. Results show what each group has done, but it is also required to measure how TWC is developed individually in those teams. In order to do so this work has explored different possibilities and adapted CTMTC methodology for these projects, including also some other tools to take into account students self-perception about teamwork behavior.

The application of the methodology was tested in an experiment that involves several projects. From the gathered results it is possible to assert that the methodology was properly adapted, that it makes possible to measure individual development of teamwork. Also experiment let us know that the groups require some more training about the methodology, so they include team normative when doing their job, which could help solving problems between group members. It would be also useful to include more members in each team so more difficult projects can be addressed.

The experiment has also limitations. The number of projects should be increased and also the number of components in a team, so we can check not only team work behavior in the whole sample but look in each of the project teams. In addition, it would be desirable to explore a complete project and not only when it is not already finished.

As future work it would be helpful to analyze team members and advisor opinions about the methodology, which could help us to improve it. Moreover, it would be desirable to compare projects from different academic years and what are the difference when the methodology is applied and when it is not.

References

1. Colomo-Palacios, R., Casado-Lumbreras, C., Soto-Acosta, P., García-Peñalvo, F.J., Tovar-Caro, E.: Competence gaps in software personnel: A multi-organizational study. Comput. Hum. Behav. **29**, 456–461 (2013)
2. Blumenfeld, P.C., Soloway, E., Marx, R.W., Krajcik, J.S., Guzdial, M., Palincsar, A.: Motivating project-based learning: sustaining the doing, supporting the learning. Educ. Psychol. **26**, 369–398 (1991)
3. Johnson, L., Adams, S.: Challenge Based Learning: The Report from the Implementation Project. The New Media Consortium (2011)
4. Conde, M.Á., Rodríguez-Sedano, F.J., Sánchez-González, L., Fernández-Llamas, C., Rodríguez-Lera, F.J., Matellán-Olivera, V.: Evaluation of teamwork competence acquisition by using CTMTC methodology and learning analytics techniques. In: Proceedings of the Fourth International Conference on Technological Ecosystems for Enhancing Multiculturality, pp. 787–794. ACM, Salamanca, Spain (2016)
5. Lerís, D., Fidalgo, Á., Sein-Echaluce, M.L.: A comprehensive training model of the teamwork competence. Int. J. Learn. Intellect. Capital **11**, 1–19 (2014)
6. Conde, Miguel Á., Hernández-García, Á., García-Peñalvo, Francisco J., Fidalgo-Blanco, Á., Sein-Echaluce, M.: Evaluation of the CTMTC methodology for assessment of teamwork competence development and acquisition in higher education. In: Zaphiris, P., Ioannou, A. (eds.) LCT 2016. LNCS, vol. 9753, pp. 201–212. Springer, Cham (2016). https://doi.org/10.1007/978-3-319-39483-1_19
7. Viles Diez, E., Zárraga-Rodríguez, M., Jaca García, C.: Herramienta para evaluar el funcionamiento de los equipos de trabajo en entornos docentes. Intangible Capital **9**, 281–304 (2013)
8. NCB: Bases para la competencia en dirección de proyectos http://www.lpzconsulting.com/images/CP-_Trabajo_en_Equipo.pdf. Última vez accedido 23 Feb 2018
9. Séin-Echaluce, M.L., Fidalgo Blanco, Á., García-Peñalvo, F.J., Conde, M.Á.: A knowledge management system to classify social educational resources within a subject using teamwork techniques. In: Zaphiris, P., Ioannou, A. (eds.) LCT 2015. LNCS, vol. 9192, pp. 510–519. Springer, Cham (2015). https://doi.org/10.1007/978-3-319-20609-7_48

10. Fidalgo-Blanco, Á., Sein-Echaluce, M.L., García-Peñalvo, F.J., Conde, M.Á.: Using learning analytics to improve teamwork assessment. Comput. Hum. Behav. **47**, 149–156 (2015)
11. Fidalgo, A., Leris, D., Sein-Echaluce, M.L., García-Peñalvo, F.J.: Indicadores para el seguimiento de evaluación de la competencia de trabajo en equipo a través del método CTMT. In: Congreso Internacional sobre Aprendizaje Innovación y Competitividad - CINAIC 2013, Madrid, Spain (2013)
12. Sein-Echaluce, M.L., Fidalgo-Blanco, Á., García-Peñalvo, F.J.: Students' knowledge sharing to improve learning in engineering academic courses. Int. J. Eng. Educ. (IJEE) **32**, 1024–1035 (2016)
13. Conde, M.A., Colomo-Palacios, R., García-Peñalvo, F.J., Larrucea, X.: Teamwork assessment in the educational web of data: a learning analytics approach towards ISO 10018. Telematics and Informatics (In press)
14. Cockburn, A.: Agile Software Development. Addison-Wesley, Boston (2002)
15. Tasa, K., Taggar, S., Seijts, G.H.: The development of collective efficacy in teams: a multilevel and longitudinal perspective. J. Appl. Psychol. **92**, 17–27 (2007)
16. Pérez-Martínez, J.E., García-Martín, J., Sierra-Alonso, A.: Teamwork competence and academic motivation in computer science engineering studies In: 2014 IEEE Global Engineering Education Conference (EDUCON), Istanbul, Turkey, pp. 778–783 (2014)
17. Sánchez-González, L., Ferrero-Castro, R., Conde-González, M.Á., Alfonso-Cendón, J.: A learning experiment based in collaborative project implementation for the development of entrepreneurship. In: 2016 International Symposium on Computers in Education (SIIE), pp. 1–6 (2016)
18. Garcia-Martin, J., Alcover-de-la-Hera, C.M., Manzano-Garcia, P., Rodríguez-Mazo, F., Perez-Martinez, J.E.: Measuring the influence of cooperative learning and project based learning on problem solving skill. In: Krogh, L., Jensen, A.A. (eds.) Visions Challenges and Strategies: PBL Principles and Methodologies in a Danish Global Perspective, pp. 281–297. Aalborg University Press (2013)

Collaborative Learning with Virtual Entities

Liane M. R. Tarouco[✉], Clóvis Silveira, and Aliane L. Krassmann

Graduate Program of Informatics in Education, Universidade Federal do Rio
Grande do Sul, Porto Alegre, Brazil
liane@penta.ufrgs.br, csclovis@gmail.com,
alkrassmann@gmail.com

Abstract. This paper describes strategies to support collaborative learning
using virtual entities simulating the performance of competent peers in the
interaction with students, in order to extend the Zone of Proximal Development.
It is exemplified how those entities can be materialized in learning management
systems and immersive learning environments, and some limitations and challenges are discussed, signaling the potential of this research field for education.

Keywords: Collaborative learning · Zone of Proximal Development
Conversational agents · Chatbots · Virtual entities

1 Introduction

Vygotsky's [1] interactionist theory suggests that learning is a social process and that a
student's development is influenced by his peers during the cognitive growth process.
The ZPD (Zone of Proximal Development) is a basic concept of this theory defined as
the distance between the real level of development, which is usually determined by the
ability to solve problems independently, and the potential level of development,
determined by the ability to solve problems under the guidance of an "adult" or in
collaboration with more able partners. Based on this concept, social interactions are
understood to be relevant to student knowledge production, particularly those that
allow for dialogue, cooperation, and the exchange of mutual information and the
confrontation of divergent points of view.

According to Dillenbourg [2], peers do not learn because they are two, but because
they perform activities that trigger specific learning mechanisms. This includes activities accomplished individually, since individual cognition is not suppressed in peer
interaction. In addition, the interaction between individuals generates extra activities
(explanation, disagreement, mutual regulation) that triggers additional cognitive processes (knowledge elicitation, internalization, reduced cognitive load, etc.).

These assumptions form the basis for collaborative learning, and a number of
studies [3–7] show that cooperation, when compared to individual effort, usually results
in greater achievement, longer content retention periods, production of critical and
meta-cognitive thinking, as well as increased creativity for problem solving and a
greater degree of student persistence, as well as reducing the time required for learning.

Traditionally, these interactions are established between human peers (students,
tutors, teachers, etc.). However, there are cases where the interaction among these peers

© Springer International Publishing AG, part of Springer Nature 2018
P. Zaphiris and A. Ioannou (Eds.): LCT 2018, LNCS 10924, pp. 480–493, 2018.
https://doi.org/10.1007/978-3-319-91743-6_35

is scarce, difficult, or even impracticable. In distance education courses, for example, geographical, administrative and/or financial limitations make it difficult to provide an interlocutor for collaborative learning to take place whenever it is convenient for the student. Therefore, the use of collaboration resources involving virtual entities has been tested by several research groups [8–10].

In order to contribute to the topic, this paper presents strategies to support collaborative learning by involving virtual entities, which simulate the performance of competent peers during interaction with students, in order to stimulate the ZPD. This interaction has special relevance for distance education activities, where geographically dispersed students participate asynchronously more often than synchronously.

The article is structured as follows: Sect. 2 presents the assumptions of collaborative learning, connecting them to the ZPD concept. In Sect. 3 virtual entities are explored as tools to support collaborative learning, going into further detail in Subsect. 3.1 regarding conversational virtual entities, which in turn is subdivided according to the types of environments in which such software can be integrated, including learning management systems and immersive virtual environments. Section 4 presents an analysis of real student interactions with virtual entities, highlighting their potential to leverage collaborative learning. Finally, Sect. 5 presents some conclusions, limitations, and challenges in the field.

2 Collaborative Learning

Collaborative learning is an active and student-centered process, who expresses ideas, articulates thinking, develops representations, elaborates cognitive structures and engages in a social validation process regarding his/her new knowledge in collaboration with peers. It describes a situation in which certain forms of interaction among people must occur in order for cognitive mechanisms to be activated. This interaction generates explanations, disagreements, and mutual regulations that trigger cognitive mechanisms, such as knowledge explicitness and negotiation, leading to internalization. Such process allows learning through the experience of others.

In the collaborative construction of knowledge, a group can engage in thinking together about a problem or task and produce a knowledge artifact. This artifact can be a verbal clarification, a textual solution or a theoretical formalization that integrates different perspectives on the topic and represents the shared negotiated result.

The intervention of the tutor or other interlocutor to incite students to think, reflect, and elaborate through instigating questions is desirable and beneficial, and this sequence of interactions has the potential to expand the ZPD [1]. However, for this to happen, it is desirable for the interlocutor to have relevant knowledge and experience in relation to the student. That way, he will be able to create situations of cognitive imbalance that will promote the need for adaptation and/or accommodation, and will be capable of taking the student to a higher level of balance, as foreseen in Piaget's constructivist theory [11].

The effectiveness of tutoring was demonstrated by Bloom [12], identifying large differences in student performance under one-on-one tutoring with individualized instruction compared to group instruction methods, which was termed the "2 Sigma

Problem". Since individualized care entails high costs, solutions using technology to make learning activity more interactive have been researched.

In this sense, virtual entities configure themselves as solutions in the category of intelligent tutors. Despite being limited in relation to human tutoring, they have the potential to improve students' academic performance, providing a service that is close to what would be provided by a real individual tutor.

3   Virtual Entities

The impossibility of having a human tutor permanently available to perform interaction tasks led to the search for automated solutions, using virtual entities, which can be made available through the internet without interruption. They can be materialized in different ways, such as sensors, scripts, avatars, agents, and various other resources. This article presents virtual entities solutions specifically involving the use of conversational agents, discussing pedagogical strategies that may guide their use in different types of environments, as well as the technologies used for its implementation. The infrastructure and assumptions to ensure the quality of conversational virtual entities will be detailed in the following section.

3.1   Conversational Virtual Entities

Conversational agents (also called chatbots or virtual assistants) are applications that simulate dialogue through a natural language interaction (by text or voice) between a human, who provides the input, and the agent that responds to him (providing answers or formulating questions). According to Dale [13], the use of chatbots is one of the major trends in technology today, being available for interaction with users of large corporations such as Apple (Siri), Amazon (Alexa), Microsoft (Cortana) and Google (Now).

One of the most popular solutions to support the implementation of chatbots, Alicebot, was developed by [14], using the A.L.I.C.E (Artificial Linguistic Internet Computer Entity) inference machine. Alicebot is an open source project that also disseminated the use of AIML (Artificial Intelligence Markup Language). Over the years, a variety of online softwares and services for the construction of these conversational virtual entities has emerged from this implementation, such as PandoraBots, Program-Z, Program-O, and Program AB.

Within this technology, the chatbot software interprets the submitted query, searches in a knowledge base for a response that contains the query elements, and selects, according to some criteria, a response to send to the user. But there are a diversity of other techniques to design chatbots, such as markov chains, Chat Script and parsing [15].

In the beginning, Wallace et al. [14] predicted chatbots acting as "speaking books for children", or chatbots for foreign language teaching and general education. Since then, the use of conversational agents as educational tools has been continually explored [16]. According to Fryer et al. [17] and Crown et al. [18], they offer numerous benefits to education, essentially through the provision of information in the form of dialogue, becoming a potential source of sustained motivation for learning. Ghose and Barua [19] highlight its ability to retrieve information instantly and simply, without the student having to browse or search multiple web pages to find answers to frequently asked questions.

Against the foregoing, conversational virtual entities have the potential to function as a virtual companions for the student, and just as in the situation of humans, can perform interventions that affect the ZPD in several ways, such as:

1. Guidance regarding the activities to be undertaken (especially relevant in distance learning where students often report feeling lost and somewhat disoriented).
2. Answer questions related to the conceptual field in action.
3. Formulate questions to the student in order to instigate reflection and meta-knowledge.
4. Suggest external sources (sites, videos, etc.) with additional information related to the context being addressed.

With these strategies in mind, it is possible to create a learning environment based on Vygotsky's theory of social interaction, capable of fostering collaborative learning using virtual entities as substitutes for real partners or tutors. In this way, social interactions become important elements for the production of knowledge in a collaborative manner, through dialogue, exchange of information and confrontation between divergent points of view.

In order to perform its function with quality, the conversational virtual entity needs to have an extensive knowledge base to support the interventions/reactions. In this sense, its construction demands some care, as discussed below.

- **Orientation for the conceptual field in action.** As defined by Vergnaud [20], the theory of conceptual fields assumes that the heart of cognitive development is conceptualization. Vergnaud's definition of the conceptual field involves a set of problems and situations whose treatment requires concepts, procedures, and representations of different but closely related types. Thus, the creation of the knowledge base of the conversational agent needs to take into account the concepts and procedures inherent to the context in which they will be needed.
- **Information about the student's developmental activity and progress up to the moment of interaction** (activities already carried out, experiment object of the activity and interactions carried out by the student with the experiment). The role of the conversational agent may vary over the course of the student. At an early stage, the agent should provide information about what the student should accomplish, and be able to answer questions regarding to the related concepts. The operation of these functionalities requires a support infrastructure, which implies the existence of a knowledge base related to the conceptual field in action and the possibility of extending the search for a response beyond its content, accessing web search engines. Later on, the agent should be able to provide the student with information about the status of their assignments (responding to any pending activities or other information related to the progress of the learning process). In addition, in the activity completion phase, the agent should promote reflection through answers that, in turn, are able to instigate reflection on student.

In the educational context, there are mostly two types of virtual environments currently being used to support activities and provide materials, both in face-to-face and in distance learning courses: virtual learning environments or Learning Management Systems (LMS), which mainly use web technology, and immersive virtual environments, where interactive 3D scenarios with different purposes are built. In sequence, conversational virtual entities and discussions regarding their use on each of these types of environments is presented.

Conversational Virtual Entities and Learning Management Systems
Education is increasingly being based on the technological resources to carry out student-teacher mediation. Some distance learning courses can be fully accomplished online, through virtual learning environments or LMS. In an attempt to make them more interactive, many educational approaches provide conversational agents combined with these environments, in a parallel way via web or integrated with them (inserted into the code itself). Among the examples is Doroty, who assists the training of apprentice user in computer networks [21], and Blaze, created to enhance students' cognitive abilities while solving mathematical problems from examples [22].

An example of how collaborative learning can be incited through the use of conversational agents is illustrated in Graesser et al. [8], by introducing AutoTutor, which provides feedback to the student (positive, neutral, and negative). It asks the student for more information, request suggestions, completes information gaps, identifies and corrects answers, replies student questions and summarizes the answers.

Within the framework of the AVATAR Project (Virtual Learning and Remote Academic Work) of the Universidade Federal do Rio Grande do Sul (UFRGS) [23], which aims to implement ways of facilitating learning through virtual laboratories and virtual worlds with the use of the OpenSimulator platform, agent ATENA (Tutor Agent for Teaching and Navigation of the Environment) was initially developed, which will be presented in the sequence. In addition to this agent, a new conversational agent with web access was deployed for use in distance learning courses in the area of educational technology. This agent was called METIS[1] (Mediator in Educational Technology Informatics and Socializer) (Fig. 1). This course uses the MOODLE virtual learning environment, and the access to the agent was offered parallel via web. In this case, the agent was not incorporated into the environment, but offered as a "conversation window". Although it has already been tested with students, it is still being refined. The agent is able to interact in Portuguese and has in its knowledge base a set of information related to educational technologies.

As the screenshot in Fig. 1 shows, a visual representation (avatar) was assigned to agent METIS and another to the user, seeking to associate a more personalized "human-like" character with the agent and thus make this interaction more motivating. In the extracted example, the student sends the message "could you explain to me what a software license is?" and the agent responds by adding, besides the textual answer explaining the concept, a related video resource. This additional feature is presented in the format of a frame inserted in the chat window itself, and it can be extended by the user to full screen mode through a click. Likewise, other multimedia resources can be

---

[1] METIS web interface at: http://avatar.cinted.ufrgs.br/metis/.

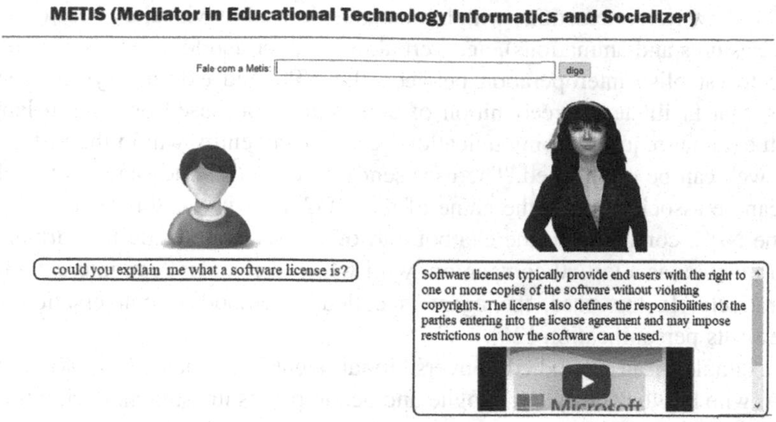

METIS (Mediator in Educational Technology Informatics and Socializer)

Fig. 1. Web interface of the METIS conversational agent

added to the responses, via links to digital repositories, electronic libraries, web queries, audio, and images. Therefore, this virtual entity encourages the student to seek for more information, acting as a more capable companion that can expand the ZPD. The agent was developed using the Program-O open source software and has an interface in Cascading Style Sheets (CSS), which allows the screen to be adjusted according to the device, facilitating its use by mobile devices.

Conversational Virtual Entities in Immersive Virtual Environments

Immersive 3D virtual environments, also called virtual worlds or metaverses, are open environments where the user, represented by his own avatar, can move and interact with other users, changing and creating structures [24]. They differ from other pedagogical tools because of their interactive and immersive feature, which allows the student to manipulate 3D digital artifacts included in the environment, which, in its turn, are capable of displaying dynamic behaviors, thus providing a process of active knowledge construction. According to Morgado et al. [25], immersive virtual worlds enable not only constructivist and connectivist approaches, but the possibility of integrating experiences and contexts (both real and virtual) that support mobile, social and multichannel learning.

In this context there are the Non Player Characters (NPCs), virtual entities in the form of program-controlled avatars (or scripts) that can perform various functions, acting as receptionists, guides, personal assistants, companions, mentors, and tutors. Through scripts and sensors, actions can be programmed to be executed by the NPC, which may be triggered by the proximity of the avatar (representing the user) or as a reflection of some action that the user has performed. In popular platforms such as Second Life (proprietary) and OpenSimulator (open source), the LSL (Linden Scripting Language) is the most used. In the OpenSimulator environment there is also a language called OSSL (OpenSimulator Scripting Language) that offers additional functions for this environment. These languages allow to associate scripts triggered by the occurrence of events.

NPCs allow rich interactions with humans, as they allow visual expression (bodily, through gestures and animations), and verbal, textual, or auditory expression. It is also possible to establish interoperation between the NPC and external systems, such as chatbots, that facilitate the recognition of communication based on natural language. Through external requests, communication between any entity within the virtual world and the web can be established. The user sends and receives messages to the chatbot, which can be associated with the name of the NPC, as if it was this character talking. Thus, the NPC, connected to the chatbot and other systems outside the virtual world, starts to function as a virtual companion, with which the student can interact and learn collaboratively. In this case, the agent is called an embodied conversational agent because of its personification [26].

An example of an embodied conversational agent implemented via NPC is agent ATENA, who has the ability to dialogue and accompanies the student during their time in the virtual scenario. This agent was prepared to work in the conceptual field of Physics (at the high school level), and its development is one of the actions of the AVATAR Project. Figure 2 shows ATENA approaching the user's avatar, to introduce herself, describe the environment, the activities that can be carried out in the environment, and recommend sources of information so that the student can be prepared for the experimental activities that were planned. In each room in the virtual world, new instances of the ATENA agent, acting as virtual companions, are available to interact with the student. The first implemented experiments involved the conceptual field of electricity [23].

The AVATAR Project is focused on science education, an area that has serious gaps in terms of laboratories for the development of student experiments. In addition, there are many training courses for science teaching that are developed in distance education modality, and in such courses there are no laboratories to carry out experiments in sufficient quantity and proximity. These two factors show the importance of offering virtual labs so that students can somehow perform at least some experiments essential to their training.

However, as in the case of real laboratories, there is a need for guidance for students to know what can and should be done in the laboratory, to provide explanations and guidance on experiments and underlying concepts, and to instigate reflection on what was observed in the experiments. To fill this gap, "human surrogates" must be added [27], whose purpose is to carry out interventions aimed at expanding the ZPD (explaining, guiding, questioning, discussing, responding, etc.).

Several instances of agent ATENA are arranged in the virtual world, and as the user moves, his presence is detected by sensors and the information is sent to the nearest agent, to initiate guidance or suggestion dialog. When the user touches a virtual device, ATENA also receives a signal and presents herself to provide guidance on the use of the experiments. These virtual entities have been outlined to function as virtual companions, accompanying the user in their activity in the immersive virtual world [28].

Figure 3 shows the modules that support ATENA operation, presenting succinctly the functionalities and services used so that the agent can better act as a virtual companion, which can serve as an exemplar architecture to other similar approaches.

This type of architecture has also been used in other works such as the one proposed by Burden [24] that contains two main modules: (a) avatar control and interface,

Fig. 2. AVATAR Project virtual laboratories with the ATENA conversational agent

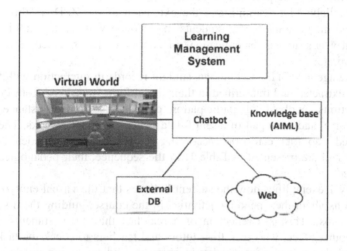

Fig. 3. Architecture of conversational virtual entities in immersive virtual environments

usually using the virtual world platform resources; (b) web environment, connecting with chatbot software and external web services.

Agents that are personified and applied on the basis of interactionist theory have been the subject of numerous empirical investigations over the years, which analyzed variables associated with agent design and investigated the resulting effects on performance metrics, learning, motivation, and perception [29]. Lester et al. [30] proved the existence of the "persona effect", where even in simpler forms the mere presence of a realistic character in interaction with students can have a significant positive effect on the perception of the learning experience in a virtual environment. Mayer and Moreno's [31] multimedia learning theory suggests that students can process information more efficiently when material and feedback are presented as a mixture of visual and auditory stimuli, which also points to advantages of agents that take on a more human shape.

Xie and Luo [32] also investigated the use of virtual companions within the conceptual field of physics, but focusing on electricity. They used multiple types of agents in their study, categorized into six classes: control orientation, problem solving, character orientation, information orientation, navigational orientation, and creative orientation. They also used NPCs and the OpenSimulator platform. The virtual agent in each room provides different types of assistance as indicated in the predicted categories, helping students to complete the proposed tasks (Fig. 4).

The authors conclude that virtual entities presented in the form of embodied conversational agents, with the role of virtual companions, have promising effects on the completion of tasks and the satisfaction perceived by the students [32].

4   Student Interactions with Conversational Virtual Entities

In order to illustrate the potential of the conversational virtual entities for the development of collaborative learning and the extension of the ZPD, in this section we present some interactions of real students in dialogue with virtual entities. In these dialogues, it was searched for indications of conditions for the occurrence of collaborative learning.

From the agent METIS system logs, student records in interaction with this virtual entity were extracted and transcribed in their literal form (translated from Portuguese). The interactions involved the participation of students from a distance education graduate course, and were part of a set of data collected over 12 weeks. The messages were divided into four categories according to their context, as identified by the researchers, and are presented in Table 1. In the sequence, their pedagogical potential are discussed.

Category 1 exemplifies how the student believes that the virtual entity can answer their questions about their pending activities in the course, guiding them so that their focus is not lost. This is a reflection of a real fact that many students in distance education courses face, who seek their tutors and teachers to check the tasks they are missing, and due to absence or delay in answers, end up giving up on the contact attempt or even the course. A virtual entity can provide this type of response immediately, guiding the student and helping to reduce dropout rates for lack of assistance and guidance.

Category 2 shows that the student understands that the virtual entity can give him instructions and information about subjects related to course content, and in fact assist him in performing tasks. In other words, it reflects the case of the student who has doubts about the content and would like to dialogue to remedy them. The lack of peers for dialogue, even with colleagues when there is a geographical distance, can make a small doubt get worse and become a demotivating factor that contributes to drop out rates.

Category 3 illustrates the student's curiosity to know what the virtual entity knows and is able to do, and test its limits to see how much he can count on its help. A student even seems to doubt whether the agent is a human or machine by questioning "are you a person or a program?" This fact shows the credibility and the realistic aspect of the virtual entity, showing its potential to act as a human surrogate, where the user thinks that he or she may be interacting with a human being [27].

In the Category 4 messages it is possible to observe that the student demonstrates satisfaction with the dialogue and recognizes the effort of the virtual entity in trying to

Fig. 4. Interaction between the student's avatar and the virtual entity in the virtual world [32]

Table 1. Messages from students interacting with METIS virtual entity

---

Category 1 - Questions regarding the course activities

Student A - "If we terminate an activity and forgot to post it or if we think we have posted a document, how can you redo the activity?"

Student B - "I'm having trouble with video activity"

Student C - "How can you help me in relation to the course?"

Student D - "I'd like to know what activities I should do?"

Category 2 - Questions regarding the course content

Student E - "Help me make a video."

Student C- "How do I make a webquest?"

Student F - "digital games about recycling - do you know any?"

Student G - "Hi Metis! Can the infograph generate comparison between data?"

Category 3 - Curiosities regarding the agent's capability

Student H - "What is your purpose?"

Student I - "what kind of help can you give me?"

Student J - "Are you a person or a program?"

Student K - "Can you do a search for me?"

Category 4 - Satisfaction, acknowledgement, unburden and interest

Student L - "It's good to learn with you."

Student M - "Thanks for the help"

Student N - "I am concerned, but I am trying"

Student O - "I think you are very interesting"

assist him. A student also seems to feel safe to vent his concerns about the course by mentioning "I'm concerned but I am trying", and another exposes his opinion that the agent is interesting. Thus, affectivity issues are present, showing how the virtual entity can also act in the emotional field, stimulating and motivating the student, reducing the feeling of isolation and lack of integration commonly experienced by students in distance education courses.

To summarize, the messages presented in Table 1 show that students interacted with the virtual entity as if it was a virtual companion or tutor, able to assist and provide answers to conceptual and operational questions about the course. Therefore, indications that investing in the development of automated resources to simulate credible human partners can bring good results in terms of improving motivation were revealed. Also, it has been shown that this type of resource has the potential to foster collaborative learning.

The evidences presented in this section shows how virtual entities can help students on widening their potential development as proposed by Vygotsky [1]. Thus, it is possible to use technology to create a virtual companion to dialogue, provide guidance, and act in collaboration with the student, with better cost-benefits, since virtual entities can be available twenty-four hours a day and assist more users, even simultaneously.

5 Conclusions, Limitations, and Challenges

Nowadays, LMS and immersive 3D virtual environments are on the rise of technology enhanced learning, supporting the most diverse levels and modes of instruction. However, teachers, guardians or colleagues are not always accessible at the moment a particular student accesses the system, making it difficult the interaction with peers, which is an important and necessary part of the learning process.

The accelerated development of technology has created opportunities to promote collaborative learning through new automated elements called virtual entities. This paper have presented some strategies to support collaborative learning by involving these virtual entities. Evidence was presented that these resources, when conceived for pedagogical purposes, can elicit knowledge, provide information on the conceptual field being studied, guide external sources of information, elucidate doubts, resolve disagreements, provide mutual regulation and instigation for reflection, as well as provide emotional support, simulating the performance of competent peers and stimulating the full potential of the student, as advocated by Vygotsky [1] theory of ZPD (Zone of Proximal Development).

From the research and experiments reported in this work, it should be noted that some difficulties are also observed in the use of conversational agents as virtual companions. They include the communication between agents and humans, due to limitations in the natural language comprehension capacity of the conversational agents. Although different variants are incorporated into the knowledge base for the conceptual field in focus, it is possible for the student to elaborate a question or statement that is not understood by the agent, and in these cases the student is asked to reformulate their statement. Hill et al. [33] reveal that an obstacle to computers is not only understanding the words, but the infinite variability of expressions and meanings placed in the use of language.

Another implication is the maintenance of a dialogue control to allow continuity to interactions with subsequent responses by referencing or complementing previous responses, as suggested by Neves et al. [34]. Also, Fryer et al. [17] point out that there is a difficulty in maintaining interest in the tool after the "novelty effect" has subsided. And, the study by Mou and Xu [35] showed that when interacting with a machine some people may feel more confident while others feel confused or even intimidated.

However, in spite of the limitations pointed out, this research shows that the interactions of students with a virtual entity, as elucidated in Table 1 (Sect. 4), are representative of students' potential interest and motivation when engaged in a collaborative learning process interacting with virtual companions.

To solve the difficulties pointed out, some challenges are brought up, as the development of functionalities to automate the expansion of the knowledge base of conversational virtual entities through the treatment of linguistic corpus selected for the desired conceptual field. An effort in this regard is being made in the scope of AVATAR Project[2], where beyond the textual treatment of the linguistic corpus to identify key concepts, it involves a system for generating categories in AIML to integrate in the agent knowledge base using the Alicebot solution. Additionally, in order to expand the chatbot's knowledge search capacity, experiments are being developed with the implementation of interfacing with web search systems and external databases. This way, the virtual entity can help the student by going beyond the initially envisaged knowledge scope for the conceptual field under study, seeking answers to broader questions presented by the student, drawing on the technologies of virtual assistants that are already available in most smartphones, such as Apple's Siri and Google Now.

Acknowledgements. We gratefully thank CAPES - Coordenação de Aperfeiçoamento de Pessoal de Nível Superior for financial support to Project AVATAR.

References

1. Vygotsky, L.S.: Mind in Society: The Development of Higher Psychological Processes. Harvard University Press, Cambridge (1978)
2. Dillenbourg, P.: What do you mean by collaborative learning? In: Dillenbourg, P. (ed.) Collaborative-Learning: Cognitive and Computational Approaches, pp. 1–19. Elsevier, Oxford (1999)
3. Harsley, R., Fossati, D., Di Eugenio, B., Green, N.: Interactions of individual and pair programmers with an intelligent tutoring system for computer science. Paper Presented at the Proceedings of the Conference on Integrating Technology into Computer Science Education, ITiCSE, pp. 285–290 (2017). https://doi.org/10.1145/3017680.3017786
4. Cho, Y.H., Lim, K.Y.: Effectiveness of collaborative learning with 3D virtual worlds. Br. J. Edu. Technol. **48**(1), 202–211 (2017)

---

[2] Project AVATAR official website available at http://www.ufrgs.br/avatar.

5. Purcher, P., Hofler, M., Pirker, J., Tomes, L., Ischebeck, A., Gutl, C.: Individual versus collaborative learning in a virtual world. Paper Presented at the 2016 39th International Convention on Information and Communication Technology, Electronics and Microelectronics, MIPRO 2016 - Proceedings, pp. 824–828 (2016). https://doi.org/10.1109/mipro.2016.7522253
6. Berns, A., Rodriguez, F., Gomez, R.: Collaborative learning in 3-D virtual environments. Global Perspectives on Computer-Assisted Language Learning Glasgow, 10–13 July 2013, Papers, 17 (2013)
7. Ibáñez, M.B., García Rueda, J.J., Maroto, D., Delgado Kloos, C.: Collaborative learning in multi-user virtual environments. J. Netw. Comput. Appl. **36**(6), 1566–1576 (2013). https://doi.org/10.1016/j.jnca.2012.12.027
8. Graesser, A.C., Chipman, P., Haynes, B.C., Olney, A.: AutoTutor: an intelligent tutoring system with mixed-initiative dialogue. IEEE Trans. Educ. **48**(4), 612–618 (2005)
9. Soliman, M., Guetl, C.: Implementing Intelligent Pedagogical Agents in virtual worlds: tutoring natural science experiments in OpenWonderland. In: 2013 IEEE Global Engineering Education Conference (EDUCON), pp. 782–789. IEEE (2013)
10. Kim, Y.: Desirable characteristics of learning companions. Int. J. Artif. Intell. Educ. **17**(4), 371–388 (2007)
11. Piaget, J.: Piaget's theory. In: Inhelder, B., Chipman, H.H., Zwingmann, C. (eds.) Piaget and His School, pp. 11–23. Springer, Heidelberg (1976). https://doi.org/10.1007/978-3-642-46323-5_2
12. Bloom, B.S.: The 2 Sigma problem: the research for methods of group instruction as effective as one-to-one tutoring. Educ. Res. **13**(6), 4–16 (1984)
13. Dale, R.: The return of the chatbots. Nat. Lang. Eng. **22**(5), 811–817 (2016)
14. Wallace, R.S., Tomabechi, H., Aimless, D.: Chatterbots Go Native: considerations for an eco-system fostering the development of artificial life forms in a human world (2003). http://www.pandorabots.com/pandora/pics/chatterbotsgonative.doc. Accessed Feb 2018
15. Abdul-Kader, S.A., Woods, J.: Survey on chatbot design techniques in speech conversation systems. Int. J. Adv. Comput. Sci. Appl. **6**(7), 72–80 (2015)
16. Kerly, A., Hall, P., Bull, S.: Bringing chatbots into education: towards natural language negotiation of open learner models. Know.-Based Syst. **20**(2), 177–185 (2007)
17. Fryer, L.K., Ainley, M., Thompson, A., Gibson, A., Sherlock, Z.: Stimulating and sustaining interest in a language course: an experimental comparison of Chatbot and Human task partners. Comput. Hum. Behav. **75**, 461–468 (2017)
18. Crown, S., Fuentes, A., Jones, R., Nambiar, R., Crown, D.: Anne G. Neering: interactive chatbot to engage and motivate engineering students. Comput. Educ. J. **21**(2), 24–34 (2011)
19. Ghose, S., Barua, J.J.: Toward the implementation of a topic specific dialogue based natural language chatbot as an undergraduate advisor. In: 2013 International Conference on Informatics, Electronics & Vision (ICIEV). IEEE (2013)
20. Vergnaud, G.: The theory of conceptual fields. Hum. Dev. **52**(2), 83–94 (2009). https://doi.org/10.1159/000202727
21. Leonhardt, M.D., Tarouco, L.: Aplicando Linguagem Natural ao Gerenciamento de Redes de Computadores através do Chatbot Doroty. XXV Congresso da Sociedade Brasileira de Computação. UNISINOS – São Leopoldo – RS (2005)
22. Aguiar, E.V.B., Tarouco, L.M.R., Reategui, E.: Supporting problem-solving in mathematics with a conversational agent capable of representing gifted students' knowledge. In: The Hawaii International Conference on System Sciences - HICSS-47, Waikiloa, USA (2014)

23. Herpich, F., Filho, T.A.R., Tibola, L.R., Ferreira, V.A., Tarouco, L.M.R.: Learning principles of electricity through experiencing in virtual worlds. In: Beck, D., et al. (eds.) iLRN 2017. CCIS, vol. 725, pp. 229–242. Springer, Cham (2017). https://doi.org/10.1007/978-3-319-60633-0_19
24. Burden, D.J.: Deploying embodied AI into virtual worlds. Knowl.-Based Syst. **22**(7), 540–544 (2009)
25. Morgado, L., Varajão, J., Coelho, D., Rodrigues, C., Sancin, C., Castello, V.: The Journal of Virtual Worlds and Education, Volume 1 Issue 1. The Center for Virtual Worlds Education and Research Rochester, New York 14619 (2010)
26. Cassell, J. (ed.): Embodied Conversational Agents. MIT Press, Cambridge (2000)
27. Hughes, C.E.: Human surrogates: remote presence for collaboration and education in smart cities. Paper Presented at the EMASC 2014 - Proceedings of the 1st International Workshop on Emerging Multimedia Applications and Services for Smart Cities, Workshop of MM 2014, 1–2 (2014). https://doi.org/10.1145/2661704.2661712
28. Sgobbi, F.S., Tarouco, L., Mühlbeier, A.R.K.: Virtual agents' support for practical laboratory activities. In: 5th European Immersive Education Summit, Paris, France (2015)
29. Veletsianos, G., Russell, G.S.: Pedagogical agents. In: Spector, J., Merrill, M., Elen, J., Bishop, M. (eds.) Handbook of Research on Educational Communications and Technology, pp. 759–769. Springer, New York (2014). https://doi.org/10.1007/978-1-4614-3185-5_61
30. Lester, J.C., Converse, S.A., Kahler, S.E., Barlow, S.T., Stone, B.A., Bhogal, R.S.: The persona effect: affective impact of animated pedagogical agents. In: Proceedings of the ACM SIGCHI Conference on Human Factors in Computing Systems, pp. 359–366. ACM (1997)
31. Mayer, R.E., Moreno, R.: A split-attention effect in multimedia learning: evidence for dual processing systems in working memory. J. Educ. Psychol. **90**(2), 312 (1998)
32. Xie, T., Luo, L.: Impact of prompting agents on task completion in the virtual world. Int. J. Online Eng. (iJOE) **13**(06), 35–48 (2017)
33. Hill, J., Ford, W.R., Farreras, I.G.: Real conversations with artificial intelligence: a comparison between human–human online conversations and human–chatbot conversations. Comput. Hum. Behav. **49**, 245–250 (2015)
34. Neves, A.M.M., Barros, F.A., Hodges, C.: iAIML: a mechanism to treat intentionality in AIML chatterbots. In: 18th IEEE International Conference on Tools with Artificial Intelligence, 2006, ICTAI 2006. IEEE (2006). https://doi.org/10.1109/ictai.2006.64
35. Mou, Y., Xu, K.: The media inequality: comparing the initial human-human and human-AI social interactions. Comput. Hum. Behav. **72**, 432–440 (2017)

Author Index

Printed in the United States
By Bookmasters